Lawrenceville Press

An Introduction to Programming Using Microsoft® Visual Basic® .NET

Beth Brown
Bruce Presley

All orders including educational, Canadian, foreign, FPO, and APO may be placed by contacting:

Lawrenceville Press, Inc.
P.O. Box 704
Pennington, NJ 08534-0704
(609) 737-1148
(609) 737-8564 fax

This text is available in hardcover and softcover editions.

16 15 14 13 12 11 10 9 8 7 6 5 4 3 2 1

The text is written and published by Lawrenceville Press, Inc. and is in no way connected with the Microsoft® Corporation.

Microsoft® and Visual Basic® are either registered trademarks or trademarks of the Microsoft Corporation in the United States and/or other countries. Screen Shots and Icons reprinted with permission from Microsoft® Corporation.

Exam*View* is a registered trademark of FSCreations, Inc.

Names of all other products mentioned herein are used for identification purposes only and may be trademarks of their respective owners.

Preface

We have strived to make this the most comprehensive and easy to understand Visual Basic .NET text available. Our primary objective in this text is to present material in clear language with easy to follow examples. To meet this objective, we use our teaching experiences as well as the feedback, comments, and suggestions from other experienced teachers to determine how best to present programming concepts.

For the best classroom experience for both the student and the teacher, our comprehensive text book includes hands-on reviews, critical-thinking exercises, and projects of varying difficulty levels. Additionally, our Teacher's Resource Package correlates directly to the text book and offers teaching hints for explaining difficult concepts, additional lessons and exercises, and a comprehensive question bank for creating tests, quizzes, and reviews. The Teacher's Resource Package also has a Resource CD with material that includes the programs, Case Studies, and vocabulary from the text book, as well as answers to all the exercises.

It is our belief that learning to program offers the student an invaluable opportunity to develop problem-solving skills. The process of defining a problem, breaking it down into a series of smaller problems, and finally writing a computer program to solve it exercises a student's logical abilities. Additionally, the student is made aware of the capabilities and limitations of a computer and soon realizes that the programmer—the human element—is more important than the machine.

An Introduction to Programming Using Microsoft Visual Basic .NET is written for a one-term or two-term course. No previous programming experience is required or assumed. It is the goal of this text to provide students the best possible introduction to programming using Visual Basic .NET, whether they will continue on to more advanced computer science courses or end their programming education with this introductory course.

Topic Organization

Chapter 1 presents a brief history of computers and programming languages. Networks, number systems, and the social and ethical implications of computers are also discussed.

Chapter 2 introduces students to the Windows XP operating system. Chapters for other operating systems are available for downloading at lpdatafiles.com.

Chapter 3 introduces OOP and the Visual Basic .NET IDE. The importance of good programming style is emphasized throughout the text.

Chapter 4 introduces variables and constants. Automatic type conversion and scope are also discussed. The Visual Basic .NET debugger is also introduced. The Case Study that ends the chapter produces a Calculator application.

The emphasis of Chapter 5 is on decision structures. Concepts presented include random numbers, pseudocode, and counters. Static variables and logic errors are also discussed. In the Case Study, a Pizza Order application is created.

Chapter 6 presents looping structures. The String class and its members are presented, as well as the Char structure. Accumulators and string comparison considerations are also explained. In the Case Study, a Word Guess game is created.

Sub, function, and event Procedures are discussed in Chapter 7. Adding graphics to an application is also explained. An advanced calculator application is created in the Case Study.

Chapter 8 covers the Math class and business functions. Windows application standards such as focus, access keys, and tab order are also discussed. The Case Study presents a Loan Analyzer application.

Arrays, structures, and enumerated types are explained in Chapter 9. Two dimensional matrices are also discussed. Lucy's Cuban Cafe application is created in the Case Study.

In Chapter 10, color, graphics, and animation are covered. The ColorDialog, Graphics class, and Image Editor are discussed. In the Case Study, a Click It! game is created.

In Chapter 11 classes are created. Instantiation, encapsulation, inheritance, and polymorphism are explained. A Triangle Calculator application is created in the Case Study.

Files are discussed in Chapter 12. The FileInfo, FileStream, StreamReader, and StreamWriter classes are discussed. An advanced Word Guess application is created in the Case Study.

Chapter 13 introduces sorting and searching. Algorithms for bubble sort, selection sort, insertion sort, and binary search are introduced. The DateTime structure is used for creating timing code.

Chapter 14 discusses MDI applications that include dialog boxes. The Case Study for this chapter is a Bingo application.

Chapter 15 introduces ASP.NET for creating Web applications.

Design and Features

Programming Concepts This text emphasizes learning the fundamental concepts of programming so that this knowledge can be applied to other programming languages.

Problem Solving From the very beginning, students are taught to implement programming solutions with proper programming techniques.

Programming Style Throughout the text, proper programming style is emphasized so that students can make their applications easy to read, modify, and debug.

Demonstration Applications and Runs Many demonstration applications are included, complete with sample runs, so that students are shown both proper programming techniques and the output actually produced by an application.

Format Each Visual Basic .NET statement is clearly defined, shown in sample code, and then used in an application.

Expectations An outline of the significant topics that will be covered is presented at the beginning of each chapter.

Reviews Numerous reviews are presented throughout each chapter which provide immediate reinforcement to newly learned concepts. Reviews based on previous work are marked with a ↺ symbol. Solutions to the reviews are given on the Resource CD.

Case Studies Most chapters end by stating a problem and then developing the appropriate algorithm. The process of specification, design, coding, and debugging and testing is clearly outlined for producing the problem's solution.

Chapter Summaries Each chapter ends by summarizing the concepts, statements, and controls covered in the chapter.

Vocabulary Sections Each chapter contains a vocabulary section that defines new terms. A separate section lists Visual Basic .NET controls, keywords, statements, and classes.

Critical Thinking Written response exercises that require critical thinking from the student are included at the end of each chapter.

Exercises Each chapter includes a large set of exercises of varying difficulty, making them appropriate for students with a range of abilities. Most exercises include a demonstration run to help make clear what output is expected from the student's application. Exercises based on previous work are marked with a ↺ symbol. Advanced exercises are indicated as such, and require a carefully thought-out algorithm as part of their solution, similar in form to that used in solving a Case Study. Answers to the exercises are included on the Resource CD.

Indexes In addition to a standard index, an index of the applications in the text is also included.

Appendix Students learn about Visual Basic .NET help in an appendix.

Teacher's Resource Package

The Lawrenceville Press *Teacher's Resource Package* that correlates to this text provides all the additional material required to offer students an excellent introductory Visual Basic .NET programming course. These materials place a strong emphasis on developing the student's problem-solving skills. The Package divides each of the chapters in the text into lessons that contain the following features:

- **Assignments** Suggested reading and problem assignments.

- **Teaching Notes** Helpful information that we and our reviewers have learned from classroom experience.

- **Discussion Topics** Additional material that supplements the text and can be used in leading classroom discussions.

- **Worksheets** Problems that supplement the exercises in the text by providing additional reinforcement of concepts.

A Resource CD, included with the Package, contains the following:

- **Supplements** An application that presents material from the text in a slide presentation format.

- **Application files** All applications presented in the text, as listed in the Applications Index.

- **Data files** Files required by some of the exercises in the text.

- **Exam***View*® **Test Generator** Question banks and the popular **Exam***View*® software are included so that multiple tests and assessment materials can be created for each chapter.

- **Answer files** Answers to the reviews, exercises, worksheets, and tests.

Student CDs with data files and programs from the text are available for purchase in packs of 10.

As an added feature, the Package is contained in a three-ring binder. This not only enables pages to be removed for duplication, but also allows you to keep your own notes in the Package.

An Introduction to Programming Using Microsoft Visual Basic .NET

Previous editions of our programming texts have established them as leaders in their field, with more than two million students having been introduced to computing using one of our texts. With this new Visual Basic .NET text, we have made significant improvements over our earlier programming texts. These improvements are based on the many comments we received, a survey of instructors who are teaching the text, and our own classroom experience.

An Introduction to Programming Using Microsoft Visual Basic .NET is available in softcover and hardcover editions. As an additional feature the softcover edition has an improved sewn lay-flat binding that keeps the text open at any page and gives the book additional strength.

Acknowledgments

Jan Marrelli has contributed much to this text. Jan authored Chapter 15, edited the entire text, contributed exercises, and worked extensively on the vocabulary sections.

Thanks to Elaine Malfas for her work on this project. Elaine's art direction, editing, and layout suggestions have added clarity to the presentation in this text.

We thank Nanette Hert of Saint Andrew's School for reviewing the text and testing the materials in her classroom. She has also contributed exercises, produced answer files, and assisted with other aspects of producing such a comprehensive text.

A special thanks and much appreciation are due Mary Misiaszek of LaSalle Academy. She reviewed the entire text and made many suggestions that were implemented. Mary authored the critical thinking questions presented in the text and contributed exercises.

Finally, we would like to thank our students, for whom and with whom this text was written. Their candid evaluation and their refusal to accept anything less than perfect clarity in explanation have been the driving forces behind the creation of *An Introduction to Programming Using Microsoft Visual Basic .NET.*

We value the expertise of John Olivari at Courier Book Companies, Inc. who supervised the printing of this text.

The success of this and all of our texts is due to the efforts of Heidi Crane, Vice President of Marketing at Lawrenceville Press. Joseph Dupree and Christina Albanesius run our Customer Relations Department and handle the thousands of orders we receive in a friendly and efficient manner. Richard Guarascio and Michael Porter are responsible for the excellent service Lawrenceville Press offers in the shipping of orders.

About the Authors

Beth A. Brown, a graduate in computer science from Florida Atlantic University, is director of development at Lawrenceville Press where she has coauthored many programming and applications texts and their Teacher's Resource Packages. Ms. Brown currently works with computer teachers at the middle school and high school level in both the United States and Canada.

Bruce W. Presley, a graduate of Yale University, taught computer science and physics and served as the director of the Karl Corby Computer and Mathematics Center at the Lawrenceville School in Lawrenceville, New Jersey. Mr. Presley was a member of the founding committee of the Advanced Placement Computer Science examination and served as a consultant to the College Entrance Examination Board. Presently Mr. Presley, author of more than thirty computer textbooks, is president of Lawrenceville Press.

Table of Contents

Chapter 1
Computers and Programming Languages

1.1	Mechanical Devices	1–1
1.2	Electro-Mechanical Devices	1–3
1.3	First Generation Computers	1–4
1.4	The Stored Program Computer	1–5
1.5	Second Generation Computers	1–6
1.6	High-Level Programming Languages	1–6
1.7	Third Generation Computers	1–7
1.8	Mainframes	1–7
1.9	Fourth Generation Computers	1–8
1.10	The Personal Computer	1–8
1.11	Networks	1–10
1.12	Number Systems	1–12
1.13	Storing Data in Memory	1–13
1.14	The Social and Ethical Implications of Computers	1–14
1.15	Protecting Computer Software and Data	1–15
1.16	The Ethical Responsibilities of the Programmer	1–16
	Chapter Summary	1–16
	Vocabulary	1–18
	Review Questions	1–20
	Exercises	1–22

Chapter 2
Introducing Windows XP

2.1	What is an Operating System?	2–1
2.2	What is a Windows Application?	2–3
	Review 1	2–5
2.3	Using Menus and Toolbars	2–6
2.4	Dialog Boxes	2–7
	Review 2	2–8
2.5	Using the Keyboard	2–9
2.6	Working with Files	2–10
2.7	Storage Devices	2–12
2.8	Using My Computer	2–13
	Review 3	2–15
2.9	Managing and Organizing Files and Folders	2–15
2.10	Formatting and Copying Diskettes	2–17
	Review 4	2–19
2.11	Finding Files and Folders	2–19
	Chapter Summary	2–20
	Vocabulary	2–22
	Windows XP Commands and Buttons	2–23
	Review Questions	2–24
	Exercise	2–25

Chapter 3
Introducing Visual Basic .NET

3.1   Visual Basic .NET Windows
      Programming 3–1
3.2   The Visual Basic .NET IDE 3–2
3.3   Creating a New Project 3–2
      Review 1 3–4
3.4   The Windows Form 3–4
3.5   The Label Control 3–5
3.6   Saving and Running an Application 3–6
      Review 2 3–7
3.7   The MainMenu Control 3–8
3.8   Closing and Opening a Project and
      Quitting Visual Basic .NET 3–9
      Review 3 3–10
3.9   Program Code 3–10
3.10   The Event Procedure 3–11
      Review 4 3–12
      Review 5 3–14
3.11   Assignment Statements 3–14
3.12   Using AutoList 3–15
      Review 6 3–16
3.13   The RadioButton Control 3–17
3.14   Commenting Code 3–18
      Review 7 3–18
3.15   Arithmetic Operators and Numeric
      Expressions 3–19
3.16   The Button Control 3–20
      Review 8 3–20
      Chapter Summary 3–22
      Vocabulary 3–24
      Visual Basic .NET 3–25
      Critical Thinking 3–26
      Exercises 3–28

Chapter 4
Variables and Constants

4.1   Variables 4–1
4.2   Variable Assignment 4–2
      Review 1 4–2
4.3   Obtaining a Value from the User 4–3
      Review 2 4–4
      Review 3 4–5
4.4   Using Named Constants 4–5
4.5   Choosing Identifiers 4–6
      Review 4 4–6
4.6   Built-In Data Types 4–6
4.7   Automatic Type Conversion 4–8
4.8   Scope 4–8
      Review 5 4–9
4.9   Special Division Operators 4–10
      Review 6 4–10

4.10   Programming Errors 4–11
4.11   Debugging an Application 4–12
      Review 7 4–13
      Case Study 4–14
      Review 8 4–17
      Chapter Summary 4–17
      Vocabulary 4–19
      Visual Basic .NET 4–20
      Critical Thinking 4–21
      Exercises 4–24

Chapter 5
Controlling Program Flow with Decision Structures

5.1   The If...Then Statement 5–1
5.2   Roundoff Error 5–2
      Review 1 5–2
5.3   The If...Then...Else Statement 5–3
      Review 2 5–3
      Review 3 5–3
5.4   Nested If...Then...Else Statements 5–4
5.5   The If...Then...ElseIf Statement 5–4
      Review 4 5–4
5.6   The Select...Case Statement 5–5
      Review 5 5–5
5.7   The Select...Case Is Statement 5–5
      Review 6 5–6
5.8   Generating Random Numbers 5–6
      Review 7 5–7
5.9   Algorithms 5–9
5.10   Static Variables 5–10
      Review 8 5–10
5.11   Logical Operators 5–12
      Review 9 5–13
      Review 10 5–15
      Review 11 5–15
5.12   Displaying a Message Box 5–15
      Review 12 5–16
      Review 13 5–16
5.13   Counter Variables 5–16
      Review 14 5–16
      Review 15 5–16
5.14   The CheckBox Control 5–17
5.15   The Line-Continuation Character 5–18
      Review 16 5–18
      Case Study 5–19
      Review 17 5–23
      Chapter Summary 5–23
      Vocabulary 5–24
      Visual Basic .NET 5–25
      Critical Thinking 5–26
      Exercises 5–30

Chapter 6
Controlling Program Flow with Looping Structures

6.1   Looping 6–1
6.2   The Do…Loop Statement 6–1
6.3   Infinite Loops 6–2
      Review 1 6–3
6.4   Using an Input Box 6–4
6.5   Accumulator Variables 6–5
6.6   Using Flags 6–6
      Review 2 6–6
      Review 3 6–8
6.7   The For…Next Statement 6–8
      Review 4 6–9
      Review 5 6–10
6.8   The String Class 6–10
      Review 6 6–12
      Review 7 6–12
      Review 8 6–13
6.9   String Concatenation 6–13
      Review 9 6–14
6.10 The Char Structure 6–14
6.11 Unicode 6–15
      Review 10 6–16
6.12 Comparing Strings 6–16
      Review 11 6–17
6.13 The Like Operator 6–17
      Case Study 6–18
      Review 12 6–21
      Chapter Summary 6–21
      Vocabulary 6–23
      Visual Basic .NET 6–24
      Critical Thinking 6–25
      Exercises 6–27

Chapter 7
Procedures

7.1   Sub Procedures 7–1
7.2   The PictureBox Control 7–2
      Review 1 7–3
7.3   Value Parameters 7–4
7.4   Procedure Documentation 7–6
      Review 2 7–6
7.5   Reference Parameters 7–7
      Review 3 7–9
      Review 4 7–11
7.6   Control Object Parameters 7–11
      Review 5 7–12
7.7   The Event Handler Procedure 7–12
7.8   The Tag Property 7–13
      Review 6 7–14

7.9   Function Procedures 7–17
      Review 7 7–18
      Case Study 7–20
      Review 8 7–27
      Review 9 7–27
      Review 10 7–27
      Chapter Summary 7–27
      Vocabulary 7–29
      Visual Basic .NET 7–29
      Critical Thinking 7–30
      Exercises 7–33

Chapter 8
Mathematical and Business Functions

8.1   The Math Class 8–1
8.2   The IsNumeric() Function 8–1
      Review 1 8–2
8.3   The Round() Method 8–2
      Review 2 8–2
8.4   Formatting Numeric Output 8–3
8.5   Business Functions 8–3
8.6   Processing Business Data 8–4
      Review 3 8–6
      Review 4 8–7
      Review 5 8–7
8.7   The ListBox Control 8–8
      Review 6 8–9
8.8   The ComboBox Control 8–10
      Review 7 8–12
      Review 8 8–13
8.9   Windows Application Standards 8–13
      Review 9 8–14
      Review 10 8–16
      Review 11 8–16
      Case Study 8–16
8.10 Trigonometric Methods 8–24
      Review 12 8–24
      Review 13 8–24
      Review 14 8–25
      Review 15 8–25
8.11 Inverse Trigonometric Methods 8–26
      Review 16 8–26
8.12 Logarithmic and Exponential Methods 8–27
      Review 17 8–27
      Chapter Summary 8–28
      Vocabulary 8–29
      Visual Basic .NET 8–30
      Critical Thinking 8–31
      Exercises 8–34

Chapter 9
Arrays and Structures

9.1 Arrays 9–1
9.2 Using Arrays 9–2
    Review 1 9–2
9.3 Array Parameters 9–3
9.4 Arrays with Meaningful Indexes 9–4
    Review 2 9–7
    Review 3 9–7
9.5 Searching an Array 9–8
9.6 Dynamic Arrays 9–8
    Review 4 9–11
    Review 5 9–11
9.7 Two-Dimensional Arrays 9–11
9.8 Structures 9–15
9.9 Structure Arrays 9–16
    Review 6 9–16
9.10 Enumerated Types 9–16
    Review 7 9–18
    Case Study 9–18
9.11 Arrays of Objects 9–23
    Review 8 9–24
    Chapter Summary 9–24
    Vocabulary 9–26
    Visual Basic .NET 9–26
    Critical Thinking 9–27
    Exercises 9–31

Chapter 10
Color and Graphics

10.1 Using Color 10–1
    Review 1 10–2
10.2 The ColorDialog Control 10–2
    Review 2 10–3
10.3 Using Images 10–4
    Review 3 10–5
10.4 Image Editor 10–5
10.5 The Image Editor Toolbar 10–6
    Review 4 10–7
10.6 The Timer Control 10–8
    Review 5 10–9
10.7 Animation 10–9
    Review 6 10–10
10.8 The Graphics Class 10–12
10.9 Pen Styles 10–14
    Review 7 10–14
10.10 Drawing Solid Shapes 10–16
    Review 8 10–17
10.11 The Point Structure 10–17
10.12 Drawing Curves and Polygons 10–17
    Review 9 10–19

10.13 Handling Mouse Events 10–19
    Review 10 10–20
    Case Study 10–21
    Review 11 10–25
    Chapter Summary 10–26
    Vocabulary 10–27
    Visual Basic .NET 10–27
    Critical Thinking 10–29
    Exercises 10–31

Chapter 11
Creating Classes

11.1 Classes 11–1
11.2 Designing a Class 11–2
11.3 The Class Module 11–3
    Review 1 11–4
11.4 Encapsulation 11–5
11.5 Field, Data, and Property Members 11–6
    Review 2 11–7
11.6 Methods 11–9
    Review 3 11–10
11.7 Constructors 11–13
    Review 4 11–13
11.8 Overloading Methods 11–14
    Review 5 11–15
11.9 Inheritance and Polymorphism 11–16
11.10 Reusing Code 11–17
    Review 6 11–18
    Case Study 11–21
    Review 7 11–27
    Chapter Summary 11–28
    Vocabulary 11–30
    Visual Basic .NET 11–30
    Critical Thinking 11–31
    Exercises 11–34

Chapter 12
Using Files

12.1 What is a File? 12–1
12.2 The FileInfo Class 12–1
    Review 1 12–2
12.3 The File Stream 12–3
12.4 The FileStream and StreamReader
    Classes 12–4
12.5 Advanced TextBox Features 12–5
    Review 2 12–7
12.6 The OpenFileDialog Control 12–8
    Review 3 12–9
12.7 The StreamWriter Class 12–10
12.8 The SaveFileDialog Control 12–12
    Review 4 12–13

Review 5 12–15

12.9 Reading and Writing Data 12–15
Review 6 12–16
Case Study 12–19
Review 7 12–23
Chapter Summary 12–23
Vocabulary 12–25
Visual Basic .NET 12–25
Critical Thinking 12–26
Exercises 12–28

Chapter 13
Sorting and Searching

13.1 Bubble Sort 13–1
13.2 The DateTime Structure 13–3
Review 1 13–3
13.3 A More Efficient Bubble Sort 13–4
Review 2 13–4
13.4 Selection Sort 13–5
Review 3 13–7
13.5 Insertion Sort 13–7
Review 4 13–10
13.6 Binary Search 13–10
Review 5 13–14
Chapter Summary 13–15
Vocabulary 13–15
Visual Basic .NET 13–15
Critical Thinking 13–16
Exercises 13–17

Chapter 14
Advanced Applications

14.1 MDI Applications 14–1
14.2 Creating an MDI Application 14–2
14.3 Using Child Forms 14–3
Review 1 14–4
14.4 Creating a Window Menu 14–6
Review 2 14–6
14.5 Advanced TextBox Methods 14–8
Review 3 14–8
14.6 Creating Dialog Boxes 14–10
Review 4 14–11
14.7 Creating a Help Menu 14–13
Review 5 14–13
Case Study 14–15
Review 6 14–26
Chapter Summary 14–27
Vocabulary 14–28
Visual Basic .NET 14–28
Critical Thinking 14–29
Exercises 14–31

Chapter 15
Introducing ASP.NET Web Applications

15.1 Web Applications 15–1
15.2 Creating a Web Application 15–2
Review 1 15–3
15.3 Web Forms 15–4
15.4 Page Layout Modes 15–4
15.5 Web Forms Controls 15–5
15.6 Saving and Running a Web
Application 15–6
Review 2 15–6
15.7 Validation Controls 15–8
Review 3 15–9
15.8 Application Code 15–10
15.9 Event Procedures 15–11
Review 4 15–11
15.10 Adding a Web Form to a Project 15–12
Review 5 15–13
Chapter Summary 15–15
Vocabulary 15–16
Visual Basic .NET 15–17
Critical Thinking 15–18
Exercises 15–20

Appendix A
Using Help

A.1 Finding a Help Topic A–1
A.2 Using Dynamic Help A–2

Indexes

Index of Programs I–1
Index I–2

Computers and Programming Languages

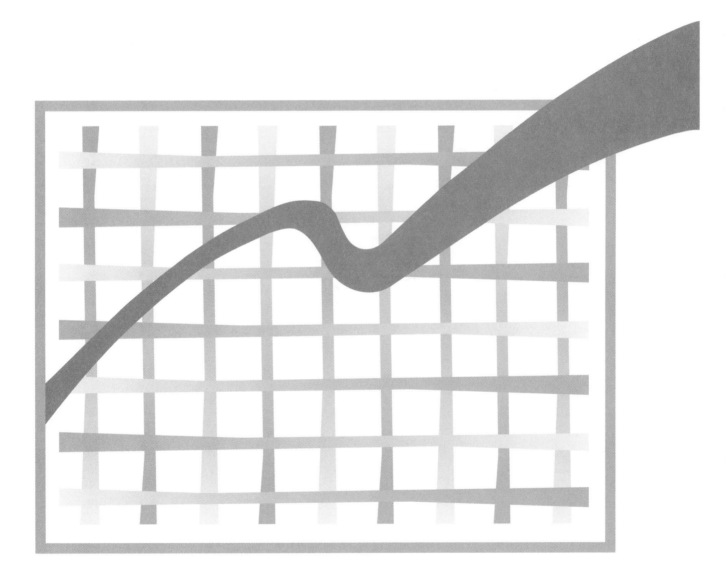

Chapter 1 Expectations

After completing this chapter you will be able to:

1. Discuss the history of computers.

2. Understand how a microcomputer works.

3. Understand the binary number system.

4. Understand how data is stored in memory.

5. List several computer programming languages.

6. Discuss the basics of a network.

7. Understand the importance of antivirus software and the illegal practice of piracy.

8. Understand the ethical responsibilities of the programmer.

$\mathbf{T}$his chapter discusses the history of computers and how computers process and store data. High-level programming languages, networks, object-oriented programming, and important social and ethical issues relating to computers are also discussed.

1.1 Mechanical Devices

Pascaline

One of the earliest mechanical calculating devices was the *Pascaline*, invented in 1642 by the French philosopher and mathematician Blaise Pascal. The Pascaline was a complicated set of gears that operated similarly to a clock. It was designed to only perform addition. Unfortunately, due to manufacturing problems, Pascal never got the device to work properly.

Blaise Pascal
1623 – 1662

The Pascaline was a mechanical calculating device invented by Blaise Pascal in 1642

Stepped Reckoner

Later in the 17th century Gottfried Wilhelm von Leibniz, a famous mathematician, invented a device that was supposed to be able to add and subtract, as well as multiply, divide, and calculate square roots. His device, the *Stepped Reckoner*, included a cylindrical wheel called the *Leibniz wheel* and a moveable carriage that was used to enter the number of digits in the multiplicand. However, because of mechanically unreliable parts, the device tended to jam and malfunction.

Gottfried Wilhelm von Leibniz
1646 – 1716

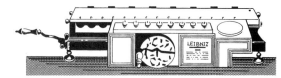

The Stepped Reckoner was another early attempt at creating a mechanical calculating device

Difference Engine

In 1822 Charles Babbage began work on the *Difference Engine*. His hope was that this device would calculate numbers to the 20ᵗʰ place and then print them at 44 digits per minute. The original purpose of this machine was to produce tables of numbers that would be used by ships' navigators. At the time, navigation tables were often highly inaccurate due to calculation errors and a number of ships were known to have been lost at sea because of these errors. Although never built, the ideas for the Difference Engine led to the design of Babbage's Analytical Engine.

Analytical Engine

The *Analytical Engine*, designed around 1833, was supposed to perform a variety of calculations by following a set of instructions, or program, stored on punched cards. During processing, the Analytical Engine was planned to store information in a memory unit that would allow it to make decisions and then carry out instructions based on those decisions. For example, when comparing two numbers, it could be programmed to determine which was larger and then follow an appropriate set of instructions. The Analytical Engine was also never built, but its design served as a model for the modern computer.

The History of Punched Cards

Punched cards were originally used to provide instructions for weaving looms. In 1810 Joseph Jacquard, a French weaver, placed punched cards in his looms so that as the cards passed through the loom in sequence, needles passed through the holes and picked up threads of the correct color or texture.

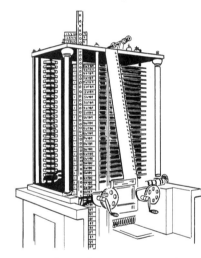

Babbage's Analytical Engine was designed as a calculating machine that used punched cards to store information

*Charles Babbage
1792 – 1871*

*Ada Byron
1815 – 1852*

Babbage's chief collaborator on the Analytical Engine was Ada Byron, Countess of Lovelace, the daughter of Lord Byron. Interested in mathematics, Lady Byron was a sponsor of the Analytical Engine and one of the first people to realize its power and significance. She also wrote of its achievements in order to gain support for it. Ada Byron is often called the first programmer because she wrote a program based on the design of the Analytical Engine.

Babbage had hoped that the Analytical Engine would be able to think. Ada Byron, however, said that the Engine could never "originate anything," meaning that she did not believe that a machine, no matter how powerful, could think. To this day her statement about computing machines remains true.

An Introduction to Programming Using Microsoft Visual Basic .NET

1.2 Electro-Mechanical Devices

By the end of the 19th century, U.S. Census officials were concerned about the time it took to tabulate the continuously increasing number of Americans. This counting was done every 10 years, as required by the Constitution. However, the Census of 1880 took nine years to compile which made the figures out of date by the time they were published.

Hollerith's tabulating machine

In response to a contest sponsored by the U.S. Census Bureau, Herman Hollerith invented a tabulating machine that used electricity rather than mechanical gears. Holes representing information to be tabulated were punched in cards, with the location of each hole representing a specific piece of information (male, female, age, etc.). The cards were then inserted into the machine and metal pins used to open and close electrical circuits. If a circuit was closed, a counter was increased by one.

Herman Hollerith
1860 – 1929

Based on the success of his tabulating machine, Herman Hollerith started the Tabulating Machine Company in 1896. In 1924, the company was taken over by International Business Machines (IBM).

Herman Hollerith's tabulating machine, invented for the Census of 1890, used electricity instead of gears to perform calculations

Hollerith's machine was immensely successful. The general count of the population, then 63 million, took only six weeks to calculate. Although the full statistical analysis took seven years, it was still an improvement over the nine years it took to compile the previous census.

Mark I

In 1944, the *Mark I* was completed by a team from International Business Machines (IBM) and Harvard University under the leadership of Howard Aiken. The Mark I used mechanical telephone relay switches to store information and accepted data on punched cards. Because it could not make decisions about the data it processed, the Mark I was not a computer but instead a highly sophisticated calculator. Nevertheless, it was impressive in size, measuring over 51 feet in length and weighing 5 tons. It also had over 750,000 parts, many of them moving mechanical parts which made the Mark I not only huge but unreliable.

Howard Aiken
1900 – 1973

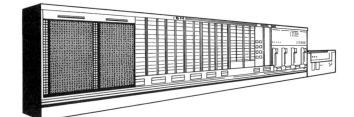

The Mark 1 was over 51 feet long and weighed over 5 tons

1.3 First Generation Computers

John Atanasoff
1903 – 1995

Clifford Berry
1918 – 1963

The first electronic computer was built between 1939 and 1942 at Iowa State University by John Atanasoff, a math and physics professor, and Clifford Berry, a graduate student. The *Atanasoff-Berry Computer* (ABC) used the binary number system of 1s and 0s that is still used in computers today. It contained hundreds of vacuum tubes and stored numbers for calculations by electronically burning holes in sheets of paper. The output of calculations was displayed on an odometer type of device.

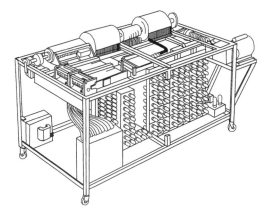

The Atanasoff-Berry Computer used the binary number system used in computers today

The patent application for the ABC was not handled properly, and it was not until almost 50 years later that Atanasoff received full credit for his invention. In 1990, he was awarded the Presidential Medal of Technology for his pioneering work. A working replica of the ABC was unveiled at the Smithsonian in Washington, D.C. on October 9, 1997.

ENIAC

In June 1943, John Mauchly and J. Presper Eckert began work on the *ENIAC* (Electronic Numerical Integration and Calculator). It was originally a secret military project which began during World War II to calculate the trajectory of artillery shells. Built at the University of Pennsylvania, it was not finished until 1946, after the war had ended. But the great effort put into the ENIAC was not wasted. In one of its first demonstrations, ENIAC was given a problem that would have taken a team of mathematicians three days to solve. It solved the problem in twenty seconds.

John Mauchly
1907 – 1980

The ENIAC was originally a secret military project

J. Presper Eckert
1919 – 1995

An Introduction to Programming Using Microsoft Visual Basic .NET

The ENIAC weighed 30 tons and occupied 1500 square feet, the same area taken up by the average three bedroom house. It contained over 17,000 vacuum tubes, which consumed huge amounts of electricity and produced a tremendous amount of heat requiring special fans to cool the room.

computer

The ABC and the ENIAC are first generation computers because they mark the beginning of the computer era. A *computer* is an electronic machine that accepts data, processes it according to instructions, and provides the results as new data. Most importantly, a computer can make simple decisions and comparisons.

1.4 The Stored Program Computer

The ABC and ENIAC required wire pulling, replugging, and switch flipping to change their instructions. A breakthrough in the architectural design of first generation computers came as a result of separate publications by Alan Turing and John von Neumann, both mathematicians with the idea of the stored program.

Alan Turing
1912 – 1954

program

In the late 30s and 40s, Alan Turing developed the idea of a "universal machine." He envisioned a computer that could perform many different tasks by simply changing a program rather than by changing electronic components. A *program* is a list of instructions written in a special language that the computer understands.

CPU

In 1945, John von Neumann presented his idea of the stored program concept. The stored program computer would store computer instructions in a CPU (Central Processing Unit). The CPU consisted of different elements used to control all the functions of the computer electronically so that it would not be necessary to flip switches or pull wires to change instructions.

John
von Neumann
1903 – 1957

EDVAC
EDSAC

machine language

Together with Mauchly and Eckert, von Neumann designed and built the *EDVAC* (Electronic Discrete Variable Automatic Computer) and the *EDSAC* (Electronic Delay Storage Automatic Computer). These computers were designed to solve many different problems by simply entering new instructions that were stored on paper tape. The instructions were in *machine language*, which consists of 0s and 1s to represent the status of a switch (0 for off and 1 for on).

UNIVAC
C-10

The third computer to employ the stored program concept was the *UNIVAC* (UNIVersal Automatic Computer) built by Mauchly and Eckert. With the UNIVAC came the first computer language called *C-10*, which was developed by Betty Holberton. Holberton also designed the first computer keyboard and numeric keypad in an effort to make the computer more user-friendly. The first UNIVAC was sold to the U.S. Census Bureau in 1951.

Francis "Betty"
Holberton
1917 – 2001

These first generation computers continued to use many vacuum tubes which made them large and expensive. They were so expensive to purchase and run that only the largest corporations and the U.S. government could afford them. Their ability to perform up to 1,000 calculations per second, however, made them popular.

1.5 Second Generation Computers

In 1947, William Shockley, John Bardeen, and Walter Brittain of Bell Laboratories invented the *transistor*. One small transistor replaced many vacuum tubes. The transistor was much smaller than vacuum tubes, less expensive, and increased calculating speeds to up to 10,000 calculations per second:

transistor

*John Bardeen,
William Shockley,
and Walter Brittain*

*Transistors made computers smaller, less expensive,
and more reliable than those with vacuum tubes*

Model 650

In the early 1960s, IBM introduced the first medium-sized computer named the *Model 650*. It was expensive, but much smaller than first generation computers and still capable of handling the flood of paperwork produced by many government agencies and businesses. Such organizations provided a ready market for the 650, making it popular in spite of its cost.

read, write

Second generation computers also saw a change in the way data was stored. Punched cards were replaced by magnetic tape and high speed reel-to-reel tape machines. Using magnetic tape gave computers the ability to *read* (access) and *write* (store) data quickly and reliably.

1.6 High-Level Programming Languages

Second generation computers had more capabilities than first generation computers and were more widely used by businesses. This led to the need for *high-level programming languages* that had English-like instructions and were easier to use than machine language. In 1957, John Backus and a team of researchers completed *Fortran*, a high-level programming language with intuitive commands such as READ and WRITE.

One of the most widely used high-level programming languages has been COBOL, designed by Grace Murray Hopper, a Commodore in the Navy at the time. *COBOL* (COmmon Business Oriented Language) was first developed by the United States Department of Defense (DOD) in 1959 to provide a common language for use on all computers. In the late 1970s, the DOD also developed Ada, named after the first programmer, Ada Byron. *Ada* is a high-level programming language that supports real-time applications. Large systems that rely on real-time processing, such as those used in the banking industry, often use Ada.

In the 1960s, John Kemeny and Thomas Kurtz developed BASIC at Dartmouth University. *BASIC* (Beginner's All-Purpose Symbolic Instruction Code) was widely used to teach programming to students during the 1970s. In the mid 1970s, *C* was developed by Dennis Ritchie at Bell Laboratories. C has been used to write a variety of applications.

*Grace Murray Hopper
1906 – 1992*

Rear Admiral Dr. Grace Murray Hopper is also known for using the term "debug" for a programming error. A program running on the Mark II had to be "debugged" when a moth flew into the computer's circuitry causing an electrical short.

In the 1980s, object-oriented programming (OOP) evolved out of the need to better develop complex programs in a systematic, organized approach. The OOP approach allows programmers to create modules that can be used over and over again in a variety of programs. These modules contain code called classes, which group related data and actions. Properly designed classes encapsulate data to hide the implementation details, are versatile enough to be extended through inheritance, and give the programmer options through polymorphism. Object-oriented languages include C++ and Java. Visual Basic .NET, released in 2002, has many features for easily developing an object-oriented program.

1.7 Third Generation Computers

The replacement of transistors by integrated circuits (ICs) began the third generation of computers. In 1961, Jack Kilby and Robert Noyce, working independently, developed the IC, also called a *chip*. One IC could replace hundreds of transistors, giving computers tremendous speed to process information at a rate of millions of calculations per second.

ICs are silicon wafers with intricate circuits etched into their surfaces and then coated with a metallic oxide that fills in the etched circuit patterns. This enables the chips to conduct electricity along the many paths of their circuits. The silicon wafers are then housed in special plastic cases that have metal pins. The pins allow the chips to be plugged into circuit boards that have wiring printed on them.

A typical chip is about 1 cm wide by 2.5 cm long

In 1964, the IBM *System 360* was one of the first computers to use integrated circuits and was so popular with businesses that IBM had difficulty keeping up with the demand. Computers had come down in size and price to such a point that smaller organizations such as universities and hospitals could now afford them.

Robert Noyce
1927 – 1990

Noyce developed the integrated circuit while working for Fairchild Semiconductor. In 1968, he left Fairchild to form the company now known as Intel Corporation.

Jack S. Kilby
1923 –

Kilby, working for Texas Instruments, developed the first integrated circuit. To demonstrate this new technology, he invented the first electronic hand-held calculator. It was small enough to fit in a coat pocket, yet as powerful as the large desktop models of the time.

1.8 Mainframes

A *mainframe* is a large computer system that is usually used for multi-user applications. They are used by large corporations, banks, government agencies, and universities. Mainframes can calculate a large payroll, keep the records for a bank, handle the reservations for an airline, or store student information for a university—tasks that require the storage and processing of huge amounts of information. The IBM System 360 was one of the first mainframes available.

Mainframe computers are large and are usually set up in their own rooms

Most people using mainframes communicate with them using *terminals*. A terminal consists of a keyboard for data input, and a monitor for viewing output. The terminal is connected to the computer, which may be located on a different floor or a building a few blocks away. Some mainframes have hundreds of terminals attached.

1.9 Fourth Generation Computers

microprocessor

In 1970, Marcian Hoff, an engineer at Intel Corporation, invented the *microprocessor*, an entire CPU on a single chip. The replacement of several larger components by one microprocessor made possible the fourth generation of computers.

The small microprocessor made it possible to build a computer called a *microcomputer* or *personal computer* that fits on a desktop. The first of these was the *Altair* built in 1975. In 1976, Stephen Wozniak and Steven Jobs designed and built the first Apple computer. The Apple Macintosh set new standards for ease of computer use with its graphical user interface. In 1981, IBM introduced the IBM–PC. The computer was an instant success because of the availability of spreadsheet, accounting, and word processor software.

Advances in technology made personal computers inexpensive and therefore available to many people. Because of these advances almost anyone could own a machine that had more computing power and was faster and more reliable than either the ENIAC or UNIVAC. As a comparison, if the cost of a sports car had dropped as quickly as that of a computer, a new Porsche would now cost about one dollar.

1.10 The Personal Computer

The physical components of the personal computer, such as the monitor and base unit, are called *hardware*:

Marcian Hoff
1937 –

Stephen Wozniak
1950 –

Steve Jobs
1955 –

- The personal computer accepts data from *input devices*. Examples of input devices include the keyboard, mouse, CD/DVD drive, and diskette drive.

- A personal computer becomes much more versatile when other input and output devices such as printers and scanners are added. Such devices are sometimes called *peripheral devices*. A *scanner* is an input device that uses a laser to create a digital image from artwork such as photos and drawings. The digitized image can then be incorporated into a document.

An Introduction to Programming Using Microsoft Visual Basic .NET

- *Output devices* display or store processed data. Monitors and printers are the most common visual output devices.

The *base unit* contains many storage devices such as a diskette drive, a CD/DVD drive, and a hard disk drive. The diskette and CD/DVD drives are accessible from outside the base unit, and the hard disk is completely contained inside the base unit.

The base unit also contains the *motherboard*, which is the main circuit board that contains the components:

CPU

ALU

nanoseconds

clock rate
megahertz, gigahertz

- The *CPU* (Central Processing Unit) processes data and controls the flow of data between the computer's other units. Within the CPU is the *ALU* (Arithmetic Logic Unit), which can perform arithmetic and logic operations. It can also make comparisons, which is the basis of the computer's decision-making power. The ALU is so fast that the time needed to carry out a single addition is measured in *nanoseconds* (billionths of a second). The speed at which a CPU can execute instructions is determined by the computer's *clock rate*. The clock rate is measured in *megahertz* (million of cycles per second) or *gigahertz* (billion of cycles per second) and can range from 450 MHz to 2.4 GHz.

memory, ROM

RAM

storage media

- The personal computer's *memory* stores data electronically. *ROM* (Read Only Memory) contains the most basic operating instructions for the computer. The data in ROM is a permanent part of the computer and cannot be changed. *RAM* (Random Access Memory) is memory where data and instructions are stored temporarily. Data stored in RAM can be written to any type of *storage media*, such as a floppy diskette, a hard disk, a zip disk, or a CD-R.

SRAM
cache

- *SRAM* (Static Random Access Memory) is high-speed memory referred to as *cache* (pronounced "cash"). This memory is used to store frequently used data so that it can be quickly retrieved by an application.

bus
data bus
address bus

control bus

- A *bus* is a set of circuits that connect the CPU to other components. The *data bus* transfers data between the CPU, memory, and other hardware devices on the motherboard. The *address bus* carries memory addresses that indicate where the data is located and where the data should go. A *control bus* carries control signals.

All data flows through the CPU:

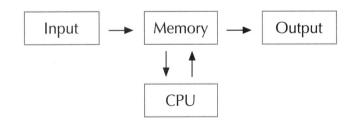

Because one of the tasks of the CPU is to control the order in which tasks are completed, it is often referred to as the "brain" of the computer. However, this comparison with the human brain has an important flaw. The CPU only executes tasks according to the instructions it has been given; it cannot think for itself.

software
operating system software

applications software

Personal computers also contain *software* that instructs the computer what to do. *Operating system software* is run automatically when the computer is turned on and enables the user to communicate with the computer by using input devices such as the mouse and keyboard. *Applications software* is written by programmers to perform a specific task, such as a word processor. Software is also called a program or an application.

1.11 Networks

A *network* is a combination of software and hardware that work together to allow computers to exchange data and to share software and devices, such as printers. Networks are widely used by businesses, universities, and other organizations because a network:

- allows users to reliably share and exchange data

- can reduce costs by sharing devices such as printers

- can be set up to allow users access to only specific files

- simplifies the process of creating backup copies of files

- allows users to communicate with e-mail

Networks are classified by their size, architecture, and topology. One common size classification is *LAN* (Local-Area Network), which is a network used to connect devices within a small area such as a building or a campus. The *WAN* (Wide-Area Network) is used to connect computers over large geographical distances. A WAN can be one widespread network or it can be a number of LANs linked together.

The computers and other devices in a LAN contain a circuit board called a *network interface card*:

network interface card

A cable plugs into the network interface card to connect one device to another to form the LAN.

Network architecture includes the type of computers on the network and determines how network resources are handled. Two main types of network architecture are called client/server and peer-to-peer. A *client/server network* consists of a group of computers, called *clients*, connected to a server. A *server* is a powerful computer used to manage network functions such as communications and data sharing. A *peer-to-peer network* does not have a server. Each computer on the network is considered equal in terms of responsibilities and resource sharing.

Topology is the logical arrangement of the nodes on a network. A *node* is a device, such as a computer or printer, that is connected to the network and is capable of communicating with other network devices.

network architecture

client/server

peer-to-peer

topology

Wireless Networks

Wireless networks do not use cables. Instead they use high frequency radio waves or infrared signals to transmit data. WLANs (wireless local-area networks) are becoming more common as the cost decreases and performance improves.

Transmission Media

Computers must be connected in order to transmit data between the nodes. The type of connection used is called the *transmission media*.

Types of transmission media include twisted-pair wiring, coaxial cable, and fiber optic cable.

The amount of data and the speed at which the data can travel over the transmission media is called its *bandwidth* and is measured in bits per second (bps). Each type of transmission media has different length or range restrictions, data transmission rates, and costs.

---

bus topology   A popular LAN topology is the *bus topology* where each node is attached to a single shared communication cable that is often referred to as the bus:

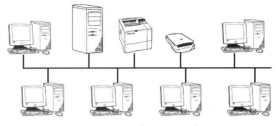

LAN using a bus topology

star topology, hub   In a *star topology*, each node is attached to a *hub*, which is a device that joins communication lines at a central location on the network:

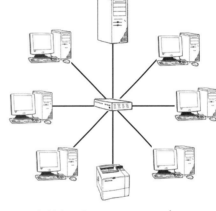

LAN using a star topology

A *ring topology* connects each node to form a closed loop. Data travels in one direction and is sent from node to node, with each node examining the data and either accepting it or passing it on to the next node in the ring. A LAN with a ring topology can usually cover a greater distance than a bus or star topology:

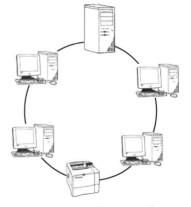

LAN using a ring topology

It is important to note that topology refers to the logical connection between the nodes and not the physical setup. For example, a ring topology may be set up in an arrangement other than a circle as long as the nodes form a closed loop.

Ethernet

One widely used LAN configuration, or protocol, is Ethernet, which was developed by Bob Metcalfe in 1976. This protocol significantly contributed to the growth of LANs in the late 1970s and 1980s. Ethernet uses a bus or star topology and connects the network devices by twisted-pair wiring, coaxial cable, or fiber optic cable. A newer version of Ethernet is Fast Ethernet, which operates at 100 Mbps and Gigabit Ethernet which operates at 1 Gbps (Gigabit per second).

Baseband and Broadband Technology

Most LANs use baseband technology which means the transmission media carries one signal at a time. Broadband technology allows for data transmission of more than one signal at a time. Broadband technology is found in WANs.

1.12   Number Systems

binary number system

The electrical circuits on an IC have one of two states, off or on. Therefore, the *binary number system* (base 2), which uses only two digits (0 and 1), was adopted for use in computers. To represent numbers and letters, a code was developed with eight binary digits grouped together to represent a single number or letter. Each 0 or 1 in the binary code is called a *bit* (BInary digiT) and an 8-bit unit is called a *byte*.

bit, byte

base 10

Our most familiar number system is the decimal, or *base 10*, system. It uses ten digits: 0 through 9. Each place represents a power of ten, with the first place to the left of the decimal point representing 10^0, the next place representing 10^1, the next 10^2, and so on (remember that any number raised to the zero power is 1). In the decimal number 485, the 4 represents 4×10^2, the 8 represents 8×10^1, and the 5 represents 5×10^0. The number 485 represents the sum $4 \times 100 + 8 \times 10 + 5 \times 1$ (400 + 80 + 5) as shown below:

Decimal Number	Base 10 Equivalent
485	$4 \times 10^2 + 8 \times 10^1 + 5 \times 10^0 = 400 + 80 + 5$

base 2

The binary, or *base 2*, system works identically except that each place represents a power of two instead of a power of ten. For example, the binary number 101 represents the sum $1 \times 2^2 + 0 \times 2^1 + 1 \times 2^0$ or 5 in base ten. Some decimal numbers and their binary equivalents are shown below:

Decimal Number	Binary Number	Base 2 Equivalent		
0	0	$= 0 \times 2^1 + 0 \times 2^0$	$= 0 \times 2 + 0 \times 1$	$= 0 + 0$
1	1	$= 0 \times 2^1 + 1 \times 2^0$	$= 0 \times 2 + 1 \times 1$	$= 0 + 1$
2	10	$= 1 \times 2^1 + 0 \times 2^0$	$= 1 \times 2 + 0 \times 1$	$= 2 + 0$
3	11	$= 1 \times 2^1 + 1 \times 2^0$	$= 1 \times 2 + 1 \times 1$	$= 2 + 1$
4	100	$= 1 \times 2^2 + 0 \times 2^1 + 0 \times 2^0$	$= 1 \times 4 + 0 \times 2 + 0 \times 1$	$= 4 + 0 + 0$

base 16

The hexadecimal system is used to represent groups of four binary digits. The *hexadecimal*, or *base 16*, system is based on 16 digits: 0 through 9, and the letters A through F representing 10 through 15 respectively. Each place represents a power of sixteen. For example, the hexadecimal number 1F represents the sum $1 \times 16^1 + 15 \times 16^0$. Some decimal numbers and their hexadecimal equivalents are shown below:

Decimal Number	Binary Number	Hexadecimal Number	Base 16 Equivalent		
0	0000 0000	0	$= 0 \times 16^0$	$= 0 \times 1$	$= 0$
10	0000 1010	A	$= 10 \times 16^0$	$= 10 \times 1$	$= 10$
15	0000 1111	F	$= 15 \times 16^0$	$= 15 \times 1$	$= 15$
20	0001 0100	14	$= 1 \times 16^1 + 4 \times 16^0$	$= 1 \times 16 + 4 \times 1$	$= 16 + 4$
25	0001 1001	19	$= 1 \times 16^1 + 9 \times 16^0$	$= 1 \times 16 + 9 \times 1$	$= 16 + 9$
30	0001 1110	1E	$= 1 \times 16^1 + 14 \times 16^0$	$= 1 \times 16 + 14 \times 1$	$= 16 + 14$

For clarity, a non-base 10 number should have the base subscripted after the number. For example, to show the difference between 100 in base 10 and 100 in base 2 (which represents 4), the base 2 number should be written as 100_2.

An Introduction to Programming Using Microsoft Visual Basic .NET

Unicode

Every letter of an alphabet (Latin, Japanese, Cherokee, and so on) and symbols of every culture (=, @, ½, and so on) have been given a representation in a digital code called Unicode. *Unicode* uses a set of sixteen 1s and 0s to form a 16-bit binary code for each symbol. For example, the uppercase letter V is Unicode 00000000 01010110, which can be thought of as the base 10 number 86 (86_{10}). Lowercase v has a separate code of 00000000 01110110, or 11810. Refer to Chapter 6 for additional Unicode symbols.

1.13   Storing Data in Memory

Computer memory, file sizes, and storage device capacities are measured in bytes. For example, a computer might have 128MB of RAM. In computers and electronics *MB* stands for *megabytes* where mega represents 2^{20} or 1,048,576 bytes and *GB* stands for *gigabytes*, which is 2^{30} or 1,073,741,820 bytes. Simple files, such as a text document, can be measured *kilobytes*, for example 256K. The *K* comes from the word *kilo* and represents 2^{10} or 1,024. Therefore, a 64K file uses 65,536 bytes (64×2^{10}) of storage.

> ### Storage Media
>
> The capacity of storage media varies. For example, a diskette has a storage capacity of 1.44 MB, a CD has a storage capacity of at least 650 MB, and a DVD has a storage capacity of over 4 GB.

Data stored in memory is referred to by an address. An *address* is a unique binary representation of a location in memory. Therefore, data can be stored, accessed, and retrieved from memory by its address. For data to be addressable in memory, it must usually be at least one byte in length. For example, to store JIM in memory each character is converted to Unicode and stored in two bytes of memory with each memory location designated by its address:

	J	I	M
binary code	00000000 01001010	00000000 01001001	00000000 01001101
memory address	01	10	11

Because JIM is a character string, it will probably be stored in adjacent memory addresses.

word

Bits grouped in units of 16 to 64 (2 to 8 bytes) are called *words*. Data stored in a word is also located by an address. The size of a word depends on the computer system.

The binary representation of an integer number is usually stored in four bytes of memory. Because an integer is stored in four bytes, the range of integers that can be stored is –2,147,483,648 to 2,147,483,647. An *overflow error* occurs when the number of bits that are needed to represent the integer is greater than the size of four bytes.

overflow error

real numbers

Real numbers, also called *floating point numbers*, are numbers that contain decimal points. The binary representation of a real number is usually 4 to 8 bytes of memory. The binary number 111.10 is equivalent to the real decimal number 7.5 and is stored in memory as the binary number 0.11110×2^3. In this form, the bits that represent the mantissa (fractional part) are stored in one section of a word and the exponent, in this example 3 (11_2), is stored in another section of the word:

mantissa
exponent

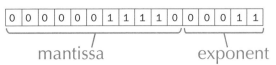

The overflow problem discussed for integers can also occur in real numbers if the part of the word storing the exponent is not large enough. A *roundoff error* occurs when there are not enough bits to hold the mantissa.

1.14 The Social and Ethical Implications of Computers

information age

The society in which we live has been so profoundly affected by computers that historians refer to the present as the *information age*. This is due to the computer's ability to store and manipulate large amounts of information (data). Because of computers, we are evolving out of an industrial and into an information society. Such fundamental societal changes cause disruptions which must be planned for. For this reason it is crucial that we consider both the social and ethical implications of our increasing dependence on computers.

netiquette

By ethical implications we mean asking what are the morally right and wrong ways to use computers. For example, when working on a network, users should follow a certain etiquette referred to as *netiquette*:

- Do not attempt to access the account of another user without authorization.

- Do not share your password, and change it periodically.

- Use appropriate subject matter and language, and be considerate of other people's beliefs and opinions.

privacy

An ethical issue associated with computers is the invasion of privacy. Every time you use a credit card, make a phone call, withdraw money, reserve a flight, or register at school a computer records the transaction. These records can be used to learn a great deal about you—where you have been, when you were there, and how much money you spent. Should this information be available to everyone? To protect both the privacy of an individual and the accuracy of data stored about individuals, a number of laws have been passed.

The **Fair Credit Reporting Act of 1970** addresses data collection by credit, insurance, and employment agencies. The act gives individuals the right to see information maintained about them. If a person is denied credit they are allowed to see the files used to make the credit determination. If any of the information is incorrect, the person has the right to have it changed. The act also restricts who may access credit files to only those with a court order or the written permission of the individual whose credit is being checked.

The **Privacy Act of 1974** restricts the way in which personal data can be used by federal agencies. Individuals must be permitted access to information stored about them and may correct any information that is incorrect. Agencies must insure both the security and confidentiality of any sensitive information. Although this law applies only to federal agencies, many states have adopted similar laws.

The **Financial Privacy Act of 1978** requires that a government authority have a subpoena, summons, or search warrant to access an individual's financial records. When such records are released, the financial institution must notify the individual of who has had access to them.

The **Electronic Communications Privacy Act of 1986** (ECPA) makes it a crime to access electronic data without authorization. It also prohibits unauthorized release of such data.

The **Electronic Freedom of Information Act of 1996** requires federal government agencies to make certain agency information available for public inspection and is designed to improve public access to agency records.

The **Safety and Freedom through Encryption Act of 1999** (SAFE) gives Americans the freedom to use any type of encryption to protect their confidential information. It also prohibits the government from monitoring people's communications without their knowledge or consent.

1.15   Protecting Computer Software and Data

piracy

Because computer software can be copied electronically, it is easy to duplicate. Such duplication is usually illegal because the company producing the software is not paid for the copy. The illegal copying of software is called *piracy*. Developing, testing, marketing, and supporting software is an expensive process. If the software developer is then denied rightful compensation, the future development of all software is jeopardized.

Software companies are increasingly vigilant in detecting and prosecuting those who illegally copy their software. Persons found guilty of using illegally copied software can be fined, and their reputation damaged. Therefore, when using software it is important to use only legally acquired copies, and to not make illegal copies for others.

Another problem that is growing as computer use increases is the willful interference with or destruction of computer data. Because computers can transfer and erase data at high speeds, it makes them especially vulnerable to acts of vandalism. These acts are usually illegal and can cause very serious and expensive damage. The Electronic Communications Privacy Act of 1986 specifically makes it a federal offense to access electronic data without authorization.

virus

A *virus* is a program that is designed to reproduce itself by copying itself into other programs stored on a computer without the user's knowledge. Viruses have varying effects, such as displaying annoying messages, causing programs to run incorrectly, and erasing the contents of the hard disk. Precautions need to be taken to avoid viruses:

- Install antivirus software. Antivirus software will detect many types of viruses by scanning incoming e-mail messages before they are opened. If a virus is detected, the software will display a warning and try to remove the virus.

- Update the antivirus software frequently. New viruses are created daily and new virus definitions must be downloaded on a regular basis in order for the antivirus software to be effective.

- Many computer viruses have been spread as e-mail attachments. Therefore, always save an attachment file and then virus-check the file before opening it. This precaution should be taken for all messages from known and unknown sources, since many viruses target address books and fool users into thinking the e-mail is from someone familiar.

- Virus-check a diskette before copying or opening files stored on the diskette.

Contaminated diskettes are one way that viruses are spread from computer to computer

1.16 The Ethical Responsibilities of the Programmer

It is extremely difficult, if not impossible, for a computer programmer to guarantee that a program will *always* operate properly. The programs used to control complicated devices contain millions of instructions, and as programs grow longer the likelihood of errors increases. A special cause for concern is the increased use of computers to control potentially dangerous devices such as aircraft, nuclear reactors, or sensitive medical equipment. This places a strong ethical burden on the programmer to insure, as best as he or she can, the reliability of the computer software.

As capable as computers have proven to be, we must be cautious when allowing them to replace human beings in areas where judgement is crucial. As intelligent beings, we can often detect that something out of the ordinary has occurred which has not been previously anticipated and then take appropriate actions. Computers will only do what they have been programmed to do, even if it is to perform a dangerous act.

Chapter Summary

The earliest computing devices were mechanical and were unreliable. The advent of electricity brought about electromechanical machines, and later first generation computers that used vacuum tubes. The architectural design of computers changed with the idea of a machine that could perform many different tasks by simply changing its program. With the development of the transistor came second generation computers that were smaller and faster. High-level programming languages were developed so that more people could write programs using English-like instructions. Third generation computers used integrated circuits. Fourth

An Introduction to Programming Using Microsoft Visual Basic .NET

generation computers include an entire CPU on a single chip. In the 1980s, object-oriented programming (OOP) evolved out of the need to better develop complex programs in a systematic, organized approach.

The physical components of the personal computer are called hardware. The personal computer accepts data from input devices, and then output devices display or store processed data. Peripheral devices, such as printers and scanners, enhance the versatility of personal computers.

The base unit of a personal computer contains many components including the CPU, ROM, RAM, SRAM, a motherboard, the data bus, the address bus, and the control bus. A CPU directs the processing of information throughout the computer. Within the CPU is the ALU. The speed at which a CPU can execute instructions is determined by the computer's clock rate, measured in megahertz (million of cycles per second). Since RAM storage is temporary, data is written to storage media, such as a floppy diskette, hard disk, zip disk, or CD-R.

Personal computers contain software that instructs the computer what to do. Operating system software is run automatically when the computer is turned on and enables the user to communicate with the computer. Applications software is written to perform specific tasks.

A network is a combination of software and hardware that allow computers to exchange data and to share software and other devices such as printers. Common network size classifications are LAN (Local-Area Network) and WAN (Wide-Area Network). LAN topologies include bus, star, and ring. Network architecture includes the type of computers on the network and determines how network resources are handled. Two main types of network architecture are client/server and peer-to-peer.

The electrical circuits of an IC have one of two states, off or on. Therefore, the binary number system is used to represent the two states: 0 for off and 1 for on. Each 0 or 1 in binary code is called a bit and a 8-bit unit is called a byte. Our most familiar number system is the decimal or base 10 system. The binary number is a base 2 system and the hexadecimal system is base 16.

Every letter of an alphabet and every symbol of a culture have been given a representation in a digital code called Unicode. Unicode uses a set of sixteen 1s and 0s to form a 16-bit binary code for each symbol.

Computer memory, file sizes, and storage device capacities are measured in bytes. In computers and electronics MB stands for megabytes, GB stands for gigabtyes, and K stands for kilobytes.

The binary representation of an integer number is usually stored in four bytes of memory. Real numbers are numbers that contain decimal points and the binary representation of a real number is usually stored in 4 to 8 bytes of memory.

The society in which we live has been so profoundly affected by computers that historians refer to the present as the information age. The increasing dependence on computers requires examining the social implications of our increasing dependence on computers. For example, when working on a network users should follow a certain etiquette referred to as netiquette. Ethical issues related to computer use are privacy, piracy, viruses, and the reliability of software.

Ada A high-level programming language that supports real-time applications.

Address A unique binary representation of a location in memory.

Address bus Carries memory addresses that indicate where the data is located and where the data should go.

ALU (Arithmetic Logic Unit) The part of the CPU that handles arithmetic and logic operations.

Applications software Programs written to perform specific tasks.

Base unit Unit that contains the motherboard, diskette drive, and hard disk drive.

BASIC A high-level programming language that was developed by John Kemeny and Thomas Kurtz.

Binary number system Number system used by modern computers—uses only digits 0 and 1. Also called Base 2.

Bit (BInary digiT) A single 0 or 1 in binary code.

Bus A set of circuits that connect the CPU to other components.

Bus topology A LAN topology where each node of a network is connected to a single shared communication cable called a bus.

Byte A group of 8 bits.

C A high-level programming language that was developed by Dennis Ritchie.

Cache memory High-speed memory used to store frequently used data so that it can be quickly retrieved by an application. See also SRAM.

Client/Server network A group of computers, called clients, connected to a server.

Clock rate The speed at which a CPU can execute instructions, measured in megahertz.

COBOL A high-level programming language that was designed by Grace Murray Hopper.

Computer An electronic machine that accepts data, processes it according to instructions, and provides the results as new data.

Control bus Carries control signals.

CPU (Central Processing Unit) A component inside the base unit that processes data and controls the flow of data between the computer's other units.

Data bus Transfers data between the CPU, memory, and other hardware devices on the motherboard.

Fortran A high-level programming language that was developed by John Backus.

GB (gigabyte) 1,073,741,820 bytes.

Gigahertz One billion cycles per second.

Hardware The physical components of the personal computer.

Hexadecimal system Number system based on 16 digits. Also called base 16.

High-level programming language A programming language that uses English-like instructions.

Hub A device that joins communication lines at a central location on the network.

Information age A term used by historians to refer to the present.

Input device Used by the computer to accept data.

IC (Integrated Circuit) A silicon wafer with intricate circuits etched into its surface and then coated with a metallic oxide that fills in the etched circuit patterns. Also called a chip.

K (kilobyte) 1,024 bytes.

LAN (Local Area Network) A network that connects devices within a small area.

Machine language Instructions in binary code (0s and 1s).

Mainframe Computer system that is usually used for multi-user applications.

MB (megabyte) 1,048,576 bytes.

Megahertz One million cycles per second.

Memory A component on the motherboard that stores data electronically.

Microcomputer A computer that fits on a desktop and uses a microprocessor. Also called a personal computer.

Microprocessor An entire CPU on a single chip.

Motherboard The main circuit board inside the base unit.

Nanosecond One billionth of a second.

Netiquette Network etiquette.

Network A combination of software and hardware that allows computers to exchange data and to share applications software and devices.

Network architecture Includes the type of computers on the network and determines how network resources are handled.

Network interface card A circuit board in the base unit of a networked computer.

Node A device, such as a computer or printer that is connected to the network and is capable of communicating with other network devices.

Operating system software Software that allows the user to communicate with the computer.

Output devices Display or store processed data.

Overflow error An error that occurs when the number of bits that are needed to represent the integer is greater than four bytes.

Personal computer A computer that fits on a desktop and uses a microprocessor.

Peer-to-Peer network A group of computers that share responsibilities and resources equally without a server.

Peripheral device A device attached to a personal computer.

Piracy The illegal copying of software.

Program List of instructions written in a special language that the computer understands.

RAM (Random Access Memory) Temporary memory where data and instruction can be stored.

Read Accessing data from a storage medium.

Real numbers Numbers that contain decimal points. Also called floating point numbers.

Ring topology A LAN topology where each node of a network is connected to form a closed loop.

ROM (Read Only Memory) Data that is a permanent part of the computer and cannot be changed.

Roundoff error An error that occurs when there are not enough bits to hold the mantissa.

Scanner An input device that uses a laser to create a digital image from artwork.

Server A powerful computer used to manage network functions such as communications and data sharing.

Software Instructions that tell the computer what to do.

SRAM (Static Random Access Memory) High-speed memory referred to as cache.

Star topology A LAN topology where each node of a network is connected to a hub, which is a device that joins communication lines at a central location on the network.

Storage media Used to store data.

Terminal A keyboard and monitor used to communicate with a mainframe.

Topology The logical arrangement of the nodes on a network.

Transistor An electronic device that replaced the vacuum tube making computers smaller and less expensive and increasing calculating speeds.

Unicode A digital code that uses a set of sixteen 1s and 0s to form a 16-bit binary code for each symbol.

Virus A program designed to reproduce itself by copying itself into other programs stored on a computer without the user's knowledge.

Word Bits grouped in units of 16 to 64.

Write Storing data on a storage medium.

WAN (Wide Area Network) A network that connects computers over large geographical distances.

Sections 1.1 — 1.9

1. Describe the Pascaline and explain what mathematical operation it was designed to perform.

2. a) What mathematical operations was the Stepped Reckoner supposed to perform?
   b) Why did it tend to malfunction?

3. What did Ada Byron mean when she said that the Analytical Engine could never "originate anything"?

4. a) For what purpose did Herman Hollerith invent his tabulating machine?
   b) What were punched cards used for in the tabulating machine?

5. Why wasn't the Mark 1 considered a computer?

6. What number system did the Atanasoff-Berry Computer use?

7. For what purpose was the ENIAC originally designed?

8. What is a computer?

9. In what way did Alan Turing and John von Neumann improve upon the design of the ENIAC?

10. a) What is a program?
    b) What is machine language?
    c) List the first three computers designed to use a stored program.

11. How did the invention of the transistor affect the development of computers?

12. How did the use of magnetic tape improve data storage?

13. a) What is a high-level programming language?
    b) Who designed COBOL?
    c) List three high-level programming languages.
    d) Why was object-oriented programming developed?
    e) List two object-oriented programming languages.

14. Explain what ICs are and why they have been important in the development of computers.

15. a) What is a mainframe?
    b) What is the usual way for a person to communicate with a mainframe?

16. Why was the invention of the microprocessor important to the development of computers?

17. List some of the advantages of a microcomputer compared with the ENIAC or UNIVAC.

Sections 1.10 — 1.16

18. a) What is hardware?
    b) What are input and output devices used for?
    c) What is a peripheral device?

19. List and describe five components found on the motherboard.

20. List three examples of storage media.

21. Describe the flow of data between the components of a computer.

22. In what way was the design of Babbage's Analytical Engine similar to the modern computer?

23. a) Describe one difference between operating system software and applications software.
    b) What is another name for software?

24. What is a network?

25. List four benefits of using a network.

26. a) What are the two most common size classifications for networks?
    b) What size classification is used to connect devices over large geographical distances?

27. a) What does network architecture include?
    b) What is a client?
    c) What is a server?

28. a) What is topology?
    b) What is a node?
    c) What topology uses a hub?
    d) What topology connects each node to form a closed loop?

29. Why was the binary number system adopted for use in computers?

30. Explain what a bit and a byte are.

31. a) What is the decimal equivalent of 111_2?
    b) What is the decimal equivalent of $2C_{16}$?

32. What is Unicode?

33. a) How many bytes of data can 32 MB of RAM store?
    b) How many bytes of data can a 3 GB hard drive store?

34. What are bits grouped in units of 16 to 64 called?

35. When would an overflow error occur?

36. What are real numbers?

37. When would a roundoff error occur?

38. What is meant by the information age?

39. List two examples of netiquette.

40. How are computers used to invade privacy?

41. List and then explain three laws passed to protect an individual's privacy.

42. What is piracy?

43. List three precautions that can be taken to avoid getting a virus.

44. a) What ethical responsibilities does a programmer have when writing a program that will impact human lives?
    b) Can the programmer absolutely guarantee that a program will operate properly? Why?

The exercises in this chapter require written information. If a word processor is used, be sure to use an appropriate header, footer, and file name.

Exercise 1

Expand on the information presented in this chapter by researching one of the following topics:

- The History of Computers
- Individuals in the Computer Industry
- The History of a Computer Company
- Current Mainframe Computers

a) Use the Internet, magazines, and books to find at least three sources of information.

b) Write a two page report that summarizes your research.

c) On a separate sheet, titled References, cite each source.

Exercise 2

In this exercise you will research your classroom computer and network by answering a series of questions.

a) What type of input devices are attached to your computer?

b) What peripheral devices are attached to your network?

c) What visual output device is attached to your computer?

d) List the storage media that can be used with your computer.

e) How much RAM does your computer have?

f) What is the computer's clock rate?

g) List one application that is available on your computer.

h) Is your computer network a LAN or a WAN?

i) What type of topology is used in your computer network?

j) What network operating system is used?

k) What kind of Internet connection does your network use?

Exercise 3

In this exercise you will research the cost of purchasing a personal computer.

a) Use the Internet, magazines, and newspapers to find advertisements for three similar personal computers.

b) Summarize the features of the three computer systems. Along with the technical specifications, be sure to note warranty and service information.

c) Write a one paragraph conclusion that explains what computer system would be the best buy.

Exercise 4

In this exercise you will research the computer courses in your school to find out what software and what programming languages are taught in what courses.

    a) Obtain a school calendar, talk to teachers, or use the school's web site to find course information.

    b) List all the computer courses available in the school.

    c) For each course listed in part (b), list what software or what programming language is taught in the course.

    d) For each course listed in part (b), list any object-oriented programming languages that are taught.

Exercise 5

In this exercise you will research a social or ethical issue associated with computer use, such as privacy, piracy, or viruses, to find real-life examples of how these issues have impacted companies or individuals.

    a) Use the Internet, magazines, and books to find at least three sources of information.

    b) Write a two page report that summarizes your research.

    c) On a separate sheet, titled References, cite each source.

An Introduction to Programming Using Microsoft Visual Basic .NET

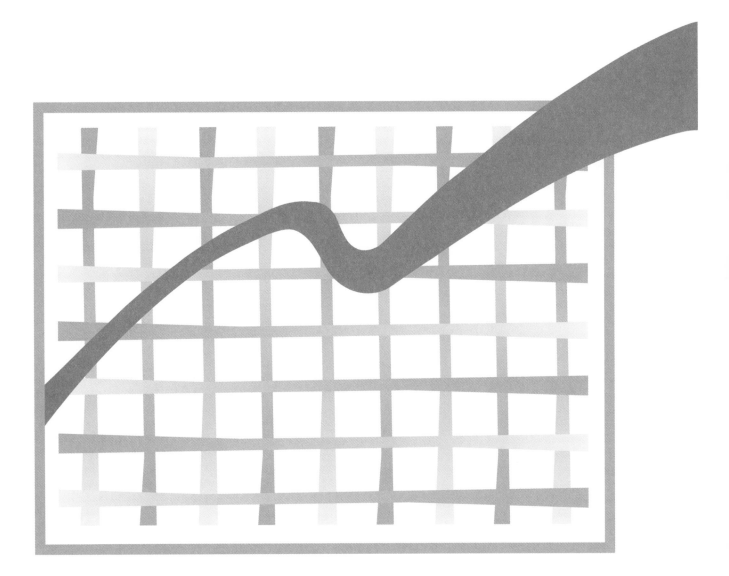

Chapter 2 Expectations

After completing this chapter you will be able to:

1. Define what an operating system is.
2. Understand the features of the Windows XP operating system.
3. Use a windows application.
4. Understand windows, menus, toolbars, and dialog boxes.
5. Understand the features of the keyboard.
6. List storage devices.
7. Understand how to use and properly handle diskettes.
8. Format, copy, write protect, and backup a diskette.
9. Navigate through the contents of the computer.
10. Copy, move, delete, and rename files and folders.
11. Create files and folders.
12. Recover deleted files.
13. Locate files.

This chapter introduces the Windows XP operating system. Windows XP applications and using menus, toolbars, and dialog boxes are discussed. The chapter also discusses how to work with, organize, and search for files.

2.1 What is an Operating System?

All computers run software called the *operating system*. The operating system allows the computer to run other software and to perform basic tasks, such as communicating between the computer and the user, keeping track of files and folders, and controlling peripheral devices.

When a computer is turned on, the operating system software is automatically loaded into the computer's memory from the hard disk in a process called *booting*.

Examples of operating systems include Windows XP, Linux, and Mac OS X. This chapter discusses the Windows XP operating system. Windows XP has a graphical user interface or GUI (pronounced "gooey") that displays open applications and documents in areas on the screen called *windows*. Placing each open application into its own window allows Windows XP to multitask. *Multitasking* is an operating system feature that allows more than one application to run at a time.

When the Windows XP operating system is running, the computer screen is referred to as the *Desktop*:

Cold Boot vs. Warm Boot

A cold boot is when a computer is started by turning the computer on and a warm boot is when the computer is restarted while already on.

windows

multitasking

Desktop

Desktop Appearance

The Desktop's properties can be changed by right-clicking the Desktop and selecting **Properties** from the menu, which displays the Display Properties dialog box. This dialog box contains options that can be used to change the Desktop's theme, background, and screen saver.

Icons

windows

Desktop

start menu   Quick Launch toolbar   taskbar   notification area

- **Icons** represent the applications and files available on the computer. Double-clicking an icon opens that file or application.

- The **taskbar** displays buttons that represent each open file or application. In the example above, there are two open applications, My Pictures and WordPad. Clicking a button either displays or minimizes the window containing the file or application. The taskbar also contains the start menu, Quick Launch toolbar, and the notification area.

- The **start menu** is used to run applications and is discussed in Section 2.2.

- The **Quick Launch toolbar** is used to start frequently used applications with just one click.

- The **notification area** contains a clock and other icons that display the status of certain activities such as printing.

2.2 What is a Windows Application?

Applications, also called software, applications software, or programs, are written by professional programmers to perform specific tasks. A *Windows application* runs under the Windows operating system. There are several versions of the Windows operating system including Windows 2000, Windows ME, and Windows XP.

In Windows XP, click start on the taskbar to display a menu:

The Start Menu

The appearance of the start menu may vary because it can be customized and because it displays the most commonly used applications.

In the start menu, some items are commands that perform specific tasks, such as starting an application. For example, clicking Microsoft Word starts the Microsoft Word application. Clicking a menu item with an arrow, such as All Programs and My Recent Documents displays a submenu of commands. For example, in the All Programs menu, clicking Microsoft Visual Studio .NET displays a submenu with the Microsoft Visual Studio .NET command for starting the Microsoft Visual Studio .NET application:

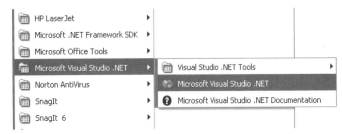

interface

Most Windows applications have a similar interface. The *interface* of an application is the way it looks on the screen and the way in which a user provides input to the application. For example, an application window looks similar to:

Using the Mouse

Sliding the mouse to move the pointer on the screen is called *pointing*. An object on the screen can be selected by pointing to it and pressing the left mouse button and releasing it quickly. This type of selection is called *clicking*.

Double-clicking means to point to an object and press the left mouse button twice in rapid succession.

Right-clicking means to point to an object and press and release the right mouse button quickly.

WordPad

The WordPad application comes with the Windows XP operating system and is a simple word processor program.

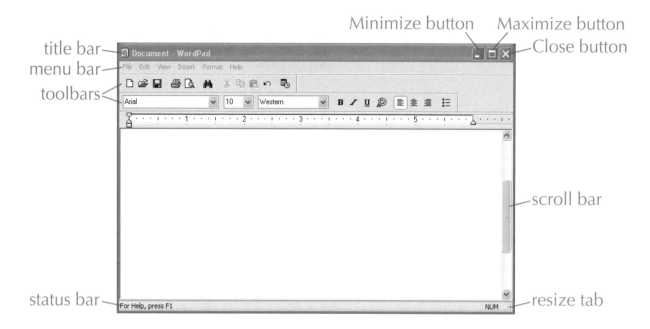

- The **title bar** displays the name of the application and the open document. Drag the title bar to move the window, if needed.

- The **menu bar** contains the names of drop-down menus, which contain commands.

- The **toolbars** contain buttons that represent different actions.

- The **status bar** displays information about the application or document.

- The **Minimize button** (▬) is clicked to reduce the application window to a button on the taskbar.

- The **Maximize button** (□) is clicked to expand the window to fill the screen.

- The **Restore button** (▣) is displayed instead of the Maximize button when a window has been maximized. Click this button to restore the window to its previous size.

- The **Close button** (✕) is clicked to close the window.

- The **scroll bar** is dragged to bring unseen parts of the document into view.

- The **resize tab** is dragged to size the window.

Review 1

In this review you will view the Windows XP Desktop, start an application, and minimize, maximize, and restore a window.

① *BOOT THE COMPUTER*

> In addition to the step below, a log on procedure may be required.
>
> a. Turn on the computer and the monitor. After a few seconds, the computer automatically loads Windows XP.

② *IDENTIFY THE PARTS OF THE DESKTOP*

> a. Identify the icons on the Desktop. How many icons appear on your Desktop?
> b. Locate the taskbar. Are there any open programs?
> c. Locate the Quick Launch toolbar. How many icons appear on the Quick Launch toolbar?
> d. Locate the notification area. What is the current time?
> e. Locate start and move the pointer to it.

③ *VIEW THE START MENU AND OPEN AN APPLICATION*

> a. Click start. A menu is displayed. Note that some of the items have an arrow.
> b. In the start menu, click All Programs. A submenu of items available on your computer is displayed.
> c. In the submenu, click Accessories. Another submenu is displayed.
> d. In the submenu, click WordPad. The WordPad application is started and displayed in a window.

④ *MANIPULATE THE WINDOW*

> a. In the WordPad window, locate the features of a window.
> b. If the window is maximized, click the Restore button (⧉) to decrease the size of the window, otherwise click the Maximize button (□).
> c. Click the Minimize button (▬). The window is reduced to a button on the taskbar.
> d. On the taskbar, click Document - WordPad. The window is again displayed.
> e. Click the Restore or Maximize button. The window is returned to its original size.

⑤ *CLOSE THE WINDOW*

> In the upper-right corner of the window, click the Close button (✕). The window is removed from the Desktop and the WordPad application is closed.

2.3 Using Menus and Toolbars

An application window contains menus and toolbars. Each menu name can be clicked to display a menu of commands. For example, clicking File displays a menu similar to:

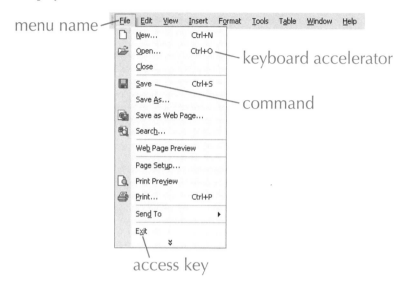

Click a command to execute it. Click outside the displayed menu or press the Esc key to remove the menu from the screen.

expanding a menu   The arrows (⌄) at the bottom of a menu indicate that there are more commands available. Pointing to the arrows expands the menu to display more commands. The commands in an unexpanded menu are the most commonly used commands.

Dimmed commands indicate that they cannot be selected at this time. Other commands may have an ellipsis (…) after the command name, which indicates that a dialog box will appear when the command is selected. A dialog box is used to supply the information needed to execute a command.

keyboard accelerator   A *keyboard accelerator* is a sequence of keys that executes a command or displays a menu without using a mouse. For example, the New command can be executed by pressing and holding the Ctrl key while pressing the N key. This keyboard accelerator is displayed Ctrl+N in the menu, as shown in the menu. The Alt key can be used in combination with the *access key*   appropriate access key to select a menu name. An *access key* is indicated by the underlined character in a command or menu name. Access keys are displayed by pressing the Alt key.

toolbars   *Toolbars* contain buttons that represent different actions, such as saving a document. Click a button to perform an action. Point to a button to *ScreenTip*   display a *ScreenTip*, which is the action that the button will perform:

If a toolbar displays a ⌄ button at the far right, clicking this button displays more buttons. Toolbars may vary in appearance since the most frequently used buttons are displayed.

An Introduction to Programming Using Microsoft Visual Basic .NET

2.4 Dialog Boxes

A dialog box is how a user communicates with an application. Dialog boxes can contain different elements:

- **Radio buttons** enable the user to choose from a set of options.

- **Check boxes** allow the user to select options.

- **Text boxes** allow the user to enter values.

- **Buttons** initiate an action when clicked.

- The **Help button** (?) is used to display information about dialog box elements. Clicking the Help button changes the pointer to ?, then clicking an element in the dialog box displays information.

- The **Close button** (X) removes a dialog box without applying any options. Selecting Cancel or pressing the Esc key also removes the dialog box without applying any options.

The default button in a dialog box is displayed with a thicker border and can be selected by pressing the Enter key. In the dialog box above, Print is the default button.

Additional elements that can be displayed in a dialog box include:

- **Lists** display a list of items to choose from. Click the arrow in the list to display items.

- **Shortcuts** are icons that perform actions. In the dialog box above, the shortcuts change a folder location.

Review 2

In this review you will start the WordPad application, display ScreenTips, and display a menu.

① *START THE WORDPAD APPLICATION*

② *DISPLAY SCREENTIPS*

    a. On the toolbar, point to the left-most button. A ScreenTip is displayed. What action does this button perform?

    b. On the toolbar, point to the various buttons and note the ScreenTips.

③ *DISPLAY A MENU*

    a. On the menu bar, click File. The File menu is displayed. Note the commands in the menu.

    b. In the File menu, which commands will display a dialog box when the command is selected?

    c. What is the keyboard accelerator for the Open command?

    d. Press the Esc key. The File menu is removed.

④ *CLOSE THE WINDOW*

    In the upper-right corner of the window, click the Close button (☒). The window is removed from the Desktop and the WordPad application is closed.

2.5 Using the Keyboard

The keyboard is used to enter text into a document by pressing a character key. There are also keys on the keyboard that are used to perform a specific action, such as moving the insertion point or deleting text:

insertion point

repeat keys

The *insertion point* is a blinking line that indicates where the next typed character will be placed. The insertion point can be moved without erasing or entering text using the arrow keys. These keys can only be used to move the insertion point within existing text. Pressing an arrow key once moves the insertion point either up or down one line, or one character to the left or right. The arrow keys are *repeat keys*, meaning that the insertion point will continue to move as long as an arrow key is held down.

The Ctrl key (Control) can be used with the arrow keys to move the insertion point quickly in the document. Pressing the Ctrl key and the right arrow key moves the insertion point to the beginning of the word to its right.

Pressing the Home key or End key moves the insertion point to the beginning or end of the line of text, respectively.

The Delete key is used to erase the character directly to the left of the insertion point. When a character is deleted, the characters to the right are moved over to fill the gap.

The Backspace key is used to erase the character directly to the left of the insertion point. Characters to the right are moved over to fill the gap.

The Esc (Escape) key is used to cancel (escape from) the current operation. The specific effect that pressing the Esc key will have depends on the operation being performed.

The Enter key is used to end a paragraph or to terminate a line of text. When Enter is pressed, the current paragraph is ended and a new one is created. Blank lines can be added in a document by pressing Enter, which creates a new, blank paragraph.

The keyboard can be used to move a document in the window by pressing the Page Up or Page Down keys. These keys move the document one window towards the top or bottom of the document, respectively. The insertion point can be moved quickly to the first character in a document by pressing Ctrl+Home, or to the last character by pressing Ctrl+End.

2.6 Working with Files

file
A *file* is a collection of related data stored on a lasting medium such as a hard disk, a CD, or a diskette. Once a file has been saved, it can be loaded into memory for further editing at a later time.

file name
A file must be given a name to identify it. A *file name* is a unique name for a file stored on disk. File names can contain letters, numbers, spaces, and the underscore character (_). File names cannot contain colons (:), asterisks (*), question marks (?), and some other special characters. Examples of valid file names are Notes, CHAPTER 5, and 2nd Memo. A descriptive file name is helpful. For example, a file containing a letter to your friend Greta should be named Greta Letter or Letter to Greta rather than just Letter.

extension
Applications automatically add an extension to the file name. An *extension* indicates what application the file was created in. For example, Microsoft Word automatically adds the .doc extension to the file name and Microsoft Visual Basic .NET adds the .vbproj extension to a project file name.

Since Windows applications have a similar interface, the way users work with files to perform common tasks such as saving and printing is the same in most Windows applications. This section uses the WordPad application to illustrate this concept.

saving a file
To save a file, select Save from the File menu or click the Save button (🖫) on the toolbar. The Save As dialog box is displayed the first time a document is saved:

The Save in list displays a location. The folders at that location are displayed in the contents box below the Save in list. Double-click a folder in the contents box to place that folder name in the Save in list and display that folder's contents. When the correct folder is displayed in the Save in list, type a descriptive file name in the File name box and select Save. The shortcuts can also be used to change the folder location.

overwrite

Any changes made to a document after saving are not automatically stored in the file on disk. The file must be saved again, which *overwrites* the original file with the changed file.

printing a document

To print a document, select Print from the File menu. The Print dialog box is displayed:

Print	? X
General	

Select Printer
- Add Printer
- Acrobat Distiller
- Acrobat PDFWriter
- HP 4050N PCL
- HP 4050N PS
- HP 5000N PCL
- HP
- HP
- HP

Status: Ready   □ Print to file   [Preferences]
Location:
Comment: [Find Printer...]

Page Range
- ⊙ All
- ○ Selection   ○ Current Page
- ○ Pages: 1-65535

Enter either a single page number or a single page range. For example, 5-12

Number of copies: 1

☑ Collate

[Print] [Cancel] [Apply]

The Print dialog box varies depending on the printer

Select Print to print the document. To print more than one copy of the document, type a number in the Number of copies box and then select Print.

The Print button (🖨) on the toolbar may also be used to print a document. However, clicking the Print button prints one copy of the document using the default settings without displaying the Print dialog box.

closing a document

When finished working on a document, it should be saved and then closed. *Closing a document* means that its window is removed from the screen and the file is no longer in the computer's memory. To close a document, select Close from the File menu or click the Close button (⊠) in the upper-right corner of the document window. A warning dialog box is displayed if the document has been modified since it was last saved.

opening a file

📂

Opening a file transfers a copy of the file contents to the computer's memory and then displays it in a window. To open a file, select Open from the File menu or click the Open button (📂) on the toolbar. The Open dialog box is displayed:

Default Settings

A default setting is the setting that is automatically selected unless it is changed by the user. For example, in the Print dialog box on this page, the default setting for the number of copies is 1, which means one copy of the document will be printed unless the user specifies a different number in the Number of copies box.

The **Open** dialog box:

| Open | ? X |

Look in: My Documents

My Recent Documents

Desktop

My Documents

My Computer

My Network Places

- My Music
- My Pictures
- Visual Studio Projects

File name:

Files of type: Rich Text Format (*.rtf)

Open   Cancel

The Look in list displays a location. The folders at that location are displayed in the contents box below the Look in list. Double-click a folder in the contents box to place that folder name in the Look in list and display that folder's contents. When the correct folder is displayed in the Look in list, click the file name in the contents box and then select Open to open the file. The shortcuts can also be used to change the Look in location.

quitting an application

Quitting an application means that the application window is removed from the Desktop and the program is no longer in the computer's memory. To quit a Windows application, select Exit from the File menu or click the Close button (⊠) in the upper-right corner of the application window.

2.7 Storage Devices

Computer typically include several devices for the long-term storage of files. Most personal computers have a diskette drive, a CD/DVD drive, and a hard disk drive. Each drive uses a different kind of storage media:

Storage Media

Other storage media include the Iomega Zip disk, with a capacity of 250 MB, the SuperDisk diskette, with a capacity of 120 MB, and a data tape, with a capacity of up to 40 GB or more.

diskette   CD/DVD   hard disk

diskette

CDs and DVDs

hard disks

A *diskette*, sometimes called a floppy disk, is made of a Mylar (thin polyester film) disk that is coated with magnetic material and then loosely encased in hard plastic. Each diskette has a capacity of 1.44 MB. *CDs* and *DVDs* are made of a Mylar disk with a reflective coating that is sealed in clear, hard plastic. A CD can store over 650 MB of data. A DVD can store over 4 GB and is used for video and audio, and other media that require large file sizes. CD/DVD drives can be read-only or read-write. *Hard disks* are made of an aluminum disk coated with a magnetic material. Unlike diskettes and CD/DVDs, hard disks are permanently installed inside a hard disk drive. Each hard drive may have multiple disks inside, and therefore have large storage capacities of many gigabytes.

handling diskettes

The handling of diskettes is important because they store data in a magnetic format that is vulnerable to dirt, heat, and magnets. To avoid damaging the data on diskettes:

* Keep diskettes away from electrical and magnetic devices such as computer monitors, vacuums, and any type of magnet.

* Do not expose diskettes to either extreme cold or heat.

* Store diskettes away from dust, dirt, and moisture.

* Never touch the diskette's magnetic surface.

handling CDs and DVDs

CDs and DVDs should also be handled carefully to avoid damaging the data:

* Always handle the CD/DVD by the center hole or by the edges.

* Never bend a CD/DVD.

* Always store a CD/DVD in a case.

2.8 Using My Computer

My Computer is an application that comes with Windows XP and is used to view the contents of the hard disk drive and of the computer's removable storage devices. My Computer can also be used to manage files and folders, view details about disk capacity, and format a diskette. Double-click the My Computer icon on the Desktop to display the My Computer window:

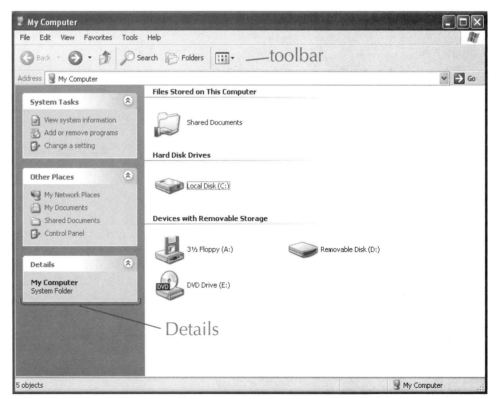

The My Computer window lists the locations that files may be stored in on the computer. For example, in the window on the previous page, the hard disk drive is Local Disk (C:) and the diskette drive is 3½ Floppy (A:). Clicking a drive icon expands the Details section to include information about the capacity of the drive, including the amount of free space.

folders

To view the contents of a drive, double-click the drive icon. The contents can include files and folders. *Folders* are used to organize commonly related files. For example, double-clicking Local Disk (C:) displays a list of folders and files stored on the hard drive.

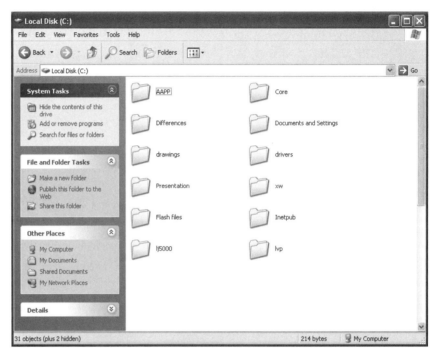

Disk Cleanup

In the My Computer window, right-clicking the hard disk drive and selecting **Properties** from the menu displays the hard drive's Properties dialog box. Clicking the Disk Cleanup button in the hard drive's Properties dialog box runs a wizard that frees up space on the hard drive by removing temporary Internet files, removing files that are not used on the computer, and emptying the Recycle Bin. The Recycle Bin is discussed in Section 2.9.

The folders can be double-clicked to display their contents. When the contents of a drive are displayed, the File and Folder Tasks section is also displayed in My Computer.

The My Computer toolbar contains buttons for navigation:

Back button   returns to the previously displayed folder or previous window.

Forward button   displays the next folder in a previously displayed sequence of folders.

Up button   displays the folder one level up.

Search button   can be used to locate files and folders and is discussed in Section 2.9.

Folders button   displays the Folders pane which can be used to display a list of all the folders stored on the computer and on the removable storage devices.

Views button   changes the way folders and files are displayed.

Review 3

In this review you will use My Computer to view files and folders.

(1) *DISPLAY MY COMPUTER*

Double-click the My Computer icon. The My Computer window is displayed.

(2) *VIEW FILES AND FOLDERS*

    a. In the My Computer window, double-click the Local Disk (C:) icon. The contents of the (C:) drive is displayed in a new window.

    b. Navigate through the contents of the drive by double-clicking folders and using the buttons on the My Computer toolbar.

(3) *CHANGE THE VIEW*

    a. On the My Computer toolbar, click the Views button (▦▾) and select Details. What additional information is displayed?

    b. On the My Computer toolbar, click the Views button (▦▾) and select Large Icons. The folder and file icons are redisplayed.

(4) *CLOSE THE WINDOW*

In the upper-right corner of the window, click the Close button (✕). The window is removed from the Desktop and the My Computer window is closed.

2.9 Managing and Organizing Files and Folders

In the My Computer window, selecting a file or folder expands the list of commands in the File and Folder Tasks section. For example, clicking a folder or file displays commands that vary depending if a folder or file was clicked:

> ### Windows Explorer
>
> Windows Explorer is an application that comes with Windows XP that can be used to do many of the same file and folder management tasks that can be performed in My Computer.

A folder was clicked   A file was clicked

rename a file or folder

Rename this folder selects the folder name. A new name can be typed, and pressing Enter makes the change. Rename this file works similarly.

copy a file or folder
move a file or folder

Copy this file or Copy this folder leaves the original file or folder in its present location and places an exact copy in a new location. Move this file or Move this folder removes it from its present location and places it in a new location.

The steps for copying a file or folder in My Computer are:

1. Select the file or folder to copy by clicking its icon.

2. In the File and Folder Tasks section, click Copy this file or Copy this folder, which displays the Copy Items dialog box:

Copy Items dialog box showing:

Select the place where you want to copy 'toe'. Then click the Copy button.

- Desktop
  - My Documents
  - My Computer
    - 3½ Floppy (A:)
    - Local Disk (C:)
    - Removable Disk (D:)
    - DVD Drive (E:)
    - Shared Documents

To view any subfolders, click a plus sign above.

Make New Folder | Copy | Cancel

3. In the Copy Items dialog box, select the drive or folder you want to copy to and then select Copy.

moving a file or folder

A file or folder can be moved from one location to another in a similar manner to copying a file, except Move this file or Move this folder should be clicked.

delete a file or folder

To delete a file or folder, select it and then click Delete this file or Delete this folder. A dialog box is displayed:

Confirm File Delete dialog box:

Are you sure you want to send 'toe' to the Recycle Bin?

Yes | No

Recycle Bin

Selecting Yes moves the file to the Recycle Bin. The *Recycle Bin* is a storage area on the computer's hard drive that stores deleted files until they are permanently deleted or recovered. Note that items deleted from a floppy disk or a network drive are not moved to the Recycle Bin, instead they are permanently deleted. Deleting a folder works similarly, and deletes all of the folder contents.

Double-click the Recycle Bin icon on the Desktop to show the contents of the Recycle Bin. Deleted files still take up disk space until they are permanently deleted. To permanently delete these files, select Empty Recycle Bin from the File menu and then select Yes in the warning dialog box. To recover a file that has been moved to the Recycle Bin, right-click the file and select Restore from the menu. A recovered file is returned to the location it was deleted from. It is important to note that Windows XP automatically empties the Recycle Bin periodically.

make a new folder

Clicking an empty area of the My Computer window so that no files or folders are selected displays the following File and Folder Tasks:

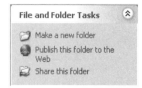

Select Make a new folder to display a new folder in the window. The new folder name is already selected so that a descriptive name can be typed and Enter pressed.

2.10 Formatting and Copying Diskettes

Formatting a diskette prepares it to receive data. From the My Computer application, the steps for formatting a diskette are:

1. Place the diskette to be formatted into the diskette drive.

2. Right-click the 3½ Floppy (A:) icon. A menu is displayed.

3. Select Format. The Format dialog box is displayed:

Open
Explore
Search...

Sharing and Security...

Copy Disk...
Add to Zip

Format...

Cut
Copy

Create Shortcut
Rename

Properties

Format 3½ Floppy (A:)

Capacity:
3.5", 1.44MB, 512 bytes/sector

File system
FAT

Allocation unit size
Default allocation size

Volume label

Format options
☐ Quick Format
☐ Enable Compression
☐ Create an MS-DOS startup disk

Start   Close

4. Select Start.

5. A warning dialog box appears stating that formatting will erase all the data on the disk. Select OK. The formatting process will take anywhere from a few seconds to a few minutes.

6. Select OK to remove the dialog box that appears after the formatting is complete and then select Close to remove the Format dialog box.

| Open |
| Explore |
| Search... |
| Sharing and Security... |
| Scan with Norton AntiVirus |
| Copy Disk... |
| Add to Zip |
| Format... |
| Cut |
| Copy |
| Create Shortcut |
| Rename |
| Properties |

The entire contents of a diskette can be copied to another diskette. The steps for copying a diskette are:

1. In the My Computer window, right-click the 3½ Floppy (A:) icon. A menu is displayed.

2. Select Copy Disk. The Copy Disk dialog box is displayed:

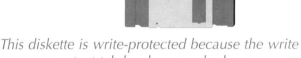

3. Click the appropriate drive icons in the Copy from and Copy to boxes if they are not already selected.

4. Place the diskette to be copied from (source diskette) into the drive and then select Start.

5. When prompted, place the diskette that will be copied to (destination diskette) into the drive and then select OK.

6. Select Close when copying is complete.

A diskette can be *write-protected*, which means that data cannot be written to it. To write-protect a diskette, turn to the back of the diskette and slide the write-protect tab upward. The write-protect tab is located in the upper-left corner on the back of the diskette:

write-protect tab

This diskette is write-protected because the write protect tab has been pushed up

A *backup* is a copy of a file or diskette. Although it is easy to create backups of a file or diskette, many people do not take the time to do so. However, the few minutes it takes to backup a file could save hours if the file is damaged or deleted and must be recreated.

Backup diskettes should be kept in a different location than the original copies to reduce the chance of both copies being destroyed. For example, if you keep your data diskettes in the computer lab, keep the backup copy at home. Businesses often store their backup copies in special fireproof safes, in safe deposit boxes at a bank, or with a company that provides safe "off-site" storage for computer data.

Copying Files to a CD

My Computer contains a CD Writing Wizard that can be used to copy files to a CD. In order to copy files to a CD, the computer must contain a CD-R drive and a writeable CD must be inserted into the drive.

To start the CD Writing Wizard, select the file(s) to be copied and then select Copy the selected items in the File and Folder Tasks section, click the CD drive, select Copy, and then click Write these file to CD to display the CD Writing Wizard.

Compressed (Zipped) Files and Folders

Compressing, or zipping, files and folders reduces the file size. Compressed files require less storage space.

Windows XP includes utilites that can be used to compress files and folders. Applications such as WinZip can also be used to compress files and folders.

An Introduction to Programming Using Microsoft Visual Basic .NET

Review 4

In this review you will use My Computer to format a diskette. The following instructions assume that the diskette drive is the A: drive and that you have a diskette for formatting. Note that any data that is on the diskette will be lost.

① *DISPLAY MY COMPUTER*

Double-click the My Computer icon. The My Computer window is displayed.

② *FORMAT A DISKETTE*

   a. Place the diskette to be formatted into the diskette drive.

   b. Right-click the 3½ Floppy (A:) icon. A menu is displayed.

   c. Select Format. A dialog box is displayed.

   1. Select Start.

   2. If a warning dialog box appears, select OK. It may take from a few seconds to a few minutes to format the diskette. A dialog box stating that formatting is complete is displayed.

   3. Select OK.

   4. Select Close. The Format dialog box is removed.

③ *CLOSE THE MY COMPUTER WINDOW*

In the upper-right corner of the window, click the Close button (✖). The My Computer window is removed.

④ *REMOVE THE DISKETTE FROM THE DRIVE*

2.11   Finding Files and Folders

The My Computer window can be used to find files and folders. In the My Computer window, selecting a drive and then Search for files or folders in the System Tasks section displays the What do you want to search for? section in the left pane of the My Computer window:

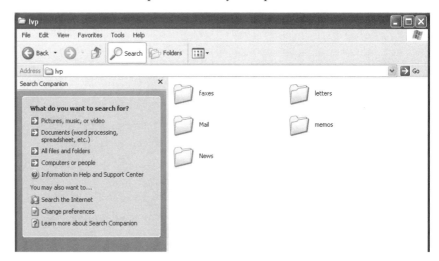

Selecting All files and folders displays the Search pane:

If the complete name of a file or folder is known but not the location, the location can be found by typing the complete name in the All or part of the file name box, clicking the Look in list and selecting the appropriate drive, and then selecting Search.

If only a word or phrase in the name of a file or folder is known, the location can be found by typing the known word or phrase in the A word or phrase in the file box, clicking the Look in list and selecting the appropriate drive, and then selecting Search. The Search button on the toolbar can also be used to search for files and folders.

Chapter Summary

All computers run software called the operating system. The operating system allows the computer to run other software and to perform basic tasks, such as communicating between the computer and the user, keeping track of files and folders, and controlling peripheral devices.

When a computer is turned on, the operating system software is automatically loaded into the computer's memory from the hard disk in a process called booting.

This chapter discussed the Windows XP operating system. When the Windows XP operating system is running, the computer screen is referred to as the Desktop. Multitasking is an operating system feature that allows more than one application to run at a time. Windows XP handles multitasking by placing each running application into its own window.

Applications, also called software, applications software, or programs, are written by professional programmers to perform specific tasks. A Windows application runs under the Windows operating system. Most Windows applications have a similar interface. The interface of an application is the way it looks on the screen and the way in which a user provides input to the application.

An application window contains menus and toolbars. Each word on the menu bar can be clicked to display a menu of commands. The arrows at the bottom of a menu indicate that there are more commands available.

A keyboard accelerator allows a command or menu to be selected by pressing a sequence of keys. Toolbars contain buttons that represent different actions, such as saving a document. Pointing to a button displays a ScreenTip, which describes the action that button will perform.

A dialog box is how a user communicates with an application. Dialog boxes can contain different elements including buttons, text boxes, check boxes, radio buttons, and lists.

The keyboard is used to enter text into a document by pressing a character key. The insertion point is a blinking line that indicates where the next typed character will be placed. There are also keys on the keyboard that are used to perform a specific action. The arrow keys are repeat keys, meaning that the insertion point will continue to move as long as an arrow key is held down.

A file is a collection of related data stored on a lasting medium such as a hard disk, a CD, or a diskette. A file name is a unique name for a file stored on disk. An extension indicates what application the file was created in. Computer typically include several devices for the long-term storage of files.

Since Windows applications have a similar interface, the way users work with files to perform common tasks such as saving and printing is the same in most Windows applications.

My Computer is an application that comes with Windows XP and is used to view the contents of the hard disk drive and of the computer's removable storage devices. Folders are used to organize commonly related files. In the My Computer window, selecting a file or folder expands the list of commands in the File and Folder Tasks section to include commands such as Rename this folder, Copy this file and Delete this file. Deleted files are moved to the Recycle Bin, which is a storage area on the computer's hard drive that stores deleted files until they are permanently deleted or recovered.

The My Computer window can be used to format diskettes. The My Computer window can also be used to find, copy, or move files and folders. A search for a file or folder can be performed in My Computer by selecting Search for files or folders in the System Tasks section.

Vocabulary

Access key A key that is indicated by the underlined character in a command or menu name.

Application Written by professional programmers to perform specific tasks. Also called software, applications software, or programs.

Backup A copy of a file or diskette.

Closing a document Removing the document's window from the screen and the file from the computer's memory.

CD A storage media made of a Mylar disk with a reflective coating that is sealed in clear, hard plastic. A CD can store over 650 MB of data.

Copying Leaves the original file or folder in its present location and places an exact copy in a new location.

Desktop The computer screen that is displayed when Windows XP is running.

Diskette A storage media that is made of a Mylar disk that is coated with magnetic material and then loosely encased in hard plastic. Also called a floppy disk.

DVD A storage media made of a Mylar disk with a reflective coating that is sealed in clear, hard plastic. A DVD can store over 4 GB of data.

Extension Characters added to the end of a file name to indicate what application the file was created in.

File A collection of related data stored on a lasting medium such as a hard disk.

File name A unique name for a file stored on disk.

Folder Used to organize commonly related files.

Hard disk A storage media made of an aluminum disk coated with a magnetic material. A hard disk is permanently installed inside a hard disk drive.

Icons Represent the applications and files available on the computer.

Insertion point A blinking line that indicates where the next typed character will be placed.

Interface The way an application looks on the screen and the way in which a user provides input to the application.

Keyboard accelerator A sequence of keys that select a command or menu.

Moving Removes a file or folder from its present location and places an exact copy in a new location.

Multitasking An operating system feature that allows more than one application to run at a time.

My Computer An application that comes with Windows XP and is used to view the contents of the hard disk drive and of the computer's removable storage devices. It can also be used to manage files and folders and format a diskette.

Notification area Contains a clock and other icons that display the status of activities such as printing.

Opening a file Transfers a copy of the file contents to the computer's memory and then displays it in a window.

Operating System Software that allows the computer to run other software and to perform basic tasks, such as communicating between the computer and the user.

Overwrite Replaces the original file when changes are made to a document and it is saved again.

Quitting an application The application window is removed from the screen and the program is no longer in the computer's memory.

Quick Launch toolbar Used to start frequently used applications with just one click.

Taskbar Contains the start menu, Quick Launch toolbar, the notification area, and a button for each open file or application.

Toolbar Contains buttons that represent different actions, such as saving a document.

Window An area on the screen that displays open applications and documents.

Windows application An application that runs under the Windows operating system.

Write-protected diskette A diskette that has the write-protect tab pushed up, which means that data cannot be written to it.

Windows XP Commands and Buttons

Back button Returns to the previously displayed folder or previous window. Found on the My Computer toolbar.

Close button Used to close the document window or remove the application from the screen. Found in the upper-right corner of a window.

Copy Disk **command** Copies the contents of a diskette. Found in the menu displayed by right-clicking the 3½ Floppy (A:) icon.

Copy this file **command** Copies a selected file to a new location. Found in the File and Folder Tasks section of the My Computer window.

Copy this folder **command** Copies a selected folder to a new location. Found in the File and Folder Tasks section of the My Computer window.

Delete this file **command** Moves a selected file to the Recycle Bin. Found in the File and Folder Tasks section of the My Computer window.

Delete this folder **command** Moves a selected folder to the Recycle Bin. Found in the File and Folder Tasks section of the My Computer window.

Folders button Displays the Folders pane which can be used to display a list of all the folders stored on the computer and on the removable storage devices. Found on the My Computer toolbar.

Format **command** Prepares a diskette to receive data. Found in the menu displayed by right-clicking the 3½ Floppy (A:) icon.

Forward button Displays the next folder in a previous displayed sequence of folders.

Help button Displays information about the dialog box elements. Found in the upper-right corner of a dialog box.

Make a new folder **command** Creates a new folder. Found in the File and Folder Tasks section of the My Computer window.

Maximize button Expands the window to fill the screen. Found in the upper-right corner of a window.

Minimize button Reduces an application's window to its name on the taskbar. Found in the upper-right corner of a window.

Move this file **command** Moves a file to a new location. Found in the File and Folder Tasks section of the My Computer window.

Move this folder **command** Moves a folder to a new location. Found in the File and Folder Tasks section of the My Computer window.

Rename this file **command** Selects the existing file name so that a new name can be typed. Found in the File and Folder Tasks section of the My Computer window.

Rename this folder **command** Selects the existing folder name so that a new name can be typed. Found in the File and Folder Tasks section of the My Computer window.

Restore button Restores the window to its previous size. Found in the upper-right corner of a window.

Restore **command** Restores a file in the Recycle Bin to its previous location.

Search button Used to locate files and folders. Found on the My Computer toolbar.

Search for files or folders **command** Used to find files and folders. Found in the System Tasks section of the My Computer window.

start menu Used to run applications. Found on the taskbar.

Up button Displays the folder on level up. Found on the My Computer toolbar.

Views button Changes the way folders and files are displayed. Found on the My Computer toolbar.

Review Questions

Sections 2.1 — 2.5

1. a) What is an operating system?
    b) What is booting?
    c) What is a window?
    d) What is the Desktop?

2. What is multitasking?

3. a) What area of the Desktop displays the current time?
    b) On the Desktop, what do icons represent?
    c) List the step required for a user to quickly switch between running applications.

4. a) What is another name for applications?
    b) List three versions of the Windows operating system.

5. a) What does the interface of an application refer to?
    b) How is a window moved?
    c) What does the toolbar contain?
    d) What does the status bar display?
    e) What button is used to expand a window to fill the screen?

6. a) How can a menu be removed from the screen?
    b) What do arrows at the bottom of a menu indicate?
    c) Can a dimmed command be selected?
    d) What is a keyboard accelerator?
    e) How is an access key indicated in a menu?
    f) How can you find out what action a button on the toolbar will perform?

7. a) What is a dialog box used for?
    b) What is a radio button?
    c) Which element in a dialog box initiates an action when clicked?

8. a) What does the insertion point indicate?
    b) Where does the insertion point move if the Home key is pressed?
    c) What character is erased when the Delete key is pressed?

Sections 2.6 — 2.11

9. a) What is a file?
    b) Can a file name contain spaces?
    c) What does the extension at the end of a file name indicate?

10. a) What happens when a document is closed?
    b) What happens when a file is opened?
    c) What happens when an application is quit?

11. a) List three examples of storage devices.
    b) What is the storage capacity of a CD?
    c) List two guidelines for handling diskettes.
    d) List two guidelines for handling CDs.

12. a) What is My Computer?
    b) What information is displayed in the Details section in My Computer?

13. a) List the steps required to view the contents of a drive.
    b) What are folders used for?

14. a) List three commands listed in the File and Folder Tasks section of My Computer when a file is selected.
    b) Where is a file moved to when it is deleted from the hard disk?
    c) List the steps required to recover a deleted file.
    d) Is a file deleted from a diskette moved to the Recycle Bin?
    e) Why would a new folder be created?

15. What is formatting a diskette?

16. a) What is a backup?
    b) Why would a backup be created?

17. Is it possible to search for a file if only a word or phrase in the file name is known?

The exercise in this chapter requires written information. If a word processor is used, be sure to use an appropriate header, footer, and file name.

Exercise 1

In this exercise you will research your classroom operating system and computer by answering a series of questions.

a) What operating system is running on your computer?

b) List three icons on your Desktop.

c) List two icons on your Quick Launch toolbar.

d) What is displayed in the notification area?

e) List three programs in your start menu.

e) What storage devices are available on your computer?

f) What type of media is used with the storage devices listed in part (e)?

g) In My Computer, create folders in the appropriate drive to organize your files and then move any existing files into the appropriate folders.

Chapter 3
Introducing Visual Basic .NET

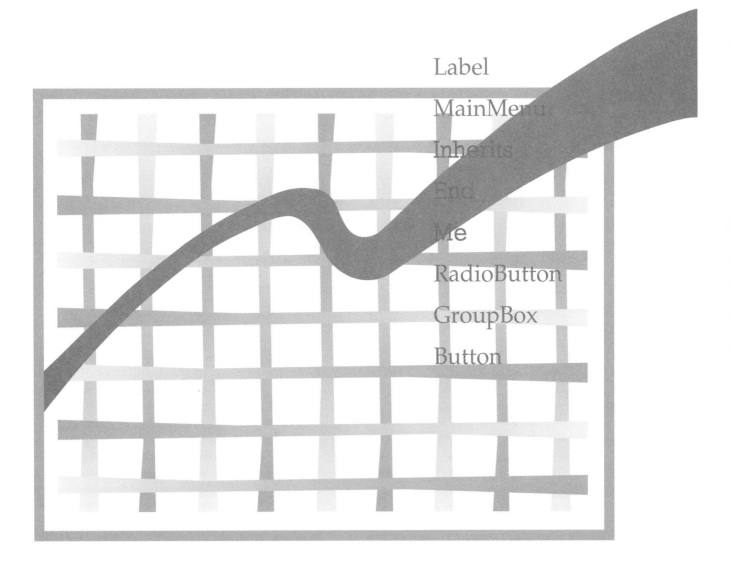

Label

MainMenu

Inherits

End

Me

RadioButton

GroupBox

Button

Chapter 3 Expectations

After completing this chapter you will be able to:

1. Define an object-oriented language.
2. Use the Visual Basic .NET IDE.
3. Understand controls and add objects to a form.
4. Create an event-driven application.
5. Understand event procedures.
6. Change property values at design time and at run time.
7. Add comments to program code.
8. Write assignment statements.
9. Understand arithmetic operators and numeric expressions.
10. Understand good programming style guidelines.

Visual Basic .NET is used to create applications for Microsoft Windows. It includes tools that allow a programmer to build a Windows application without having to write many lines of code. The concepts explained in this chapter include procedures, assignment, and numeric expressions. The Form, Label, MainMenu, RadioButton, and Button controls are also introduced.

3.1 Visual Basic .NET Windows Programming

application

Visual Basic .NET is used to create Windows, Web, and command-line (console) applications. An *application* makes the computer a useful tool by enabling the user to perform a task, such as word processing. A Windows application has an interface with visual objects for communicating with the user. Buttons, check boxes, and text boxes are common objects in a Windows application.

OOP language
class, object

The Visual Basic .NET language is an object-oriented programming (OOP) language. *OOP languages* enable the programmer to define a *class* with a set of data and actions. The class is then used to generate *objects*. Performing tasks with objects is the basis of an OOP application. Visual Basic .NET also enables rapid application development with many predefined classes. For example, the interface below uses predefined classes to generate two objects. The Form object and the Label object, both with a graphical element, create the Message application:

event
event-driven application

A Windows application is event-driven. An *event* can occur when the user interacts with an object, such as clicking a button. An *event-driven application* executes code in response to events. For example, the Message application remains on the screen until the Close button (☒) in the upper-right corner of the window is clicked by the user.

3.2 The Visual Basic .NET IDE

Visual Basic .NET applications are created in an *integrated development environment*, or *IDE*. When the IDE is started, the Start Page is shown:

- The menu bar at the top of the IDE contains the names of drop-down menus that contain commands.

- The toolbars below the menu bar contain buttons that represent different actions.

- The Start Page is a help window for getting started with application development.

Starting Visual Studio .NET

Visual Basic .NET is part of the Visual Studio package. Visual Studio can be started by using Programs in the Start menu.

3.3 Creating a New Project

Developing an application requires several related files. In Visual Basic .NET, these files are collectively maintained as a *project*. To create a new Windows project, select New Project on the Start Page or click the New Project button ( ) on the toolbar. The New Project dialog box is displayed:

The Project Command

Select File → New → Project to display the New Project dialog box.

Displaying the Toolbox

Select View → Toolbox or click the Toolbox button (🛠) on the Toolbar to display the Toolbox. If the Toolbox is docked to the left of the Design window, point to the Toolbox and then click the AutoHide button (📌) to keep it displayed.

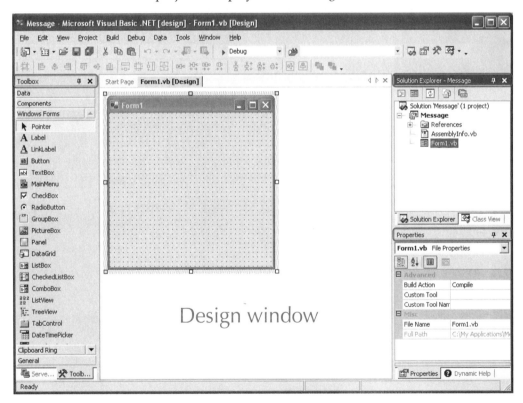

Select Visual Basic Projects in the Project Types list and click the Windows Application icon in the Templates list. In the Name box, type a descriptive application name. Type the project location in the Location box or select Browse to choose the location of the project from a dialog box. Select OK. The new project is displayed in the *Design window*:

Design window

- The **Design window** displays the application interface where objects are added, deleted, and sized.

- The **Toolbox** contains controls that are used to create objects.

- The **Solution Explorer window** is used to switch between the Design and Code windows.

- The **Properties window** lists the properties of a selected object.

In this review you will create a project named Message.

① *START VISUAL BASIC .NET*

② *CREATE A NEW PROJECT*

    a. On the toolbar, click the New Project button (⊞▾). The New Project dialog box is displayed.

        1. In the Projects Type list, select Visual Basic Projects, if it is not already selected.

        2. In the Templates list, click the Windows Application icon if it is not already selected.

        3. In the Name box, replace the existing text with Message.

        4. In the Location box, type the appropriate project location path or click Browse to choose the appropriate folder.

        5. Select OK. A project is created and the Form Design window is displayed.

    b. Locate the Toolbox with controls for creating objects, the Solution Explorer window, and the Properties window.

3.4 The Windows Form

A Windows application interface includes at least one form. A form is a graphical object that contains a title bar, a system menu (⊞), and Minimize (▬), Maximize (◻), and Close (✕) buttons.

sizing a form

A new Visual Basic .NET Windows application automatically includes one Form object. The project Design window displays the Form object, which can be clicked to select it. A *selected object* displays handles that appear as squares. Drag a side handle to separately size the height or width of an object. A corner handle is dragged to size both height and width together. Pointing to a corner handle displays the ↖ pointer:

Designing an Interface

Interface design becomes an important step in developing an application of any complexity. Using pencil and paper and field testing different interfaces are usually part of the design process.

---

properties

A Form object has *properties* that define its appearance, behavior, position, and other attributes. For example, the Text property of a form defines what is displayed in its title bar. Property values are displayed in the Properties window.

Text property

setting a property

A property value is set by typing or selecting a new value. For example, selecting the form, clicking the Text property in the Properties window, and then typing Message displays the following:

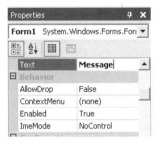

Pressing Enter or clicking outside the Properties window applies the new Text property value to the form:

3.5 The Label Control

The Toolbox in the Visual Basic .NET IDE contains controls. A *control* is used to add objects to a form. *Control objects* display information or get user input. An application interface typically contains many control objects on the Form object. For example, a Label object displays text that cannot be changed by the user. The Message application interface uses a label to display Hello, world!:

The Message Form object contains a Label object

Control Class Objects

An *object* is a unit of code and data that is described by other code called a *class*. One class can be used to create multiple objects. Visual Basic .NET provides many built-in classes called *controls* for creating graphical objects, such as a Label, that can be used in an application interface.

Double-Clicking

A control object can be added to a form by double-clicking the control in the Toolbox.

To add an object to a form, click a control in the Toolbox and then click the form. For example, clicking the Label control in the Toolbox and then pointing to the form displays:

The pointer shape displays an icon similar to the selected control. Clicking the form adds a new control object. The grid on the form can be used for precise placement of objects.

Drag a control object (not a handle) to move it to a new location on the form. Multiple objects are moved together by selecting them as a group and then dragging one of the selected objects. This technique is useful when multiple objects need to be moved while maintaining their relative position. The arrow keys can also be used to move selected objects. Pressing the Ctrl key when clicking an object selects it in addition to already selected objects.

The Label control has the properties:

- **Name** identifies a control for the programmer. It is good programming style to begin Label object names with lbl.

- **Text** is the text displayed in the label.

- **Font** contains the ... button that is clicked to display the Font dialog box where the font name, font style, and font size of label text is selected.

- **TextAlign** is the alignment of text in a label. Alignment can be set to TopLeft (the default), TopCenter, TopRight, MiddleLeft, MiddleCenter, MiddleRight, BottomLeft, BottomCenter, and BottomRight.

Label object properties are set in the Properties window, just as Form object properties were set. For example, the properties of the Message label are set to lblMessage for Name, Hello, world! for Text, bold size 20 for Font, and MiddleCenter for TextAlign:

Marquee Selection

Multiple control objects can be selected together using a technique called marquee selection. Clicking Pointer in the Toolbox and then dragging on the form displays a selection box called a marquee. Any objects within the boundaries of the marquee are selected.

The Name Property

The Name property is displayed as (Name) in the Properties window.

Message

Hello, world!

For most objects, the Name property should always be set to a descriptive name. A proper object name begins with the appropriate prefix and then describes the purpose of the object. For example, the label in the Message application is lblMessage. This name begins with the appropriate prefix (lbl) and is descriptive of the label's purpose. Following proper

naming conventions is good programming style.

3.6 Saving and Running an Application

An application should be saved frequently to avoid losing changes. To save a project, select Save from the File menu or click the Save button (🖫) on the toolbar.

To run an application from the IDE, click the Start button (▶) on the toolbar or select Start (F5) from the Debug menu. The IDE remains on the screen and a new window is generated from the application form. The form no longer displays a grid. Controls cannot be modified, but they can be tested to see if events such as clicking a button, produce the desired effect. A Windows application can be run at any time for testing at different stages of development.

To terminate a running application, click the Stop Debugging button (■) on the toolbar or select Stop Debugging from the Debug menu. The Close button (✕) in the upper-right corner of the window can also be clicked to close the application.

compile   Running an application means that a program is first converted to a language the computer understands in a process called *compiling*. During compilation, an output window is displayed with messages about the program. The output window can be closed by clicking the Close button in the upper-right corner of the window after the program has run.

Review 2

In this review you will add a Label object to the Message form and then run the application. The Message project should still be open from Review 1.

① *SET THE FORM PROPERTIES*

    a. Click the Form to select it.

    b. In the Properties window, the Text property is already selected.

    c. Type Message and press Enter. The title bar now displays "Message."

② *ADD A LABEL OBJECT TO THE FORM*

    a. In the Toolbox, click the Label control.

    b. Click the grid of the form. A Label object is added to the form:

③ *SET THE LABEL PROPERTIES*

    a. Click the Label object to select it, if it is not already selected. Handles are displayed.

    b. Scroll the Properties window to display the Name property in the Design section.

    c. Click Name and enter lblMessage.

    d. Scroll the Properties window to display the Text property in the Appearance section.

    e. Click Text and enter Hello, world! The Label object now displays "Hello, world!" Note that the text is displayed in the upper-left corner of the object.

    f. Just below Text, click TextAlign and then click the TextAlign arrow. A group of icons is displayed.

        1. Click the icon in the middle center. The TextAlign property is set to MiddleCenter. The label text is now displayed in the center of the Label object.

    g. Scroll the Properties window to display the Font property in the Appearance section.

h. Click Font and then click the ▦ button. A dialog box is displayed.

    1. In the Font style list, select Bold.

    2. In the Size list, select 20.

    3. Select OK. The label text is displayed larger and may not be entirely shown because of the Label object size.

④ *SIZE THE OBJECTS*

a. Select the Label object, if it is not already selected.

b. Drag the corner handle to size the label so that the text is completely displayed on one line.

c. Select the form. Size the form so that it is a smaller rectangular shape.

d. Drag the label so that it is in the center of the form.

Check – Your application interface should look similar to:

⑤ *SAVE AND RUN MESSAGE*

a. Select File → Save. The Message application is saved using the location specified at the time the application was created.

b. On the toolbar, click the Start button (▶). An Output window is displayed and Message is started. The Message application displays text.

c. Click the Close button (✖) in the application window. The application is closed and the IDE is again active.

3.7 The MainMenu Control

A Windows application typically includes menus that contain commands. For example, the Message application can be modified to include a Program menu with an Exit command:

Message with a Program menu and an Exit command

Choosing Command Names

Command names should be short and descriptive. Grouping command names, creating smart menus, and other menu options are advanced topics that can be explored using online help.

To add a menu to an interface, click the MainMenu control in the Toolbox and then click the form. A menu is automatically added to the upper-left corner of a form and the MainMenu component is shown in the component tray at the bottom of the Design window. Typing a menu name displays boxes for typing a command and another menu:

The menu name Program has been typed

When a command or menu name is typed, another box is automatically added to allow for more commands and menus. Only the command and menu names actually typed are included in the menu. Each menu and command name typed is a MenuItem object with the properties:

MenuItem object

- **Name** identifies an object for the programmer. It is good programming style to begin MenuItem object names with mnu.

- **Text** is the menu or command name and is set by typing the appropriate name in a MainMenu box in the Design window.

editing MenuItem objects

A menu is modified in the Design window by clicking a MenuItem object and typing a new name. A MenuItem is deleted by right-clicking the item and selecting Delete from the menu. A new MenuItem is inserted above an existing one by right-clicking the existing item and selecting Insert New from the menu.

3.8 Closing and Opening a Project and Quitting Visual Basic .NET

When finished working with a project, it should be saved and closed. To close a project, select Close Solution from the File menu. A warning dialog box is displayed if the project has been modified since it was last saved. Closing a project removes it from the IDE. To quit Visual Basic .NET, select Exit from the File menu.

closing a project

quitting Visual Basic .NET

opening a project

To open a project, select Project from the Open submenu in the File menu. The Open Project dialog box is displayed:

The Look in list displays a location. The folders at that location are displayed in the contents box below the Look in list. Double-click a folder in the contents box to place that folder name in the Look in list and display that folder's contents. When the project folder is displayed in the Look in list, click the project name in the contents box and then select Open to open the project.

displaying the Form Design window   After opening a project, it may be necessary to double-click the form name in the Solution Explorer window to display the form in the Design window.

Review 3

In this review you will add a Program menu with an Exit command to the Message application. Open the Message project in Visual Basic .NET and display the application interface if it is not already displayed.

① *ADD A MENU TO THE FORM*

    a. In the Toolbox, click the MainMenu control.

    b. Click the grid of the form. A menu is added to the upper-left corner of the form and a MainMenu component is displayed in the component tray.

② *ADD A MENU NAME AND A COMMAND*

    a. In the menu, click Type Here. The text is selected.

    b. Type Program and then press Enter. Additional MainMenu boxes are displayed.

    c. Click Program to select it.

    d. Scroll the Properties window to display the Name property and then enter mnuProgram.

    e. Click the MenuItem object below the Program menu and then type Exit and press Enter.

    f. Click Exit to select it and then change its Name property to mnuExit.

③ *RUN MESSAGE*

    a. Save the modified Message application.

    b. On the toolbar, click the Start button (▶). Note the Program menu.

    c. Click the Program menu and select Exit. Nothing happens because code has not been written for this part of the interface.

    d. Close the application.

3.9 Program Code

An application contains a set of instructions called *program code* that tells the computer how to perform tasks. Each line of code is called a *statement*   *statement*. Programs can contain tens to hundreds, even millions of lines of program code, or statements.

In a Visual Basic .NET project, some code is automatically generated for a form and the objects on the form. This code is added to initialize the objects and set property values.

Code window

The Code window is displayed by clicking the View Code button () in the Solution Explorer window or selecting Code from the View menu. The Code window for a new application looks similar to:

Displaying the Solution Explorer Window

Click the Solution Explorer button ( ) on the toolbar or select View ➞ Solution Explorer to display the Solution Explorer window.

Icons are used in the Code window to indicate if a block of code is expanded to show all its statements (–) or if the block is hidden (+). The statements for the Windows Form Designer generated code are hidden because this code should not be modified from the Code window.

Inherits

The code for a project's form is a class. The **Inherits** statement indicates that the Form1 class contains, or has "inherited", all the attributes of the Form class. Statements can be added below the **Inherits** statement to extend the Form1 class and add functionality to the objects on the form.

switching between Design and Code windows

The buttons in the Solution Explorer window can be used to switch between Design and Code windows. The tabs in the IDE can also be used. The Design window is indicated by [Design] in the tab.

3.10   The Event Procedure

procedure
event handler

A *procedure* is a block of code written to perform specific tasks. An *event procedure*, also called an *event handler*, is a type of procedure that performs tasks in response to user interaction with an object. Event procedures add functionality to an application. For example, when the user clicks a menu command, specific actions should occur.

Click event procedure

A *Click event procedure* executes in response to a mouse click. For example, clicking a command executes the Click event procedure for that MenuItem object. In the Message application, an Exit Click event procedure should quit the application. To add an event procedure to the Code window, select the object name in the Class Name list and then select the event from the Method Name list,

adding an event procedure

The procedure added has a blank area for statements:

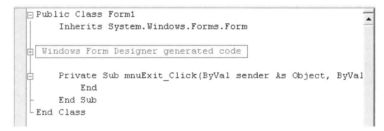

The procedure heading that is automatically added by Visual Basic .NET contains a set of parentheses with arguments after a descriptive procedure name. The arguments are not completely displayed in the screen above. They are values used by the procedure and will be discussed in Chapter 7. It is important not to modify the procedure heading, including deleting any of the arguments.

Private
Sub
End Sub
body

In an event procedure, **Private** indicates that the procedure cannot be accessed outside of the Form1 class. **Sub** declares the procedure and **End Sub** is required to end the procedure. Between **Sub** and **End Sub** is the *body* with statements that execute when the event occurs.

End

The **End** statement is used to stop program execution. The mnuExit Click event procedure is completed by adding an **End** statement:

```
Public Class Form1
     Inherits System.Windows.Forms.Form

   Windows Form Designer generated code

     Private Sub mnuExit_Click(ByVal sender As Object, ByVal
         End
     End Sub
End Class
```

good programming style

Body statements are indented for better readability. The IDE automatically indents code, but the Tab key can be used as well. Properly indenting code is good programming style.

printing code

The program code of an application is printed by selecting Print from the File menu, which displays the Print dialog box. Selecting OK prints the application code.

Naming Objects

Event procedures require object names as part of the procedure name. For example, mnuExit_Click() is the name of the click event procedure for the Exit command. Therefore, objects must be appropriately named before creating any event procedures. Visual Basic .NET will not automatically change an object's name in an event procedure if its Name property is set after the code is created.

Printing Object Properties

Expanding the Windows Form Designer generated code section before printing will include object properties in the printout.

Review 4

In this review you will add an event procedure to the Message application. The Message Design window should still be displayed.

① DISPLAY THE CODE WINDOW

    a. In the Solution Explorer window, click the View Code button (▤). The Message Code window is displayed.

    b. In the Solution Explorer window, click the View Designer button (▤). The Design window is once again displayed. Note the tabs in the IDE for switching between the windows.

    c. In the IDE, click the Form1.vb tab. The Code window is again displayed.

(2) *ADD THE EXIT COMMAND CLICK EVENT PROCEDURE*

    a. From the Class Name list, select mnuExit:

    b. From the Method Name list, select Click:

The mnuExit_Click event procedure has been added to the program code:

```
Private Sub mnuExit_Click(ByVal sender As Object, ByVal

    End Sub
End Class
```

(3) *ADD A STATEMENT TO THE PROGRAM CODE*

    a. Click the body of the mnuExit_Click event procedure if the insertion point is not already there. Use the Tab key to indent the insertion point if it is not already properly indented.

    b. Type End. The event procedure looks like:

```
Private Sub mnuExit_Click(ByVal sender As Object, ByVal
        End
    End Sub
End Class
```

(4) *TEST THE EXIT COMMAND*

    a. Save the modified Message application.

    b. On the toolbar, click the Start button (▶). Message is started.

    c. On the Message menu bar, select Program → Exit. Message is quit.

(5) *PRINT THE CODE*

    a. Be sure the Code window is displayed and then select File → Print. A dialog box is displayed.

        1. Select OK. The program code is printed.

(6) *CLOSE THE PROJECT*

    Select File → Close Solution. The project is removed from the IDE and the Start Page is displayed.

Create a My Name application that displays your name centered, bold, and size 14. Include a Program menu with an Exit command that terminates the application when clicked. Size the controls appropriately. Use the Message application as a guide. The application interface should look similar to that shown on the right after clicking the Program menu.

3.11 Assignment Statements

An *assignment statement* is used in a procedure to change a value at run time. One use of assignment is to set an object property at run time. In this case, an assignment statement takes the form:

Object.Property = Value

dot (.)

equal sign (=)

where *Object* is the control object name, *Property* is the name of a property for that object, and *Value* is a valid property setting. A dot (.) is required between *Object* and *Property* to access the property. The equal sign (=) assigns the property on the left of the equal sign the value on the right of the equal sign. For example, the statement

lblMessage.Text = "Smile!"

sets the Text property of the lblMessage Label object to Smile! Note that text must be enclosed in quotation marks in an assignment statement.

Assignment statements allow a single label to display different text at run time. The Message application can be modified to demonstrate this. First, two menu commands are added to the interface:

Message with Hello World and Smile commands

Next, event procedures are added for the two new commands. Note that assignment statements are used to change the label text:

```
Private Sub mnuExit_Click(ByVal sender As Object, ByVal
    End
End Sub

Private Sub mnuHelloWorld_Click(ByVal sender As Object,
    lblMessage.Text = "Hello, world!"
End Sub

Private Sub mnuSmile_Click(ByVal sender As Object, ByVa
    lblMessage.Text = "Smile!"
End Sub
End Class
```

As shown by the code, when Smile is clicked the label is assigned "Smile!" and when Hello World is clicked the label is assigned "Hello, World!" Both procedures use the same label to display a different message depending on the user's input.

3.12 Using AutoList

The Visual Basic .NET IDE makes coding easier with AutoList. When a dot (.) is typed in a statement, an AutoList of options is displayed:

```
Private Sub mnuHelloWorld_Click(ByVal s
    Me.lblMessage.|
End Sub          SetBounds             ▲
                 Show
                 Size
                 SuspendLayout
                 TabIndex
                 TabStop
                 Tag
                 Text
                 TextAlign
                 Top                   ▼
```

AutoList includes properties for the current object

The options displayed in an AutoList depend on what was typed just before the dot. For example, typing an object name and then a dot displays an AutoList with options that include control properties. In the example above, a label name was typed followed by a dot. The AutoList includes the properties of a Label control, such as the Text property selected above.

Me

Also in the example above, **Me** was used in the assignment statement so that object names are displayed when a dot is typed. **Me** refers to the Form object.

typing =

An AutoList is sometimes displayed when an equal sign (=) is typed. For example, typing the equal sign in the following assignment statement displays an AutoList with the possible assignment values:

```
Private Sub mnuTopCenter_Click(ByVal sender As System.O
    Me.lblPosition.TextAlign=|    I
End Sub                ContentAlignment.BottomCenter
                       ContentAlignment.BottomLeft
                       ContentAlignment.BottomRight
                       ContentAlignment.MiddleCenter
                       ContentAlignment.MiddleLeft
                       ContentAlignment.MiddleRight
                       ContentAlignment.TopCenter
                       ContentAlignment.TopLeft
                       ContentAlignment.TopRight
```

Selecting from an AutoList

The arrow keys or the mouse can be used to select an item in an AutoList. Once the item is selected, pressing Enter or Tab places the item in the statement.

Selecting from an AutoList can reduce typing errors in code. AutoList is also a good way to choose values in an assignment statement.

In this review you will add commands to the Message interface and write code for their corresponding event procedures. Message was last modified in Review 4.

① *OPEN MESSAGE*

② *ADD COMMANDS*

    a. In the upper-left corner of the Message form in the Design window, click the Program menu name. The Program menu is displayed.

    b. Right-click Exit. A menu is displayed.

    c. Select Insert New. A blank MenuItem is inserted above Exit and selected.

    d. Type Hello World and press Enter.

    e. Click Hello World and then scroll the Properties window to display the Name property. Enter mnuHelloWorld.

    f. Right-click Exit and select Insert New from the displayed menu. A blank MenuItem is inserted above Exit.

    g. Type Smile and press Enter.

    h. Click Smile and then scroll the Properties window to display the Name property. Enter mnuSmile.

③ *ADD THE HELLO WORLD CLICK EVENT PROCEDURE*

    a. Display the Code window. The program contains one event procedure.

    b. From the Class Name list, select mnuHelloWorld.

    c. From the Method Name list, select Click. The mnuHelloWorld_Click event procedure is added to the program code.

    d. Click the body of the mnuHelloWorld_Click event procedure if the insertion point is not already there. Use the Tab key to indent the insertion point if it is not already properly indented.

    e. Type Me. (Be sure to type the dot.) An AutoList is displayed.

    f. Type l (the letter L) to scroll to list items that begin with that letter.

    g. Press the down-arrow key until lblMessage is selected.

    h. Type a dot (period). lblMessage is added to the statement and a new AutoList is displayed.

    i. Type t (the letter T) to display list items that begin with that letter.

    j. Press the down-arrow key until Text is selected.

    k. Type = to add Text to the statement.

    l. Type "Hello, world!" The event procedure should look similar to:

```
Private Sub mnuHelloWorld_Click(ByVal sender As Object,
    Me.lblMessage.Text = "Hello, world!"
End Sub
```

④ *ADD THE SMILE CLICK EVENT PROCEDURE*

    Use the techniques from step 2 above to create the mnuSmile_Click event procedure, which should look similar to:

```
Private Sub mnuSmile_Click(ByVal sender As Object, ByVa
    Me.lblMessage.Text = "Smile!"
End Sub
```

 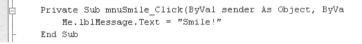

a. Save the modified Message project.

b. Run the application. Test the Smile and Hello World commands by selecting each one. Note how the assignment statements change the message displayed in the label.

c. In the Message application, select Program → Exit. The application is closed.

⑥ PRINT THE CODE AND THEN CLOSE THE PROJECT

a. Be sure the Code window is displayed and then print the code.

b. Close the project.

3.13   The RadioButton Control

A group of radio buttons is often used in an application to enable the user to choose from a set of options. Only one radio button in a set can be selected at a time. For example, the Hello World International application provides radio buttons so that the user can choose the language of the message:

Formatting an Interface

The Format menu contains commands for aligning, sizing, and spacing objects. The objects to be arranged should first be selected as a group and then the appropriate command selected.

Hello World International after clicking Spanish

RadioButton

The RadioButton control has the properties:

- **Name** identifies a control for the programmer. It is good programming style to begin RadioButton object names with rad.

- **Text** is the text displayed next to the button.

- **Checked** can be set to either True or False to display the radio button as selected or not selected, respectively. Only one radio button in a group can be checked at any given time. Therefore, changing the Checked value of one button to True automatically changes the other buttons in the group to False.

click event

A Click event procedure is usually coded for each RadioButton object. The Click event procedure executes when the user clicks a button. For example, the Spanish Click event procedure includes an assignment statement that changes the Text property of the label to "Hola, mundo!".

group box

A GroupBox object is used to group related radio buttons. In the application above, the radio buttons for choosing a language were placed in the same group box. A GroupBox object must be added to a form before adding RadioButton objects. Radio buttons are then added to the group box by clicking the RadioButton control and then clicking the group box. Dragging a group box moves it and all the controls within it together.

adding radio buttons

moving a group box

`[xy] GroupBox`

The GroupBox control has the properties:

- **Name** identifies a control for the programmer. It is good programming style to begin GroupBox object names with grp.

- **Text** is the text displayed at the top of the group box.

3.14 Commenting Code

Comments are used to explain and clarify program code for other programmers. Comments have no effect on the way an application runs. The single quotation mark (') must begin a comment. Anything after the single quotation mark is considered a comment for that line of the program only. Multiline comments can be created by placing a quotation mark at the beginning of each line.

programming style   Comments are good programming style and should be used wherever code may be ambiguous. Comments are also used to include information such as the programmer's name and date of modifications.

Review 7

Follow the instructions below to create the Hello World International application.

① *CREATE A NEW PROJECT*

   a. Create a new Visual Basic .NET Windows project naming it Hello World International.

   b. Click the form to select it. Text is selected in the Properties window.

   c. Enter Hello World International for the form text. The application's title bar now displays "Hello World International."

② *COMPLETE THE INTERFACE*

   Refer to the form below to add a label, a group box, and three radio buttons. Be sure to add the group box before adding the radio buttons to the group box object. Size and move objects as necessary. Be sure to make the label large enough to display greetings of different lengths. Use the table below the form when setting object properties.

Object	Name	Text	Font	Text Align	Checked
Label1	lblGreeting	Hello, world!	Bold 20	MiddleCenter	
GroupBox1	grpLanguage	Select a language			
RadioButton1	radEnglish	English			True
RadioButton2	radSpanish	Spanish			False
RadioButton3	radFrench	French			False

a. Display the Code window.

b. Add comments that include your name and today's date, similar to:

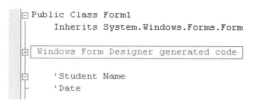

```
Public Class Form1
      Inherits System.Windows.Forms.Form

    Windows Form Designer generated code

        'Student Name
        'Date
```

c. From the Class Name list, select radEnglish.

d. From the Method Name list, select Click. A radEnglish_Click event procedure is added to the program code.

e. Add the following assignment statement to the radEnglish_Click event procedure:

```
Me.lblGreeting.Text = "Hello, world!"
```

f. Create a radSpanish_Click event procedure and add an assignment statement to change the label text to Hola, mundo!

g. Create a radFrench_Click event procedure and add an assignment statement to change the label text to Bonjour le monde!

④ RUN THE APPLICATION

Save the modified Hello World International project and then run the application. Select each radio button to test the application. The label changes. Close the application.

⑤ PRINT THE CODE AND THEN CLOSE THE PROJECT

3.15 Arithmetic Operators and Numeric Expressions

arithmetic operators

Visual Basic .NET includes a set of built-in arithmetic operators for exponentiation (^), multiplication (*), division (/), addition (+), and subtraction (–). Arithmetic operators are used to form a *numeric expression*. A numeric expression can be used anywhere a number is allowed. For example, the assignment statement below includes a numeric expression:

```
Me.lblAnswer.Text = 2 + 6 * 3
```

A numeric expression is not enclosed in quotation marks because quotation marks indicate text. When the above statement is executed at run time, the expression is evaluated by the computer and then the value assigned to the Text property of the Label object. Since a label displays text, the value is automatically converted to text.

operator precedence

Visual Basic .NET evaluates a numeric expression using a specific order of operations, or *operator precedence*. Exponentiation is performed first, multiplication and division next, and then addition and subtraction. Two operators of the same precedence, for example + and –, are evaluated in order from left to right. For example, the numeric expression, 2 + 6 * 3, evaluates to 20 because multiplication is performed first and then the addition.

parentheses

Operator precedence can be changed by including parentheses in a numeric expression. The operations within parentheses are evaluated first. For example, the result of $(2 + 6) * 3$ is 24 because 2 and 6 were added before multiplication was performed. It is also good programming style to include parentheses when there is any ambiguity or question about the numeric expression so a programmer reading the code will not have any doubts about what is intended.

programming style

3.16 The Button Control

A button is commonly used in Windows application interfaces. For example, the Calculations application below contains four Button objects and four Label objects. The labels initially display no text. When a button is clicked, the result of the numeric expression displayed on the button is assigned to the Text property of the label next to the button. For example, when 3+4 * 2 is clicked, the application interface looks like:

The Button control has the properties:

- **Name** identifies a control for the programmer. It is good programming style to begin Button object names with btn.
- **Text** is the text displayed on the button.

click event

A Click event procedure is usually coded for a Button object and executes when the user clicks the button. For example, the Click event procedure coded for the button that displays 3+4 * 2 looks like:

```
Private Sub btnExpression3_Click(ByVal sender As System
    Me.lblExpression3.Text = 3 + 4 * 2
End Sub
```

When the button is clicked, the statement in the Click event procedure evaluates the numeric expression and assigns the result to the label's Text property. Note that the expression is not enclosed in quotation marks.

Review 8

In this review, the Calculations application discussed in Section 3.16 will be created.

① CREATE A NEW PROJECT

a. Create a new Visual Basic .NET Windows project naming it Calculations.

b. Set the Text property of the Form object to Calculations. The form title bar now displays "Calculations."

An Introduction to Programming Using Microsoft Visual Basic .NET

② COMPLETE THE INTERFACE

Refer to the form below to add four buttons and four labels. Size and move objects as necessary. Use the table below the form when setting object properties.

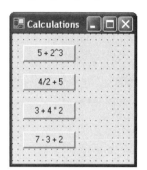

Control	Name	Text	Text Align
Button1	btnExpression1	5 + 2^3	
Label1	lblExpression1	empty	MiddleCenter
Button2	btnExpression2	4/2 + 5	
Label2	lblExpression2	empty	MiddleCenter
Button3	btnExpression3	3 + 4 * 2	
Label3	lblExpression3	empty	MiddleCenter
Button4	btnExpression4	7 − 3 + 2	
Label4	lblExpression4	empty	MiddleCenter

③ WRITE THE APPLICATION CODE

a. Display the Code window.

b. Add comments that include your name and today's date.

c. From the Class Name list, select btnExpression1.

d. From the Method Name list, select Click. The btnExpression1_Click event procedure is added.

e. Add the following assignment statement to the btnExpression1_Click event procedure:

   Me.lblExpression1.Text = 5 + 2 ^ 3

f. Add the remaining event procedures and statements so that the program code looks like:

```
Private Sub btnExpression1_Click(ByVal sender As System
    Me.lblExpression1.Text = 5 + 2 ^ 3
End Sub

Private Sub btnExpression2_Click(ByVal sender As System
    Me.lblExpression2.Text = 4 / 2 + 5
End Sub

Private Sub btnExpression3_Click(ByVal sender As System
    Me.lblExpression3.Text = 3 + 4 * 2
End Sub

Private Sub btnExpression4_Click(ByVal sender As System
    Me.lblExpression4.Text = 7 - 3 + 2
End Sub
```

④ RUN THE APPLICATION

Save the modified Calculations project and then run the application. Test each of the buttons and then close the application.

⑤ PRINT THE CODE AND THEN CLOSE THE PROJECT

⑥ QUIT VISUAL BASIC .NET

Visual Basic .NET is an object-oriented programming language that is used to create event-driven applications for Microsoft Windows. Event-driven programs wait for an event to occur and then respond to it by executing a corresponding event handler.

The Visual Basic .NET IDE (Integrated Development Environment) is used to create or modify an application. An application consists of several related files that are collectively maintained as a project. A project is created by selecting New Project on the Start page or clicking the New Project button on the toolbar.

An application interface is displayed in the Design window of the IDE. A form is a graphical object that contains a title bar, system menu, and Minimize, Maximize, and Close buttons. The Toolbox contains controls that are used to add objects to a form. An object can be sized by dragging a handle, and moved by dragging the object. The Properties window lists the properties of a selected object. A property value is set by clicking the property and then typing or selecting a new value. The Solution Explorer window is used to switch between the Design and Code windows.

A Label object displays text. The Label control has the properties Name, Text, Font, and TextAlign. It is good programming style to change the Name property of an object to a descriptive name. A Label object name should begin with the prefix lbl.

An application is saved by selecting Save or clicking the Save Project button on the toolbar. An application is closed by selecting Close Solution, and the IDE is quit by selecting Exit. Selecting Open opens an existing project.

An application is run by clicking the Start button on the toolbar or selecting Start. A running application can be terminated by clicking the Stop Debugging button on the toolbar or selecting Stop Debugging. Clicking the Close button in the upper-right corner of the application also quits the application.

A MainMenu object displays a menu at run time. Each menu and command name typed is a MenuItem object with the properties Name and Text. A MenuItem object name should begin with the prefix mnu. New MenuItem objects can be added and existing items modified and deleted in the Design window.

A set of instructions for an application is called program code. A statement is a single line of code. Some code is automatically generated when controls are added to a form. Application code is displayed in the Code window by clicking the View Code button in the Solution Explorer window or selecting Code.

A procedure is a block of code written to perform specific tasks. The event procedure, also called an event handler, executes to a corresponding event. An event procedure is added to the Code window by selecting the object name in the Class Name list and then the event name from the Method Name list.

The **End** statement quits an application. **Private** indicates that a procedure cannot be accessed outside of the form class. **Sub** declares the procedure, and **End Sub** indicates the end of a procedure.

An assignment statement is used in a procedure to change a value at run time. Assignment can be used to change property values at run time. The IDE displays an AutoList of properties when a dot (.) is typed. Using an AutoList for selecting properties can reduce typing errors.

⊙ RadioButton

A set of RadioButton objects allow the user to choose from a set of options. The RadioButton control has the properties Name, Text, and Checked. A RadioButton object name should begin with the prefix rad. A Click event procedure is usually coded for each button. Related radio buttons must be grouped in a group box. The GroupBox control has the properties Name and Text.

GroupBox

Comments are used to explain and clarify program code for other programmers. They can also be used to include the programmer's name and document modifications to a program. A comment is included in code by preceding text with a single quotation mark (').

Visual Basic .NET includes a set of built-in operators for exponentiation ($^$), multiplication ($*$), division ($/$), addition ($+$), and subtraction ($-$). Arithmetic operators are used to form a numeric expression. Numeric expressions are evaluated using a specific operator precedence. Parentheses can be used to change operator precedence.

Button

Button objects are commonly used in Windows applications. The Button control has the properties Name and Text. A Button object name should begin with the prefix btn. A Click event procedure is usually coded for a button.

Application A program which makes the computer a useful tool.

Assignment statement Uses the equal sign to give the object property on the left of the equal sign the value on the right of the equal sign.

Body The statements in a procedure.

Click event procedure A procedure that executes in response to a mouse Click event.

Code window The part of the IDE that displays the Form1 module window where program statements are entered.

Comment Text that explains and clarifies program code for other programmers. Comments are preceded by a single quotation mark.

Compiler Converts a program to a language that the computer understands.

Control Used to create a control class object that the user can interact with.

Design window Displays the application interface and allows control class objects to be added, deleted, and sized.

Event Occurs when the user interacts with an object.

Event-driven application Executes code in response to events.

Event handler See Event procedure.

Event procedure Block of code that executes in response to an event.

Form A control class object that is an application interface. Contains a title bar, system menu, and Minimize, Maximize, and Close buttons.

IDE (Integrated Development Environment) Used to create or modify a Visual Basic .NET application.

Interface What appears on the screen when an application is running.

Menu bar The part of the IDE that contains the names of menus that contain commands. Can also be added to an application with a MainMenu control.

Numeric expression Formed with arithmetic operators.

Operator precedence The order in which operators are evaluated in a numeric expression.

Procedure A block of code written to perform specific tasks.

Program code A set of instructions in an application.

Project The set of files that make up a Visual Basic .NET application.

Project Explorer window The part of the IDE that lists the files in the current project.

Properties window The part of the IDE that lists the properties values of an object.

Property The part of a control object that defines its appearance, behavior, position, and other attributes.

Select Clicking an object, which displays handles.

Statement A line of code.

Solution Explorer window Used to switch between the Design and Code windows.

Toolbox The part of the IDE that contains controls that are used to add objects to a form.

Visual Basic .NET Object-oriented programming language used to create Windows, Web, and command-line (console) applications.

^ Arithmetic operator for exponentiation.

* Arithmetic operator for multiplication.

/ Arithmetic operator for division.

+ Arithmetic operator for addition.

– Arithmetic operator for subtraction.

() Used to change operator precedence in a numeric expression.

' Precedes a comment.

" Used to enclose text in an assignment statement.

= Used in an assignment statement to give the property on the left of the equal sign the value on the right of the equal sign.

Button control Used to add a Button control class object to a form. Properties include Name and Text. Events include Click.

Close Solution command Closes a project. Found in the File menu.

Delete command Deletes a menu item. Found in the menu displayed by right-clicking the menu item in the Form Design window.

End Statement used to stop program execution.

End Sub Statement used to end a procedure.

Exit command Closes the Visual Basic .NET IDE. Found in the File menu.

Form class Used to create a control class object that is an application interface. Properties include Text.

GroupBox control Used to add a GroupBox control class object to a form for grouping a set of radio buttons. Properties include Name and Text.

Inherits Statement used to indicate that a class contains all the attributes of another class.

Insert command Inserts a new menu item above an existing one. Found in the menu displayed by right-clicking the existing menu item in the Form Design window.

Label control Used to add a Label control class object to a form. Properties include Name, Text, Font, and TextAlign.

MainMenu control Used to add an application component that contains menu items. Properties include Name.

Me Keyword used in a statement to refer to the current Form object.

MenuItem objects The items added to a MainMenu component. Properties include Name and Text. Events include Click.

New Project button Clicked to create a new project. Found on the toolbar. New Project on the Start Page can be used instead.

Print command Prints the program code of an application. Found in the File menu.

Private Keyword used in a statement to indicate that a procedure cannot be accessed outside of the form class.

Project command Opens an existing project. Found in the Open submenu in the File menu. Open Project on the Start Page can be used instead.

RadioButton control Used to add a RadioButton control class object to a form. Properties include Name, Text, and Checked. Events include Click.

Save command Saves the current project. Found in the File menu. The Save Project button on the toolbar can be used instead of the command.

Start command Runs an application. Found in the Debug menu. The button on the toolbar can be used instead of the command.

Stop Debugging command Stops the current application. Found in the Debug menu. The button on the toolbar can be used instead of the command.

Sub Statement used to declare a procedure.

View Code button Displays the Code window. Found in the Solution Explorer window. The Code command from the View menu can be used instead of the button.

View Designer button Clicked to view the Design window. Found in the Solution Explorer window.

1. List the parts of the Visual Basic .NET IDE and explain how they relate an application project.

2. Indicate what would be displayed if each of these expressions were assigned to a label:
   a) $10 + 3 - 6$
   b) $2 \wedge 3 + 5 * 4$
   c) $4 + 3 * 2$
   d) $2 + 9 \wedge (1 / 2)$
   e) $15 * 2 + 4$
   f) $15 * (2 + 4)$
   g) $2 + 4 / 2 + 1$
   h) $5 - 3 \wedge 2 + 1$
   i) $15 / 3 + 2$
   j) $"6 + 3 - 2"$
   k) $2 + 9 \wedge 1 / 2$
   l) $5 - 3 \wedge (2 + 1)$

3. Explain the term "event-driven."

4. List the controls presented in this chapter and explain if and how the user can interact with each one.

5. List at least one difference in the way a form looks between the Design window and run time.

6. List two ways an application can be terminated.

7. Explain the difference between the Name and Text properties of a control.

8. Make three sketches that show labels based on the statements below:

   ```
   Me.lblOutput1.TextAlign = ContentAlignment.MiddleCenter
   Me.lblOutput1.Text = "Have a nice day!"

   Me.lblOutput2.TextAlign = ContentAlignment.BottomLeft
   Me.lblOutput2.Text = "Thanks for playing"

   Me.lblOutput3.Text = "2 – 4 ^ 3"
   Me.lblOutput4.Text = 2 – 4 ^ 3
   ```

9. Why is it better to type the statement **Me**.lblMessage.Text = "Hello world!" rather than just lblMessage.Text = "Hello world!"

10. Write the statements needed for the Click event procedures of radSum and radDifference based on the following application. Assume the first label is named lblMessage and the second is named lblResult:

11. Explain the error(s) in the following comments:

```
'This is my first program
9/9/03
'Display greeting        Me.lblMessage.Text = "Hi There!"
```

12. Determine if each of the following statements is true or false. If false, explain why.

a) The properties of an object can only be set in the Properties window.

b) A MenuItem object can have a Click event procedure.

c) A MainMenu object can have only one MenuItem object.

d) The only purpose of a GroupBox object is to display a title for a set of RadioButton objects.

Exercise 1 ——————————————————————————————— Address

Create an Address application that displays your name, city, and state in three separate labels. The interface should look similar to:

Exercise 2 ——————————————————————————————— School

a) Create a School application that displays your school's name and mascot centered in two separate labels. Choose a different font, style, and size for the school name. The interface should look similar to:

b) Modify the School application to include a Program menu with an Exit command.

Exercise 3 ——————————————————————————— Band Information

Create a Band Information application that displays the members of a selected band. Include at least three of your favorite bands. The interface should look similar to:

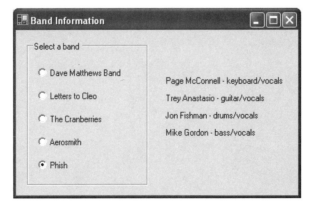

Exercise 4 ——————————————————— School Information

Create a School Information application that displays the city and state of a selected school. Include at least five of your favorite schools. The interface should look similar to:

Exercise 5 ——————————————————— Addition Properties

a) Create an Addition Properties application that shows the associative property of addition, $(a + b) + c = a + (b + c)$, in a label. The interface should look similar to:

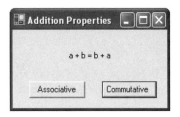

b) Modify the Addition Properties application to display the associative property of addition when one button is clicked and the commutative property, $a + b = b + a$, when another button is clicked. The interface should look similar to the following after clicking **Commutative**:

c) Modify the Addition Properties application to include a **Program** menu with **Associative**, **Commutative**, and **Exit** commands.

Exercise 6 —————————————————— Hello and Good-bye

a) Create a Hello and Good-bye application that displays a label centered, bold, and size 18 that reads Hello! or Good-bye! depending on the button clicked. The interface should look similar to the following after clicking Hello:

b) Modify the Hello and Good-bye application to include a Program menu with Hello, Good-bye, and Exit commands.

Exercise 7 —————————————————— Circle Circumference

a) Create a Circle Circumference application that displays in a label the circumference $(2\pi r)$ of a circle with radius 10. Use the value 3.14 for π. The interface should look similar to the following after clicking Answer:

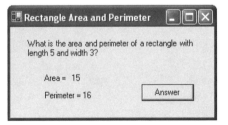

b) Modify the Circle Circumference application to include a Program menu with an Exit command.

Exercise 8 —————————————————— Rectangle Area and Perimeter

a) Create a Rectangle Area and Perimeter application that displays the area (length * width) and perimeter $(2l + 2w)$ of a rectangle of length 5 and width 3. The interface should look similar to the following after clicking Answer:

b) Modify the Rectangle Area and Perimeter application to include a Program menu with an Exit command.

Exercise 9 ———————————————— Long Jump Average

a) Create a Long Jump Average application that calculates and displays the average jump length of an athlete whose jumps were 3.3m, 3.5m, 4.0m, and 3.0m. The interface should look similar to the following after clicking Average:

b) Modify the Long Jump Average application to include a Program menu with an Exit command.

Exercise 10 (advanced) ———————————————— Position

Create a Position application that changes the position of text in a label according to the command selected by the user. The application should include a Program menu with an Exit command and a Position menu with TopLeft, TopCenter, TopRight, MiddleLeft, MiddleCenter, MiddleRight, BottomLeft, BottomCenter, and BottomRight commands. The interface should look similar to the following after selecting TopLeft from the Position menu:

Hints: Be sure the label is large enough to show changes in text position. Also, use the AutoList for selecting the assignment value for the TextAlign property.

An Introduction to Programming Using Microsoft Visual Basic .NET

Chapter 4
Variables and Constants

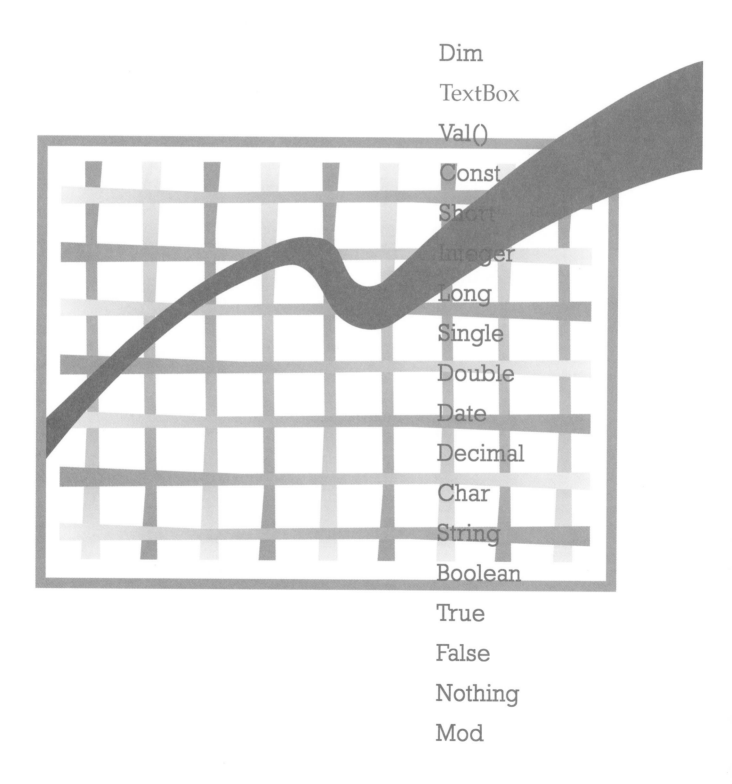

Dim

TextBox

Val()

Const

Short

Integer

Long

Single

Double

Date

Decimal

Char

String

Boolean

True

False

Nothing

Mod

Chapter 4 Expectations

After completing this chapter you will be able to:

1. Declare variables in program code.

2. Understand variable assignment statements.

3. Use named constants.

4. Choose legal Visual Basic .NET identifiers that also follow good programming style.

5. Appropriately use data types.

6. Understand syntax, logic, and run-time errors.

7. Use the Visual Basic .NET debugger.

8. Understand scope.

9. Understand specification, design, coding, testing, and debugging.

10. Use TextBox objects to get user input.

11. Understand automatic type conversion.

12. Use special division operators.

The concepts explained in this chapter include variables, constants, and scope. The TextBox control for obtaining user input is also explained. Techniques for debugging a program are introduced.

4.1 Variables

Variables are used in a program so that values can be represented with meaningful names. For example, when a variable named Length is used in a program, it is clear that its value is a distance. The use of variables is *programming style* good programming style because code is easier to modify and easier for a programmer to understand. A *variable* is a named memory location that *declaration statement* stores a value. A variable must be declared before it is used. A *declaration statement* takes the form:

Dim *variable_name* **As** *type*

Dim A **Dim** statement must include the name for the variable and the type of data the variable will store. For example, the statement

Dim sngLength **As Single**

Single declares a variable sngLength to store data of type **Single**. A **Single** is a numeric value that can contain a decimal portion. The variable name begins with sng for good programming style to indicate that the value stored is a **Single**. Other data types are described in Section 4.6.

A variable can be thought of as a named box (memory location) containing a value. A numeric variable is automatically initialized to 0 in Visual Basic .NET:

Dimension

Dim stands for dimension. A declared variable has "dimension" because it has been assigned space in memory.

sngLength

A declaration statement can also include a specific value for initialization. For example, the statement

Dim sngRadius **As Single** = 12.3

initializes a variable named sngRadius with the value 12.3. This statement can be thought of as:

sngRadius

multiple declarations in a single statement

Multiple variables with the same data type can be declared in a single statement, similar to:

```
Dim sngRadius, sngDiameter As Single
```

programming style

Grouping variables together in a single declaration is good programming style when the variables represent related items. Declarations should not be grouped together in a single statement just because the variables are of the same type.

4.2 Variable Assignment

The value stored in a variable can be changed at run time through assignment. A variable assignment statement must be written so that the variable name is on the left side of the equal sign and the value is on the right. For example, the statements below initialize a variable to the value 10 and then change its value to 12.3:

```
Dim sngRadius As Single = 10        'declaration and initialization
sngRadius = 12.3                    'change value
```

An expression may also be used on the right side of an assignment statement. For example, in the statement

```
sngCircleArea = 3.14 * sngRadius ^ 2    'sngCircleArea = 475.05
```

the expression on the right is evaluated first and the result assigned to sngCircleArea. Note that the expression itself includes a variable. A variable can be used wherever a value can be used.

One common error is to reverse the variable name and the value in an assignment statement:

```
12.3 = sngRadius  'Error!
```

It is important to realize that a variable can store only one value at any given time. For example, after the following statements have executed

```
Dim sngX As Single
sngX = 5.5
sngX = 8
```

the value stored in sngX is 8 because 8 was the last value assigned to sngX and sngX can hold only one value.

Review 1

In this review you will create the Circle Area application that uses variables.

① *CREATE A NEW PROJECT*

Create a Windows application named Circle Area.

② *CREATE THE INTERFACE*

Refer to the form on the next page to size and place objects. Use the table below the form to set properties.

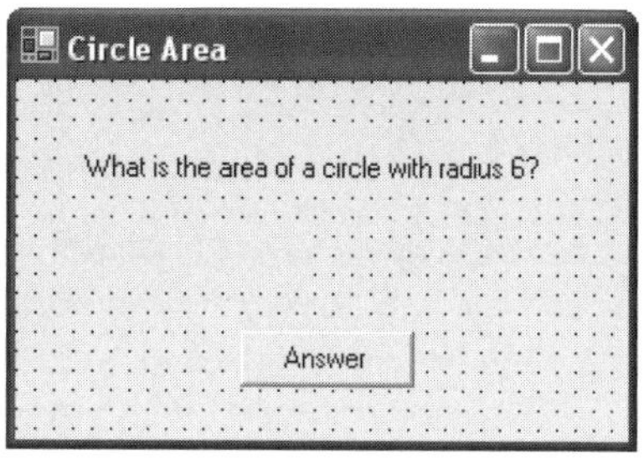

Object	Name	Text	TextAlign
Form1		Circle Area	
Label1	lblQuestion	What is the area of a circle with radius 6?	MiddleCenter
Label2	lblAnswer	*empty*	MiddleLeft
Button1	btnAnswer	Answer	

③ WRITE THE APPLICATION CODE

  a. Display the Code window.

  b. Add comments that include your name and today's date.

  c. The area of a circle is calculated by multiplying π (3.14) and the radius of the circle squared (πr^2). Create a btnAnswer_Click event procedure and then add the statements:

```
Dim sngRadius As Single = 6
Dim sngCircleArea As Single

sngCircleArea = 3.14 * sngRadius ^ 2
Me.lblAnswer.Text = sngCircleArea   'Display answer
```

④ RUN THE APPLICATION

  a. Save the modified Circle Area project and then run the application. Click Answer to test the application. 113.04 should be displayed.

  b. Close the Circle Area application.

4.3 Obtaining a Value from the User

TextBox object

An application is more flexible when values can be entered, or input, at run time. A TextBox object is one way to allow users to enter values. For example, the Circle Area application could include a text box for the user to type a radius value:

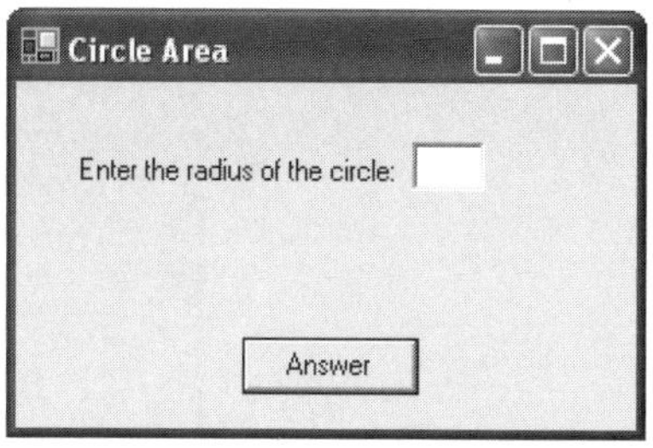

prompt

A label is often placed near a text box to describe its contents or purpose. This label is also called the *prompt*.

abl TextBox

The TextBox control has the properties:

- **Name** identifies a control for the programmer. It is good programming style to begin TextBox object names with txt.

- **Text** is what is displayed in the text box.

- **Alignment** sets the alignment of text relative to the text box.

TextChanged event

A TextChanged event procedure is sometimes coded for a TextBox object. This procedure is executed when the user types in the text box.

assignment

At run time, the TextBox Text property stores whatever characters are currently in the text box. This property can be used in an assignment statement to retrieve the data typed by the user. The following statement assigns the data in a text box named txtRadius to the variable sngRadius:

```
sngRadius = Me.txtRadius.Text
```

If the text box does not contain data that matches the variable type, a run-time error occurs and the program is halted. To prevent this, the Val() function should be used when assigning data from a text box to a numeric variable. A *function* is a procedure that performs a task and returns a value. Val() takes a string and returns a number corresponding to the numeric characters in the string. If the first character of the string is not a number, Val() returns a 0. The statements below demonstrate Val():

```
Dim sngHeight As Single
sngHeight = Val("62.5 inches")      'sngHeight is assigned 62.5
sngHeight = Val("Twenty inches")    'sngHeight is assigned 0
sngHeight = Val("Six feet 2 inches") 'sngHeight is assigned 0
```

To convert text from a text box to a number, the Val() function should be used in a statement similar to:

Val()

```
sngRadius = Val(Me.txtRadius.Text)  'return a Single value
```

> ### What is a function?
>
> A function is a type of procedure that performs a task and returns a value. Functions are used by including the function name in a statement. When the line of code containing the function name is executed, the statements that make up the function are executed. A function may require data to perform its task. The data is "passed" to the function as arguments enclosed in parentheses after the function name.

Review 2 ↻

In this review you will add a text box to Circle Area. Open the Circle Area project created in Review 1, if it is not already displayed.

① MODIFY THE INTERFACE

a. Change the lblQuestion Text property to Enter the radius of the circle: Appropriately size the label so that it is large enough to completely display the new text.

b. Add a text box to the form. Move and size the object so that the interface looks similar to:

c. Name the TextBox object txtRadius and set the Text property so that it is empty.

    a. Display the Code window and then modify the btnAnswer_Click procedure as shown:

```
Dim sngRadius As Single
Dim sngCircleArea As Single

sngRadius = Val(Me.txtRadius.Text)
sngCircleArea = 3.14 * sngRadius ^ 2
Me.lblAnswer.Text = sngCircleArea   'Display answer
```

    b. Run the application. Type 2 in the text box and then click **Answer**. The area 12.56 is displayed.

    c. Type 3 in the text box, but do not click **Answer**. Note the previous answer is still displayed.

    d. Close the Circle Area application.

③ *ADD A TEXT CHANGED EVENT PROCEDURE*

    a. Create a txtRadius_TextChanged event procedure and then add the statement:

```
'Clear the current answer when the user begins to type a new radius value
Me.lblAnswer.Text = ""
```

    b. Run the application. Type 2 in the text box and then click **Answer**. The area 12.56 is displayed.

    c. Type 3 in the text box. The previous answer is cleared. Click **Answer** to display a new value.

    d. Close the Circle Area application.

④ *PRINT THE CODE AND THEN CLOSE THE PROJECT*

Review 3

Create a Rectangle Area application that prompts the user for a length and width and then displays the area of a rectangle when **Answer** is clicked. Use appropriate variables and include TextChanged event procedures that clear the answer label. The application interface should look similar to that shown on the right after typing 5 and 2 and clicking **Answer**.

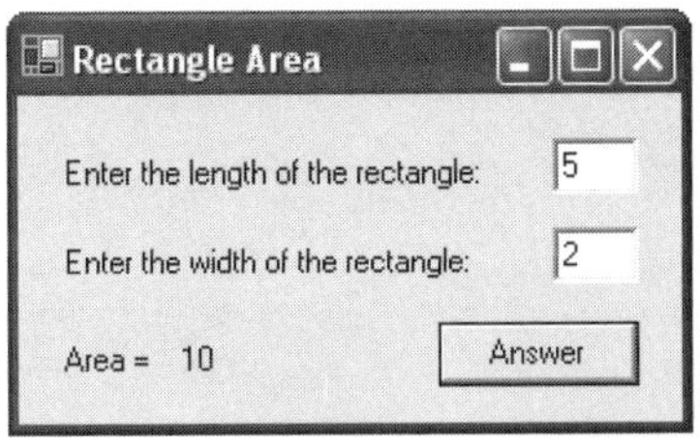

4.4 Using Named Constants

When should a constant be used?

Constants should be used wherever they can add clarity to code. However, there are some values that should not be replaced with named constants. For example, in an expression that calculates the area of a triangle (½bh), the value 0.5 is best used instead of a named constant. This determination can be made when naming the constant. A value that does not have an obvious name should not be a declared constant.

A *constant* is a named memory location which stores a value that cannot be changed from its initial assignment. The use of named constants is good programming style because they give a value a meaningful name and make code easier for a programmer to read. For example, the following statement declares a constant sngPI with the value 3.14:

Const sngPI **As Single** = 3.14

A constant can be used wherever a value can be used. For example:

sngCircleArea = sngPI * sngRadius ^ 2

The value of a constant is typed only in the declaration, eliminating the possibility of typing the wrong value elsewhere in a program. This also means that if the program is modified later, the constant value need only be changed in one place. For example, to use the value of π to several decimal places, the constant declaration should be changed to:

Const sngPI **As Single** = 3.14159265

This value of sngPI will then be used throughout the program.

programming style

As a matter of good programming style, constants should be in all uppercase except for the prefix that indicates the data type. It is also good programming style to place constant declarations before variable declarations at the beginning of a procedure:

```
Private Sub ...
    Const sngPI As Single = 3.14
    Dim sngRadius As Single
    Dim sngCircleArea As Single
...
```

One common error is to try to change the value of a constant, as in the following statement:

```
Const sngPI As Single = 3.14
sngPi = 22/7      'Error
```

Case Sensitivity

Visual Basic .NET does not distinguish identifiers by case. For example, dblradius and dblRadius are the same variable. The IDE autotmatically changes the case of an identifier to match that of the first occurrence.

4.5 Choosing Identifiers

Legal Visual Basic .NET identifiers for use as variable and constant names must begin with a letter and contain only letters, digits, and the underscore (_) character. Periods, spaces and other special characters are not allowed.

keyword

There are several identifiers that Visual Basic .NET reserves for use as keywords. A *keyword* has special meaning, and therefore cannot be used for a variable or named constant identifier. For example, **Single**, **End**, and **Sub** are keywords. In this text, keywords appear in a different font, just as the word **Single** is formatted. Refer to Appendix A for a complete list of Visual Basic .NET keywords.

Review 4 ♻

Modify the Circle Area application from Review 2 so that a named constant sngPI is declared for π and this named constant is used rather than the number 3.14 in the btnAnswer_Click event procedure.

4.6 Built-In Data Types

Data Type Storage Requirements

Each data type requires bytes of memory:

Type	Bytes
Short	2
Integer	4
Long	8
Single	4
Double	8
Date	8
Decimal	16
Char	2
String	2 per character
Boolean	2

A variable or constant declaration includes a data type that corresponds to the data stored. Visual Basic .NET includes several data types, including **Single** and the other types listed below:

Type	Used to represent
Short	integers from -32,768 to 32,767
Integer	integers from -2,147,483,648 to 2,147,483,647
Long	large integers (no decimals)
Single	numbers possibly containing a decimal
Double	large numbers possibly containing a decimal
Date	a date in m/d/yyyy format
Decimal	numbers that may have many significant digits
Char	a single character
String	a set of characters
Boolean	True or False

Short, Integer, Long   The **Short**, **Integer** and **Long** types represent positive or negative integers. The difference between the types is the range of values that can be represented. In most cases, the **Integer** type is the appropriate type for representing whole numbers.

Single, Double floating point   The **Single** and **Double** types represent positive or negative real numbers. These types are often referred to as *floating point*, meaning that they can represent values with numbers after the decimal point. The difference between the types is the range of values that can be represented. A **Single** can store values up to $3.4e^{38}$ and a **Double** up to $1.8e^{308}$.

Date   The **Date** type should be used to represent a date. Dates can be in the range 1/1/0001 through 12/31/9999. The value assigned to a Date data type must be enclosed within # signs, as in the statement below:

     Dim dtmBirthDate **As Date** = #1/1/1996#

Decimal   The **Decimal** type is appropriate for storing values representing currency. **Decimal** variables store many digits without rounding.

Char   The **Char** type represents a single character. A character can include a letter of the alphabet, a digit, and in general any character that can be typed or displayed, such as $, %, and space. A **Char** assignment requires double-quotation marks ("):

     Dim chrMiddleInitial **As Char**
     chrMiddleInitial = "A"

String   The **String** type represents a set of characters, also called a *string*. A string can include the letters of the alphabet, digits, and in general any character that can be typed or displayed, such as $, %, and spaces. A **String** assignment requires double-quotation marks ("):

     Dim strLastName **As String** = "Lutz"

Boolean   The **Boolean** type can be either **True** or **False**. A **Boolean** variable is useful for representing on/off and yes/no values. Boolean assignment statements use the keywords **True** and **False**.

programming style   Variable identifiers should be descriptive and begin with an appropriate prefix, as listed below:

Type	Prefix	Type	Prefix
Short	srt	Double	dbl
Integer	int	Decimal	dec
Long	lng	Char	chr
Single	sng	String	str
Date	dtm	Boolean	bln

variable initialization   Visual Basic .NET automatically initializes variables to a default value when they are declared. Variables of numeric types, such as **Short**, **Integer**, **Long**, **Single**, **Double**, and **Decimal** are initialized to 0. **Date** variables are initialized to 12:00:00 AM. **Boolean** variables are initialized to **False**. **Char** and **String** variables are initialized to nothing, which is equal to the keyword **Nothing**. This keyword can be used in place of an

Nothing empty string ("") for clearing labels, and so on.

4.7 Automatic Type Conversion

In an assignment statement, Visual Basic .NET automatically converts data to match the type of the variable it is being assigned to. For example, a value with a decimal portion is automatically rounded to a whole number when assigned to an **Integer** variable:

```
Dim intX As Integer
intX = 6.7        'intX is assigned the value 7
```

Visual Basic .NET will try to convert from one data type to another as long as the data is valid for the receiving data type. For example, assigning 12.3 to an **Integer** variable intX is valid because the number can be converted to 12. However, an error will be generated when abc is assigned to an **Integer** variable.

Type Casting

An *implicit conversion* takes place automatically when data of one type is assigned to a variable of a different type. An *explicit conversion* uses a type conversion keyword to convert data from one type to another and is also called *casting*.

4.8 Scope

declaration placement

Variables used throughout a procedure should be declared in a group of statements at the beginning of the procedure for good programming style. Other variables may be better placed near the group of statements that use them, as will be seen in a later chapter.

The placement of a declaration is also important because it determines the variable scope. The *scope* of a variable is the set of statements that can use the variable. For example, a variable declared at the beginning of a procedure is accessible to any statement in that procedure. This means that any statement in the procedure can refer to the variable, change its value, and so on. Statements outside the procedure do not have access to the variable. A declaration at the beginning of a procedure is also called a *local declaration* because the variable can be used "locally" only.

local declaration

The placement of a declaration also defines the scope of a constant. However, because the value of a constant does not change throughout a program run, it is usually safe to allow a broader scope. In this case, constant declarations are placed at the beginning of a program, outside any procedures. This type of declaration is called a *module-level*, or *global*, declaration because the constant can be used anywhere in the module. For example, the code below includes both global variables and constants and local variables:

module-level declaration
global declaration

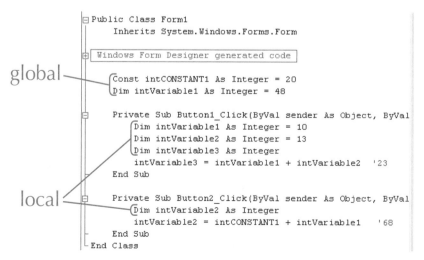

```
Public Class Form1
    Inherits System.Windows.Forms.Form

    Windows Form Designer generated code

global    Const intCONSTANT1 As Integer = 20
          Dim intVariable1 As Integer = 48

    Private Sub Button1_Click(ByVal sender As Object, ByVal
          Dim intVariable1 As Integer = 10
          Dim intVariable2 As Integer = 13
          Dim intVariable3 As Integer
          intVariable3 = intVariable1 + intVariable2    '23
    End Sub

local     Private Sub Button2_Click(ByVal sender As Object, ByVal
          Dim intVariable2 As Integer
          intVariable2 = intCONSTANT1 + intVariable1     '68
    End Sub
End Class
```

programming style   It is good programming style to keep the scope of variable and constant declarations as narrow as possible. For example, variables should not be declared globally if there is no need.

Review 5

In this review you will create the ScopeDemo application that demonstrates the concept of scope.

① *CREATE A NEW PROJECT*

Create a Windows application named ScopeDemo.

② *COMPLETE THE INTERFACE*

Refer to the form below to add, position, and size objects. Use the table below to set properties.

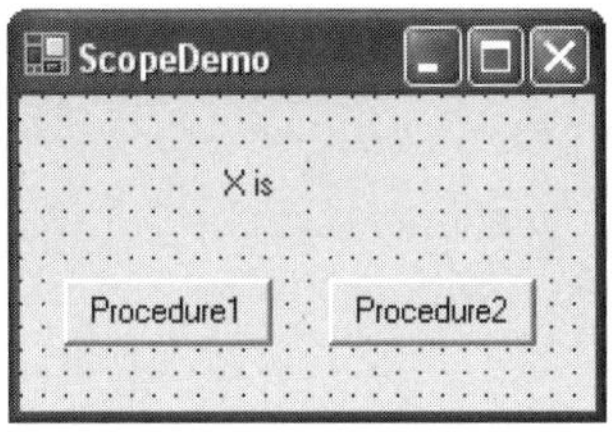

Object	Name	Text	TextAlign
Form1		ScopeDemo	
Label1	lblXis	X is	MiddleLeft
Label2	lblAnswer	*empty*	MiddleLeft
Button1	btnProc1	Procedure1	
Button2	btnProc2	Procedure2	

③ *WRITE THE APPLICATION CODE*

a. Display the Code window.

b. Add comments that include your name and today's date.

c. Create event procedures and add the global variable intX as shown below:

```
Public Class Form1
    Inherits System.Windows.Forms.Form

    Windows Form Designer generated code

    Dim intX As Integer = 10

    Private Sub btnProc1_Click(ByVal sender As Object, ByVa
        Dim intX As Integer = 3
        Me.lblAnswer.Text = intX
    End Sub

    Private Sub btnProc2_Click(ByVal sender As Object, ByVa
        Me.lblAnswer.Text = intX
    End Sub
End Class
```

④ *RUN THE APPLICATION*

a. Run the application. Click Procedure1. 3 is displayed. Click Procedure2. 10 is displayed. Note that the intX variable in the btnProc1 procedure is local to that procedure. The intX value displayed by the btnProc2 procedure uses the global variable.

b. Close the ScopeDemo application.

4.9 Special Division Operators

In addition to the standard built-in operators (^, *, /, +, –), Visual Basic .NET includes two other division operators. The \ operator performs Integer division, and the **Mod** operator performs modulus division.

integer division

Integer division truncates the decimal portion of the quotient, which results in an integer. For example, in the assignment statement below

```
Dim intX As Integer
intX = 20 \ 7          'intX is assigned 2
```

intX is assigned 2 because the whole portion of the quotient is 2:

$$\underset{7\overline{)20}}{\overset{\textstyle 2 \ \text{r6}}{}} \quad 20\setminus 7$$

$$\frac{14}{6}$$

modulus division

Modulus division returns the remainder resulting from division. For example, in the assignment statement below

```
Dim intX As Integer
intX = 20 Mod 7        'intX is assigned 6
```

intX is assigned 6 because the remainder of 20 divided by 7 is 6:

$$\frac{2 \ \text{r6}}{7\overline{)20}} \quad 20 \ \text{Mod} \ 7$$

$$\frac{14}{6}$$

Modulus division is used in applications where the separate digits of a number are needed, for finding the number of minutes left over after hours have been accounted for, and for other integer-related tasks.

order of operations

In numeric expressions, integer division is performed after multiplication and division. Modulus division is performed next, and then addition and subtraction. For example, the expression 5 * 2 **Mod** 3 \ 2 evaluates to 0 because 5 * 2 is performed first, then 3 \ 2, and then 10 **Mod** 1. Operator precedence can be changed using parentheses. Parentheses can also be used to make an expression clearer for a reader.

Review 6

Skyhook International sells skyhooks that ship 3 per box. Padded envelopes are used to ship individual skyhooks. Create a Skyhook International application that prompts the user for the number of skyhooks ordered, and then displays the number of boxes and envelopes required for the shipment when Ship is clicked. The application interface should look similar to that shown on the right after typing 26 and selecting Ship.

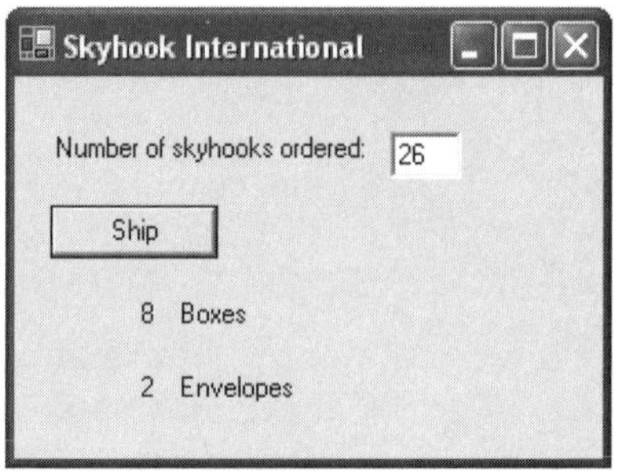

An Introduction to Programming Using Microsoft Visual Basic .NET

4.10 Programming Errors

Syntax errors, logic errors, and run-time errors are the three types of errors that can occur in a program. A statement that violates the rules of Visual Basic .NET is a *syntax error*. For example, the second statement

syntax error

```
Const intCONSTANT1 As Integer = 20
intCONSTANT1 = 12                    'Syntax error!
```

is not syntactically correct because constant assignment is illegal outside the declaration. Syntax errors display a blue wavy underline. Hovering with the mouse over the line displays help text:

```
Const intCONSTANT1 As Integer = 20
intCONSTANT1 = 12    'Syntax error!
```
Constant cannot be the target of an assignment.

logic or semantic error

A *logic error*, also called a *semantic error*, is more difficult to detect. Logic errors are caused by statements that are syntactically correct, but produce undesired or unexpected results, as in the following example:

```
Dim sngLength As Integer
Dim sngArea As Single

sngLength = 3.2                 '3 is actually assigned
sngArea = sngLength * sngLength 'expected value is 10.24
```

The statements assign the value 9 to sngArea rather than the expected 10.24. Although sngLength has a sng prefix to indicate a **Single** it was accidentally declared as an **Integer**. Therefore, 3.2 is converted to 3 in the statement sngLength = 3.2.

programming style

Logic errors must be found by the programmer through testing of the application and by careful reading of the program code. Good programming style in the form of accurate and careful commenting, proper indentation, and descriptive identifiers can help in finding and preventing logic errors.

run-time error
exception

Syntax and logic errors that go undetected may generate a *run-time error* when the program is run. A run-time error, also called an *exception*, halts the program at the statement that cannot be executed. The Code window with the statement causing the error is highlighted and a dialog box describing the error is displayed:

Clicking **Continue** removes the dialog box and places the insertion point in the statement causing the error.

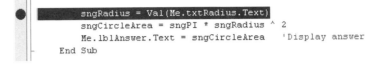
4.11 Debugging an Application

breakpoint

The source of logic errors can be hard to determine without tools for debugging a program. *Debugging* is the process of getting an application to work correctly. One debugging technique uses breakpoints. A *breakpoint* is a statement that has been marked as a stopping point. The code below shows a breakpoint, which is marked with a solid red circle to its left:

```
●          sngRadius = Val(Me.txtRadius.Text)
           sngCircleArea = sngPI * sngRadius ^ 2
           Me.lblAnswer.Text = sngCircleArea    'Display answer
      End Sub
```

Watch window

A breakpoint is created by clicking in the gray area to the left of a statement. When the application is run, program execution stops at the first breakpoint and the IDE goes into break mode. In break mode, the Watch window can be used to examine values. Right-clicking a variable, constant, or object name displays a menu with an **Add Watch** command. Selecting this command adds the variable, constant, or object name to the Watch window with its current value:

Debug toolbar

Watch window

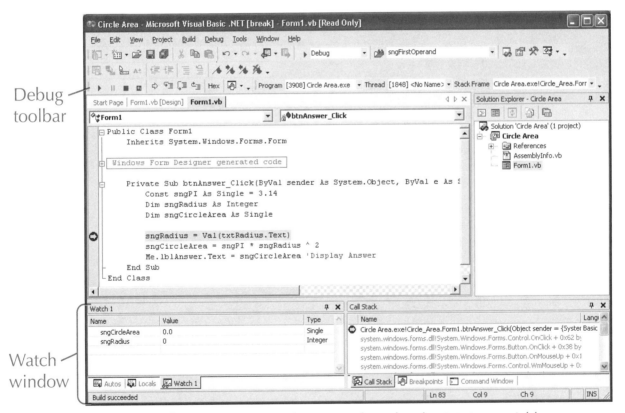

When program execution stopped at a breakpoint, two variables were added to the Watch window

Program execution is continued from a breakpoint by clicking the Step Into button (⬚) on the Debug toolbar or pressing the F11 key, which executes one statement at a time. The Debug toolbar is automatically displayed when a program with a breakpoint is executed. **Step Into** from the Debug menu can also be used to step through a program. Values in the Watch window are automatically updated while stepping through a program.

An Introduction to Programming Using Microsoft Visual Basic .NET

In this review you will use a breakpoint and the Watch window in the Circle Area application last modified in Review 4.

① **OPEN THE CIRCLE AREA PROJECT**

② **ADD A BREAKPOINT TO THE CODE**

    a. Display the Code window.

    b. Click the pointer in the gray area to the left of sngRadius = Val(**Me**.txtRadius.Text). The Code window should look similar to:

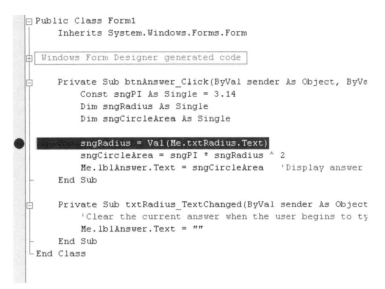

③ **RUN THE APPLICATION**

    a. Run the application. The Circle Area application is displayed.

    b. Type 2 in the text box and then click **Answer**. The breakpoint is reached and the Code window is again displayed. Note the breakpoint statement is now selected in yellow.

    c. Right-click sngCircleArea in the statement below the breakpoint. A menu is displayed.

    d. Select **Add Watch**. sngCirclArea is added to the Watch window with its current value of 0.0 displayed.

    e. Add sngRadius to the Watch window. Note its value.

    f. On the toolbar, click the Step Into button ( ). The next statement is executed. In the Watch window, the value of sngRadius changes to 2.0.

    g. Step into the next statement. sngCircleArea has been assigned 12.56, the result of the circle area expression.

    h. Continue stepping through the application until the Circle Area window is again displayed.

    i. Close the application. The Watch window is closed and the Code window is again displayed.

④ **CLEAR THE BREAKPOINT**

    Click the dot to the left of the breakpoint to remove the breakpoint.

⑤ **QUIT VISUAL BASIC .NET**

This and all subsequent chapters end with a Case Study. *Case Studies* are used to learn problem-solving techniques. Each Case Study illustrates the sequence of steps and thinking that goes into the construction of a substantial application. Learning to program is much more than simply learning a particular language. It is learning how to produce robust, clear, working code. It is learning a *process* for creating an application.

The four steps in creating an application are specification, design, coding, and testing and debugging. In this first Case Study, each of these steps is explained.

specification

spec

The first step in creating an application is clearly defining what the application is to accomplish. This definition is called the *specification*, or *spec*, because it specifies what the application should do. In real-world situations, the specification is developed by talking with the application user and other computer professionals. In this text, the specification will be provided.

The specification for this Case Study is:

The calculator application prompts the user for two numbers (operands) and then displays the result of an expression formed with the operands and an operator ($^\wedge$, *, /, \, Mod, +, −) selected by the user. Selecting an operator automatically displays the result of the expression.

design

Application *design* includes how the interface looks and how the code is written to accomplish the specification. The best way to design the interface is to draw interface designs on paper. The code design is a description of each object's event procedures. In this text, Case Study interface and code designs will be presented.

The interface design for this Case Study is:

The program code design describes how to accomplish the spec. The code design for this Case Study is:

Global variables of type **Single** can be used to store the values entered by the user and the value of the expression. This is good programming style because all the radio button Click event procedures need access to the values. Each radio button Click event procedure evaluates an expression and then assigns the value to a label. TextChanged event procedures will be coded to clear the radio buttons and label.

coding   *Coding* is creating the interface and writing the program code. The interface and code for this Case Study are:

Object	Name	Text
Form1		Calculator
Label1	lblOp1Prompt	First Operand:
Label2	lblOp2Prompt	Second Operand:
TextBox1	txtOperand1	*empty*
TextBox2	txtOperand2	*empty*
GroupBox1	grpOperators	Select an Operator
RadioButton1	radExponentiation	^
RadioButton2	radMultiplication	*
RadioButton3	radDivision	/
RadioButton4	radIntDivision	\
RadioButton5	radModDivision	Mod
RadioButton6	radAddition	+
RadioButton7	radSubtraction	–
Label3	lblResult	Result:
Label4	lblExpressionValue	*empty*

```
Public Class Form1
    Inherits System.Windows.Forms.Form

    Windows Form Designer generated code

    Private Sub txtOperand1_TextChanged(ByVal sender As Object,
    ByVal e As System.EventArgs) Handles txtOperand1.TextChanged

        Me.radAddition.Checked = False
        Me.radDivision.Checked = False
        Me.radExponentiation.Checked = False
        Me.radIntDivision.Checked = False
        Me.radModDivision.Checked = False
        Me.radMultiplication.Checked = False
        Me.radSubtraction.Checked = False
        Me.lblExpressionValue.Text = Nothing

    End Sub


    Private Sub txtOperand2_TextChanged(ByVal sender As Object,
    ByVal e As System.EventArgs) Handles txtOperand2.TextChanged

        Me.radAddition.Checked = False
        Me.radDivision.Checked = False
        Me.radExponentiation.Checked = False
        Me.radIntDivision.Checked = False
        Me.radModDivision.Checked = False
        Me.radMultiplication.Checked = False
        Me.radSubtraction.Checked = False
        Me.lblExpressionValue.Text = Nothing

    End Sub
```

```vb
Private Sub radExponentiation_Click(ByVal sender As Object,
ByVal e As System.EventArgs) Handles radExponentiation.Click

    Dim sngAnswer As Single
    sngAnswer = Val(Me.txtOperand1.Text) ^ Val(Me.txtOperand2.Text)
    Me.lblExpressionValue.Text = sngAnswer

End Sub


Private Sub radMultiplication_Click(ByVal sender As Object,
ByVal e As System.EventArgs) Handles radMultiplication.Click

    Dim sngAnswer As Single
    sngAnswer = Val(Me.txtOperand1.Text) * Val(Me.txtOperand2.Text)
    Me.lblExpressionValue.Text = sngAnswer

End Sub


Private Sub radDivision_Click(ByVal sender As Object,
ByVal e As System.EventArgs) Handles radDivision.Click

    Dim sngAnswer As Single
    sngAnswer = Val(Me.txtOperand1.Text) / Val(Me.txtOperand2.Text)
    Me.lblExpressionValue.Text = sngAnswer

End Sub


Private Sub radIntDivision_Click(ByVal sender As Object,
ByVal e As System.EventArgs) Handles radIntDivision.Click

    Dim sngAnswer As Single
    sngAnswer = Val(Me.txtOperand1.Text) \ Val(Me.txtOperand2.Text)
    Me.lblExpressionValue.Text = sngAnswer

End Sub


Private Sub radModDivision_Click(ByVal sender As Object,
ByVal e As System.EventArgs) Handles radModDivision.Click

    Dim sngAnswer As Single
    sngAnswer = Val(Me.txtOperand1.Text) Mod Val(Me.txtOperand2.Text)
    Me.lblExpressionValue.Text = sngAnswer

End Sub


Private Sub radAddition_Click(ByVal sender As Object,
ByVal e As System.EventArgs) Handles radAddition.Click

    Dim sngAnswer As Single
    sngAnswer = Val(Me.txtOperand1.Text) + Val(Me.txtOperand2.Text)
    Me.lblExpressionValue.Text = sngAnswer

End Sub


Private Sub radSubtraction_Click(ByVal sender As Object,
ByVal e As System.EventArgs) Handles radSubtraction.Click

    Dim sngAnswer As Single
    sngAnswer = Val(Me.txtOperand1.Text) – Val(Me.txtOperand2.Text)
    Me.lblExpressionValue.Text = sngAnswer

End Sub

End Class
```

testing and debugging *Testing* is the process of running the application and entering data to test different possibilities to reveal any bugs. *Debugging* is the process of getting an application to work correctly.

This Case Study should be tested by entering values that are positive, negative, and zero. What will happen when 0 is entered in the second text box? One way to prevent this error is discussed in the next chapter.

Running this Case Study, entering two numbers, and then selecting the * operator displays the following:

Review 8

Add appropriate breakpoints to the Calculator Case Study. In break mode add sngAnswer to the Watch window. Step through the program and watch the value of the variable change.

Chapter Summary

Variables and constants are used in a program so that values can be represented with meaningful names. Using variables and constants is good programming style because code is easier to read and modify. Both are named memory locations that require a declaration. A variable is declared with a **Dim** statement and a constant with a **Const** statement. A variable can be given a value in a declaration. The value of a variable is changed in an assignment statement. The value of a constant cannot change from its initial assignment in a declaration.

Variable and constant identifiers must begin with a letter and contain only letters, digits, and the underscore character. A keyword, such as **End** or **Single**, has special meaning and cannot be used as an identifier. Identifiers should include an appropriate prefix to identify the data type.

abl TextBox

A TextBox is an object that allows the user to enter a value at run time. The TextBox control has the properties Name, Text, and Alignment. A TextBox object name should begin with txt. A label is usually placed near a text box to describe its purpose. A TextChanged event procedure is usually coded for a text box.

The information entered into a text box at run time can be accessed with the Text property of the TextBox object. The Val() function is used to convert the data in the Text property to a numeric value.

Visual Basic .NET includes several built-in data types, including **Short**, **Integer**, **Long**, **Single**, **Double**, **Date**, **Decimal**, **Char**, **String**, and **Boolean**. A variable or constant declaration should include the appropriate data type for the information to be stored. Visual Basic .NET automatically converts data to match the type of the variable it is being assigned to. If a conversion is not possible, a run-time error is generated.

The scope of a declaration is the set of statements that can access the declared variable or constant. A declaration at the beginning of a procedure is accessible to the statements in the procedure only. This type of declaration is called a local declaration. Global declarations are outside the procedures in a program and are accessible to all the procedures. A global declaration is also called a module-level declaration. It is good programming style to keep the scope of a variable or constant as narrow as possible. For example, a variable used in one procedure only should be declared locally in that procedure, not globally to the module.

Visual Basic .NET includes an integer division operator (\) that returns the whole portion of the quotient, and a modulus division operator (**Mod**) that returns the remainder of a division operation.

A statement that violates the rules of Visual Basic .NET contains a syntax error and is displayed with a blue wavy underline in the Code window. A logic error, also called a semantic error, are caused by syntactically correct statements that produce undesired or unexpected results. Syntax and logic errors that go undetected can cause a run-time error, also called an exception.

Debugging is the process of getting an application to work correctly. One debugging technique uses breakpoints, which is a statement marked as a stopping point. When the IDE is in break mode, the Debug toolbar with a Step Into button and a Watch window for viewing the value of variables is displayed.

The sequence of steps and thinking that goes into the construction of a substantial application are specification, design, coding, and testing and debugging.

Breakpoint A statement that has been marked as a stopping point.

Constant A named memory location which stores a value that cannot be changed from its initial assignment.

Debugging The process of getting an application to work correctly.

Declaration statement A statement used to create a variable or constant.

Coding Creating the interface and writing the program code.

Design How an application's interface will look and how the program code will be written.

Exception See Run-time error.

Floating point A data type that can represent values with numbers after the decimal point.

Function A procedure that performs a task and then returns a value.

Global declaration A declaration outside the procedures of a program. Also called module-level declaration.

Integer division Division performed with the \ operator to return only the whole portion of the quotient.

Keyword Identifier reserved by Visual Basic .NET.

Local declaration A declaration at the beginning of a procedure.

Logic error An error caused by syntactically correct statements that produce unexpected results. Also called semantic error.

Module-level declaration See Global declaration.

Modulus division Division performed with the **Mod** operator to return only the remainder portion of the division operation.

Prompt A label placed near a text box describing the expected input from the user.

Run-time error A syntax or logic error that halts a program at run time. Also called an exception.

Scope The set of statements that can be accessed by a declared variable or constant.

Semantic error See Logic error.

Specification Definition of what an application should do.

String A set of characters.

Syntax error An error caused by a statement that violates the rules of Visual Basic .NET.

Testing The process of running an application and entering data to test different possibilities to reveal any bugs.

Text box An object that allows the user to enter a value.

Variable A named memory location that stores a value.

Watch window The part of the IDE that can be used to examine values.

\   Arithmetic operator used to perform integer division.

Boolean A data type used to represent True or False.

Char A data type representing a single character.

Const Statement used to declare a constant.

Date A data type representing dates and times.

Decimal A data type representing currency.

Dim Statement used to declare a variable.

Double A data type representing very large positive or negative real numbers.

False One of two possible Boolean values.

Integer A data type representing positive or negative integers.

Long A data type representing very large positive or negative integers.

Mod Arithmetic operator used to perform modulus division.

Nothing Keyword that can be used in place of an empty string for clearing labels, and so on.

Short A data type representing positive or negative integers.

Single A data type representing positive or negative real numbers.

Step Into button Clicked to step through a program in break mode. Found on the Debug toolbar.

String A data type representing a string.

TextBox control Used to add a TextBox control class object to a form. Properties include Name, Text, and Alignment. Events include TextChanged.

True One of two possible Boolean values.

Val() A function that takes a string and returns a number corresponding to the numeric characters.

1. What would be the final value of the variable sngResult after each set of statements below are executed?

    a) **Dim** sngNumber **As Single** = 10
        Dim sngResult **As Single**
        sngNumber = 2 * 3
        sngResult = sngNumber * 2

    b) **Dim** sngNumber **As Single**
        Dim sngResult **As Single** = 5
        sngNumber = 2
        sngResult = sngResult + sngNumber

2. List three legal and three illegal variable identifiers illustrating the rules for identifiers in Visual Basic .NET. Indicate why each illegal name is incorrect.

3. State the appropriate data type and a descriptive variable identifier that begins with an appropriate prefix for each of the following:
    a) number of students in a class
    b) class average
    c) name of the school
    d) grade, given as letter
    e) distance to the moon
    f) whether a bill has been paid or not
    g) the cost of a pizza
    h) the date of the last day of school

4. Write variable declarations to separately represent the first, middle, and last names of a student, the age of a student, and the GPA (Grade Point Average) of a student. Be sure to use good programming style when naming the variables.

5. Discuss the various ways a variable can get a value.

6. Why is the Val() function used when the data from a text box is assigned to a numeric variable?

7. What is the primary purpose of a TextBox object?

8. Why do text boxes have labels near them?

9. Assume the statement **Dim** intValue **As Integer** = 3 is executed in a Click event procedure for a button. After that button is clicked, another button is clicked which contains the statements:

    Dim intValue **As Integer**
    Me.lblOutput.Text = intValue

    a) Is the scope of intValue local or global?
    b) What is shown in the label? Why?

10. For each of the following determine if the code contains a syntax error, logical error, or run-time error, and then correct the code.

a) **Dim** intNum = 6

b) intNum = Value(**Me**.txtNum.Text)

c) lblOutput = strMessage

d) **Dim** intTest1 **As Integer**
Dim intTest2 **As Integer**
Dim sngAvg **As Single**
intTest1 = Val(**Me**.txtTest1.Text)
intTest2 = Val(**Me**.txtText2.Text)
sngAvg = intTest1 + intTest2 / 2

e) **Dim** intNumberTests **As Integer**
Dim intTest1 **As Integer** = 80
Dim intTest2 **As Integer** = 88
Dim sngAvg **As Single**
sngAvg = (intTest1 + intTest2) / intNumberTests

f) **Const** intMAXSIZE **As Integer** = 22   'Maximum allowable class size
Dim intMaxSize **As Integer**   'Current class size
intMaxSize = Val(**Me**.txtMax.Text)
Me.lblEmptySeats.Text = intMAXSIZE – intMaxSize

11. What is assigned to decTaxRate in the following statement if seven percent is typed in the txtTaxRate text box?

decTaxRate = Val(**Me**.txtTaxRate.Text)

12. Write each equation as a Visual Basic .NET expression, assuming all variables are declared and π is a constant named PI.

a) $A = lw$ (geometry)

b) $P = \dfrac{R - C}{N}$ (business)

c) $A = \dfrac{h(b_1 + b_2)}{N}$ (geometry)

d) $V = \dfrac{4}{3}\pi r^3$ (geometry)

e) $A = \dfrac{F + S + T}{3}$ (algebra)

f) $P = \dfrac{5F}{4d^2}$ (physics)

g) $A = P + Prt$ (business)

h) $M = \dfrac{Pr(1+r)^n}{(1+r)^n - 1}$ (algebra)

i) $x = \dfrac{-b\sqrt{b^2 - 4ac}}{2a}$ (business)

13. For the expressions in parts (a) through (h) of question 12, write a Visual Basic .NET expression that solves for the variable listed:

a) l
b) R
c) b_1
d) r
e) T
f) F
g) P
h) P

14. Determine if each of the following statements is true or false. If false, explain why.

a) Constant declarations must be placed in the beginning of a program.
b) Visual Basic .NET sees no difference between the variables intNEW and intNew.
c) Since **End** is a keyword, intEnd would not be allowed as a variable.
d) In the variable assignment statement intX = 4.5, intX is assigned the value 4.
e) In the variable assignment statement sngX = 14 Mod 4 * 2, sngX is assigned the value 4.
f) The Visual Basic .NET IDE informs the programmer of a syntax error.
g) A breakpoint temporarily stops the execution of a program, but pressing the right-arrow key continues execution.

15. What is assigned to intY when intX is 1998? When intX is 1776? When intX is 38? Explain, in general, the result of this expression:

```
Dim intX As Integer
Dim intY As Integer
intY = (intX \ 10) Mod 10
```

Exercise 1 ———————————————————————— Object Height

The height of an object at any given time dropped from a starting height of 100 meters is given by the equation $h = 100 - 4.9 * t^2$ where t is the time in seconds. Create an Object Height application that prompts the user for a time less than 4.5 seconds and then displays the height of the object at that time when Height is clicked. The application interface should look similar to:

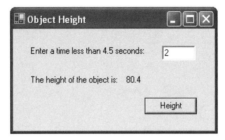

Exercise 2 ———————————————————————— Temperature Conversion

a) Create a Temperature Conversion application that prompts the user for a temperature in degrees Fahrenheit and then displays the temperature in degrees Celsius when Celsius is clicked. Use the formula $C = 5/9(F-32)$ to make the conversion. Test the program with values 212, 32, 98.6, and –40. The application interface should look similar to:

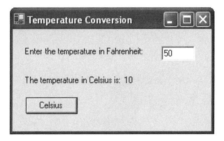

b) Modify the Temperature Conversion application to include a Program menu with Celsius, Fahrenheit, and Exit commands. Use the formula in part (a) above to determine the formula for converting from Celsius to Fahrenheit. Modify the prompt to display Enter the temperature: Modify the temperature label appropriately. Remove the Celsius button and corresponding code and size the form appropriately.

Exercise 3 ⟳ ———————————————————— Rectangle Area and Perimeter

Modify the Rectangle Area and Perimeter application created in Chapter 3 Exercise 8 to prompt the user for the length and width of the rectangle and then display the area and perimeter of the rectangle when Answer is clicked. The application interface should look similar to:

```
┌──────────────────────────────────────────┐
│ ▣ Rectangle Area and Perimeter  [_][□][X] │
│ Program                                    │
│  ┌──────────────────────────────────────┐ │
│  │  Enter the length: [10]   Enter the width: [5] │
│  │                                        │ │
│  │      Area =  50                        │ │
│  │                        ┌──────────┐    │ │
│  │      Perimeter = 30    │  Answer  │    │ │
│  │                        └──────────┘    │ │
│  └──────────────────────────────────────┘ │
└──────────────────────────────────────────┘
```

Exercise 4 ———————————————————————————————— Pizza Cost

The cost of making a pizza at a local shop is as follows:

- Labor cost is $0.75 per pizza, regardless of size
- Rent cost is $1.00 per pizza, regardless of size
- Materials is $0.05*diameter*diameter (diameter is measured in inches)

Create a Pizza Cost application that prompts the user for the size of a pizza and then displays the cost of making the pizza when Cost is clicked. The application interface should look similar to:

```
┌──────────────────────────────────────────┐
│ ▣ Pizza Cost            [_][□][X]          │
│                                            │
│  Enter the size of the pizza in inches:    │
│                                  [10]      │
│                                            │
│  The total cost of the pizza is $  6.75    │
│                                            │
│              ┌──────────┐                  │
│              │   Cost   │                  │
│              └──────────┘                  │
└──────────────────────────────────────────┘
```

Exercise 5 ————————————————————————————————————— Energy

Einstein's famous formula, $e=mc^2$, gives the amount of energy released by the complete conversion of matter of mass m into energy e. If m represents the mass in kilograms and c represents the speed of light in meters per second (3.0×10^8 m/s), then the result is in the energy units Joules. It takes 360000 Joules to light a 100-watt light bulb for an hour. Create an Energy application that prompts the user for a mass in kilograms and then displays the energy and the number of light bulbs that could be powered when Energy is clicked. The application interface should look similar to:

$C = 5/9*(f-32)$

```
┌──────────────────────────────────────────┐
│ ▣ Energy                [_][□][X]          │
│                                            │
│  Enter the mass in kg::  [.01]             │
│                                            │
│  The energy produced                       │
│  in Joules =              9E+14            │
│                                            │
│  The number of 100-watt                    │
│  light bulbs powered =    2.5E+09          │
│                                            │
│              ┌──────────┐                  │
│              │  Energy  │                  │
│              └──────────┘                  │
└──────────────────────────────────────────┘
```

Exercise 6 ⟳ ——————————————————————————Long Jump Average

Modify the Long Jump Average application created in Chapter 3 Exercise 9 to prompt the user for the lengths of four long jumps and then display the average jump length when Average is clicked. The application interface should look similar to:

Exercise 7 —————————————————————————————— Change

Create a Change application that prompts the user for an amount less than 100 and then displays the minimum number of coins necessary to make the change when Coins is clicked. The change can be made up of quarters, dimes, nickels, and pennies. The application interface should look similar to:

Exercise 8 ————————————————————————— Digits of a Number

a) Create a Digits of a Number application that prompts the user for a two-digit number and then displays the digits separately when Digits is clicked. The application interface should look similar to:

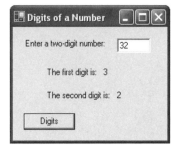

b) Modify the Digits of a Number application to include a Program menu with a Digits command.

An Introduction to Programming Using Microsoft Visual Basic .NET

Exercise 9 ———————————————————————— Time Conversion

Create a Time Conversion application that prompts the user for a time in minutes and then displays the time in seconds or hour:minute format depending on the radio button clicked. Be sure to consider times where the number of minutes left over is less than 10. For example, 184 minutes in hour:minute format is 3:04 (Hint: use the modulus operator). The application interface should look similar to the following after clicking Minutes to hour:minute format:

An Introduction to Programming Using Microsoft Visual Basic .NET

Controlling Program Flow with Decision Structures

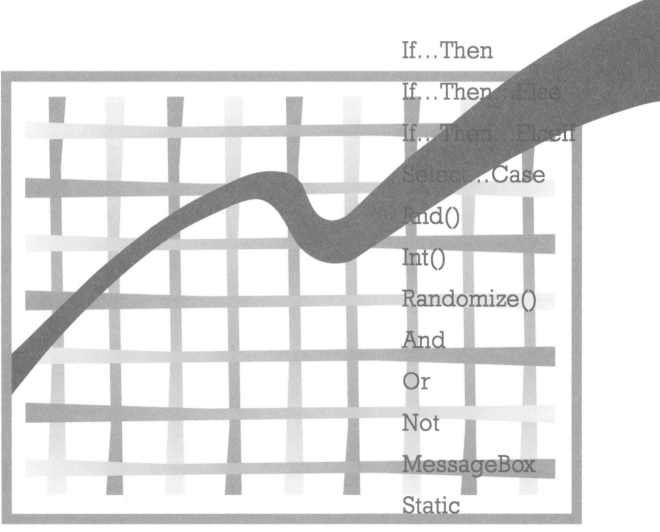

If...Then

If...Then...Else

If...Then...ElseIf

Select...Case

Rnd()

Int()

Randomize()

And

Or

Not

MessageBox

Static

CheckBox

Chapter 5 Expectations

After completing this chapter you will be able to:

1. Use the If...Then, If...Then...Else, and If...Then...ElseIf statements.

2. Understand Nested If...Then...Else statements.

3. Understand roundoff error.

4. Use the Select...Case and Select...Case Is statements.

5. Generate random numbers.

6. Return the integer portion of a number without rounding.

7. Understand variable lifetime.

8. Use And, Or, and Not in Boolean expressions.

9. Understand algorithms and pseudocode.

10. Use message boxes in applications.

11. Use counters in applications.

The concepts explained in this chapter include using decision structures to control the flow of a program, roundoff error, and counter variables. Creating algorithms, using logical operators, and generating random numbers are also discussed. The CheckBox control and displaying message boxes are explained.

5.1 The If...Then Statement

decision structure

The **If**...**Then** statement is a *decision structure* that executes a set of statements when a condition is True. The **If**...**Then** statement takes the form:

```
If condition Then
    statements
End If
```

For example, in the following **If**...**Then** statement intGuess = 7 is the *condition*. Note that the equal sign in the condition is used to compare values, rather than make an assignment:

```
If intGuess = 7 Then
    Me.lblMessage.Text = "You guessed it!"
End If
```

If the value of intGuess is 7, the assignment statement changing the Text property of the label is executed. If the value of intGuess is not equal to 7 (i.e. it is greater than or less than 7), then the assignment statement is not executed and program flow continues to the **End If**, which is required to end the **If**...**Then** statement.

Boolean expression
relational operators

The condition of an **If**...**Then** statement is a *Boolean expression*, which evaluates to either True or False. *Relational operators* can be used to form Boolean expressions. In the previous **If**...**Then** statement, the equal to relational operator (=) was used. There are five other relational operators in addition to the = operator:

Operator	Meaning
=	equal to
<	less than
<=	less than or equal to
>	greater than
>=	greater than or equal to
<>	not equal to

Boolean variable

A Boolean variable may also be used as the *condition* of an **If**...**Then** statement because its value is either True or False.

The Number Guess application demonstrates an If...**Then** statement:

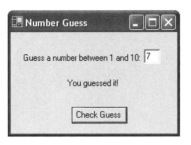

```
Public Class Form1
    Inherits System.Windows.Forms.Form

    Windows Form Designer generated code

    Private Sub btnCheckGuess_Click(ByVal sender As Object,
        Const intSECRETNUMBER As Integer = 7
        Dim intGuess As Integer
        intGuess = Val(Me.txtNumber.Text)
        If intGuess = intSECRETNUMBER Then
            Me.lblMessage.Text = "You guessed it!"
        End If
    End Sub
End Class
```

Running the application, typing 5 in the text box, and then clicking Check Guess displays no message. Typing 7 and clicking Check Guess displays the message "You guessed it!"

5.2 Roundoff Error

The condition of an If...**Then** statement should never make an equality comparison between floating point numbers because of the possibility of roundoff error. A *roundoff error* occurs when a floating point number cannot be exactly represented in binary notation by the computer. For example, the decimal number 0.8 is a repeating decimal in binary form (0.1100110011...). Since there are only a finite number of bits in memory that can be used to represent a number, a repeating decimal must be rounded off, preventing an exact representation.

For example, consider the following statements:

If (4.80 * 100 – 480) = 0 **Then**
    Me.lblComparison.Text = "Zero"
End If

The condition seems to be True. However, the number 4.80 cannot be exactly represented in binary. Therefore, when 4.80 is multiplied by 100 the result is slightly different from 480. This difference is due to roundoff error. In this case, subtracting 480 from 4.80 * 100 results in a very small number that is not equal to 0 (–1.77635683940025E-14). The following statements are one way to take into consideration possible roundoff error:

Const sngVERYSMALLVALUE **As Single** = 0.000001
If (4.80 * 100 – 480) < sngVERYSMALLVALUE **Then**
    Me.lblComparison.Text = "Nearly zero."
End If

Review 1

Create a Test Grade application that prompts the user for a test grade and then displays "Good job!" for a test grade greater than or equal to 70 when Check Grade is clicked. The application interface should look similar to that shown on the right after typing 88 and clicking Check Grade. Be sure to include a TextChanged event procedure for the text box.

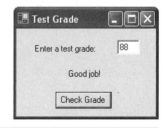

An Introduction to Programming Using Microsoft Visual Basic .NET

5.3 The If...Then...Else Statement

The If...Then statement can include an optional Else clause that is executed when the If condition evaluates to False. The If...Then...Else statement takes the following form:

```
If condition Then
    statements
Else
    statements
End If
```

Indenting Code

Properly indenting code becomes even more important as decision structures become large and complex.

The Number Guess application could be modified to include an If...Then...Else statement:

```
If intGuess = intSECRETNUMBER Then
    Me.lblMessage.Text = "You guessed it!"
Else
    Me.lblMessage.Text = "Try again."
End If
```

Running the application, typing a number other than 7, and then clicking Check Guess displays the message "Try again." Typing 7 and then clicking Check Guess displays the message "You guessed it!"

programming style

The indentation used in the If...Then...Else statement is good programming style and has no effect on the execution of the statement. The indentation makes it easier for a programmer reading the code to follow the logic of the statement. This is especially important as If...Then...Else statements become large.

Review 2

Modify the Test Grade application created in Review 1 so that "Good job!" is displayed for a grade greater than or equal to 70 and Study more. is displayed for a grade less than 70.

Review 3

Modify the Circle Area application created in Chapter 4 to display the message Negative radii are illegal. when a negative radius value is entered otherwise the the area of the circle should be displayed. The interface should look similar to that shown on the right after typing −5 and clicking Answer.

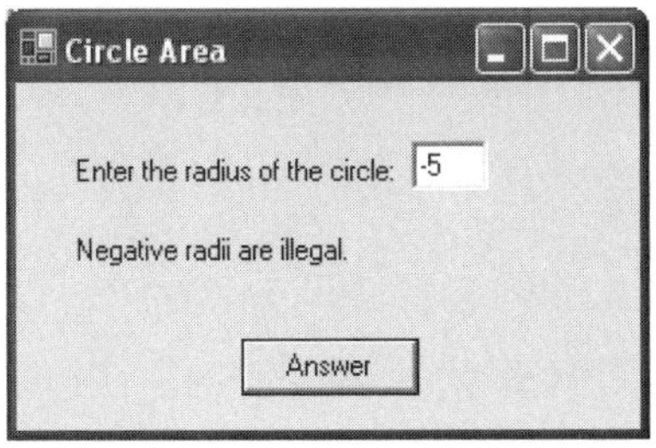

5.4 Nested If...Then...Else Statements

nested

An If...**Then**...**Else** statement can contain another If...**Then**...**Else** or If...**Then** statement, which is said to be *nested*. For example, the Number Guess application could be modified to give the user more of a hint:

```
If intGuess = intSECRETNUMBER Then          'correct
    Me.lblMessage.Text = "You guessed it!"
Else
    If intGuess < intSECRETNUMBER Then       'too low
        Me.lblMessage.Text = "Too low."
    Else                                     'too high
        Me.lblMessage.Text = "Too high."
    End If
End If
```

programming style

Nested statements should be indented for good programming style.

5.5 The If...Then...ElseIf Statement

The If...**Then**...**ElseIf** statement (note there is no space in **ElseIf**) is used to decide among three or more actions and takes the form:

```
If condition Then
    statements
ElseIf condition Then
    statements
...
Else
    statements
End If
```

There can be multiple **ElseIf** clauses, and the last **Else** clause is optional. For example, there are three possible decisions in the If...**Then**...**ElseIf** statement below:

```
If intGuess = intSECRETNUMBER Then              'correct
    Me.lblMessage.Text = "You guessed it!"
ElseIf intGuess < intSECRETNUMBER Then          'too low
    Me.lblMessage.Text = "Too low."
Else                                            'too high
    Me.lblMessage.Text = "Too high."
End If
```

The logic used in developing an If...**Then**...**ElseIf** statement is important. For example, when testing a range of numbers, If conditions must be properly ordered because *statements* are executed only for the first True condition and then program flow continues to the **End If**.

programming style

When choosing between nested If...**Then**...**Else** statements and a single If...**Then**...**ElseIf** statement, the If...**Then**...**ElseIf** is easier to read and understand and is considered better programming style.

Review 4

Create a Number Guess application like the one shown in Section 5.1. Write the Number Guess code so that 7 is the secret number and an If...**Then**...**ElseIf** statement is used to determine the message to display.

An Introduction to Programming Using Microsoft Visual Basic .NET

5.6 The Select...Case Statement

The Select...Case statement is a decision structure that uses the result of an expression to determine which block of code to execute. The Select...Case statement is sometimes preferable to the If...Then...ElseIf statement because code may be easier to read. The Select...Case statement takes the form:

> **Select** *expression*
>   **Case** *value*
>   *statements*
>   ...
>   **Case Else**
>   *statements*
> **End Select**

To

expression must evaluate to a built-in data type. There can be multiple **Case** clauses, and the **Case Else** clause is optional. The *value* type should match the *expression* type and can be a single value, a list separated by commas, or a range separated by the keyword **To**. **End Select** is required to end the Select...Case statement.

The Select...Case statement below uses the value of a score to determine the message to display:

```
Select Case intScore
    Case 0, 10        'Score is 0 or 10
        Me.lblMessage.Text = "Nice try."
    Case 20 To 25     'Score is 20, 21, 22, 23, 24, or 25
        Me.lblMessage.Text = "Great!"
    Case Else         'Score other than 0, 10, 20, 21, 22, 23, 24, or 25
        Me.lblMessage.Text = "Invalid score."
End Select
```

Review 5

Modify the Test Grade application last modified in Review 2 to use a Select...Case statement to display A for grades 93 through 100, B for 85 through 92, C for 78 through 84, D for 69 through 77, F for 0 through 68, and "Invalid grade." for any other number instead of the "Good job!" and "Study more." messages.

5.7 The Select...Case Is Statement

The Select...Case Is statement compares the result of an expression to a range of values when a relational operator is part of the *value*. For example, the following statement uses ranges to determine the message to display:

```
Select Case intScore
    Case Is < 10                            'less than 10
        Me.lblMessage.Text = "Nice try."
    Case Is < 25                            'less than 25
        Me.lblMessage.Text = "Good."
    Case Is >= 25                           'greater than or equal to 25
        Me.lblMessage.Text = "Great!"
End Select
```

Modify the Test Grade application last modified in Review 5 to use a **Select…Case Is** and ranges of values to determine which grade to display.

5.8 Generating Random Numbers

Rnd()

Games, simulators, screen savers, and many other types of applications require random numbers. Visual Basic .NET includes a built-in Rnd() function that generates a random number that is greater than or equal to 0 and less than 1. For example, the Random Numbers application generates and displays six random numbers when Random Numbers is clicked:

A random number is generated and displayed in a label with a statement similar to:

Me.lblRandNum1.Text = Rnd()

generating random numbers in a range

Using Rnd() alone generates random numbers greater than or equal to 0 and less than 1. To generate random numbers in a greater range, Rnd() is multiplied by the upper limit of the range. This produces numbers from 0 to one less than the upper limit. For example, to generate random numbers greater than or equal to 0 and less than 10, a statement similar to the following is used:

Me.lblRandNum1.Text = Rnd() * 10

A lower limit for a range of random numbers can be specified using the following expression:

(*HighNumber* – *LowNumber* + 1) * Rnd() + *LowNumber*

HighNumber is the maximum value desired and *LowNumber* is the minimum value. For example, the following statement generates a number greater than or equal to 10 and less than 31 ((30 – 10 + 1) * Rnd() + 10) and then assigns it to a label:

Me.lblRandNum1.Text = 21 * Rnd() + 10

The Fix() Function

Fix() is a Visual Basic .NET built-in function that is similar to Int(). Int() and Fix() work the same for positive numbers. However, for negative numbers Int() returns the first negative integer less than or equal to its argument, while Fix() returns the first negative integer that is greater than or equal to its argument. For example, Fix(-5.4) returns –5 and Int(-5.4) returns –6.

Using this type of expression, the Random Numbers application can be modified to display six floating point numbers in the range 10 to 30:

Int()

Numbers generated by Rnd() are real numbers with a decimal portion. To produce random integers (whole numbers), the Int() function can be used to return the integer portion of a number without rounding. The Int() function requires a number in parentheses after the function name. For example, the following statement uses the Int() function to generate a random integer in the range 10 to 30 and then assigns it to a label:

Me.lblRandNum1.Text = Int(21 * Rnd()) + 10

Using this type of expression, the Random Numbers application can be modified to display six integers in the range 10 to 30:

How Random Numbers are Generated

The Randomize() statement uses the value returned by the computer's clock as a seed. A seed is a value used by the Rnd() function to generate a pseudorandom (not truly random) sequence of numbers.

Randomize()

Programs using Rnd() should also include one Randomize() statement in the beginning of the event procedure before the Rnd() function is used. Randomize() initializes the Rnd() function so that different random numbers are generated from run to run.

Review 7

In this review you will create the Random Numbers application discussed in Section 5.8.

① CREATE A NEW PROJECT

Create a Windows application named Random Numbers.

② CREATE THE INTERFACE

Refer to the form below to add, position, and size objects. Use the table below to set properties.

Object	Name	Text
Form1		Random Numbers
Label1	lblRandNum1	*empty*
Label2	lblRandNum2	*empty*
Label3	lblRandNum3	*empty*
Label4	lblRandNum4	*empty*
Label5	lblRandNum5	*empty*
Label6	lblRandNum6	*empty*
Button1	btnRandomNumbers	Random Numbers

③ WRITE THE APPLICATION CODE

a. Display the Code window.

b. Add comments that include your name and today's date.

c. Create a btnRandomNumbers_Click event procedure and then add the statements:

```
Me.lblRandNum1.Text = Rnd()
Me.lblRandNum2.Text = Rnd()
Me.lblRandNum3.Text = Rnd()
Me.lblRandNum4.Text = Rnd()
Me.lblRandNum5.Text = Rnd()
Me.lblRandNum6.Text = Rnd()
```

④ RUN THE APPLICATION

a. Save the modified Random Numbers project.

b. Run the application. Click Random Numbers. Write down on a piece of paper the six numbers generated.

c. Run the application again and click Random Numbers. Note that the numbers are the same as before.

d. Close the Random Numbers application.

⑤ ADD THE RANDOMIZE() STATEMENT

a. In the btnRandomNumbers_Click event procedure, add a Randomize() statement:

```
Randomize()
Me.lblRandNum1.Text = Rnd()
Me.lblRandNum2.Text = Rnd()
Me.lblRandNum3.Text = Rnd()
Me.lblRandNum4.Text = Rnd()
Me.lblRandNum5.Text = Rnd()
Me.lblRandNum6.Text = Rnd()
```

b. Save the modified Random Numbers application and then run the application a few times. Note that the numbers are always different.

An Introduction to Programming Using Microsoft Visual Basic .NET

Modify the btnRandomNumbers_Click event procedure to generate random integers between 10 and 30, similar to:

```
Randomize ()
Me.lblRandNum1.Text = Int(21 * Rnd()) + 10
Me.lblRandNum2.Text = Int(21 * Rnd()) + 10
Me.lblRandNum3.Text = Int(21 * Rnd()) + 10
Me.lblRandNum4.Text = Int(21 * Rnd()) + 10
Me.lblRandNum5.Text = Int(21 * Rnd()) + 10
Me.lblRandNum6.Text = Int(21 * Rnd()) + 10
```

⑦ RUN THE APPLICATION

Save the modified Random Numbers project and then run the application a few times.

⑧ PRINT THE CODE AND THEN CLOSE THE PROJECT

5.9 Algorithms

Applications with complex specifications require a method of design called an algorithm. An *algorithm* is a set of steps that tell how to solve a problem. For example, the algorithm for the Number Guess application looks similar to:

1. Determine a secret number.

2. Get a number from the player.

3. Compare the player's number with the secret number.

4. If the player's number is the same as the secret number go to step 5, otherwise tell the player if the number entered was too low or too high and then go back to step 2.

5. Display a message telling the player the secret number was guessed.

pseudocode   An algorithm can be further refined by writing it in *pseudocode*, which is both English and program code. For example, the Number Guess algorithm can be written in the following pseudocode:

```
Sub btnCheckGuess_Click()
    SecretNumber = 7
    Get guess from text box
    If guess = SecretNumber Then
        Display "You guessed it!"
    ElseIf guess < SecretNumber Then
        Display "Too low."
    Else
        Display "Too high."
    End If
End Sub
```

Creating an algorithm and then writing pseudocode allows a programmer to think through a program before actually typing code. This helps a programmer focus on the overall structure of a program and may reduce errors in logic.

5.10 Static Variables

lifetime

As discussed in Chapter 4, the scope of a variable is the set of statements that can use the variable. In addition to scope, variables have a lifetime in which they exist in memory. The *lifetime* of a local variable is the duration of the procedure in which it was declared. A global variable's lifetime is the duration of the program.

The lifetime of a local variable can be extended by using a **Static** declaration statement, which takes the form:

Static *variable_name* **As** *type = initial_value*

scope

programming style

A static variable is declared using the keyword **Static** instead of **Dim**. It should also be explicitly initialized in the declaration. A *static variable's* scope is local to the procedure in which it is declared, but its lifetime is the duration of the program. When either a static and global variable can be used, the static variable is a better choice because it is good programming style to keep the scope of a variable as narrow as possible.

event procedures

Static variables are necessary in event procedures with variables that should be retained in memory throughout program execution. A variable declared in a Click event procedure is redeclared and reinitialized each time the Click event occurs unless the variable is declared as static. For example, the following declaration assigns a random number to a static variable. Unless the variable is assigned a new value, this value is retained throughout program execution:

Static intSecretNumber **As Integer** = Int(50*Rnd())+1

Review 8

In this review you will create the Guessing Game application. Guessing Game is similar to the Number Guess application, except that it can be played again and again by the same user because a new random number between 1 and 50 is generated for the secret number each time the application is started. The algorithm for Guessing Game is:

1. Generate a random secret number between 1 and 50.

2. Get a number from the player.

3. Compare the player's number with the secret number.

4. If the player's number equals the secret number go to step 5, otherwise tell the player if the number entered was too low or too high and then go back to step 2.

5. Display a message telling the player the secret number was guessed.

The Guessing Game algorithm can be refined into the following pseudocode:

```
Sub btnCheckGuess_Click()
    Generate a random number between 1 and 50 once when program starts
    Get guess from text box
    If guess = secret number Then
        Display "You guessed it!"
    ElseIf guess < secret number Then
        Display "Too low."
    Else
        Display "Too high."
    End If
End Sub
```

An Introduction to Programming Using Microsoft Visual Basic .NET

① *CREATE A NEW PROJECT*

Create a Windows application named Guessing Game.

② *CREATE THE INTERFACE*

Refer to the form below to add, position, and size objects. Use the table below to set properties.

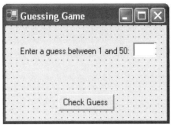

Object	Name	Text
Form1		Guessing Game
Label1	lblPrompt	Enter a guess between 1 and 50:
TextBox1	txtPlayerGuess	*empty*
Label2	lblMessage	*empty*
Button1	btnCheckGuess	Check Guess

③ *WRITE THE APPLICATION CODE*

a. Display the Code window.

b. Add comments that include your name and today's date.

c. Create two global variables and then create a btnCheckGuess_Click event procedure with the statements:

```
Public Class Form1
    Inherits System.Windows.Forms.Form

    Windows Form Designer generated code

    Const intMIN As Integer = 1
    Const intMAX As Integer = 50

    Private Sub btnCheckGuess_Click(ByVal sender As System.Object, ByVal e As System.EventArgs)
        Randomize()
        Static intSecretNumber As Integer = Int((intMAX - intMIN + 1) * Rnd()) + intMIN
        Dim intGuess As Integer

        intGuess = Val(Me.txtPlayerGuess.Text)
        If intGuess = intSecretNumber Then          'correct
            Me.lblMessage.Text = "You guessed it!"
        ElseIf intGuess < intSecretNumber Then       'too low
            Me.lblMessage.Text = "Too low."
        Else
            Me.lblMessage.Text = "Too high."          'too high
        End If
    End Sub
End Class
```

d. Create a txtPlayerGuess_TextChanged event procedure that assigns **Nothing** to the label.

④ *RUN THE APPLICATION*

Save the modified Guessing Game application and then play the game a few times to test it.

⑤ *PRINT THE CODE AND THEN CLOSE THE PROJECT*

5.11   Logical Operators

And
Or

A Boolean expression can be formed using the logical operators **And** and **Or**. A *logical operator* joins two expressions to create an expression that evaluates to either True or False. For example, the following statement tests for invalid guesses:

```
If intGuess < 1 Or intGuess > 50 Then          'invalid guess
    Me.lblMessage.Text = "Invalid guess."
ElseIf intGuess = intSecretNumber Then          'correct guess
    Me.lblMessage.Text = "You guessed it!"
...
```

The condition of the If...Then...ElseIf statement evaluates the first expression, intGuess < 1. The second expression, intGuess > 50, is then evaluated. If *either* expression is true when the logical operator **Or** is used, then the entire expression is true and "Invalid guess." is displayed.

When the logical operator **And** is used, an expression evaluates to True only when both expressions are True. The tables below show how the logical operators **And** and **Or** are evaluated:

And

Expression1	Expression2	Result
True	True	True
True	False	False
False	True	False
False	False	False

Or

Expression1	Expression2	Result
True	True	True
True	False	True
False	True	True
False	False	False

As another example, consider an application that computes a discount depending on the quantity and type of purchase:

```
If strItem = "Pencil" And intQuantity > 50 Then    'more than 50 pencils
    decDiscount = 1                                 '$1.00 discount
End If
```

This If...Then statement executes the decDiscount = 1 statement if *both* strItem is Pencil *and* intQuantity is greater than 50.

Not

A third logical operator is **Not**. An expression including **Not** is evaluated according to the following rules:

Not

Expression	Result
True	False
False	True

For example, the following statements change the label because strItem is not Pencil:

```
Dim strItem As String
strItem = "Pen"

If Not strItem = "Pencil" Then    'any item EXCEPT Pencil
    Me.lblMessage.Text = "No discount given."
End If
```

In logical expressions, **Not** is evaluated before **And**. **Or** is evaluated last. For example, the expression **Not** 5 < 6 **Or** 2 > 4 **And** 3 < 6 evaluates to False because **Not** 5 < 6 is performed first, then 2 > 4 **And** 3 < 6, and then False **Or** False. Operator precedence can be changed by using parentheses.

An Introduction to Programming Using Microsoft Visual Basic .NET

In this review you will create the Rock Paper Scissors application. Rock Paper Scissors is a popular game used for decision making between two individuals. The rules of the game are Rock dulls Scissors, Scissors cut Paper, and Paper covers Rock. In this computer-game version, the user plays against the computer. The Rock Paper Scissors algorithm is:

1. The player selects either Rock, Paper, or Scissors.

2. A random number between 1 and 3 is generated to represent the computer's choice. A 1 corresponds to Rock, a 2 to Paper, and a 3 to Scissors.

3. Compare the player's choice to the computers choice.

4. Display an appropriate message.

The Rock Paper Scissors algorithm can be refined into the following pseudocode:

```
Sub btnPlay_Click()
    Get user's choice from radio buttons
    Generate a random number between 1 and 3
    If user = radRock and comp = Rock Then
        draw
    Elself user = radRock and comp = Paper Then
        computer wins
    Elself user = radRock and comp = Scissors Then
        user wins
    End If
    If user = radPaper and comp = Rock Then
        user wins
    Elself user = radPaper and comp = Paper Then
        draw
    Elself user = radPaper and comp = Scissors Then
        computer wins
    End If
    If user = radScissors and comp = Rock Then
        computer wins
    Elself user = radScissors and comp = Paper Then
        user wins
    Elself user = radScissors and comp = Scissors Then
        draw
    End If
End Sub
```

① CREATE A NEW PROJECT

Create a Windows application named Rock Paper Scissors.

② CREATE THE INTERFACE

Refer to the form below to add, position, and size objects. Use the table below to set properties.

Object	Name	Text	TextAlign	Checked
Form1		Rock Paper Scissors		
GroupBox1	grpThrow	Choose Your Throw		
RadioButton1	radRock	Rock		False
RadioButton2	radPaper	Paper		False
RadioButton3	radScissors	Scissors		False
Label1	lblWinner	*empty*	MiddleCenter	
Button1	btnGo	Go!		

③ WRITE THE APPLICATION CODE

a. Display the Code window.

b. Add comments that include your name and today's date.

c. Create a btnGo_Click event procedure and then add the statements:

```
Const intROCK As Integer = 1
Const intPAPER As Integer = 2
Const intSCISSORS As Integer = 3
Dim intComputerThrow As Integer

'Generate computer throw
Randomize()
intComputerThrow = Int(3 * Rnd()) + 1

If Me.radRock.Checked And intComputerThrow = intROCK Then
    Me.lblWinner.Text = "Computer throws Rock. It's a Draw!"        'Rock Rock
ElseIf Me.radRock.Checked And intComputerThrow = intPAPER Then
    Me.lblWinner.Text = "Computer throws Paper. Computer wins!"   'Rock Paper
ElseIf Me.radRock.Checked And intComputerThrow = intSCISSORS Then
    Me.lblWinner.Text = "Computer throws Scissors. You win!"        'Rock Scissors
End If

If Me.radPaper.Checked And intComputerThrow = intROCK Then
    Me.lblWinner.Text = "Computer throws Rock. You win!"            'Paper Rock
ElseIf Me.radPaper.Checked And intComputerThrow = intPAPER Then
    Me.lblWinner.Text = "Computer throws Paper. It's a Draw!"        'Paper Paper
ElseIf Me.radPaper.Checked And intComputerThrow = intSCISSORS Then
    Me.lblWinner.Text = "Computer throws Scissors. Computer wins!" 'Paper Scissors
End If

If Me.radScissors.Checked And intComputerThrow = intROCK Then
    Me.lblWinner.Text = "Computer throws Rock. Computer wins!"     'Scissors Rock
ElseIf Me.radScissors.Checked And intComputerThrow = intPAPER Then
    Me.lblWinner.Text = "Computer throws Paper. You win!"           'Scissors Paper
ElseIf Me.radScissors.Checked And intComputerThrow = intSCISSORS Then
    Me.lblWinner.Text = "Computer throws Scissors. It's a Draw!"    'Scissors Scissors
End If
```

Save the modified Rock Paper Scissors application and then play the game a few times to test it. Close the application.

Review 10 ↺

Modify the Rock Paper Scissors application created in Review 9 to use nested **If...Then...ElseIf** statements to determine the outcome of game.

Review 11 ↺

Modify the Rock Paper Scissors application created in Review 9 to use a **Select...Case** statement and **If...Then...ElseIf** statements to determine the outcome of game. Hint: Use the intComputerThrow value as the *expression* in the **Select...Case** statement.

5.12   Displaying a Message Box

A message box is a predefined dialog box that displays a message for the user. A message can be displayed to alert the user to invalid data or as a reminder of options required for an application to continue. For example, the Guessing Game application could be modified to alert the user to a guess that is out of range:

> *Message Box Parameters*
>
> A message box can have a title bar by including a string as the second parameter. For example, the following statement displays a message box with a "Game" title bar: MessageBox.Show("Good guess!", "Game")

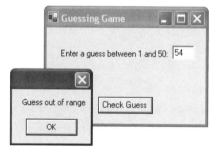

Show   The MessageBox class includes a Show() method for displaying a message box and is used in a statement that takes the form:

MessageBox.Show(*message*)

message is a variable, constant, or a string enclosed in quotation marks. For example, the If...Then...ElseIf statement alerts the user to a number outside the allowed range:

```
If intGuess < 1 Or intGuess > 50 Then       'invalid guess
    MessageBox.Show("Guess out of range.")
ElseIf intGuess = intSecretNumber Then       'correct
    Me.lblMessage.Text = "You guessed it!"
ElseIf intGuess < intSecretNumber Then       'too low
    Me.lblMessage.Text = "Too low."
Else                                          'too high
    Me.lblMessage.Text = "Too high."
End If
```

Review 12

Modify the Guessing Game application created in Review 8 to display a message box with an appropriate message if the user's guess is less than the minimum allowed number or greater than maximum.

Review 13

Modify the Test Grade application last modified in Review 6 so that "Invalid grade." is displayed in a message box if the grade entered is less than 0 or greater than 100.

5.13 Counter Variables

updating a counter

A *counter* is a variable storing a number that is incremented by a constant value. Counters are useful for keeping track of the number of times a user clicks a button, enters a guess, or types a password. The statement for incrementing a counter, often called *updating* a counter, takes the form:

counter = counter + constant

counter is the numeric variable that is updated. *constant* is the number that is added to the current value of *counter*. A counter should be initialized when it is declared and then updated by an unchanging amount. For example, the following statement updates a counter by 1:

intNumTries = intNumTries + 1

In this statement, intNumTries is the name of the counter variable. Each time the statement is executed, 1 is added to the current value of intNumTries and then this new value is assigned to intNumTries.

Static variable

A counter in an event procedure should be declared as a **Static** variable so that it is initialized only once.

Review 14

Modify the Guessing Game application last modified in Review 12 to include a counter that keeps track of the number of guesses made by the user. Have the program display the total number of guesses in a message box after the user correctly guesses the secret number.

Review 15

Modify the Rock Paper Scissors application created in Review 9 to include three counters that maintain the number of wins by the player, the number of wins by the computer, and the number of draws. The scores should be updated and displayed in labels at the end of each game.

5.14 The CheckBox Control

Check boxes allow the user to select options. Unlike radio buttons, more than one check box can be selected at a time. For example, in the Morning To Do application, CheckBox objects give the user options:

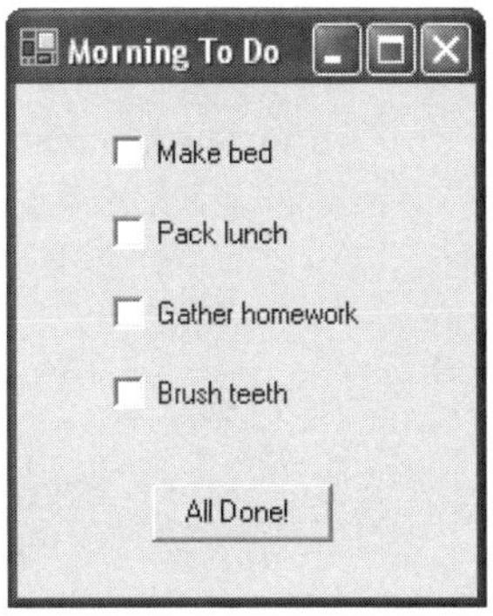

☑ CheckBox

The CheckBox control has the properties:

- **Name** identifies a control for the programmer. It is good programming style to begin CheckBox object names with chk.

- **Text** is the text displayed next to the box.

- **Checked** can be set to either True or False to display the check box with or without a check, respectively.

group box   Related check boxes are sometimes placed together in a GroupBox object. As with radio buttons, a group box should be added to the form before adding check boxes.

If...Then for determining the state of a check box   An **If...Then** statement can be used in a program to determine if a check box is selected or cleared. For example, the following statement displays a message that depends on the state of the check box:

```
If Me.chkLunch.Checked Then      'check box selected
    MessageBox.Show("Don't forget your bottled water!")
Else                             'check box cleared
    MessageBox.Show("Take lunch money!")
End If
```

Click event   A Click event procedure is sometimes coded for a check box. This procedure executes when a check box is clicked and usually includes code to determine the state of the check box and then perform actions depending on whether the check box was selected or cleared.

5.15 The Line-Continuation Character

(underscore)

Visual Basic .NET statements that are long can be typed onto two or more lines when the line-continuation character is used. The underscore (_) is the line-continuation character and must have a space before it and nothing after it and cannot occur within quotation marks. For example, a condition typed on two lines:

```
If Not (Me.chkBed.Checked And Me.chkLunch.Checked _
And Me.chkHomework.Checked And Me.chkTeeth.Checked) Then
    MessageBox.Show("Did you forget something?")
Else
    End
End If
```

programming style

Properly dividing a statement into two or more lines can make code easier to read for the programmer, which is good programming style.

Review 16

In this review you will create the Morning To Do application.

① **CREATE A NEW PROJECT**

Create a Windows application named Morning To Do.

② **CREATE THE INTERFACE**

Refer to the form below to add, position, and size objects. Use the table below to set properties.

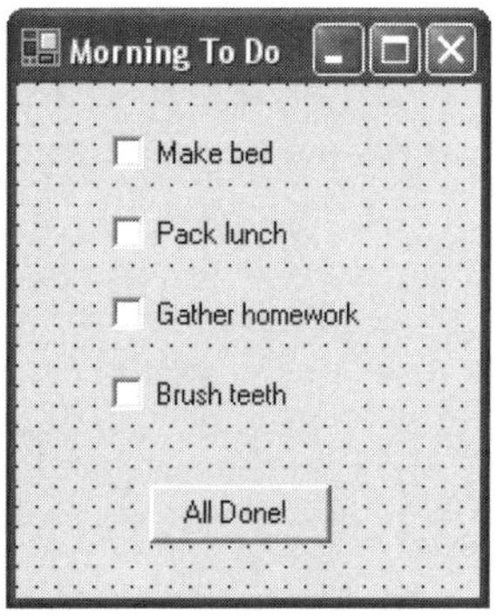

Object	Name	Text	Checked
Form1		Morning To Do	
CheckBox1	chkBed	Make bed	False
CheckBox2	chkLunch	Pack lunch	False
CheckBox3	chkHomework	Gather homework	False
CheckBox4	chkTeeth	Brush teeth	False
Button1	btnAllDone	All Done!	

③ **WRITE THE APPLICATION CODE**

a. Display the Code window.

b. Add comments that include your name and today's date.

c. Create a chkLunch_Click event procedure and then add the statements:

```
If Me.chkLunch.Checked Then
    MessageBox.Show("Don't forget bottled water!")
End If
```

d. Create a btnAllDone_Click event procedure and then add the statements:

```
If Not (Me.chkBed.Checked And Me.chkLunch.Checked _
And Me.chkHomework.Checked And Me.chkTeeth.Checked) Then
    MessageBox.Show("Did you forget something?")
Else
    End
End If
```

④ RUN THE APPLICATION

a. Save the modified Morning To Do application and then run it. Select the Pack Lunch check box and note the message box.

b. Select all the check boxes and then select All Done! The application is ended.

c. Run the application again. Select only two or three of the check boxes and then select All Done! A message box is displayed. Select the remaining check boxes and then select All Done!

⑤ PRINT THE CODE AND THEN CLOSE THE PROJECT

Case Study

In this Case Study a Pizza Order application will be created.

specification   The specification for this Case Study is:

The Pizza Order application allows a user to place an order for pizza by selecting toppings (pepperoni, mushrooms, onions, hot peppers) and a pizza size (regular or large). An order number and the pizza price are displayed when Place Order is clicked. The price is calculated as follows:

Regular:	$6.00
Large:	$10.00
one topping:	$1.00 additional
two toppings:	$1.75 additional
three toppings:	$2.50 additional
four toppings:	$3.25 additional

Clicking New Order clears the selected options on the form, selects Regular, and removes the current price and order number. The order number should automatically increment when the next order is placed during program execution.

design   When designing the interface for this Case Study the options for selecting the pizza size and toppings need to be considered. For each pizza order there can be only one size, but many toppings. Therefore, check boxes should be used to select the toppings (more than one can be selected at a time) and radio buttons should be used to select the size (only one can be selected at a time):

The code design should start with an algorithm and pseudocode:

1. Increment order number.

2. Determine toppings price based on the selected number of toppings.

3. Determine pizza price based on the selected size and then add toppings price.

4. Display pizza price and order number.

5. When a new order is started, select the Regular radio button and clear the check boxes and labels.

The algorithm is implemented with the following pseudocode:

```
Sub btnPlaceOrder_Click()
    Const REGULAR As Decimal = 6
    Const LARGE As Decimal = 10
    Const ONETOPPING As Decimal = 1
    Const TWOTOPPINGS As Decimal = 1.75
    Const THREETOPPINGS As Decimal = 2.5
    Const FOURTOPPINGS As Decimal = 3.25
    Static OrderNumber As Integer = 0
    Dim NumToppings As Integer
    Dim ToppingsPrice As Decimal
    Dim PizzaPrice As Decimal

    Increment OrderNumber

    For each topping check box selected, increment NumToppings

    Use NumToppings to select ONETOPPING, TWOTOPPINGS,
    THREETOPPINGS, or FOURTOPPINGS

    If radRegular.Checked Then
        PizzaPrice = REGULAR + ToppingsPrice
    Else
        PizzaPrice = LARGE + ToppingsPrice
    End If

    lblOrderNumber.Text = OrderNumber
    lblPrice.Text = PizzaPrice
End Sub


Sub btnNewOrder_Click()
    Clear check boxes
    Select the Regular radio button
    Clear labels
End Sub
```

An Introduction to Programming Using Microsoft Visual Basic .NET

coding　　The interface and code for this Case Study are:

Object	Name	Text
Form1		Pizza Order
GroupBox1	grpToppings	Select toppings
CheckBox1	chkPepperoni	Pepperoni
CheckBox2	chkMushrooms	Mushrooms
CheckBox3	chkOnions	Onions
CheckBox4	chkHotPeppers	Hot Peppers
GroupBox2	grpPizzaSize	Select pizza size
RadioButton1	radRegular	Regular
RadioButton2	radLarge	Large
Button1	btnPlaceOrder	Place Order
Button2	btnNewOrder	New Order
Label1	lblOrder	*empty*
Label2	lblOrderNumber	*empty*
Label3	lblPrice	*empty*
Label4	lblPizzaPrice	*empty*

The Checked property of the radRegular radio button must be set to True.

```
Public Class Form1
    Inherits System.Windows.Forms.Form

    Windows Form Designer generated code

    Private Sub btnPlaceOrder_Click(ByVal sender As Object, _
    ByVal e As System.EventArgs) Handles btnPlaceOrder.Click

        Const decREGULAR As Decimal = 6
        Const decLARGE As Decimal = 10
        Const decONETOPPING As Decimal = 1
        Const decTWOTOPPINGS As Decimal = 1.75
        Const decTHREETOPPINGS As Decimal = 2.5
        Const decFOURTOPPINGS As Decimal = 3.25
        Static intOrderNumber As Integer = 0
        Dim intNumToppings As Integer
        Dim decToppingsPrice As Decimal
        Dim decPizzaPrice As Decimal

        'increment order number
        intOrderNumber = intOrderNumber + 1
```

```vb
'Count number of toppings selected
If Me.chkPepperoni.Checked Then
    intNumToppings = intNumToppings + 1
End If
If Me.chkMushrooms.Checked Then
    intNumToppings = intNumToppings + 1
End If
If Me.chkOnions.Checked Then
    intNumToppings = intNumToppings + 1
End If
If Me.chkHotPeppers.Checked Then
    intNumToppings = intNumToppings + 1
End If

'Determine toppings price
Select Case intNumToppings
    Case 1
        decToppingsPrice = decONETOPPING
    Case 2
        decToppingsPrice = decTWOTOPPINGS
    Case 3
        decToppingsPrice = decTHREETOPPINGS
    Case 4
        decToppingsPrice = decFOURTOPPINGS
End Select

'Determine pizza price
If Me.radRegular.Checked Then          'regular pizza size
    decPizzaPrice = decREGULAR + decToppingsPrice
Else                                   'large pizza size
    decPizzaPrice = decLARGE + decToppingsPrice
End If

'Display order number and pizza price
Me.lblOrder.Text = "Order Number:"
Me.lblOrderNumber.Text = intOrderNumber
Me.lblPrice.Text = "Price: $"
Me.lblPizzaPrice.Text = decPizzaPrice

End Sub


Private Sub btnNewOrder_Click(ByVal sender As Object, _
ByVal e As System.EventArgs) Handles btnNewOrder.Click

    Me.chkPepperoni.Checked = False
    Me.chkMushrooms.Checked = False
    Me.chkOnions.Checked = False
    Me.chkHotPeppers.Checked = False
    Me.radRegular.Checked = True
    Me.radLarge.Checked = False
    Me.lblOrder.Text = Nothing
    Me.lblOrderNumber.Text = Nothing
    Me.lblPrice.Text = Nothing
    Me.lblPizzaPrice.Text = Nothing

End Sub

End Class
```

Running Pizza Order, selecting options, and then clicking Place Order displays:

testing and debugging   This Case Study should be tested by generating several different pizza orders and checking the price displayed by hand.

Review 17

Modify the Pizza Order Case Study to include Pickup and Delivery radio buttons in a new group box. If Delivery is selected, $1.50 should be added to the total price of the pizza. Pickup should add nothing to the total price of the pizza and should be selected when the program starts and when a new order is started.

Chapter Summary

Decision structures are used to control program flow. In this chapter the If...Then, If...Then...Else, If...Then...ElseIf, Select...Case, and Select...Case Is statements were used to control program flow. Each of these decision structures evaluates a *condition* to determine program flow. The *condition* in the If...Then statements is a Boolean expression that evaluates to True or False. The If...Then...ElseIf statement is used to decide among three, four, or more actions. The Select...Case statements are also used to decide among many actions. Indentation used in decision structures is good programming style and makes it easier to follow the logic of the statement.

The If...Then statements should never make an equality comparison between floating point numbers because of the possibility of roundoff error. A Boolean expression may be a Boolean variable or an expression formed using relational operators (=, <, <=, >, >=, <>). A Boolean expression may also include logical operators (And, Or, Not).

The Rnd() function generates a random number greater than or equal to 0 and less than 1. The Int() function is used to return the integer portion of a number. The Randomize() statement is used to initialize the Rnd() function so that different random numbers are generated from program run to program run.

An algorithm is a set of steps that tell how to solve a problem. An algorithm refined using both English and program code is called pseudocode. Creating an algorithm and writing pseudocode before using the computer helps reduce logic errors.

Static variables have a local scope but a lifetime the duration of the program. Static variables are necessary in event procedures with variables that should be retained in memory throughout a program run.

A message box is used to provide information to the user, such as when invalid data has been entered. The MessageBox class includes a Show method that displays a predefined dialog box using a string as its message.

A counter is a variable storing a number that is incremented by a constant value. A counter in an event procedure should be declared as a Static variable so that it is initialized only once.

A check box is an object that allows the user to select one or more options from a set of options. The CheckBox control has the properties Name, Text, and Checked. A CheckBox object name should begin with the prefix chk. A Click event is sometimes coded for a check box. The procedure should include an If...Then statement to determine if the check box has been selected or cleared. Related check boxes are sometimes placed together in a group box.

The line-continuation character (_) is used to divide a statement over two or more lines.

Vocabulary

Algorithm   A set of steps that tell how to solve a problem.

Boolean expression   An expression that evaluates to either True or False.

Counter   A variable used to store a value that is updated by a constant value.

Decision structure   A statement that uses a condition to determine which set of statements to execute.

Lifetime   The duration in which a declared variable exists in memory.

Logical operators   Operators (And, Or, and Not) that may be used to form a Boolean expression.

Message box   A predefined dialog box that displays a message for the user.

Nested statements   One or more statements within a statement.

Pseudocode   An algorithm written in both English and program code.

Relational operators   Operators (=, <, <=, >, >=, and <>) that can be used to form a Boolean expression.

Roundoff error   Occurs when a floating point number cannot be exactly represented in binary notation by the computer.

Static variable   A variable with a local scope but a lifetime the duration of the program.

Update   To increment a counter variable.

_ (underscore) The line-continuation character.

= (equal to) Relational operator used to determine if one value is equal to another.

< (less than) Relational operator used to determine if one value is less than another.

<= (less than or equal to) Relational operator used to determine if one value is less than or equal to another.

> (greater than) Relational operator used to determine if one value is greater than another.

>= (greater than or equal to) Relational operator used to determine if one value is greater than or equal to another.

<> (not equal to) Relational operator used to determine if one value is not equal to another.

And Logical operator used to form a Boolean expression. An expression formed using **And** is True only when the expressions it joins are all True.

CheckBox control Used to add a CheckBox control class object to a form. Properties include Name, Text, and Checked. Events include Click.

If...Then Statement that executes code when a condition is True.

If...Then...Else Statement that executes code in the **Else** clause when a condition is False.

If...Then...ElseIf Statement that is used to decide among three or more actions.

Int() A function that returns the integer portion of a number without rounding.

MessageBox class Used to display a predefined dialog box that displays a message and an OK button. Methods include Show().

Not Logical operator used to form a Boolean expression. An expression formed using **Not** is True only when the expression it is used with is False.

Or Logical operator used to form a Boolean expression. An expression formed using **Or** is True when any of the expressions it joins are True.

Randomize() Statement used to initialize the Rnd() function so that different random numbers are generated from run to run.

Rnd() A function used to generate a random number greater than or equal to 0 and less than 1.

Select...Case Statement that executes code depending on the result of an expression.

Select...Case Is Statement that executes code depending on a comparison of a range of values to the result of an expression.

Static Statement used to declare a static variable.

1. Assuming the comment is correct, determine the logic error in the following statement:

    ```
    If intGrade > 90 Then
        Me.lblGrade.Text = "You have an A"    'Displays an A for scores greater than or equal to 90
    End If
    ```

2. What is displayed in the label after the following statement executes? Does the label assignment reflect what was intended? If not, how should the statement be rewritten to produce the intended result?

    ```
    Dim intScore As Integer = 25
    If intScore >= 100 Then
        Me.lblMessage.Text = "You won!"
    ElseIf intScore < 100 Then
        Me.lblMessage.Text = "Good try."
    ElseIf intScore < 50 Then
        Me.lblMessage.Text = "Practice more."
    End If
    ```

3. A *binary search* is a divide-and-conquer technique for efficiently searching a list of numbers that are sorted from lowest to highest. A strategy that incorporates the binary search technique can be used by the Guessing Game player when making guesses about the secret number:

    1. Guess the number halfway between the lowest and highest numbers.

    2. If the number guessed matches the secret number, then the player wins.

    3. If the number guessed is too high, then take the number guessed minus one and make this the highest number and go back to Step 1.

    4. If the number guessed is too low, then take the number guessed plus one and make this the lowest number and go back to Step 1.

    For example, assuming the random number generated in the Guessing Game application is 15, the game would play out as follows when the player uses a divide-and-conquer technique:

Current Low	Current High	Player Types	Message Displayed
1	50	26 (i.e., (1+50)/2=25.5)	Too high.
1	25	13 (i.e., (1+25)/2=13)	Too low.
14	25	20 (i.e., (14+25)/2=19.5)	Too high.
14	19	16 (i.e., (14+19)/2=16.5)	Too high.
14	15	14 (i.e., (14+15)/2=14.5)	Too low.
15	15	15 (i.e., (15+15)/2=15)	You guessed it!

    In another program run, assuming the random number generated is 20, the game would play out as follows using the same divide-and-conquer technique:

Current Low	Current High	Player Types	Message Displayed
1	50	26 (i.e., (1+50)/2=25.5)	Too high.
1	25	13 (i.e., (1+25)/2=13)	Too low.
14	25	20 (i.e., (14+25)/2=19.5)	You guessed it!

    When this approach is taken, it has been proven that a player will not be required to make more than Log_2 n guesses, in this case Log_2 50, or at most 6 guesses. Try this technique yourself. Explain in your own words why this works. Would this strategy be possible if hints were not given after each guess?

4. Check boxes, radio buttons, and text boxes all accept user input.

   a) List the primary differences in the way the three accept input.

   b) Give an example of how each would be used in a specific application.

5. Given the statements

   Dim intQuantity **As Integer** = 20
   Dim decPrice **As Decimal** = 5

   determine the value, True or False, for each of the following expressions:

   a) intQuantity > 10 **And** decPrice > 5
   b) intQuantity = 15 **Or** decPrice = 5
   c) intQuantity >= 20 **And** decPrice >=2 **And** intQuantity * decPrice >= 40
   d) **Not** decPrice = 5
   e) intQuantity < 100 **Or** decPrice > 4 **And Not** intQuantity = 20

6. Write an appropriate decision statement for each of the following:

   a) Display Great Job in a label named lblMessage if sngGrade is 90 or above.

   b) Display High Scorer in a label named lblHigh for intTotalPoints between 100 and 200, inclusive.

   c) Display Number must be less than 100. in a message box if the value in txtGrade is greater than 100.

7. a) Which is the appropriate word for the first blank below, *odd* or *even*? Which is the appropriate word for the second blank?

   ```
   If intNumber Mod 2 = 0 Then
       MessageBox.Show ("Your number is _____")
   Else
       MessageBox.Show ("Your number is _____")
   End If
   ```

   b) Rewrite the If…Then…Else statement from part (a) as a **Select**…**Case** statement.

8. List the errors in the statement below and then rewrite the statement so that it will execute as expected:

   ```
   If 50 <= intNumberTickets <= 100 And_
       Me.radStudent.Checked
       MessageBox.Show = ("Will get student discount and volume discount.)
   ElseIf 50 <= intNumberTickets <= 100
       MessageBox.Show = ("Will get volume discount.)
   ElseIf Me.radStudent.Checked
       MessageBox.Show = ("Will get student discount.)
       Case Else
           MessageBox.Show = ("No discount.)
       End If
   End If
   End If
   End If
   ```


9. Rewrite the following statement so that it does <u>not</u> include a nested If…Then statement:

   ```
   If Me.chkValue1.Checked Then
       If Me.chkValue2.Checked Then
           MessageBox.Show("Both have been applied.")
       End If
   End If
   ```

10. Assume txtTest1, txtTest2, and txtTest3 contain numeric values. Write an **If…Then…Else** statement that displays in a label the average of the three numbers only if all of the numbers are between 0 and 100, otherwise a message box with an appropriate message should be displayed and the text boxes cleared.

11. Assume txtNum1 and txtNum2 contain numeric values. Write an **If…Then…ElseIf** statement that displays a message box with one of the following messages as appropriate:
    First number is larger
    Second number is larger
    Both numbers are equal

12. Write a statement that generates a random whole number between 5 and 50, inclusive.

13. a) List the errors in the statement below and then rewrite the statement so that it will execute as expected:
    ```
    Select Case intNum
        Case 2 Or 3, intNum > 10
            MessageBox.Show("1st Case")
        Case 20 <= intNum < 30
            MessageBox.Show("2nd Case")
    End Case
    ```

    b) Rewrite the **Select…Case** statement in part (a) using an **If…Then…ElseIf** statement.

14. Assume txtMonth contains all uppercase text that is a month of the year, for example, SEPTEMBER. Another text box, txtYear, contains the year. Write a **Select…Case** statement that displays in a message box the number of days in the month entered. Hint: An efficient statement does not require 12 case values. The days in February can be determined by using the following pseudocode:
    ```
    If year Mod 4 <> 0 Then
        use 28 days for February
    ElseIf  year Mod 400 = 0 Then
        use 29 days for February
    ElseIf year Mod 100 = 0 Then
        use 28 days for February
    Else
        use 29 for days in February
    End If
    ```

15. Write a Click event procedure for btnPurchase which calculates the cost of tickets and gives free tickets on every 100th purchase. The txtNumberTickets text box contains the number of tickets for a purchase and each ticket price is $8.00. A counter variable should be updated by one each time Purchase is clicked. On the 100th purchase, a message box should display "Congratulations, the tickets are free!" The counter should then be reset to zero. If the purchase is not the 100th, a message box should display the cost of the tickets. Use appropriate constants and variables.

16. Write a Click event procedure for btnMessage that displays one of the messages below in a message box:

You win $100	2% of the time
You win $10	10% of the time
You win $1	50% of the time
Thanks for trying.	The rest of the time.

Hint: Use a random number between 1 and 100 and a **Select…Case** to determine the message to display.

17. Determine if each of the following statements is true or false. If false, explain why.

a) A decision structure must have an **Else** clause.

b) It is good programming style to line up the **If**, the **Else**, and the **End If** in a decision structure, and to indent the lines in between.

c) The **Select…Case** statement must have the **Case Else** clause.

d) The **Select…Case** statement can only be used if you have more than two cases.

e) Using Rnd() without including Randomize() will produce an error.

f) The value of local variables are always retained in memory for the duration of a program execution.

g) Message boxes can only be used in decision statements.

h) Counter variables are useful for keeping track of the number of times a specific event occurs.

i) intSum, assigned as intSum = 1 + 2 + 3, is a counter variable.

Exercise 1 ———————————————————————— Number of Digits

Create a Number of Digits application that prompts the user for a number less than 100 and then when Check Number is clicked displays whether the number is one digit or two digits:

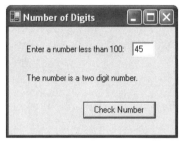

Exercise 2 ———————————————————————————— Payroll

An employee should receive pay equal to time and a half for every hour worked over 40 hours.

a) Create a Payroll application that prompts the user for the number of hours worked and the hourly rate of pay and then calculates the gross weekly wages (before taxes) when Pay is clicked:

b) Modify the Payroll application so that there is an 18% deduction from gross pay, unless the employee is exempt. If an employee is exempt, "NO TAXES DEDUCTED" should be displayed in a message box and then the wages displayed. The application interface should look similar to the following for an employee that is not exempt:

Exercise 3 ———————————————————————————— Printing Prices

Printing prices are typically based on the number of copies to be printed. For example:

0 - 499 copies	$0.30 per copy
500 - 749 copies	$0.28 per copy
750 - 999 copies	$0.27 per copy
1000 copies or more	$0.25 per copy

Create a Printing Prices application that prompts the user for the number of copies to print and then when Price is clicked displays the price per copy and the total price:

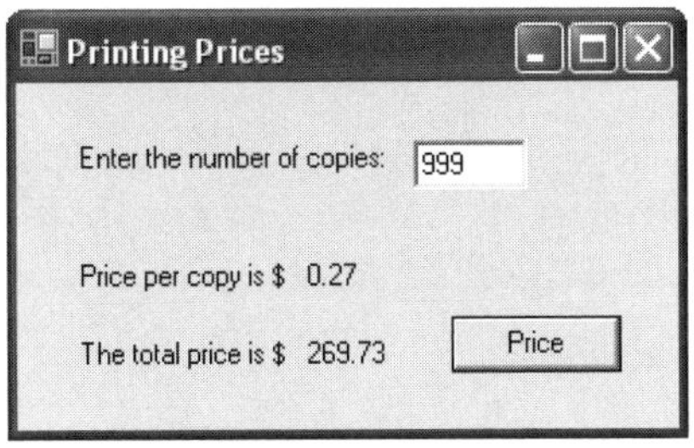

Exercise 4 ———————————————————————————— Package Check

A delivery service does not accept packages heavier than 27 kilograms or larger than 0.1 cubic meters (100,000 cubic centimeters). Create a Package Check application that prompts the user for the weight of a package and its dimensions, and when Check Package is clicked displays an appropriate message if the package does not meet the requirements (e.g., too large, too heavy, or both):

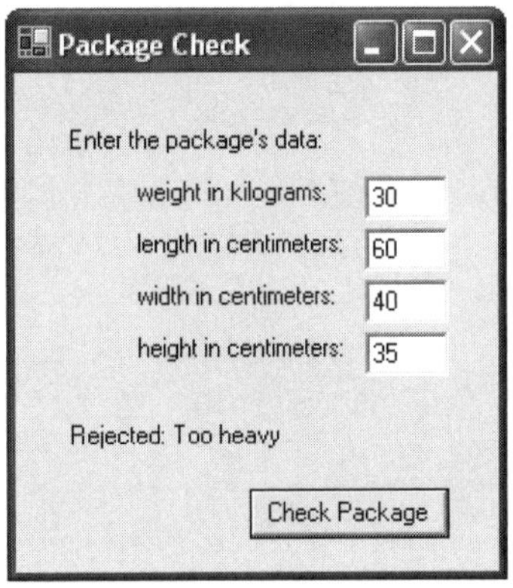

Exercise 5 —————————————— Computer Troubleshooting

Create a Computer Troubleshooting application that asks the user if the ailing computer beeps on startup and if the hard drive spins. If it beeps and the drive spins, have the application display "Contact tech support." If it beeps and the drive doesn't spin, have the application display "Check drive contacts." If it doesn't beep and the hard drive doesn't spin, have the application display "Bring computer to repair center." Finally, if it doesn't beep and the hard drive spins, have the application display "Check the speaker connections." The application interface should look similar to:

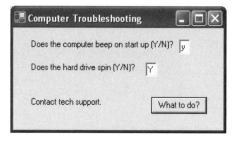

Exercise 6 ————————————————————— Car Models

An auto company produced some models of cars that may be difficult to drive because the car wheels are not exactly round. Cars with model numbers 119, 179, 189 through 195, 221, and 780 have been found to have this defect. Create a Car Models application that prompts a customer for the model number of their car to find out if it is defective. When Evaluate is clicked, the message "Your car is not defective." should be displayed if the user typed a model number without a defect. Otherwise, the message "Your car is defective. Please have it fixed." should be displayed:

Exercise 7 ————————————————————————— Grades

Create a Grades application that allows the user to enter one letter grade (uppercase or lowercase) after another and continuously displays the number of students who passed (D or better) and the number who failed. The application interface should look similar to the following after entering 15 grades and clicking Enter Grade:

An Introduction to Programming Using Microsoft Visual Basic .NET

Exercise 8 —————————————————————————————— Phone Bill

Create a Phone Bill application that determines a phone bill by prompting the user for calling options (call waiting, call forwarding, and caller ID). The monthly basic service charge is $25.00 and each additional calling option is $3.50. The application interface should look similar to the following after selecting options and clicking Calculate:

Exercise 9 —————————————————————————————— Welcome

Many programs are password protected and require the user to enter a user ID and password to get access to the application. A welcome dialog box usually looks similar to:

The password is kept secret by showing a special character, often an asterisk (*), in place of each letter typed in the text box. This can be specified from the Design window by typing * in the PasswordChar property of the text box object.

a) Create a Welcome application that prompts the user for an ID and a password. If the ID and password are correct, display a message box stating so and then end the application. If the ID is not correct display an "Incorrect ID." message box and then clear the ID text box and allow the user to enter another ID. If the password is not correct display an "Incorrect password." message box and then clear the Password text box and allow the user to enter another password. If the ID and password are both not correct display an "Incorrect ID and password." message box and then clear both text boxes and allow the user to enter another ID and password. If the user has made three incorrect attempts then display a "Sorry, access denied." message box and then end the application.

b) *Advanced* Modify the application to check for three different users and their passwords.

Exercise 10 ———————————————————————————— Math Tutor

Create a Math Tutor application that displays math problems by randomly generating two numbers, 1 through 10, and an operator (*, +, –, /) and prompts the user for an answer. The application should check the answer and display a message, display the correct answer, and generate a new problem. The application interface should look similar to the following after typing a correct answer and clicking Check Answer:

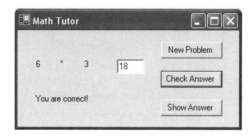

Exercise 11 ———————————————————————————— Sandwich Order

Create a Sandwich Order application that creates a sandwich order by prompting the user for the size of the sandwich (small or large) and the fixings (lettuce, tomato, onion, mustard, mayonnaise, cheese). A small sandwich is $2.50 and a large sandwich is $4.00. Mustard and mayonnaise are free, lettuce and onion are $0.10 each, tomato is $0.25, and cheese is $0.50. The defaults should be a small sandwich with no fixings. The application interface should look similar to the following after selecting options and clicking Place Order:

An Introduction to Programming Using Microsoft Visual Basic .NET

Exercise 12 ———————————————————— Guess the Blocks

Create a Guess the Blocks application to simulate a modified version of the game Mastermind. In this game, three different colored blocks are lined up and hidden from the player. The player then tries to guess the colors and the order of the blocks. There are four colored blocks (red, green, blue, yellow) to choose from. After guessing the color of the three hidden blocks the program displays how many of the colors are correct and how many of the colors are in the right position. Based on this information the player makes another guess and so on until the player has determined the correct order and color of the hidden blocks. Use R for Red, G for Green, B for Blue, and Y for Yellow. The application interface should look similar to the following after making a guess and clicking Check Guess:

Exercise 13 ↻ ———————————————— Rock Paper Scissors

Modify the Rock Paper Scissors application created in Review 9 to include a Program menu with New Game and Exit commands. The New Game command should clear the labels and set all the radio buttons to False.

Exercise 14 (advanced) ———————————————— Game 21

Create a Game 21 application to simulate a simplified version of the game "21" against the computer. A deck with cards numbered 1 through 10 is used and any number can be repeated. The program starts by dealing the user two randomly picked cards and itself three randomly picked cards that are not revealed until Check Scores is clicked. The user may then draw one card. If the user and computer scores are both over 21, or if both are equal but under 21, the game is declared a draw. Otherwise, the winner is the one with the highest score less than or equal to 21. If one score is over 21 and the other is 21 or less, the player with 21 or less is declared the winner. The result should be displayed in a message box. The application interface should include a Program menu with Play Game and Exit commands. The application should look similar to the following after cards have been dealt and drawn and Check Scores clicked:

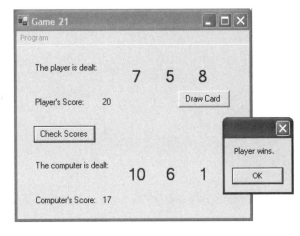

An Introduction to Programming Using Microsoft Visual Basic .NET

Chapter 6
Controlling Program Flow with Looping Structures

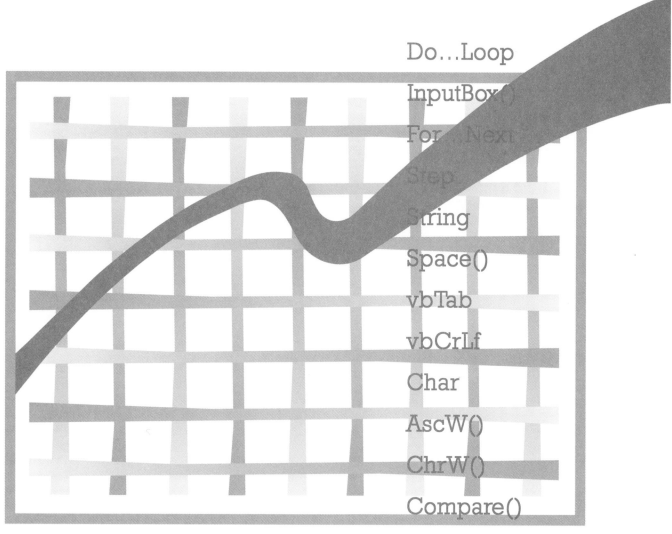

Do…Loop

InputBox()

For…Next

Step

String

Space()

vbTab

vbCrLf

Char

AscW()

ChrW()

Compare()

Like

Chapter 6 Expectations

After completing this chapter you will be able to:

1. Understand the Do...Loop statement and infinite loops.

2. Use input boxes in applications.

3. Understand accumulators and flags.

4. Understand the For...Next statement and how to use Step.

5. Use the String class and its properties and methods.

6. Understand string concatenation and comparison.

7. Use the Char structure and its methods.

8. Understand Unicode.

9. Understand pattern matching.

The concepts explained in this chapter include looping structures to control program flow, accumulator variables, and flags. The **String** class, **Char** structure, Unicode, and the **Like** operator are discussed. The input box is introduced for getting user input.

6.1 Looping

Applications often need to perform repetitive tasks, such as summing a set of numbers entered one at a time by the user or repeatedly prompting the user for a value until valid data is entered. These tasks use the same set of statements that are executed again and again until a specific condition is met. A set of statements that perform a task over and over again based on a condition is called a *loop*. Repeating a set of statements is called *looping*, or *iteration*.

loop
iteration

6.2 The Do...Loop Statement

looping structure

The **Do...Loop** statement is a *looping structure* that can either evaluate a condition after executing a loop once or before executing a loop at all. The first type of **Do...Loop** structure takes the form:

```
Do
    statements
Loop While condition
```

statements is the loop and is executed at least once. *condition* is a Boolean expression used to determine if the loop is to be repeated. If *condition* is True, *statements* is executed again and then the *condition* reevaluated. The loop is repeated until *condition* evaluates to False. For example, in the statements

```
Dim intNumber As Integer = 0
Do
    intNumber = intNumber + 2        'Increment by 2
Loop While intNumber < 10
```

the **Do...Loop** structure executes the loop five times. On the fifth iteration, intNumber is 10 making the loop condition intNumber < 10 False.

Another form of **Do**...**Loop** evaluates a condition before executing the loop and takes the form:

Do While *condition*
    statements
Loop

In this case, if *condition* is True, *statements* is executed and then *condition* reevaluated. The loop is repeated until *condition* evaluates to False.

The first form of **Do**...**Loop** executes the loop at least once. The second form of **Do**...**Loop** may execute zero or more times. This is because, if *condition* is initially False, the loop never executes.

6.3 Infinite Loops

The condition of a loop is used to determine when the loop should stop executing. A **Do**...**Loop** continues until its condition is False. What happens, though, if the condition never becomes False? The result is an *infinite loop*—one which continues forever.

A logic error can lead to an infinite loop. For example, the following statements create an infinite loop. Can you see why?

Dim intNumber **As Integer** = –1
Do While intNumber < 0
    intNumber = intNumber – 1
Loop

Because intNumber is initialized to –1 and never incremented to a positive number in the loop, the condition of the loop structure is always True. However, in this case, intNumber is eventually assigned a number that results in an overflow and a run-time error is generated:

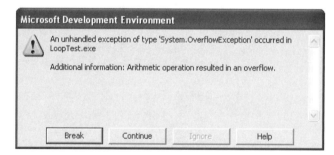

An assignment statement similar to the following will not generate an overflow error:

Dim intNumber **As Integer** = –1
Do While intNumber < 0
    intNumber = –1
Loop

ending an infinite loop   Instead, the program will simply stop responding to user events such as mouse clicks. When this happens, right-clicking the program name on the Windows Taskbar and selecting Close from the menu displays the following dialog box:

An Introduction to Programming Using Microsoft Visual Basic .NET

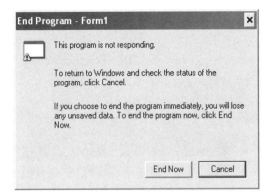

Selecting End Now closes the dialog box and ends the application.

Review 1

In this review you will create the Prime Number application. A prime number is an integer greater than 1 that is evenly divisible by only 1 and itself. For example, 2, 3, and 7 are prime numbers, but 4, 6, and 9 are not. **Mod** can be used to determine if one number evenly divides into another, and a loop can be used to generate divisors between 1 and the number entered. The pseudocode for determining a prime number is:

```
Get TestNum from user
Divisor = 1
If TestNum <= 1 Then
        Display message that TestNum is not prime
Else
        Do
                Increment Divisor by 1
        Loop While TestNum Mod Divisor <> 0
        If Divisor = TestNum Then
                Display message that TestNum is prime
        Else
                Display message that TestNum is not prime
        End If
End If
```

① *CREATE A NEW PROJECT*

Create a Windows application named Prime Number.

② *CREATE THE INTERFACE*

Refer to the form below to add, position, and size objects. Use the table below to set properties.

Object	Name	Text
Form1		Prime Number
Label1	lblIntegerPrompt	Enter an integer:
TextBox1	txtInteger	*empty*
Label2	lblPrimeResult	*empty*
Button1	btnTest	Test

a. Display the Code window.

b. Add comments that include your name and today's date.

c. Create a btnTest_Click event procedure and then add the statements:

```
'Get number from user
Dim intTestNum As Integer = Val(Me.txtInteger.Text)

'Test number
Dim intDivisor As Integer = 1
If intTestNum <= 1 Then            '1 and negatives are not prime numbers
    Me.lblPrimeResult.Text = "Not a prime number."
Else
    Do
        intDivisor = intDivisor + 1
    Loop While intTestNum Mod intDivisor <> 0
    If intDivisor = intTestNum Then
        Me.lblPrimeResult.Text = "Prime number."
    Else
        Me.lblPrimeResult.Text = "Not a prime number."
    End If
End If
```

d. Create a txtInteger_TextChanged event procedure and then add the statements:

```
'Clear the previous test result
Me.lblPrimeResult.Text = Nothing
```

④ RUN THE APPLICATION

a. Save the modified Prime Number project.

b. Run the application. Type 7 and then click Test. The number is prime.

c. Try other prime and nonprime numbers to test the application.

d. Close the Prime Number application.

⑤ PRINT THE CODE AND THEN CLOSE THE PROJECT

6.4 Using an Input Box

An input box is a predefined dialog box that has a prompt, a text box, and OK and Cancel buttons. It is used to get information from the user and looks similar to:

InputBox()

The InputBox() function displays an input box and is used in a statement that takes the form:

stringVar = InputBox(*prompt, title*)

prompt is a **String** variable or a string enclosed in quotation marks that is displayed as a prompt in the input box. *title* is an optional **String** variable or a string enclosed in quotation marks that is displayed in the title bar of the input box. When OK is selected, the data in the text box is assigned to *stringVar*, a **String** variable. For example, the following statement prompts the user for a name and then assigns the text entered to a label:

Me.lblUserName.Text = InputBox("Enter your name", "Name")

testing input

If the user selects Cancel or leaves the text box blank, **Nothing** is returned by the InputBox() function. Testing for **Nothing** is good programming style and can be done using code similar to:

```
Dim strTextEntered As String
strTextEntered = InputBox("Enter your name", "Name")

'Test data entered
If strTextEntered = Nothing Then        'Cancel or empty text box
    Me.lblUserName.Text = "Canceled."
Else                                    'text entered
    Me.lblUserName.Text = strTextEntered
End If
```

Val()

If the user is expected to enter a numeric value in an input box, the Val() function can be used to convert the entry to a number after checking for a **Nothing**.

Me.Text

The title of an input box can reflect the text in the application title bar by using **Me**.Text for the title argument of the InputBox() function.

6.5 Accumulator Variables

An *accumulator* is a variable storing a number that is incremented by a changing value. The statement for updating an accumulator takes the form:

accumulator = *accumulator* + *value*

accumulator is the numeric variable that is updated. *value* is the number that is added to the current value of *accumulator*. An accumulator is often

running total
sum

within a loop structure and is useful for keeping a running total or sum, as in the statement:

intTotalScore = intTotalScore + intNewScore

In this statement, intTotalScore is the name of the accumulator variable. Each time the statement is executed, the value of intNewScore is added to the current value of intTotalScore and then this new value assigned to intTotalScore.

6.6 Using Flags

sentinel   A *flag*, also called a *sentinel*, is a condition used to signify that a loop should stop executing. This approach provides a clear and easy-to-change method for ending a loop. For example, in the loop below the value –1 "flags" the loop to stop executing:

```
Const intFlag As Integer = -1
Dim intNewNumber As Integer
Dim intTotal As Integer = 0
Dim strTempNumber As String

Do
    strTempNumber = InputBox("Enter a positive number (-1 to finish)")
    If strTempNumber = Nothing Then      'Cancel or empty text box
        intNewNumber = intFlag
    Else                                  'number entered
        intNewNumber = Val(strTempNumber)
        If intNewNumber <> intFlag Then
            intTotal = intTotal + intNewNumber
        End If
    End If
Loop While intNewNumber <> intFlag
```

Review 2

In this review you will create the Average Score application. The average of a set of scores is calculated by dividing the sum of the scores by the number of scores. The pseudocode for computing an average score is:

```
Do
    Prompt user for a score
    If empty string entered Then
        Score = Flag
    Else
        Score = Val(UserEntry)
        If Score <> Flag Then
            Increment Count by 1
            Add score to sum of scores
        End If
    End If
Loop While Score <> Flag
Average Score = (Sum of Scores)/Count
```

① *CREATE A NEW PROJECT*

Create a Windows application named Average Score.

② *CREATE THE INTERFACE*

Refer to the form below to add, position, and size objects. Use the table on the next page to set properties.

Object	Name	Text
Form1		Average Score
Label1	lblInstructions	*See interface*
Button1	btnEnterScores	Enter Scores
Button2	btnAverageScore	Average Score
Label2	lblScoresMessage	*empty*
Label3	lblNumberofScores	*empty*
Label4	lblAverageMessage	*empty*
Label5	lblAverage	*empty*

③ *WRITE THE APPLICATION CODE*

   a. Display the Code window.

   b. Add comments that include your name and today's date.

   c. Add two global variable declarations:

```
Dim intNumberOfScores As Integer
Dim intSumOfScores As Integer
```

   d. Create a btnEnterScores_Click event procedure and then add the statements:

```
Const strTitle As String = "Grades"
Const strPrompt As String = "Enter a score (–1 to finish):"
Const intFlag As Integer = –1     'loop flag
Dim intNewScore As Integer
intNumberOfScores = 0             'initialize global counter
intSumOfScores = 0                'initialize global accumulator

'Clear labels
Me.lblAverageMessage.Text = Nothing
Me.lblAverage.Text = Nothing
Me.lblScoresMessage.Text = Nothing
Me.lblNumberofScores.Text = Nothing

'Get scores
Do
  Dim strTempScore = InputBox(strPrompt, strTitle)
  If strTempScore = Nothing Then          'Cancel or empty text box
    intNewScore = intFlag
  Else                                    'score or flag entered
    intNewScore = Val(strTempScore)
    If intNewScore <> intFlag Then
      intNumberOfScores = intNumberOfScores + 1     'update scores count
      intSumOfScores = intSumOfScores + intNewScore 'update scores sum
    End If
  End If
Loop While intNewScore <> intFlag

Me.lblScoresMessage.Text = "Scores entered:"
Me.lblNumberofScores.Text = intNumberOfScores
```

e. Create a btnAverageScore_Click event procedure and then add the statements:

```
Dim sngAverage As Single
Me.lblAverageMessage.Text = "Average score:"
If intNumberOfScores > 0 Then
    sngAverage = intSumOfScores / intNumberOfScores        'compute average
    Me.lblAverage.Text = sngAverage
Else
    Me.lblAverage.Text = 0
End If
```

④ *RUN THE APPLICATION*

a. Save the modified Average Score project.

b. Run the application. Test it with several sets of scores and then close Average Score.

⑤ *PRINT THE CODE AND THEN CLOSE THE PROJECT*

Review 3

Create a Unique Random Numbers application that prompts the user for a number greater than 3 and then generates three unique random numbers between 1 and the number entered. Use a loop to repeatedly generate three random numbers until all three numbers are different. Include a counter in the loop to count the number of loop iterations required. The application interface should look similar to that shown on the right after entering 5, and clicking Generate Numbers.

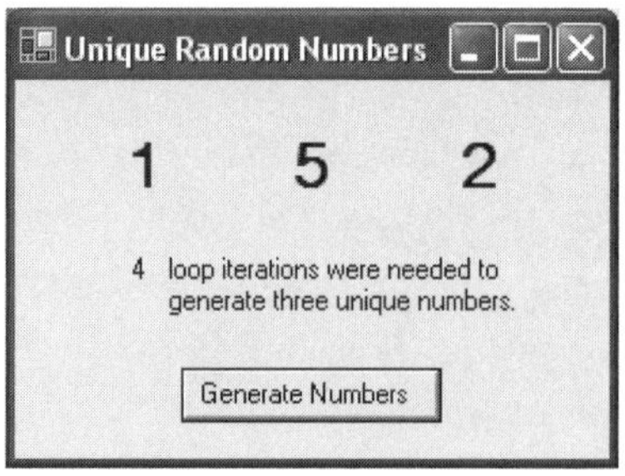

6.7 The For...Next Statement

The For...Next statement is a looping structure that executes a set of statements a fixed number of times. Unlike a Do...Loop that executes while a condition is True, For...Next executes until a counter reaches an ending value. The For...Next statement takes the form:

```
For counter = start To end
    statements
Next counter
```

counter, start, and *end* are **Integer** variables, values, or expressions. *counter* is initialized to *start* (*counter = start*) only once when the loop first executes, and compared to *end* before each loop iteration. *counter* is automatically incremented by 1 after each iteration of the loop (*statements*).

With each iteration of the following For...Next, a message box is displayed. In this case, 10 message boxes in all will be displayed with numbers counting from 1 to 10:

```
Dim intNumber As Integer
For intNumber = 1 To 10
    MessageBox.Show(intNumber)
Next intNumber
```

programming style   While it is possible to modify the value of the counting variable in the **For...Next** loop or to terminate the loop prematurely, this is considered poor programming style. It is also important to note that the counter variable is incremented after the last loop iteration and the variable can be accessed outside of the loop. Therefore, in the previous example, intNumber has the value 11 after the last loop iteration.

Step   A **For...Next** statement can include the keyword **Step** to change the way the counter is incremented. For example, the following **For...Next** loop increments a counter by 2 with each iteration to sum all the even numbers between 2 and 8:

```
Dim intCount As Integer
Dim intStart As Integer = 2
Dim intEnd As Integer = 8
Dim intStep As Integer = 2
Dim intSum As Integer = 0

For intCount = intStart To intEnd Step intStep
    intSum = intSum + intCount              'update sum
Next intCount
Me.lblEvenSum.Text = intSum                 '2+4+6+8
```

Step may also be used to decrement a counter. For example, the statements below count down from 10 to 1 with each number being displayed in a message box:

```
Dim intNumber As Integer
For intNumber = 10 To 1 Step –1
    MessageBox.Show(intNumber)
Next intNumber
```

Review 4

In this review you will create the Factorial application. The factorial of a number is the product of all the positive integers from 1 to the number. For example, 3 factorial, written as 3!, is 3 * 2 * 1, or 6. The pseudocode for computing the factorial of a number is:

```
Get a number from the user
Factorial = 1
For Counter = 1 To Number
        Factorial = Factorial * Counter
Next Counter
```

① CREATE A NEW PROJECT

Create a Windows application named Factorial.

② CREATE THE INTERFACE

Refer to the form below to add, position, and size objects. Use the table on the next page to set properties.

Object	Name	Text
Form1		Factorial
Label1	lblNumberPrompt	Enter a number:
TextBox1	txtNumber	*empty*
Button1	btnComputeFactorial	Compute Factorial
Label2	lblFactorialMessage	*empty*
Label3	lblFactorial	*empty*

③ *WRITE THE APPLICATION CODE*

    a. Display the Code window.

    b. Add comments that include your name and today's date.

    c. Create a btnComputeFactorial_Click event procedure and then add the statements:

```
Dim lngFactorial As Long = 1

Dim intNumber As Integer
intNumber = Val(Me.txtNumber.Text)          'Get number from user
Dim intCount As Integer
For intCount = 1 To intNumber
    lngFactorial = lngFactorial * intCount
Next intCount

Me.lblFactorialMessage.Text = "Factorial is:"
Me.lblFactorial.Text = lngFactorial
```

    d. Create a txtNumber_TextChanged event procedure and then add the statements:

```
Me.lblFactorialMessage.Text = Nothing
Me.lblFactorial.Text = Nothing
```

④ *RUN THE APPLICATION*

    a. Save the modified Factorial project and then run the application. Test the application with several different numbers, including 0 and 1. Note that numbers higher than 20 generate a run-time error because the **Long** variable type cannot hold numbers that large.

    b. Close the Factorial application.

⑤ *PRINT THE CODE AND THEN CLOSE THE PROJECT*

Review 5

Create an Odd Numbers Sum application that displays the sum of the odd numbers from 1 to a maximum value entered by the user.

6.8 The String Class

members
object

String properties

The **String** data type is a class. A class includes properties and methods called *members*. When a class is used to create a variable, the variable is called an *object*. An object accesses a member of its class with a dot (.) between the object name and the member name. Property members of the **String** class are:

- **Chars(*index*)** returns the character at a specified position in a **String** object, with the first character of a string at index 0.

- **Length** returns the number of characters in a **String** object.

The code below demonstrates the **String** class properties:

```
Dim strSeason As String = "Summer"
Dim chrLetter As Char
Dim intNumChars As Integer

chrLetter = strSeason.Chars(4)        'e
intNumChars = strSeason.Length        '6
```

method

A *method* is a procedure in a class. The **String** class contains several method members for manipulating strings:

- **ToUpper** converts a **String** object to all uppercase characters.

- **ToLower** converts a **String** object to all lowercase characters.

- **Trim** removes all spaces from the beginning and end of a **String** object.

- **TrimEnd** removes all spaces from the end of a **String** object.

- **TrimStart** removes all spaces from the beginning of a **String** object.

- **PadLeft(***len***, ***char***)** adds a specified character to the beginning of a **String** object until the string is a specified length. *len* is the padded length of the string and *char* is a character in quotation marks or a **Char** variable.

- **PadRight(***len***, ***char***)** adds a specified character to the end of a **String** object until the string is a specified length. *len* is the padded length of the string and *char* is a character in quotation marks or a **Char** variable.

StrConv() Function

The built-in StrConv() function can be used to change each word in a string to proper case, as in the statements:

```
Dim strN As String
strN = "ben franklin"
Dim strPN As String
'Ben Franklin
strPN = StrConv(strN, _
    vbStrConv.ProperCase)
```

The code below demonstrates the **String** methods:

```
Dim strSeason As String = "SummerTime"
Dim strNewString As String

strNewString = strSeason.ToUpper          'SUMMERTIME
strNewString = strSeason.ToLower          'summertime

strSeason = "   SummerTime   "
strNewString = strSeason.Trim             'SummerTime
strNewString = strSeason.TrimEnd          '   SummerTime
strNewString = strSeason.TrimStart        'SummerTime

strSeason = "SummerTime"
strNewString = strSeason.PadLeft(15, "x")   'xxxxxSummerTime
strNewString = strSeason.PadLeft(9, "x")    'SummerTime
strNewString = strSeason.PadRight(13, "x")  'SummerTimexxx
```

substring

The **String** class also contains methods that return a portion of a string called a *substring*. Other methods modify or insert substrings. These methods include:

- **Substring(***startPos***, ***numOfChars***)** returns a substring of the **String** object. *startPos* indicates the position of the character that starts the substring, with the first character of a string at position 0. *numOfChars* indicates the length of the substring.

- **Remove(***startPos***, ***numOfChars***)** deletes a substring from the **String** object. *startPos* indicates the position of the character to start deleting, with the first character of a string at position 0. *numOfChars* indicates the number of characters to delete.

- **Replace(*oldString, newString*)** exchanges every occurrence of a substring in the **String** object with a new string. *oldString* is an existing substring. *newString* is the string to replace *oldString*.

- **Insert(*startPos, substring*)** inserts a substring in the **String** object. *startPos* indicates the position to place *substring*, with the first character of a string at position 0.

- **IndexOf(*substring*)** returns the position of the first occurrence of *substring* in the **String** object, with the first character of a string at position 0. –1 is returned if the *substring* is not found.

programming style

When using the Substring() and Remove() methods, it may be necessary to first use the Length property to determine how many characters are in a string. In these methods, if *numOfChars* exceeds the number of characters in the string, a run-time error will occur. It is good programming style to add code to prevent run-time errors.

The following code demonstrates the **String** methods:

```
Dim strSeason As String = "SummerTime"
Dim strNewString As String
Dim intPos As Integer

strNewString = strSeason.Substring(6, 4)           'Time
strNewString = strSeason.Remove(0, 6)              'Time
strNewString = strSeason.Replace("Time", " is fun!")   'Summer is fun!
strNewString = strSeason.Insert(6, " is a fun ")   'Summer is a fun Time
intPos = strSeason.IndexOf("mer")                  '3
```

Review 6

Create a Letter Count application that displays the number of times a specific letter occurs in a word or phrase. Uppercase and lowercase characters should be counted. The application interface should look similar to that on the right after typing saxophone, the letter o, and clicking Count Letter.

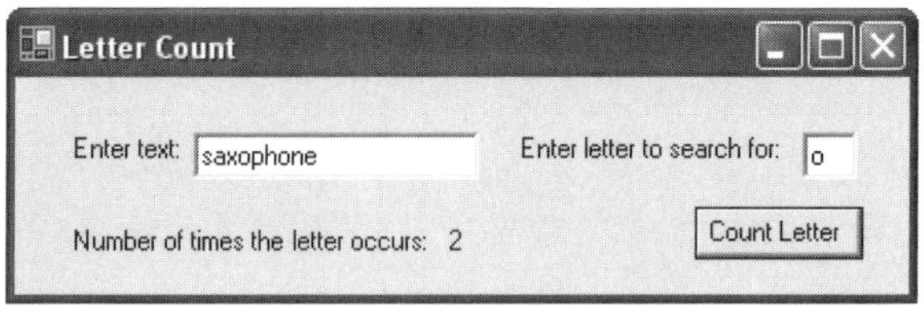

Review 7

Create a String Test application that displays the first letter, last letter, and middle letter of a word or phrase. The application interface should look similar to that shown on the right after typing Hemingway and clicking Display Data.

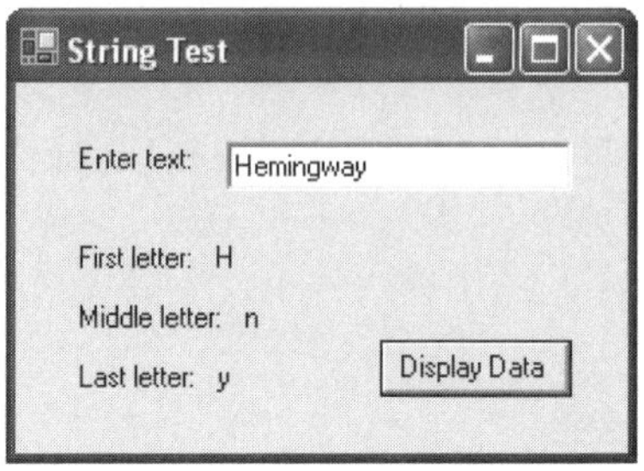

An Introduction to Programming Using Microsoft Visual Basic .NET

Create a Find String application that displays the first position of a word or phrase in another word or phrase. Use text boxes to prompt the user for a string and a search substring. The application interface should look similar to that shown on the right after typing the strings and clicking Find String.

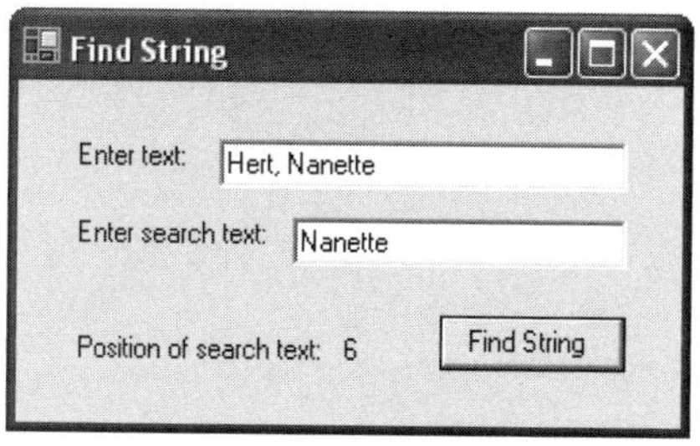

6.9 String Concatenation

Two or more strings can be joined together in a process called *concatenation*. Strings that have been joined are said to be *concatenated*. The **String** class method for concatenation is:

- **Concat(***string1, string2, ...***)** concats two or more strings into one string. *string1*, *string2*, and so on can be strings in quotation marks or **String** variables.

shared method   The Concat() method is a *shared method* which means that it must be used with the **String** type, not with a particular variable. The code below demonstrates the Concat() method:

```
Dim strSeason As String = "SummerTime"
Dim strMessage As String = " is a fun time!"
Dim strNewString As String

'SummerTime is a fun time!
strNewString = String.Concat(strSeason, strMessage)
```

&   The & operator can also be used to concatenate strings. The & operator is used in an expression similar to the following:

newString = string1 & string2

newString is a **String** variable that will store the result of the expression. *string1* and *string2* are **String** variables or strings enclosed in quotation marks. The following code demonstrates &:

```
Dim strFirstName As String, strLastName As String
Dim strFullName As String

strFirstName = "Elaine"
strLastName = "Malfas"
strFullName = strFirstName & " " & strLastName      'Elaine Malfas
```

Space()   The Space() function is a built-in function that returns a string of spaces. The Space function takes the form:

Space(*numOfSpaces*)

numOfSpaces is an **Integer** variable or a value indicating the number of spaces for the returned string. The following code demonstrates Space():

```
Dim strBlanks As String
strBlanks = "10" & Space(10) & "spaces"             '10       spaces
```

vbTab
vbCrLf

Visual Basic .NET contains two built-in constants that are useful for formatting strings. The vbTab constant can be used to place a string into the next field of eight characters. The vbCrLf constant represents a carriage return-linefeed combination and is used to move text to a new line. The following statements demonstrate vbTab and vbCrLf:

```
Dim strMessage As String
strMessage = "Hello" & vbTab & "and" & vbCrLf & "Good-bye"
MessageBox.Show(strMessage)
```

Review 9

Create a Full Name application that prompts the user for a first name and last name in two separate input boxes when Start is clicked and then displays in a label the first name and last name concatenated with a space between. The application interface should look similar to that shown on the right after clicking Start and entering the two names.

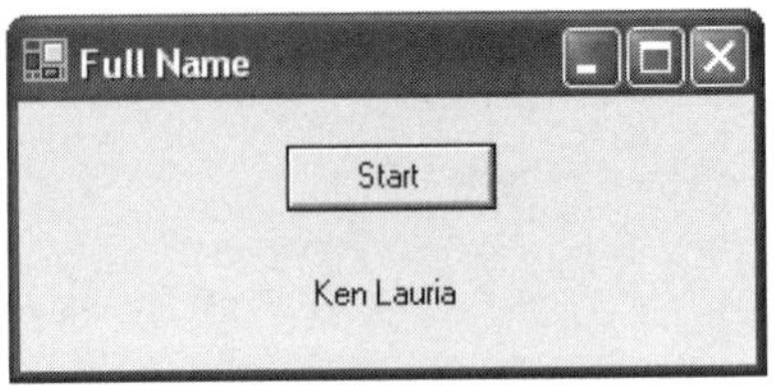

6.10   The Char Structure

structure

The **Char** data type is a structure. A *structure* is a simple form of a class. Like a class, a structure has properties and methods. The differences between structures and classes are discussed later in the text.

ToUpper()
ToLower()

The ToUpper() and ToLower() **Char** methods are similar to the **String** class methods ToUpper() and ToLower(). However, the **Char** methods are shared methods that must be used with the **Char** type. The code below demonstrates the methods:

```
Dim chrLetter1 As Char = "b"
Dim chrLetter2 As Char = "E"
Dim chrNewLetter As Char

chrNewLetter = Char.ToUpper(chrLetter1)    'B
chrNewLetter = Char.ToLower(chrLetter2)    'e
```

An Introduction to Programming Using Microsoft Visual Basic .NET

6.11 Unicode

Every letter of an alphabet (Latin, Japanese, Cherokee, and so on) and symbols of every culture (=, @, ½, and so on) have been given a representation in a digital code called Unicode. *Unicode* uses a set of sixteen 1s and 0s to form a 16-bit binary code for each symbol. For example, the uppercase letter V is Unicode 00000000 01010110, which can be thought of as the base 10 number 86 (86_{10}). Lowercase v has a separate code of 00000000 01110110, or 118_{10}. Below is a table of some Unicode symbols and their corresponding decimal and binary equivalents.

Visual Basic .NET includes two built-in functions for converting between characters and Unicode:

- **AscW(*char*)** returns the integer Unicode value of *char*. *char* is a character in quotation marks or a **Char** variable.

- **ChrW(*integer*)** returns the character corresponding to *integer*.

The following code demonstrates the conversion functions:

```
Dim chrTestChar As Char
Dim intCharCode As Integer

chrTestChar = ChrW(65)        'A
chrTestChar = ChrW(37)        '%
intCharCode = AscW("A")       '65
intCharCode = AscW("%")       '37
```

Decimal	Binary	Unicode Symbol
32	00000000 00000000	*space*
33	00000000 00100001	!
34	00000000 00100010	"
35	00000000 00100011	#
36	00000000 00100100	$
37	00000000 00100101	%
38	00000000 00100110	&
39	00000000 00100111	'
40	00000000 00101000	(
41	00000000 00101001	)
42	00000000 00101010	*
43	00000000 00101011	+
44	00000000 00101100	,
45	00000000 00101101	-
46	00000000 00101110	.
47	00000000 00101111	/
48	00000000 00110000	0
49	00000000 00110001	1
50	00000000 00110010	2
51	00000000 00110011	3
52	00000000 00110100	4
53	00000000 00110101	5
54	00000000 00110110	6
55	00000000 00110111	7
56	00000000 00111000	8
57	00000000 00111001	9
58	00000000 00111010	:
59	00000000 00111011	;
60	00000000 00111100	<
61	00000000 00111101	=
62	00000000 00111110	>
63	00000000 00111111	?

Decimal	Binary	Unicode Symbol
64	00000000 00000000	@
65	00000000 01000001	A
66	00000000 01000010	B
67	00000000 01000011	C
68	00000000 01000100	D
69	00000000 01000101	E
70	00000000 01000110	F
71	00000000 01000111	G
72	00000000 01001000	H
73	00000000 01001001	I
74	00000000 01001010	J
75	00000000 01001011	K
76	00000000 01001100	L
77	00000000 01001101	M
78	00000000 01001110	N
79	00000000 01001111	O
80	00000000 01010000	P
81	00000000 01010001	Q
82	00000000 01010010	R
83	00000000 01010011	S
84	00000000 01010100	T
85	00000000 01010101	U
86	00000000 01010110	V
87	00000000 01010111	W
88	00000000 01011000	X
89	00000000 01011001	Y
90	00000000 01011010	Z
91	00000000 01011011	[
92	00000000 01011100	\
93	00000000 01011101	]
94	00000000 01011110	^
95	00000000 01011111	_

Decimal	Binary	Unicode Symbol
96	00000000 00000000	
97	00000000 01100001	a
98	00000000 01100010	b
99	00000000 01100011	c
100	00000000 01100100	d
101	00000000 01100101	e
102	00000000 01100110	f
103	00000000 01100111	g
104	00000000 01101000	h
105	00000000 01101001	i
106	00000000 01101010	j
107	00000000 01101011	k
108	00000000 01101100	l
109	00000000 01101101	m
110	00000000 01101110	n
111	00000000 01101111	o
112	00000000 01110000	p
113	00000000 01110001	q
114	00000000 01110010	r
115	00000000 01110011	s
116	00000000 01110100	t
117	00000000 01110101	u
118	00000000 01110110	v
119	00000000 01110111	w
120	00000000 01111000	x
121	00000000 01111001	y
122	00000000 01111010	z
123	00000000 01111011	{
124	00000000 01111100		
125	00000000 01111101	}
126	00000000 01111110	~

Review 10

Create a Secret Message Decoder application that uses a loop to prompt the user for six uppercase letters in six input boxes when Start is clicked. After the user enters the letters, a coded message is displayed in a label. The code is the set of base 10 numbers corresponding to the lowercase of the letters entered. The application interface should look similar to that shown on the right clicking Start and entering H, O, M, B, R, E.

6.12   Comparing Strings

A program will often need to alphabetically compare strings. For example, a list of names may need to be displayed in alphabetical order or a user's name may need to be compared to a list of permitted users. Relational operators (=, >, <, >=, <=, <>) can be used to compare strings. However, they use the Unicode values of the strings to determine the relationship between the strings. This can give unexpected results because uppercase and lowercase letters have different values. For example, "j" and "J" are two different Unicode values.

The String Equals() Method

Equals(*string1, string2*) returns True if *string1* and *string2* are the same, including case. Otherwise, False is returned.

The Compare() method in the **String** class should be used to alphabetically compare strings:

- **Compare(*string1, string2, Case-insensitive*)** returns 0 if *string1* and *string2* are the same. A positive number is returned if *string1* is greater than *string2* and a negative number if *string1* is less than *string2*. *Case-insensitive* should be True if the case of the strings should not be considered. A False will compare the case of the strings as well.

The following code demonstrates the **String** Compare() method:

```
Dim strName As String = "Chris"
Dim strNewName As String

strNewName = "chris"
Select String.Compare(strName, strNewName, True)
  Case 0
    Me.lblMessage.Text = "The same."          'this text displayed
  Case Is < 0
    Me.lblMessage.Text = "Alphabetically before."
  Case Is > 0
    Me.lblMessage.Text = "Alphabetically after."
End Select
```

Create a Compare Words application that prompts the user for two words and then textually compares the words to determine if they are equal or if the first word comes alphabetically before or after the second word. The application interface should look similar to that shown on the right after entering miniature and MINIATURE and clicking **Compare Words**.

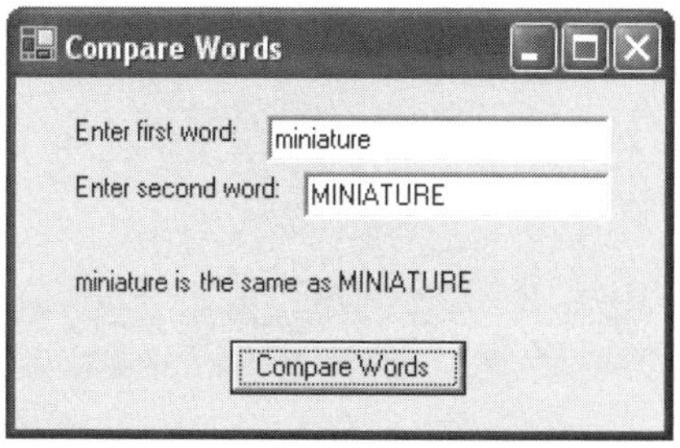

6.13 The Like Operator

pattern matching

The **Like** operator is also used to perform a textual comparison between two strings. However, **Like** can be used to perform pattern matching. *Pattern matching* allows wildcard characters, character lists, and character ranges to match strings. The **Like** operator is used in a statement and takes the form:

result = *string* **Like** *pattern*

result is a **Boolean** variable that is assigned True if *string* matches *pattern* and False otherwise. *string* is a **String** variable or a string enclosed in quotation marks. *pattern* can be in many forms:

```
? used in place of any single character
* used in place of many characters
# used in place of any single number
[] used to enclose a list of characters
– used to indicate a range of characters in a character list
, used to separate characters in a character list
```

The following code demonstrates **Like**:

```
Dim strWord As String
Dim strPattern As String
strWord = "Run"
strPattern = "?un"
Me.lblMessage.Text = strWord Like strPattern        'displays True

strWord = "Run"
strPattern = "?um"
Me.lblMessage.Text = strWord Like strPattern        'displays False

strWord = "Letter to Suzy"
strPattern = "Letter to *"
Me.lblMessage.Text = strWord Like strPattern        'displays True

strWord = "Case 9876"
strPattern = "Case 987#"
Me.lblMessage.Text = strWord Like strPattern        'displays True

strWord = "Case 9876"
strPattern = "Case ##6#"
Me.lblMessage.Text = strWord Like strPattern        'displays False
```

```
strWord = "C"
strPattern = "[A,B,C,D,E,F]"
Me.lblMessage.Text = strWord Like strPattern          'displays True

strWord = "B"
strPattern = "[A–F]"
Me.lblMessage.Text = strWord Like strPattern          'displays True
```

Case Study

In this Case Study a Word Guess application will be created.

specification   The specification for this Case Study is:

> A Word Guess application that allows a user to guess the letters in a secret word. NOODLE is the secret word that is represented as a row of dashes on the form, with one dash for each letter. The user is prompted for a letter automatically and can enter a lowercase letter or an uppercase letter as a guess. If the letter is in the secret word, the appropriate dash(es) on the form is replaced by the letter guessed. The user may try to guess the word at any time. If the secret word is guessed, the word is displayed on the form along with the number of guesses made. If the wrong word is guessed, the user loses.

design   The interface design should have a label with a font sized large enough to show the secret word prominently on the form. Since the user is to be prompted automatically, an input box will be used, so there is no need for a text box. A button allows the user to start the game:

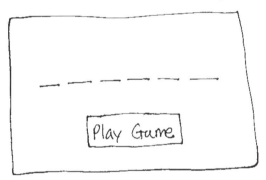

The code design starts with an algorithm and pseudocode:

1. Display the same number of dashes as in the secret word.
2. Prompt the user for a letter, but also allow the user to enter a flag if ready to guess the entire word.
3. Increment a guess counter.
4. If a letter was entered determine if the letter is in the secret word and then display the letter entered in the proper position on the form.
5. If the flag was entered, prompt the user for the entire word.
6. Repeat step 1 until the word has been guessed or the user gives up by clicking Cancel in the input box or leaves the input box empty.

```
Sub btnPlayGame_Click()
    Const SECRETWORD As String = "NOODLE"
    Const FLAG As Char = "!"
    Static NumGuesses As Integer = 0
    Dim LetterGuess As Char
    Dim WordGuess As String
    Dim LetterPos As Integer
    Dim TempWord As String
    Dim EndGame As Boolean

    Dim WordGuessedSoFar = ""
    Dim Length = SECRETWORD.Length
    WordGuessedSoFar = WordGuessedSoFar.PadLeft(Length, "–")
    Show WordGuessedSoFar in a label

    Get LetterGuess from user, ending game if Cancel is clicked
    Do While LetterGuess <> Flag And WordGuessedSoFar <> SecretWord _
    And Not EndGame
        Increment number of guesses
        Compare each letter of SecretWord to LetterGuess
        If LetterGuess matches a letter in SecretWord Then
            Replace appropriate dash in WordGuessedSoFar with LetterGuess
        If WordGuessedSoFar <> SecretWord Then
            Get LetterGuess from user, ending game if Cancel clicked
    Loop

    If WordGuessedSoFar = SecretWord Then
        Display message with number of guesses
    Else If LetterGuess = FLAG Then
        Show input box prompting for WordGuess
        If WordGuess = SecretWord Then
            Display message with number of guesses
        Else
            Display "you lose" message
    Else
        Display "game over" message
End Sub
```

Note that the string of dashes is created by padding an empty string with the same number of dashes as characters in the secret word. This allows more flexibility in the program because creating a new secret word means just changing one variable assignment.

coding   The interface and code for this Case Study are:

Object	Name	Text	TextAlign	Font
Form1		Word Guess		
Label1	lblSecretWord	*empty*	MiddleCenter	Size 36
Button1	btnPlayGame	Play Game		

```
Public Class Form1
    Inherits System.Windows.Forms.Form

    Windows Form Designer generated code

    Private Sub btnPlayGame_Click(ByVal sender As Object, ByVal e As System.EventArgs) _
    Handles btnPlayGame.Click

        Const strSECRETWORD As String = "NOODLE"
        Const chrFLAG As Char = "!"
        Const strGuessPrompt As String = "Enter a letter or " & chrFLAG & " to guess word:"
        Dim intNumGuesses As Integer = 0
        Dim chrLetterGuess As Char
        Dim strWordGuess As String
        Dim intLetterPos As Integer
        Dim strTempWord As String
        Dim blnEndGame As Boolean = False

        'Set same number of dashes as letters in strSECRETWORD
        Dim strWordGuessedSoFar As String = ""
        Dim intLength As Integer = strSECRETWORD.Length
        strWordGuessedSoFar = strWordGuessedSoFar.PadLeft(intLength, "-")
        Me.lblSecretWord.Text = strWordGuessedSoFar      'Initialize game

        'Get first guess
        Dim strTempLetterGuess = InputBox(strGuessPrompt, Me.Text)
        'Test data entered
        If strTempLetterGuess = Nothing Then      'Cancel or empty text box
            blnEndGame = True
        Else                                      'user entered a letter
            chrLetterGuess = strTempLetterGuess
        End If

        Do While chrLetterGuess <> chrFLAG And strWordGuessedSoFar <> strSECRETWORD _
        And Not blnEndGame
            intNumGuesses = intNumGuesses + 1
            For intLetterPos = 0 To strSECRETWORD.Length - 1
                If strSECRETWORD.Chars(intLetterPos) = Char.ToUpper(chrLetterGuess) Then
                    'remove dash at position of letter guessed
                    strTempWord = strWordGuessedSoFar.Remove(intLetterPos, 1)
                    'insert guessed letter
                    strWordGuessedSoFar = strTempWord.Insert(intLetterPos, Char.ToUpper(chrLetterGuess))
                    Me.lblSecretWord.Text = strWordGuessedSoFar        'update interface
                End If
            Next intLetterPos

            'Get next letter if word hasn't been guessed
            If strWordGuessedSoFar <> strSECRETWORD Then
                'Get user guess
                strTempLetterGuess = InputBox(strGuessPrompt, Me.Text)
                'Test data entered
                If strTempLetterGuess = Nothing Then      'Cancel or empty text box
                    blnEndGame = True
                Else                                      'user entered a letter
                    chrLetterGuess = strTempLetterGuess
                End If
            End If
        Loop
```

```
        If strWordGuessedSoFar = strSECRETWORD Then          'user guessed all letters
            MessageBox.Show("You guessed it in " & intNumGuesses & " guesses!")
        ElseIf chrLetterGuess = chrFLAG Then                 'user tries to guess word
            strWordGuess = InputBox("Enter a word:", Me.Text)
            If strWordGuess.ToUpper = strSECRETWORD Then
                MessageBox.Show("You guessed it in " & intNumGuesses & " guesses!")
                Me.lblSecretWord.Text = strSECRETWORD
            Else
                MessageBox.Show("Sorry you lose.")
            End If
        Else                                                 'end game
            MessageBox.Show("Game over.")
        End If

    End Sub

End Class
```

Running Word Guess and guessing two correct letters displays:

testing and debugging   This Case Study should be tested by entering correct and incorrect characters and correct and incorrect word guesses.

Review 12

Modify Word Guess to display the player's score on the form. The player should start with a score of 100, and have 10 points taken off for each incorrect guess. The score should be updated and displayed as the game is played.

Chapter Summary

Looping structures are used to control program flow and allow for iteration. In this chapter the Do…Loop and For…Next statements were used to control program flow. The Do…Loop executes a set of statements as long as a condition is True. The For…Next executes a set of statements a fixed number of times. Another form of Do…Loop evaluates a condition before executing the loop.

An infinite loop is a loop which continues forever. An infinite loop may result in a run-time error. If a program stops responding, Close can be selected from the menu displayed by right-clicking the program name on the Windows Task bar.

An input box is used to get information from the user. The InputBox() function returns the text entered by the user or an empty string if Cancel was clicked.

An accumulator is a variable that stores a value that accumulates, or gets added to by a varying amount during run time. A sentinel is a constant that holds a special value that "flags" a loop to stop executing. A sentinel provides a clear and easy-to-change method for ending a loop.

The String class includes several properties and methods for converting and manipulating strings. Some methods return, modify, or insert substrings. Two or more strings can be joined together in a process called concatenation. The Concat() method is a shared method and is used with the String type itself. The & operator can also be used to concatenate two or more strings.

The Char type is a structure that includes the ToUpper() and ToLower() shared methods for converting a character to uppercase or lowercase, respectively.

The Space() function returns a string of spaces. The vbTab and vbCrLf built-in constants are used to format a string.

Unicode uses a 16-bit binary code to represent letters and symbols from every language and culture. The AscW() and ChrW() functions can be used to convert between Unicode and characters. Strings can be alphabetically compared with the Compare() String method. The Like operator uses pattern matching and wildcards to compare strings.

Vocabulary

Accumulator A variable used to store a number that is updated by a changing amount.

Concatenation The process of joining two or more strings into one string.

Concatenated Strings that have been joined.

Flag A condition used to signify that a loop should stop executing.

Infinite loop A loop that continues forever.

Input box A predefined dialog box that accepts input from the user.

Iteration Also called looping.

Loop A set of statements that repeatedly perform a task based on a condition.

Looping Repeating one or more statements.

Looping structure A statement that executes a loop as long as a condition is True.

Members Properties and methods of a class.

Method A procedure in a class.

Object A variable that is declared with a data type that is a class.

Pattern matching Allows wildcard characters (?, *, #), character lists, and character ranges ([A–M, Z]) to match strings using the Like operator.

Shared method A method that is used with a class, not with a particular object of that class.

Sentinel See Flag.

Structure A simple form of a class.

Substring A portion of a string.

Textual comparison Comparing characters without distinguishing case.

Unicode A digital code that represents every letter of an alphabet and symbols of every culture. Each code uses 16 bits or 2 bytes.

Visual Basic .NET

& Used to concatenate two or more strings.

AscW() Function that returns the integer Unicode value that corresponds to a character argument.

Char structure Used to manipulate characters. Methods include ToLower() and ToUpper().

ChrW() Function that returns the character corresponding to an integer representing a Unicode value.

Do…Loop Statement that repeatedly executes a loop as long as a condition is True.

For…Next Statement that executes a loop a fixed number of times.

InputBox() Function used to generate a predefined dialog box that has a prompt, a text box, and OK and Cancel buttons.

Like Operator used to perform textual comparison on strings and pattern matching using characters such as ?, *, #, [].

Space() Function used to generate a string of spaces.

Step Keyword used in a For…Next statement to increment or decrement the counter by a set amount.

vbTab Built-in constant that places a string in the next field of eight characters.

vbCrLf Built-in constant that represents a carriage return-linefeed combination.

String class Used to manipulate strings. Properties include Chars and Length. Methods include Concat(), Compare(), IndexOf(), Insert(), PadLeft(), PadRight(), Remove(), Replace(), Substring(), Trim(), ToUpper(), ToLower(), TrimEnd(), and TrimStart().

1. What is the primary purpose of a loop?

2. a) What is an infinite loop?
    b) What causes an infinite loop?

3. a) What are the two predefined dialog boxes discussed so far?
    b) How are they similar?
    c) How do they differ?

4. Contrast and compare accumulator variables and counter variables. Discuss uses for each.

5. What are the two ways strings can be combined to create a new string?

6. Complete the code below that sums the digits in a number. For example, 1234 in txtNumber displays "The sum of the digits in 1234 is 10" in a message box.

    ```
    strNumber = Me.txtNumber.Text
    For intI = _____ To strNumber. _____ − 1
        intSum = _____ + _____(strNumber.Substring(____, ____))
    Next intI
    MessageBox.Show("The sum of the digits in " & strNumber & " is " & _____)
    ```

7. Write code to average the sum of every third integer from 2 through 99 (i.e. 2 + 5 + ...) using
    a) a Do...Loop.
    b) a For...Loop.

8. A *variable trace* is a table listing the values of variables at the points of assignment. A variable trace is a way to manually debug a program and to also verify the logic involved in code. A trace often includes control object properties because these are effectively variables of an object class. For example, a variable trace table has been created for the following segment of code. Note that each row lists the values through each loop iteration:

    ```
    Dim intI As Integer = 0
    Dim intX As Integer = 0
    Do While intI < 10
        If intI Mod 3 = 0 Then
            intX = intX + intI
            Me.lblOutput.Text = Me.lblOutput.Text & intX & ","
        End If
        intI = intI + 1
    Loop
    ```

intX	lblOutput.Text	intI
0	0,	1
0	0,	2
0	0,	3
3	0,3,	4
3	0,3,	5
3	0,3,	6
9	0,3,9,	7
9	0,3,9,	8
9	0,3,9,	9
18	0,3,9,18,	10

    Create a variable trace table for the following code, tracing the values of intI, intJ, and lblOutput:

    ```
    For intI = 0 To 2
        For intJ = 1 To 3
            Me.lblOutput.Text = Me.lblOutput.Text & intI + 2 * intJ & ","
        Next intJ
    Next intI
    Me.lblOutput.Text = Me.lblOutput.Text & intI & "," & intJ
    ```

9. Write code that prompts the user for a starting value and an ending value, and then displays a table of each number in the range and its square in a label. Be sure to account for the fact that the user may not necessarily type a smaller number first.

10. Write code that prompts the user for words in an input box and concatenates them together with a space between until a period is entered. The concatenated words should then be displayed in a label.

11. Consider the statement: str1 = "TesT iT" What value is assigned to the variables in the statements?
    a) strNew1 = str1.ToLower
    b) strNew3 = str1.Substring(0, 4)
    c) strNew4 = (str1.ToUpper).Substring(3, 4)
    d) intStrPos1 = str1.IndexOf("T")
    e) intStrPos2 = str1.IndexOf("IT")

12. Correct the errors in the code:
```
Dim chrFirst As Char = "f"
Dim chrMiddle As Char = "m"
Dim chrLast As Char = "l"
'Create monogram
Me.lblMonogram.Text = chrFirst.ToUpper & chrMiddle.ToUpper & chrLast.ToUpper
```

13. Write code that prompts the user for a date in the form mm/dd/yy and then displays the date in form Month dd, year. For example, 12/25/03 displays December 25, 2003.

14. What is displayed by the message box?
```
strNums = "01234567890123456789001234567890"
MessageBox.Show(strNums & vbCrLf & vBTab & "This" & vbTab & _
"Is" & vbCrLf & "So Wonderful" & "and Marvelous")
```

15. What is displayed in the label?
```
strOriginal = "Visual Basic .NET is so much fun!"
intLength = strOriginal.Length
For intI = 0 To intLength − 1
   strChar = strOriginal.Substring(intI, 1)
   If intI Mod 2 = 0 Then
      strOutput = strOutput & strChar.ToUpper
   Else
      strOutput = strOutput & strChar.ToLower
   End If
Next intI
Me.lblOutput.Text = strOutput
```

16. a) Write an algorithm to count the number of words in a sentence.
    b) Write an algorithm to count the number of letters in a sentence.

17. An *input validation loop* is a loop that checks user input for the valid data. If valid data is not entered, the loop reiterates until valid data is entered. Write code that checks the data in txtNumStudents for a value between 1 and 30 inclusive and displays an appropriate prompt in an InputBox if valid data is not typed. This check loop should continue until a valid value is typed. Be sure to consider what happens if Cancel is selected in the Input box.

18. Determine if each of the following is true or false. If false, explain why.
    a) Sentinel values must always be the value –1.
    b) Accumulator variables can only be **Integer** variables.
    c) A **Do…Loop** that evaluates the condition before executing a loop may never execute.
    d) The Unicode value for an uppercase letter is the same for the corresponding lowercase letter.
    e) **String**.Compare("Test", "TEST", False) returns a negative value.
    f) A wildcard character is a ?, *, or #, which matches an unknown character or group of characters.
    g) The statement intSum = intSum + 1 uses intSum as an accumulator variable.
    h) vbTab is a variable that allows the programmer to control the spaces in a string.

An Introduction to Programming Using Microsoft Visual Basic .NET

Exercise 1 ———————————————————— Grooming Services

Create an Grooming Services application that allows the user to select pet grooming services. A shampoo is $15, a flea dip is $5, a trim is $15, and a full shave is $20. The displayed price should reflect the total of the services currently selected. If a service is cleared, the price should change immediately to reflect the correct price. Hint: Use Click event procedures for each check box to update an accumulator. The application interface should look similar to the following after selecting the Shampoo and Flea Dip check boxes:

Exercise 2 ———————————————————— CD Calculator

A certificate of deposit (CD) is a type of investment that matures at a specified interest rate for a specified period. Create a CD Calculator application that prompts the user for the initial investment amount, the annual interest rate, and the desired ending value and then displays the number of years required for the CD to be worth the specified ending value when interest is compounded annually. The CD value at the end of each year can be calculated by the formula CD Value = CD Value + (CD Value * Interest Rate). To determine the number of years it will take for the CD to reach the desired ending value, repeatedly execute the formula until the CD Value is greater than or equal to the desired ending value. The application interface should look similar to:

Exercise 3 ——————————————— Sum Numbers

Create a Sum Numbers application that calculates the sum of a range of numbers entered by the user and displays in a label an expression with the numbers in the range. The application interface should look similar to:

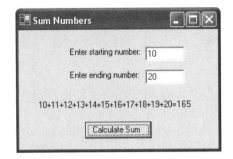

Exercise 4 ——————————————— Bowling Scores

a) Create a Bowling Scores application that prompts the user to enter as many bowling scores as desired and then displays the high score and the low score. The application interface should look similar to the following after clicking Enter Scores, entering a set of scores, and then clicking Statistics:

b) Modify the application to display the average bowling score in a label.

Exercise 5 ——————————————— Initials

Create an Initials application that prompts the user to enter his or her first and last names and then displays the initials of the name in uppercase. The application interface should look similar to:

An Introduction to Programming Using Microsoft Visual Basic .NET

Exercise 6 ——————————————————————————————— Monogram

Create a Monogram application that prompts the user to enter his or her first, middle, and last names and then displays a monogram with the first and middle initials in lowercase and the last initial in uppercase. The application interface should look similar to:

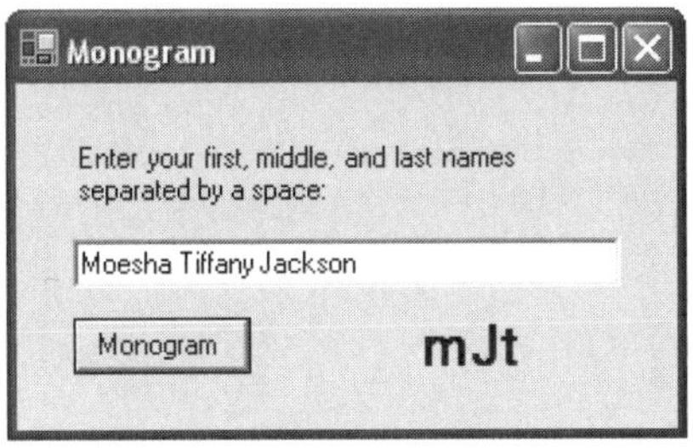

Exercise 7 ——————————————————————————————— Average

Create an Average application that calculates the average of a set of numbers from 1 to a number entered by the user. For example, if the user enters 5, the average of 1, 2, 3, 4, and 5 would be calculated. The application interface should looks similar to:

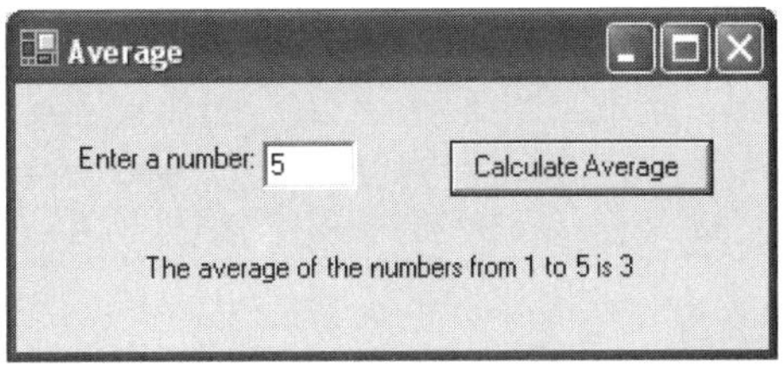

Exercise 8 ——————————————————————————— Replace String

Create a Replace String application that displays a new string in a label. The new string should take a sentence entered by the user and replace every occurrence of a substring with a new string supplied by the user. The application interface should look similar to:

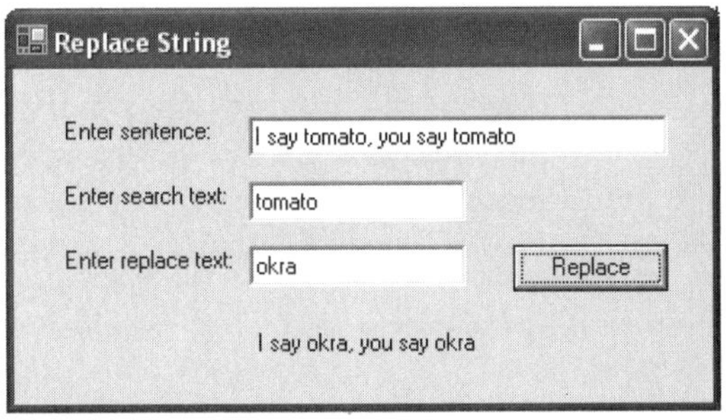

Exercise 9 — Remove String

Create a Remove String application that displays a new string in a label. The new string should take a sentence entered by the user and remove every occurrence of a substring supplied by the user. The application interface should look similar to:

Exercise 10 — Acronym

An acronym is a word formed from the first letters of a few words, such as GUI for graphical user interface. Create an Acronym application that displays an acronym for the words entered by the user. The application should first display an input box asking the user how many words will make up the acronym, then display separate input boxes to get each word, and finally display the acronym in all uppercase. The application interface should look similar to the following after clicking Create Acronym, entering 2, and then entering jelly bean as the words:

Exercise 11 — Name Backwards

As a young boy Franklin Roosevelt signed his letters to his mother backwards: tlevesoor nilknarf. Create a Name Backwards application that prompts the user to enter his or her name and then displays the name backwards in all lowercase in a label. The application interface should look similar to:

An Introduction to Programming Using Microsoft Visual Basic .NET

Exercise 12 ——————————————————————— Count Vowels

Create a Count Vowels application that counts the number of vowels in a word or phrase. The application interface should look similar to:

```
┌─────────────────────────────────────┐
│ 🖼 Count Vowels          [_][□][✕]   │
├─────────────────────────────────────┤
│                                     │
│  Enter text: │zucchini          │    │
│                                     │
│     The number of vowels in zucchini is: 3 │
│                                     │
│         ┌──────────────┐            │
│         │ Count Vowels │            │
│         └──────────────┘            │
└─────────────────────────────────────┘
```

Exercise 13 ——————————————————————————— Unicode

Create a Unicode application that prompts the user for a word and then displays the Unicode base 10 number for each letter in the word. The application interface should look similar to:

```
┌─────────────────────────────────────┐
│ 🖼 Unicode               [_][□][✕]   │
├─────────────────────────────────────┤
│                                     │
│  Enter a word: │Aretha         │     │
│                                     │
│   A = 65  r = 114  e = 101  t = 116  h = 104  a = 97 │
│                                     │
│      ┌────────────────────────┐     │
│      │ Display Unicode base 10 │     │
│      └────────────────────────┘     │
└─────────────────────────────────────┘
```

Exercise 14 ————————————————————————————— Coder

a) Create a Coder application that encodes or decodes a message using Unicode. The application interface should look similar to the following after selecting Enter Message, entering Meet me for lunch in an input box, and then selecting Encode:

```
┌─────────────────────────────────────┐
│ 🖼 Coder                 [_][□][✕]   │
├─────────────────────────────────────┤
│                                     │
│         ┌───────────────┐           │
│         │ Enter Message │           │
│         └───────────────┘           │
│   ┌─ Select conversion ───────────┐ │
│   │                               │ │
│   │    ⦿ Encode     ○ Decode      │ │
│   │                               │ │
│   └───────────────────────────────┘ │
│                                     │
│   77 101 101 116 32 109 101 32 102 111 │
│       114 32 108 117 110 99 104      │
└─────────────────────────────────────┘
```

b) *Advanced*. Modify Coder to produce the code by converting each letter in the original message to its corresponding Unicode number, add 2 to each number, and then convert these numbers back to characters to display a coded message. Keep all spaces between the words in their original places and realize that the letters "Y" and "Z" are to be converted to A and B.

Exercise 15 ——————————————————————————————————— Palindrome

A palindrome is a word or phrase that is spelled the same backwards and forwards, such as madam, dad, or Race car. Create a Palindrome application that uses a loop to determine if the word or phrase entered by the user is a palindrome. The application interface should look similar to:

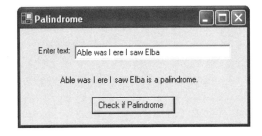

Exercise 16 ——————————————————————————————————— Student Group

Create a Student Group application that prompts the user to enter a student name and then displays what group a student is assigned to depending on the first letter in the student's last name. Last names beginning with A through I are in Group 1, J through S are in Group 2, T through Z are in Group 3. The application interface should look similar to the followinf after entering text and clicking Determine Group:

Exercise 17 ——————————————————————————————————— Slot Machine Game

Create a Slot Machine Game application that acts as a simple slot machine. The user starts with 100 tokens. With each "pull" of the handle, the user loses 1 token and the computer "spins" three wheels, each consisting of the numbers 1, 2, and 3. If all three numbers are 1, the user gets 4 tokens; if all are 2, the user gets 8 tokens; if all are 3, the user gets 12 tokens. The number of tokens that the user has should be displayed on the form and the result of the spin should be displayed in a message box. The application interface should look similar to the following after Pull has been clicked several times:

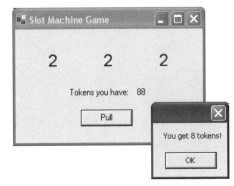

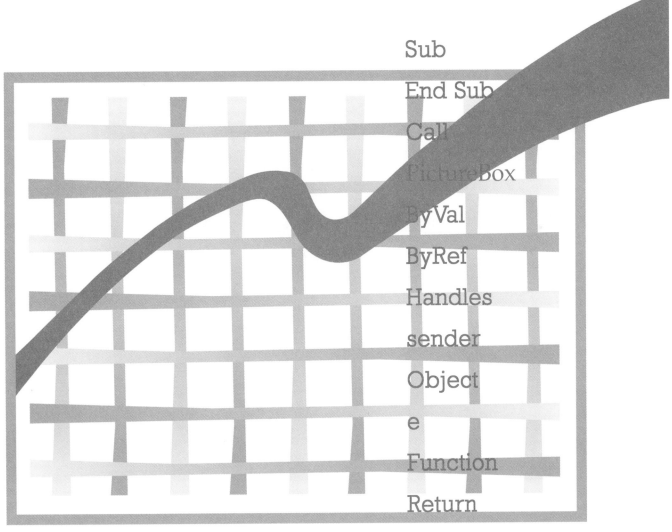

Sub

End Sub

Call

PictureBox

ByVal

ByRef

Handles

sender

Object

e

Function

Return

End Function

Chapter 7 Expectations

After completing this chapter you will be able to:

1. Create Sub procedures and use the **Call** statement.

2. Add images to applications and use the **Image** class to change a graphic at run time.

3. Describe arguments, parameters, and how to pass data to a procedure.

4. Use **ByVal** and **ByRef** for parameters.

5. Document the preconditions and postconditions of a procedure.

6. Use control object parameters.

7. Create event handlers for multiple events.

8. Understand the sender parameter.

9. Use the Tag property to identify objects at run time.

10. Create function procedures and use the **Return** statement.

Concepts explained in this chapter are procedures, functions, value and reference parameters, and **Object** variables. Program documentation is also discussed and the PictureBox control is introduced.

7.1 Sub Procedures

In Visual Basic .NET there are several types of procedures. One type is called the *Sub procedure*, which is a set of statements that perform specific tasks. An event procedure is a Sub procedure written for a specific object event. A Sub procedure can also perform tasks not specifically related to an event, and takes the form:

Sub *ProcedureName*()
   statements
End Sub

ProcedureName is a name describing the task performed by the procedure. *statements* is one or more statements that perform the task. **Sub** declares the procedure and **End Sub** ends the procedure.

programming style

The use of Sub procedures is good programming style because a program is divided into smaller, more manageable blocks of code. There is also less code redundancy because the statements for a specific task need only appear once in a single Sub procedure. A program is also more flexible because changes to the statements for a task need only be made in the Sub procedure, not every procedure using the Sub procedure. For example, the following Sub procedure displays a message to the user:

Sub FormNotComplete()
   MessageBox.Show("Please complete all text boxes.")
End Sub

The FormNotComplete() procedure can be used whenever a message of this type needs to be displayed. If a different message is needed, only the statement in the Sub procedure is changed.

calling a procedure

A Sub procedure must be *called* from another procedure in order to execute. The **Call** statement takes the form:

Call *ProcedureName*()

ProcedureName() is the Sub procedure name followed by parentheses. The parentheses indicate a procedure.

writing a procedure   A procedure is added to program code in the Code window by typing Sub followed by the procedure name and then pressing Enter. When this is done, the IDE automatically adds an **End Sub** statement and places the insertion point in the body of the procedure. Statements can then be typed for the procedure.

7.2 The PictureBox Control

Images can make an application more interesting or improve usability. For example, the Greetings application includes three picture boxes:

Creating Graphics

Creating and using images is discussed in Chapter 10.

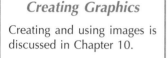

File Formats

BMP, JPG, and GIF are bitmap images. JPG supports millions of colors and is usually the format of photographs and GIF is used for images with few colors such as clip art and logos. PNG is an improved format over GIF and JPG. ICO is the format for icon images. EMF and WMF are Windows metafiles that are vector-based graphics.

The PictureBox control has the properties:

- **Name** identifies a control for the programmer. It is good programming style to begin PictureBox object names with pic.

- **Image** contains the ... button that is clicked to display the Open dialog box where an image file can be selected. Image files can be BMP, JPG, GIF, PNG, ICO, EMF, and WMF formats. Right-clicking Image and then selecting Reset clears the picture box.

- **SizeMode** can be set to either Normal, StretchImage, AutoSize, or CenterImage. AutoSize is often the best choice because the picture box is automatically sized to fit the image. Normal places an image in the upper-left corner of the picture box. If the image is too big, it it clipped. If the image is too small, blank area is displayed. StretchImage sizes an image to fit the picture box, which may distort some images.

- **Visible** can be set to either True or False. Visible is often used at run time to display or hide an image.

- **Size** is the picture box size in pixels. The size of a pixel depends on the screen resolution. Size changes automatically when SizeMode is AutoSize.

Click event   A Click event procedure can be coded for a picture box. The Click event procedure is executed when the user clicks the displayed image. In the Greetings application, the user clicks an image to display a greeting in the language of that country. For example, the picNorway_Click event procedure contains the statement **Me**.lblGreeting.Text = "Goddag!"

image file location
changing an image at run time   Images for a project should be copied to the bin folder located in the project folder. The image in a picture box can be changed at run time by using the **Image** class in a statement similar to:

Me.picCountryFlag.Image = Image.FromFile("CanadaFlag.gif")

FromFile()   The FromFile() method in the **Image** class creates an image object.

In this review you will create the Friends application with **Sub** procedures. Note that the image files should be placed in the bin folder located in the project folder after creating the project.

① *CREATE A NEW PROJECT*

Create a Windows application named Friends.

② *CREATE THE INTERFACE*

Refer to the form below to add, position, and size objects. Use the table below to set properties.

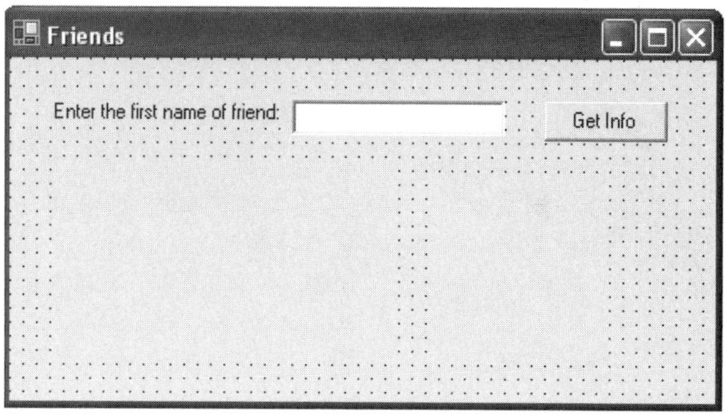

Object	Name	Text	Image	Size
Form1		Friends		
Label1	lblPrompt	*see interface*		
TextBox1	txtFriendName	*empty*		
Label2	lblFriendInfo	*empty*		
PictureBox1	picFriendPhoto		*empty*	100, 100
Button1	btnGetInfo	Get Info		

③ *WRITE THE APPLICATION CODE*

a. Display the Code window.

b. Add comments that include your name and today's date.

c. Create a btnGetInfo_Click event procedure and then add the following statements. Note that a blue wavy underline will appear below the procedure names because they do not yet exist:

```
Dim strFriendName As String
strFriendName = Me.txtFriendName.Text

'Show friend info
Select Case strFriendName.ToUpper
    Case "SHANA"
        Call SHANAInfo()
    Case "LUIZ"
        Call LUIZInfo()
    Case "CRIS"
        Call CRISInfo()
    Case Else
        MessageBox.Show("Sorry, no information available.")
End Select
```

d. After the btnGetInfo_Click event procedure, type **Sub** SHANAInfo and then press Enter. An **End Sub** statement is added and the insertion point is placed in the body of the new procedure. Add the following statements to the procedure. Note that your filename path may need to be different:

```
Sub SHANAInfo()

    Me.picFriendPhoto.Image = Image.FromFile("shana.bmp")
    Me.lblFriendInfo.Text = "Shana's birthday is June 24. Her favorite animal" & _
    " is the dolphin, her favorite color is blue, and she likes to do extreme inline skating."

End Sub
```

e. Create a LUIZInfo() procedure:

```
Sub LUIZInfo()

    Me.picFriendPhoto.Image = Image.FromFile("luiz.bmp")
    Me.lblFriendInfo.Text = "Luiz's birthday is August 21. His favorite animal" & _
    " is the tiger, his favorite color is green, and he likes to do gymnastics."

End Sub
```

f. Create a CRISInfo() procedure:

```
Sub CRISInfo()

    Me.picFriendPhoto.Image = Image.FromFile("cris.bmp")
    Me.lblFriendInfo.Text = "Cris' birthday is September 20. His favorite animal" & _
    " is any kind of bird, his favorite color is yellow, and he likes to play the guitar."

End Sub
```

④ *RUN THE APPLICATION*

a. Save the modified Friends project and then run the application. Type Shana and then click Get Info. A picture and information are displayed. Display information for Luiz, Cris, and then a name that does not have a procedure.

b. Close the Friends application.

⑤ *PRINT THE CODE AND THEN CLOSE THE PROJECT*

7.3 Value Parameters

parameter passing

A procedure often needs data in order to complete its task. Data is given, or *passed*, to a procedure by enclosing it in parentheses in the procedure call. For example, the statement below calls a procedure named GiveHint() and passes it two values, intSecretNumber and intGuess:

```
Call GiveHint(intSecretNumber, intGuess)
```

argument

A variable or value passed to a procedure is called an *argument*. In the statement, intSecretNumber and intGuess are the arguments to be used by the procedure.

A procedure that requires arguments is declared with *parameters* and takes the following form:

```
Sub ProcedureName(ByVal parameter1 As type, …)
    statements
End Sub
```

ProcedureName is the name describing the procedure. **ByVal** indicates that the parameter is a value parameter, *parameter1* is the name of the parameter, and *type* is the data type of the expected value. A value parameter is only used as a local variable by the called procedure. This means that after the procedure has executed, the value of the argument in the procedure call has not changed. There can be many parameters separated by commas. *statements* is the body of the procedure.

The GiveHint() procedure has two parameters. When GiveHint() is called, the first argument is assigned to intFirstNum and the second argument is assigned to intSecondNum:

```
Sub GiveHint(ByVal intFirstNum As Integer, ByVal intSecondNum As Integer)
    If intFirstNumber > intSecondNumber Then
        MessageBox.Show("Too low.")
    Else
        MessageBox.Show("Too high.")
    End If
End Sub
```

GiveHint() does not rely on any other information except what it is passed, and its parameters have names meaningful to GiveHint() but not necessarily to the calling procedure. Generic procedures such as this one can be easily reused in other programs, making coding more efficient.

The following points are important to keep in mind when working with procedures that have value parameters:

- The order of the arguments passed corresponds to the order of the parameters. For example, the first argument in a procedure call corresponds to the first parameter in a procedure declaration.

- The number of arguments in a procedure call must match the number of parameters in the procedure declaration.

- Arguments passed by value can be in the form of constants, variables, values, or expressions. For example, the GiveHint() procedure call may take any of the following forms:

  ```
  Call GiveHint(intSecretNumber, intGuess)
  Call GiveHint(2*5, 10*2)
  Call GiveHint(10, intGuess)
  Call GiveHint(10, 20)
  ```

- Variable arguments passed by value are not changed by the procedure. For example, consider the following code. Assume the Demo() procedure executes first:

  ```
  Sub Demo()
      Dim intCounter As Integer = 1
      Call ShowCount(intCounter)
      Me.lblNumber.Text = intCounter          'displays 1
  End Sub

  Sub ShowCount(ByVal intCounter As Integer)
      intCounter = intCounter + 1
      MessageBox.Show(intCounter)             'displays 2
  End Sub
  ```

  When the **Call** ShowCount(intCounter) statement executes, 1 is passed to the intCounter parameter in ShowCount(). A **ByVal** parameter is used like a local variable for the duration of the procedure. When the procedure finishes executing, the **ByVal** parameter is no longer maintained in memory. The code above demonstrates that intCounter in ShowCount() has no relation to intCounter in Demo().

7.4 Procedure Documentation

Just as comments are used to clarify statements, comments should also be used to describe, or *document*, procedures. Procedure documentation should include a brief description of what the procedure does followed by any preconditions and postconditions. The assumptions or initial

precondition
postcondition

requirements of a procedure are called its *preconditions*. The *postcondition* is a statement of what must be true at the end of the execution of a procedure if the procedure has worked properly. A procedure may not have a precondition, but every procedure must have a postcondition.

A precondition is indicated by pre:, and a postcondition is indicated by post:. The GiveHint() procedure below includes proper documentation. Note that there is no precondition:

```
'~~~~~~~~~~~~~~~~~~~~~~~~~~~~~~~~~~~~~~~~~~~~~~~~~~~~
'Determines if intFirstNum is larger than intSecondNum and then displays an
'appropriate message.
'
'post: A message is displayed in a message box.
'~~~~~~~~~~~~~~~~~~~~~~~~~~~~~~~~~~~~~~~~~~~~~~~~~~~~
Sub GiveHint(ByVal intFirstNum As Integer, ByVal intSecondNum As Integer)

    If intFirstNum > intSecondNum Then
        MessageBox.Show("Too low.")
    Else
        MessageBox.Show("Too high.")
    End If

End Sub
```

Review 2

In this review you will modify the Guessing Game application to include a **Sub** procedure.

① *OPEN THE GUESSING GAME PROJECT*

Open the Guessing Game project, which was last modified in Chapter 5, Review 14.

② *MODIFY THE PROGRAM CODE*

a.   Display the Code window.
b.   Add the GiveHint() procedure after the existing procedures:

```
'~~~~~~~~~~~~~~~~~~~~~~~~~~~~~~~~~~~~~~~~~~~~~~~~~~~~
'Determines if intFirstNum is larger than intSecondNum and then displays an
'appropriate message.
'
'post: A message is displayed in a message box.
'~~~~~~~~~~~~~~~~~~~~~~~~~~~~~~~~~~~~~~~~~~~~~~~~~~~~
Sub GiveHint(ByVal intFirstNum As Integer, ByVal intSecondNum As Integer)

    If intFirstNum > intSecondNum Then
        MessageBox.Show("Too low.")
    Else
        MessageBox.Show("Too high.")
    End If

End Sub
```

An Introduction to Programming Using Microsoft Visual Basic .NET

c. Change the If...Then...ElseIf statement in the btnCheckGuess_Click() procedure to include a procedure call:

```
...
If intGuess < intMIN Or intGuess > intMAX Then         'invalid guess
    MessageBox.Show("Guess out of range.")
ElseIf intGuess = intSecretNumber Then                 'correct
    Me.lblMessage.Text = "You guessed it!"
    MessageBox.Show(intCount)
Else                                                   'too low or too high
    Call GiveHint(intSecretNumber, intGuess)
End If
```

③ *RUN THE APPLICATION*

Save the modified Guessing Game project and then run the application. Test the application.

④ *PRINT THE CODE AND THEN CLOSE THE PROJECT*

7.5 Reference Parameters

A procedure that sends values back to the calling procedure uses reference parameters. *Reference parameters* can alter the value of the actual variables used in the procedure call. A procedure with reference parameters takes the following form:

```
Sub ProcedureName(ByRef parameter1 As type, ...)
    statements
End Sub
```

ProcedureName is the name describing the procedure. **ByRef** indicates that the parameter is by reference, *parameter1* is the name of the parameter, and *type* is the data type of the parameter. There can be many parameters separated by commas. A procedure can have both reference (**ByRef**) and value (**ByVal**) parameters. *statements* is the body of the procedure.

The TwoDigits() procedure returns the first and second digits of a two-digit number in separate variables:

```
'~~~~~~~~~~~~~~~~~~~~~~~~~~~~~~~~~~~~~~~~~~~~~~~~~~~~
'The digits of a two-digit number are returned in separate parameters.
'
'pre: intNum is a number less than 100 and greater than -100.
'post: intFirstDigit is a number between 0 and 9 inclusive.
'intSecondDigit is a number between 0 and 9 inclusive.
'~~~~~~~~~~~~~~~~~~~~~~~~~~~~~~~~~~~~~~~~~~~~~~~~~~~~
Sub TwoDigits(ByVal intNum As Integer, ByRef intFirstDigit As Integer, _
ByRef intSecondDigit As Integer)

    intFirstDigit = intNum \ 10
    intSecondDigit = intNum Mod 10

End Sub
```

> ### *Actual Parameters*
>
> Reference parameters are sometimes called actual parameters because they can change the value of the actual variable arguments used in the procedure call.

When TwoDigits() is called, the value of the first argument is assigned to a new memory location also called intNum. The next two arguments give their *address* to intFirstDigit and intSecondDigit. The *address* of a variable is the location in memory where its value is stored. A **ByRef** parameter uses the same memory location as the argument:

address

```
Private Sub btnDisplayDigits_Click(ByVal sender As Object, _
ByVal e As System.EventArgs) Handles btnDisplayDigits.Click

    Dim intNum As Integer = 27
    Dim intTensDigit As Integer
    Dim intOnesDigit As Integer

    Call TwoDigits(intNum, intTensDigit, intOnesDigit)
    Me.lblTensDigit.Text = intTensDigit    '2
    Me.lblOnesDigit.Text = intOnesDigit    '7

End Sub

'~~~~~~~~~~~~~~~~~~~~~~~~~~~~~~~~~~~~~~~~~~~~~~~~~~~~~~~~~
'The digits of a two-digit number are returned in separate
'parameters.
'
'pre: intNum is a number less than 100 and greater than -100.
'post: intFirstDigit is a number between 0 and 9 inclusive.
'intSecondDigit is a number between 0 and 9 inclusive.
'~~~~~~~~~~~~~~~~~~~~~~~~~~~~~~~~~~~~~~~~~~~~~~~~~~~~~~~~~
Sub TwoDigits(ByVal intNum As Integer, _
ByRef intFirstDigit As Integer, ByRef intSecondDigit As Integer)

    intFirstDigit = intNum \ 10
    intSecondDigit = intNum Mod 10

End Sub
```

LowestToHighest()

The LowestToHighest() procedure also uses reference parameters:

```
'~~~~~~~~~~~~~~~~~~~~~~~~~~~~~~~~~~~~~~~~~~~~~~~~~~~
'Determines if intLowest is the lesser of two values and then swaps
'intLowest and intHighest if necessary.
'
'post: intLowest is the lesser of the two arguments passed.
'intHighest is the greater of the two arguments passed.
'~~~~~~~~~~~~~~~~~~~~~~~~~~~~~~~~~~~~~~~~~~~~~~~~~~~
Sub LowestToHighest(ByRef intLowest As Integer, _
ByRef intHighest As Integer)

    Dim intTemp As Integer
    If intLowest > intHighest Then        'swap values
        intTemp = intLowest
        intLowest = intHighest
        intHighest = intTemp
    End If

End Sub
```

When LowestToHighest() is called, the values of the passed arguments are switched if the first argument's value is greater than the second. For example, when the following statements are executed

```
intNum1 = 30
intNum2 = 12
Call LowestToHighest(intNum1, intNum2)
Me.lblOrderedNumbers.Text = intNum1 & " " & intNum2    '12 30
```

LowestToHighest() is passed the addresses of intNum1 and intNum2. Since intLowest has a greater value than intHighest, intTemp is assigned 30, then intLowest is assigned 12, and finally intHighest is assigned 30, the value of intTemp.

The following points are important to keep in mind when working with procedures with reference parameters:

- The order of the arguments corresponds to the order of the parameters.

- **ByRef** parameters accept only variable arguments. For example, a run-time error is generated when LowestToHighest() is called with constants, as in the statement:

  Call LowestToHighest(5, 1)   'Bad Call Statement

- Variable arguments passed by reference may be changed by the procedure.

Review 3

In this review you will create the Number Breakdown application, which displays the separate digits of a number that contains up to three digits.

① *CREATE A NEW PROJECT*

Create a Windows application named Number Breakdown.

② *CREATE THE INTERFACE*

Refer to the form below to add, position, and size objects. Use the table below to set properties.

Object	Name	Text
Form1		Number Breakdown
Label1	lblPrompt	Enter a number less than 1,000:
TextBox1	txtNumber	*empty*
Label2	lblDigits	*empty*
Button1	btnBreakDown	Break Down

③ *WRITE THE APPLICATION CODE*

a. Display the Code window.

b. Add comments that include your name and today's date.

c. Create a btnBreakDown_Click event procedure and then add the statements:

```
Dim intNumberEntered As Integer
Dim intOnesDigit As Integer
Dim intTensDigit As Integer
Dim intHundredsDigit As Integer

intNumberEntered = Val(Me.txtNumber.Text)
If intNumberEntered < 10 Then
   Me.lblDigits.Text = "The first digit is: " & intNumberEntered
ElseIf intNumberEntered < 100 Then
   Call TwoDigits(intNumberEntered, intTensDigit, intOnesDigit)
   Me.lblDigits.Text = "The first digit is: " & intTensDigit & _
      vbCrLf & "The second digit is: " & intOnesDigit
ElseIf intNumberEntered < 1000 Then
   Call ThreeDigits(intNumberEntered, intHundredsDigit, intTensDigit, intOnesDigit)
   Me.lblDigits.Text = "The first digit is: " & intHundredsDigit & _
      vbCrLf & "The second digit is: " & intTensDigit & _
      vbCrLf & "The third digit is: " & intOnesDigit
Else
   Me.lblDigits.Text = "Invalid entry."
End If
```

d. Add the TwoDigits procedure:

```
'~~~~~~~~~~~~~~~~~~~~~~~~~~~~~~~~~~~~~~~~~~~~~~~~~~~
'The digits of a two-digit number are returned in separate parameters
'
'pre: intNum is a number less than 100 and greater than -100.
'post: intFirstDigit is a number between 0 and 9 inclusive.
'intSecondDigit is a number between 0 and 9 inclusive.
'~~~~~~~~~~~~~~~~~~~~~~~~~~~~~~~~~~~~~~~~~~~~~~~~~~~
Sub TwoDigits(ByVal intNum As Integer, ByRef intFirstDigit As Integer, _
ByRef intSecondDigit As Integer)

   intFirstDigit = intNum \ 10
   intSecondDigit = intNum Mod 10

End Sub
```

e. The ThreeDigits procedure uses integer division to determine the third digit (the hundreds digit) of the number and then calls TwoDigits to get the first two digits of a number. Add the ThreeDigits procedure after the TwoDigits procedure:

```
'~~~~~~~~~~~~~~~~~~~~~~~~~~~~~~~~~~~~~~~~~~~~~~~~~~~
'The digits of a three-digit number are returned in separate parameters
'
'pre: intNum is a number less than 1000 and greater than -1000.
'post: intFirstDigit is a number between 0 and 9 inclusive.
'intSecondDigit is a number between 0 and 9 inclusive.
'intThirdDigit is a number between 0 and 9 inclusive.
'~~~~~~~~~~~~~~~~~~~~~~~~~~~~~~~~~~~~~~~~~~~~~~~~~~~
Sub ThreeDigits(ByVal intNum As Integer, ByRef intFirstDigit As Integer, _
ByRef intSecondDigit As Integer, ByRef intThirdDigit As Integer)

   intFirstDigit = intNum \ 100
   intNum = intNum Mod 100
   Call TwoDigits(intNum, intSecondDigit, intThirdDigit)

End Sub
```

f. Add a TextChanged event procedure for the text box.

④ *RUN THE APPLICATION*

Save the modified Number Breakdown project and then run the application. Test the application using single, double, and triple-digit numbers, and invalid data, such as four-digit numbers.

⑤ *PRINT THE CODE AND THEN CLOSE THE PROJECT*

Review 4

Create a Sort Numbers application that prompts the user for two numbers and then displays the numbers sorted from lowest to highest when Sort is clicked. The program should use the LowestToHighest procedure from Section 7.5. The application interface should look similar to that shown on the right after entering 5 and 2 and then clicking Sort.

Sort Numbers
Enter first number: 5
Enter second number: 2
Sort   2, 5

7.6 Control Object Parameters

control class

Control objects, such as labels, are a data type called a *control class*. A control class has a visual element that is displayed on the form and properties for storing data. Control classes include CheckBox, Label, RadioButton, Button, TextBox, and PictureBox. A control object can be passed as an argument to a procedure. For example, a call that passes a reference to an actual label on the form looks similar to:

control object argument

```
Call GiveHint(Me.lblMessage, intSecretNumber, intGuess)
```

control object parameters

Control object parameters should be declared **ByRef** in a procedure using the appropriate control class name. For example, GiveHint() has a Label parameter:

```
'~~~~~~~~~~~~~~~~~~~~~~~~~~~~~~~~~~~~~~~~~~~~~~~
'Determines if intFirstNum is larger than intSecondNum and then
'displays an appropriate message.
'
'post: A message is displayed in a label.
'~~~~~~~~~~~~~~~~~~~~~~~~~~~~~~~~~~~~~~~~~~~~~~~
Sub GiveHint(ByRef lblHint As Label, ByVal intFirstNum As Integer, _
    ByVal intSecondNum As Integer)

    If intFirstNum > intSecondNum Then
        lblHint.Text = "Too low."
    Else
        lblHint.Text = "Too high."
    End If

End Sub
```

Note that the keyword **Me** is not used in the assignment statements because the label being referred to is the one passed to the parameter. This allows a procedure to be written without actually knowing the names of the objects on the form. A procedure written this way can be used again and again in other programs without being modifed. Development time for larger and more complex programs can be reduced by using generic procedures like this one after thoroughly testing and debugging.

Modify the Guessing Game application last modified in Review 2 to include an Object parameter in the GiveHint() procedure so that a hint is displayed to the user in a label on the form rather than in a message box. Use the procedure in Section 7.6. The application interface should look similar to that shown on the right after guessing a number that is too low and clicking Check Guess.

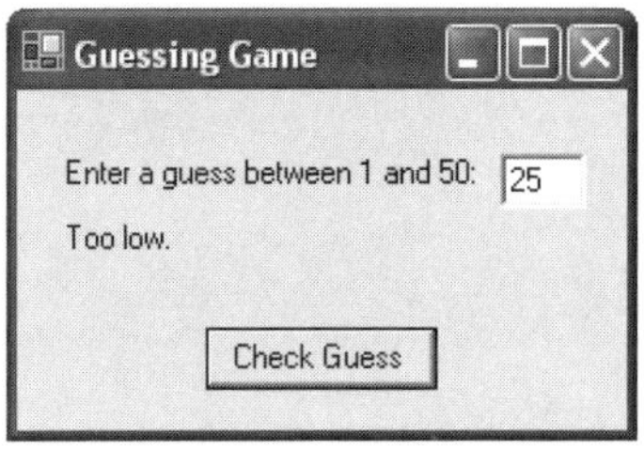

```
Guessing Game                    _ □ ✕

Enter a guess between 1 and 50:  25
Too low.


              Check Guess
```

7.7 The Event Handler Procedure

Event procedures are used in every program. They are also called event handler procedures because they execute in response to events. For example, the following event procedure executes when a check box named chkRelish is clicked:

procedure name

```
Private Sub chkRelish_Click(ByVal sender As Object, _
ByVal e As System.EventArgs) Handles chkRelish.Click

    If chkRelish.Checked Then        'Relish selected
        decprice = decprice + 0.25
    Else                             'Relish cleared
        decprice = decprice - 0.25
    End If

End Sub
```

event

Event procedure declarations include the **Handles** keyword followed by the events to be "handled." This keyword, <u>not</u> the procedure name, determines when an event procedure executes. Changing an event procedure name has no effect on procedure execution.

Event procedures always include two parameters, as shown in the chkRelish_Click heading. *sender* is the object that raised the event, and *e* is information about the event and will be explained later in the text. *Object* *sender* is type **Object**, a data type that can be used to represent any value.

handling multiple events An event procedure handles multiple events when event names, separated by commas, are added after the **Handles** keyword. For example, the Hot Dog application uses a single Click event procedure to handle click events for three different check boxes. Note that an assignment statement uses the *sender* parameter to access the properties of the object that caused the event:

```
Public Class Form1
    Inherits System.Windows.Forms.Form

  ┌─────────────────────────────────────┐
  │ Windows Form Designer generated code │
  └─────────────────────────────────────┘

    '~~~~~~~~~~~~~~~~~~~~~~~~~~~~~~~~~~~~~~~~~~~~~~~~~~~~~~~~~~~~~~~~~~~~~~
    'Updates the price of a hot dog.
    '
    'post: The price has been updated in the label on the form.
    '~~~~~~~~~~~~~~~~~~~~~~~~~~~~~~~~~~~~~~~~~~~~~~~~~~~~~~~~~~~~~~~~~~~~~~
    Private Sub Topping_Click(ByVal sender As Object, ByVal e As System.EventArgs) _
    Handles chkRelish.Click, chkKraut.Click, chkCheese.Click

        Const decTOPPING As Decimal = 0.25  'toppings prices
        Static decPrice As Decimal = 2      'hot dog base price

        Dim chkSelectedTopping As CheckBox = sender 'object that raised event
        If chkSelectedTopping.Checked Then          'topping selected
            decPrice = decPrice + decTOPPING
        Else                                        'topping cleared
            decPrice = decPrice - decTOPPING
        End If

        Me.lblCurrentPrice.Text = "$" & decPrice    'display updated price

    End Sub

End Class
```

- The procedure name was changed to a more generic name. This was done by modifying the name of the chkRelish_Click event procedure after it was added to the Code window.

- Additional events to be handled by the procedure were typed after the **Handles** keyword. An AutoList is displayed when a comma is typed after the **Handles** keyword in the procedure heading.

- *sender* was assigned to a CheckBox variable so that its properties can be accessed.

7.8 The Tag Property

Every control has a Tag property. The Tag property of an object can be set in the Properties window to any string expression and is useful for identifying, or "tagging," objects for the programmer. When an event procedure is handling more than one object, the string in the Tag property can be used to determine which object raised the event. This is important when different actions should be taken for different objects. For example, the Hot Dog II application prices a hot dog by an amount that varies depending on the selected check box:

```
Public Class Form1
    Inherits System.Windows.Forms.Form

  Windows Form Designer generated code

    '~~~~~~~~~~~~~~~~~~~~~~~~~~~~~~~~~~~~~~~~~~~~~~~~~~~~~~~~~~~~~~
    'Updates the price of a hot dog.
    '
    'pre: sender has a valid Tag expression.
    'post: The price has been updated in the label on the form.
    '~~~~~~~~~~~~~~~~~~~~~~~~~~~~~~~~~~~~~~~~~~~~~~~~~~~~~~~~~~~~~~
    Private Sub Toppings_Click(ByVal sender As Object, ByVal e As System.EventArgs) _
    Handles chkRelish.Click, chkKraut.Click, chkCheese.Click

        Const decRELISH As Decimal = 0.1
        Const decKRAUT As Decimal = 0.25
        Const decCHEESE As Decimal = 0.5
        Static decPrice As Decimal = 2                'hot dog base price

        Dim chkSelectedTopping As CheckBox = sender  'object that raised event
        If chkSelectedTopping.Checked Then           'topping selected
            Select Case chkSelectedTopping.Tag
                Case "Relish"
                    decPrice = decPrice + decRELISH
                Case "Kraut"
                    decPrice = decPrice + decKRAUT
                Case "Cheese"
                    decPrice = decPrice + decCHEESE
            End Select
        Else                                         'topping cleared
            Select Case chkSelectedTopping.Tag
                Case "Relish"
                    decPrice = decPrice - decRELISH
                Case "Kraut"
                    decPrice = decPrice - decKRAUT
                Case "Cheese"
                    decPrice = decPrice - decCHEESE
            End Select
        End If

        Me.lblCurrentPrice.Text = "$" & decPrice     'display updated price

    End Sub
End Class
```

The Tag property for each of the check boxes was set to a descriptive string. This property value is then used to determine which action to take.

Review 6

In this review, you will create the Shell Game application. The Shell Game displays pictures of three shells. Under one shell is a "hidden" pearl. The user guesses which shell is hiding the pearl by clicking a shell. The hidden pearl is then displayed along with a message telling the player if a correct guess was made. The pearl is hidden again after each try so that the game can be played again and again. An algorithm for implementing this kind of guessing game is:

1. Generate a random number between 1 and 3. Use this number to determine which shell is "hiding" the pearl.

2. Show a pearl picture below the shell that corresponds to the random number.

3. Using one procedure that handles click events for all three shells, determine if the user clicked the shell that corresponds to the random number.

4. Display a message to the player. The player won, if the shell clicked corresponds to the generated random number.

5. Make the pearl picture no longer visible so that the game can be played again without quitting and running the application again.

An Introduction to Programming Using Microsoft Visual Basic .NET

The algorithm can then be refined into the following pseudocode:

```
Sub picShell_Click(sender, e) Handles Shell1.Click, Shell2.Click, Shell3.Click
    Generate a random number between 1 and 3 inclusive
    Show the pearl that corresponds to the random number
    If picShellClicked.Tag = randomNumber then
        Display "You won!"
    Else
        Display "Sorry, you lose."
    End If
    Hide the displayed pearl
End Sub
```

① CREATE A NEW PROJECT

Create a Windows application named Shell Game.

② CREATE THE INTERFACE

Refer to the form below to add, position, and size objects. Use the table below to set properties. To create the three shells and pearls, create one set and then copy and paste. Next, appropriately change the properties of the pasted objects.

Object	Name	Text	Image	Visible	Tag	Size
Form1		Shell Game				
PictureBox1	picShell1		shell.gif	True	1	110, 110
PictureBox2	picPearl1		pearl.gif	False	1	32, 32
PictureBox3	picShell2		shell.gif	True	2	110, 110
PictureBox4	picPearl2		pearl.gif	False	2	32, 32
PictureBox5	picShell3		shell.gif	True	3	110, 110
PictureBox6	picPearl3		pearl.gif	False	3	32, 32

③ WRITE THE APPLICATION CODE

a. Display the Code window.

b. Add comments that include your name and today's date.

c. Create a picShell1_Click event procedure.

d. Modify the procedure name, document the procedure, add events after the **Handles** keyword, and add statements so that the procedure is like:

```
'~~~~~~~~~~~~~~~~~~~~~~~~~~~~~~~~~~~~~~~~~~~~~~~~~~~~~~~~~~~~~
'Determines which shell was clicked and displays a message if shell clicked is the
'same as a randomly chosen shell.
'
'pre: Shell picture objects have valid Tag properties.
'post: The hidden shell is shown and a message box is displayed to the user.
'~~~~~~~~~~~~~~~~~~~~~~~~~~~~~~~~~~~~~~~~~~~~~~~~~~~~~~~~~~~~~
Private Sub picShell_Click(ByVal sender As Object, ByVal e As System.EventArgs) _
Handles picShell1.Click, picShell2.Click, picShell3.Click

    'Determine which shell was clicked by user
    Dim picShellClicked As PictureBox = sender
    Dim intShellClicked As Integer = Val(picShellClicked.Tag)

    'Pick the shell that hides the pearl
    Randomize()
    Dim intShellWithPearl As Integer = Int(3 * Rnd()) + 1

    'Show the pearl
    Select Case intShellWithPearl
        Case 1
            Me.picPearl1.Visible = True
        Case 2
            Me.picPearl2.Visible = True
        Case 3
            Me.picPearl3.Visible = True
    End Select

    'Display message to player
    If intShellClicked = intShellWithPearl Then
        MessageBox.Show("You won!")
    Else
        MessageBox.Show("Sorry, you lose.")
    End If

    'Hide pearl again
    Select Case intShellWithPearl
        Case 1
            Me.picPearl1.Visible = False
        Case 2
            Me.picPearl2.Visible = False
        Case 3
            Me.picPearl3.Visible = False
    End Select

End Sub
```

④ RUN THE APPLICATION

a. Save the modified Shell Game project.

b. Run the application. Click a shell. Select OK in the message box and play a few more times.

c. Close the Shell Game application.

⑤ PRINT THE CODE AND THEN CLOSE THE PROJECT

7.9 Function Procedures

A function procedure, often just called a *function*, performs a specific task and then returns a value. Several built-in functions have been discussed in previous chapters, including Int() and Rnd(). A function procedure takes the following form:

Function *ProcedureName*(**ByVal** *parameter1* **As** *type*, ...) **As** *Returntype*
   statements
   Return *value*
End Function

ProcedureName describes the task performed by the function. **ByVal** indicates that the parameter is by value, *parameter1* is the name of the parameter, and *type* is the data type of the parameter. There can be many parameters separated by commas. *Returntype* indicates the data type of the value returned by the function. *statements* is one or more statements needed to perform the task. The **Return** statement returns a value to the calling statement. There can be more than one **Return**, but the function ends after the first **Return** statement executes. **Function** declares the function procedure and **End Function** ends the function procedure.

programming style   A function often has at least one parameter for data that is required to perform its task. However, parameters are **ByVal** because a function performs a task and returns a single value. It should not alter the arguments it has been passed.

calling a function   Functions are called from within a statement that will make use of the return value, as in the assignment statement below:

Me.lblStudentGrade.Text = LetterGrade(sngAverage)

The lblStudentGrade label displays the character returned by the LetterGrade() function:

```
'~~~~~~~~~~~~~~~~~~~~~~~~~~~~~~~~~~~
'Returns a letter grade corresponding to sngScore.
'
'post: A letter grade has been returned.
'~~~~~~~~~~~~~~~~~~~~~~~~~~~~~~~~~~~
Function LetterGrade (ByVal sngScore As Single) As Char

    If sngScore >= 90 Then
        Return "A"
    ElseIf sngScore >= 80 Then
        Return "B"
    ElseIf sngScore >= 70 Then
        Return "C"
    ElseIf sngScore >= 60 Then
        Return "D"
    Else
        Return "F"
    End If

End Function
```

Functions are useful for validating user input. For example, an application that prompts the user for a value between 1 and 10 could use the following **Boolean** function to determine if user input is valid:

```
'~~~~~~~~~~~~~~~~~~~~~~~~~~~~~~~~~~~~~~~~~~~~~~~~~~
'Returns True if intLowerLimit <= intUserNum <= intUpperLimit.
'
'post: True returned if intLowerLimit <= intUserNum <= intUpperLimit
'otherwise False returned.
'~~~~~~~~~~~~~~~~~~~~~~~~~~~~~~~~~~~~~~~~~~~~~~~~~~
Function ValidEntry (ByVal intUserNum As Integer, ByVal intUpperLimit As Integer, _
ByVal intLowerLimit As Integer) As Boolean

    If intUserNum > intUpperLimit Or intUserNum < intLowerLimit Then
        Return False
    Else
        Return True
    End If

End Function
```

The following code uses ValidEntry() to check user input:

```
...
intGuess = Me.txPlayerGuess.Text
If Not ValidEntry(intGuess, intMAX, intMIN) Then
    MessageBox.Show("Invalid guess. Please try again.")
...
```

Note how the Boolean value returned by the function is used as the condition of the **If…Then** statement.

A function is a better choice over a Sub procedure when a well-defined task that results in a single value if to be performed. The following points are important to keep in mind when working with functions:

- The order of the arguments corresponds to the order of the parameters.

- Only **ByVal** parameters should be declared in a function because a function should not alter the arguments it has been passed.

- A function returns a single value and therefore must be used in a statement such as an assignment statement that makes use of the returned value.

Review 7

In this review you will create the Letter Grade application.

① **CREATE A NEW PROJECT**

Create a Windows application named Letter Grade.

② **CREATE THE INTERFACE**

Refer to the form on the next page to add, position, and size objects. Use the table below the form to set properties.

An Introduction to Programming Using Microsoft Visual Basic .NET

Object	Name	Text
Form1		Letter Grade
Label1	lblPrompt	Enter a test score:
TextBox1	txtScore	*empty*
Button1	btnLetterGrade	Letter Grade
Label2	lblLetterGrade	*empty*

③ **WRITE THE APPLICATION CODE**

    a. Display the Code window.

    b. Add comments that include your name and today's date.

    c. Create a btnLetterGrade_Click event procedure and then add the statements:

```
Const sngLowestScore As Single = 0
Const sngHighestScore As Single = 100
Dim sngScoreEntered As Single

sngScoreEntered = Val(Me.txtScore.Text)

If Not ValidEntry(sngScoreEntered, sngHighestScore, sngLowestScore) Then
    MessageBox.Show("Enter a score between " & sngLowestScore & " and " _
                & sngHighestScore)
    Me.txtScore.Text = Nothing
    Me.lblLetterGrade.Text = Nothing
Else
    Me.lblLetterGrade.Text = "Your grade is " & LetterGrade(sngScoreEntered)
End If
```

    d. Add the ValidEntry function:

```
'~~~~~~~~~~~~~~~~~~~~~~~~~~~~~~~~~~~~~~~~~~~~~~~~~
'Returns True if intLowerLimit <= intUserNum <= intUpperLimit.
'
'post: True returned if intLowerLimit <= intUserNum <= intUpperLimit
'otherwise False returned.
'~~~~~~~~~~~~~~~~~~~~~~~~~~~~~~~~~~~~~~~~~~~~~~~~~
Function ValidEntry (ByVal intUserNum As Integer, ByVal intUpperLimit As Integer, _
ByVal intLowerLimit As Integer) As Boolean

    If intUserNum > intUpperLimit Or intUserNum < intLowerLimit Then
        Return False
    Else
        Return True
    End If

End Function
```

e. Add the LetterGrade function:

```
'~~~~~~~~~~~~~~~~~~~~~~~~~~~~~~~~~~~~~~~~
'Returns a letter grade corresponding to sngScore.
'
'post: A letter grade has been returned.
'~~~~~~~~~~~~~~~~~~~~~~~~~~~~~~~~~~~~~~~~
Function LetterGrade (ByVal sngScore As Single) As Char

    If sngScore >= 90 Then
        Return "A"
    ElseIf sngScore >= 80 Then
        Return "B"
    ElseIf sngScore >= 70 Then
        Return "C"
    ElseIf sngScore >= 60 Then
        Return "D"
    Else
        Return "F"
    End If

End Function
```

f. Add an appropriate TextChanged event procedure.

④ RUN THE APPLICATION

a. Save the modified Letter Grade project.

b. Run the application. Test the application by entering several valid and invalid scores.

c. Close the Letter Grade application.

⑤ PRINT THE CODE AND THEN CLOSE THE PROJECT

Case Study

The Chapter 4 Case Study was a simple calculator. In this Case Study a Calculator II application will be created. This calculator will provide an interface similar to standard calculators and will be able to perform calculations involving many operands.

specification   The specification for this Case Study is:

A Calculator II application that is an onscreen calculator with buttons for digits 0 through 9, the decimal point (.), operators +, −, *, /, and = . The = button displays the result of a calculation. The user should be able to enter a series of numbers and operators which are evaluated as they are entered. For example, clicking 2, +, 3, and * displays 5. Continuing on and clicking 4 and then = displays 20. A Clear button should change the display to 0. After clearing, the number entered is considered the first operand. An Off button should close the application.

design   The interface design for this Case Study is based on the appearance of a standard calculator:

The code design starts with an algorithm:

1. When the user clicks the decimal point button or a digit other than 0, replace the 0 on the display with the digit or decimal point clicked.
2. As the user clicks buttons, concatenate the digits and the decimal point to the display until an operator button is clicked.
3. When an operator button is clicked, convert the calculator display to a number and store this number as the first operand. Store the operator clicked for use in a calculation after the second operand is entered.
4. When a digit or decimal point button is clicked, display this value to replace the current display.
5. As the user clicks buttons, concatenate the digits and the decimal point to the display until an operator or equal sign button is clicked.
6. When an operator or equal sign button is clicked, convert the calculator display to a number and store this number as the second operand. Perform a calculation using the stored operator and the two operands. Display the result on the calculator display and also store the result as the first operand for use in another operation, if necessary.
7. If another operator button is clicked, store the operator and then start again with step 4.
8. If Clear is clicked, reinitialize the operands to 0 and clear the operator, show a 0 on the display, and then start again with step 1.
9. If Off is clicked, end the application.

From the algorithm, event procedures, variables, and functions can be identified by carefully reading the description. For example, "clicks," "clicking," and "clicked" indicates a Click event procedure. The words "store" and "stored" indicate a variable. An action to be performed could mean the need for a function. In this case, "perform a calculation" indicates the need for a function that takes two operands and an operator and returns the result of a calculation.

Analyzing the algorithm further reveals some aspects of the code:

- The same or similar actions are needed for the digit buttons and the decimal point button so a single event procedure should handle a Click event for the ., 0, 1, 2, 3, 4, 5, 6, 7, 8, and 9 buttons.

- The same or similar actions are needed for the operator buttons so a single event procedure should handle a Click event for the =, +, −, x, and / buttons.

- Variables representing the first operand, the second operand, and the last operator clicked need to be global because both the digit and operator Click event procedures require access to the variables.

- The Click event procedure handling digit clicks needs a flag to determine if the digit or decimal point clicked should be concatenated to the current display or if the current display should be replaced by the clicked value.

Based on the algorithm and analysis of the algorithm, the pseudocode for this application appears like:

```
Dim Operand1 As Single = 0
Dim Operand2 As Single = 0
Dim Operator As String = Nothing
Dim NewOperand As Boolean = True

Sub btnNumber_Click(sender, e) Handles btn0.Click, btn1.Click, _
btn2.Click, btn3.Click, btn4.Click, btn5.Click, btn6.Click, _
btn7.Click, btn8.Click, btn9.Click, btnDot.Click
    Dim btnNumberClicked As Button = sender
    If NewOperand Then
        Change calculator display to digit clicked
        NewOperand = False
    Else
        Concatenate digit clicked to current display
    End If
End Sub

Sub btnClear_Click(sender, e)
    Change calculator display to 0
    Operand1 = 0
    Operand2 = 0
    Operator = Nothing
    NewOperand = True
End Sub

Sub btnOff(sender, e)
    End
End Sub

Sub btnOperator_Click(sender, e) Handles btnPlus.Click, btnMinus.Click, _
btnTimes.Click, btnDivide.Click, btnEqual.Click
    Dim btnOperatorClicked As Button = sender
    If (Operand1 = 0 And Operator = Nothing) Or Operator = "=" Then
        Operand1 = value displayed
    Else
        Operand2 = value displayed
        Operand1 = Calculate(Operand1, Operand2, Operator)
        Change calculator display to Operand1
    End If
    Operator = operator clicked
    NewOperand = True
End Sub
```

```
Function Calculate(ByVal sngFirstOperand As Single _
ByVal sngSecondOperand As Single, ByVal strOperator As String) As Single
    Select Case strOperator
        Case "+"
            Return(sngFirstOperand + sngSecondOperand)
        Case "-"
            Return(sngFirstOperand - sngSecondOperand)
        Case "X", "x", "*"
            Return(sngFirstOperand * sngSecondOperand)
        Case "/"
            Return(sngFirstOperand / sngSecondOperand)
    End Select
End Function
```

coding—level 1

Complex applications often require many Sub procedures and functions to perform tasks that together meet the overall program specification. Each new Sub procedure and function should be developed with the specification, design, coding, and testing and debugging steps used in creating a larger application. Solidly written and tested Sub procedures and functions can then be used in an application without introducing bugs and side effects.

In this Case Study, a function is needed to perform a calculation with two operands. Its pseudocode appears above. Next, the function needs to be coded and then tested and debugged. This can be done in an application created just for testing the function:

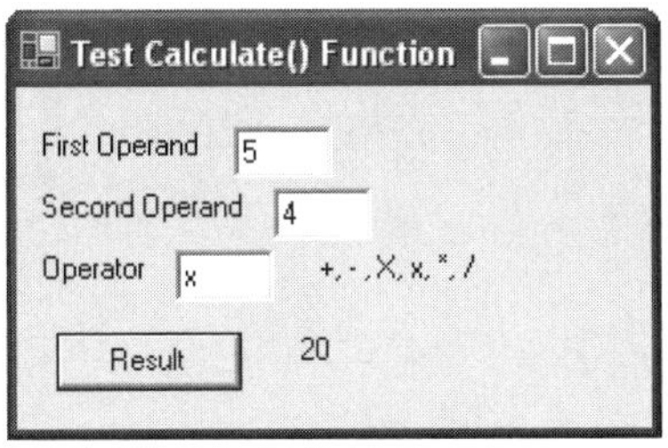

```
Public Class Form1
    Inherits System.Windows.Forms.Form

    Windows Form Designer generated code

    Private Sub btnResult_Click(ByVal sender As Object, _
    ByVal e As System.EventArgs) Handles btnResult.Click

        Dim sngOp1 As Single = Val(Me.txtFirstOperand.Text)
        Dim sngOp2 As Single = Val(Me.txtSecondOperand.Text)
        Dim strOperator As String = Me.txtOperator.Text
        Me.lblResult.Text = Calculate(sngOp1, sngOp2, strOperator)

    End Sub

    '~~~~~~~~~~~~~~~~~~~~~~~~~~~~~~~~~~~~~~~~~~~~~~~~~~~~~~~~~~~~~~~~~~~~~
    'Returns the result of a calculation.
    '
    'post: The result of a calculation involving two operands has
    'been performed.
    '~~~~~~~~~~~~~~~~~~~~~~~~~~~~~~~~~~~~~~~~~~~~~~~~~~~~~~~~~~~~~~~~~~~~~
    Function Calculate(ByVal sngFirstOperand As Single, _
    ByVal sngSecondOperand As Single, ByVal strOperator As String) As Single

        Select Case strOperator
            Case "+"
                Return (sngFirstOperand + sngSecondOperand)
            Case "-"
                Return (sngFirstOperand - sngSecondOperand)
            Case "X", "x", "*"
                Return (sngFirstOperand * sngSecondOperand)
            Case "/"
                Return (sngFirstOperand / sngSecondOperand)
        End Select

    End Function

End Class
```

First Operand 5
Second Operand 4
Operator x   +, -, X, x, *, /
Result 20

The next level of coding is for the Calculator II application itself. The interface for the Case Study is:

Object	Name	Text	Tag
Form1		Calculator II	
TextBox1	txtDisplay	0	
Button1	btn0	0	0
Button2	btnDot	.	.
Button3	btn1	1	1
Button4	btn2	2	2
Button5	btn3	3	3
Button6	btn4	4	4
Button7	btn5	5	5
Button8	btn6	6	6
Button9	btn7	7	7
Button10	btn8	8	8
Button11	btn9	9	9
Button12	btnEqual	=	=
Button13	btnPlus	+	+
Button14	btnMinus	–	–
Button15	btnTimes	X	X
Button16	btnDivide	/	/
Button17	btnClear	Clear	
Button18	btnOff	Off	

coding—level 2   The final coding for this Case Study is shown on the next page. Note that the Calculate() function should be copied from the function tested previously:

```
Public Class Form1
    Inherits System.Windows.Forms.Form

    Windows Form Designer generated code

    Dim sngOp1 As Single = 0
    Dim sngOp2 As Single = 0
    Dim strOperator As String = Nothing
    Dim blnNewOp As Boolean = True


    '~~~~~~~~~~~~~~~~~~~~~~~~~~~~~~~~~~~~~~~~~~~~~~~~~~~~~~~~~~~~~~~~~~~
    'Updates the calculator display.
    '
    'pre: Global variable blnNewOp is True when the current display should be changed to a new
    'number and False when the current display should be updated with a new digit. The Tag
    'property of the button clicked contains the number corresponding to the number on the button.
    'post: The calculator display contains a new number or an additional digit has
    'been added to the existing display.
    '~~~~~~~~~~~~~~~~~~~~~~~~~~~~~~~~~~~~~~~~~~~~~~~~~~~~~~~~~~~~~~~~~~~
    Private Sub btnNumber_Click(ByVal sender As System.Object, ByVal e As System.EventArgs) _
    Handles btnDot.Click, btn0.Click, btn1.Click, btn2.Click, btn3.Click, btn4.Click, _
    btn5.Click, btn6.Click, btn7.Click, btn8.Click, btn9.Click

        Dim btnNumberClicked As Button = sender 'Contains properties of clicked button
            If blnNewOp Then
                Me.txtDisplay.Text = btnNumberClicked.Tag
                blnNewOp = False
            Else
                Me.txtDisplay.Text = Me.txtDisplay.Text & btnNumberClicked.Tag
            End If

    End Sub


    '~~~~~~~~~~~~~~~~~~~~~~~~~~~~~~~~~~~~~~~~~~~~~~~~~~~~~~~~~~~~~~~~~~~
    'Clears the calculator display.
    '
    'post: The calculator display contains a 0 and global variables have been reinitialized.
    '~~~~~~~~~~~~~~~~~~~~~~~~~~~~~~~~~~~~~~~~~~~~~~~~~~~~~~~~~~~~~~~~~~~
    Private Sub btnClear_Click(ByVal sender As System.Object, ByVal e As System.EventArgs) _
    Handles btnClear.Click

        Me.txtDisplay.Text = "0"
        sngOp1 = 0
        sngOp2 = 0
        blnNewOp = True
        strOperator = Nothing

    End Sub


    '~~~~~~~~~~~~~~~~~~~~~~~~~~~~~~~~~~~~~~~~~~~~~~~~~~~~~~~~~~~~~~~~~~~
    'Closes the application.
    '
    'post: The calculator program is ended.
    '~~~~~~~~~~~~~~~~~~~~~~~~~~~~~~~~~~~~~~~~~~~~~~~~~~~~~~~~~~~~~~~~~~~
    Private Sub btnOff_Click(ByVal sender As Object, ByVal e As System.EventArgs) _
    Handles btnOff.Click

        End

    End Sub
```

```
'~~~~~~~~~~~~~~~~~~~~~~~~~~~~~~~~~~~~~~~~~~~~~~~~~~~~~~~~~~~~~~~~
'Updates the value of the operands and shows the result of a calculation
'on the calculator display if two operands have been entered.
'
'post: The value of the first operand is assigned the value on the calculator display if an operator
'has not been previously clicked or the equal sign was the last operator clicked. If an operator as
'previously clicked, the second operand is assigned the value on the calculator display and the
'result of the calculation is shown on the calculator display.
'~~~~~~~~~~~~~~~~~~~~~~~~~~~~~~~~~~~~~~~~~~~~~~~~~~~~~~~~~~~~~~~~
Private Sub btnOperator_Click(ByVal sender As Object, ByVal e As System.EventArgs) _
Handles btnPlus.Click, btnMinus.Click, btnTimes.Click, btnDivide.Click, btnEqual.Click

    'No operator previously clicked or a calculation just performed
    If (sngOp1 = 0 And strOperator = Nothing) Or strOperator = "=" Then
        sngOp1 = Val(Me.txtDisplay.Text)
    Else                              'second operand entered and a second operator clicked
        sngOp2 = Val(Me.txtDisplay.Text)
        sngOp1 = Calculate(sngOp1, sngOp2, strOperator)
        Me.txtDisplay.Text = sngOp1
    End If

    'Store operator for use when the next operator is clicked
    Dim btnOperatorSelected As Button = sender      'contains properties of clicked button
    strOperator = btnOperatorSelected.Tag
    blnNewOp = True

End Sub


'~~~~~~~~~~~~~~~~~~~~~~~~~~~~~~~~~~~~~~~~~~~~~~~~~~~~~~~~~~~~~~~~
'Returns the result of a calculation.
'
'post: The result of a calculation involving two operands has been performed.
'~~~~~~~~~~~~~~~~~~~~~~~~~~~~~~~~~~~~~~~~~~~~~~~~~~~~~~~~~~~~~~~~
Function Calculate(ByVal sngFirstOperand As Single, ByVal sngSecondOperand As Single, _
ByVal strOperator As String) As Single

    Select Case strOperator
        Case "+"
            Return (sngFirstOperand + sngSecondOperand)
        Case "–"
            Return (sngFirstOperand – sngSecondOperand)
        Case "X"
            Return (sngFirstOperand * sngSecondOperand)
        Case "/"
            Return (sngFirstOperand / sngSecondOperand)
    End Select

End Function

End Class
```

Running Calculator II displays the following:

This Case Study should be tested by trying several calculations and verifying by hand that the result is correct.

Review 8

Modify the Calculator II Case Study to include a button for integer division (\).

Review 9

Modify the Calculator II Case Study to display "ERROR" if a division by 0 is attempted. "ERROR" should also be displayed if more than one decimal point is entered for a single number.

Review 10

Write a RndInt() function that has intLowNum and intHighNum parameters and returns a random integer in the range intLowNum to intHighNum. Test and debug the function in a project named Test RndInt() Function. Properly document the function.

Chapter Summary

A Sub procedure is a set of statements that performs a specific task. Sub procedures simplify a program by dividing it into smaller, more manageable blocks of code. There is also less code redundancy and more program flexibility. A Call statement is used to execute a procedure.

PictureBox

A PictureBox object displays an image. The PictureBox control has the properties Name, Image, SizeMode, Visible, and Size. A PictureBox object name should begin with the prefix pic. A Click event is sometimes coded for a picture box. An image can be loaded at run time by using the FromFile method in the Image class.

A procedure can be passed data for use in completing its task. The data passed is called the arguments and a procedure that requires arguments is declared with parameters. ByVal parameters create a local copy of the argument passed and cannot alter the actual value of the variable. ByRef parameters use the actual variable passed and can alter the value of the variable. Objects can also be passed as arguments to procedures. Control object parameters should be declared using the appropriate control class names.

Comments are used to properly document a procedure. Documentation should include a brief description of what the procedure does followed by any preconditions and postconditions.

An event handler procedure always has two parameters. The *sender* parameter can be assigned to a variable of the appropriate control object type so that the properties of the object can be accessed. The Handles keyword in the procedure declaration indicates the events to be handled by the procedure. Adding additional control object events allows one procedure to handle several related objects. Every control has a Tag property. The Tag property can be set to any string expression and is useful for identifying objects in an event procedure.

A function is a procedure that returns a value. Functions often have at least one parameter for data that is required to perform its task. However, parameters are ByVal because a function performs a task and returns a value. It should not alter the arguments it has been passed. Functions are called from within a statement that make use of the return value. A Return statement within a function is terminates the function and returns a value to the calling statement.

Vocabulary

Address A variable's location in memory where its value is stored.

Argument A variable or value passed to a procedure.

Control class The data type used to create a control object.

Documentation Comments that describe a procedure and any preconditions or postconditions of the procedure.

Function procedure A procedure that performs a specific task and then returns a value. Also referred to as "function."

Parameter A variable declared in a procedure to accept the value or address of an argument.

Pass Giving data to a procedure.

Postcondition A statement of what must be true at the end of the execution of a procedure if the procedure has worked properly. Also referred to as "post."

Precondition The initial requirements of a procedure. Also referred to as "pre."

Reference parameter A variable declared in a procedure to accept the address of an argument. Reference parameters can alter the value of the variable arguments used in the procedure call.

Sub procedure A set of statements that perform specific tasks. Event procedures and general procedures are Sub procedures.

Value parameter A variable declared in a procedure to accept a copy of an argument. Value parameters cannot alter the value of the actual arguments used in the procedure call.

Visual Basic .NET

ByRef Keyword used to declare a reference parameter in a procedure.

ByVal Keyword used to declare a value parameter in a procedure or function.

Call Statement used to execute a procedure.

End Function Statement used to end the Function statement.

End Sub Statement used to end the Sub statement.

Function Statement used to declare a function procedure.

Handles Keyword that determines which events cause an event procedure to execute.

Image Class that contains the FromFile() method for changing an image at run time.

Object A data type that can be used to represent any value.

PictureBox control Used to create a control class object that can display an image. Properties include Name, Image, SizeMode, Visible, and Size.

Return Statement used in a function procedure to send a value back to the calling statement.

sender Parameter in an event procedure that is the object that raised the corresponding event.

Sub Statement used to declare a procedure.

Tag Control class property that can be set to a string expression for identifying objects.

1. Explain the similarities and differences between:
   a) parameters and arguments
   b) Sub procedures and function procedures
   c) the keywords **ByVal** and **ByRef**

2. Determine if a Sub procedure or a function procedure should be used for each of the following tasks. State any parameters needed and if they are **ByVal** or **ByRef**. If a function procedure should be used, indicate the data type of the value returned by the function.
   a) Encode a string.
   b) Find the largest and the smallest of four whole numbers.
   c) Display an appropriate message in a message box for a numerical average.
   d) Display the rules to a game application.

3. Write code that:
   a) displays sun.jpg, located on the A: drive, in a picture box named picDay and sets the SizeMode property of the picture box so that the image is sized to fit the picture box.
   b) calls a procedure named LookFor() that has two value parameters named intFirst and intSecond and a reference parameter named strFoundIt.
   c) contains the Sub procedure heading for the **Call** statement in part (b).
   d) calls a procedure named ShowMe(), which has no arguments.
   e) contains the Sub procedure heading for the **Call** statement in part (d).
   f) calls a function named FindAverage() that has parameters intTest1, intTest2 and intTest3 and assigns the return value to a variable named sngAverage.
   g) contains the function procedure heading for the function used in part (f).
   h) contains an event procedure heading for btnChoose_Click that handles the click events for btnDelivered, btnPickUp, and btnSpeedy.

4. What is the SizeMode property (Normal, StretchImage, AutoSize, or CenterImage) of a PictureBox object set to for each of the following situations to occur?
   a) Size of image is as designed, but outer edges have been clipped.
   b) Size of image is as designed, but blank area is displayed to the right and below the picture.
   c) Size of image is as designed, but blank area surrounds the picture.
   d) Size of image is shrunk to fit picture box and image is distorted.
   e) Size of image is as designed, but bottom and right edges are not visible.
   f) Image is as designed, but Size of PictureBox is automatically changed to display entire image.

5. Three images named car1.gif, car2.gif, and car3.gif are stored in the CarPics folder on drive A:.
   a) Write a procedure that randomly displays one of the three images in a picture box.
   b) Write the **Call** statement for the procedure in part(a). Be sure the statement passes a reference to the PictureBox object.

6. Given the function:

```
Function Testing(ByVal intNum As Integer)

    If intNum > 100 Then
        Return Testing * 4
    Else
        Return Testing – 20
    End If
    Return 500

End Function
```

What do the following Call statements display?

a) **Me**.lblAnswer.Text = Testing(60)

b) **Me**.lblAnswer.Text = Testing(100)

c) **Me**.lblAnswer.Text = Testing(200)

7. What is displayed by the following application code when Display is clicked?

```
Private Sub btnDisplay_Click(ByVal sender As System.Object, _
ByVal e As System.EventArgs) Handles btnDisplay.Click

    Dim intA As Integer = 0
    Dim intB As Integer = 0
    Dim intC As Integer = 0

    Call FirstSub(intA, intC, Me.lblOutput)
    Me.lblOutput.Text = Me.lblOutput.Text & intA & " " & intB & " " & intC & vbCrLf
    Call SecondSub(intA, intC, intB, Me.lblOutput)
    Me.lblOutput.Text = Me.lblOutput.Text & intA & " " & intB & " " & intC & vbCrLf
    Call ThirdSub(intA, intB, intC, Me.lblOutput)
    Me.lblOutput.Text = Me.lblOutput.Text & intA & " " & intB & " " & intC & vbCrLf

End Sub


Sub FirstSub(ByRef intX As Integer, ByRef intY As Integer, ByRef lblOutput As Label)

    intX = 2
    intY = intX
    lblOutput.Text = lblOutput.Text & intX & " " & intY & vbCrLf

End Sub


Sub SecondSub(ByVal intX As Integer, ByRef intY As Integer, ByRef intZ As Integer, _
ByRef lblOutput As Label)

    intX = intX – 1
    intY = intZ
    lblOutput.Text = lblOutput.Text & intX & " " & intY & " " & intZ & vbCrLf

End Sub


Sub ThirdSub(ByVal intX As Integer, ByRef intY As Integer, ByVal intZ As Integer, _
ByRef lblOutput As Label)

    intX = 5
    intY = 5
    intZ = 5
    lblOutput.Text = lblOutput.Text & intX & " " & intY & " " & intZ & vbCrLf

End Sub
```

8. Determine if each of the following is true or false. If false, explain why.
   a) A Sub procedure must always be declared with parameters.
   b) A function can only have one **Return** statement.
   c) A procedure can call another procedure.
   d) A constant can be a **ByVal** parameter only.
   e) Once an image is assigned to a picture box it cannot be changed.
   f) A PictureBox object can respond to a Click event.
   g) A **Call** statement must be used in order to execute any type of procedure.
   h) A **ByRef** parameter only exists for the duration of a procedure.
   i) A **ByRef** parameter uses the same memory location as the argument it is passed.
   j) The parameters sender and e are optional in an event handler procedure.
   k) A Click event procedure can be coded to handle multiple events for more than one control object.
   l) Only the Button control has a Tag property.
   m) Every procedure must have documentation before it can be compiled.
   n) Every type of procedure ends with **End Sub**.

Exercise 1 ———————————————————————— Diskette Tips

Create a Diskette Tips application that displays one of the following messages when Tip is clicked:

Keep diskettes away from electrical and magnetic devices.

Do not expose diskettes to either extreme cold or heat.

Store diskettes away from dust, dirt, and moisture.

Never touch the diskette's magnetic surface.

The program code should include a DisplayTip() procedure that uses RndInt() from Review 10 to randomly display one of the tips in a label. The application interface should look similar to the following after clicking Tip:

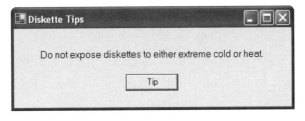

Exercise 2 ———————————————————————— Add Coins

Create an Add Coins application that prompts the user for the number of quarters, dimes, nickels, and pennies and then displays the total dollar amount. The program code should include a TotalDollars() function with intQuarters, intDimes, intNickels, and intPennies parameters. The application interface should look similar to:

Exercise 3 ———————————————— Reduce Fraction

Create a Reduce Fraction application that takes an integer numerator and denominator of a fraction and then displays the fraction reduced or a message stating the fraction cannot be reduced. A fraction may be reduced by finding the largest common factor and dividing both the numerator and denominator by this factor. The program code should include a Reduce() procedure with intNum and intDenom parameters that are changed, if possible, to the reduced values. The application interface should look similar to:

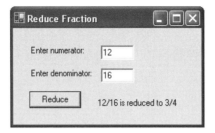

Exercise 4 ———————————————— Test Build

Create a Test Build application that breaks up and then rebuilds numbers 100 through 125 and displays them in a label. The application interface should look similar to the following after clicking Break Up and Rebuild:

Number	Break Up			Rebuild
100	1	0	0	100
101	1	0	1	101
102	1	0	2	102
103	1	0	3	103
104	1	0	4	104
105	1	0	5	105
106	1	0	6	106
107	1	0	7	107
108	1	0	8	108
109	1	0	9	109
110	1	1	0	110
111	1	1	1	111
112	1	1	2	112
113	1	1	3	113
114	1	1	4	114
115	1	1	5	115
116	1	1	6	116
117	1	1	7	117
118	1	1	8	118
119	1	1	9	119
120	1	2	0	120
121	1	2	1	121
122	1	2	2	122
123	1	2	3	123
124	1	2	4	124
125	1	2	5	125

The program code should include:

- the ThreeDigits() and TwoDigits() procedures from Review 3.
- a Build() procedure that has intFirstDigit, intSecondDigit, and intThirdDigit parameters and returns, in an intBuiltNumber parameter, a value that consists of the number represented by the three digits.

An Introduction to Programming Using Microsoft Visual Basic .NET

Exercise 5 ——————————————— Alarm System

An office building uses an alarm system that is turned off by entering a master code and then pressing Enter. The master code is 62498. Create an Alarm System application that displays a message box with an appropriate message after a code is typed and then Enter is clicked. The application interface should look similar to the following after clicking five number buttons:

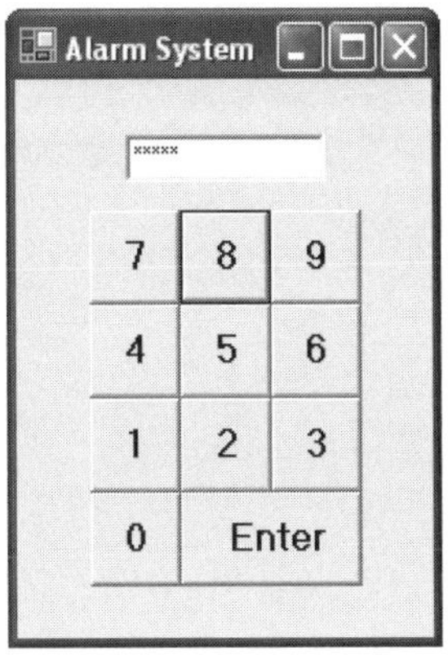

Exercise 6 ——————————————— Metric Conversion

The following formulas can be used to convert English units of measurement to metric units:

inches * 2.54 = centimeters
feet * 30 = centimeters
yards * 0.91 = meters
miles * 1.6 = kilometers

Create a Metric Conversion application that prompts the user for a number and then converts it from inches to centimeters, feet to centimeters, yards to meters, and miles to kilometers and vice versa when a button is clicked. The program code should include separate functions to perform the conversions. The application interface should look similar to:

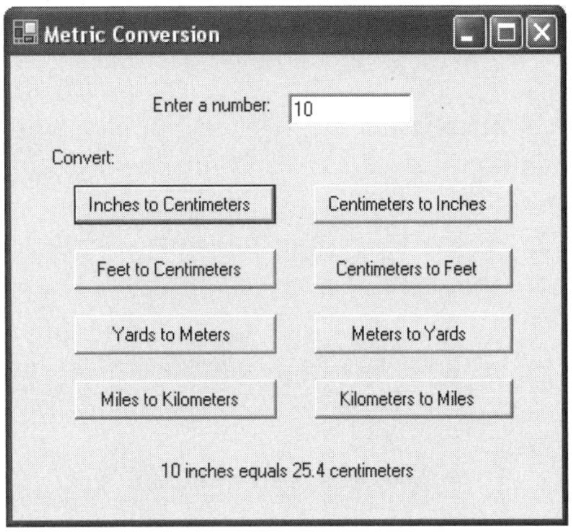

Exercise 7 ─────────────────────────────── Test Entries

Validating user input is often required in programs. Create a Test Entries application that prompts the user for an integer, decimal number, and letter and then determines if the values are valid. The application interface should look similar to:

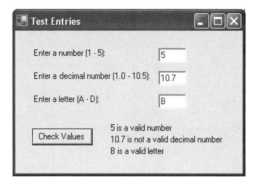

The program code should include:

- a ValidInt() function that has intHighNum, intLowNum, and intNumber parameters and returns True if intNumber is in the range intLowNum to intHighNum, and False otherwise.
- a ValidSingle() function that has sngHighNum, sngLowNum, and sngNumber parameters and returns True if sngNumber is in the range sngLowNum to sngHighNum, and False otherwise.
- a ValidChar() function that has chrHighChar, chrLowChar, chrCharacter parameters and returns True if chrCharacter is in the range chrLowChar to chrHighChar, and False otherwise.

Exercise 8 ─────────────────────────── Lumberyard Helper

The basic unit of lumber measurement is the board foot. One board foot is the cubic content of a piece of wood 12 inches by 12 inches by 1 inch thick. For example, a board that is 1 inch thick by 8 feet long by 12 inches wide is 8 board feet:

$$((1 * (8 * 12) * 12) / (12 * 12 * 1)) = 8$$

Milled wood is cut to standardized sizes called board, lumber, and timber. A board is one-inch thick or less, timber is more than four inches thick, and lumber is anything between one and four inches thick. Create a Lumberyard Helper application that prompts the user for the thickness, length, and width of a piece of wood and then displays the board feet and the classification of the cut. The application interface should look similar to:

The program code should include a BoardFeet() function that has sngThickness, sngLength, and sngWidth parameters and returns the number of board feet and a CutClassification() function that has a sngThickness parameter and returns the classification of the cut.

Exercise 9 ———————————————————— Hi-Lo Game

In the Hi-Lo Game, the player begins with a score of 1000. The player enters the number of points to risk and chooses High or Low. The player's choice of high or low is compared to a random number between 1 and 13, inclusive. If the number is between 1 and 6 inclusive, it is considered "low." If it is between 8 and 13 inclusive, it is considered "high." The number 7 is neither high nor low, and the player loses the points at risk. If the player guesses correctly, he or she receives double the points at risk. If the player guesses incorrectly, he or she loses the points at risk. Create a Hi-Lo Game application that prompts the user for the number of points. The player then clicks either High or Low to play. The program code should include RndInt() from Review 10 to generate the random number between 1 and 13 inclusive. The application interface should look similar to:

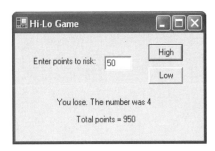

Exercise 10 ———————————————————— Dice Game

Create a Dice Game application. The player begins with a score of 1000. After entering the number of points to risk, the player clicks Roll Dice. The points on each die is displayed. If the total is even, the player loses the points at risk. If the total is odd, the player receives double the points at risk. The program code should include a RollDice() procedure with picDie1, picDie2, and intTotal parameters that generates a two random numbers in the range 1 to 6 to determine the die faces to display in the picture boxes. RollDie() then updates the intTotal parameter. The die1.gif, die2.gif, die3.gif, die4.gif, die5.gif, and die6.gif data files for this text are required to complete this exercise. The program code should also include RndInt() from Review 10. The Dice Game application should look similar to:

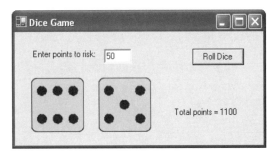

Exercise 11 ✪ ─────────────────────────Shell Game

The Shell Game application from Review 6 gives the user just one chance at choosing the shell with the pearl. Modify the Shell Game application to give the user a better chance of finding the pearl:

- After the user selects a shell but before the hidden pearl is displayed, remove (hide) one of the other two shells that does not contain the pearl.
- Use an input box to ask the user if he or she wants to keep the original guess or choose the remaining shell as the new guess.
- Display the result in a message box.

Improve the Shell Game application by appropriately separating tasks into procedures and functions, including using the RndInt() from Review 10 to generate a random number from 1 to 3 for the shell that hides the pearl. The application interface should look similar to the following after playing one game:

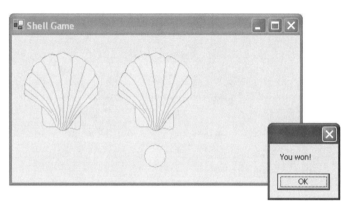

Exercise 12 ──────────────────────────── Nim

The game of Nim starts with a random number of stones between 15 and 30. Two players alternate turns and on each turn may take either 1, 2, or 3 stones from the pile. The player forced to take the last stone loses. Create a Nim application that allows the user to play against the computer. In this version of the game, the application generates the number of stones to begin with, the number of stones the computer takes, and the user goes first. The application interface should look similar to:

The program code should:

- prevent the user and the computer from taking an illegal number of stones. For example, neither should be allowed to take three stones when there are only 1 or 2 left.
- include ValidEntry() from Section 7.9 to check user input.
- include RndInt() from Review 10 to generate a random number from 1 to 3 for the computer's turn to remove stones from the pile.
- include separate procedures for the user's turn and the computer's turn.

An Introduction to Programming Using Microsoft Visual Basic .NET

The game of Mastermind is played as follows: one player (the codemaker) chooses a secret arrangement of colored pegs and the other player (the codebreaker) tries to guess it. After each guess, the codemaker reports two numbers:

1. The number of pegs that are the correct color in the correct position.
2. The number of pegs that are the correct color regardless of whether they are in the correct position.

Create a Mastermind application where the computer is the codemaker and the player is the codebreaker. For simplicity, do not allow the secret arrangement of colored pegs to have duplicate colors and do not allow the codebreaker to guess duplicate peg colors. The application interface should look similar to the following after making several guesses:

```
┌─ Mastermind ──────────────────────────────────────── _ □ X ┐
│                                                             │
│  ┌──────────────┐    ┌─Peg 1──┐ ┌─Peg 2──┐ ┌─Peg 3──┐      │
│  │ Check Guess  │    │        │ │        │ │        │      │
│  └──────────────┘    │ ○ Yellow│ │ ○ Yellow│ │ ○ Yellow│    │
│                      │        │ │        │ │        │      │
│  Pegs correct: 0  Colors correct: 2 ○ Blue │ │ ● Blue │ │ ○ Blue │
│  Pegs correct: 1  Colors correct: 2        │ │        │ │        │
│  Pegs correct: 2  Colors correct: 2 ○ Red  │ │ ○ Red  │ │ ● Red  │
│                      │        │ │        │ │        │      │
│                      │ ○ Green │ │ ○ Green │ │ ○ Green │    │
│                      │        │ │        │ │        │      │
│                      │ ● White │ │ ○ White │ │ ○ White │    │
│                      └────────┘ └────────┘ └────────┘      │
└─────────────────────────────────────────────────────────────┘
```

The program code should:

- include a ChooseColors() procedure that has intPeg1Color, intPeg2Color, and intPeg3Color parameters to generate unique colors for the secret arrangement of the colored pegs. Use numbers 1 through 5 to represent colors and use RndInt() from Review 10 to generate a random number.

- generate the secret arrangement of the colored pegs in the btnCheckGuess_Click() procedure. intPeg1Color, intPeg2Color, and intPeg3Color should be static variables that get assigned a color the first time the player makes a guess. Code similar to the following can be used to make peg color assignments:

```
If intPeg1Color = 0 Then        'First time variable used
    Call ChooseColors(intPeg1Color, intPeg2Color, intPeg3Color)
End If
```

- use separate functions to determine the number of correct colors and the number of correct pegs each time the player makes a guess.

Exercise 14 ——————————————————————— Funny Sentences

Create a Funny Sentences application that prompts the user for a noun, verb, and adjective and then displays a sentence using these words. The program code should include a MakeSentence() procedure that has strNoun, strVerb, strAdjective, and lblLabel parameters and displays the sentence in the label. Use numbers 1 through 5 to represent five different sentences of your choosing and use RndInt() from Review 10 to generate a random number. The application interface should look similar to:

Exercise 15 (advanced) ——————————————— Arithmetic Drill

Computers are used to test a student's ability to solve arithmetic problems. Create an application that tests a student on addition, subtraction, or multiplication using random integers between 1 and 100. The student begins by choosing the type of problem and is then asked 10 problems with 3 chances to answer each correctly. If after 3 chances the answer is still incorrect, the correct answer is displayed. A score is calculated by awarding 10 points for a correct answer on the first try, 5 points on the second try, 2 points on the third try, and 0 points if all three attempts are wrong. Your program code should contain procedures, functions, and static variables. RndInt() from Review 10 should be used as well.

Exercise 16 (advanced) ——————————————— Pet Adoption

A new pet adoption agency has opened up in your neighborhood and needs an application to keep track of pets in need of a home. The agency currently has 15 puppies, 10 kittens, 3 canaries, and 2 iguanas. Create an application that keeps a running total of how many pets are available by subtracting animals that have been adopted and adding new animals in need of a home to the total.

Exercise 17 (advanced) ———————————Card Game

The Card Game application that deals three cards to the user (player) and three cards to the computer. The cards dealt are randomly selected and are in the range 1 to 10, inclusive. The winner is the one with the highest score. After each game, a message should be displayed (You won!, Computer won!, or It's a draw!) and a score updated and displayed (1 point for each win). The user can repeatedly play the game. The scores are maintained until the user quits the application. The application interface should look similar to the following after playing the game five times:

Use the pseudocode below when designing the application:

```
Sub btnPlayGame_Click()
    Deal 3 cards to player
    Deal 3 cards to computer

    If Winner = Player Then
        UpdateScore(PlayerScore)
        ShowScore
    ElseIf Winner = Computer Then
        UpdateScore(CompScore)
        ShowScore
    Else
        UpdateScore(DrawScore)
        ShowScore
    End If
End Sub
```

The interface should display six picture boxes that show the cards dealt. These picture box images should display cardback.gif when the application starts. The cardback.gif, card1.gif, card2.gif, card3.gif, card4.gif, card5.gif, card6.gif, card7.gif, card8.gif, card9.gif, and card10.gif data files for this text are required to complete this exercise.

The program code should include:

- a DealCard() procedure with picCard and intTotal parameters that generates a random number in the range 1 to 10 to determine the card to display in a picture box. DealCard() then updates the total and returns this value in a parameter.
- RndInt() from Review 10.
- a Winner() function that compares the totals of the two hands and returns the winner. An UpdateScore() procedure adds 1 to the winner's score, and the ShowScore() procedure displays the current scores in a label.

An Introduction to Programming Using Microsoft Visual Basic .NET

Mathematical and Business Functions

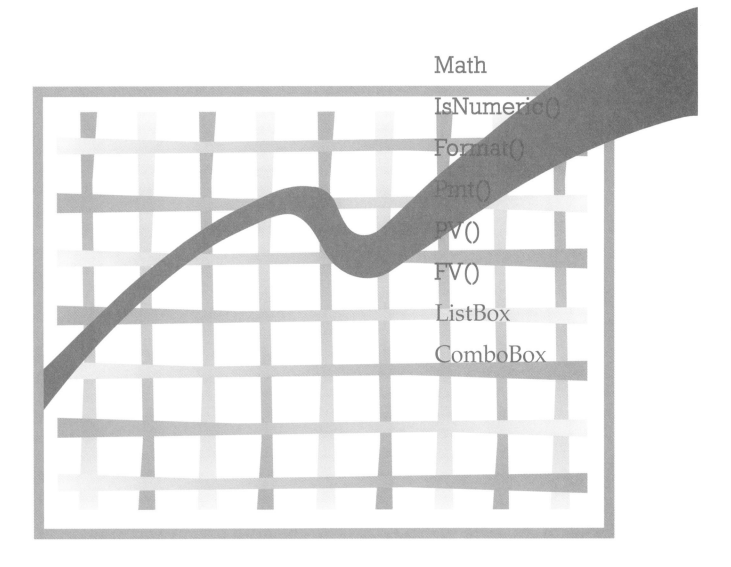

Math

IsNumeric()

Format()

Print()

PV()

FV()

ListBox

ComboBox

Chapter 8 Expectations

After completing this chapter you will be able to:

1. Use the **Math** class and its methods and member constants.

2. Use the IsNumeric() function.

3. Format numeric output.

4. Use the Pmt(), PV(), and FV() business functions.

5. Process business data.

6. Understand Windows application standards, including focus, access keys, tab order, and disabled objects.

7. Convert degrees to radians and the reverse.

Most of the earliest uses for computers were for performing mathematical calculations. In this chapter, the Visual Basic .NET **Math** class is introduced. Built-in functions for formatting numbers and making business calculations are also introduced. The ListBox and ComboBox controls are explained. Application design that includes Windows standards is also discussed.

8.1 The Math Class

The Visual Basic .NET **Math** class includes method members that perform common math functions. Three of these methods are:

- **Abs(*num*)** returns the absolute value of a number. *num* is a numeric variable or value.

- **Sqrt(*num*)** returns a **Double** value that is the square root of a number. *num* is a positive numeric variable or value. A negative number generates a run-time error.

- **Sign(*num*)** returns the **Integer** value 1, –1, or 0 when a number is positive, negative, or 0 respectively. *num* is a numeric variable or value.

The following code demonstrates the **Math** methods discussed above:

```
Dim intNumber As Integer

intNumber = -5
Me.lblResult.Text = Math.Abs(intNumber)        '5

intNumber = 16
Me.lblResult.Text = Math.Sqrt(intNumber)       '4

intNumber = 8
Me.lblResult.Text = Math.Sign(intNumber)       '1
```

8.2 The IsNumeric() Function

The IsNumeric() function is a Visual Basic .NET built-in function that returns True if its argument can be evaluated as a number and False if it cannot. The IsNumeric() function takes the form:

```
IsNumeric(argument)
```

argument is a numeric or string expression or variable. The code on the next page demonstrates IsNumeric():

```
Dim strString As String
strString = "123"
Me.lblAnswer.Text = IsNumeric(strString)        'True

strString = "abc"
Me.lblAnswer.Text = IsNumeric(strString)        'False

Me.lblAnswer.Text = IsNumeric("2+4")            'False
Me.lblAnswer.Text = IsNumeric(2 + 4)            'True
```

Note that "123" evaluates to a number because the string contains only numbers. However, "2+4" is False because the string contains characters other than numbers. In this case, since the + character is not a number, the expression evaluates to a string.

Review 1

Create a Mathematical Functions application that prompts the user for a number and then depending on which button is clicked, displays the absolute value, square root, or whether the number is positive, negative, or zero. Use the IsNumeric() function to verify user input is numeric. Display an appropriate message if the user enters nonnumeric data. The application interface should look similar to that shown on the right after typing 9 and clicking Square Root.

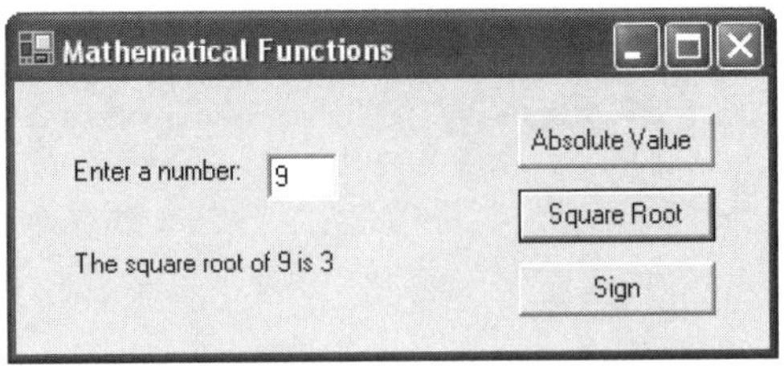

Rules of Rounding

A number with a decimal portion greater than or equal to 0.5 is rounded up and a number with a decimal portion less than 0.5 is rounded down. When the decimal portion is exactly 0.5, an odd number is rounded up and an even number remains the same.

8.3 The Round() Method

The Math class contains the Round() method for rounding numeric data to a specified number of decimal places:

- **Round(*num, places*)** returns a **Double** representing a value rounded to a specified number of decimal places. *num* is a numeric variable or value. *places* is a numeric variable or value.

The following code demonstrates Round():

```
Dim sngNumber As Single = 3.4567
Me.lblRoundedValue.Text = Math.Round(sngNumber, 2)        '3.46
```

Review 2

Create a Round the Number application that prompts the user for a number and number of decimal places and then displays that number rounded to the specified decimal place when Round is clicked. The application interface should look similar to that shown on the right after typing 23.45788 and 3 and clicking Round.

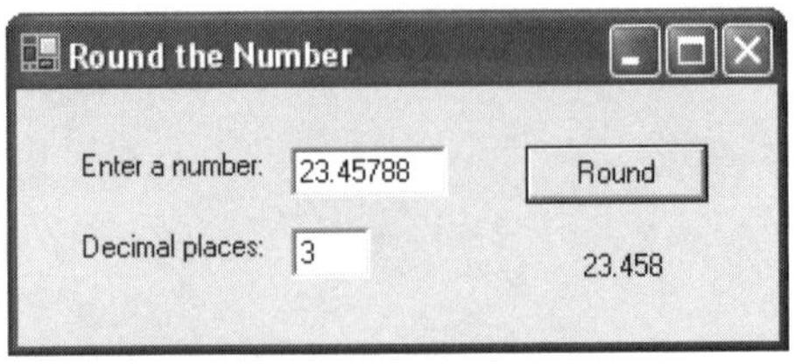

Round the Number

Enter a number: 23.45788

Round

Decimal places: 3

23.458

8.4 Formatting Numeric Output

Applications that display numeric data are more user-friendly when the numbers are formatted for the values they represent. For example, a value that represents a percentage should display a percent sign (%). The Visual Basic .NET built-in Format() function converts a number to a formatted string. This string can be displayed on the interface. However, the actual value used in a calculation is just a number with no formatting.

Format()

The Format() function takes the form:

Format(*number*, "*format type*")

number is a numeric variable or value and *format type* is a predefined Visual Basic .NET format. The following code demonstrates Format() and some format types:

```
Me.lblAnswer.Text = Format(8789, "General Number")   '8789
Me.lblAnswer.Text = Format(8789, "Currency")         '$8,789.00
Me.lblAnswer.Text = Format(8789, "Fixed")            '8789.00
Me.lblAnswer.Text = Format(8789, "Standard")         '8,789.00
Me.lblAnswer.Text = Format(89, "Percent")            '8900.00%
Me.lblAnswer.Text = Format(8789, "Scientific")       '8.79E+3
Me.lblAnswer.Text = Format(8, "Yes/No")              'Yes
Me.lblAnswer.Text = Format(0, "True/False")          'False
Me.lblAnswer.Text = Format(1, "On/Off")              'On
```

The Yes/No, True/False, and On/Off formats display No, False, or Off when *number* is 0 and Yes, True, and On otherwise.

8.5 Business Functions

annuity

An *annuity* is a set of payments made on a regular basis for a specified period. When an annuity is a loan it is sometimes called an installment loan. An annuity can also refer to an investment, such as a retirement plan. Visual Basic .NET includes built-in business functions that return information about an annuity. These functions include a payment function called Pmt(), a present value function called PV(), and a future value function called FV(). The Pmt() function takes the form:

Pmt()

Pmt(*rate, term, principal*)

rate is the monthly interest rate, *term* is the total number of monthly payments to be made, and *principal* is the amount borrowed. For example, the Pmt() function would be used to determine the monthly payment on a mortgage loan. The statements below calculate the monthly payments for a 30-year, $100,000 loan with an interest rate of 6%:

```
Dim sngPayments As Single
sngPayments = Pmt(0.06/12, 360, –100000)       'calculate payment
Me.lblPayment.Text = Format(sngPayments, "Currency")   '$599.55
```

rate and *term* must be in the same units. Since the payments are monthly, the interest rate is calculated as monthly by dividing 6% by 12. The number of payments is 360, 30 years * 12 months. The principal is negative because it is the amount borrowed or owed.

PV()

PV() returns the present value of an annuity. The PV() function takes the form:

PV(*rate, term, amount*)

rate is the monthly interest rate, *term* is the total number of monthly payments, and *amount* is the dollars paid per payment. For example, PV() would be used to determine the cost of financing a car. The statements below calculate the cost of financing when $250 per month over a 4-year period is applied to a loan with an interest rate of 8%:

Amortization

Amortization is a method of computing equal peridoc payments for an installment loan. Each installment, or payment, is the same and consists of two parts: a portion to pay interest due on the principal and the remainder which reduces the principal.

```
Dim sngAmountSpent As Single
Dim sngFinancing As Single
Dim sngPresentValue As Single
sngAmountSpent = 250 * 12 * 4                          '12000
sngPresentValue = PV(0.08/12, 48, –250)               '10240.48
sngFinancing = sngAmountSpent – sngPresentValue       '1759.52
Me.lblPV.Text = Format(sngFinancing, "Currency")      '$1,759.52
```

This means that when you apply $250 a month for 4 years to an 8% loan, $1,759.52 is spent on financing, and $10,240.48 is available for purchasing the car.

As another example of PV(), the following statements determine the maximum amount that should be borrowed for a 15-year mortgage at 10% when the desired monthly payment should not go over $650:

```
Dim sngBorrowAmount As Single
sngBorrowAmount = PV(0.10/12, 180, –650)
Me.lblAmount.Text = Format(sngBorrowAmount, "Currency")   '$60,487.34
```

FV()

FV() returns the value of an annuity. The FV() function takes the form:

FV(*rate, term, amount*)

rate is the monthly interest rate, *term* is the total number of monthly payments to be made, and *amount* is the dollars invested per month. For example, assume $500 per month is invested in a retirement plan that earns 8% interest per year. The statements below determine how much the retirement plan will be worth after 20 years:

```
Dim sngFutureValue As Single
sngFutureValue = FV(0.08/12, 240, -500)          'calculate future value
Me.lblRetirement.Text = Format(sngFutureValue, "Currency")  '$294,510.21
```

8.6 Processing Business Data

Business applications that prompt the user for currency values and percentage rates should be written to accept a variety of formats. For example, a user may type $45,000.00 or 45000 for an amount. Each of these inputs reflect a currency amount, but a run-time error will occur if code is not written to handle the dollar sign and comma. The same is true for data that could include the percent sign (%).

processing currency values
Val()

The IsNumeric() function returns True when a string begins with $. For example, $45 returns True. However, the Val() function returns 0 for $45 because $ is not recognized. When the user is expected to enter a currency value, the Replace() **String** method can be used to find and replace the dollar sign and commas with empty strings before converting

An Introduction to Programming Using Microsoft Visual Basic .NET

the entry to a numeric value. The following procedure processes data in a text box and returns a number. The blnIsValid variable is True only when a valid number greater than 0 is in the text box:

```
'~~~~~~~~~~~~~~~~~~~~~~~~~~~~~~~~~~~~~~~~~~
'Processes data in a text box to read a dollar amount, if any.
'
'post: decDollars contains a number if numeric data with or
'without a $ and commas was entered in the text box. blnIsValid is
'True if a valid dollar amount has been entered in the text box.
'~~~~~~~~~~~~~~~~~~~~~~~~~~~~~~~~~~~~~~~~~~
Sub GetDollarAmount(ByVal txtUserData As TextBox, _
ByRef decDollars As Decimal, ByRef blnIsValid As Boolean)

    Dim strTestAmount As String

    blnIsValid = False                      'assume nonnumeric data
    If txtUserData.Text <> Nothing Then
        strTestAmount = txtUserData.Text                'data typed
        strTestAmount = strTestAmount.Replace("$", "")  'delete $
        strTestAmount = strTestAmount.Replace(",", "")  'delete commas
        If IsNumeric(strTestAmount) Then                'numeric data
            decDollars = Val(strTestAmount)
            blnIsValid = True
        End If
    End If

End Sub
```

processing percentages The way in which a percentage value is entered must also be considered. For example, a decimal value such as 0.10 may be typed or just 10. Percentage values are sometimes entered with %, which must be removed from an entry. The TrimEnd() **String** method can be used to remove a percent sign from a string. The TrimEnd() method removes spaces when no other character is specified. However, it will also remove a specified character as shown in the procedure below:

```
'~~~~~~~~~~~~~~~~~~~~~~~~~~~~~~~~~~~~~~~~~~
'Processes data in a text box to read a percentage amount, if any.
'
'post: sngPercent contains a decimal number if numeric data with
'or without a % was entered in the text box. blnIsValid is True if a
'valid percent has been entered in the text box.
'~~~~~~~~~~~~~~~~~~~~~~~~~~~~~~~~~~~~~~~~~~
Sub GetPercentAmount(ByVal txtUserData As TextBox, _
ByRef sngPercent As Single, ByRef blnIsValid As Boolean)

    Dim strTestAmount As String

    blnIsValid = False                      'assume nonnumeric data
    If txtUserData.Text <> Nothing Then
        strTestAmount = txtUserData.Text
        strTestAmount = strTestAmount.TrimEnd("%")   'delete %
    End If
    If IsNumeric(strTestAmount) Then                'numeric data
        If Val(strTestAmount) > 1 Then              'convert data
            sngPercent = Val(strTestAmount) / 100
        Else
            sngPercent = Val(strTestAmount)
        End If
        blnIsValid = True
    End If

End Sub
```

In this review you will create the Loan Payment application.

① *CREATE A NEW PROJECT*

Create a Windows application named Loan Payment.

② *CREATE THE INTERFACE*

Refer to the form below to add, position, and size objects. Use the table below to set properties.

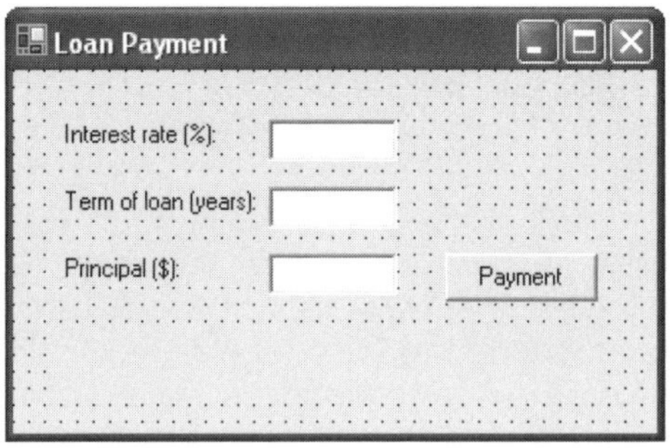

Object	Name	Text
Form1		Loan Payment
Label1	lblRatePrompt	*see interface*
TextBox1	txtRate	*empty*
Label2	lblTermPrompt	*see interface*
TextBox2	txtTerm	*empty*
Label3	lblPrincipalPrompt	*see interface*
TextBox3	txtPrincipal	*empty*
Label4	lblMonthlyPayment	*empty*
Button1	btnPayment	Payment

③ *WRITE THE APPLICATION CODE*

a. Display the Code window.

b. Add comments that include your name and today's date.

c. Create a btnPayment_Click event procedure and then add the statements:

```
Dim sngRate, sngPrincipal As Single
Dim intTerm As Integer
Dim sngPayment As Single
Dim blnValidData As Boolean

'Get interest rate
GetPercentAmount(Me.txtRate, sngRate, blnValidData)

'Get term if interest rate is valid
If blnValidData Then
   intTerm = Val(Me.txtTerm.Text)
   If intTerm <= 0 Then
      blnValidData = False
   End If
End If

'Get principal if interest rate and term are valid
If blnValidData Then
    GetDollarAmount(Me.txtPrincipal, sngPrincipal, blnValidData)
End If
```

```
'Calculate payment if all data entered by user is valid
If blnValidData Then
    sngPayment = Pmt(sngRate / 12, intTerm * 12, -sngPrincipal)
    Me.lblMonthlyPayment.Text = "The monthly payment for a loan of  " & _
    Format(sngPrincipal, "Currency") & " at " & Format(sngRate, "Percent") _
    & " for " & intTerm & " years is " & Format(sngPayment, "Currency")
Else
    Me.lblMonthlyPayment.Text = "Enter valid data."
End If
```

    d. Add the GetPercentAmount() and GetDollarAmount() procedures shown in Section 8.6.

    e. Create an event procedure that handles TextChanged events for all three text boxes. Change the procedure name to NewDataEntered and add the statement:

        Me.lblMonthlyPayment.Text = **Nothing**

④ *RUN THE APPLICATION*

    a. Save the modified Loan Payment project and then run and test the application.

    b. Close the Loan Payment application.

⑤ *PRINT THE CODE AND THEN CLOSE THE PROJECT*

Review 4

Create a Credit Card Loan application that prompts the user for the interest rate of the card, the total amount charged, and the minimum payment desired. Clicking **Number of Payments** displays the number of payments required to pay off the credit card loan, the total amount that will be paid, and the amount that will be paid to interest. The application interface should look similar to that shown on the right.

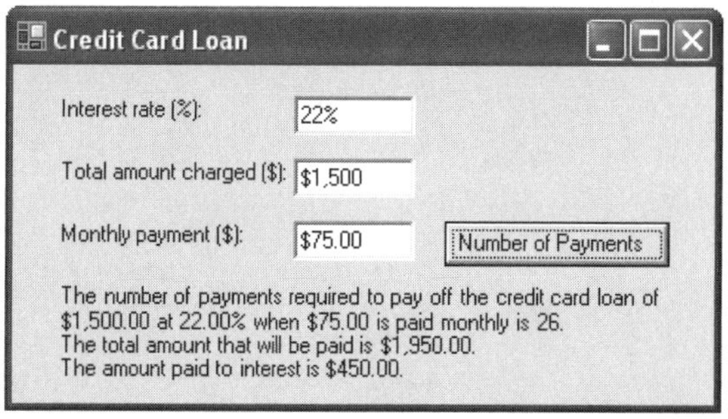

Review 5

Create a Watch Your Money Grow application that prompts the user for the interest rate, term, and the amount invested each month and then displays the value of the investment (future value) when **Future Value** is clicked. The application interface should look similar to that shown on the right.

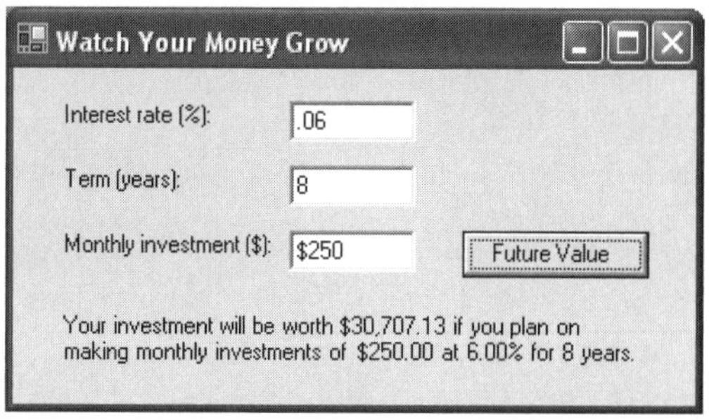

8.7 The ListBox Control

A list box is used to display a list of items. A scroll bar automatically appears in the list box if the number of list items exceeds the height of the list box. For example, in the Tuition Calculator application, a list box contains course level names:

ListBox

A ListBox control has the properties:

- **Name** identifies a control for the programmer. It is good programming style to begin ListBox object names with lst.

- **Items** contains the ... button that is clicked to display the String Collection Editor dialog box where a set of strings is typed.

- **Sorted** is set to True to display the list items in alphabetical order. This property is available only in the Design window.

- **SelectedItem** is the selected list item. This property is available only at run time.

- **SelectedIndex** is the index of the selected list item. This property is available only at run time.

indexed items

The items in a list box have an index value, with 0 being the index of the first item, 1 the index of the next, and so on. An index value of –1 means that none of the list items are selected.

SelectedIndexChanged event

A SelectedIndexChanged event procedure is sometimes coded for a list box. This procedure executes when a list item is clicked. The specific item clicked is determined with the SelectedItem or the SelectedIndex properties. The **Select...Case** statement below uses the SelectedItem property to determine the selected item:

```
Select Case Me.lstCourseLevels.SelectedItem
    Case "Undergraduate"
        decCreditHour = 75
    Case "Graduate"
        decCreditHour = 145
    Case "Thesis and Dissertation"
        decCreditHour = 160
End Select
```

adding items at run time

The ListBox control class contains methods that can be used to display output at run time. Up to this point, labels have primarily been used to display output. However, a list box is a good choice for output that should be displayed as one item after another. The height of the list box is of little concern because a scroll bar is automatically displayed when the list gets longer than the box.

An Introduction to Programming Using Microsoft Visual Basic .NET

Items.Add()	The Items.Add() method is used to add an item to a list at run time and takes the form:

lstControl.Items.Add(*Item*)

lstControl is the name of the list box object and *Item* is a value or string. The item is added to the end of the list, or in the proper position if the list is sorted. The following code demonstrates Items.Add():

```
For intNum = 2 To 20 Step 2
    Me.lstByTwos.Items.Add(intNum & " x 5 = " & intNum * 5)
Next intNum
```

&, vbTab	Note that the & was used for concatenation. The vbTab constant can also be used to form strings with consistent spacing.
Items.Remove()	The Items.Remove() method is used to delete a specified item from the list and takes the form:

lstControl.Items.Remove(*Item*)

lstControl is the name of the list box object and *Item* is a value or string.

Items.Clear()	The Items.Clear() method is used to delete the contents of the list box and takes the form:

lstControl.Items.Clear()

lstControl is the name of the list box object.

Review 6

In this review you will create the Tuition Calculator application.

① *CREATE A NEW PROJECT*

Create a Windows application named Tuition Calculator.

② *CREATE THE INTERFACE*

a. Refer to the form below to add, position, and size objects. Use the table below to set properties.

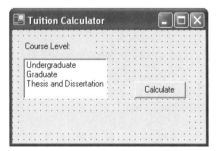

Object	Name	Text
Form1		Tuition Calculator
Label1	lblCourseLevelList	Course Level:
ListBox1	lstCourseLevels	
Label2	lblTuition	*empty*
Button1	btnCalculate	Calculate

b. Click the list box to select it and then click the Items property in the Properties window. Click the **...** button to display a dialog box. Type the following items, pressing Enter after each except the last:

> Undergraduate
> Graduate
> Thesis and Dissertation

③ *WRITE THE APPLICATION CODE*

a. Display the Code window.

b. Add comments that include your name and today's date.

c. Create a btnCalculate_Click event procedure and then add the statements:

```
Const decUNDERGRADUATEPERHOUR As Decimal = 75
Const decGRADUATEPERHOUR As Decimal = 145
Const decTHESISPERHOUR As Decimal = 160
Dim decTuition As Decimal

Select Case Me.lstCourseLevels.SelectedItem
  Case "Undergraduate"
    decTuition = decUNDERGRADUATEPERHOUR
  Case "Graduate"
    decTuition = decGRADUATEPERHOUR
  Case "Thesis and Dissertation"
    decTuition = decTHESISPERHOUR
End Select

Me.lblTuition.Text = "Tuition is  " & Format(decTuition, "Currency") & _
" per credit hour."
```

d. Create a lstCourseLevels_SelectedIndexChanged event procedure and then add the following statement to clear the label when a different list item is clicked:

```
Me.lblTuition.Text = Nothing
```

④ *RUN THE APPLICATION*

a. Save the modified Tuition Calculator project and then run the application. Test the application by clicking each of the list items and then Calculate.

b. Close the Tuition Calculator application.

c. Print the application code.

8.8 The ComboBox Control

A combo box displays a text box for typing an entry and an arrow that can be clicked to choose an item from a list. A scroll bar automatically appears in the list when necessary. For example, the Tuition Calculator application can be modified to include a combo box for the user to enter or select the number of credit hours:

An Introduction to Programming Using Microsoft Visual Basic .NET

ComboBox

A ComboBox control has the properties:

- **Name** identifies a control for the programmer. It is good programming style to begin ComboBox object names with cbo.

- **Items** contains the ⋯ button that is clicked to display the String Collection Editor dialog box where a set of strings is typed for the list box of the combo box.

- **Text** is the text displayed in the text box of the combo box.

- **Sorted** is set to True to display the list items in alphabetical order. This property is available only in the Design window.

- **SelectedItem** is the currently selected list item. This property is available only at run time.

- **SelectedIndex** is the index of the selected list item. This property is available only at run time.

The items in the list box of a combo box have an index value, with 0 being the index of the first item, 1 the index of the next, and so on. An index value of –1 means that none of the list items are selected. The Text property contains the item typed by the user in the text box.

TextChanged event
SelectedIndexChanged event

The entry in a combo box changes when the user either types a value or selects a value from the list. Typing a value raises a TextChanged event, and selecting a value raises a SelectedIndexChanged event. Two different event procedures can be written for these events or a single event procedure can be written to handle both events. An If...**Then**...**Else** statement can be used to determine if a value was entered or an item selected, as in the statement below:

```
If Me.cboCreditHours.SelectedIndex >= 0 Then    'list item selected
    MessageBox.Show(Me.cboCreditHours.SelectedItem)
Else
    MessageBox.Show(Me.cboCreditHours.Text)    'value typed
End If
```

Items.Add()

The ComboBox control class also contains methods for adding and clearing list items at run time. The Items.Add() method is used to add an item to a list at run time and takes the form:

```
cboControl.Items.Add(Item)
```

cboControl is the name of the combo box object and *Item* is a value or a string. The item is added to the end of the list, or in the proper position if the list is sorted. The following statement demonstrates Items.Add():

```
Me.cboCreditHours.Items.Add("18")
```

Items.Remove()

The Items.Remove() method is used to delete a specified item from the list and takes the form:

```
cboControl.Items.Remove(Item)
```

cboControl is the name of the combo box object and *Item* is a value or a string.

Items.Clear()

The Items.Clear() method is used to delete the contents of the list in the combo box takes the form:

```
cboControl.Items.Clear()
```

cboControl is the name of the combo box object.

In this review you will modify the Tuition Calculator application to include a combo box.

① *OPEN THE TUITION CALCULATOR PROJECT*

Display the Tuition Calculator Design window if it is not already displayed.

② *MODIFY THE INTERFACE*

a. Refer to the form below to add, position, and size a label and combo box object. Use the table below to set properties.

Object	Name	Text
Label1	lblCreditHours	Credit Hours:
ComboBox1	cboCreditHours	*empty*

b. Use the ComboBox Items property to add the list items 3, 6, 9, 12, and 15 to the combo box.

③ *MODIFY THE APPLICATION CODE*

a. Display the Code window.

b. Modify the btnCalculate_Click event procedure:

```
Const decUNDERGRADUATEPERHOUR As Decimal = 75
Const decGRADUATEPERHOUR As Decimal = 145
Const decTHESISPERHOUR As Decimal = 160
Dim intCreditHours As Integer
Dim decTuition As Decimal

If Me.cboCreditHours.SelectedIndex >= 0 Then       'list item selected
    intCreditHours = Val(Me.cboCreditHours.SelectedItem)
Else
    intCreditHours = Val(Me.cboCreditHours.Text)     'value typed
End If

Select Case Me.lstCourseLevels.SelectedItem
    Case "Undergraduate"
        decTuition = decUNDERGRADUATEPERHOUR * intCreditHours
    Case "Graduate"
        decTuition = decGRADUATEPERHOUR * intCreditHours
    Case "Thesis and Dissertation"
        decTuition = decTHESISPERHOUR * intCreditHours
End Select

Me.lblTuition.Text = "Tuition is:  " & Format(decTuition, "Currency")
```

c. Modify lstCourseLevels_SelectedIndexChanged() to handle SelectedIndexChanged events for lstCourseLevels and cboCreditHours and the TextChanged event for cboCreditHours. Change the procedure name to DataChanged.

④ *RUN THE APPLICATION*

Save the modified Tuition Calculator project and then run the application. Test the application by selecting different combinations of course levels and credit hours.

⑤ *PRINT THE CODE AND THEN CLOSE THE PROJECT*

Review 8

Modify the Loan Payment application created in Review 3 so that combo boxes prompt the user for the interest rate and term. The interest rate combo box should contain 6%, 6.5%, 7%, 7.5%, 8%, 8.5%, and 9%. Modify GetPercentAmount() accordingly. The term combo box should contain 3, 5, 10, 15, 20, and 30. Modify the NewDataEntered() procedure to handle the five possible TextChanged and SelectedIndexChanged events. The application interface should look similar to that shown on the right after entering the loan information and clicking **Payment**.

8.9 Windows Application Standards

Windows applications have a standard look and feel about them. An application that has features similar to other Windows applications is easier for the user to learn and understand. For example, the application below has several features found in a Windows application:

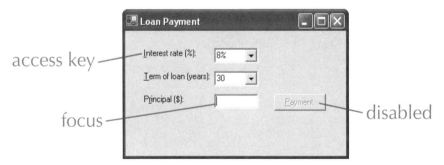

The text box contains the insertion point. This indicates it has the focus. An object with *focus* will receive the user input from the keyboard. The underlined r in the P<u>r</u>incipal ($) label is an access key. An *access key* is the key pressed while holding down the Alt key to select an object. For example, Alt+T moves the insertion point to the <u>T</u>erm of loan (years) combo box. The *tab order* has been set so that the focus will move from one object to the next in a logical order when the Tab key is pressed. <u>P</u>ayment appears dimmed because it is disabled. A *disabled object* cannot be selected by the user. In this case, <u>P</u>ayment is not appropriate to select at this time because all the loan information has not be entered.

focus

access key

tab order

disabled object

A button that has the focus appears with a dashed line around it. A text box that has the focus contains an insertion point and any text typed will be displayed in that text box. When a list box or combo box has the focus, the arrow keys can be used to select a list item. Labels cannot receive focus.

&   An ampersand (&) is used in the Text property for an object to define an access key. For example, typing &Payment for a button's Text property displays Payment on the button and allows the user to press Alt+P at run time to select the button. Access keys are not displayed until the user presses the Alt key.

tab order   Tab order allows for easier and faster data entry. For example, when the Loan Payment application is started, the interest rate combo box should have the focus. Pressing the Tab key should logically move the focus to the term combo box, and then the principal text box, and finally the payment button. The tab order is determined by the order in which objects are added to a form. However, this order can be changed by set-

TabIndex   ting the TabIndex property of the objects, with the first object to be selected given TabIndex 0.

Although labels cannot receive focus, their tab order is important. When the access key of a label is selected, the object that comes after the label in tab order receives the focus. For example, in the Loan Payment application, the Interest rate (%) label has tab order 0 and the cboRate combo box has tab order 1. When Alt+I is pressed, the label cannot receive focus, so the combo box gets the focus, which is exactly what the user expects.

Enabled   The Enabled property for an object can be set to False to make the object appear dimmed. Disabled objects cannot be selected. For example, in the Loan Payment application, the rate, term, and principal are required to calculate a payment. Therefore, the button is disabled until valid data is entered.

Visible   The Visible property for an object can be used to hide an object. An object with False for the Visible property does not appear on the form at run time. This is useful when an object is not relevant at the current time.

hiding a set of objects   Setting the Visible property of a group box to False hides the group box and every object within the group box.

Review 9

In this review you will add access keys and set the tab order of the Loan Payment application.

① *OPEN THE LOAN PAYMENT PROJECT*

    a. Open the Loan Payment project, which was last modified in Review 8.

    b. Display the Design window.

② *DISABLE A BUTTON*

    a. Set the Enabled property of btnPayment to False.

    b. Run the application. Note that the Payment button is dimmed and nothing happens when it is clicked.

    c. Close the application and display the Design window.

③ ADD ACCESS KEYS

    a. Set the Text property of lblRatePrompt to &Interest rate (%):

    b. Use the table below to set other Text properties:

Object	Text
lblTermPrompt	&Term of loan (years):
lblPrincipalPrompt	P&rincipal ($):
btnPayment	&Payment

④ RUN THE APPLICATION AND TEST THE TAB ORDER AND ACCESS KEYS

    a. Run the application. Press the Tab key a few times. Notice how the focus does not go from one object to another in a logical order.

    b. Press Alt+I. Note how the interest rate combo box does not receive the focus like expected.

    c. Close the application and display the Design window.

⑤ SET THE TAB ORDER

    a. Set the TabIndex property of lblRatePrompt to 0 if it is not already 0.

    b. Use the table shown below to set other TabIndex properties:

Object	TabIndex
cboRate	1
lblTermPrompt	2
cboTerm	3
lblPrincipalPrompt	4
txtPrincipal	5
lblMonthlyPayment	6
btnPayment	7

⑥ MODIFY THE APPLICATION CODE

    a. Display the Code window.

    b. Modify the NewDataEntered() procedure to enable the Payment button when appropriate:

```
Private Sub NewDataEntered(ByVal sender As System.Object, _
ByVal e As System.EventArgs) Handles txtPrincipal.TextChanged, _
cboRate.SelectedIndexChanged, cboTerm.SelectedIndexChanged, _
cboRate.TextChanged, cboTerm.TextChanged

  Me.lblMonthlyPayment.Text = Nothing
  Me.btnPayment.Enabled = False

  If Me.cboRate.Text <> Nothing And Me.cboTerm.Text <> Nothing And _
  Me.txtPrincipal.Text <> Nothing Then
    Me.btnPayment.Enabled = True
  End If

End Sub
```

⑦ RUN THE APPLICATION

    a. Save the modified Loan Payment project and then run the application. Press the Alt key to display access keys. Press the Tab key several times. The focus moves in a logical order.

    b. Enter all the necessary loan information. Note how Payment is enabled. Use the appropriate access key to select Payment.

⑧ PRINT THE CODE AND THEN CLOSE THE PROJECT

Review 10 ⟳

Modify the Credit Card Loan application created in Review 4 so that the focus is in the first text box when the application is started and the focus moves to the next object in the application in a logical order when the Tab key is pressed. Set appropriate access keys. Modify the interface so that the Number of Payments button is disabled at startup and add code to enable the button when valid data has been entered.

Review 11 ⟳

Modify the Tuition Calculator application which was last modified in Review 7 so that the focus is in the list box when the application is started and the focus moves to the next object in the application in a logical order when the Tab key is pressed. Set appropriate access keys. Modify the interface so that the Calculate button is disabled at startup and add code to enable the button when valid data has been entered.

Case Study

In this Case Study a Loan Analyzer application will be created.

specification   The specification for this Case Study is:

A Loan Analyzer application that provides the user with a loan payment and a loan amount for car and house loans. Terms available are 2, 3, 5, and 7 years for an auto loan and 10, 15, and 30 years for a mortgage. The user should be asked loan specifics only as necessary to prevent confusion. A final calculation should then display either a loan payment amount or a total loan amount.

design   The interface for this Case Study should provide easy-to-understand options for choosing either an auto loan or a home loan. Pictures are the best choice for getting this input since there are only two possible choices and images can clearly convey the options. Only one type of information can be calculated at a time, so radio button are the best option for getting this data. Because the term options are limited, a list box is the best choice for getting this input. A combo box is the best choice the interest rate because rates can vary, but there are some typical values. A New Loan button clears all options except the icons. A Calculate button displays the result of a calculation based on the information entered.

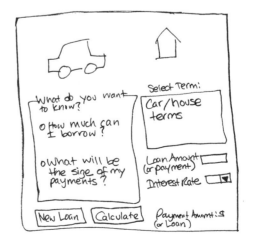

The code design starts with an algorithm:

1. Starting the application shows only an Auto icon and a House icon. All other objects should not be visible.
2. Clicking an image displays the What do you want to know? options. Term options can be added to the Select Term list, but the list should not be displayed until the user selects the type of information wanted. A New Loan button should also appear to allow the user to clear the form and start over.
3. Selecting the type of information wanted displays the loan options. A Calculate button should also appear, but should not be enabled until all the required data has been entered or selected. If How much can I borrow? is selected, a text box should prompt for a payment amount. If What will be the size of my payments? is selected, a text box should prompt for a loan amount.
4. After required data has been entered, clicking Calculate uses either the Pmt() or PV() function to determine the information wanted by the user. This information should then be displayed in a label.
5. If New Loan is clicked, all options except the images are made not visible.

Analyzing the algorithm further reveals some aspects of the code:

- The Visible property should be used in the Design window to hide many of the options. At run time, the Visible option can be set to True to display options as they are required.

- The Enabled property should be used to disable Calculate until all the required data is entered or selected.

- The same or similar actions are needed for the radio buttons so a single event procedure should handle a Click event for How much can I borrow? and What will be the size of my payments?

- When either the term, amount, or interest rate data is entered, selected, or changed, the other options need to be checked for required data to determine if Calculate should be displayed. This should all be done in a single event procedure that handles selected index changes and text changes.

Based on the algorithm and analysis of the algorithm, the pseudocode for this application appears like that shown on the next page:

```
Sub Image_Click(sender, e) Handles picAuto.Click, picHome.Click
    Show the group box of radio button options
    Show the New Loan button
    Show the disabled Calculate button

    ImageClicked = sender
    Select Case ImageClicked.Tag
        Case auto
            lstTerm.Items.Add("2 years")
            lstTerm.Items.Add("3 years")
            lstTerm.Items.Add("5 years")
            lstTerm.Items.Add("7 years")
        Case home
            lstTerm.Items.Add("10 years")
            lstTerm.Items.Add("15 years")
            lstTerm.Items.Add("30 years")
    End Select
End Sub


Sub btnNewLoan_Click(sender, e)
    Hide all objects except picture boxes
    Clear result label
End Sub


Sub WhatDoYouWantToKnow_Click(sender, e) Handles radHowMuch.Click,
radPaymentSize.Click
    Show term prompt and term list
    Show textbox for principal or payment with appropriate prompt
    Show interest rate prompt and combo box
End Sub


Sub InfoEntered(sender, e) Handles lstTerm.SelectedIndexChanged,
txtPrincipalOrPayment.TextChanged,  cboInterestRate.SelectedIndexChanged,
cboInterestRate.TextChanged
    Clear result label
    Disable Calculate button
    If txtPrincipalOrPayment.Text <> Nothing _
    And cboInterestRate.Text <> Nothing Then
        Enable Calculate button
    End If
End Sub
```

```
Sub btnCalculate
    Term = Val(lstTerm.SelectedItem)
    Get Principal or payment
    If Principal or payment is valid Then
        Get Interest rate
    End If
    If Interest rate is valid Then 'perform calculation
        If radHowMuch.Checked
            Use PV() function to calculate loan amount. Show message.
        Else
            Use Pmt() function to calculate payment amount. Show message.
        End If
    Else
        Display message that data is invalid
    End If
End Sub
```

coding   The interface and code for this Case Study are:

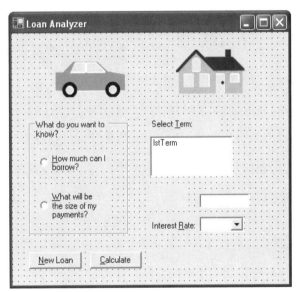

Object	Name	Text	Tag	TabIndex
Form1		Loan Analyzer		
PictureBox1	picAuto		auto	
PictureBox2	picHome		home	
GroupBox1	grpWhatToKnow			0
RadioButton1	radHowMuch	*see interface*	how much	1
RadioButton2	radPaymentSize	*see interface*	payment size	2
Button1	bntNewLoan	&New Loan		3
Label1	lblTermPrompt	Select &Term:		4
ListBox1	lstTerm			5
Label2	lblPrincipalOrPaymentPrompt	*empty*		6
TextBox1	txtPrincipalOrPayment	*empty*		7
Label3	lblInterestRatePrompt	Interest &Rate:		8
ComboBox1	cboInterestRate	*empty*		9
Button2	btnCalculate	&Calculate		10
Label4	lblResult	*empty*		11

The Visible property should be set to False for every object except the picture boxes, radio buttons, and the form. The Calculate button should also be disabled.

```vb
Public Class Form1
    Inherits System.Windows.Forms.Form

    Windows Form Designer generated code

    '~~~~~~~~~~~~~~~~~~~~~~~~~~~~~~~~~~~~~~~~~~~~~~~~~~~~~~~~~~~~~
    'Displays options for choosing the loan information.
    'Adds appropriate list items to the Term list box.
    '
    'post: Options are displayed.
    '~~~~~~~~~~~~~~~~~~~~~~~~~~~~~~~~~~~~~~~~~~~~~~~~~~~~~~~~~~~~~
    Private Sub Image_Click(ByVal sender As Object, ByVal e As System.EventArgs) _
    Handles picAuto.Click, picHome.Click

        'Display options for choosing loan information
        Me.grpWhatToKnow.Visible = True
        Me.btnNewLoan.Visible = True
        Me.btnCalculate.Visible = True
        Me.btnCalculate.Enabled = False            'calculate button shown, but disabled

        Me.lstTerm.Items.Clear()                   'clear any existing list items

        Dim picImageClicked As PictureBox = sender 'contains properties of clicked image
        Select Case picImageClicked.Tag            'add appropriate terms to list box
            Case "auto"
                Me.lstTerm.Items.Add("2 years")
                Me.lstTerm.Items.Add("3 years")
                Me.lstTerm.Items.Add("5 years")
                Me.lstTerm.Items.Add("7 years")
            Case "home"
                Me.lstTerm.Items.Add("10 years")
                Me.lstTerm.Items.Add("15 years")
                Me.lstTerm.Items.Add("30 years")
        End Select

    End Sub


    '~~~~~~~~~~~~~~~~~~~~~~~~~~~~~~~~~~~~~~~~~~~~~~~~~~~~~~~~~~~~~
    'Hides loan information options. Clear label text.
    '
    'post: Loan options are hidden and label text set to en empty string.
    '~~~~~~~~~~~~~~~~~~~~~~~~~~~~~~~~~~~~~~~~~~~~~~~~~~~~~~~~~~~~~
    Private Sub btnNewLoan_Click(ByVal sender As System.Object, _
    ByVal e As System.EventArgs) Handles btnNewLoan.Click

        Me.grpWhatToKnow.Visible = False
        Me.radHowMuch.Checked = False
        Me.radPaymentSize.Checked = False
        Me.lblTermPrompt.Visible = False
        Me.lstTerm.Visible = False
        Me.lblPrincipalOrPaymentPrompt.Visible = False
        Me.txtPrincipalOrPayment.Visible = False
        Me.lblInterestRatePrompt.Visible = False
        Me.cboInterestRate.Visible = False
        Me.btnNewLoan.Visible = False
        Me.btnCalculate.Visible = False
        Me.lblResult.Text = Nothing

    End Sub
```

```
'~~~~~~~~~~~~~~~~~~~~~~~~~~~~~~~~~~~~~~~~~~~~~~~~~~~~~~~~~~~~~~~~~~~~~~~~~
'Displays options for entering loan information.
'
'post: Options are displayed.
'~~~~~~~~~~~~~~~~~~~~~~~~~~~~~~~~~~~~~~~~~~~~~~~~~~~~~~~~~~~~~~~~~~~~~~~~~
Private Sub WhatDoYouWantToKnow_Click(ByVal sender As Object, _
ByVal e As System.EventArgs) Handles radHowMuch.Click, radPaymentSize.Click

    'Display term options
    Me.lblTermPrompt.Visible = True
    Me.lstTerm.Visible = True

    'Display either principal or payment options
    Dim radOptionClicked As RadioButton = sender     'contains properties of clicked button
    Select Case radOptionClicked.Tag
      Case "how much"
        Me.lblPrincipalOrPaymentPrompt.Text = "Desired payment:"
      Case "payment size"
        Me.lblPrincipalOrPaymentPrompt.Text = "Loan Amount:"
    End Select
    Me.lblPrincipalOrPaymentPrompt.Visible = True
    Me.txtPrincipalOrPayment.Visible = True
    Me.txtPrincipalOrPayment.Text = Nothing

    'Display interest rate options
    Me.lblInterestRatePrompt.Visible = True
    Me.cboInterestRate.Visible = True            '
    Me.cboInterestRate.Text = Nothing

End Sub


'~~~~~~~~~~~~~~~~~~~~~~~~~~~~~~~~~~~~~~~~~~~~~~~~~~~~~~~~~~~~~~~~~~~~~~~~~
'Clears the last loan results. Checks for numeric loan information and enables the
'Calculate button if required data has been entered or selected.
'
'post: The Results label is blank. The Calculate button is enabled if data has been entered
'or selected.
'~~~~~~~~~~~~~~~~~~~~~~~~~~~~~~~~~~~~~~~~~~~~~~~~~~~~~~~~~~~~~~~~~~~~~~~~~
Private Sub InfoEntered(ByVal sender As Object, ByVal e As System.EventArgs) Handles _
lstTerm.SelectedIndexChanged, txtPrincipalOrPayment.TextChanged, _
cboInterestRate.SelectedIndexChanged, cboInterestRate.TextChanged

    Me.lblResult.Text = Nothing
    Me.btnCalculate.Enabled = False

    If Me.txtPrincipalOrPayment.Text <> Nothing And _
    Me.cboInterestRate.Text <> Nothing Then
        Me.btnCalculate.Enabled = True
    End If

End Sub
```

```
'~~~~~~~~~~~~~~~~~~~~~~~~~~~~~~~~~~~~~~~~~~~~~~~~~~~~~~~~~~~~~~~~~
'Displays either the monthly payment for a loan or a loan amount that can be borrowed.
'
'pre: Data has been entered or selected for the term, principal or payment, and the
'interest rate.
'post: The result of a calculation based on the selected term, principal or payment,
'and interest rate is displayed, if data entered is valid. Otherwise, an invalid data message
'displayed.
'~~~~~~~~~~~~~~~~~~~~~~~~~~~~~~~~~~~~~~~~~~~~~~~~~~~~~~~~~~~~~~~~~
Private Sub btnCalculate_Click(ByVal sender As Object, ByVal e As System.EventArgs) _
Handles btnCalculate.Click

    Dim intTerm As Integer
    Dim sngPrincipalOrPayment, sngInterestRate As Single
    Dim sngResult As Single
    Dim blnValidData As Boolean

    'Get term
    intTerm = Val(Me.lstTerm.SelectedItem)

    'Get principal or payment
    GetDollarAmount(Me.txtPrincipalOrPayment, sngPrincipalOrPayment, blnValidData)

    'Get interest rate if principal or payment is valid
    If blnValidData Then
        GetPercentAmount(Me.cboInterestRate, sngInterestRate, blnValidData)
    End If

    'Calculate result if principal or payment and interest rate are valid
    If blnValidData Then
        If Me.radHowMuch.Checked Then
            sngResult = PV(sngInterestRate / 12, intTerm * 12, -sngPrincipalOrPayment)
            Me.lblResult.Text = "Loan amount: " & Format(sngResult, "Currency")
        Else
            sngResult = Pmt(sngInterestRate / 12, intTerm * 12, -sngPrincipalOrPayment)
            Me.lblResult.Text = "Payment amount: " & Format(sngResult, "Currency")
        End If
    Else
        Me.lblResult.Text = "Data not valid."
    End If

End Sub


'~~~~~~~~~~~~~~~~~~~~~~~~~~~~~~~~~~~~~~~~~~~~~~~~~~~~~~~~~~~~~~~~~
'Processes data in a text box to read a dollar amount, if any.
'
'post: decDollars contains a number if numeric data with or without a $ was entered in the
'text box. blnIsValid is True if a valid dollar amount has been entered in the text box.
'~~~~~~~~~~~~~~~~~~~~~~~~~~~~~~~~~~~~~~~~~~~~~~~~~~~~~~~~~~~~~~~~~
Sub GetDollarAmount(ByVal txtUserData As TextBox, ByRef decDollars As Decimal, _
ByRef blnIsValid As Boolean)

    Dim strTestAmount As String
    blnIsValid = False                        'assume nonnumeric data
    If txtUserData.Text <> Nothing Then
        strTestAmount = txtUserData.Text                      'data typed
        strTestAmount = strTestAmount.Replace("$", "")        'delete $
        strTestAmount = strTestAmount.Replace(",", "")        'delete commas
        If IsNumeric(strTestAmount) Then                      'numeric data
            decDollars = Val(strTestAmount)
            blnIsValid = True
        End If
    End If

End Sub
```

An Introduction to Programming Using Microsoft Visual Basic .NET

```
'~~~~~~~~~~~~~~~~~~~~~~~~~~~~~~~~~~~~~~~~~~~~~~~~~~~~~~~~~~~~~
'Processes data in a combo box to read a percentage amount, if any.
'
'post: sngPercent contains a decimal number if numeric data with or without a % was
'entered in the combo box. blnIsValid is True if a valid percent has been entered in the
'combo box.
'~~~~~~~~~~~~~~~~~~~~~~~~~~~~~~~~~~~~~~~~~~~~~~~~~~~~~~~~~~~~~
Sub GetPercentAmount(ByVal cboUserData As ComboBox, ByRef sngPercent As Single, _
ByRef blnIsValid As Boolean)

    Dim strTestAmount As String
    blnIsValid = False                              'assume nonnumeric data
    If cboUserData.Text <> Nothing Then
      strTestAmount = cboUserData.Text
      strTestAmount = strTestAmount.TrimEnd("%")    'delete %
    End If
    If IsNumeric(strTestAmount) Then                'numeric data
      If Val(strTestAmount) > 1 Then                'convert data
        sngPercent = Val(strTestAmount) / 100
      Else
        sngPercent = Val(strTestAmount)
      End If
      blnIsValid = True
    End If

End Sub

End Class
```

Running Loan Analyzer, clicking the Auto picture, and entering data displays the following:

This Case Study should be tested by selecting different items to calculate and different rates, terms, and payments or loan amounts. Entering invalid rates, terms, and loan amounts (text instead of numbers) will test the error handling in the code.

8.10 Trigonometric Methods

The Visual Basic .NET **Math** class also includes trigonometric method members. These methods include Sin(), Cos(), and Tan():

- **Sin(*angle*)** returns the sine of an angle. *angle* is a numeric variable or value, and is in radians.

- **Cos(*angle*)** returns the cosine of an angle. *angle* is a numeric variable or value, and is in radians.

- **Tan(*angle*)** returns the tangent of an angle. *angle* is a numeric variable or value, and is in radians.

The following code demonstrates the **Math** methods discussed above:

Dim sngRadians **As Single**

```
sngRadians = 0.79                                '45 Degrees
Me.lblSine.Text = Math.Sin(sngRadians)           '0.710353

sngRadians = 0.79                                '45 Degrees
Me.lblCosine.Text = Math.Cos(sngRadians)         '0.703845

sngRadians = 0.79                                '45 Degrees
Me.lblTangent.Text = Math.Tan(sngRadians)        '1.009246
```

converting between degrees and radians

PI

The Sin(), Cos(), and Tan() functions require an argument in radians. An angle in degrees can be converted to radians using a formula that requires π. The **Math** class includes a member constant PI with the value 3.14159265358979323846, which can be used in the conversion formula:

```
sngRadians = (Math.PI / 180) * sngDegrees
```

This formula works because 180 degrees equals π radians. To convert from radians to degrees, the following formula is used:

```
sngDegrees = sngRadians * (180 / Math.PI)
```

Review 12

Write a DegreesToRadians() function that has a sngDegrees parameter and returns the angle in radians. Test and debug the function in a project named Test DegreesToRadians() Function. Properly document the function, including the following:

```
'~~~~~~~~~~~~~~~~~~~~~~~~~~~~~~~~~~~~~~~~~~~~~~~~
'Converts the value sngDegrees in degrees to a value in radians.
'
'pre: 0 <= sngDegrees <= 360
'post: The radian equivalent of sngDegrees returned.
'~~~~~~~~~~~~~~~~~~~~~~~~~~~~~~~~~~~~~~~~~~~~~~~~
```

Review 13

Write a RadiansToDegrees() function that has a sngRadians parameter and returns the angle in degrees. Test and debug the function in a project named Test RadiansToDegrees() Function. Properly document the function, including the following:

```
'~~~~~~~~~~~~~~~~~~~~~~~~~~~~~~~~~~~~~~~~~~~~~~~~
'Converts the value sngRadians in radians to a value in degrees.
'
'pre: 0 <= sngRadians <= 2PI
'post: The degree equivalent of sngRadians returned.
'~~~~~~~~~~~~~~~~~~~~~~~~~~~~~~~~~~~~~~~~~~~~~~~~
```

An Introduction to Programming Using Microsoft Visual Basic .NET

Review 14 ↻

Create a Trigonometric Functions application that prompts the user for an angle in degrees and then displays the sine, cosine, or tangent of the angle rounded to 2 decimal places depending on the function selected from a list box. Include the DegreesToRadians() function from Review 12 in the code. The application interface should look similar to that shown on the right after typing 50 and clicking Tangent in the list box.

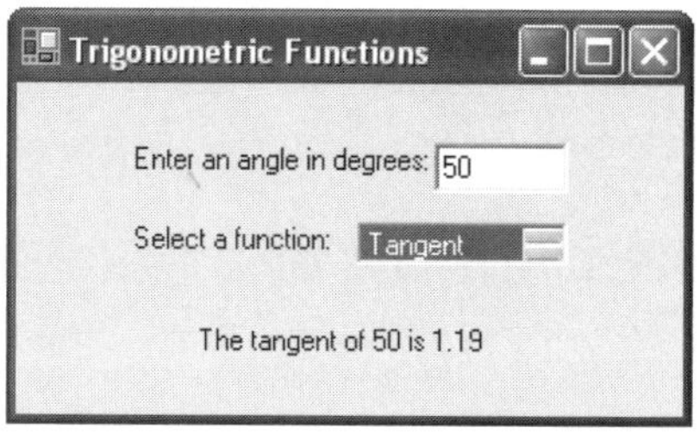

Trigonometric Functions

Enter an angle in degrees: 50

Select a function: Tangent

The tangent of 50 is 1.19

Review 15 ↻

In this review you will create the Sine Cosine Table application.

① **CREATE A NEW PROJECT**

Create a Windows application named Sine Cosine Table.

② **CREATE THE INTERFACE**

Refer to the form below to add, position, and size objects. Use the table below to set properties.

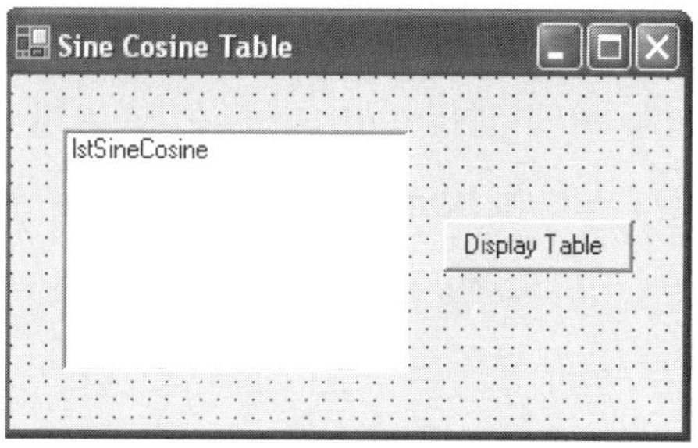

Sine Cosine Table

lstSineCosine

Display Table

Object	Name	Text	Items
Form1		Sine Cosine Table	
ListBox1	lstSineCosine		*empty*
Button1	btnDisplayTable	Display Table	

③ **WRITE THE APPLICATION CODE**

a. Display the Code window.

b. Add comments that include your name and today's date.

c. Create a btnDisplayTable_Click event procedure and then add the following statements:

```
Me.lstSineCosine.Items.Add("Angle" & vbTab & "Sin" & vbTab & "Cos")

Dim sngAngleRadians As Single
Dim sngSin As Single
Dim sngCos As Single

Dim intAngle As Integer
For intAngle = 0 To 360 Step 15
   sngAngleRadians = DegreesToRadians(intAngle)
   sngSin = Math.Round(Math.Sin(sngAngleRadians), 2)
   sngCos = Math.Round(Math.Cos(sngAngleRadians), 2)
   Me.lstSineCosine.Items.Add(intAngle & vbTab & sngSin & vbTab & sngCos)
Next intAngle
```

d. Add the DegreesToRadians() function from Review 12.

    a. Save the modified Sine Cosine Table project and then run the application.

    b. Close the Sine Cosine Table application.

⑤ PRINT THE CODE AND THEN CLOSE THE PROJECT

8.11 Inverse Trigonometric Methods

arcsine, arccosine, and arctangent

Mathematical work often requires finding the angle that corresponds to a trigonometric value. This is called the *inverse trigonometric function*. The inverse of sine is called *arcsine*, the inverse of cosine is called *arccosine*, and the inverse of tangent is called *arctangent*. The Visual Basic .NET **Math** class includes these inverse trigonometric method members:

- **Asin(*num*)** returns the radian angle that corresponds to a sine. *num* is a numeric variable or value.

- **Acos(*num*)** returns the radian angle that corresponds to a cosine. *num* is a numeric variable or value.

- **Atan(*num*)** returns the radian angle that corresponds to a tangent. *num* is a numeric variable or value.

The following code demonstrates the **Math** methods discussed above:

```
Dim sngNumber As Single

sngNumber = 0.710353
Me.ArcSine.Text = Math.Asin(sngNumber)          '0.79 Radians

sngNumber = 0.703845
Me.ArcCosine.Text = Math.Acos(sngNumber)        '0.79 Radians

sngNumber = 1.009246
Me.lblArcTangent.Text = Math.Atan(sngNumber)    '0.79 Radians
```

Review 16

Create an Inverse Trigonometric Functions application that prompts the user for a value and then displays the arcsine, arccosine, or arctangent in degrees rounded to 2 decimal places depending on the button clicked. Include the RadiansToDegrees() function from Review 13 in the code. The application interface should look similar to that shown on the right after typing 0.703845 and clicking Arccosine.

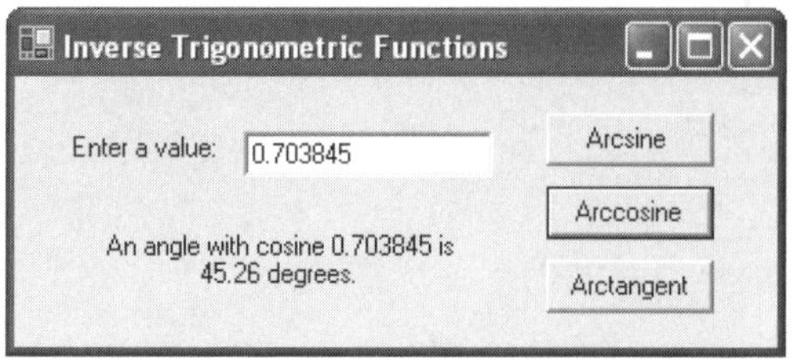

8.12 Logarithmic and Exponential Methods

The Visual Basic .NET **Math** class also includes methods for logarithmic and exponential operations. These methods include:

- **Log(*num*)** returns the natural logarithm (base *e*) of a number. *num* is a variable or value that is greater than 0.

- **Log(*num, base*)** returns the logarithm of a number in a specified base. *num* is a numeric variable or value that is greater than 0. *base* is a numeric variable or value that is greater than 0.

- **Log10(*num*)** returns the base 10 logarithm of a number. *num* is a numeric variable or value that is greater than 0.

- **Exp(*power*)** returns *e* raised to a power (e^x). *power* is a numeric variable or value. Exp() is the inverse function of Log().

- **Pow(*num, power*)** returns a number raised to a power. *num* and *power* are numeric variables or values.

Note that the Log() function can have either one or two arguments. When only one argument is used, the natural logarithm is returned. When two numbers are used, the logarithm is returned in the specified base. A function that performs a different action depending on the number of

overloaded function   arguments it receives is called an *overloaded function*.

E   The **Math** class also includes a member constant E with the value 2.7182818284590452354.

The following code demonstrates the **Math** methods logarithmic and exponential functions:

```
Dim sngNum1 As Single = 10
Dim sngNum2 As Single = 8
Me.lblLogE.Text = Math.Log(sngNum1)                'base e, 2.3025
Me.lblLogX.Text = Math.Log(sngNum1, sngNum2)       'base 8, 1.1073
Me.lblLog10.Text = Math.Log10(sngNum1)             'base 10, 1
sngNum1 = 2
sngNum2 = 4
Me.lblExp.Text = Math.Exp(sngNum1)                 'e², 7.389
Me.lblPow.Text = Math.Pow(sngNum1, sngNum2)        '2⁴, 16
```

Review 17

Create a Logarithmic and Exponential Functions application that prompts the user for a number and then displays the natural logarithm of the number or e raised to that number depending on the button clicked. The application interface should look similar to that shown on the right after typing 1 and clicking Natural Logarithm.

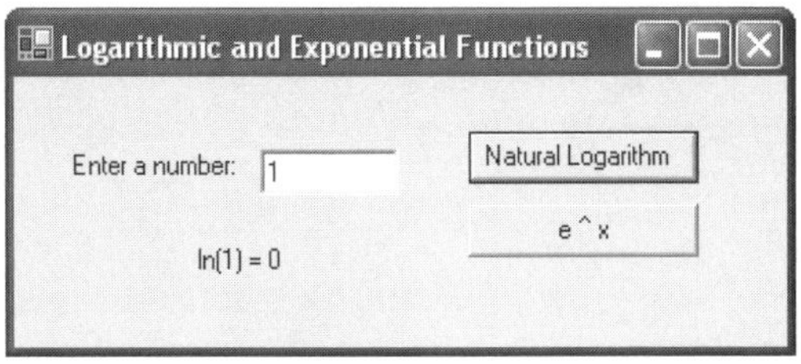

This chapter introduced the Visual Basic .NET **Math** class and built-in mathematical and business functions.

The **Math** class members include the Abs(), Sqrt(), Sign(), Round(), Sin(), Cos(), Tan(), Asin(), Acos(), Atan(), Log(), Log10(), Exp(), and Pow() methods. The **Math** class also includes constants PI and E.

Built-in functions include IsNumeric() and Format(). The IsNumeric() and Val() functions can be used with **String** methods to allow the user to enter data that includes a dollar sign.

The Pmt(), PV(), and FV() built-in functions are used for payment, present value, and future value business calculations.

ListBox

A ListBox object can contain several items for the user to choose from. The ListBox control has the properties Name, Items, Sorted, SelectedItem, and SelectedIndex. A ListBox object name should begin with the prefix lst. The items in a list box have an index value beginning with 0 and a SelectedIndexChanged event procedure is sometimes coded for a list box.

A list box is a good choice for displaying items that should appear one after the other. The ListBox control class contains the Items.Add(), Items.Remove(), and Items.Clear() methods for controlling the contents of a list box at run time.

ComboBox

A ComboBox object combines a text box and a list box. The ComboBox control has the properties Name, Items, Text, Sorted, SelectedItem, and SelectedIndex. A ComboBox object name should begin with the prefix cbo. The items in the list box of the combo box have an index value beginning with 0. Because a user can type or select a value in a combo box, both TextChanged and SelectedIndexChanged events need to be considered. The ComboBox control class also contains Items.Add(), Items.Remove(), and Items.Clear() methods for controlling the contents of the list box part of the combo box at run time.

An object that has focus receives the user input. An ampersand (&) may be used in an object's Text property to define an access key. The tab order for the objects in an application can be set with the TabIndex property. The Enabled property can be set to False so that the user cannot select an object. The Visible property can be used to hide an object.

Vocabulary

Access key The underlined character in an application that indicates which key can be pressed while holding down the Alt key to select an object.

Annuity A set of payments made on a regular basis for a specified period.

Arccosine The inverse of cosine.

Arcsine The inverse of sine.

Arctangent The inverse of tangent.

Disabled An object that cannot be selected by the user.

Focus Describes an object that will receive user input from the keyboard.

Overloaded Function A function that performs a different action depending on the number and type of the arguments it receives.

Visual Basic .NET

& Used in the Text property of an object to define an access key. Also used to concatenate items to form a single item to be added to a list box or combo box.

ComboBox control Used to create a ComboBox control class object. Properties include Name, Items, Text, Sorted, SelectedItem, and SelectedIndex. Methods include Items.Add(), Items.Clear(), and Items.Remove(). Events include TextChanged, SelectedIndexChanged.

E Math class constant with the value 2.7182818284590452354.

Enabled Control object property used to disable an object so that it cannot be selected.

Format() Function used to convert a number to a formatted string.

FV() Function that returns the future value of an annuity.

IsNumeric() Function that returns True if its argument can be evaluated as a number and False if it is not.

ListBox control Used to create a ListBox control class object. Properties include Name, Items, Sorted, SelectedItem, and SelectedIndex. Methods include Items.Add(), Items.Remove(), and Items.Clear(). Events include SelectedIndexChanged.

Math class Used to perform common math functions. Methods include Abs(), Acos(), Asin(), Atan(), Cos(), Exp(), Log(), Log100(), Pow(), Round(), Sign(), Sin(), Sqrt(), and Tan(). Other members include PI and E.

PI Math class constant with the value 3.14159265358979323846.

Pmt() Function that returns the payment for an annuity.

PV() Function that returns the present value of an annuity.

TabIndex Control object property used to set the tab order for an application interface.

Visible Control object property used to hide or display an object.

1. Write the conventional three-letter prefix for each control and variable type:
   - a) Button
   - b) Char
   - c) CheckBox
   - d) Decimal
   - e) Single
   - f) Integer
   - g) GroupBox
   - h) Label
   - i) Long
   - j) MainMenu
   - k) PictureBox
   - l) RadioButton
   - m) String
   - n) TextBox
   - o) ListBox
   - p) ComboBox

2. List the similarities and differences between radio buttons and list boxes.

3. Why might a programmer decide to use a combo box over a list box?

4. What are the two ways a user can enter data into a combo box?

5. a) Why might a programmer decide to set an object's Enabled property to False instead of setting Visible to False?
   b) Why might a programmer decide to set an object's Visible property to False instead of setting Enabled to False?

6. A button displays Exit.
   a) What functionality does the underlined x indicate?
   b) How was this functionality added to the button?
   c) What must the user do to display the underlining at run time?

7. How do you know when a:
   a) text box has the focus?
   b) button is disabled?
   c) button has the focus?
   d) list box has the focus?

8. List three ways the user can change which object has the focus in a running application.

9. Explain how access keys can be used to give the focus to a combo box.

10. a) Why should a programmer consider the tab order of objects on an interface?
    b) Without any programmer intervention, how is the tab order of objects determined?
    c) How is tab order changed?

11. List three ways to determine the square root of the value stored in a variable intNum.

12. a) What does it mean to say a function is overloaded?

    b) Name the overloaded function covered in this chapter and give an example of how both versions can be used.

13. State the numeric expression needed to evaluate the following:

    a) The money you will have in 10 years if you invest $100 monthly at 6%.

    b) The monthly payment for a $15,000 4-year car loan at 8%.

    c) The lump sum equivalent to receiving $1,000 a month for 10 years invested at 10%.

    d) The total amount paid on a 30-year mortgage with monthly payments of $800.

    e) The total interest amount paid on a 30-year mortgage with monthly payments of $800 at 7.25%.

14. Write a statement that includes the appropriate function(s) to:

    a) store a number in intValue that indicates the absolute value of intGuess.

    b) assign the square root of ($b^2 - 4ac$) to sngDeter.

    c) replace the current value of sngValue with its value rounded to 2 decimal places.

    d) determine if the data in txtNum1 and txtNum2 are numbers. If the data is numeric, btnCalculate should be enabled, otherwise, "Enter valid data." should be displayed in a message box. What must be done in the Design window for the code to work as expected?

    e) determine the logarithm of sngNum in base sngBase as long as both sngNum and sngBase are positive.

15. Use the following interface to answer parts (a), (b), and (c):

    a) If Second was selected, its _____ would have a value of 1.

    b) If the list was not sorted, where would the statement Me.lstTest.Items.Add("Fourth") place the new item?

    c) If the list was sorted, where would the statement Me.lstTest.Item.Add("Fourth") place the new item?

16. Write an event procedure that executes when the user selects an item in lstStudentName. The code should determine if the radio button radRemove is selected. If it is, the selected list item should be removed from the list box.

17. Write code that adds the value typed in a combo box to the combo box list and then clears the text box of the combo box. Include code that checks the Text property for a valid entry before trying to add the item to the list.

18. An application contains a txtNumSand object, which prompts the user for the number of sandwiches, and a lstSize object, which contains Small, Medium, and Large list items. Write code that executes when a list item is clicked. Include a statement that displays the total cost of the sandwiches in lblCost or the message "Invalid number." The cost of a sandwich is stored in constants named decCOSTSMALL, decCOSTMEDIUM, and decCOSTLARGE.

19. Write a btnCalculate_Click event procedure that adds to lstResult the numbers 1 through 10 and next to each number either their square root rounded to 1 decimal place or their square, depending on the selected radSquareRoots or radSquares radio button. Make the first list item an appropriate title.

20. Use the following interface to answer parts (a) and (b):

a) Write event handlers for each button. The Move button should move a selected item from the Available Items list to the Ordered Items list. The Remove button should move an item from the Ordered Items list back to the Available Items list. The buttons should be enabled only when items are available for moving in their respective lists.

b) When the application starts, should there be items in lstAvailable, lstOrdered, or both? Explain.

21. Determine if each of the following are true or false. If false, explain why.
   a) An object with Enabled set to False is not displayed on the form.
   b) IsNumeric(3–7) evaluates to True.
   c) The Sqrt() function returns the square root of any number.
   d) Format(0.079, "Percent") would display 79%.
   e) Val($100) returns 100.
   f) The Items.Add() method always adds the new item to the bottom of a list box or combo box.
   g) The Sorted property of a list box or combo box cannot be set at run time.
   h) A SelectedIndex value of 0 means no item has been selected in a list box or combo box.
   i) A Click event is raised when the user selects an item in either a combo box or list box.
   j) If a list box or combo box cannot display all the items added to the list, a vertical scroll bar is automatically displayed.
   k) The Text property of a combo box contains the value of the selected list item.
   l) It is possible to have both Calculate and Choose buttons on the same form.
   m) TabIndex values should start at 0.
   n) The trigonometric methods use degree as the angle of measurement.
   o) It is possible for certain functions to accept a varying number of arguments.

An Introduction to Programming Using Microsoft Visual Basic .NET

Exercise 1 —————————————————————————— Perfect Square

A perfect square is an integer whose square root is a whole number. For example, 4, 9, and 16 are perfect squares. Create a Perfect Square application that determines if the number entered by the user is a perfect square. The program code should include a PerfectSquare() Boolean function that has an intNumber parameter (Hint: Use the Int() function in determining if a square root is a whole number). The application interface should look similar to:

Exercise 2 —————————————————————————— Payment Calculator

Create a Payment Calculator application the prompts the user for a loan amount, interest rate, loan term in years, and payments term (daily, monthly, or yearly). Keep in mind the payments must be converted so that the number used in the calculation is in the appropriate units. For this conversion, assume that there are 30 days in each month and there are 360 days in a year. The application should display the payments, total amount paid over the length of the loan, and the total amount of interest paid. The application interface should look similar to:

Exercise 3 ──────────────────────────Loan Calculator

Create a Loan Calculator application the prompts the user for the monthly payment, interest rate, and term of a loan in years. The application should display the loan amount, total amount paid, and the total amount of interest paid. The application interface should look similar to:

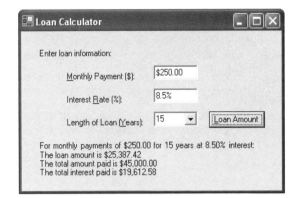

Exercise 4 ──────────────────── Investment Calculator

Create an Investment Calculator application that prompts the user for the amount invested monthly, interest rate, and term of the investment in years. The application should display the value of the investment at 5 year intervals in a list box and look similar to:

An Introduction to Programming Using Microsoft Visual Basic .NET

Exercise 5 ——————————————————Pythagorean Triples

A Pythagorean triple is a set of three integers that solves the equation $a^2 + b^2 = c^2$. Create a Pythagorean Triples application that displays all Pythagorean triples with values of A and B less than 100. The program code should include a PerfectSquare() function like the one created in Exercise 1. The application interface should look similar to the following after clicking <u>C</u>ompute:

A	B	C
3	4	5
4	3	5
5	12	13
6	8	10
7	24	25
8	6	10
8	15	17
9	12	15
9	40	41
10	24	26
11	60	61
12	5	13
12	9	15
12	16	20

Exercise 6 ——————————————— Square Root Roundoff Error

Create a Square Root Roundoff Error application that compares the square of the square root of a number with the number itself for all integers from 1 to 100. This difference in values is due to the computer's rounding error. The application interface should look similar to the following after clicking <u>C</u>ompute:

```
1 - (Sqrt(1))^2 = 0.00E+00
2 - (Sqrt(2))^2 = -4.44E-16
3 - (Sqrt(3))^2 = 4.44E-16
4 - (Sqrt(4))^2 = 0.00E+00
5 - (Sqrt(5))^2 = -8.88E-16
6 - (Sqrt(6))^2 = 8.88E-16
7 - (Sqrt(7))^2 = -8.88E-16
8 - (Sqrt(8))^2 = -1.78E-15
9 - (Sqrt(9))^2 = 0.00E+00
```

Exercise 7 ——————————————— Bookstore Order Form

Create a Bookstore Order Form application the prompts the user to select different items and quantities to purchase and then displays the order information in a list box that is on top of a cart.gif graphic, included in the data files for this text. The application interface should look similar to:

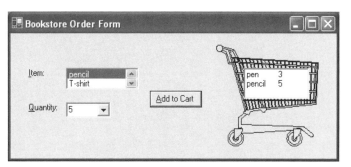

Exercise 8 ——————————————————————————Pythagorean Theorem

The Pythagorean Theorem is $a^2 + b^2 = c^2$ where a and b are the lengths of two sides of a right triangle and c is the length of the side opposite the right angle (the hypotenuse). Create a Pythagorean Theorem application that prompts the user for the lengths of sides a and b and then displays the length of the hypotenuse when Hypotenuse is clicked. The application interface should look similar to:

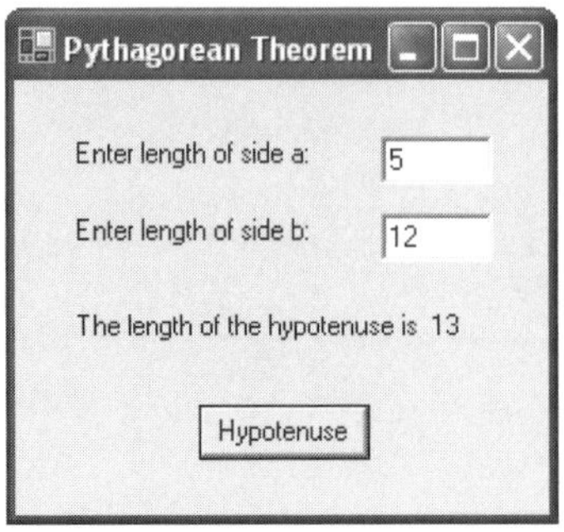

Exercise 9 ⟳ trigonometry required ————————— Angle Conversion

Create an Angle Conversion application that converts an angle in degrees to radians and vice versa. The application should include the options 30, 0.52, 45, 0.79, 60, and 1.05 in a combo box. Refer to the functions created in Reviews 12 and 13. The application interface should look similar to:

An Introduction to Programming Using Microsoft Visual Basic .NET

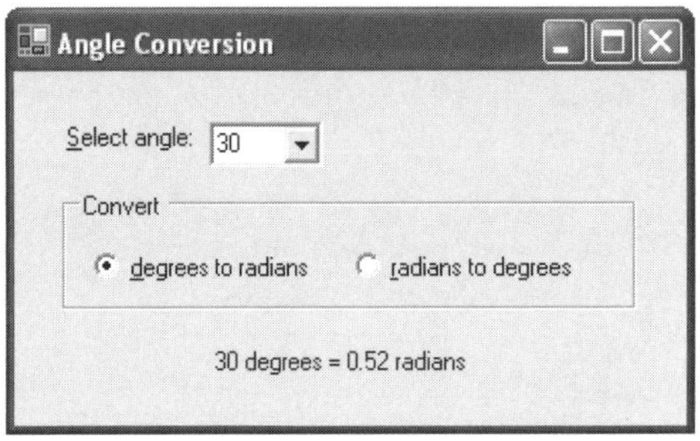

Exercise 10 trigonometry required ———— My Random Numbers

Create a My Random Numbers application that produces a sequence of random numbers without using the Rnd() function. To do this, let X vary from 1 to 100 in steps of 1. Obtain Sin(X) and multiply this by 1000, which results in a value Y. Then take the absolute value of Y and divide Int(Y) by 16, and let the remainder serve as the random number. The application interface should look similar to the following after clicking Random Numbers:

Exercise 11 ————————————————————————— Triangle Area

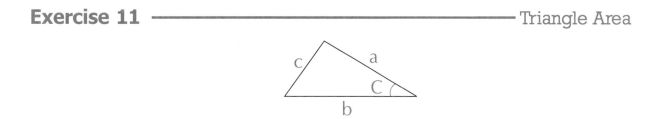

a) The formula Area = $\sqrt{s(s-a)(s-b)(s-c)}$ computes the area of a triangle where a, b, and c are the lengths of the sides and s is the semiperimeter (half the permieter). Create a Triangle Area application that prompts the user with text boxes for lengths of sides a, b, and c and then displays the area of the triangle in a label.

b) *Trigonometry required.* The trigonometric formula Area = ½ * a * b * Sin C computes the area of a triangle where C is the angle formed by sides a and b, in degrees. Modify Triangle Area to use this formula. The application interface should look similar to:

Exercise 12 trigonometry required ——————— SOH–CAH–TOA

SOH-CAH-TOA is a mnemonic for the trigonometric formulas that can be used to find the sine, cosine, and tangent of an angle in a right triangle:

Sine = Opposite/Hypotenuse   Cosine = Adjacent/Hypotenuse   Tangent = Opposite/Adjacent

For example, the sine of angle A is calculated by dividing the opposite side a by the hypotenuse c. Likewise, the cosine of angle A is b/c, and the tangent of angle A is a/b:

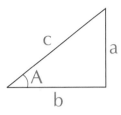

Create a SOH-CAH-TOA application that prompts the user for the lengths of the three sides of a triangle and then calculates the sine, cosine, and tangent of angle A depending on which button is clicked. The application should use the RadiansToDegrees() function from Review 13 to determine angle A in degrees. The code should also include a CheckSides() Boolean function that checks that the sides entered form a right triangle (Hint: Refer to Exercise 8) and if not, displays a message box and clears the text boxes to allow for new entries. The application interface should look similar to:

The formula $y = ne^{kt}$ can be used for estimating growth where:

> y   is the final amount
>
> n   is the initial amount
>
> k   is a constant
>
> t   is the time

For example, this formula could be used for estimating population growth in a region or for estimating cell grown in a lab experiment. Create a Bacteria Growth application that calculates how many bacteria will be present based on this formula. The application interface should look similar to:

The formula $V_n = P(1 + r)^n$ is can be used to estimate depreciation or appreciation where:

> V_n is the value at the end of n years
>
> P   is the initial value of the equipment
>
> r   is the rate of appreciation (positive) or depreciation (negative)
>
> n   is the time in years

For example, this formula could be used to determine the current value of a mainframe that a company has owned for 10 years. From this formula you can also determine how long it will take a piece of equipment to depreciate to a specific value using the formula: $n = \log(V_n / P) / \log(1 + r)$. Create a Depreciation application that calculates how long it will take a piece of equipment to depreciate using this formula. The application interface should look similar to:

Exercise 15 trigonometry required (advanced) ———— Triangle

Create an application that solves a triangle (compute the unknown sides and angles) for the following situations:

- given two sides and the included angle
- given two angles and any side
- given three sides

The application should prompt the user to select one of the three choices, and based on the selected option prompts the user to enter the appropriate known information. Angles should be entered in degrees and displayed in degrees.

Exercise 16 (advanced) ———————————————— Decay

The formula used in Exercise 14 for depreciation problems can also be used in decay problems. In decay problems, k is negative. Create an application that allows the user to select from the following options:

- calculate the final amount: ne^{kt}
- calculate the initial amount: y / e^{-kt}
- calculate the constant (called the half-life): $(\log (y/n)) / (t * \log e)$
  (where $\log e = 0.4343$)

The application should prompt the user to select one of the three choices and based on the selected option prompts the user to enter the appropriate known information. For example, a radioactive mass of 200 grams will reduce to 100 grams in 10 years. Based on this information, the half-life is calculated to be –0.06931.

Chapter 9
Arrays and Structures

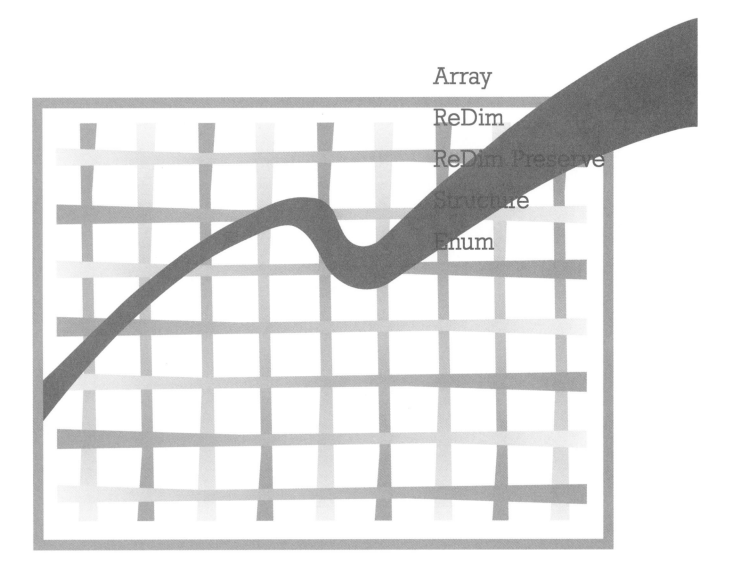

Array

ReDim

ReDim Preserve

Structure

Enum

Chapter 9 Expectations

After completing this chapter you will be able to:

1. Understand arrays.

2. Write array declarations that include initial values.

3. Understand how to access array elements and determine the length of an array.

4. Use **ByRef** array parameters and pass array arguments.

5. Understand how to implement an array with meaningful indexes.

6. Search an array using a linear search algorithm.

7. Understand dynamic arrays.

8. Declare an array with 0 elements and then use the **ReDim** and **ReDim Preserve** statements to change the array size.

9. Understand a two-dimensional array.

10. Declare a **Structure** and use it as a parameter, argument, and array element.

11. Declare an enumerated type.

12. Use control objects as array elements.

Concepts explained in this chapter are composite data types including arrays and structures. Enumerated types are also discussed. Dynamic arrays and the linear search algorithm is explained.

9.1 Arrays

Up to this point, only variables that hold a single value at a time have been used in applications. With this approach, many separate variables are required to represent a collection of related values such as names of students in a class or game scores for a team's season. A better way to represent related values is with an array that stores multiple values and has a name that describes the set of values.

composite data type

An *array* is a set of elements that are all the same data type. Because it is made up of a collection of elements, an array is called a *composite data type*. A **String** array with five elements could be visualized as:

0	1	2	3	4
Elaine	Jan	Tristan	Sage	CK

strStuNames

index

The elements of an array have an index value, with 0 being the index of the first item, 1 the index of the second, and so on. In the example above, Sage is the fourth element of the array and has index 3.

An array is declared with a **Dim** statement that includes the array name followed by the index of the last element in parentheses and then the data type of the elements. For example, the statement

Dim strStuNames(4) **As String**   '5 elements

declares a strStuNames array that has five **String** elements with indexes 0, 1, 2, 3, and 4. Note that the size of the array is indicated with the index of the last element. The elements are automatically initialized to the default value of the element data type. In this case, each element is initialized to **Nothing**.

array initialization

An array declaration may also include initial values for each element in a statement similar to:

Dim strStuNames() **As String** = {"Elaine", "Jan", "Tristan", "Sage", "CK"}

Note that an index is not included in the parentheses because the number of values in the brackets indicate the size. Strings must be enclosed in quotation marks, but numeric and boolean values are not.

Scaler Variable

An array stores many values. A variable that stores only one value is referred to as a scaler. For example, an **Integer** variable is a scaler because it can store only one value at a time.

9.2 Using Arrays

accessing an element

An array element is accessed by including its index in parentheses after the array name. For example, the following statement displays the element at index 4 in a label:

```
Me.lblStudentName.Text = strStuNames(4)   'CK
```

assignment

Assignment to an array element works similarly. For example, the following statement assigns "Sage" to the element at index 3:

```
strStuNames(3) = "Sage"
```

run-time error

A run-time error occurs when an invalid index is used. For example, the following assignment statement causes a run-time error:

```
Dim strNames(9) As String
strNames(10) = "Constance"
```

Subscript

Index is sometimes referred to as *subscript*.

The error message produced in this case is "Index was outside the bounds of the array"

Array class

Arrays are objects of the **Array** class that includes many properties and methods. One property is Length, which returns the number of elements in an array, as in the statement:

```
Me.lblNumElements.Text = strStuNames.Length      '5
```

A For...**Next** loop is often used to access the elements of an array because the loop counter can be used as the array index. For example, in the following statements, a For...**Next** loop and an input box are used to assign values to the elements of an array:

```
For intName = 0 To strStuNames.Length – 1
   strStuNames(intName) = InputBox("Enter student's first name:", "Students")
Next intName
```

Note that the loop iterates from 0 to one less than the length of the array because Length is a count of the number of elements, not the greatest index value.

Review 1

In this review you will create the Student Names application.

① *CREATE A NEW PROJECT*

Create a Windows application named Student Names.

② *CREATE THE INTERFACE*

Refer to the form on the next page to add, position, and size objects. Use the table below the form to set properties.

Object	Name	Text
Form1		Student Names
ListBox1	lstStuNames	
Button1	btnAddNames	Add Names

③ WRITE THE APPLICATION CODE

a. Display the Code window.

b. Add comments that include your name and today's date.

c. Create a btnAddNames_Click event procedure and then add the statements:

```
Const intNUMNAMES As Integer = 5
Dim strStuNames(intNUMNAMES – 1)
Dim intName As Integer

'get student names from user
For intName = 0 To strStuNames.Length – 1
    strStuNames(intName) = InputBox("Enter student's first name:", "Students")
Next intName

'add names to list box
For intName = 0 To strStuNames.Length – 1
    Me.lstStuNames.Items.Add(strStuNames(intName))
Next intName
```

④ RUN THE APPLICATION

a. Save the modified Students Names project.

b. Run the application. Click Add Names and then add one name to each input box. Note how the names are added to the list from the array.

c. Close the Student Names application.

⑤ PRINT THE CODE AND THEN CLOSE THE PROJECT

9.3 Array Parameters

Procedures can be passed an array when a parameter is declared with the array name followed by an empty set of parentheses. Arrays can get very large so it is usually more efficient if the parameter is **ByRef** because this parameter type refers to the actual array and does not make a copy of the array for use in the procedure. The SumOfValues() function on the next page has a **ByRef** array parameter and returns the sum of the array elements:

```
'~~~~~~~~~~~~~~~~~~~~~~~~~~~~~~~~~~~~~~~~~~~
'Returns the sum of the values in intNumArray().
'
'post: Sum of the values in intNumArray() is returned. 0
'returned if array has no elements.
'~~~~~~~~~~~~~~~~~~~~~~~~~~~~~~~~~~~~~~~~~~~
Function SumOfValues (ByRef intNumArray() As Integer) As Integer

    Dim intSum As Integer = 0

    Dim intIndex As Integer
    For intIndex = 0 To intNumArray.Length – 1
        intSum = intSum + intNumArray(intIndex)
    Next intIndex
    Return intSum

End Function
```

passing an array

A procedure call uses just the array name. For example, the statement below passes intDataArray() to the SumOfValues() function:

```
intTotal = SumOfValues(intDataArray)
```

passing an array element

A single array element may also be used as an argument. Passing a single element to a procedure means that only that element can be included in the procedure call. For example, the following statement passes the fourth element of intDataArray() to DisplayElement():

```
Call DisplayElement(intDataArray(3), Me.lblOutput)
```

DisplayElement() displays the value of a passed element in a label:

```
'~~~~~~~~~~~~~~~~~~~~~~~~~~~~~~~~~~~~~~~~~~~
'Sets the Text property of lblLabel to intNumber.
'
'post: intNumber displayed in a label.
'~~~~~~~~~~~~~~~~~~~~~~~~~~~~~~~~~~~~~~~~~~~
Sub DisplayElement (ByVal intNumber As Integer, _
ByRef lblLabel As Label)

    lblLabel.Text = intNumber

End Sub
```

Note that the procedure declares a parameter with a data type that matches the element data type.

9.4 Arrays with Meaningful Indexes

Many algorithms make use of the index value of an array element for simplifying the storage and retrieval of data. For example, an intTestScores array with 101 elements indexed from 0 to 100 could store a count of all the scores of 90 in the element with index 90, the scores of 82 in element 82, and so on. The Dice Rolls and Letter Occurrences applications described in this section implement similar algorithms.

Dice Rolls application

The Dice Rolls application counts the frequency of dice roll outcomes. Each roll of the dice is simulated by generating a random number from 1 to 6 for each of two dice. The outcome of each roll is used to update the intCounts array, which is a set of counters. For example, if 3 is rolled, then intCounts(3) is incremented. The Dice Rolls interface and code are:

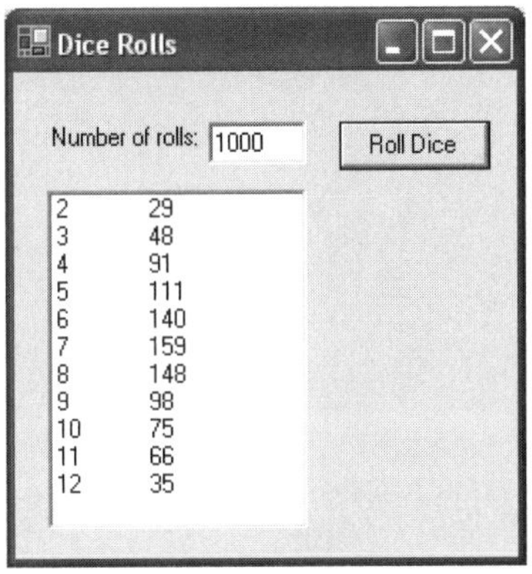

```
Private Sub btnRollDice_Click(ByVal sender As Object, _
ByVal e As System.EventArgs) Handles btnRollDice.Click

    Dim intNumRolls As Integer = Val(Me.txtRolls.Text)

    Dim intCounts(12) As Integer
    Call CountTrials(intNumRolls, intCounts)
    Call DisplayRollsCounts(intCounts, Me.lstRollsOutcomes)

End Sub


'~~~~~~~~~~~~~~~~~~~~~~~~~~~~~~~~~~~~~~~~~~~~~~~~~
'Simulates intNumRolls rolls of two dice and keeps a count of the
'outcomes.
'
'pre: intCounts() has elements with at least index values 2 through 12.
'post: intNumRolls dice rolls simulated. Counts of intNumRolls
'simulated dice rolls stored in intCounts().
'~~~~~~~~~~~~~~~~~~~~~~~~~~~~~~~~~~~~~~~~~~~~~~~~~
Sub CountTrials(ByVal intNumRolls As Integer, _
ByRef intCounts() As Integer)

    Dim intRollOutcome As Integer

    Randomize()
    Dim intRoll As Integer
    For intRoll = 1 To intNumRolls
        intRollOutcome = (Int(6 * Rnd()) + 1) + (Int(6 * Rnd()) + 1)
        intCounts(intRollOutcome) = intCounts(intRollOutcome) + 1
    Next intRoll

End Sub


'~~~~~~~~~~~~~~~~~~~~~~~~~~~~~~~~~~~~~~~~~~~~~~~~~
'Displays the contents of intCounts() in a list box.
'
'pre: intCounts() has elements with at least index values 2 through 12.
'post: Elements of intCounts() displayed in a list box.
'~~~~~~~~~~~~~~~~~~~~~~~~~~~~~~~~~~~~~~~~~~~~~~~~~
Sub DisplayRollsCounts(ByRef intCounts() As Integer, _
ByRef lstList As ListBox)

    Dim intRollOutcome As Integer
    For intRollOutcome = 2 To 12
        lstList.Items.Add(intRollOutcome & vbTab & _
        intCounts(intRollOutcome))
    Next intRollOutcome

End Sub
```

```
Private Sub txtRolls_TextChanged(ByVal sender As Object, _
ByVal e As System.EventArgs) Handles txtRolls.TextChanged

    Me.lstRollsOutcomes.Items.Clear()

End Sub
```

Letter Occurrences application

The Letter Occurrences application counts the occurrences of letters in a string. The storage of the letter counts is simplified by using an array with index values that correspond to the Unicode values of letters A (Unicode 65) through Z (Unicode 90). The Letter Occurrences interface and code are:

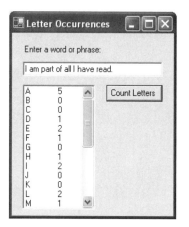

The Letter Occurrences application after typing a phrase
(a John Kieran quote) and clicking Count Letters

```
Private Sub btnCountLetters_Click(ByVal sender As Object, _
ByVal e As System.EventArgs) Handles btnCountLetters.Click

    Const intUNICODEZ As Integer = AscW("Z")
    Dim intLetterCounts(intUNICODEZ) As Integer

    Dim strPhrase As String = Me.txtPhrase.Text
    Call CountLetters(strPhrase, intLetterCounts)
    Call DisplayLetterCounts(intLetterCounts, Me.lstLetterCounts)

End Sub
```

```
'~~~~~~~~~~~~~~~~~~~~~~~~~~~~~~~~~~~~~~~~~~~~~~~~~~~~~~~
'Counts the occurrences of letters a through z in a string, regardless of case.
'
'pre: intLetterCounts() has elements with at least index values 65 through 90
'corresponding to the Unicode value for A through the Unicode value for Z.
'post: Counts of letters in a phrase stored in intLetterCounts().
'~~~~~~~~~~~~~~~~~~~~~~~~~~~~~~~~~~~~~~~~~~~~~~~~~~~~~~~
Sub CountLetters(ByVal strPhrase As String, _
ByRef intLetterCounts() As Integer)

    Dim intLetterIndex As Integer
    Dim chrUppercaseLetter As Char

    Dim intCharacter As Integer
    For intCharacter = 0 To strPhrase.Length - 1
        chrUppercaseLetter = Char.ToUpper(strPhrase.Chars(intCharacter))
        If chrUppercaseLetter >= "A" And chrUppercaseLetter <= "Z" Then
            intLetterIndex = AscW(chrUppercaseLetter)
            intLetterCounts(intLetterIndex) = intLetterCounts(intLetterIndex) + 1
        End If
    Next intCharacter

End Sub
```

An Introduction to Programming Using Microsoft Visual Basic .NET

```
'~~~~~~~~~~~~~~~~~~~~~~~~~~~~~~~~~~~~~~~~~~~~~~~~~~
'Displays the contents of intLetterCounts() in a list box.
'
'post: Elements of intLetterCounts() displayed in a list box.
'~~~~~~~~~~~~~~~~~~~~~~~~~~~~~~~~~~~~~~~~~~~~~~~~~~
Sub DisplayLetterCounts(ByRef intLetterCounts() As Integer, _
ByRef lstList As ListBox)

    Dim intLetter As Integer
    For intLetter = AscW("A") To AscW("Z")
        lstList.Items.Add(ChrW(intLetter) & vbTab & intLetterCounts(intLetter))
    Next intLetter

End Sub

Private Sub txtPhrase_TextChanged(ByVal sender As Object, _
ByVal e As System.EventArgs) Handles txtPhrase.TextChanged

    Me.lstLetterCounts.Items.Clear()

End Sub
```

The CountLetters() procedure converts each letter of the phrase to uppercase to simplify counting. In DisplayLetterCounts(), the loop control variable, intLetter, is converted to a character to act as a label in the list.

Review 2

The Dice Rolls application in Section 9.5 displays statistics for rolling two dice. Modify the Dice Rolls application to display statistics on rolling three dice. The application interface should look similar to that shown on the right after typing 1000 and clicking Roll Dice.

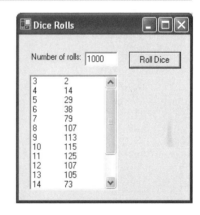

Review 3

Create a Number Occurrences application that displays the counts of the occurrences of each digit in a number entered by the user (Hint: treat the number entered as a string). The application interface should look similar to that shown on the right after typing the number 12664590 and clicking Count Numerals.

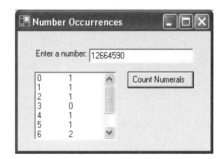

9.5 Searching an Array

linear search

There are many ways to search an array for a specific value. The simplest searching algorithm is called *linear search* and works by proceeding from one array element to the next until the specified value is found or until the entire array has been searched. The function FindItemIndex() implements the linear search algorithm:

```
'~~~~~~~~~~~~~~~~~~~~~~~~~~~~~~~~~~~~~~~~~~~~~~~~~~
'Returns the index of the first occurrence of intSearchItem in
'intDataArray() or −1 if intSearchItem not found.
'
'post: Index of the first occurrence of intSearchItem returned, or
'−1 returned if intSearchItem not found.
'~~~~~~~~~~~~~~~~~~~~~~~~~~~~~~~~~~~~~~~~~~~~~~~~~~
Function FindItemIndex(ByRef intDataArray() As Integer, _
ByVal intSearchItem As Integer) As Integer

   'Empty array
   If intDataArray.Length = 0 Then
      Return −1          'Item not found
   End If

   'Find search item
   Dim intIndex As Integer = 0
   Do While (intDataArray(intIndex) <> intSearchItem) _
   And (intIndex < intDataArray.Length − 1)
      intIndex = intIndex + 1
   Loop
   If intDataArray(intIndex) = intSearchItem Then
      Return intIndex    'Item found
   Else
      Return −1          'Item not found
   End If

End Function
```

The loop used in FindItemIndex does not explicitly check the last item in intDataArray(). However, if intSearchItem has not yet been found the If...**Then** compares it to the last array item.

9.6 Dynamic Arrays

ReDim

A *dynamic array* varies in size during run time and is used in situations where the size of an array is unknown at the start of a program or when it would be more efficient to vary array size throughout the program execution. The size of an existing array is changed at run time with a **ReDim** statement. The code below demonstrates **ReDim**:

```
Dim intDataArray(−1) As Integer        'array contains 0 elements
ReDim intDataArray(4)                  'array now contains 5 elements
```

array with zero elements

An array with size −1 contains zero elements. The **ReDim** statement sizes the array to contain five elements.

ReDim can be executed again and again to change the size of an array throughout program execution. However, each time a **ReDim** statement is executed, all the values in the array are lost. To keep the existing values in an array when sizing it, a **ReDim Preserve** statement must be used.

Preserve

For example, the following statements demonstrate **Preserve**:

```
Dim intDataArray() As Integer = {25, 50}    'array with 2 elements
ReDim intDataArray(3)                        'array with 4 elements
Me.lblElement.Text = intDataArray(1)     '0 because value not preserved
intDataArray(1) = 300
ReDim Preserve intDataArray(4)               'array with 5 elements
Me.lblElement.Text = intDataArray(1)     '300 because value preserved
```

The application below demonstrates dynamic arrays:

The Dynamic Array Demo application after adding values and then finding a value

```
Private Sub btnProcess_Click(ByVal sender As Object, _
ByVal e As System.EventArgs) Handles btnProcess.Click

   Static intDataArray(-1) As Integer      'array with zero elements
   Dim intIndex As Integer

   Dim intNumEntered As Integer = Val(Me.txtValue.Text)
   If Me.radAdd.Checked Then
      Call AddItem(intDataArray, intNumEntered)
      Call DisplayData(intDataArray, Me.lstOutput)
   ElseIf Me.radRemove.Checked Then
      Call RemoveItem(intDataArray, intNumEntered)
      Call DisplayData(intDataArray, Me.lstOutput)
   ElseIf Me.radFind.Checked Then
      intIndex = FindItemIndex(intDataArray, intNumEntered)
      Me.lstOutput.Items.Add("Item at index " & intIndex)
   End If

End Sub


'~~~~~~~~~~~~~~~~~~~~~~~~~~~~~~~~~~~~~~~~~~~~~~~~~~
'Adds new element intNumToAdd as the last element of intDataArray().
'
'pre: intDataArray() contains zero or more elements.
'post: intDataArray() contains a new element intNumToAdd as the
'last element of the array.
'~~~~~~~~~~~~~~~~~~~~~~~~~~~~~~~~~~~~~~~~~~~~~~~~~~
Sub AddItem(ByRef intDataArray() As Integer, _
ByVal intNumToAdd As Integer)

   'Use Length to size array because that value is one greater than the
   'current highest index value
   ReDim Preserve intDataArray(intDataArray.Length)
   intDataArray(intDataArray.Length - 1) = intNumToAdd

End Sub
```

```
'~~~~~~~~~~~~~~~~~~~~~~~~~~~~~~~~~~~~~~~~~~~~~~~
'Removes the first occurrence of intNumToRemove from intDataArray()
'and sizes the array with one less element.
'
'post: If intNumToRemove found, intDataArray() has one less element
'and intNumToRemove is deleted from array.
'~~~~~~~~~~~~~~~~~~~~~~~~~~~~~~~~~~~~~~~~~~~~~~~
Sub RemoveItem(ByRef intDataArray() As Integer, _
ByVal intNumToRemove As Integer)

    Dim intItemIndex As Integer
    intItemIndex = FindItemIndex(intDataArray, intNumToRemove)
    'move remaining elements up one position in array
    If intItemIndex > -1 Then
        Dim intIndex As Integer
        For intIndex = intItemIndex To intDataArray.Length - 2
            intDataArray(intIndex) = intDataArray(intIndex + 1)
        Next intIndex
        ReDim Preserve intDataArray(intDataArray.Length - 2)
    End If

End Sub


'~~~~~~~~~~~~~~~~~~~~~~~~~~~~~~~~~~~~~~~~~~~~~~~
'Returns the index of the first occurrence of intSearchItem in
'intDataArray() or -1 if intSearchItem not found.
'
'post: Index of the first occurrence of intSearchItem returned, or
'-1 returned if intSearchItem not found.
'~~~~~~~~~~~~~~~~~~~~~~~~~~~~~~~~~~~~~~~~~~~~~~~
Function FindItemIndex(ByRef intDataArray() As Integer, _
ByVal intSearchItem As Integer) As Integer

    'Empty array
    If intDataArray.Length = 0 Then
        Return -1          'Item not found
    End If

    'Find search item
    Dim intIndex As Integer = 0
    Do While (intDataArray(intIndex) <> intSearchItem) _
    And (intIndex < intDataArray.Length - 1)
        intIndex = intIndex + 1
    Loop
    If intDataArray(intIndex) = intSearchItem Then
        Return intIndex    'Item found
    Else
        Return -1          'Item not found
    End If

End Function
```

An Introduction to Programming Using Microsoft Visual Basic .NET

```
'~~~~~~~~~~~~~~~~~~~~~~~~~~~~~~~~~~~~~~~~~~~~~~~
'Clears a list box and then displays intDataArray() elements in the list box.
'
'pre: intDataArray.Length > 0
'post: List box cleared of any previous items. intDataArray()
'elements displayed in the list box.
'~~~~~~~~~~~~~~~~~~~~~~~~~~~~~~~~~~~~~~~~~~~~~~~
Sub DisplayData(ByRef intDataArray() As Integer, _
ByRef lstList As ListBox)

    lstList.Items.Clear()

    Dim intIndex As Integer
    For intIndex = 0 To intDataArray.Length – 1
        lstList.Items.Add(intIndex & vbTab & intDataArray(intIndex))
    Next intIndex

End Sub
```

Note that in the btnProcess_Click event procedure, intDataArray() is declared as a static array so it would not be reinitialized each time Process is clicked. The RemoveItem() procedure finds the first location of the element to be removed and then overwrites it by moving the elements ahead of it up by one index. Finally, the "extra" element is removed from the array by sizing the array down by one.

Review 4

Modify the Dynamic Array Demo application so that "Item not found" is displayed in the list box rather than "Item at index –1" when a search item is not found.

Review 5

Create a Find Name application that allows the user to add, delete, and find names. The application interface should look similar to the Dynamic Array Demo interface.

9.7 Two-Dimensional Arrays

An array with two dimensions can be used to represent data that corresponds to a grid. For example, a checkerboard, the streets in a city, and seats in a theater can all be represented with a grid. A tic-tac-toe board represented in a two-dimensional array can be visualized as:

	0	1	2
0	X	O	X
1	X	X	O
2	O	O	O

chrTTTBoard

A two-dimensional array is declared with a **Dim** statement that includes the array name followed by the index of the last element of each dimension separated by commas in parentheses and then the data type of the elements. For example, the statement

```
Dim chrTTTBoard(2, 2) As Char     '9 elements
```

declares a 3 x 3 chrTTTBoard with rows 0 through 2 and columns 0 through 2 for a total of nine **Char** elements. An element is accessed by including the appropriate row and column indexes in parentheses after the array name. For example, the following statement assigns the letter X to the first row (0) in the third column (2):

```
chrTTTBoard(0, 2) = "X"
```

Array class

The Length property returns the total number of elements in all the dimensions of an array. For example, 9 is the length of the chrTTTBoard array. The **Array** class contains other properties and methods useful when working with arrays with more than one dimension:

- **Rank** returns the number of dimensions in the array.

- **GetLength(***dimension***)** returns the number of elements in a dimension of an array. *dimension* is the dimension of the array, with 0 being the first dimension, 1 being the second, and so on.

accessing elements

Nested **For…Next** loops are often used to access the elements of a two-dimensional array because one loop counter indicates the row of the array and the other counter indicates the column. For example, in the following statements, nested **For…Next** loops are used to display the contents of a two-dimensional array in a list box:

```
Dim intRow, intCol As Integer
Dim chrTTTBoard(2, 2) As Char
For intRow = 0 To chrTTTBoard.GetLength(0) – 1
    For intCol = 0 To chrTTTBoard.GetLength(1) – 1
        Me.lstElements.Items.Add(chrTTTBoard(intRow, intCol))
    Next intCol
Next intRow
```

ReDim

A ReDim statement can be used to change the size of individual dimensions, but the number of dimensions in an array cannot be changed once delcared.

two-dimensional array parameters

Two-dimensional array parameters should be declared **ByRef** with the array name followed by an empty set of parentheses that includes a comma indicating two dimensions. For example, **ByRef** intNumArray(,) **As Integer** would be the parameter for a procedure.

Tic-Tac-Toe

The Tic-Tac-Toe application allows two players to play a computerized game of tic-tac-toe. The application keeps track of whether X or O is the next player and with each move checks to see if there is a winner or if the game is a draw. The application uses a two-dimensional array to keep track of the board. The Tic-Tac-Toe interface and code are:

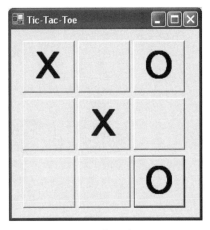

Tic-Tac-Toe after four moves

```
'~~~~~~~~~~~~~~~~~~~~~~~~~~~~~~~~~~~~~~~~~~~~~~~~~~~~~
'Two player game of Tic-Tac-Toe.
'
'pre: Buttons representing the board have Tags that correspond to:
'        0,0  0,1  0,2
'        1,0  1,1  1,2
'        2,0  2,1  2,2
'post: Tic-Tac-Toe has been played until a winner or a draw is
'declared.
'~~~~~~~~~~~~~~~~~~~~~~~~~~~~~~~~~~~~~~~~~~~~~~~~~~~~~
Private Sub btnMoveMade_Click(ByVal sender As Object, _
ByVal e As System.EventArgs) Handles btn00.Click, btn01.Click, _
btn02.Click, btn10.Click, btn11.Click, btn12.Click, btn20.Click, _
btn21.Click, btn22.Click

    Dim btnSquareClicked As Button = sender
    Static chrTTT(2, 2) As Char        'Store player moves
    Static chrPlayer As Char = "X"     'X goes first

    'Check for existing X or O
    If btnSquareClicked.Text <> Nothing Then
        MessageBox.Show("Invalid move.")
    Else
        'Show move
        btnSquareClicked.Text = chrPlayer

        'Store move in chrTTT()
        Dim strIndex As String
        strIndex = btnSquareClicked.Tag
        Dim intX As Integer = Val(strIndex.Chars(0))
        Dim intY As Integer = Val(strIndex.Chars(2))
        Call StoreMove(intX, intY, chrPlayer, chrTTT)

        'Check for winner
        If IsWinner(chrTTT) Then
            MessageBox.Show("Game over!")
        Else                                    'Next player's turn
            If chrPlayer = "X" Then
                chrPlayer = "O"
            Else
                chrPlayer = "X"
            End If
        End If
    End If

End Sub
```

```
'~~~~~~~~~~~~~~~~~~~~~~~~~~~~~~~~~~~~~~~~~~~~~~~~
'Store Tic-Tac-Toe move in chrTTT().
'pre: intX and intY is a valid index. chrTTT() is a 3 x 3 array.
'post: Tic-Tac-Toe move stored in chrTTT().
'~~~~~~~~~~~~~~~~~~~~~~~~~~~~~~~~~~~~~~~~~~~~~~~~
Sub StoreMove(ByVal intX As Integer, ByVal intY As Integer, _
ByVal chrPlayer As Char, ByRef chrTTT(,) As Char)

    chrTTT(intX, intY) = chrPlayer

End Sub


'~~~~~~~~~~~~~~~~~~~~~~~~~~~~~~~~~~~~~~~~~~~~~~~~
'Determines if there is a winner.
'pre: chrTTT() is a 3 x 3 array.
'post: True returned if a winner is found or if all squares are filled.
'~~~~~~~~~~~~~~~~~~~~~~~~~~~~~~~~~~~~~~~~~~~~~~~~
Function IsWinner(ByRef chrTTT(,) As Char) As Boolean
    'Check all rows
    Dim intRow As Integer
    For intRow = 0 To 2
        If chrTTT(intRow, 0) = chrTTT(intRow, 1) And _
        chrTTT(intRow, 1) = chrTTT(intRow, 2) And _
        (chrTTT(intRow, 0) = "X" Or chrTTT(intRow, 0) = "O") Then
            Return True      'Winner
        End If
    Next intRow

    'Check all columns
    Dim intCol As Integer
    For intCol = 0 To 2
        If chrTTT(0, intCol) = chrTTT(1, intCol) And _
        chrTTT(1, intCol) = chrTTT(2, intCol) And _
        (chrTTT(0, intCol) = "X" Or chrTTT(0, intCol) = "O") Then
            Return True      'Winner
        End If
    Next intCol

    'Check one diagonal
    If chrTTT(0, 0) = chrTTT(1, 1) And chrTTT(1, 1) = chrTTT(2, 2) _
    And (chrTTT(0, 0) = "X" Or chrTTT(0, 0) = "O") Then
        Return True      'Winner
    End If

    'Check other diagonal
    If chrTTT(0, 2) = chrTTT(1, 1) And chrTTT(1, 1) = chrTTT(2, 0) _
    And (chrTTT(0, 2) = "X" Or chrTTT(0, 2) = "O") Then
        Return True      'Winner
    End If

    'Check for empty squares
    Dim blnMovesLeft As Boolean = False
    For intRow = 0 To 2
        For intCol = 0 To 2
            If chrTTT(intRow, intCol) = Nothing Then
                blnMovesLeft = True
            End If
        Next intCol
    Next intRow
    If Not blnMovesLeft Then
        Return True      'All squares filled
    End If

    Return False      'No winner found

End Function
```

9.8 Structures

A structure is a composite data type that groups related variables. Unlike arrays that have elements of the same data type, structures have members that can be different data types. For example, the following is a declaration for a structure named Student:

```
Structure Student
    Dim FirstName As String
    Dim LastName As String
    Dim MiddleInitial As Char
    Dim GPA As Single
    Dim Credits As Integer
End Structure
```

Structure Members

A structure is a simple form of a class and can have members that include methods, properties, constants, and events.

programming style

Note that structure name and its member names do not contain prefixes because the structure is defining a new data type. The names used for structures should be descriptive without exposing specific types as a matter of good programming style.

In general, a **Structure** takes the form:

```
Structure StructureName
    member declarations
End Structure
```

StructureName is a name describing the data grouped by the structure. *member declarations* is one or more statements that declare variables of any data type to store information. **Structure** declares the structure and **End Structure** ends the structure. A structure must be declared outside of any procedures and is usually placed at the beginning of a program with other global declarations.

declaring a structure variable

accessing structure members

A structure variable declaration can appear anywhere in a program. Variables declared using a structure should have the prefix stc for good programming style. A structure variable accesses members of its structure with a dot (.) between the variable name and the member name. For example, the following statements declare a variable of type Student and then assign a value to its GPA member:

```
Dim stcNewStudent As Student
stcNewStudent.GPA = 3.4
```

structure parameters

A procedure can include a structure parameter that is either **ByRef** or **ByVal**. A structure argument is passed to a procedure by including the variable name. A single member of a structure is passed to a procedure by using the structure name followed by a dot and then the member name. The procedure heading must declare a variable using the data type for the single member. For example, both of the following statements are valid procedure calls:

```
Call ShowStudentData(stcNewStudent)
Call ShowName(stcNewStudent.FirstName, stcNewStudent.LastName)
```

9.9   Structure Arrays

UDTs

Structures and arrays are sometimes referred to as user-defined types (UDTs) because the programmer decides the characteristics of the type.

An array of structures can be used to store related information for a group of elements. For example, information for the students in a school could be stored in an array with elements of type Student:

```
Structure Student
    Dim FirstName As String
    Dim LastName As String
    Dim MiddleInitial As Char
    Dim GPA As Single
    Dim Credits As Integer
End Structure
```

...

```
Dim stcStudents(99) As Student          '100 students
```

Note that an array of structures can be declared anywhere in the program and does not need to be global like the **Structure** declaration itself.

accessing structure array members

The members of each element are accessed by using the index of the element and then a dot with a member name:

```
stcStudents(3).FirstName = "Faith"    'Faith assigned to fourth student
```

Review 6

Create a Customers application that prompts the user with input boxes for the first name, last name, and account balance of 5 customers and then displays the customer with the highest account balance and display the average account balance. Store the customer data in an array of structures. The application interface should look similar to that shown on the right after clicking Enter Customer Information and entering data for five customers.

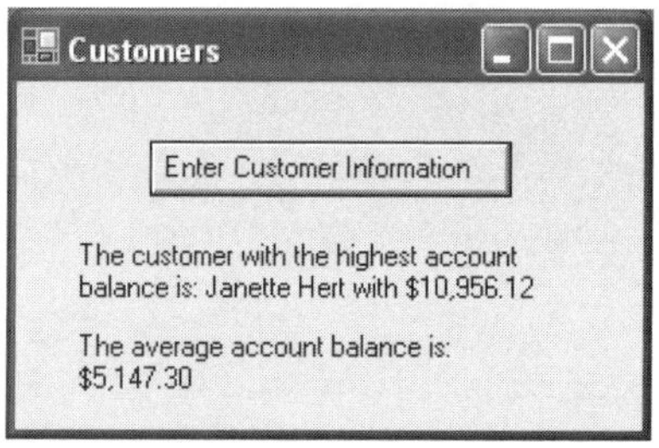

9.10   Enumerated Types

An *enumerated type* is a data type that defines a related set of named constants. A variable that should be limited to a set of values can be declared using a predefined enumerated type. For example, student level is either freshman, sophomore, junior, or senior, based on the years in school. A **String** variable can be used to store a student level, but this type of variable can hold any string, not just the four possible levels, which could lead to hard-to-find bugs. Instead an enumerated type can be declared and then a variable of this type can be used to store a level:

```
Enum Level
    Freshman
    Sophomore
    Junior
    Senior
End Enum
```

A variable declared as type Level is limited to storing the values defined in the enumerated type. Visual Basic .NET enforces this in the IDE with an AutoList. For example, in a Level variable assignment statement an AutoList is displayed when the equal sign is typed:

```
Dim Year As Level
Year=|
        ⊞ Level.Freshman
        ⊞ Level.Junior
        ⊞ Level.Senior
        ⊞ Level.Sophomore
```

The values allowed for assignment to this variable are displayed in alphabetical order by the AutoList.

declaring an enumerated type

declaring an enumerated type variable

An enumerated type must be declared outside of any procedures and is usually placed at the beginning of a program with other global declarations. Variables declared as an enumerated type can appear anywhere in the program.

The members of an enumerated type correspond to a set of integer constants, starting with 0 if no other values are assigned in the **Enum** statement. The **Enum** Level members correspond to Freshman = 0, Sophomore = 1, Junior = 2, and Senior = 3. Therefore, the following statements display 1 in the label:

```
Year = Level.Sophomore
Me.lblShowLevel.Text = Year         '1 is displayed!
```

Select...Case

A **Select**...**Case** statement is often used to determine what action to take based on the value of an enumerated type variable. In the Code window, an AutoList is displayed after **Case** is typed:

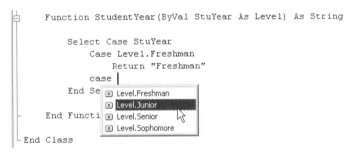

```
    Function StudentYear(ByVal StuYear As Level) As String

        Select Case StuYear
            Case Level.Freshman
                Return "Freshman"
            case |
        End Se ⊞ Level.Freshman
               ⊞ Level.Junior
    End Functi ⊞ Level.Senior
               ⊞ Level.Sophomore
└ End Class
```

In this example, the **Select**...**Case** statement is part of a function that returns the string equivalent of an enumerated type member.

explicit assignment

Enumerated type members can be explicitly assigned constant values, as in the statement:

```
Enum Summer
    June = 6
    July = 7
    August = 8
End Enum
```

Create a Students application that maintains an array of student information using an appropriate data type for the array members. The application should prompt the user with text boxes for the first name, middle initial, last name, GPA, and credits for a student. A list box should prompt the user for the student's year. Add Student adds the student to the array. Show Student displays an input box prompting the user for a last name and then displays student information in a message box. The application should use a modified FindItemIndex() from Section 9.6. The interface should look similar to that shown on the right after adding students and then displaying information about a student.

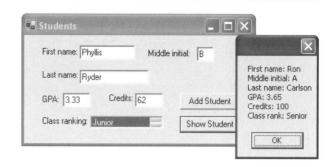

Case Study

In this Case Study an application for generating orders for Lucy's Cuban Cafe will be created.

specification   The specification for this Case Study is:

Lucy's Cuban Cafe is a small restaurant that offers nine menu items: Arroz con Pollo for $9.95, Ropa Vieja for $9.95, Masitas for $8.95, Cuban Sandwich for $6.95, Moros for $2.75, Yuca for $2.75, Cafe con Leche for $1.75, Flan for $2.50, and Pudin de Pan for $2.95. The Lucy's Cuban Cafe application should maintain a list of the items ordered and a running total price for the order. The user should be able to create a new order, which clears the list and the total.

design   The interface for this Case Study should provide easy-to-use options for selecting menu items. Since there are only nine items, buttons can be used. A list box displays any number of items ordered and a label displays the total price of an order. A New Order button clears the list box and total price.

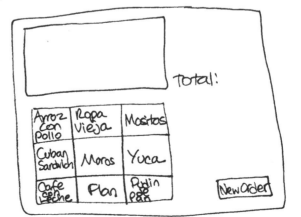

The code design starts with an algorithm:

1. Starting the application shows only a New Order button. All other objects are not visible.
2. Clicking New Order loads the menu items into an array and displays item names on the interface buttons.
3. Clicking a menu item button adds that item and its price to the list and updates the current total price label.
4. Clicking New Order removes any items from the list box and removes the price from the total price label.

Analyzing the algorithm further reveals some aspects of the code:

- The Visible property should be used in the Design window to hide options.

- The same or similar actions are performed by the New Order and menu item buttons.

- The data for the menu items could be stored as structure elements in an array, with the structure containing the item name and price.

Based on the algorithm and analysis of the algorithm, the pseudocode for this application appears like:

```
Structure MenuItem
    ItemName
    Price
End Structure

MAXFOODITEMS = 9

Sub ProcessOrder (sender, e) Handles btnNewOrder.Click, btnItem0.Click,
btnItem1.Click, btnItem2.Click, btnItem3.Click, btnItem4.Click, btnItem5.Click,
btnItem6.Click, btnItem7.Click, btnItem8.Click
    Static LucyMenu(MAXFOODITEMS) As MenuItem
    Static TotalPrice As Decimal
    Dim intMenuItem As Integer

    Dim ButtonClicked As Button = sender
    Select Case ButtonClicked.Tag
        Case "NewOrder"
            LoadMenu(LucyMenu)
            LoadButtons(LucyMenu)
            TotalPrice = 0
            Clear list box items and label
            Show list box
        Case Else
            intMenuItem = ButtonClicked.Tag
            AddToList(LucyMenu(intMenuItem), list box)
            TotalPrice = TotalPrice + LucyMenu(intMenuItem).Price
            ShowTotal
    End Select
End Sub
```

```
Sub LoadMenu(ByRef Menu() As MenuItem)
    Menu(0).ItemName = "Arroz con Pollo"
    Menu(0).Price = 9.95

    ... Repeat block for remaining eight menu items ...
End Sub

Sub LoadButtons(ByRef Menu() As MenuItem)
    btnItem0.Text = Menu(0).ItemName
    Show button

    ... Repeat block for remaining eight menu items ...
End Sub

Sub AddToList(ByVal Item As MenuItem, ByRef lstOrderList As ListBox)
    lstOrderList.Items.Add(Item.ItemName & vbTab & _
    Format(Item.Price, "Currency")
End Sub

Sub ShowTotal(ByVal Amount As Decimal, ByRef lblAmount As Label)
    lblAmount.Text = "Total:" & Format(Amount, "Currency")
End Sub
```

coding   The interface and code for this Case Study are:

Object	Name	Text	Tag
Form1		Lucy's Cuban Cafe	
ListBox1	lstItemsOrdered		
Label1	lblTotal	*empty*	
Button1	btnItem0	*empty*	0
Button2	btnItem1	*empty*	1
Button3	btnItem2	*empty*	2
Button4	btnItem3	*empty*	3
Button5	btnItem4	*empty*	4
Button6	btnItem5	*empty*	5
Button7	btnItem6	*empty*	6
Button8	btnItem7	*empty*	7
Button9	btnItem8	*empty*	8
Button10	btnNewItem	New Item	NewItem

The Visible property is set to False for every object except the New Item
button. The label is bold, size 10.

```
Public Class Form1
    Inherits System.Windows.Forms.Form

    Windows Form Designer generated code

Structure MenuItem
    Dim strItemName As String
    Dim decPrice As Decimal
End Structure

Const intMAXFOODITEMS As Integer = 9    'Number of item buttons on interface


'~~~~~~~~~~~~~~~~~~~~~~~~~~~~~~~~~~~~~~~~~~~~~~~~~~~~~~~~~~~~~~~~~~~~
'Processes orders by showing selected items in a list and maintaining a current total.
'
'post: A total price is displayed and selected items are displayed in a list if menu
'items have been selected. The list is clear and no price is displayed if a new order is started.
'~~~~~~~~~~~~~~~~~~~~~~~~~~~~~~~~~~~~~~~~~~~~~~~~~~~~~~~~~~~~~~~~~~~~
Private Sub ProcessOrder(ByVal sender As System.Object, ByVal e As System.EventArgs) _
Handles btnNewOrder.Click, btnItem0.Click, btnItem1.Click, btnItem2.Click, btnItem3.Click, _
btnItem4.Click, btnItem5.Click, btnItem6.Click, btnItem7.Click, btnItem8.Click

    Static stcLucyMenu(intMAXFOODITEMS) As MenuItem
    Static decTotalPrice As Decimal
    Dim intMenuItem As Integer

    Dim btnButtonClicked As Button = sender
    Select Case btnButtonClicked.Tag
        Case "NewOrder"
            'Load menu items and display on buttons
            Call LoadMenu(stcLucyMenu)
            Call LoadButtons(stcLucyMenu)
            'initialize price and clear total from interface
            decTotalPrice = 0
            Me.lblTotal.Text = Nothing
            'clear list of existing items and show list
            Me.lstItemsOrdered.Items.Clear()
            Me.lstItemsOrdered.Visible = True
        Case Else
            intMenuItem = Val(btnButtonClicked.Tag)
            Call AddToList(stcLucyMenu(intMenuItem), Me.lstItemsOrdered)
            decTotalPrice = decTotalPrice + stcLucyMenu(intMenuItem).decPrice
            Call ShowTotal(decTotalPrice, Me.lblTotal)
    End Select

End Sub


'~~~~~~~~~~~~~~~~~~~~~~~~~~~~~~~~~~~~~~~~~~~~~~~~~~~~~~~~~~~~~~~~~~~~
'Stores item names and prices in Menu() array.
'
'post: Menu item names and prices are stored in an array.
'~~~~~~~~~~~~~~~~~~~~~~~~~~~~~~~~~~~~~~~~~~~~~~~~~~~~~~~~~~~~~~~~~~~~
Sub LoadMenu(ByRef Menu() As MenuItem)

    Menu(0).strItemName = "Arroz con Pollo"
    Menu(0).decPrice = 9.95

    Menu(1).strItemName = "Ropa Vieja"
    Menu(1).decPrice = 9.95

    Menu(2).strItemName = "Masitas"
    Menu(2).decPrice = 8.95

    Menu(3).strItemName = "Cuban Sandwich"
    Menu(3).decPrice = 6.95

    Menu(4).strItemName = "Moros"
    Menu(4).decPrice = 2.75
```

```
        Menu(5).strItemName = "Yuca"
        Menu(5).decPrice = 2.75

        Menu(6).strItemName = "Cafe con Leche"
        Menu(6).decPrice = 1.75

        Menu(7).strItemName = "Flan"
        Menu(7).decPrice = 2.5

        Menu(8).strItemName = "Pudin de Pan"
        Menu(8).decPrice = 2.95

    End Sub


    '~~~~~~~~~~~~~~~~~~~~~~~~~~~~~~~~~~~~~~~~~~~~~~~~~~~~~~~~~~~~~~
    'Displays menu item names on interface.
    'post: Menu item names are displayed on buttons.
    '~~~~~~~~~~~~~~~~~~~~~~~~~~~~~~~~~~~~~~~~~~~~~~~~~~~~~~~~~~~~~~
    Sub LoadButtons(ByRef Menu() As MenuItem)

        Me.btnItem0.Text = Menu(0).strItemName
        Me.btnItem0.Visible = True

        Me.btnItem1.Text = Menu(1).strItemName
        Me.btnItem1.Visible = True

        Me.btnItem2.Text = Menu(2).strItemName
        Me.btnItem2.Visible = True

        Me.btnItem3.Text = Menu(3).strItemName
        Me.btnItem3.Visible = True

        Me.btnItem4.Text = Menu(4).strItemName
        Me.btnItem4.Visible = True

        Me.btnItem5.Text = Menu(5).strItemName
        Me.btnItem5.Visible = True

        Me.btnItem6.Text = Menu(6).strItemName
        Me.btnItem6.Visible = True

        Me.btnItem7.Text = Menu(7).strItemName
        Me.btnItem7.Visible = True

        Me.btnItem8.Text = Menu(8).strItemName
        Me.btnItem8.Visible = True

    End Sub


    '~~~~~~~~~~~~~~~~~~~~~~~~~~~~~~~~~~~~~~~~~~~~~~~~~~~~~~~~~~~~~~
    'Adds selected menu item to a list.
    'post: Selected menu item name and price of item are displayed in a list.
    '~~~~~~~~~~~~~~~~~~~~~~~~~~~~~~~~~~~~~~~~~~~~~~~~~~~~~~~~~~~~~~
    Sub AddToList(ByVal Item As MenuItem, ByRef lstOrderList As ListBox)

        lstOrderList.Items.Add(Item.strItemName & vbTab & Format(Item.decPrice, "Currency"))

    End Sub


    '~~~~~~~~~~~~~~~~~~~~~~~~~~~~~~~~~~~~~~~~~~~~~~~~~~~~~~~~~~~~~~
    'Displays a total price for the current order in a label.
    'post: A price is displayed in a label.
    '~~~~~~~~~~~~~~~~~~~~~~~~~~~~~~~~~~~~~~~~~~~~~~~~~~~~~~~~~~~~~~
    Sub ShowTotal(ByVal decAmount As Decimal, ByRef lblAmount As Label)

        lblAmount.Text = "Total: " & Format(decAmount, "Currency")

    End Sub

End Class
```

An Introduction to Programming Using Microsoft Visual Basic .NET

Running Lucy's Cuban Cafe, clicking New Order, and selecting a few menu items displays the following:

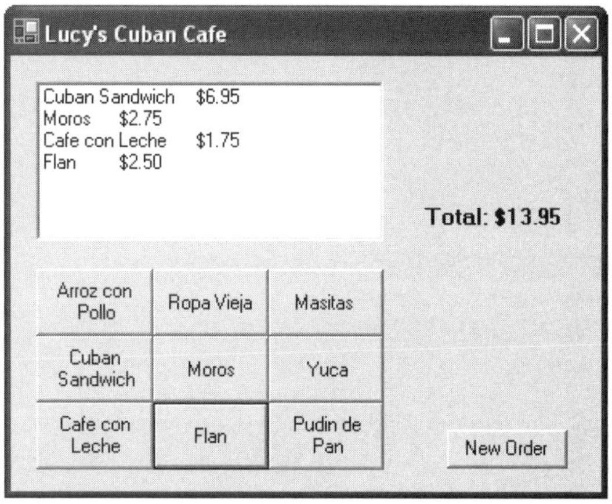

This Case Study should be tested by selecting each of the menu items at least once and verifying that the items appear correctly in the list and that the total is updated correctly. The New Order button should also be clicked to verify that it performs as expected.

> ***Lucy's Cuban Cafe***
>
> Lucy serves only authentic Cuban food at her restaurant. The menu items are in Spanish and translate to English as Arroz con Pollo (Chicken and Yellow Rice), Ropa Vieja (Shredded Beef), Masitas (Pork and Plantains), Cuban Sandwich (Cuban Bread with Meat and Cheese), Moros (Black Beans and Rice), Yuca (Cassava), Cafe con Leche (Coffee with Milk), Flan (Baked Custard), and Pudin de Pan (Bread Pudding).

9.11 Arrays of Objects

An array can store a reference to a set of control class objects, such as a set of buttons on a form. For example, the following statement declares an array of the menu buttons in the Lucy's Cuban Cafe application:

```
Dim btnItems() As Button = {Me.btnItem0, Me.btnItem1, Me.Item2 _
Me.btnItem3, Me.btnItem4, Me.btnItem5, Me.btnItem6, Me.btnItem7 _
Me.btnItem8}
```

An array of objects must be declared with the appropriate control class data type. In addition to the Button data type used in the declaration, there are CheckBox, Label, TextBox, RadioButton, and PictureBox classes.

An array of control class objects can simplify code that sets the same property for multiple objects of the same type. For example, the Case Study LoadButtons() procedure could be rewritten to include a Button array parameter:

```
Sub LoadButtons(ByRef Menu() As MenuItem, _
ByRef btnItems() As Button)

  Dim intItem As Integer

  'set each button to an item name
  For intItem = 0 To Menu.Length – 1
    btnItems(intItem).Text = Menu(intItem).strItemName
    btnItems(intItem).Visible = True
  Next intItem

End Sub
```

Modify the Lucy's Cuban Cafe application to include a button that displays English when the application is started. Clicking this button displays the menu items in English and the language button then displays Spanish to allow the user to switch the application back to Spanish language item names. Refer to the sidebar above to determine the English names of the menu items. The application changes will include modifying the MenuItem structure to contain appropriate members for storing English and Spanish names, using arrays of objects to simplify code, modifying ProcessOrder(), LoadMenu(), LoadButtons(), and AddToList() procedures, and sizing the list box and buttons appropriately.

Chapter Summary

An array is a composite data type that stores a set of variables with the same data type. Each variable of an array is called an element. The elements of an array have an index value, with the first element being index 0, the second being index 1, and so on. Arrays are objects of the **Array** class, which has member Length that returns the number of elements.

An array is declared using a **Dim** statement that includes the array name followed by the index of the last element in parentheses and then the data type of the elements. Array elements can include built-in types, such as **Single** and **String**, structures, or control class objects, such as Button. An array can be initialized when it is declared by including in brackets the values of the elements separated by commas.

An array element is accessed by including the index in parentheses after the array name. A **For...Next** loop is used to access the elements of an array. A "Subscript out of range" run-time error occurs if an invalid index is used. Subscript is another word for index.

An array parameter can be declared by value or by reference and uses the array name followed by an empty set of parentheses. An array argument uses just the array name. A single array element may also be used for parameters and arguments. A single element is passed by including the array name followed by the index of the element in parentheses.

An array's structure can be thought of as a set of storage boxes where the name of each box (the index) indicates the data stored in that box. Many algorithms make use of this aspect of an array's structure to simplify storage.

A simple algorithm for searching an array is called linear search, which proceeds from one array element to the next until the specified value is found or until the entire array has been searched.

A dynamic array varies in size during run time and is used in situations where the size of an array is unknown at the start of a program or when it would be more efficient to vary the size of an array throughout program execution. An array declared with a size of –1 contains 0 elements. A **ReDim** statement changes the size of an existing array. A **ReDim Preserve** statement changes the size of an array and leaves existing values.

A two-dimensional array is often used to represent data that relates to a grid and is declared using a **Dim** statement that includes the array name followed by the size of each dimension separated by commas in parentheses and then the data type of the elements. Nested **For…Next** loops are used to access the elements of a two-dimensional array. Elements of a two-dimensional array are accessed using both the row and column indexes. The Rank and GetLength members of the **Array** class are often used with two-dimensional arrays.

A structure is a composite data type grouping related variables that can be of different types. Structures must be declared outside of any procedures and are usually placed at the beginning of a program with other global declarations. Variables declared using a structure should have the prefix stc for good programming style. Structure members are accessed using a dot between the structure variable name and the member name. An array of structures can be used to store related information for a group of elements.

An enumerated type is a data type that defines a related set of named constants. Enumerated types are used to declare variables that should store a value from a limited set of values. Enumerated types must be declared outside of any procedures and are usually placed at the beginning of a program with other global declarations. The members of an enumerated type can be assigned specific constant values.

Vocabulary

Array A composite data type consisting of a set of elements that are all the same data type.

Composite data type A data type that is made up of a collection of elements.

Dynamic array An array that varies in size during run time.

Enumerated type A data type that defines a related set of named constants.

Index The number used to identify an array element.

Linear search A simple algorithm for searching an array for a specific value.

Structure A composite data type that groups related variables that can be of different data types.

Visual Basic .NET

() Parentheses are used to enclose an index that refers to an array element.

{} Brackets are used to enclose initial array element values.

Array class Used to manipulate array elements. Properties include GetLength, Length, and Rank.

End Structure Statement used to end a structure data type.

Enum Statement used to declare an enumerated data type.

Preserve Keyword used in a ReDim statement to keep the existing values of an array when it is sized.

ReDim Statement used to change the size of an array at run time.

Structure Statement used to declare a structure data type.

1. Write declarations for an array storing 15 test grades (integer values), an array storing 100 prices (decimal values), and an array storing 50 true/false test answers (Boolean values).

2. a) What is the purpose of using a **ReDim** statement?
   b) What happens if the keyword **Preserve** does not follow **ReDim**?

3. What are the similarities and differences between **Structure** declarations and **Enumerated** type declarations?

4. a) Why is it <u>not</u> possible to create a two-dimensional array that stores movie titles in its first dimension and gross money earned in its second dimension?
   b) Write a declaration for a structure named MovieInfo that stores a movie title and a gross money earned amount.
   c) Where must the structure in part (b) be declared in a program?
   d) Using the structure declared in part (b), write a declaration for an array named TopActionMovies that stores information for 50 movies.
   e) Write an assignment statement for the first element of the TopActionMovies array declared in part (d) so that *Star Wars* which grossed $460,395,655 is stored.

5. Write an array declaration for:
   a) decPrices() which initially stores 1.50, 2.25, 3.15, 4.30.
   b) strNames() which initially contains no elements.
   c) intScores() which has 30 rows and 5 columns.

6. The array intValues can be visualized as:

   ```
   4   6   2   0
   10  9   1   12
   ```

   a) What will intValues.Length return?
   b) What will intValues.Rank return?
   c) What will intValues.GetLength(0) return?
   d) What will intValues.GetLength(1) return?
   e) What is stored at intValues(2, 2)?
   f) What is stored at intValues(1, 2)?
   g) What will lstOutput display after the following code segment executes:

   ```
   For intI = 0 To 3
      For intJ = 0 To 1
         Me.lstOutput.Items.Add(intValues(intJ, intI))
      Next intJ
   Next intI
   ```

7. For each of the following, determine the error(s):

a) 'procedure header which accepts an array declared as (2, 3) for an argument
```
Sub GetName(ByRef strNames(2, 3) As String)
```

b) `Dim decCost(7) As Decimal`   'an array with 7 items

c) 'The winner is the last element in an array that holds 20 names
```
Me.lblOutput.Text = "The winner is " & strName(20)
```

d) 'nested for-next loop to output a 2-dimenstional array
```
For intRow = 0 To intArray.GetLength(1)
    For intCol = 0 To intArray.GetLength(2)
        Me.lblArray.Text = Me.lblArray.Text & intArray(intRow, intCol) & "  "
    Next intCol
    Me.lblArray.Text = Me.lblArray.Text & vbCrLf
Next intRow
```

e)
```
Private Sub btnPlay_Click(ByVal sender As System.Object, ByVal e As System.EventArgs) _
Handles btnPlay.Click

    Enum Card
        Ace = 1
        Duece = 2
        King = "Highest Value"
    End Enum
    Card.Ace = 14
    Dim MyDeck As Card
    MyDeck = Card.Ace
        …

End Sub
```

f) 'uses a month array and a day array
'FindNumDays() uses a liner search to return number of days
```
Dim strMonth() As String = {"January", "February", "March", "April", "May", "June", "July", _
"August", "September", "October", "November", "December"}
Dim intDays() As Integer = {31, 28, 31, 30, 31, 30, 31, 31, 30, 31, 30, 31}
Dim strInputMonth As String = InputBox("Enter name of month to see how many days it has.")
If strInputMonth <> Nothing Then
    Dim intDaysResult As Integer = FindNumDays(strInputMonth, strMonth, intDays)
    If intDaysResult = 0 Then
        MessageBox.Show("Input was not a proper month.")
    Else
        MessageBox.Show(strInputMonth & " has " & intDaysResult & " days.")
    End If
Else
    MessageBox.Show("Need to enter name of month.")
End If

Function FindNumDays(ByVal strInput As String, ByRef strString As String, _
ByRef intNum As Integer)
    Dim intI As Integer
    For intI = 0 To strString.Length – 1
        If strInput.ToUpper = strString(intI) Then
            Return intNum
        End If
    Next intI
End Function
```

An Introduction to Programming Using Microsoft Visual Basic .NET

8. a) Show the contents of lstOutput after the following statements execute:

```
Dim intValues() As Integer = {2, 4, 6, 8}
ReDim Preserve intValues(6)
Dim intI As Integer
For intI = 6 To 0 Step –1
    Me.lstOutput.Items.Add(intValues(intI))
Next intI
```

   b) Is intValues() in part (a) an example of a dynamic array or a nondynamic array?

9. Show the contents of the intGrid array after the following statements execute:

```
Dim intGrid(3, 2) As Integer
Dim intValue, intI, intJ As Integer
For intI = 0 To 3
    For intJ = 0 To 2
        intValue = intI + intJ
        intGrid(intI, intJ) = intValue
    Next intJ
Next intI
```

10. Write an event handler procedure for the following interface:

   The Tag properties of the buttons are assigned the same values as the Text properties of the buttons. The procedure responds to the clicking of the buttons and uses array intTotalTimesSelected() to keep track of the number of times each button has been clicked. Use meaningful array indexes. For example, if the 3 button has been clicked 5 times then the value of intTotalTimesSelected(3) will be 5.

11. a) Write a function RowSum() that returns the sum of the values in the elements of a specific row for a two-dimensional array. The header is:

   Function RowSum(**ByRef** intArray(,) **As Integer, ByVal** intRow **As Integer**) **As Integer**

   b) Write a function ColSum() that returns the sum of the values in the elements of a specific column for a two-dimensional array. The header is:

   Function ColSum(**ByRef** intArray(,) **As Integer, ByVal** intCol **As Integer**) **As Integer**

   c) Write a decision structure that calls RowSum() in part (a) only if the value of the row number is valid. If the row number is not valid, a message box with an appropriate message is displayed.

12. Use the following code to answer the questions below:

```
Enum AnimalType
    Bird
    Cat
    Dog
    Fish
End Enum

Structure PetType
    Dim Name As String
    Dim Animal As AnimalType
End Structure

Dim Pets(9) As PetType
```

    a) What is the result of: Pets(2).Animal = AnimalType.Dog

    b) What integer value does Fish correlate to?

    c) What will the following code display:

```
Dim MyPet As AnimalType
For MyPet As AnimalType.Bird To AnimalType.Fish
    MessageBox.Show(MyPet)
Next MyPet
```

13. Assume an interface has seven Label objects. Write statements that create an array of the Label objects and then sets each to a random number between 1 and 7.

14. Determine if each of the following is true or false. If false, explain why.

    a) The length of a one-dimensional array is one more than the index of the last element.

    b) An array declaration must have a number in the parentheses.

    c) "Index was outside the bounds of the array" is a syntax error message that is displayed when an invalid index is used.

    d) An array being passed in a **Call** statement must have its size indicated in parantheses.

    e) An array used as a parameter must have its size in parentheses.

    f) Arrays must be passed into procedures by reference.

    g) A dynamic array is an array that has been assigned values in its declaration statement.

    h) **ReDim** reinitializes all the elements in an array to **Nothing**.

    i) In a dimension statement, the size of an array must be a positive number.

    j) All columns in a two-dimensional array must be of the same type.

    k) Structures can have members of different types.

    l) To pass a structure requires that each individual member be listed.

    m) A linear search looks at one element after another until the desired element is found or the entire array has been searched.

    n) A structure can be declared in the procedure that uses it.

    o) The **Preserve** keyword is used when the programmer wants to make sure the array size is not changed.

    p) An enumerated type cannot be defined in the procedure that uses it.

    q) The first member declared in an enumerated type has a default value of 0 (zero).

    r) An array can contain elements from the application interface that are all the same control class type.

Exercise 1 ⟳ ————————————————————————— Student Names

Modify the Student Names application created in Review 1 so that the names are displayed in the list box in the reverse order in which they were entered.

Exercise 2 ————————————————————— Max and Min Numbers

Create a Max and Min Numbers application that generates an array of 10 random numbers between 1 and 99 and then displays the array elements in a list box when Numbers is clicked. The application should display the highest number in the array when Max is clicked and the lowest number in the array when Min is clicked. The application interface should look similar to:

Exercise 3 ———————————————————————— Generated Numbers

Create a Generated Numbers application that stores in an array with indexes 1 through 100 numbers generated by the index values when Generate is clicked. Generate the number to be stored at each index by summing the index and its individual digits. For example, 25 should be stored at index 17 because 17 + 1 + 7 = 25 and 4 should be stored at index 2 because 2 + 0 + 2. The application interface should look similar to:

Your program code should use a FillArray() procedure to generate the numbers and a DisplayArray() procedure that displays each index and its element in the list box.

Exercise 4 ✿ ─────────────────────────────── Word Guess

Modify the Word Guess Case Study from Chapter 6 to keep track of the letters guessed in an array with meaningful indexes. Include in the modifications code that displays a message box if the user enters the same guess twice.

Exercise 5 ─────────────────────────────── Dynamic Numbers

a) Create a Dynamic Numbers application that prompts the user for an array size and then loads the array with random numbers between 1 and 99 and displays the index and contents of each array element in a list box when **Create Array** is clicked. The application interface should look similar to:

b) *Advanced.* An array is said to be sorted if its elements are in either increasing or decreasing order. One way the selection sort algorithm works is by repeatedly taking the lowest item from an array and adding it to a new array, so that all the elements in the new array are sorted from low to high. Modify the Dynamic Numbers application so that it also displays the array sorted from low to high in the list box. Your program code should use:

- FindLowest() function that returns the index of the lowest value in the array.

- Sort() procedure that repeatedly finds the lowest value in an array A, removes it, and adds it to an array T. When all the values of A have been moved, the elements of T are copied to A with an assignment statement and a loop. Use the FindLowest() function and refer to the AddItem() and RemoveItem() procedures from the text.

Exercise 6 ——————————————— Matching Index and Element

Create a Matching Index and Element application that prompts the user with an input box for an array size and then randomly fills each element of the array with a number that is in the range of 0 to one less the length of the array and displays the array elements in a list box. Have the application count the indexes of the array that match its corresponding element value. For example, if the random number generated is 2 and stored in index 2, then update the count. The application interface should look similar to the following, after clicking Generate/Match and entering 10 in the input box:

Exercise 7 ———————————————Even and Odd Numbers

Create an Even and Odd Numbers application that generates an array of 10 random numbers between 1 and 99 and displays in a list box the index and array value of each element, the even number array values, and the odd number array values when Generate is clicked. The application interface should look similar to:

Your program code should use:

- FillArray() procedure to generate and store the random numbers in the array.
- DisplayArray() procedure that displays the index and its element in the list box.
- EvenNumbers() procedure that adds the even numbers to the list box.
- OddNumbers() procedure that adds the odd numbers to the list box.

Exercise 8 ——————————————————— Duplicate Values

Create a Duplicate Values application that prompts the user with input boxes for numbers between 1 and 99 until a duplicate value is entered. When a duplicate value is entered, the numbers entered before the duplicate value are displayed in a list box and a message in a label displays how many numbers where entered. The application interface should look similar to the following after the user has clicked Input Numbers and entered 67, 87, 90, and 67 in input boxes:

Exercise 9 ⟳ ————————————————————— Mastermind

Modify the Mastermind application from Chapter 7 Exercise 13 to use arrays with the following features:

- Permit the number of pegs (from 1 to 10) to be specified at the start of the application.

- Permit the number of colors (from 1 to 9) to be specified at the start of the program.

- Permit both the guess and the secret code to contain duplicates. This will require extra care when counting the number of pegs of the correct color. For example, if the secret code is 1, 2, 3, 4, 5 and the guess is 2, 1, 1, 2, 2 then the program should only report two correct colors (a single 1 and a single 2).

Exercise 10 ——————————————————————— Lockers

Create a Lockers application that simulates a progressive cycle of closing and opening every nth locker in a hall of 100 lockers, with n starting at the 2nd locker and continuing through to the 100th locker. The application should represent the locker status (opened or closed) as a Boolean array with True representing opened. When the application first starts, all of the lockers should be open and their status displayed in a list box when Initialize is clicked. When the user clicks Simulate, the status of every 2nd locker should be switched (if it is open then close it and if it is closed, open it). Then, the status of every 3rd locker should be switched. Continue this process for every 4th through the 100th locker. Display the concluding locker statuses in a list box. The application interface should look similar to that shown on the next page after clicking Initialize and then Simulate:

An Introduction to Programming Using Microsoft Visual Basic .NET

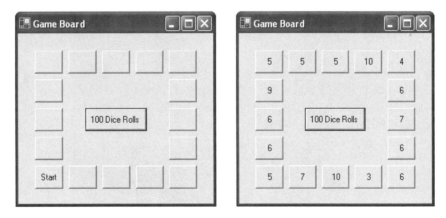

Can you identify what pattern the open lockers represent in the concluding array?

Exercise 11 ——————————————————— Game Board

a) Create a Game Board application that represents a game board with 16 spots. Use buttons to represent the 16 spots. The application should simulate 100 dice rolls when the user clicks **100 Dice Rolls** and store in an array with meaningful indexes the total number of times each spot was landed on based on the dice roll (moving around the board clockwise from the Start location). The total count should be displayed on each button. The application interface should look similar to the following after clicking **100 Dice Rolls**:

b) *Advanced.* Modify the application so that spot 13 is a "Go Back" location. If spot 13 is landed on, count it as being landed on but go back to spot 5, count it as being landed on and continue from spot 5. Also, if doubles are consecutively rolled then go back to spot 5.

Exercise 12 ——————————————————————————— Golf Game

a) Create a Golf Game application that uses a two-dimensional array representing 4 golfers playing 9 holes of golf (4 x 9 array) to store 36 randomly generated golf scores (integer values 1 through 9) and displays the contents of the array in a list box when Play Golf! is clicked. The golfer with the lowest number of strokes on a hole wins that hole. Display how many holes each player won overall. The application interface should look similar to:

	Hole 1	Hole 2	Hole 3	Hole 4	Hole 5	Hole 6	Hole 7	Hole 8	Hole 9
Player 1	1	4	4	3	3	9	5	5	7
Player 2	6	4	2	3	7	3	3	4	8
Player 3	2	2	4	1	9	9	3	8	8
Player 4	7	5	6	8	3	1	2	3	1

Player 1 Won: Hole 1 Hole 5

Player 2 Won: Hole 3

Player 3 Won: Hole 2 Hole 4

Player 4 Won: Hole 6 Hole 7 Hole 8 Hole 9

b) *Advanced*. Modify the Golf Game application to include an option that prompts the user for the golf scores.

Exercise 13 ——————————————————————————— Hidden Prizes

Create a Hidden Prizes application that uses buttons to represent a 5 x 5 board. The user is allowed five guesses to find the two randomly selected buttons that contain the text Comp and uter that are "hidden" when Hide the Prizes! is clicked. If the user finds both of the hidden words "You're a winner!" is displayed in a message box, otherwise "You lose." is displayed and the the text Comp and uter are shown. The application interface should look similar to:

The game of Life was devised by a mathematician as a model of a very simple world. The Life world is a grid of cells, a 10 x 10 grid in this case. Each cell may be empty or contain a single creature. Each day, creatures are born or die in each cell according to the number of neighboring creatures on the previous day. A neighbor is a cell that adjoins the cell either horizontally, vertically, or diagonally. The rules are:

- If the cell is alive on the previous day then
  if the number of neighbors was 2 or 3 the cell remains alive
  else the cell dies (of either loneliness or overcrowding)
- If the cell is not alive on the previous day then
  if the number of neighbors was exactly 3 the cell becomes alive
  else it remains dead

Start Game initializes the world by randomly generating 20 cells and displaying them on a grid:

Next Generation displays a new generation each time it is clicked:

Next Generation can be clicked until there are no more live cells. Clicking New Life displays a new Life world.

The Penny Pitch game is popular in amusement parks. Pennies are tossed onto a board that has certain areas marked with different prizes. For example, clicking New Game randomly marks a 5 x 5 board of 25 buttons with prizes of puzzle, game, ball, poster, and doll:

Poster		Ball	Puzzle	
Game	Puzzle	Game		Doll
	Ball		Doll	Ball
Poster	Game	Poster	Doll	Puzzle

Each prize appears on 3 randomly chosen squares so that 15 squares contain prizes. Clicking Toss Pennies simulates ten pennies being randomly pitched onto the board. Each penny is represented by an "x" character on a square. If all of the squares that say Ball in them are covered by a penny, the player wins a ball. This is also true for the other prizes. Clicking Toss Pennies shows where the ten pennies landed and displays a list of the prizes won or "No prizes.":

Poster	x	Ball	Puzzle	x
Game	Puzzle x	Game x	x	Doll x x
	Ball		Doll	Ball
x	x			
Poster	Game x	Poster	Doll	Puzzle

No prizes.

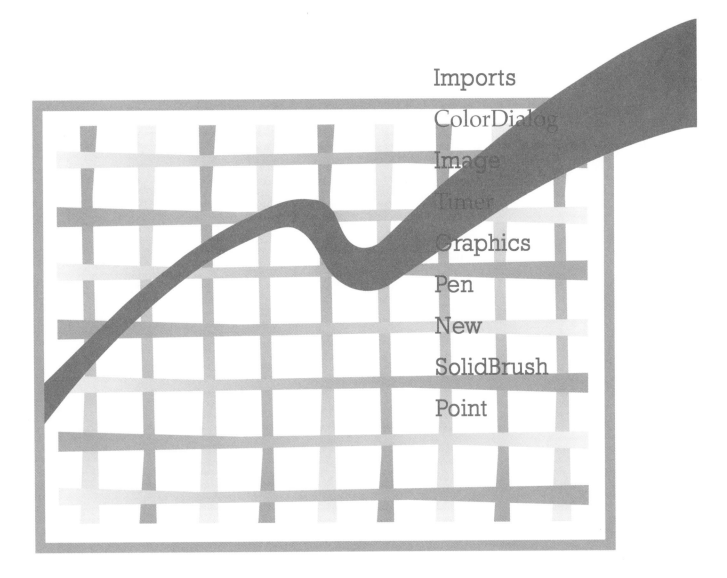

Imports

ColorDialog

Image

Timer

Graphics

Pen

New

SolidBrush

Point

Chapter 10 Expectations

After completing this chapter you will be able to:

1. Control the background and foreground color of control objects.

2. Include a Color dialog box in an application.

3. Display an image on a control object.

4. Create images using Image Editor.

5. Understand image file formats.

6. Use a Timer control to create animation.

7. Use the **Graphics** class and its properties and methods.

8. Use **Pen, SolidBrush,** and **Point** objects.

9. Create an event procedure that responds to a mouse event.

Colors and graphics are used to make applications easier to use and more interesting. In this chapter, the Visual Basic .NET **Graphics** class is introduced. The Timer control for creating simple animation in an application is also introduced. The Visual Basic .NET Image Editor for creating graphics is explained.

10.1 Using Color

Color can be used to enhance an application's interface. For example, buttons can be Lime (a green color) and a form can be Plum (a purple color). Visual Basic .NET provides more than 100 defined colors to choose from, as well as a palette of system colors. When setting colors in the Design window, a tabbed list is provided. The Web colors provide the most choices:

Inheritance

A child control "inherits" properties and other features from a parent control. Inheritance is an important object-oriented concept that means a new class can be created from an existing class and then the new class can be extended or customized. Inheritance allows for code reusability.

---

changing color in the Design window

Control objects have BackColor and ForeColor properties that can be set from the Properties window:

- **BackColor** is the background color of an object, which refers to the object area not including any text. Clicking the arrow in the property displays a list of colors to choose from.

- **ForeColor** is the color of the text displayed on an object. Clicking the arrow in the property displays a list of colors to choose from.

transparent

Web colors include Transparent. Objects on a form can be set to this "color" so that the form BackColor shows through the object.

Controls, including Button, CheckBox, and Label, are derived from the Form control. Form is said to be the *parent* control and the other controls are said to be *child* controls. When a parent control property value is changed, the corresponding child property value is also changed unless the child property is explicitly set. For example, changing the BackColor of a form means that the background color of objects on the form will also be changed to that color. New objects will inherit the form BackColor. To have objects with a background color different from the form's, the BackColor property must be individually set.

changing color at run time
Imports System.Drawing

BackColor and ForeColor can be changed at run time in assignment statements. An **Imports** System.Drawing statement must be included at the top of a program in that uses the Visual Basic .NET color constants:

Imports System.Drawing

other code ...

Me.btnDisplay.BackColor = Color.Honeydew   'button color
Me.BackColor = Color.Lime   'form color

A list of color constants is displayed in an AutoList when Color. is typed in the Code window.

Review 1

Create a Change Background Color application that changes the background color of the form only to the color indicated on the clicked button. The form should initially be white. The buttons should be a blue with white text. The application interface should look similar to that shown on the right.

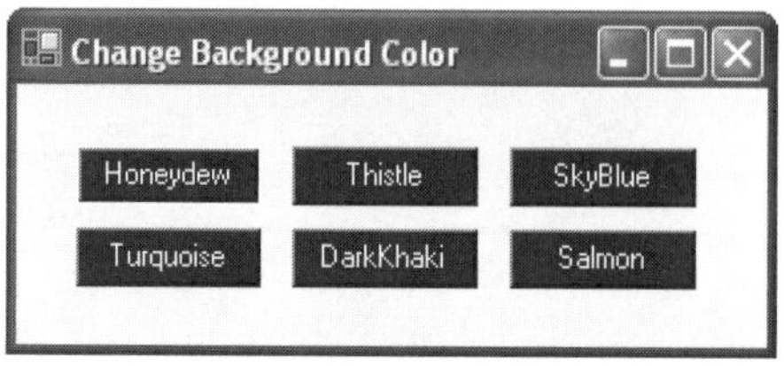

10.2   The ColorDialog Control

The Color dialog box is a predefined dialog box that has many colors for the user to choose from:

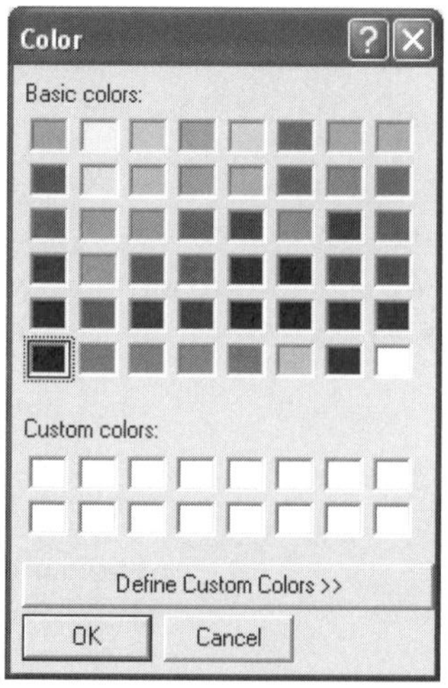

When this dialog box is displayed, the color clicked by the user can be assigned to the BackColor or ForeColor of an object.

To add a Color dialog box to an application, click the ColorDialog control in the Toolbox, and then click the form. A component is displayed in the component tray at the bottom of the Design window. The ColorDialog control is a component that has no graphical element.

ColorDialog

The ColorDialog control has the properties:

- **Name** identifies an object for the programmer. It is good programming style to begin ColorDialog component names with clr.

- **Color** is the color selected in the dialog box.

- **AllowFullOpen** is set to True to allow the user to create a custom color or False to allow the user to select only from the colors displayed.

An application that contains this component displays the dialog box with a statement similar to:

ColorDialog1.ShowDialog()

ShowDialog()   *ColorDialog1* is the name of the component added to the interface. ShowDialog() is the method of the ColorDialog class that displays the dialog box.

The Color property of a ColorDialog component contains the color selected by the user. For example, the first statement below displays a Color dialog box. The application waits until the user makes a selection before continuing to the next statement. The second statement sets the form background color to that selected by the user:

```
Me.clrChangeBackColor.ShowDialog()              'show dialog box
Me.BackColor = Me.clrChangeBackColor.Color      'set form color
```

Cancel   If the user selects Cancel in the Color dialog box, the default color in the Color dialog box is returned. The first time a Color dialog box is displayed in an application, the default color is black. The Color dialog box defaults to the last selected color after it is first displayed.

Review 2

Modify the Change Background Color application created in Review 1 to include a Choose Color button that displays a Color dialog box and then changes the background color to that selected in the dialog box. The interface should look similar to that shown on the right.

10.3 Using Images

There are different ways to include images in an application. A picture box, as discussed in Chapter 7, can be used to display an image in a box on the form. Objects can also include a background image. For example, a form can have an image displayed behind its objects:

tiled
Transparent

Note that an image is *tiled* on a form, which means that it is repeated to fill the form. Objects on the form can be set to a BackColor of Transparent to better show the tiled form image. The BackColor of the label in the Message application has been set to transparent.

BackgroundImage

Most control objects have a BackgroundImage property that can be set in the Properties window:

- **BackgroundImage** contains the **...** button that is clicked to display the Open dialog box where an image file can be selected. Image files can be BMP, JPG, GIF, PNG, ICO, EMF, and WMF formats. Right-clicking this property and then selecting Reset clears the current image.

The Label control does not have a BackgroundImage property.

Image property

The Image property is available with the Button and Label controls. Setting this property places a single image that is not tiled as the background of a button or label:

- **Image** contains the **...** button that is clicked to display the Open dialog box where an image file can be selected. Image files can be BMP, JPG, GIF, PNG, ICO, EMF, and WMF formats. Right-clicking Image and then selecting Reset clears the picture box.

changing images at run time

To change an image at run time, use the **Image** class in a statement similar to:

```
Me.btnFace.Image = Image.FromFile("happyface.bmp")      'button image
Me.BackgroundImage = Image.FromFile("happyface.bmp")  'form image
```

FromFile()

The FromFile() method in the **Image** class creates an image object from a specified file.

Create a Change Image application that changes the background of a form to the image shown on the clicked button. The form should initially be the default color with no image. The buttons should be LightGreen with a single image and not contain any text. Use the heart.bmp, happyface.bmp, star.bmp, and clock.bmp files that are data files for this text. The application interface should look similar to that shown on the right after the clicking the star button.

10.4   Image Editor

bitmap image

Visual Basic .NET includes Image Editor for customizing and creating bitmap images for use in applications. A *bitmap image* consists of a grid of bits. In the Image editor, each bit can be one of 16 colors. To create a new image, select File from the New submenu in the File menu. The New File dialog box is displayed. Click the Bitmap File icon and then Open. A new bitmap image file is displayed in the Design window:

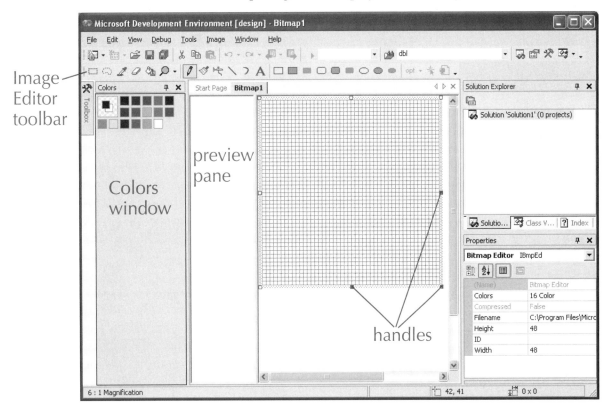

- The IDE displays a **Image Editor toolbar** with buttons to add different colors, shapes, and effects to an image.

- The **Colors window** displayed in the IDE contains colors that can be selected as bit colors.

- The Design window includes a **preview pane** that displays the image sized as it will actually appear.

- The Design window also shows a grid with three filled **handles**. Drag a handle to increase or decrease the number of bits.

- The **Properties window** includes Height and Width properties that can be set to a specific number of bits.

The default file format for a new Image Editor file is the bitmap format. File names of bitmap images (BMP) have the file extension .bmp. However, an image can be saved as a GIF or JPG image file. Select Save As from the File menu to display the Save File As dialog box. In the Save as type list, select the appropriate file type. Images used in an application should be copied to the bin folder located in the project folder.

closing an image

To close an image, select Close from the File menu. The image and its window are closed.

10.5 The Image Editor Toolbar

The Image Editor toolbar provides tools for coloring bits to form the shapes of a graphic:

freehand drawing tools   shape tools   Style Settings

Rectangle Selection Tool   Erase Tool   Text Tool

- The **Rectangle Selection Tool** is for selecting bits. Drag across the grid to select bits and then drag the selected bits to a new position on the grid.

- The **Erase Tool** is for removing color from bits. Drag across the grid to remove color from the bits under the tool.

- The **Pencil Tool**, **Brush Tool**, and **Airbrush Tool** are for freehand drawing. Drag across the grid to fill the bits under the tool icon with the selected color. The number of bits filled at a time depends on the tool selected and the style settings.

- The **Line Tool** adds a line. Drag from one bit to another.

- The **Curve Tool** adds a curved line. Drag from one bit to another and then move the mouse pointer to form a curve. When the curve is formed, double-click to shape the curve.

- The **Text Tool** displays a dialog box where the text to show is typed. The text can be moved as an object as long as the dialog box is displayed.

- The **Rectangle** and **Ellipse Tools** create filled or outlined shapes. Drag from one bit to another to create a shape.

- The **Style Settings** button is clicked to display width, size, or shape options. The options depend on the tool selected.

The color selected in the Colors window is what is used by a selected tool.

In this review you will create an image and then add it to Change Image created in Review 3.

① CREATE A NEW IMAGE FILE

Select File → New → File. A dialog box is displayed. Select the Bitmap File icon and then Open. A window is displayed with a new bitmap file. The grid currently displays no colors.

② USE THE IMAGE EDITOR TOOLBAR

a. Place the mouse pointer over each of the buttons in the Image Editor toolbar and note the names of the tools that appear.

b. Click a tool and then choose a style setting by clicking the arrow in the Style Settings button, if the Style Settings button is available.

c. Experiment with the selected tool by dragging on the grid. Select Edit → Undo if you want to remove the drawing.

d. Experiment with other tools.

e. Close the image without saving it.

③ CREATE AND SAVE AN IMAGE

a. Create a new image. In the Properties window, change the Height and Width to 48, if they are not already that size. Use the Ellipse Tool and the Line Tool on the Image Editor toolbar to create a fish image similar to:

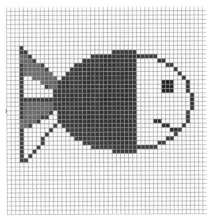

b. Save the image in the bin folder of the Change Image project folder as a bitmap naming it fish.

c. Select File → Close. The image is closed.

④ USE THE IMAGE IN AN APPLICATION

a. Open the Change Image project created in Review 3.

b. Add a new button named btnFish to the application interface. Set the Image property of the button to display fish.bmp. Set the Text property so that no text is displayed.

c. Add code so that Fish.bmp is displayed as the form background when the fish button is clicked.

d. Run and test the modified application.

⑤ PRINT THE CODE AND THEN CLOSE THE PROJECT

10.6 The Timer Control

Applications often perform actions at regular intervals. For example, a game application might display a "Time's up!" message if the user hasn't answered a question in 10 seconds.

A timer object is used to execute code at specified intervals. To add a timer to an application, click the Timer control in the Toolbox, and then click the form. A component is displayed in the component tray at the bottom of the Design window. The Timer control is a component that has no graphical element.

Timer

The Timer control has the properties:

- **Name** identifies a control for the programmer. It is good programming style to begin Timer object names with tmr.

- **Interval** is the amount of time that passes before the Tick event procedure is executed. Interval is specified in milliseconds between 0 and 64,767 where 1,000 milliseconds equals 1 second.

- **Enabled** is set to True to allow a Tick event to occur at the end of each interval. Setting Enabled to False stops Tick events from occurring. Note that Enabled is set to False by default.

Tick event

A Tick event procedure is coded for each timer object added to an application. A Tick event occurs after the time specified in the Interval property elapses. For example, if a timer is enabled and its Interval property is set to 1000, then a Tick event occurs every second (1000 milliseconds). After the Tick event procedure executes, timing automatically starts over again.

The following Tick event procedure switches the ForeColor of a button back and forth from HotPink to Chocolate every second when Enabled is True and Interval of tmrColorChange is set to 1000:

```
Private Sub tmrColorChange_Tick(ByVal sender As Object, _
ByVal e As System.EventArgs) Handles tmrColorChange.Tick

    Static blnSwitch As Boolean = True
    If blnSwitch Then
        Me.btnCheck.ForeColor = Color.HotPink
        blnSwitch = False
    Else
        Me.btnCheck.ForeColor = Color.Chocolate
        blnSwitch = True
    End If

End Sub
```

Start() and Stop() methods

The Timer control also has two methods available:

- **Start()** starts a timer and can be used instead of the Enabled property. This method is used in a statement that takes the form *Timer*.Start().

- **Stop()** stops a timer. This method is used in a statement that takes the form *Timer*.Stop().

These methods can be used from any procedure in the application.

Review 5

Create a Blinky application that cycles through three background form colors that change every 2 seconds. The Go button should switch between two green colors every 1 second and the Stop button should switch between two red colors every 1 second. Clicking Go starts the timer and Stop stops the timer. The application interface should look similar to that shown on the right.

10.7   Animation

Animation can be added to an application with a timer and a set of images. Similar images displayed quickly one after the other in a picture box gives the impression of continuous motion. For example, the Skate! application changes the image of a picture box every 180 milliseconds using a set of six similar images. The images appear so quickly that a skater appears to skate down a hill. The Skate! images are:

The Skate! interface has a PictureBox control and a Timer control. A Tick event procedure is used to animate the images:

```
Private Sub tmrChangeImage_Tick(ByVal sender As Object, _
ByVal e As System.EventArgs) Handles tmrChangeImage.Tick

    Const intMAXIMAGES As Integer = 6
    Dim strImageArray(intMAXIMAGES - 1) As String
    'store image file names in array
    strImageArray(0) = "skateboard1.bmp"
    strImageArray(1) = "skateboard2.bmp"
    strImageArray(2) = "skateboard3.bmp"
    strImageArray(3) = "skateboard4.bmp"
    strImageArray(4) = "skateboard5.bmp"
    strImageArray(5) = "skateboard6.bmp"

    'display an image from array
    Static intImage As Integer = 0

    Me.picImage.Image = Image.FromFile(strImageArray(intImage))
    'determine next image number
    intImage = (intImage + 1) Mod intMAXIMAGES

End Sub
```

Review 6

In this review you will create the Bouncing Ball application, which repeatedly shows a ball that falls from the top of the form to the bottom and then bounces back to the top. The algorithm for Bouncing Ball is:

1. Show ball images, one at a time, that progress from the top of the form to the bottom.

2. Show ball images, one at a time, that progress from the bottom of the form to the top.

3. Repeat Step 1.

4. Repeat Step 2.

The same set of images can be used for the balls falling to the bottom of the form as for the balls bouncing up to the top of the form. A counter variable can be used to determine which ball position to show. The counter will increment by 1 for balls falling down and decrement by 1 for balls bouncing up. With this in mind, the Bouncing Ball algorithm can be refined into the following pseudocode:

```
Sub tmrAnimateBall_Tick()
    strPicArray() with elements containing file names of the balls at each position
    Static intNewPosition As Integer
    Static intStep
    BallImage=strPicArray(intNewPosition)
    Select Case intNewPosition
        Case 0
            intStep = 1
        Case LastImage
            intStep = -1
    End Case
    intNewPosition = intNewPosition + intStep
End Sub
```

① CREATE IMAGES

Create a set of bitmap (BMP) images that are each 12 by 48 pixels named ball0.bmp, ball1.bmp, ball2.bmp, ball3.bmp. The four image files should look similar to:

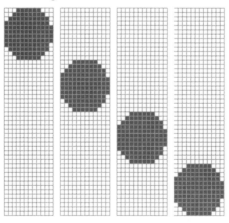

② CREATE A NEW PROJECT

Create a Windows application named Bouncing Ball.

③ CREATE THE INTERFACE

a. Refer to the form below to add, position, and size objects. Use the table below to set properties.

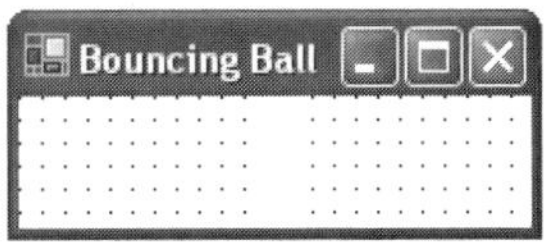

Bouncing Ball

Object	Name	Text	Size	BackColor
Form1		Bouncing Ball	160, 72	White
PictureBox1	picBall		12, 48	
Timer1	tmrAnimateBall			

Note the picture box object is in the middle of the form and extends exactly from the top to the bottom of the form.

b. Set the tmrAnimateBall Enabled property to True and the Interval property to 150.

④ WRITE THE APPLICATION CODE

a. Display the Code window.

b. Add comments that include your name and today's date.

c. Create a tmrAnimateBall_Tick event procedure and then add the statements:

```
Const intMAXIMAGES As Integer = 4
Dim strPicArray(intMAXIMAGES - 1) As String
Static intNewPosition As Integer = 0

'store image file names in array
strPicArray(0) = "ball0.bmp"
strPicArray(1) = "ball1.bmp"
strPicArray(2) = "ball2.bmp"
strPicArray(3) = "ball3.bmp"

'display an image from array
Me.picBall.Image = Image.FromFile(strPicArray(intNewPosition))

'determine next image number
Static intStep As Integer
Select Case intNewPosition
  Case 0
    intStep = 1
  Case intMAXIMAGES - 1
    intStep = -1
End Select
intNewPosition = intNewPosition + intStep
```

⑤ RUN THE APPLICATION

a. Save the modified Bouncing Ball project and then run the application.

b. Close the Bouncing Ball application.

⑥ PRINT THE CODE AND THEN CLOSE THE PROJECT

10.8   The Graphics Class

defining the drawing surface

Visual Basic .NET includes the **Graphics** class with methods for creating circles, lines, rectangles, and other shapes on a drawing surface. A drawing surface can be the surface of a form, the surface of a button, or the surface of almost any other object. The drawing surface is defined by assigning an object's surface to a **Graphics** object. The following statements create two **Graphics** objects:

```
Dim FormSurface As Graphics = Me.CreateGraphics          'form surface
Dim ButtonSurface As Graphics = Me.btnOn.CreateGraphics  'button surface
```

CreateGraphics control class method

The CreateGraphics method in the assignment statements is a control class method that encases a specific object surface area. This method is available with most control objects.

defining a drawing pen

Drawing on a surface requires a **Pen** object. The pen, pen color, and line thickness are all declared in the same statement, similar to:

```
Dim ThinAquaPen As New Pen(Color.Aqua, 2)
```

New

The keyword **New** declares a new object. A Visual Basic .NET color constant is used to define the pen color. In the Code window, these constants appear in an AutoList after typing Color followed by a dot. The color is followed by a comma and then a line thickness.

drawing on a surface

pixel

After defining a surface and a pen, **Graphics** class methods are used to draw onto the surface. A drawing surface can be thought of a grid consisting of a set of points with x values and y values. Each point is a *pixel* (picture element) and the number of pixels in a surface depends on the screen resolution. The point with coordinates (0, 0) is the pixel in the very upper-left corner of the drawing surface:

Screen Resolution

Screen resolution is expressed in pixels per inch also called dots per inch, or dpi. The DpiX and DpiY properties of a **Graphics** object return the screen resolution of the current display.

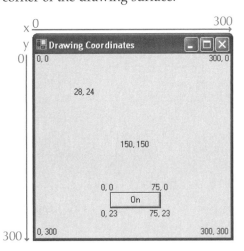

Size property

The Size property of an object stores both a height and width and can be used to determine the point in the lower-right of an object. The statements below assign the coordinates of the point in the lower-right of the On button and the coordinates of the point in the lower-right of the form to variables:

```
Dim intMaxX As Integer = Me.btnOn.Size.Width        '75
Dim intMaxY As Integer = Me.btnOn.Size.Height       '23
Dim intMaxFormX As Integer = Me.Size.Width          '300
Dim intMaxFormY As Integer = Me.Size.Height         '300
```

The **Graphics** class methods require a pen along with the shape position and size. Some of the methods are:

- **DrawLine(*pen, x1, y1, x2, y2*)** draws a line that extends from coordinates (*x1, y1*) on a **Graphics** object to coordinates (*x2, y2*).

- **DrawRectangle(*pen, x1, y1, width, height*)** draws a rectangle with the upper-left corner at coordinates (*x1, y1*) on a **Graphics** object and is *width* wide and *height* high.

- **DrawEllipse(*pen, x1, y1, width, height*)** draws an ellipse within a rectangular area that has its upper-left corner at coordinates (*x1, y1*) on a **Graphics** object and is *width* wide and *height* high.

- **DrawArc(*pen, x1, y1, width, height, startAngle, sweepAngle*)** draws an arc that starts at angle *startAngle* and continues clockwise *sweepAngle* degrees. The arc is within a rectangular area that has its upper-left corner at coordinates (*x1, y1*) on a **Graphics** object and is *width* wide and *height* high.

- **Clear(*color*)** clears the drawing surface with *color*, which can be a System.Drawing color constant or the current object color. For example, **Me**.BackColor uses the form color.

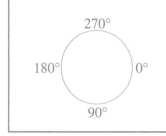

Drawing an Arc

An arc is part of an ellipse. A circle is an ellipse with the same width and height. The start angle and sweep angle of an arc can be determined with the diagram:

A Click event procedure in the Testing Graphics application demonstrates these methods:

```
Private Sub btnDrawHere_Click(ByVal sender As Object, _
ByVal e As System.EventArgs) Handles btnDrawHere.Click

    Dim ButtonSurface As Graphics = Me.btnDrawHere.CreateGraphics
    Dim OrangePen As New Pen(Color.OrangeRed, 5)
    Dim intMaxX As Integer = Me.btnDrawHere.Size.Width
    Dim intMaxY As Integer = Me.btnDrawHere.Size.Height
    ButtonSurface.DrawLine(OrangePen, 0, 0, intMaxX, intMaxY)
    ButtonSurface.DrawRectangle(OrangePen, 0, 0, intMaxX, intMaxY)

    Dim FormSurface As Graphics = Me.CreateGraphics
    Dim PurplePen As New Pen(Color.PaleVioletRed, 3)
    FormSurface.DrawRectangle(PurplePen, 0, 0, 200, 200)
    FormSurface.DrawEllipse(PurplePen, 0, 0, 200, 200)

    Dim DarkGreenPen As New Pen(Color.DarkGreen, 2)
    FormSurface.DrawArc(DarkGreenPen, 0, 0, 100, 100, 0, 180)
End Sub
```

Clicking Draw Here in the Testing Graphics application produces shapes with the **Graphics** class. Note how the shapes are relative to the drawing surface used:

GDI+

GDI+ is the graphics device interface for Windows XP that allows the programmer to use a set of classes to create shapes without having to be concerned about the specific details of the display device.

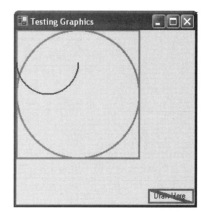

10.9 Pen Styles

DashStyle

The **Pen** class contains the DashStyle property for defining a pen style. Dashed lines, dotted lines, and dash-dot lines are a few examples of pen styles. An AutoList with Visual Basic .NET pen-style constants is displayed when setting the property:

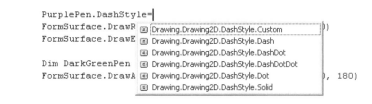

The Testing Graphics application uses the PurplePen **Pen** object with the DashStyle property set to DashDot:

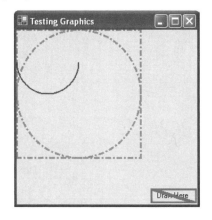

Review 7

In this review you will create the Draw Shapes application.

① *CREATE A NEW PROJECT*

Create a Windows application named Draw Shapes.

② *CREATE THE INTERFACE*

Refer to the form below to add and position a Button object. Use the table below to set properties.

Object	Name	Text	Size
Form1		Shapes	360, 245
Button1	btnDrawShapes	Draw Shapes	

③ WRITE THE APPLICATION CODE

    a. Display the Code window.

    b. Add comments that include your name and today's date.

    c. Create a btnDrawShapes_Click event procedure and then add the statements:

```
Dim FormSurface As Graphics = Me.CreateGraphics
FormSurface.Clear(Me.BackColor)

Dim intMaxX As Integer = Me.Size.Width
Dim intMaxY As Integer = Me.Size.Height

'draw thin LightSeaGreen horizontal line
Dim LightSeaGreenPen As New Pen(Color.LightSeaGreen, 2)
FormSurface.DrawLine(LightSeaGreenPen, 30, intMaxY \ 3, intMaxX - 30, intMaxY \ 3)

'draw thicker DeepPink circle (ellipse)
Dim ThickerDeepPinkPen As New Pen(Color.DeepPink, 10)
FormSurface.DrawEllipse(ThickerDeepPinkPen, intMaxX \ 2, intMaxY \ 2, 40, 40)

'draw thick DashDotDot DodgerBlue rectangle
Dim ThickDodgerBluePen As New Pen(Color.DodgerBlue, 5)
ThickDodgerBluePen.DashStyle = Drawing.Drawing2D.DashStyle.DashDotDot
FormSurface.DrawRectangle(ThickDodgerBluePen, 80, intMaxY \ 4, intMaxX \ 3, 70)

'draw thin Red arc
Dim ThinRedPen As New Pen(Color.Red, 3)
FormSurface.DrawArc(ThinRedPen, 30, 0, intMaxX - 60, intMaxY - 60, 0, 180)
```

④ RUN THE APPLICATION

    a. Save the modified Draw Shapes project and then run the application. Click **Draw Shapes**. The application interface looks similar to:

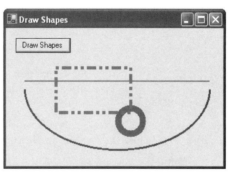

    b. Drag the lower-right corner of the form. Make the application interface smaller and then click **Draw Shapes**. The application interface looks similar to:

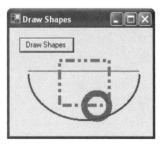

    The shapes are proportional to the drawing surface because the code statements use shape coordinates that are relative to the maximum X and Y coordinates of the drawing surface.

⑤ PRINT THE CODE AND THEN CLOSE THE PROJECT

10.10 Drawing Solid Shapes

SolidBrush
defining a drawing brush

The **Graphics** class also includes methods for creating solid shapes such as filled circles and solid rectangles. A **SolidBrush** object is needed to fill shapes. The following statement declares a **SolidBrush** object that draws in a purple color. Note that the line thickness is not indicated since the brush fills the shape:

Dim PurpleBrush **As New** SolidBrush(Color.BlueViolet)

The **Graphics** class methods that fill shapes require a brush along with the shape position and size. Some of these methods are:

* **FillRectangle(*brush, x1, y1, width, height*)** draws a solid rectangle with the upper-left corner at coordinates (*x1, y1*) on a **Graphics** object and is *width* wide and *height* high.

* **FillEllipse(*brush, x1, y1, width, height*)** draws a solid ellipse within a rectangular area that has its upper-left corner at coordinates (*x1, y1*) on a **Graphics** object and is *width* wide and *height* high.

* **FillPie(*brush, x1, y1, width, height, startAngle, sweepAngle*)** draws a filled pie shape that starts at angle *startAngle* and continues clockwise *sweepAngle* degrees. The pie shape is within a rectangular area that has its upper-left corner at coordinates (*x1, y1*) on a **Graphics** object and is *width* wide and *height* high.

A click event procedure in the Test Solid Graphics application demonstrates these methods:

```
Private Sub btnDraw_Click(ByVal sender As Object, _
ByVal e As System.EventArgs) Handles btnDraw.Click

    Dim FormSurface As Graphics = Me.CreateGraphics
    Dim PurpleBrush As New SolidBrush(Color.BlueViolet)
    FormSurface.FillPie(PurpleBrush, 0, 210, 50, 50, 0, 180)    'half circle

    Dim BeigeBrush As New SolidBrush(Color.Beige)
    FormSurface.FillRectangle(BeigeBrush, 0, 0, 200, 200)

    Dim GreenBrush As New SolidBrush(Color.GreenYellow)
    FormSurface.FillEllipse(GreenBrush, 0, 0, 200, 200)

End Sub
```

Running Test Solid Graphics shows solid shapes produced with the **Graphics** class:

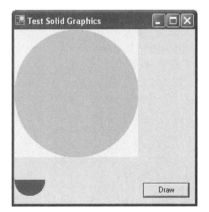

An Introduction to Programming Using Microsoft Visual Basic .NET

Create a Face application that displays a happy face when Happy is clicked and a sad face when Sad is clicked. Use a picture box and the FillRectangle, FillEllipse, and FillPie methods with different brush colors. The application interface should look similar to that shown on the right after clicking Happy.

10.11 The Point Structure

point   A *point* has an x-coordinate and a y-coordinate that together indicate a specific location. The **Point** structure has members X and Y. For example, the following three statements declare a point and set the X and Y values to 0:

```
Dim MinPoint As Point
MinPoint.X = 0
MinPoint.Y = 0
```

The X and Y values of a point can be included in the declaration when *New*   the keyword **New** is used, as in the statement:

```
Dim MinPoint As New Point(0, 0)
```

The DrawLine **Graphics** method is overloaded to accept **Point** variables in place of coordinates, as in the statements below:

```
Dim ButtonSurface As Graphics = Me.btnDrawHere.CreateGraphics
Dim OrangePen As New Pen(Color.OrangeRed, 5)

Dim MinPoint As New Point(0, 0)
Dim MaxPoint As New Point(Me.btnDrawHere.Size.Width, Me.btnDrawHere.Size.Height)

ButtonSurface.DrawLine(OrangePen, MinPoint, MaxPoint)
```

10.12 Drawing Curves and Polygons

The **Graphics** class also includes methods for creating polygons and curves on a drawing surface. The number of points that define a curve or polygon vary depending on the specific shape. Therefore, a set of points in an array is required by these methods:

* **DrawCurve(*pen, points*)** creates a curve on a **Graphics** object using the points in the *points* array.

* **DrawClosedCurve(*pen, points*)** creates a closed curve on a **Graphics** object using the points in the *points* array. The curve is automatically continued from the last point to the first point to close the curve.

- **FillClosedCurve(*brush, points*)** creates a filled, closed curve on a **Graphics** object using the points in the *points* array. The curve is automatically continued from the last point to the first to close the curve.

- **DrawPolygon(*pen, points*)** creates a closed polygon on a **Graphics** object using the points in the *points* array. A line is automatically created from the last point to the first to close the polygon.

- **FillPolygon(*brush, points*)** creates a filled, closed polygon on a **Graphics** object using the points in the *points* array. A line is automatically created from the last point to the first to close the polygon.

A click event procedure in the Test Curves and Polygons application demonstrates these methods. One set of points can be used because each shape is drawn on a separate surface. Note that the array elements are initialized with a set of point declarations:

```
Private Sub btnDraw_Click(ByVal sender As Object, ByVal e As System.EventArgs) _
Handles btnDraw.Click

    'Define drawing surfaces
    Dim DrawCurveLabel As Graphics = Me.lblDrawCurve.CreateGraphics
    Dim DrawClosedCurveLabel As Graphics = Me.lblDrawClosedCurve.CreateGraphics
    Dim FillClosedCurveLabel As Graphics = Me.lblFillClosedCurve.CreateGraphics
    Dim DrawPolygonLabel As Graphics = Me.lblDrawPolygon.CreateGraphics
    Dim FillPolygonLabel As Graphics = Me.lblFillPolygon.CreateGraphics

    'Define pen and brush
    Dim PurplePen As New Pen(Color.DarkMagenta, 1)
    Dim GreenBrush As New SolidBrush(Color.DarkGreen)

    'Define the points
    Dim CurvePoints() As Point = {New Point(10, 30), New Point(35, 35), _
    New Point(75, 80), New Point(120, 20)}

    'Draw shapes
    DrawCurveLabel.DrawCurve(PurplePen, CurvePoints)
    DrawClosedCurveLabel.DrawClosedCurve(PurplePen, CurvePoints)
    FillClosedCurveLabel.FillClosedCurve(GreenBrush, CurvePoints)
    DrawPolygonLabel.DrawPolygon(PurplePen, CurvePoints)
    FillPolygonLabel.FillPolygon(GreenBrush, CurvePoints)

End Sub
```

Running Test Curves and Polygons and clicking Draw shows curves and polygons produced with the **Graphics** class:

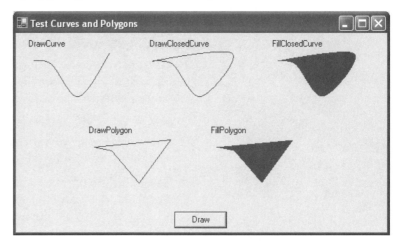

Create a Sailboat application. Clicking Draw displays a coral-colored sailboat with a black mast and white sails in medium blue waves on a light sky blue background. Use the DrawLine, FillRectangle, FillClosedCurve, DrawCurve, and FillPolygon methods. The application interface should look similar to that shown on the right after clicking Draw.

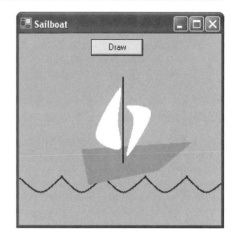

10.13 Handling Mouse Events

Event procedures can be coded for mouse events, similar to event procedures for objects on a form. Mouse events include MouseDown, which occurs when the user clicks the mouse on an application interface. By coding a MouseDown event, actions can be taken every time the user clicks an object.

Base Class Event

To add a MouseDown event procedure to the Code window, click the object name in the Class Name list and then in the Method Name list, select MouseDown. To add a MouseDown event that occurs when the user clicks the form, select Base Class Events in the Class Name list and then in the Method Name list, select MouseDown:

The MouseDown event procedure is added to the Code window with room for statements that will execute each time the user clicks the mouse on the form:

```
Private Sub Form1_MouseDown(ByVal sender As Object, _
ByVal e As System.Windows.Forms.MouseEventArgs) _
Handles MyBase.MouseDown

End Sub
```

In the procedure heading, the e parameter contains properties specific to the mouse click that raised the event. These properties store the values

X and Y properties

the x and y coordinates of the mouse click, and are accessed by typing e followed by a dot and then the property name (X or Y). The procedure below displays a message box with the mouse click coordinates:

```
Private Sub Form1_MouseDown(ByVal sender As Object, _
ByVal e As System.Windows.Forms.MouseEventArgs) _
Handles MyBase.MouseDown

    MessageBox.Show("X:" & e.X & "  Y:" & e.Y)

End Sub
```

Review 10

In this review you will create the Tracker application.

① *CREATE A NEW PROJECT*

Create a Windows application named Tracker.

② *CREATE THE INTERFACE*

The interface contains only a form. Set the Text property to Tracker:

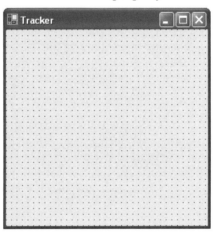

③ *WRITE THE APPLICATION CODE*

   a. Display the Code window.

   b. Add comments that include your name and today's date.

   c. Create a Form1_MouseDown event procedure and then add the statements:

```
Static PreviousPoint As Point      'remember the previous mouse click
Dim FormSurface As Graphics = Me.CreateGraphics
Dim OrangePen As New Pen(Color.OrangeRed, 3)

'get point of mouse click
Dim MouseClick As Point
MouseClick.X = e.X
MouseClick.Y = e.Y

'draw line from previous point to point clicked
FormSurface.DrawLine(OrangePen, PreviousPoint, MouseClick)

'make point clicked the next starting point
PreviousPoint = MouseClick
```

④ *RUN THE APPLICATION*

    a. Save the modified Tracker project and then run the application. Click the form. A line is created from the upper-left corner to where the mouse was clicked. Continue clicking. Lines are created from the previous click to the next.

    b. Close the Tracker application.

⑤ *PRINT THE CODE AND THEN CLOSE THE PROJECT*

Case Study

In this Case Study a game application will be created.

specification

The specification for this Case Study is:

> The Click It! game randomly displays a blue triangle, a red diamond, or a pink circle in one of six different locations of the application window. The user must click the blue triangle to score 5 points or the pink circle to score 10 points. Clicking the red diamond is a deduction of 3 points. Each image should be displayed for 1 second at a time. The game ends after one minute (60 seconds). The user's score should be displayed in a message box after the game ends.

design

The interface for this Case Study is a form with six picture boxes and a Go! button. The Go! button should be no longer displayed after it is clicked:

The code design starts with an algorithm:

1. Every second, generate a random number between 0 and 2 and use this number to determine which shape to display and generate a random number between 0 and 5 to determine which picture box to display the shape.
2. When the user clicks a picture box, determine if a shape was clicked and then update the player's score.
3. After 60 seconds display a message box with the player's score.

Analyzing the algorithm further reveals some aspects of the code:

- Timer controls are needed for timing the shape display time and the game time.

Based on the algorithm and analysis of the algorithm, the pseudocode for this application appears like:

```
Structure Shape
    Dim Image As String
    Dim Points As Integer
End Structure


Const intBOXES As Integer = 6
Const intIMAGES As Integer = 3
Dim ImageArray(intIMAGES - 1) As Shape
Dim intScore As Integer = 0
Dim intPicBox As Integer
Dim intImage As Integer


Sub btnGo_Click (sender, e) Handles btnGo.Click
    Load shapes filenames and point values into ImageArray
    Disable Go button
    Start timers
End Sub


Sub tmrShowShape_Tick(sender, e) Handles tmrShowShape.Tick
    ClearBoxes
    intPicBox = random number between 0 and intBOXES
    intImage = random number between 0 and intIMAGES
    DisplayShape(intPicBox, intImage)
End Sub


Sub ClearBoxes()
    Show default image in all picture boxes
End Sub


Sub DisplayShape(intSelectedBox, intShape)
    Display shape in selected picture box
End Sub


Sub PictureClicked(sender, e) Handles picShape1.MouseDown, _
picShape2.MouseDown, picShape3.MouseDown, picShape4.MouseDown _
picShape5.MouseDown, picShape6.MouseDown
    Dim picClicked As PictureBox = sender
    If picClicked.Tag = intPicBox Then
        intScore = intScore + ImageArray(intImage).Points
    End If
End Sub


Sub tmrGameLength_Tick(sender, e) Handles tmrGameLength.Tick
    tmrGameLength.Stop()
    tmrShowShape.Stop()
    MessageBox.Show("Score: " & intScore)
End Sub
```

coding The interface and code for this Case Study are:

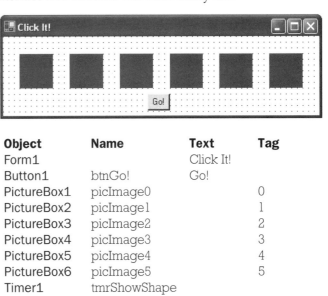

Object	Name	Text	Tag
Form1		Click It!	
Button1	btnGo!	Go!	
PictureBox1	picImage0		0
PictureBox2	picImage1		1
PictureBox3	picImage2		2
PictureBox4	picImage3		3
PictureBox5	picImage4		4
PictureBox6	picImage5		5
Timer1	tmrShowShape		
Timer2	tmrGameLength		

```
Public Class Form1
    Inherits System.Windows.Forms.Form

    Windows Form Designer generated code

    Structure Shape
        Dim Image As String      'filename of shape
        Dim Points As Integer    'points shape is worth when clicked
    End Structure

    Const intBOXES As Integer = 6       'number of picture boxes on interface
    Const intIMAGES As Integer = 3      'number of images in array
    Dim ImageArray(intIMAGES - 1) As Shape
    Dim intScore As Integer = 0         'player's score
    Dim intPicBox As Integer            'box displaying the shape
    Dim intImage As Integer             'shape displayed in box


    '~~~~~~~~~~~~~~~~~~~~~~~~~~~~~~~~~~~~~~~~~~~~~~~~~~~~~~~~~~~~~~~~
    'Starts the game.
    '
    'post: Player can start clicking on shapes to play game.
    '~~~~~~~~~~~~~~~~~~~~~~~~~~~~~~~~~~~~~~~~~~~~~~~~~~~~~~~~~~~~~~~~
    Private Sub btnGo_Click(ByVal sender As System.Object, _
    ByVal e As System.EventArgs) Handles btnGo.Click

        'load shapes
        ImageArray(0).Image = "bluetriangle.bmp"
        ImageArray(0).Points = 5
        ImageArray(1).Image = "reddiamond.bmp"
        ImageArray(1).Points = -3
        ImageArray(2).Image = "pinkcircle.bmp"
        ImageArray(2).Points = 10

        'disable button
        Me.btnGo.Enabled = False

        'start timers
        Me.tmrShowShape.Start()
        Me.tmrGameLength.Start()

    End Sub
```

```
'~~~~~~~~~~~~~~~~~~~~~~~~~~~~~~~~~~~~~~~~~~~~~~~~~~~~~~~~~~~~~
'Displays a shape in a picture box.
'
'post: A shape is displayed in a picture box. Other boxes
'contain default shape.
'~~~~~~~~~~~~~~~~~~~~~~~~~~~~~~~~~~~~~~~~~~~~~~~~~~~~~~~~~~~~~
Private Sub tmrShowShape_Tick(ByVal sender As System.Object, _
ByVal e As System.EventArgs) Handles tmrShowShape.Tick

    Call ClearBoxes()

    Randomize()
    'pick picture box to display shape
    intPicBox = Int(intBOXES * Rnd())
    'pick shape to display
    intImage = Int(intIMAGES * Rnd())

    Call DisplayShape(intPicBox, intImage)

End Sub


'~~~~~~~~~~~~~~~~~~~~~~~~~~~~~~~~~~~~~~~~~~~~~~~~~~~~~~~~~~~~~
'Return all picture boxes to display default shape.
'
'post: All picture boxes display a "starting" shape.
'~~~~~~~~~~~~~~~~~~~~~~~~~~~~~~~~~~~~~~~~~~~~~~~~~~~~~~~~~~~~~
Sub ClearBoxes()

    'clear all picture box images
    Me.picShape1.Image = Image.FromFile("greensquare.bmp")
    Me.picShape2.Image = Image.FromFile("greensquare.bmp")
    Me.picShape3.Image = Image.FromFile("greensquare.bmp")
    Me.picShape4.Image = Image.FromFile("greensquare.bmp")
    Me.picShape5.Image = Image.FromFile("greensquare.bmp")
    Me.picShape6.Image = Image.FromFile("greensquare.bmp")

End Sub


'~~~~~~~~~~~~~~~~~~~~~~~~~~~~~~~~~~~~~~~~~~~~~~~~~~~~~~~~~~~~~
'Displays in intSelectedBox picture box the shape
'corresponding to intShape.
'
'post: A shape is displayed in a picture box.
'~~~~~~~~~~~~~~~~~~~~~~~~~~~~~~~~~~~~~~~~~~~~~~~~~~~~~~~~~~~~~
Sub DisplayShape(ByVal intSelectedBox As Integer, ByVal intShape As Integer)

    Select Case intSelectedBox
        Case 0
            Me.picShape1.Image = Image.FromFile(ImageArray(intShape).Image)
        Case 1
            Me.picShape2.Image = Image.FromFile(ImageArray(intShape).Image)
        Case 2
            Me.picShape3.Image = Image.FromFile(ImageArray(intShape).Image)
        Case 3
            Me.picShape4.Image = Image.FromFile(ImageArray(intShape).Image)
        Case 4
            Me.picShape5.Image = Image.FromFile(ImageArray(intShape).Image)
        Case 5
            Me.picShape6.Image = Image.FromFile(ImageArray(intShape).Image)
    End Select

End Sub
```

```
'~~~~~~~~~~~~~~~~~~~~~~~~~~~~~~~~~~~~~~~~~~~~~~~~~~~~~~~~~~~~~~
'Determines if clicked picture box is the one with the
'shape and then updates the player's score appropriately.
'
'post: Player's score updated if shape clicked.
'~~~~~~~~~~~~~~~~~~~~~~~~~~~~~~~~~~~~~~~~~~~~~~~~~~~~~~~~~~~~~~
Private Sub PictureClicked(ByVal sender As Object, _
ByVal e As System.Windows.Forms.MouseEventArgs) Handles picShape1.MouseDown, _
picShape2.MouseDown, picShape3.MouseDown, picShape4.MouseDown, _
picShape5.MouseDown, picShape6.MouseDown

    Dim picClicked As PictureBox = sender
    If picClicked.Tag = intPicBox Then
        intScore = intScore + ImageArray(intImage).Points
    End If

End Sub


'~~~~~~~~~~~~~~~~~~~~~~~~~~~~~~~~~~~~~~~~~~~~~~~~~~~~~~~~~~~~~~
'Ends the game and displays the player's score.
'
'post: Timers have been stopped and player's score displayed.
'~~~~~~~~~~~~~~~~~~~~~~~~~~~~~~~~~~~~~~~~~~~~~~~~~~~~~~~~~~~~~~
Private Sub tmrGameLength_Tick(ByVal sender As Object, _
ByVal e As System.EventArgs) Handles tmrGameLength.Tick

    'stop game and display score in a message box
    Me.tmrGameLength.Stop()
    Me.tmrShowShape.Stop()
    MessageBox.Show("Score: " & intScore)

End Sub


End Class
```

Playing the entire Click It! game displays the interface and a message box similar to:

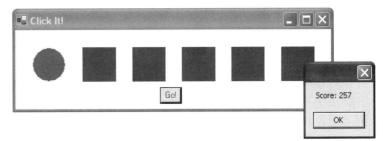

This Case Study should be tested by checking the score against actual mouse clicks.

Review 11 ⟳

Modify the Click It! tmrGameLength_Tick event procedure to include a call to NewGame(). The NewGame() procedure should execute after the player clicks OK in the message box and prepare the application for a new game. A new game requires that the score be reset to 0, the picture boxes be cleared, and the Go! button be enabled.

Color can be used to enhance an application interface. Visual Basic .NET provides more than 100 predefined colors to choose from. Control objects have BackColor and ForeColor properties that can be set to a color. The Transparent color is used to allow color behind an object to show through. BackColor and ForeColor can be set at run time in assignment statements.

ColorDialog

A ColorDialog control is an component that displays a Color dialog box at run time, but has no graphical element. The ColorDialog control has the properties Name, Color, and AllowFullOpen. A ColorDialog object name should begin with clr. The ShowDialog() method is used to display the dialog box at run time and the Color property is used to determine what color the user clicked.

Images can also be used to enhance an application interface. Images can be added to almost any control by setting the BackgroundImage property. This property tiles an image on the object. The Label control does not have a BackgroundImage property. However, the Label control has an Image property that displays a single image on a label. The Button control also has this property. An image can be loaded at run time by using the FromFile() method in the Image class.

A bitmap image can be created with the Image Editor included with Visual Basic .NET. The Image Editor toolbar contains buttons for drawing on a bitmap grid.

Timer

A Timer control is an component that raises a Tick event after a specified amount of time has elapsed. A Timer control has no graphical element. The Timer control has the properties Name, Interval, and Enabled. A Timer object name should begin with tmr. A Tick event procedure is coded for a timer object. The Interval is specified in milliseconds with 1000 ms in 1 second. Animation uses a Timer object and several similar images.

Visual Basic .NET includes the **Graphics** class with methods for creating circles, lines, rectangles, and other shapes on a drawing surface. A drawing surface is defined by assigning an object's surface to a **Graphics** object and calling the CreateaGraphics() method for the object. After creating a drawing surface, the **Pen** and **SolidBrush** classes can be used to create a pen or brush object for drawing. Next, methods are called with a pen or brush and a set of coordinates to create a shape on the drawing surface. Methods include DrawLine(), DrawRectangle(), DrawEllipse(), DrawArc(), Clear(), FillRectangle(), FillEllipse(), FillPie(), DrawCurve(), DrawClosedCurve(), FillClosedCurve(), DrawPolygon(), FillPolygon().

The **Point** structure includes X and Y members. A **Point** variable can be used in place of a set of coordinates in the **Graphics** class methods.

Events can include the MouseDown event, which is raised when the user clicks an interface object. A MouseDown event procedure includes a parameter named e that contains properties specific to the mouse click. The e parameter has properties X and Y, which are the coordinates of the mouse click.

Vocabulary

Bitmap Image A grid of bits that are filled to create an image.

Child control The objects on a form as they relate to the form.

Parent control A form as it relates to its objects.

Pixel Each point on a surface. The number of pixels in a surface depends on the screen resolution.

Point An x-coordinate and y-coordinate that together indicate a specific location.

Tiled An image that is repeated to fill an object.

Timer Used to set an interval of time.

Visual Basic .NET

Airbrush Tool button Used to display a tool for filling bits with a color. Found on the Image Editor toolbar.

Brush Tool button Used to display a tool for filling bits with a color. Found on the Image Editor toolbar.

Close command Closes an image file. Found in the File menu.

ColorDialog control Used to add an application component that displays the Color dialog box. Properties include Name, Color, and AllowFullOpen. Methods include ShowDialog().

CreateGraphics() Method used for making the surface area of a specific control object a graphics drawing surface.

Curve Tool button Used to display a tool for creating curved lines in a bitmap. Found on the Image Editor toolbar.

Ellipse Tool button Used to display a tool for creating ellipses on a bitmap. Found on the Image Editor toolbar.

Erase Tool button Used to display a tool for erasing color from bits. Found on the Image Editor toolbar.

File command Create a new bitmap file. Found in the New submenu in the File menu.

Form class Used to create a control class object that is an application interface. Properties include BackColor, ForeColor, BackgroundImage, and Size. Methods include CreateGraphics(). Events include MouseDown.

Graphics class Used to create graphic objects. Methods include Clear(), DrawCurve(), DrawArc(), DrawClosedCurve(), DrawEllipse(), DrawLine(), DrawPolygon(), DrawRectangle(), FillClosedCurve(), FillPie(), FillEllipse(), FillPolygon(), and FillRectangle().

Image Class that contains the FromFile() method for changing an image at run time.

Image Editor Used to create images from within the Visual Basic IDE.

Imports Statement used to include a namespace in an application.

Line Tool button Used to display a tool for creating lines in a bitmap. Found on the Image Editor toolbar.

New Statement used to declare a new object.

Pen class Used to create an object for drawing on a surface. Properties include DashStyle.

Pencil Tool button Used to display a tool for filling bits with a color. Found on the Image Editor toolbar.

Point Structure that has members X and Y for defining a point.

Rectangle Selection button Used to display a tool for selecting bits. Found on the Image Editor toolbar.

Rectangle Tool button Used to display a tool for creating rectangles on a bitmap. Found on the Image Editor toolbar.

SolidBrush class Used to create an object for filling shapes on a surface.

Style Setting button Used to display width, size, or shape options. Found on the Image Editor toolbar.

Timer control Used to add an application component that executes code at specific intervals. Properties include Name, Interval, and Enabled. Methods include Start() and Stop(). Events include Tick.

Text Tool button Used to display a tool for creating text on a bitmap. Found on the Image Editor toolbar.

1. a) What does it mean when a component has no graphical element?

    b) List three components.

2. a) What is meant by a predefined dialog box?

    b) List the three predefined dialog boxes discussed in the text so far.

3. What is the difference between the BackgroundImage and Image properties?

4. What happens when the BackgroundImage property of a form is right-clicked and then Reset selected?

5. Why does the Timer control have no graphical element?

6. a) Explain the parent/child relationship as it relates to the BackColor property of a form and the objects on the form.

    b) What is meant by inherits?

7. Explain how an application can display animation.

8. Give an example of when a label should be Transparent.

9. Write statements that displays a filled quarter circle in the upper-left quadrant of a label that is size 100 by 100.

10. a) What happens when the following code executes in a Tick event procedure for an enabled timer with Interval 7000?

```
Static intKeepTrack As Integer = 0
If intKeepTrack Mod 2 = 0 Then
    Me.Text = "Who's on First?"
Else
    Me.Text = "What's on Second?"
End If
intKeepTrack = intKeepTrack + 1
```

    b) What would happen if the keyword **Static** was changed to **Dim**?

11. a) Explain what happens when the following code executes in a form's mouse down event procedure.

    b) Why are < and >, rather than = are being used in the If condition?

```
Dim intHey As Integer = Me.Size.Width / 2
Dim intYou As Integer = Me.Size.Height / 2
If e.X < intHey + 10 And e.X > intHey - 10 _
And e.Y < intYou + 10 And e.Y > intYou - 10 Then
    MessageBox.Show("Bull's Eye!")
End If
```

12. a) Write statements that draw a solid blue circle with radius intR on a form starting at (50, 70).

    b) Modify the statements in part (a) to use the FillPie() method to create the solid circle.

13. a) What does the following code produce?

    ```
    Dim intX1 As Integer = 0
    Dim intY1 As Integer = Int(Me.lblShow.Height / 2)
    Dim intX2 As Integer = Me.lblShow.Width
    Dim intY2 As Integer = Int(Me.lblShow.Height / 2)
    LabelSurface.DrawLine(AquaPen, intX1, intY1, intX2, intY2)
    ```

    b) Modify the statements in part (a) to use the **Point** structure.

14. An application uses a Timer object to automatically display a message box with a message every 2 minutes.

    a) If the Interval property of a timer can be no higher than 64,767 milliseconds, how can the application use a timer to display a message every 2 minutes?

    b) Write the Tick event procedure for the application. Have the message box display "2 minutes."

15. Determine if each of the following is true or false. If false, explain why.

    a) A child control will always inherit property values from the parent control.

    b) The ForeColor of an object is the color of its text.

    c) It is impossible to change the color of a form once the program is running.

    d) A program can only have one Timer object.

    e) A Click event executes at every timer interval.

    f) If a timer should process an action every 10 seconds, then its Interval property should be set to 10.

    g) The coordinate (0, 0) is the coordinate of the center of the object.

    h) DrawCurve() would be the method to draw a pentagon.

    i) A form Click event occurs when a form is clicked.

    j) A Timer object can be turned on and off at run time by setting its Visible property.

Exercise 1 ——————————————————————— Draw House

Create a Draw House application that allows the user to select the color of the sky, sun, roof, house, and door to draw in a label by clicking radio buttons. The application interface should look similar to:

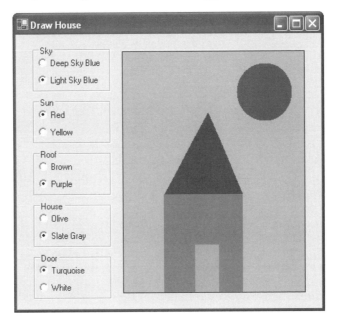

Exercise 2 ——————————————————————— Photo Album

Create a Photo Album application that allows the user to scroll through photographs and their corresponding captions by clicking an arrow button. Use the Image Editor to create an image of an arrow to be used on the button. The anemone.jpg, grayangel.jpg, sponges.jpg, starfish.jpg, and scorpionfish.jpg images are data files for this text. The application interface should look similar to the following:

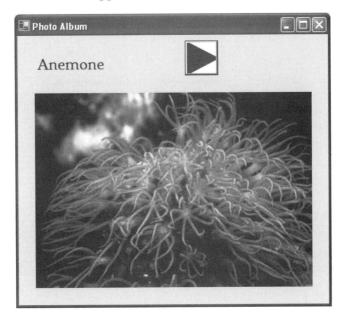

Exercise 3 ——————————————————————— Move Line

a) Create a Move Line application that displays a blue line that randomly changes position every 3 seconds after clicking Start. Clicking Stop should stop the animation. Hint: Use the size of the form and the Rnd() function to define starting and ending coordinates and the DrawLine() method to draw the lines. The form will need to be cleared before a new line is drawn. The application interface should look similar to the following after clicking Start:

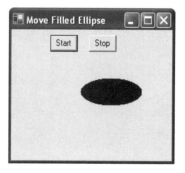

b) Modify the Move Line application to randomly display the moving line in either blue, green, or red when Start is clicked.

Exercise 4 ——————————————————————— Move Filled Ellipse

a) Create a Move Filled Ellipse application that displays a blue filled ellipse that randomly changes position every 3 seconds after clicking Start. Clicking Stop should stop the animation. Hint: Use the size of the form and the Rnd() function to define coordinates and the FillEllipse() method to draw the ellipses. The form will need to be cleared before a new ellipse is drawn. The application interface should look similar to the following after clicking Start:

b) Modify the Move Filled Ellipse application to randomly display the moving filled ellipse in either blue, green, or red when Start is clicked.

Exercise 5 ——————————————————————————— Bird Flying

Create a Bird Flying application that simulates a bird flying. Use the bird1.gif, bird2.gif, and bird3.gif images that are data files for this text. The three different animations should look similar to:

Exercise 6 ——————————————————————————— Turtle Run

Create a Turtle Run application that allows the user to control the speed of the animation by clicking a button. Use the turtle1.bmp, turtle2.bmp, and turtle3.bmp images that are data files for this text. The background color of the form should be white and the background color of the buttons should be MediumSeaGreen. The application interface should look similar to:

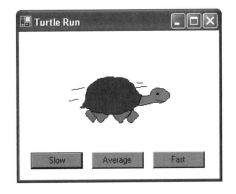

Exercise 7 ☼ ——————————————————————————— Bouncing Ball

Modify the Bouncing Ball application created in Review 6 to include a MouseDown event procedure that reverses the direction of the ball when the form is clicked. For example, if the ball is falling down from the top of the form, clicking the form makes the ball move from the bottom to the top.

Exercise 8 ——————————————————————————— Scrolling Marquee

Create a Scrolling Marquee application that displays a string one character at a time from the left to the right. Use the Image Editor to create the images. Size the grid appropriately and use the Text Tool to select font options and type the full string. Use the Save As command to save the first image and then use the Erase Tool to erase the last character. Use the Save As command to save that image. Continue the process until only character in the string is left. The application interface should look similar to the following:

Exercise 9 ───────────────────────────────── Shapes

Create a Shapes application that allows the user to enter the information needed to draw a line, ellipse, or rectangle in a MistyRose background colored label. The Select Color button should display a Color dialog box for the user to choose from. Hint: Make the color assignment to a global variable. The application interface should look similar to:

Exercise 10 ───────────────────────────────── Draw Arcs

Create a Draw Arcs application that allows the user to enter the information needed to draw an arc in a MistyRose background colored label. The application interface should look similar to:

Exercise 11 —————————————————————— Ellipse Dimensions

Create an Ellipse Dimensions application that draws a solid purple ellipse from boundary coordinates (0, 0) in the width and height determined by where the user clicks the form. Indicate in a message box the width and height dimensions of the ellipse. Every time the form is clicked, it should be cleared before drawing the new ellipse and displaying a message box. The application interface should look similar to:

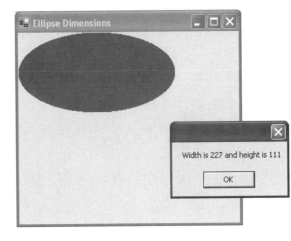

Exercise 12 —————————————————————— Curves and Polygons

Create a Curves and Polygons application that allows the user to draw in a label by clicking the mouse to define the points of the curve or polygon before clicking the button indicating the shape to draw. If the user clicks less than three times, display a message box with an appropriate message. The Select Color button should display a Color dialog box for the user to choose from. Hint: Make the color assignment to a global variable. The Clear button should clear the label. The application interface should look similar to the following after drawing many shapes and curves:

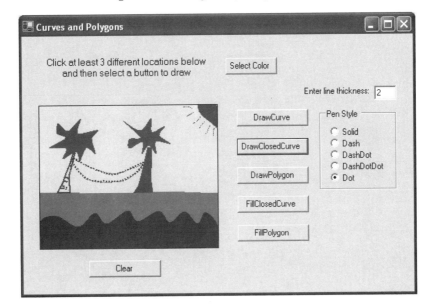

Exercise 13 —————————————————————— Count Clicks

Create a Count Clicks application that includes two label objects. Size the top label 180 x 180. Use Image Editor to create a 180 x 180 bitmap grid image similar to the one displayed named grid.bmp, and then set the Image property of the top label to the grid image. Create a MouseDown event for the top label that updates counters each time a quadrant is clicked in the top label. Your application interface should look similar to the following after clicking several times on the top label in different quadrants:

Exercise 14 ⟳ —————————————————————————— Face

Modify the Face application created in Review 8 to include a Wink button that, when clicked, winks an eye every second. The Wink button should be disabled until the Happy or Sad button is clicked. Clicking Wink starts the timer and Happy and Sad stops the timer. Your application interface should look similar to the following after clicking Happy and then Wink:

Exercise 15 (advanced) ———————————————— Pie Chart

Create a Pie Chart application that allows the user to enter four values to represent relative pie slices in a pie chart. The percentage of the total that each value represents and a pie chart drawing with different color pie slices should be displayed when the Chart button is clicked. Hint: Use the percentage of the total values to determine the degree each pie slice will sweep out of the 360 degrees available. Your application interface should look similar to:

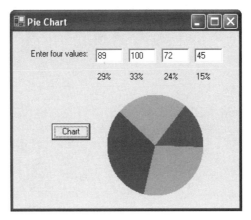

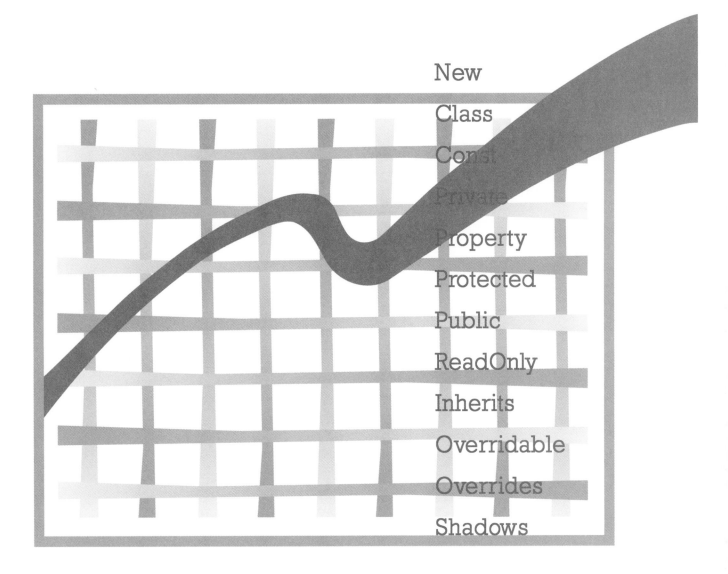

New

Class

Const

Private

Property

Protected

Public

ReadOnly

Inherits

Overridable

Overrides

Shadows

Chapter 11 Expectations

After completing this chapter you will be able to:

1. Create classes.
2. Instantiate an object.
3. Encapsulate data in a class.
4. Use access modifiers to declare class members.
5. Overload methods.
6. Use inheritance to create a derived class.
7. Make a method polymorphic by redefining it in a derived class.
8. Create base class with consideration for derived classes.
9. Reuse existing code.

Classes are the building blocks of an object-oriented program. Throughout this text, built-in classes, such as **String**, **Math**, and **Graphics**, have been used over and over again to create objects for many different types of applications. This chapter explains how to create classes and discusses instantiation, encapsulation, inheritance, and polymorphism.

11.1 Classes

Classes have been used in all the applications presented in this text. For example, a Button control is a class with a Text property. Each control in the Toolbox represents a different class. Another example is **String**. This class has methods such as ToUpper() for converting the string to all uppercase characters. These classes are precompiled code that are part of Visual Basic .NET. A Visual Basic .NET application can also include classes created by the programmer.

A program that uses classes includes declaration statements with the class name as the data type. For example, a class named **Account** could be used in a declaration statement similar to:

```
Dim CheckingAccount As New Account()  'CheckingAccount instance
```

object
instantiation

When a class is the data type, the variable is called an *object*. A statement that creates an object is *instantiating* the object. In general, instantiation takes the form:

```
Dim ClassObjectName As New ClassName(parameters)
```

ClassObjectName is a name describing the object. The keyword **New** declares a new *ClassName* object. *parameters* are sometimes used in an object declaration.

members

Classes have members, such as properties and methods. An object accesses members of its class with a dot (.) between the object name and member name. For example, the statement

```
Me.lblAcctBal.Text = CheckingAccount.Balance      'display balance
```

uses the Balance property of the **Account** class to get the current balance of the CheckingAccount object. This value is assigned to the Text property of the lblAcctBal object that is on the form object.

Classes with a Graphical Element

A class can have a graphical element. A control class, such as Button, is a class with a graphical element.

The concepts covered in this chapter are the basis of object-oriented programming. Although the terminology may seem a bit overwhelming, keep in mind that a class is simply a data type and objects are variables of a class. Classes are used to create objects. The process of creating a new object is called instantiation. Class members are accessed with a dot between the object name and member name.

11.2 Designing a Class

A class should be created for a program that requires a related set of data and actions. For example, many banks use a program to maintain customer accounts. These accounts are better implemented as objects of a class because each object has similar data and actions to be performed. A *class* is a composite data type that groups related variables and procedures. Variables in a class are either a *field member* or a *data member*. Other members called *properties* also store data, but can be directly accessed by objects of the class. Procedures in a class are called *method members*.

field and data members
property members
method members

class design
A class is designed based on a description, similar to a specification. By carefully analyzing the class specification, fields, properties, and methods can be determined. A field is piece of data that will not change. A property is an attribute of the object that can be set and viewed. A method is an action that should be performed on the object. For example, the following list of members is from the design of a class for maintaining bank accounts:

- An AcctNum property for getting and setting the account number for an existing account.
- An Activity array data member that maintains the transactions on the account.
- FirstName and LastName properties for getting and setting customer first name and last name.
- A ShowBalance property for getting the current balance.
- A Deposit() method for making a deposit transaction.
- A Withdrawal() method for making a withdrawal transaction.
- A Transactions() method for listing transactions.

Throughout the chapter, this list of members will be used to create a class named **Account**.

Creating algorithms and pseudocode are the next step in a class design. The Case Study for this chapter shows the steps for designing as well as creating a class.

11.3 The Class Module

A new class is coded in a separate file called a *Class module*. Adding a Class module to a project allows objects of that class to be instantiated in the Form1 module. To add a Class module to an open project, select Add Class from the Project menu. The Add New Item dialog box is displayed with Class selected:

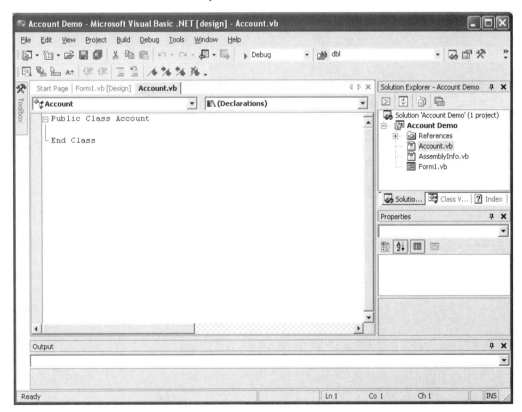

Type the class name in the Name box (be sure to keep the .vb extension) and then select Open. The class file is displayed in its own Code window in the IDE. The Class module below was named Account, which is the name automatically used for the class declaration:

class declaration   A new Class module contains a class declaration:

> **Public Class** *ClassName*
>
> **End Class**

ClassName is automatically replaced with the name of the class typed in the Add New Item dialog box. The name should be descriptive of the data and actions performed by the class. Within the declaration are the class members, which take the form:

> **Public Class** *ClassName*
>
> **Public Const** *field member declaration*
>
> **Private** *data member declaration*
>
> **Property** *PropertyName()* **As** *ReturnType*
>   *methods for getting and setting private data member value*
> **End Property**
>
> **Sub New**()
>   *statements for initializing the object*
> **End Sub**
>
> **Public Sub** *MethodName(parameters)*
>   *statements to perform a task*
> **End Sub**
>
> **Protected Sub** *MethodName(parameters)*
>   *statements to perform a task*
> **End Sub**
>
> **End Class**

There can be numerous fields, data members, properties, and methods. Declaration requirements and form for each member are discussed throughout this chapter.

programming style   Class names should begin with an uppercase letter and as a matter of good programming style not contain a prefix or postfix. The name itself should be descriptive without exposing the specific data type.

Review 1

In this review you will create a new project and add a new Class module.

① *CREATE A NEW PROJECT*

Create a Windows application named Account Demo.

② *CREATE THE INTERFACE*

Refer to the form on the next page to add, position, and size objects. Use the table below the form to set properties.

Object	Name	Text
Form1		Account Demo
Button1	btnModifyAccount	Modify Account
Button2	btnBalanceInquiry	Balance Inquiry
Button3	btnDeposit	Deposit
Button4	btnWithdrawal	Withdrawal
Button5	btnTransactions	Transactions
ListBox1	lstTransactions	

③ ADD A CLASS MODULE

    a. Display the Code window.

    b. Add comments that include your name and today's date.

    c. Select Project → Add Class. A dialog box is displayed.

        1. In the Templates list, click Class, if it is not already selected.

        2. In the Name box, type Account.vb.

        3. Select Open. The Account.vb Code window is displayed.

    d. Save the project.

11.4 Encapsulation

One important aspect of classes is that the methods of a class are the only way an object of the class can change data values. For example, the **Account** class includes Deposit() and Withdrawal() methods that update the balance, similar to a real bank that would not allow a customer to directly change an account balance without properly making a deposit or a withdrawal. The balance data is not directly accessible to an **Account** object and is said to be "encapsulated" by the class. Limiting access to data is called *data hiding*, and is the basis for *encapsulation*.

data hiding

access modifier

Private

Protected

Public

Encapsulation is accomplished by using an *access modifier* in declarations. The keywords **Private**, **Protected**, and **Public** are access modifiers used to control access to members. **Private** is used to declare a field or data as accessible to only the methods of the class. **Protected** is used to declare a member that can be used from within the class only. **Public** is used to explicitly declare a member available to an object of the class. In a Form1 module, public methods appear in an AutoList after typing an object name followed by a dot.

11.5 Field, Data, and Property Members

field members

A field is used to store a constant in a class. Fields declared as **Private Const** can be used in methods of the class only. A **Public Const** field can be used by an object of the class as well as methods of the class. For example, the following statements define public field members that can be used by both objects of the class and methods in the class:

```
Public Class Account

    Public Const MIN_REQUIRED_BALANCE As Decimal = 100   '$100
    Public Const LOW_BALANCE_FEE As Decimal = 1          '$1
    ...
```

This constant can be used within the class and objects of the class can access it. For example, a decision structure in the Form module compares the current balance to the minimum required:

```
If NewAccount.Balance < NewAccount.MINREQUIREDBALANCE Then
    ...
```

data and property members

Data members are variables used by the methods and properties in a class. A property member is used to return or change information about an object. For example, the **Account** class is designed to include an AcctNum property for getting and setting an account number. The first statement below gets an account number and assigns it to the label text. The second statement sets an account number to a new value:

```
Me.lblInfo.Text = CheckingAccount.AcctNum    'display acct number
CheckingAccount.AcctNum = "1234"             'change acct number
```

In the Class module, a property declaration takes the following form. Note that a property uses a private data member to store its value:

```
Private DataMember As DataType

Property PropertyName() As ReturnType
  Get
     Return DataMember value
  End Get
  Set(ByVal Value As DataType)
     DataMember = Value
  End Set
End Property
```

DataMember stores the property data. *PropertyName* is the name describing the information available from the property and *ReturnType* is the data type of the value returned to the calling object. Get() and Set() are property procedures. Get() returns the current *DataMember* value to the calling object, and Set() assigns *Value* to the *DataMember*. **Property** declares the property and **End Property** ends the property.

An Introduction to Programming Using Microsoft Visual Basic .NET

Get()
Set()

The **Account** class AcctNum property is coded below. The Get() procedure returns the account number to an object, and the Set() procedure allows the user to change the account number if the password is known:

```
Public Class Account
   ...
   Property AcctNum() As String
      Get
         Return AccountNumber
      End Get
      Set(ByVal Value As String)
         Const PASSWORD As String = "money"
         Dim strPasswordEntered As String = InputBox("Enter password:")
         If strPasswordEntered = PASSWORD Then
            AccountNumber = Value
         End If
      End Set
   End Property
   ...
```

ReadOnly property

A property declared as **ReadOnly** can return its data member value, but an object cannot change, or set, the property value. The **Account** class includes the read-only ShowBalance property, which contains only a Get() method:

```
Public Class Account
   ...
   Private Balance As Decimal          'data member
   ReadOnly Property ShowBalance() As Decimal
      Get
         Return Balance
      End Get
   End Property
   ...
```

writing a property

Property code should appear just after a related data member. A property is added to the Class module by typing Property followed by the property name and then pressing Enter. When this is done, the IDE automatically adds **Get** and **End Get** statements, **Set** and **End Set** statements, and an **End Property** statement. Typing ReadOnly Property adds **Get** and **End Get** statements and an **End Property** statement. Statements can then be typed for each method.

Review 2 ↻

In this review you will add data and property members to the Account class. Open the Account Demo project and display the Account window, if it is not already displayed.

① *ADD A DATA MEMBERS AND PROPERTIES*

    a. Add a comment and the AccountNumber data member:

```
Public Class Account

   'private data member and related property
   Private AccountNumber As String
```

b. Below the data member, type Property AcctNum As String and then press Enter. A new property is added:

```
Property AcctNum() As String
   Get

   End Get
   Set(ByVal Value As String)

   End Set
End Property
```

c. Modify the Get() and Set() methods to contain the statements:

```
Property AcctNum() As String
   Get
      Return AccountNumber
   End Get
   Set(ByVal Value As String)
      Const PASSWORD As String = "money"
      Dim strPasswordEntered As String = InputBox("Enter password:")
      If strPasswordEntered = PASSWORD Then
         AccountNumber = Value
      End If
   End Set
End Property
```

Note that the account number can be changed only if the user knows the password.

d. Below the property method, add two structures and their data members:

```
Private Structure Transaction
   Dim TransType As String
   Dim TransCode As Boolean          'False if no errors
   Dim EndingBalance As Decimal
End Structure
Private Activity(-1) As Transaction  'array storing transactions

Private Structure PersonalInfo
   Dim FirstName As String
   Dim LastName As String
End Structure
Private Customer As PersonalInfo
```

Note the structures are private so that they are available to the class only.

e. Below the Customer data member, add two properties:

```
Property LastName() As String
   Get
      Return Customer.LastName
   End Get
   Set(ByVal Value As String)
      Customer.LastName = Value
   End Set
End Property

Property FirstName() As String
   Get
      Return Customer.FirstName
   End Get
   Set(ByVal Value As String)
      Customer.FirstName = Value
   End Set
End Property
```

f. Below the FirstName property, add the Balance data member and the read-only ShowBalance property:

```
Private Balance As Decimal
ReadOnly Property ShowBalance() As Decimal
    Get
        Return Balance
    End Get
End Property
```

g. Save the project.

h. Display the Form1 Code window.

i. Create a global variable declaration that instantiates an **Account** object:

```
Dim CheckingAccount As New Account()
```

j. Create a btnBalanceInquiry_Click event procedure and then type CheckingAccount. and note the AutoList with the properties that have been added to the Account class:

```
CheckingAccount.|
            ┌─────────────────┐
            │ 🖗 AcctNum       │
            │ 🖗 FirstName     │
            │ ◆ GetType       │
            │ 🖗 LastName      │
            │ 🖗 ShowBalance   │
            └─────────────────┘
```

k. Delete the statement added to the event procedure and then save the project.

11.6   Methods

public methods

A method is a procedure in a class. For example, the **Account** class is designed to include Deposit() and Withdrawal() methods for making a transaction. An object of a class calls a method by passing required arguments in parentheses. In the following statements, the CheckingAccount object calls the Deposit() method. The argument passed is the amount of the deposit:

```
Dim CheckingAccount As New Account()      'Account instance
CheckingAccount.Deposit(100)              'call Deposit() method
```

In the Class module, a method declaration takes the form:

```
Public Sub MethodName (parameters)
    statements
End Sub
```

Public

Public declares a method that can be called by objects of the class. *MethodName* is the name describing the task performed. *parameters* are parameter declarations. *statements* is one or more statements that perform the task. **Sub** declares the method and **End Sub** ends the method.

function procedure

Note that a method is a procedure and can therefore also be a function procedure.

protected methods

A class also typically contains methods that perform "background" work for objects of the class. These methods should not be directly accessible to objects and are declared with the keyword **Protected**. A protected method can be used by other class members only. For example, the Deposit() and Withdrawal() methods in the **Account** class call a protected method, AddTransaction(), for recording a transaction in the Activity()

array, similar to a real bank that records all account transactions. The transaction is recorded "behind the scenes" by the protected method, without any interaction from the programmer or application user.

In the Class module, a protected method declaration requires the **Protected** keyword and takes the form:

```
Protected Sub MethodName (parameters)
    statements
End Sub
```

Review 3 ⟳

In this review you will add field and method members to the **Account** class and code events for the Account Demo application. Open the Account Demo project and display the Account window.

① ADD FIELD MEMBERS

Just below the **Public Class** Account statement, add a comment and two field members:

```
Public Class Account

    'public field members
    Public Const MIN_REQUIRED_BALANCE As Decimal = 100      '$100
    Public Const LOW_BALANCE_FEE As Decimal = 1             '$1
```

② ADD METHOD MEMBERS

a. Below the ShowBalance property declarations and before the **End Class** statement, add a comment and a protected method:

```
    'protected methods

    Protected Sub AddTransaction(ByVal Transaction As String, _
    ByVal Code As Boolean, ByVal CurrentBalance As Decimal)

        'Use Length to size array because the value is one greater than the
        'current highest index value
        ReDim Preserve Activity(Activity.Length)
        Dim intNewTransaction As Integer = Activity.Length – 1
        Activity(intNewTransaction).TransType = Transaction
        Activity(intNewTransaction).TransCode = Code
        Activity(intNewTransaction).EndingBalance = Balance

    End Sub
```

b. Below the protected method and before the **End Class** statement, add a comment and three public methods:

```
    'public methods

    Public Sub Transactions(ByRef DisplayBox As ListBox)

        Dim CurrentTransaction As Transaction

        DisplayBox.Items.Add("Error" & vbTab & "Transaction" & vbTab & "Balance")
        Dim intTransNum As Integer
        For intTransNum = 0 To Activity.Length – 1
            CurrentTransaction = Activity(intTransNum)
            DisplayBox.Items.Add(CurrentTransaction.TransCode & vbTab _
            & CurrentTransaction.TransType & vbTab & vbTab _
            & CurrentTransaction.EndingBalance)
        Next intTransNum

    End Sub
```

```
Public Sub Deposit(ByVal DepositAmt As Decimal, _
ByRef ErrorCode As Boolean)

    If DepositAmt > 0 Then          'valid deposit
       Balance = Balance + DepositAmt
       ErrorCode = False
    Else                            'deposit not valid
       ErrorCode = True
    End If
    AddTransaction("Deposit", ErrorCode, Balance)

End Sub

Public Sub Withdrawal(ByVal WithdrawalAmt As Decimal, _
ByRef ErrorCode As Boolean)

    If WithdrawalAmt <= Balance Then          'make withdrawal
       Balance = Balance – WithdrawalAmt
       ErrorCode = False
       AddTransaction("Withdrawal", ErrorCode, Balance)
       'determine if balance has fallen below required amount
       If Balance < MIN_REQUIRED_BALANCE Then  'service charge
          Balance = Balance – LOW_BALANCE_FEE
          ErrorCode = False
          AddTransaction("Low Bal Fee", ErrorCode, Balance)
       End If
    Else                                      'withdrawal not permitted
       ErrorCode = True
       AddTransaction("Withdrawal", ErrorCode, Balance)
    End If

End Sub
```

c. Save the modified project.

③ *MODIFY THE ACCOUNT DEMO APPLICATION*

a. Display the Form1 Code window.

b. In the btnBalanceInquiry_Click event procedure, add the statement:

```
MessageBox.Show("Account " & CheckingAccount.AcctNum & " has " & _
Format(CheckingAccount.ShowBalance, "Currency"))
```

c. Create a btnDeposit_Click event procedure and add the statements:

```
Dim strTextEntered As String
strTextEntered = InputBox("Enter amount of deposit:", Me.Text)

'Test data entered
Dim blnTransCode As Boolean
If strTextEntered = Nothing Then    'Cancel or empty text box
   CheckingAccount.Deposit(0, blnTransCode)
Else                                'characters entered
   CheckingAccount.Deposit(Val(strTextEntered), blnTransCode)
End If

If blnTransCode Then
   MessageBox.Show("Problem with transaction.")
End If
```

d. Create a btnWithdrawal_Click event procedure and add the statements:

```
Dim strTextEntered As String
strTextEntered = InputBox("Enter amount to withdraw:", Me.Text)

'Test data entered
Dim blnTransCode As Boolean
If strTextEntered = Nothing Then      'Cancel or empty text box
    CheckingAccount.Withdrawal(0, blnTransCode)
Else                                  'characters entered
    CheckingAccount.Withdrawal(Val(strTextEntered), blnTransCode)
End If

If blnTransCode Then
    MessageBox.Show("Problem with transaction.")
End If
```

e. Create a btnTransactions_Click event procedure and add the statements:

```
Me.lstTransactions.Items.Clear()      'clear previous items
CheckingAccount.Transactions(Me.lstTransactions)
```

f. Create a btnModifyAccount_Click event procedure and add the statements:

```
Dim strTextEntered As String

'Change first name
strTextEntered = InputBox("First name is: " & CheckingAccount.FirstName & _
vbCrLf & "Enter new first name (Cancel to keep the same):", Me.Text)
'Test data entered
If strTextEntered <> Nothing Then            'new first name
    CheckingAccount.FirstName = strTextEntered
End If

'Change last name
strTextEntered = InputBox("Last name is: " & CheckingAccount.LastName & _
vbCrLf & "Enter new last name (Cancel to keep the same):", Me.Text)
'Test data entered
If strTextEntered <> Nothing Then            'new last name
    CheckingAccount.LastName = strTextEntered
End If

'Change account number
strTextEntered = InputBox("Account number is: " & CheckingAccount.AcctNum & _
vbCrLf & "Enter new account number (Cancel to keep the same):", Me.Text)
'Test data entered
If strTextEntered <> Nothing Then            'new account number
    CheckingAccount.AcctNum = strTextEntered
End If
```

g. Run the application. Click Balance Inquiry. A message box is displayed indicating the account has $0.00. Note that there is no account number listed. Select OK to remove the dialog box.

h. Click Modify Account. Input boxes are displayed for entering account holder name and an account number. The password money will need to be used to modify the account.

i. Use the other buttons to make deposits, withdrawals, and account modifications. View the transactions by clicking Transactions.

11.7 Constructors

A *constructor* is a method that is automatically called when an object is instantiated. Statements for initializing object values can be placed in the constructor. In the Class module, a constructor method takes the form:

```
Sub New()
    statements
End Sub
```

New is the name that must be used for a constructor. *statements* is one or more statements that initialize values and perform tasks. A constructor is called only once when an object is created.

A constructor usually initializes private data members, as in the **Account** class constructor:

```
Sub New()
    Me.AccountNumber = "0000"
    Me.Balance = 0
    Me.AddTransaction("New Account", False, Balance)
End Sub
```

programming style   The keyword **Me** is used where possible in a constructor as good programming style.

Review 4

In this review you will add a constructor to the **Account** class. Open the Account Demo project if it is not already open and display the Account window.

① ADD A FIELD MEMBER

Below the existing two field members at the top of the class code, add a field member that stores a default account number:

```
Public Class Account

    'public field members
    Public Const MIN_REQUIRED_BALANCE As Decimal = 100      '$100
    Public Const LOW_BALANCE_FEE As Decimal = 1             '$1
    Public Const DEFAULT_ACCTNUM As String = "0000"
```

② ADD A CONSTRUCTOR

a. Below the ShowBalance property declaration, add a comment and the constructor method:

```
    'constructors

    Sub New()

        Me.AccountNumber = DEFAULT_ACCTNUM
        Me.Balance = 0
        Me.AddTransaction("New Account", False, Balance)

    End Sub
```

b. Save the modified project.

③ RUN THE APPLICATION

a. Run the application. Click Balance Inquiry. Note the default account number.

b. Click Transactions. Note the new account transaction.

11.8 Overloading Methods

A method that performs a different action depending on the number or type of arguments it receives is said to be *overloaded*. Constructors are commonly overloaded to give more flexibility when creating objects. For example, each of the statements below create an **Account** class object assuming four appropriate constructors are defined in the class:

```
Dim NewAcct1 As New Account()          'use default values
Dim NewAcct2 As New Account("1073")    'account number 1073
Dim NewAcct3 As New Account(200)       'beginning balance $200
'account number 2743, first name Elaine, last name Malfas
Dim NewAcct4 As New Account("2743", "Elaine", "Malfas")
```

Note that NewAcct2 and NewAcct3 are instantiated with one argument, but different constructors will be called because the arguments are different types.

The four **Account** class constructors are shown below. Note how the first constructor uses **Me.New** with arguments to call the constructor with a strAcctNum parameter:

```
'constructors
Sub New()

    'call constructor that accepts an acct number parameter
    Me.New(DEFAULT_ACCTNUM)

End Sub


'object instantiated with an acct number parameter
Sub New(ByVal strAcctNum As String)

    Me.AccountNumber = strAcctNum
    Me.Balance = 0
    Me.AddTransaction("New Account", False, Balance)

End Sub


'object instantiated with a deposit amount
Sub New(ByVal decInitialDeposit As Decimal)

    Me.AccountNumber = DEFAULT_ACCTNUM
    Me.Balance = decInitialDeposit
    Me.AddTransaction("New Account", False, Balance)

End Sub


'object instantiated with acct number and acct holder name
Sub New(ByVal strAcctNum As String, ByVal strFirstName As String, _
ByVal strLastName As String)

    Me.AccountNumber = strAcctNum
    Me.Balance = 0
    Me.FirstName = strFirstName
    Me.LastName = strLastName
    Me.AddTransaction("New Account", False, Balance)

End Sub
```

In general, methods are overloaded by writing a set of methods that each have the same name, but different parameters. Each of the constructors on the previous page have the method name New and different parameters. The parameter list for a method can vary by having parameters with different types, changing the number of parameters, or changing the data types of parameters.

Review 5

In this review you will add overloaded constructors to the **Account** class. Open the Account Demo project and display the Account window, if it is not already displayed.

① ADD THREE OVERLOADED CONSTRUCTORS

Below the existing default constructor, add three new constructor methods:

```
Sub New(ByVal strAcctNum As String)

    Me.AccountNumber = strAcctNum
    Me.Balance = 0
    Me.AddTransaction("New Account", False, Balance)

End Sub
```

```
Sub New(ByVal decInitialDeposit As Decimal)

    Me.AccountNumber = DEFAULT_ACCTNUM
    Me.Balance = decInitialDeposit
    Me.AddTransaction("New Account", False, Balance)

End Sub
```

```
Sub New(ByVal strAcctNum As String, ByVal strFirstName As String, _
ByVal strLastName As String)

    Me.AccountNumber = strAcctNum
    Me.Balance = 0
    Me.FirstName = strFirstName
    Me.LastName = strLastName
    Me.AddTransaction("New Account", False, Balance)

End Sub
```

② MODIFY THE EXISTING CONSTRUCTOR

Modify the default constructor to include just one statement:

```
Sub New()

    Me.New(DEFAULT_ACCTNUM)

End Sub
```

③ MODIFY AND THEN RUN THE APPLICATION

a. Display the Form1 Code window.

b. Modify the global variable declaration that instantiates an **Account** object:
```
Dim CheckingAccount As New Account("1234")
```

c. Save and run the application. Click Balance Inquiry. Note the account number.

d. Click Transactions. Note the new account transaction.

e. Close Account Demo.

11.9   Inheritance and Polymorphism

A new class can be created based on an existing class. For example, the **Account** class can be used in a new class named **CommercialAccount**. A commercial account should have the same features as a basic account and also include a CompanyName property. The **CommercialAccount** class looks like:

```
Public Class CommercialAccount

    Inherits Account

    Private CommercialAcctName As String
    Property CompanyName() As String
      Get
        Return CommercialAcctName
      End Get
      Set(ByVal Value As String)
        CommercialAcctName = Value
      End Set
    End Property

End Class
```

Inherits
derived class
base class

The **Inherits** statement is used in a **Class** declaration to give the new class all the features of an existing class. The new class is called the *derived class* and the inherited class is called the *base class*. The derived class can then be extended by adding new properties and methods.

polymorphism

Polymorphism is an object-oriented programming (OOP) feature that allows methods in a base class to be redefined in derived classes. This can make a single method appear *polymorphic*, changing its task to meet the needs of the object calling it. For example, a commercial account may have different withdrawal fees. Therefore, a Withdrawal() method should be included in the **CommercialAccount** class to override the method in **AccountClass**.

Overridable
Overrides

Protected

A base class should be written with derived classes in mind. Methods that are general purpose are declared with the keyword **Overridable**. A derived class can then include a method with the keyword **Overrides** and the same name as the **Overridable** base class method. Members that are general purpose should be declared **Protected** so that they accessible to the derived class.

Shadows

To override field members, a derived class can include data of the same to be used with the keyword **Shadows**. For example, the minimum required balance is usually higher for a commercial account. Therefore, a MIN_REQUIRED_BALANCE field with a different value is needed for the derived **CommercialAccount** class.

The **CommercialAccount** class is shown on the next page. Note how simple it appears because it inherits a base class:

```
Public Class CommercialAccount

  Inherits Account

  'public field members
  Shadows Const MIN_REQUIRED_BALANCE As Decimal = 500        '$500
  Shadows Const LOW_BALANCE_FEE As Decimal = 10              '$10

  'private data member and related property
  Private CommercialAcctName As String
  Property CompanyName() As String
    Get
      Return CommercialAcctName
    End Get
    Set(ByVal Value As String)
      CommercialAcctName = Value
    End Set
  End Property

  'constructor
  Sub New(ByVal strAcctNum As String, ByVal strCompanyName As String)

    Me.AccountNumber = strAcctNum
    Me.Balance = 0
    Me.CommercialAcctName = strCompanyName
    Me.AddTransaction("New Account", False, Balance)

  End Sub

  'public method
  Public Overrides Sub Withdrawal(ByVal WithdrawalAmt As Decimal, _
  ByRef ErrorCode As Boolean)

    If WithdrawalAmt <= Balance Then                  'make withdrawal
      Balance = Balance – WithdrawalAmt
      ErrorCode = False
      AddTransaction("Withdrawal", ErrorCode, Balance)
      'determine if balance has fallen below required amount
      If Balance < MIN_REQUIRED_BALANCE Then   'service charge
        Balance = Balance – LOW_BALANCE_FEE
        ErrorCode = False
        AddTransaction("Low Bal Fee", ErrorCode, Balance)
      End If
    Else                                        'withdrawal not permitted
      ErrorCode = True
      AddTransaction("Withdrawal", ErrorCode, Balance)
    End If

  End Sub

End Class
```

11.10 Reusing Code

An important aspect of object-oriented programming is code reuse. Well-developed and tested classes can be used over and over again as they are or as base classes by many different applications. To add an existing class to a project, select Add Existing Item from the Project menu. The Add Existing Item dialog box is displayed:

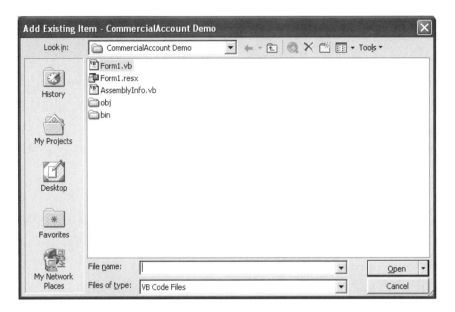

Use the **Look in** list and contents box below it to display the project folder containing the class to add to the project. When the class name is displayed in the contents box, click the class name and then select **Open** to add the class to the project. The class name will appear in the Solutions Explorer window where it can be double-clicked to open it.

reusing a form   Another way to reuse code is to use the interface from an existing application for a new application. This is useful when an application should have an interface similar to an existing application. Just as the **Add Existing Item** command was used for adding a class, this command can be used to add an existing form. In the Add Existing Item dialog box, display the project folder with the form to be copied. The form file name will be Form1.vb. Clicking the form name and then selecting **Open** copies the form to the current project. Warning dialog boxes may be displayed. **Yes** should be selected in each. Note that the form code is copied as well as the interface and overwrites any existing Form1 data.

Review 6

In this review you will create a CommercialAccount Demo application that uses the **Account** class as a base class.

① **CREATE A NEW PROJECT**

Create a Windows application named CommercialAccount Demo.

② **ADD THE INTERFACE**

The interface for this project will be copied from the Account Demo project.

a. Select **Project → Add Existing Item**. A dialog box is displayed.

1. Use the **Look in** list and contents box below it to display the contents of the Account Demo project.

2. Click Form1.vb.

3. Select **Open**. Several warning dialog boxes may be displayed. Select **Yes** in each. The form from the Account Demo project is displayed.

b. Modify the Form Text property to CommercialAccount Demo.

③ **ADD THE ACCOUNT CLASS**

The **Account** class will be copied from the Account Demo project.

Select Project ➔ Add Existing Item. A dialog box is displayed.

1. Use the Look in list and contents box below it to display the contents of the Account Demo project.

2. Click Account.vb.

3. Select Open. The Account.vb file is added to the CommercialAccount Demo project, as shown in the Solution Explorer window.

④ **MODIFY THE ACCOUNT CLASS**

a. In the Solution Explorer window, double-click the Account.vb file name. The **Account** class is displayed.

b. Change the AccountNumber and Balance declarations from **Private** to **Protected** because they need to be accessed in the derived class and update the comment and add a new one:

```
'protected data member and related property
Protected AccountNumber As String
…

'protected data member and related property
Protected Balance As Decimal
```

c. Change the Withdrawal() declaration to **Overridable** because it needs to be redeclared in the derived class:

```
Public Overridable Sub Withdrawal(ByVal WithdrawalAmt As Decimal, _
ByRef ErrorCode As Boolean)
```

⑤ **ADD A NEW CLASS MODULE**

a. Select Project ➔ Add Class. A dialog box is displayed.

1. In the Templates list, click Class, if it is not already selected.

2. In the Name box, type CommercialAccount.vb.

3. Select Open. The CommercialAccount.vb Code window is displayed.

b. Save the project.

⑥ **WRITE THE COMMERCIALACCOUNT CLASS**

a. Just below the **Public Class** CommercialAccount statement, type an **Inherits** statement:

```
Public Class CommercialAccount

    Inherits Account
```

b. Below the **Inherits** statement, add comments and two field members:

```
'public field members
Shadows Const MIN_REQUIRED_BALANCE As Decimal = 500      '$500
Shadows Const LOW_BALANCE_FEE As Decimal = 10            '$10
```

c. Below the field members, add a comment, a data member, and a property:

```
'private data member and related property
Private CommercialAcctName As String
Property CompanyName() As String
  Get
    Return CommercialAcctName
  End Get
  Set(ByVal Value As String)
    CommercialAcctName = Value
  End Set
End Property
```

d. Below the property, add a comment and a constructor:

```
'constructor
Sub New(ByVal strAcctNum As String, ByVal strCompanyName As String)

    Me.AccountNumber = strAcctNum
    Me.Balance = 0
    Me.CommercialAcctName = strCompanyName
    Me.AddTransaction("New Account", False, Balance)

End Sub
```

e. Below the constructor, add a comment and a method that overrides the **Account** Withdrawal() method:

```
'public method
Public Overrides Sub Withdrawal(ByVal WithdrawalAmt As Decimal, _
ByRef ErrorCode As Boolean)

    If WithdrawalAmt <= Balance Then              'make withdrawal
        Balance = Balance – WithdrawalAmt
        ErrorCode = False
        AddTransaction("Withdrawal", ErrorCode, Balance)
        'determine if balance has fallen below required amount
        If Balance < MIN_REQUIRED_BALANCE Then  'service charge
            Balance = Balance – LOW_BALANCE_FEE
            ErrorCode = False
            AddTransaction("Low Bal Fee", ErrorCode, Balance)
        End If
    Else                                          'withdrawal not permitted
        ErrorCode = True
        AddTransaction("Withdrawal", ErrorCode, Balance)
    End If

End Sub
```

⑦ MODIFY THE FORM CODE

a. In the Form Code window, modify the global variable declaration to instantiate a **CommercialAccount** object:

```
Dim CheckingAccount As New CommercialAccount("3985", "My Company")
```

b. Add statements to the end of the btnModifyAccount_Click event procedure to allow the company name to be modified:

```
'Change company name
strTextEntered = InputBox("Company name is: " & CheckingAccount.CompanyName & _
vbCrLf & "Enter new company name (Cancel to keep the same):", Me.Text)
'Test data entered
If strTextEntered <> Nothing Then   'new company name
    CheckingAccount.CompanyName = strTextEntered
End If
```

⑧ RUN THE APPLICATION

a. Run the application. Click Balance Inquiry. Note the account number.

b. Use the buttons to make deposits, withdrawals, and account modifications. View the transactions by clicking Transactions. Two new account transactions appear. Note how the low balance fee is different for a commercial account.

c. Close CommercialAccount Demo.

In this Case Study a triangle calculator application will be created. This application will include a **Triangle** class.

specification

The specification for this Case Study is:

> An application that displays information about a triangle based on the lengths of its sides. The user is prompted for the lengths of sides a, b, and c. The triangle area, perimeter, and type are then calculated and displayed.

design

The interface for this Case Study is a form with text boxes that prompt the user for the lengths of the triangle sides. Buttons are included to allow the user to display the area, perimeter, and triangle type:

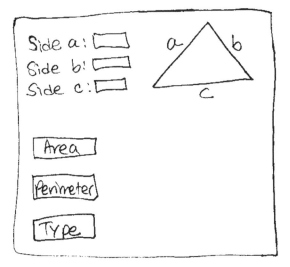

The algorithm for this Case Study is straightforward. However, since the application is about triangles, which have a clear set of related calculations and properties, a Triangle class should be implemented. The Triangle class starts with a specification:

class specification

- Triangles have three sides, commonly referred to as side a, side b, and side c. Sides a and b are the shorter sides and their sum must be greater than side c.

- The area of a triangle is computed as $\sqrt{s(s-a)(s-b)(s-c)}$

- The triangle type can be determined with the following formulas:

right triangle: $c^2 = a^2 + b^2$

acute triangle: $c^2 < a^2 + b^2$

obtuse triangle: $c^2 > a^2 + b^2$

class design From the class specification, a list of members can be determined:

- A constructor that accepts three numeric values corresponding to side a, side b, and side c, respectively, and calculates the semiperimeter.

- a, b, and c properties for getting and setting side lengths.

- An s property for getting the semiperimeter.

- A ValidTriangle() method that indicates if sides a, b, and c form a triangle.

- An Area() method that returns a value corresponding to the area of the triangle.

- The Type() method that returns a string corresponding to the triangle type.

Based on the Triangle class design, the class pseudocode appears:

```
Public Class Triangle
    Private SideA As Single
    Property a() As Single
        property get() and set()
    End Property

    Private SideB As Single
    Property b() As Single
        property get() and set()
    End Property

    Private SideC As Single
    Property c()
        property get() and set()
    End Property

    Private Semiperimeter As Single
    ReadOnly Property s() As Single
        Get
            Return Semiperimeter
        End Get
    End Property

    'constructor
    Sub New(ByVal sngSideA As Single, ByVal sngSideB As Single, _
    ByVal sngSideC As Single)
        Me.SideA = sngSideA
        Me.SideB = sngSideB
        Me.SideC = sngSideC
        Me.Semiperimeter = 0.5 * (SideA + SideB + SideC)
    End Sub

    Public Function ValidTriangle() As Boolean
        If SideA + SideB > SideC Then      'valid triangle
            Return True
        Else                               'invalid triangle
            Return False
        End If
    End Function
```

```
Public Function Area() As Single
    'Heron's formula
    Return Math.Sqrt(Semiperimeter * (Semiperimeter – SideA) * _
    (Semiperimeter – SideB) * (Semiperimeter – SideC))
End Function

Public Function Type() As String
    Select Case SideC ^ 2
        Case SideA ^ 2 + SideB ^ 2
            Return "Right triangle."
        Case Is < SideA ^ 2 + SideB ^ 2
            Return "Acute triangle."
        Case Is > SideA ^ 2 + SideB ^ 2
            Return "Obtuse triangle."
    End Select
End Function

End Class
```

The Triangle Calculator Case Study pseudocode is:

```
Private Sub Calculate(ByVal sender As Object, ByVal e As System.EventArgs) _
Handles btnArea.Click, btnPerimeter.Click, btnType.Click
    Dim sngSideA As Single = Val(Me.txtSideA.Text)
    Dim sngSideB As Single = Val(Me.txtSideB.Text)
    Dim sngSideC As Single = Val(Me.txtSideC.Text)
    Dim UserTriangle As New Triangle(sngSideA, sngSideB, sngSideC)

    If UserTriangle.ValidTriangle Then
        Dim btnButtonClicked As Button = sender
        Select Case btnButtonClicked.Tag
            Case "Area"
                Display UserTriangle.Area
            Case "Perimeter"
                Display UserTriangle.s * 2
            Case "Type"
                Display UserTriangle.Type
        End Select
    Else                        'invalid triangle
        MessageBox.Show("Measurements typed are not for a valid triangle.")
        Clear text boxes
    End If
End Sub

Private Sub SideChanged(ByVal sender As Object, _
ByVal e As System.EventArgs) Handles txtSideA.TextChanged, _
txtSideB.TextChanged, txtSideC.TextChanged
        Clear labels
End Sub
```

coding   The interface, Form1 code, and Triangle class code for this Case Study are:

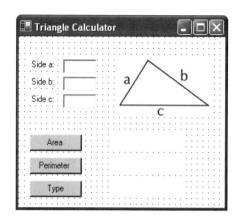

Object	Name	Text	Image
Form1		Triangle Calculator	
Label1	lblSideAPrompt	Side a:	
TextBox1	txtSideA	*empty*	
Label2	lblSideBPrompt	Side b:	
TextBox2	txtSideB	*empty*	
Label3	lblSideCPrompt	Side c:	
TextBox3	txtSideC	*empty*	
PictureBox1	picTriangle		triangle.bmp
Button1	btnArea	Area	
Button2	btnPerimeter	Perimeter	
Button3	btnType	Type	
Label4	lblArea	*empty*	
Label5	lblPerimeter	*empty*	
Label6	lblType	*empty*	

The BackColor of the form is set to White and the BackColor of the buttons set to LightGray.

Triangle class code

```
Public Class Triangle

  'private data members and related properties

  Private SideA As Single
  Property a() As Single
    Get
      Return SideA
    End Get
    Set(ByVal Value As Single)
      SideA = Value
    End Set
  End Property

  Private SideB As Single
  Property b() As Single
    Get
      Return SideB
    End Get
    Set(ByVal Value As Single)
      SideB = Value
    End Set
  End Property
```

```
Private SideC As Single
Property c()
  Get
    Return SideC
  End Get
  Set(ByVal Value)
    SideC = Value
  End Set
End Property

Private Semiperimeter As Single
ReadOnly Property s() As Single
  Get
    Return Semiperimeter
  End Get
End Property

'constructor
Sub New(ByVal sngSideA As Single, ByVal sngSideB As Single, _
ByVal sngSideC As Single)

  Me.SideA = sngSideA
  Me.SideB = sngSideB
  Me.SideC = sngSideC
  Me.Semiperimeter = 0.5 * (SideA + SideB + SideC)

End Sub

'public methods

'~~~~~~~~~~~~~~~~~~~~~~~~~~~~~~~~~~~~~~~~~~~~~~~~~~~~~~~~~~~~~~~
'Returns True if sides a, b, and c are valid for a triangle.
'
'post: True returned if the sum of sides a and b are
'greater than side c. False returned otherwise.
'~~~~~~~~~~~~~~~~~~~~~~~~~~~~~~~~~~~~~~~~~~~~~~~~~~~~~~~~~~~~~~~
Public Function ValidTriangle() As Boolean

  If SideA + SideB > SideC Then    'valid triangle
    Return True
  Else                             'invalid triangle
    Return False
  End If

End Function

'~~~~~~~~~~~~~~~~~~~~~~~~~~~~~~~~~~~~~~~~~~~~~~~~~~~~~~~~~~~~~~~
'Returns the area of a triangle.
'
'pre: sides a, b, and c correspond to a valid triangle.
'post: Area of a triangle returned.
'~~~~~~~~~~~~~~~~~~~~~~~~~~~~~~~~~~~~~~~~~~~~~~~~~~~~~~~~~~~~~~~
Public Function Area() As Single

  'Heron's formula
  Return Math.Sqrt(Semiperimeter * (Semiperimeter – SideA) * _
  (Semiperimeter – SideB) * (Semiperimeter – SideC))

End Function
```

```
'~~~~~~~~~~~~~~~~~~~~~~~~~~~~~~~~~~~~~~~~~~~~~~~~~~~~~
'Returns the type (right, acute, or obtuse) of a triangle.
'
'pre: sides a, b, and c correspond to a valid triangle.
'post: Type of a triangle returned.
'~~~~~~~~~~~~~~~~~~~~~~~~~~~~~~~~~~~~~~~~~~~~~~~~~~~~~
Public Function Type() As String

    Select Case SideC ^ 2
        Case SideA ^ 2 + SideB ^ 2
            Return "Right triangle."
        Case Is < SideA ^ 2 + SideB ^ 2
            Return "Acute triangle."
        Case Is > SideA ^ 2 + SideB ^ 2
            Return "Obtuse triangle."
    End Select

End Function

End Class
```

Form1 code

```
Public Class Form1
    Inherits System.Windows.Forms.Form

    Windows Form Designer generated code

    Private Sub Calculate(ByVal sender As Object, ByVal e As System.EventArgs) _
    Handles btnArea.Click, btnPerimeter.Click, btnType.Click

        Dim sngSideA As Single = Val(Me.txtSideA.Text)
        Dim sngSideB As Single = Val(Me.txtSideB.Text)
        Dim sngSideC As Single = Val(Me.txtSideC.Text)
        Dim UserTriangle As New Triangle(sngSideA, sngSideB, sngSideC)

        If UserTriangle.ValidTriangle Then
            Dim btnButtonClicked As Button = sender
            Select Case btnButtonClicked.Tag
                Case "Area"
                    Me.lblArea.Text = UserTriangle.Area
                Case "Perimeter"
                    Me.lblPerimeter.Text = UserTriangle.s * 2
                Case "Type"
                    Me.lblType.Text = UserTriangle.Type
            End Select
        Else            'invalid triangle
            MessageBox.Show("Measurements typed are not for a valid triangle.")
            'clear text boxes
            Me.txtSideA.Text = Nothing
            Me.txtSideB.Text = Nothing
            Me.txtSideC.Text = Nothing
        End If

    End Sub
```

An Introduction to Programming Using Microsoft Visual Basic .NET

```
'~~~~~~~~~~~~~~~~~~~~~~~~~~~~~~~~~~~~~~~~~~~~~~~~~~~~~~
'Clears the text boxes displaying calculations.
'
'post: Area, Perimeter, and Type calculations are cleared.
'~~~~~~~~~~~~~~~~~~~~~~~~~~~~~~~~~~~~~~~~~~~~~~~~~~~~~~
Private Sub SideChanged(ByVal sender As Object, ByVal e As System.EventArgs) _
Handles txtSideA.TextChanged, txtSideB.TextChanged, txtSideC.TextChanged

    Me.lblArea.Text = Nothing
    Me.lblPerimeter.Text = Nothing
    Me.lblType.Text = Nothing

End Sub

End Class
```

testing and debugging

Running Triangle Calculator, entering values for sides, and clicking Area, Perimeter, and Type displays the interface similar to:

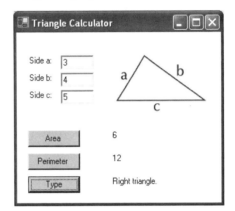

This Case Study should be tested by typing invalid values as well as values that correspond to the three triangle types.

Review 7

Modify the Triangle Calculator Case Study application to include a Height button. Clicking this button should display the height of the triangle with sides as typed by the user. The height of a triangle can be calculated with the formula h=2A/c. Implement Height() as a method of the Triangle class.

A class is a composite data type that groups related data and procedures and is the basis of object-oriented programming. A class is used to create objects. A statement declaring a new object uses the class as the data type and is said to instantiate the object. Classes have members that can include data, properties, and methods. These members are available to objects of the class. Objects are instantiated in a **Dim** statement that includes the **New** keyword.

A class should be created when an application requires a related set of data and actions. Before coding a class, a design that includes a list of members should be created. From the design, an algorithm and pseudocode should be generated.

A class is coded in a Class module, which is added to a project by selecting **Add Class** from the **Project** menu. A new class module contains a class declaration. There can be numerous fields, data members, properties, and methods in a class. In general, a class and its members takes the form:

Public Class *ClassName*

    Public Const *field member declaration*

    Private *data member declaration*

    Property *PropertyName()* **As** *ReturnType*
        methods for getting and setting private data member value
    End Property

    Sub New ()
        statements for initializing the object
    End Sub

    Public Sub *MethodName(parameters)*
        statements to perform a task
    End Sub

    Protected Sub *MethodName(parameters)*
        statements to perform a task
    End Sub

End Class

The methods of a class are the only way an object of the class can change data values. Limiting access to data is called data hiding and is the basis for encapsulation, an important aspect of object-oriented programming. Encapsulation is accomplished by using access modifiers. The **Private** access modifier is used to declare a field or data as accessible to only the methods of the class. **Protected** is used to declare a member that can be used from within the class only. **Public** is used to explicitly declare a member available to an object of the class. In a Form1 module, public methods and properties appear in an AutoList after typing an object name followed by a dot.

A field stores a constant in a class. A field is used to store a constant in a class. Fields declared as **Private Const** can be used in methods of the class only. A **Public Const** field can be used by an object of the class as well as methods of the class. Data members are variables used by the methods and properties in a class. A property is used to return or change information about an object.

A constructor is a method that is automatically called when an object is instantiated. Statements for initializing data members can be placed in the constructor. Constructors are commonly overloaded. A set of methods that each have the same name but a different set of parameters are said to be overloaded.

A new class can be based on an existing class. The **Inherits** statement is used in the class declaration to give the new class all the features of an existing class. The new class is called the derived class and the inherited class is called the base class.

Polymorphism is an object-oriented programming (OOP) feature that allows methods to be redefined in derived classes. Methods must be overridable in the base class in order to be redefined in the derived class. The **Shadows** keyword can be used to override a field member in the base class with a member of the same name in the derived class.

An important aspect of object-oriented code is code reuse. An existing class can be added to a project with the Add Existing Item command from the Project menu. Another way to reuse code is to use the Add Existing Item command to add an existing form.

Base class A class that is inherited by another class.

Class A composite data type that groups related data and procedures.

Class module A separate file used to code a new class. Appears as a separate code window containing a class declaration in the IDE.

Constructor A method that is automatically called when an object is instantiated.

Data hiding Limiting access to data in a class.

Data member A variable member in a class.

Derived class A class based on another class.

Encapsulation Data hiding in a class. Implemented with access modifier keywords.

Field member A constant member in a class.

Instantiation Creating an object of a class. A Dim statement with a class name as the data type.

Method member A member of a class that is a type of procedure.

Object An instance of a class.

Overloaded A method that performs an action depending on the number and type of arguments it receives.

Polymorphic A method that can appear to change its task to meet the needs of the object calling it.

Property A member of a class that can get (display) and set (assign) a value that is a data member of an object's class.

Visual Basic .NET

Add Class **command** Adds a new module with a Class declaration to an open project. Found in the Project menu.

Add Exiting Item **command** Adds an existing form or class to a project. Found in the Project menu.

Get() Procedure used for returning a data member value to a calling object.

Inherits Statement used in a Class declaration to give a new class all the features of an existing class.

New Keyword used in a statement to declare a new object.

Overridable Keyword used in a base class method declaration to allow a general purpose method to be redefined in a derived class.

Overrides Keyword used in a derived class method declaration to redefine a method from the base class.

Private Access modifier keyword that declares a member of a class as accessible to the class only.

Private Const Declaration used in a statement to declare a field as accessible to the class only.

Property Statement used to declare a property for a class.

Protected Access modifier keyword that declares a member of a class as accessible to the class and derived classes.

Public Access modifier keyword that declares a member of a class as accessible to class objects.

Public Class Statement used to declare a new class.

Public Const Declaration used in a statement to declare a field as accessible to the class and class objects.

ReadOnly Keyword used in a property declaration to allow a class object to get the property value, but not set the value.

Set() Procedure used to give a data member a new value from the calling object.

Shadows Keyword used in a derived class field declaration to redefine a field.

1. Programmers using an OOP language often analyze a task to distinguish between the nouns in the problem and the verbs in the problem. This helps them decide between the needed methods and classes. Fill in either *method* or *property*:
   a) Nouns (person, place, thing) help decide the _____ needed.
   b) Verbs (action) help decide the _____ needed.

2. Imagine a band festival where many Bands are playing—the TwoToos, the EggRolls, and Goop. Each band can TuneUp, PlayMusic, and TakeABow. A SetList can be read or created. If this was simulated in an object-oriented program, what would appropriate names be for:
   a) the class
   b) the objects
   c) a property
   d) the methods

3. Assume a class for a sports team named Team.
   a) List three possible object names.
   b) List three possible methods.
   c) List three possible properties.

4. What is the difference between a class and an object?

5. a) Explain the similarities and differences between field members, data members, and property members. Be sure to discuss their accessibility within the class and with objects of the class.
   b) What keyword is required to prevent a property's value from being changed?

6. State the keyword needed for each:
   a) the method in a base class that will be redefined in a derived class
   b) a field member in a base class that will be redefined in a derived class
   c) a method that is redefined in a derived class
   d) a data member that is accessible to methods of the class only
   e) a method of a class that cannot be directly called by an object of the class
   f) a method of a class that can be called an object of the class
   g) base class field members and data members that are expected to be redefined in a derived class

7. How does Visual Basic .NET know which overloaded method to use?

8. a) What is data hiding and how is it related to encapsulation?
   b) How is data hiding accomplished?

9. What are two ways to reuse code?

10. Explain the similarities and differences between inheritance and polymorphism.

11. Assume a base class named FamilyMembers and derived classes Parent and Child.
    a) List three possible methods or properties that would be in both derived classes.
    b) List three possible methods or properties that would be specific to the Parent class.
    c) List three possible methods or properties that would be specific to the Child class.

12. Write a statement to instantiate an object named CookieRookie of type IceCream.

13. What are the similarities and differences of the Set() and Get() procedures?

14. Use the following to answer the questions below:

```
Public Class Foo
    Inherits Moo

    Shadows Const Zoo As Single = 20
    Private Const Voo As String = "You"
    Private Goo As String
    Property Coo() As String
        ...
    End Property
    Public Overrides Sub Too()
        ...
    End Sub
    Protected Sub Woo()
        ...
    End Sub
End Class
```

    a) What is the derived class?
    b) What is the base class?
    c) Which method has been redefined?
    d) Which data member is new to the derived class?
    e) Which field member has been redefined?
    f) Which field member is new to the derived class?
    g) Which method can be called from the derived class only?
    h) Which is a new property for the derived class?
    i) Assume Loo is a string data member in the base class. How should its declaration appear in the base class if Loo should be accessible to members of the derived class?

15. a) Write the property procedure for an object property named Fastest. Fastest can get or set the FastOne data member in its class, which is declared as
       Private FastOne As String

    b) Write the statement needed to instantiate a Car object of the Vehicle class.
    c) What does the following code in the Vehicle class do?

       Private Const DEFAULT_FASTONE As String = "Concord"

```
Sub New()
    Me.FastOne = DEFAULT_FASTONE
End Sub
```

d) Write the statements needed in the Form1 code module to prompt the user with an input box for the name of the fastest car and then use this string to set the Fastest property of an object named Car.

e) Write a statement for the Form1 code module which displays the fastest car for an object in a message in a message box, similar to: The fastest car is _____

16. Determine if each of the following is true or false. If false, explain why.
   a) Instantiation is the process of creating a new class.
   b) Classes are coded in the Form1 code module.
   c) A class uses encapsulation to limit accessibility of certain members.
   d) An AutoList displays all the methods of the class for an object.
   e) Constants used in a class are called fields.
   f) A protected field member can be used by the class only.
   g) It is possible to have a property which has no Set() procedure.
   h) Overloaded methods allow different actions with the same number of parameters.
   i) Only constructor methods can be overloaded.
   j) The code for an inherited class needs to be in the same project as the derived class.
   k) All methods from a base class can be redefined in a derived class.
   l) A derived class can have methods and properties not found in the base class.
   m) Methods must always be Sub procedures.

Exercise 1 ———————————————————————— Employees

Create an Employees application that allows the user to enter data for as many employees as wanted and then display information for a specific employee. The application interface should look similar to the following after adding several new employees and updating and displaying employee information:

Your program code should:

- include an Employee class, as described below.
- use a dynamic array of Employee objects to maintain a set of employees.
- display input boxes for user input.
- include a FindItemIndex() function that returns the index location in the array of the employee with the indicated employee number or –1 otherwise.
- display messages indicating "Not valid." if the employee number does not exist.
- display formatted output.

The Employee class should include the following members:

- an Employee data member that is type PersonalInfo. PersonalInfo is a structure that contains EmployeeNum, FirstName, and LastName string members.
- a Payroll data member that type PayrollInfo. PayrollInfo is a structure that contains HourlyRate, RegularHours, and OvertimeHours single members.
- properties that allow for getting and setting of each piece of Employee and Payroll data.
- a constructor that has a string parameter for the employee number to initialize EmployeeNum. The constructor should also include statements that initialize HourlyRate to 5 and RegularHours to 40.

- a constructor that accepts an employee number, first name, and last name string parameters to initialize EmployeeNum, FirstName, and LastName respectively. The constructor should also include statements that initialize HourlyRate to 5 and RegularHours to 40.
- Paycheck() public function that returns the paycheck amount. The paycheck amount is calculated by multiplying regular hours worked by hourly rate and adding the overtime hours multiplied by time and a half (hourly rate x 1.5).

Exercise 2 — Students

Create a Students application that allows the user to enter data for as many students as wanted and then display information for a specific student. The application interface should look similar to the following after entering a first and last name, clicking Display Full Name, clicking Enter Score several times to enter scores, and clicking each button to display information:

The Students application should contain a class named Student with the following members:

- FirstName and LastName properties for getting and setting the student's name.
- FullName read-only property for displaying a student's full name. Hint: Concatenate the first name and last name.
- Avg, Max, and Min read-only properties for getting the average, maximum, and minimum scores entered for the student.
- A NewScore() public method for adding a new score to the student's total score. The number of scores used for the total score should also be updated.

Create a Test DynamicArray application that is similar to the Dynamic Array Demo application presented in Chapter 9. The application interface should look similar to the following after adding several values, removing values, and clicking Sum:

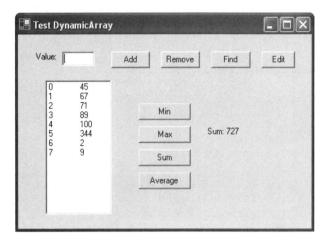

The Test DynamicArray application should contain a class named DynamicArray with the following members:

- a dynamic array data member with zero integer elements.
- Sum, Avg, Max, and Min read-only properties for getting the sum, average, max, and min of the numbers in the array.
- AddItem() and DeleteItem() public methods that add an item to or remove an item from the array, respectively.
- FindItemIndex() public function that returns the index of the item being searched for or –1 otherwise.
- Edit() public function that replaces an old element value with a new element value and returns 0 if successful and –1 if the index is invalid.
- GetStats() protected method that calculates the sum, average, maximum, and minimum values of the array contents and is called by AddItem, DeleteItem, and Edit every time a change is made to the array.
- DisplayContents() public method that displays the array contents in a list box.

The Test DynamicArray should contain the event procedure below:

```
Private Sub AButton_Click(ByVal sender As System.Object, _
ByVal e As System.EventArgs) Handles btnAdd.Click, _
btnRemove.Click, btnFind.Click, btnEdit.Click, btnMax.Click, btnMin.Click, _
btnSum.Click, btnAverage.Click

    Static Numbers As New DynamicArray()
    Dim intNum As Integer
    Dim ButtonClicked As Button = sender
    If Me.txtValue.Text = Nothing And (ButtonClicked.Tag = "Add" Or _
    ButtonClicked.Tag = "Remove" Or ButtonClicked.Tag = "Find" Or _
    ButtonClicked.Tag = "Edit") Then
        MessageBox.Show("Type a value before selecting a button.")
```

```
        Else
            intNum = Val(Me.txtValue.Text)
            Select Case ButtonClicked.Tag
                Case "Add"
                    Numbers.AddItem(intNum)
                Case "Remove"
                    Numbers.DeleteItem(intNum)
                Case "Find"
                    Dim Result As Integer = Numbers.FindItemIndex(intNum)
                    If Result = -1 Then
                        Me.lblDisplay.Text = intNum & " not found."
                    Else
                        Me.lblDisplay.Text = intNum & " found at index: " & Result
                    End If
                Case "Edit"
                    Dim intNewValue As Integer = InputBox("Enter new value ")
                    Dim Result As Integer = Numbers.Edit(intNum, intNewValue)
                    If Result = -1 Then
                        Me.lblDisplay.Text = "The value " & intNum & " not found."
                    Else
                        Me.lblDisplay.Text = "Value changed."
                    End If
                Case "Min"
                    Me.lblDisplay.Text = "Min: " & Numbers.ShowMin
                Case "Max"
                    Me.lblDisplay.Text = "Max: " & Numbers.ShowMax
                Case "Sum"
                    Me.lblDisplay.Text = "Sum: " & Numbers.ShowSum
                Case "Average"
                    Me.lblDisplay.Text = "Average: " & Numbers.ShowAverage
            End Select
            Numbers.DisplayContents(Me.lstOutput)
        End If
        Me.txtValue.Text = Nothing        'clear text box
        Me.txtValue.Select()              'move cursor to text box
    End Sub
```

Exercise 4 ———————————————— My Pizza Shop

Create a My Pizza Shop application, similar to the Pizza Order Case Study from Chapter 5. Use a Pizza class to instantiate NewPizza objects. The Pizza class should have the following members:

- RegularPrice and LargePrice fields that store values of 6 and 10 respectively (for $6 and $10).
- PizzaPrice, Toppings, and Size properties for getting and setting the pizza price, number of toppings, and pizza size.
- a constructor that takes no parameters and initializes the pizza size to Regular and the pizza price to RegularPrice.
- ToppingsPrice() public function that returns the toppings price of the pizza.
- PiePrice() public function that returns the total pizza price.

Exercise 5 —————————————————————————— Name Options

Create a Name Options applicationthat prompts the user for first, middle, and last names and provides several options for displaying the names in different ways. The project should include a Name class with the following members:

- a constructor with three parameters that initialize First, Middle, and Last data members.
- A FullName() read-only property that returns a single string containing First, Middle, and Last names separated by spaces.
- A LastCommaFirst() read-only property that returns a single string containing the Last name followed by a comma and a space and then the First name.
- A Signature() read-only property that returns a single string containing the First name followed by a space, the first initial of Middle name followed by a space, and then Last name.
- An Initials() read-only property that returns a single string containing the first inital of First name, first initial of Middle name, and then the first initial of Last name.
- A Monogram() read-only property that returns a single string containing the first initial of First name, the uppercase first inital of Last name, and then the first inital of Middle name.

Exercise 6 —————————————————————————— Metric System

Create a Metric System application with options that demonstrates all the features of a Metric class, which should include:

- InchCentFactor, FeetCentFactor, YardMeterFactor, and MileKiloFactor field members that store the conversion factors 2.54, 30, .91, and 1.6, respectively.
- InchToCent() and CentToInch() public functions that return the unit of measurement from inches to centimeters or from centimeters to inches. Inches are converted to centimeters by multiplying the value in inches by the InchCentFactor conversion factor (2.54). Centimeters are converted to inches by dividing the value in centimeters by InchCentFactor.
- FeetToCents() and CentsToFeet() public functions that return the unit of measurement from feet to centimeters or from centimeters to feet. Feet is converted to centimeters by multiplying the value in feet by the FeetCentFactor conversion factor (30). Centimeters are converted to feet by dividing the value in centimeters by FeetCentFactor.
- YardsToMeters() and MetersToYards() public functions that return the unit of measurement from yards to meters or from meters to yards. Yards are converted to meters by multiplying the value in yards by the YardMeterFactor conversion factor (.91). Meters are converted to yards by dividing the value in meters by YardMeterFactor.
- MilesToKilos() and KilosToMiles() public functions that return the unit of measurement from miles to kilometers or from kilometers to miles. Miles are converted to kilometers by multiplying the value in miles by the MileKiloFactor conversion factor (1.6). Kilometers are converted to miles by dividing the value in kilometers by MileKiloFactor.

Chapter 12
Using Files

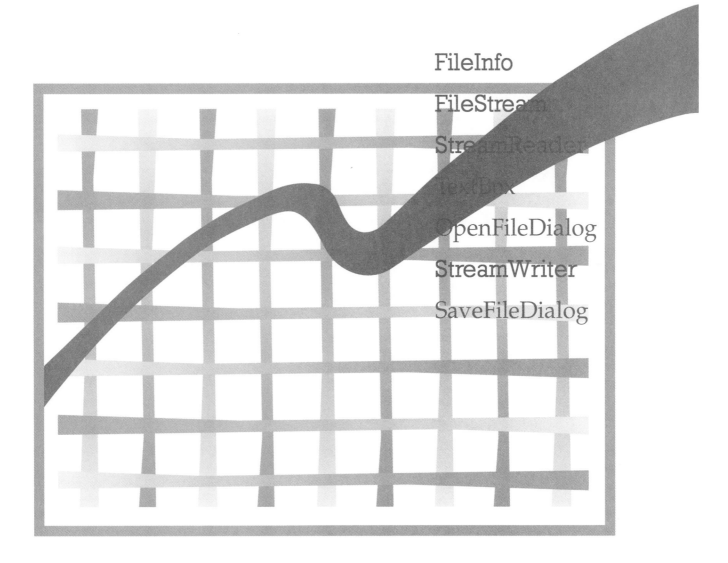

FileInfo

FileStream

StreamReader

TextBox

OpenFileDialog

StreamWriter

SaveFileDialog

Chapter 12 Expectations

After completing this chapter you will be able to:

1. Use files for data input.

2. Create, copy, and delete files at run time.

3. Understand a file stream.

4. Use a stream reader to read file contents.

5. Use a text box to display file contents.

6. Create event procedures for a KeyPress event.

7. Use the **Keys** enumerated type to determine the key pressed.

8. Include Open and Save As dialog boxes in an application.

9. Use a stream writer to create file contents.

Files are used by many applications for storing and retrieving data. In this chapter, file streams and the Visual Basic .NET classes used to handle files are introduced. Advanced features of text boxes, as well as the OpenFileDialog and SaveFileDialog controls, are discussed.

12.1 What is a File?

Up to this point, the applications created in this text have stored data in the computer's memory in the form of variables and arrays. However, storage in memory is available only when the computer is on and an application is running. A *file* is a collection of related data stored on a per-sistent medium such as a hard disk, a CD, or a diskette. *Persistent* simply means lasting.

persistent

Files often store data used by an application. A file is separate from the application using it and can be read from and written to by more than one application. Most applications require access to one or more files on disk.

Text Files

Text file names typically have a file name extension of .txt, .dat, or .log. Text files can contain characters or numeric data. However, .dat files typi-cally contain numeric data only. The application reading the file must accomodate for the type of data expected.

12.2 The FileInfo Class

The Visual Basic .NET **FileInfo** class is used to create an object for a specific file. The **FileInfo** class constructor requires a file name when an object is instantiated, as in the declaration:

Dim SchoolSuppliesList **As New** FileInfo("mylist.txt")

Property and method members of the **FileInfo** class include:

- **Exists** returns a Boolean value. True indicates the file exists and False indicates the file does not exist.

- **Length** returns a value that is the file size in bytes.

- **FullName** returns a string that is the full path and file name of the file associated with the **FileInfo** object.

- **Create()** creates a new, empty file using the name in the object declaration.

- **CopyTo(*newFilename*)** copies the existing file associated with the **FileInfo** object to *newFilename*, which cannot already exist.

- **Delete()** permanently deletes the file associated with the **FileInfo** object.

Creating a Text File

Visual Basic .NET can be used to create a text file. Select File ➔ New ➔ File to display the New File dialog box. Click the Text File icon and then select Open. A text file win-dow is displayed in the IDE where data can be typed. Select File ➔ Save to display the Save File As dialog box and navigate to the bin folder of the project folder. The file is automatically saved with a .txt extension.

Imports statement

Using the **FileInfo** class requires an **Imports** System.IO statement at the top of the code module.

The following code demonstrates the **FileInfo** properties and methods:

```
'Create object for specific file
Dim SchoolSuppliesList As New FileInfo("mylist.txt")
If Not SchoolSuppliesList.Exists Then        'if file does not exist
    SchoolSuppliesList.Create()              'create an empty file
    MessageBox.Show("New file created.")
Else                                         'display full path, name, and file size
    MessageBox.Show(SchoolSuppliesList.FullName & _
    " exists. File size: " & SchoolSuppliesList.Length)
End If

'Copy school supplies list to a new file
SchoolSuppliesList.CopyTo("newlist.txt")

'Delete file with school supplies list
SchoolSuppliesList.Delete()
```

> ### *Creating a File at Run Time*
>
> If a path is not specified in the application creating a file, the file is created in the bin folder of the project folder for the application.

Review 1

In this review you will create the My File application.

① **CREATE A NEW PROJECT**

Create a Windows application named My File.

② **CREATE THE INTERFACE**

Refer to the form below to add, position, and size objects. Use the table below to set properties.

Object	Name	Text
Form1		My File
Button1	btnCreateFile	Create File
Button2	btnDeleteFile	Delete File

③ **WRITE THE APPLICATION CODE**

   a. Display the Code window.

   b. Add comments that include your name and today's date.

   c. At the very top of the code module, add an **Imports** System.IO statement. The Code window should look similar to:

```
Imports System.IO

Public Class Form1
    Inherits System.Windows.Forms.Form

    Windows Form Designer generated code
```

   d. Add a global variable declaration:

   Const strFILENAME **As String** = "myfile.txt"

e. Create a btnCreateFile_Click event procedure and then add the statements:

```
Dim TestFile As New FileInfo(strFILENAME)
If Not TestFile.Exists Then          'if file does not exist
    TestFile.Create()                'create an empty file
    MessageBox.Show("New file created.")
Else                                 'display full path, name, and file size
    MessageBox.Show(TestFile.FullName & " exists. File size: " _
    & TestFile.Length)
End If
```

f. Create a btnDeleteFile_Click event procedure and then add the statements:

```
Dim TestFile As New FileInfo(strFILENAME)
TestFile.Delete()
MessageBox.Show(TestFile.FullName & " deleted.")
```

④ **RUN THE APPLICATION**

a. Save the modified My File project.

b. Run the application. Select **Create File**. A message box informs that a file is created. Select **Create File** again. A message box informs that the file already exists.

c. Close the My File application.

d. Run the application again. Select **Delete File**. The file is deleted.

e. Close the My File application.

⑤ **PRINT THE CODE AND THEN CLOSE THE PROJECT**

12.3   The File Stream

file position
sequential access file

In Visual Basic .NET, a file must be associated with a stream in order to perform operations on its contents, such as reading the contents, writing over the existing contents, and adding to the existing contents. The *file stream* keeps track of the *file position*, which is the point where reading or writing last occurred. File streams usually perform *sequential file access*, with all reading and writing done one character after another or one line after another. The stream can also be closed to prevent further file access.

A *stream* can be thought of as a sequence of characters. For example, a file containing a list of school supplies may look like the following when viewed in a word processor:

> 6 pens
> binder

However, when thinking about file operations, the file should be visualized as a stream:

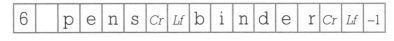

A file can be thought of as a stream of characters

line terminator
end of file

The carriage return character (Cr) followed by a line feed character (Lf) is called a *line terminator*. A –1 indicates *end of file*.

Data Streams

A stream applies to data input/output in general. For example, memory, information sent to a printer, and data sent and received from an Internet site can all be streamed.

FileStream

The Visual Basic .NET **FileStream** class is used to create a stream object for a specific file. The **FileStream** constructor requires a file name, mode, and type of access to instantiate an object, as in the declaration:

Dim fs **As New** FileStream("motto.txt", FileMode.Open, FileAccess.Read)

FileMode.Open
FileAccess.Read

The file mode indicates how the file should be opened or created. When reading from a file, the mode should be FileMode.Open, which is a constant that indicates an existing file should be opened. FileAccess.Read is a constant that indicates that the file should be opened for reading only.

Property and method members of the **FileStream** class include:

- **Length** returns a value that is the file size in bytes.

- **Position** can be set at run time to 0, which positions the file stream at the beginning of the file.

- **Close()** closes the file. Once a file stream is closed, a new one must be declared to access a file.

StreamReader

After a stream has been established, a stream reader can be used to read characters and lines of text from a file. The Visual Basic .NET **StreamReader** class contains methods for reading data from a stream. The **StreamReader** constructor requires an existing stream to instantiate an object, as in the declaration:

Dim TextFile **As New** StreamReader(fs)

Method members of the **StreamReader** class include:

- **Peek()** returns the value of the next character without actually taking it from the stream.

ChrW()
Val()

- **Read()** returns the next character in the stream as a integer value. ChrW() must be used to convert the integer to a character. If the character represents a number, Val() then be used to convert the character to a number.

- **ReadLine()** returns the next set of characters up to the line terminator in the stream as a string.

- **Close()** closes the stream reader.

end of file

The end of file can be determined by looking ahead, or peeking, to the next character in the stream. A value of –1 indicates the end of the file has been reached. The following code demonstrates this as well as some methods for the **FileStream** and **StreamReader** classes:

```
Dim fs As New FileStream("motto.txt", FileMode.Open, FileAccess.Read)
Dim TextFile As New StreamReader(fs)

Dim strLineOfText As String            'stores a line read from a file
Do While TextFile.Peek > –1            'check for the end of file
    strLineOfText = TextFile.ReadLine()
    MessageBox.Show(strLineOfText)     'display a line of text
Loop

TextFile.Close()
fs.Close()
```

programming style

Statements are included to close the stream reader and stream when no longer needed as a matter of good programming style.

It is easiest to think of a file as a stream of characters. However, it is also important to remember that each character corresponds to a Unicode value that is numeric. For example, the character "a" corresponds to 97 and the character "5" corresponds to 53. When using the Read() method, the ChrW() function is used to convert the Unicode value to a character, as in the code:

using Read()
ChrW()

```
Dim chrCharFromFile As Char  'stores a character read from a file
Do While TextFile.Peek > –1          'check for the end of file
    chrCharFromFile = ChrW(TextFile.Read)  'convert Unicode
    MessageBox.Show(chrCharFromFile)         'display character
Loop

TextFile.Close()
fs.Close()
```

Unicode

A space corresponds to 32, a tab to 9, carriage return to 13, and line feed to 10. Refer to Section 6.11 for more information about Unicode.

Val()

If a stream contains data that should be treated as numeric rather than as characters, then Val() should also be used. For example, the statement below converts a Unicode value to a character and then the character's numeric equivalent:

```
intNumFromFile = Val(ChrW(TextFile.Read))     'number expected
```

Imports statement

StreamReader parameter

Using the **FileStream** and **StreamReader** classes requires the **Imports** System.IO statement at the top of the code module. When procedures are written to manipulate a file stream, only the stream reader **ByRef** parameter is needed.

12.5 Advanced TextBox Features

A text box is the best choice for displaying several lines of text at a time, as may be necessary to display the contents of a file. For example, the application interface below has a text box that can display many lines of text. The text box is docked, so that it changes size along with the form if the user sizes the interface at run time. Also note the scroll bars for displaying additional lines of text:

abl TextBox

The TextBox control properties that are set to make a text box object appropriate for displaying file contents include:

- **Dock** is the location of docking for the text box. Setting Dock to Bottom automatically sizes the text box so that the bottom, right, and left borders are anchored to the form. Dock can also be set to Top, Left, Right, or Fill.

- **ReadOnly** is set to True when the text box should be used for output only. When ReadOnly is True, text can be displayed in the text box, but the user will not be able to type in the text box.

- **Multiline** is set to True to allow the text box to display multiple lines of text. The box can then be sized vertically.

- **WordWrap** is set to True to wrap lines of text at the right border of the text box. WordWrap can be set to False, but it is not recommended because only one line of text will be displayed and it may extend beyond the right border of the text box.

- **ScrollBars** is set to Vertical to add a vertical scroll bar to the text box. A vertical scroll bar appears only when the WordWrap and Mutliline properties are also set to True. ScrollBars can also be set to None, Horizontal, or Both.

KeyPress event

The interface shown on the previous page also includes a text box for getting the file name. A TextBox object can respond to a Keypress event, which occurs when the user types in a text box. For example, the following KeyPress event procedure performs an action when the Enter key is pressed:

```
Private Sub txtFileName_KeyPress(ByVal sender As Object, _
ByVal e As System.Windows.Forms.KeyPressEventArgs) _
Handles txtFileName.KeyPress

    'User pressed the Enter key
    If e.KeyChar = ChrW(Keys.Enter) Then
        Dim FileNameTyped As New FileInfo(Me.txtFileName.Text)
        If FileNameTyped.Exists Then
            Call ShowFileContents(Me.txtFileName.Text)
        Else
            MessageBox.Show("File does not exist.")
        End If
    End If

End Sub
```

KeyChar property

Keys enumerated type

ChrW()

In the procedure heading, the e parameter contains properties specific to the key pressed. These properties include KeyChar, used in the If...**Then** condition, which stores a **Char** corresponding to the key pressed. Also used in the If...**Then** condition is the Visual Basic .NET Keys enumerated type with members that correspond to key names. Typing Keys. in the Code window displays an AutoList with member names. The ChrW() function is used to convert the **Enum** member to a character.

In this review you will create the Read File application.

① CREATE A NEW PROJECT

Create a Windows application named Read File.

② CREATE THE INTERFACE

Refer to the form below to add, position, and size objects. Use the table and instructions below to set properties.

Object	Name	Text
Form1		Read File
Label1	lblPrompt	File name to read:
TextBox1	txtFileName	*empty*
TextBox2	txtFileContents	*empty*

Set the txtFileContents ReadOnly and Multiline properties to True. Set the ScrollBars property to Vertical. Click the Dock property arrow and then click the bottom box to set Dock to Bottom:

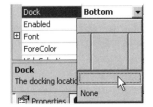

After setting properties, size the text box to extend just below the file name prompt.

③ WRITE THE APPLICATION CODE

a. Display the Code window.

b. Add comments that include your name and today's date.

c. At the very top of the code module, add an **Imports** System.IO statement.

d. Create a txtFileName_KeyPress event procedure and then add the statements:

```
'User pressed the Enter key
If e.KeyChar = ChrW(Keys.Enter) Then
    Dim FileNameTyped As New FileInfo(Me.txtFileName.Text)
    If FileNameTyped.Exists Then
        Call ShowFileContents(Me.txtFileName.Text)
    Else
        MessageBox.Show("File does not exist.")
    End If
End If
```

e. Create a ShowFileContents Sub procedure:

```
Sub ShowFileContents(ByVal strFileName As String)

    Dim fs As New FileStream(strFileName, FileMode.Open, FileAccess.Read)
    Dim TextFile As New StreamReader(fs)

    Me.txtFileContents.Text = Nothing          'clear text box of previous contents

    Dim strLineOfText As String                'stores a line read from a file
    Do While TextFile.Peek > –1                'check for the end of file
        strLineOfText = TextFile.ReadLine()
        'display line of text
        Me.txtFileContents.Text = Me.txtFileContents.Text & strLineOfText & vbCrLf
    Loop

End Sub
```

④ RUN THE APPLICATION

You will need the motto.txt file that is a data file for this text. motto.txt should be stored in the bin folder of the Read File project folder.

a. Save the modified Read File project and then run the application. Type motto.txt in the first text box. Press Enter. The file contents are displayed in the multiline text box. Try to type in the multiline text box. Input is not accepted because the text box is read only.

b. Close the Read File application.

⑤ PRINT THE CODE AND THEN CLOSE THE PROJECT

12.6 The OpenFileDialog Control

Rather than expecting the user to remember the full path and file name of a file, the Open dialog box can used. The OpenFileDialog component can be added to an application to display a predefined dialog box that allows the user to select a file by browsing:

When this dialog box is displayed, the file selected by the user can be assigned to a string variable for opening a file stream.

An Introduction to Programming Using Microsoft Visual Basic .NET

To add an Open dialog box to an application, click the OpenFileDialog control in the Toolbox, and then click the form. A component is displayed in the component tray at the bottom of the Design window. The OpenFileDialog control is a component that has no graphical element.

OpenFileDialog

The OpenFileDialog control has the properties:

- **Name** identifies an object for the programmer. It is good programming style to begin OpenFileDialog component names with opn.

- **FileName** is the file, including its path, selected in the dialog box.

An application that contains this component displays the dialog box with a statement similar to:

OpenFileDialog1.ShowDialog()

ShowDialog()

OpenFileDialog1 is the name of the component added to the interface. ShowDialog() is the method of the OpenFileDialog class that displays the dialog box.

The FileName property of an OpenFileDialog component contains the file name selected by the user. For example, the first statement below displays the Open dialog box. The application waits until the user selects Open or Cancel in the dialog box before continuing to the next statement. The second statement assigns the selected file name to a string, and the third statement creates a file stream for the selected file:

```
Me.opnOpenFile.ShowDialog()                'show dialog box
Dim strFileName As String = Me.opnOpenFile.FileName()
If strFileName <> Nothing Then
    Dim fs As New FileStream(strFileName, FileMode.Open, FileAccess.Read)
End If
```

Cancel   If the user selects Cancel in the dialog box, **Nothing** is returned.

Review 3 ⟳

In this review you will modify the Read File application to use the Open dialog box.

① *OPEN THE READ FILE PROJECT*

② *MODIFY THE INTERFACE*

    a. Delete the lblPrompt and txtFileName objects from the interface.

    b. Add a MainMenu object to the interface.

    c. Type File for the first MenuItem. Set the Name property to mnuFile.

    d. For the second menu item, type Open. Set the Name property to mnuOpen.

    e. For the third menu item, type Exit. Set the Name property to mnuExit.

    f. Size the text box to extend to just below the menu bar.

    g. Add an OpenFileDialog component to the interface. Set the Name property to opnOpenFile.

Check – The menu and interface should look similar to:

③ MODIFY THE APPLICATION CODE

a. Display the Code window.

b. Delete the txtFileName_KeyPress event procedure.

c. Create a mnuOpen_Click event procedure and add the statements to open an existing file and display its contents:

```
Me.opnOpenFile.ShowDialog()      'Open dialog box

'assign selected file name
Dim strFileName As String = Me.opnOpenFile.FileName()

'display file contents
If strFileName <> Nothing Then
   Call ShowFileContents(strFileName)
End If
```

d. Create a mnuExit_Click event procedure and then add a statement to end the application:

```
End
```

④ RUN THE APPLICATION

a. Save the modified Read File project.

b. Run the application. Select File → Open. The Open dialog box is displayed. Navigate to the bin folder of the project folder and then select motto (or motto.txt). Select Open. The file contents are displayed.

c. Select File → Exit. The Read File application is closed.

⑤ PRINT THE CODE AND THEN CLOSE THE PROJECT

12.7 The StreamWriter Class

Writing to a file also requires setting up a stream. The following statement instantiates a **FileStream** object for a new file named temp.txt that can be written to:

```
Dim fs As New FileStream("temp.txt", FileMode.Create, FileAccess.Write)
```

The FileMode.Create constant creates a new file and then opens it. If the file already exists, it is overwritten. Other file modes used when opening a file for writing include:

- **CreateNew** creates a new file only if a file by the same name does not exist and then opens the file.

- **OpenOrCreate** opens a file if it exists or creates a new file and then opens it.

- **Append** opens an existing file. Data written to the file is added to the end of existing data.

A stream writer is used to write characters and lines of text to a file stream. The Visual Basic .NET **StreamWriter** class contains methods for writing data to a stream. The **StreamWriter** constructor requires an existing stream to instantiate an object, as in the declaration:

Dim TextFile **As New** StreamWriter(fs)

Method members of the **StreamWriter** class include:

- **Write()** writes a character to the stream.

- **WriteLine()** writes a string followed by a line terminator to the stream.

- **Close()** closes the stream writer.

The code below demonstrates writing to a file:

```
Dim fs As New FileStream("temp.txt", FileMode.Create, FileAccess.Write)
Dim TextFile As New StreamWriter(fs)

Dim strLineOfText As String          'line of text to write to file
strLineOfText = "This is a text file."
TextFile.WriteLine(strLineOfText)
TextFile.WriteLine()
strLineOfText = "a"
TextFile.Write(strLineOfText)
strLineOfText = "b"
TextFile.Write(strLineOfText)

TextFile.Close()
fs.Close()
```

The stream writer and stream must be closed for the file to be properly written to.

Reading the temp.txt file after the code executes displays:

This is a text file.

ab

Using the **FileStream** and **StreamWriter** classes requires the **Imports** System.IO statement at the top of the code module. When procedures are written to manipulate a file stream, only the stream writer **ByRef** parameter is needed.

12.8 The SaveFileDialog Control

Rather than expecting the user to type the full path and file name of a file, the Save As dialog box can used. A SaveFileDialog component can be added to an application to display a predefined dialog box that allows the user to select a location by browsing:

When this dialog box is displayed, the user can navigate to the folder where the file should be saved, and then type a descriptive name in the File name box. Selecting Save saves the file using the typed name.

To add a Save As dialog box to an application, click the SaveFileDialog control in the Toolbox, and then click the form. A component is displayed in the component tray at the bottom of the Design window. The SaveFileDialog control is a component that has no graphical element.

SaveFileDialog

The SaveFileDialog control has the properties:

- **Name** identifies an object for the programmer. It is good programming style to begin SaveFileDialog component names with sav.

Cancel

- **FileName** can be changed from doc1 to another name that will be the default text displayed in the File name box of the dialog box. This text will be returned if the user selects Save without changing the name. This text is also returned if the user selects Cancel.

An application that contains this component displays the dialog box with a statement similar to:

SaveFileDialog1.ShowDialog()

ShowDialog()

SaveFileDialog1 is the name of the component added to the interface. ShowDialog() is the method of the SaveFileDialog class that displays the dialog box.

The FileName property of a SaveFileDialog component contains the file name typed by the user. For example, the first statement below displays the Save As dialog box. The application waits until the user selects Save or Cancel in the dialog box before continuing to the next statement. The remaining statements create a file stream and stream writer and write the contents of a text box to the file:

```
Me.savSaveFile.ShowDialog()           'display Save As dialog box
Dim strFileName As String = Me.savSaveFile.FileName
Dim fs As New FileStream(strFileName, FileMode.Create, FileAccess.Write)
Dim TextFile As New StreamWriter(fs)
TextFile.Write(Me.txtFileContents.Text)     'write text box contents to file
```

Note that the file stream FileMode is Create, which overwrites an existing file or creates a new file if one does not exist. This FileMode should be used because the SaveFileDialog automatically warns the user when an existing file name is selected, allowing the user to choose whether or not to overwrite an existing file.

Cancel If the user selects Cancel in the dialog box, the default file name specified in the FileName property is returned.

Review 4

In this review you will create the Write File application.

① *CREATE A NEW PROJECT*

Create a Windows application named Write File.

② *CREATE THE INTERFACE*

Refer to the form below to add, position, and size objects. Use the table and instructions on the next page to set properties.

Object	Name	Text
Form1		Write File
MenuItem1	mnuFile	File
MenuItem2	mnuNew	New
MenuItem3	mnuClose	Close
MenuItem4	mnuSave	Save
MenuItem5	mnuExit	Exit
SaveFileDialog1	savSaveFile	
TextBox1	txtFileContents	*empty*

Set the txtFileContents Dock property to Bottom. Set the Multiline property to True. Set the ScrollBars property to Vertical. Size the text box to extend just below the menu bar.

③ *WRITE THE APPLICATION CODE*

    a. Display the Code window.

    b. Add comments that include your name and today's date.

    c. At the very top of the code module, add an **Imports** System.IO statement.

    d. Create a mnuNew_Click event procedure and then add a statement to clear the file contents box:

```
Me.txtFileContents.Text = Nothing
```

    e. Create a mnuClose_Click event procedure and then add a statement to remove any text from the file contents box:

```
Me.txtFileContents.Text = Nothing
```

    f. Create a mnuSave_Click event procedure and then add statements to save the contents of the text box to a file:

```
Me.savSaveFile.ShowDialog()               'display Save As dialog box
Dim strFileName As String = Me.savSaveFile.FileName       'get file name

Dim fs As New FileStream(strFileName, FileMode.Create, FileAccess.Write)
Dim TextFile As New StreamWriter(fs)

TextFile.Write(Me.txtFileContents.Text)       'write text box contents to file

TextFile.Close()
fs.Close()
```

    g. Create a mnuExit_Click event procedure and then add a statement to end the application:

```
End
```

④ *RUN THE APPLICATION*

    a. Save the modified Write File project.

    b. Run the application. Type some text in the text box. Select File → Save. The Save As dialog box is displayed. Navigate to the bin folder of the project folder and then type a descriptive file name with the .txt extension. Select Save. The file is saved.

    c. Test the other commands.

    d. Close the Write File application.

⑤ *PRINT THE CODE AND THEN CLOSE THE PROJECT*

Modify the Write File application created in Review 4 to include an **Open** command. Selecting this command should display the Open dialog box, allowing the user to select a file. Use the ShowFileContents() procedure from Review 2 to display the file contents of the file selected by the user.

12.9 Reading and Writing Data

Applications often use files for data input. For example, a teacher might use an application that computes an average for a set of grades. If this application averaged grades from a file, there would be no need to modify the application itself, only the file containing the data needs to be updated when a different student's grades are to be computed.

The **StreamWriter** class WriteLine() method converts data to a string before writing it to a file. For example, the statements:

```
Dim x As Integer = 25
Dim b As Boolean = True
Dim d As Date = #12/22/2003#
TextFile.WriteLine(x)
TextFile.WriteLine(b)
TextFile.WriteLine(d)
```

produce the file:

```
25
True
12/22/2003 12:00:00 AM
```

Note that a default time is also written for a date. The Write() method can be used similarly to write data without a line terminator.

To read numeric data from a file, the **StreamReader** class is used to read strings and then the strings must be converted to the proper data type, as in the statements:

```
Dim x As Integer = Val(TextFile.ReadLine())     'convert to integer
Dim b As Boolean = TextFile.ReadLine()          'convert to Boolean
Dim d As Date = TextFile.ReadLine()             'convert to Date
Me.lblFileContents.Text = x & " " & b & " " & d
```

display in the label:

```
25 True 12/22/2003
```

Note that only a date is displayed.

In this review, you will create the Grade Calculator application. The specification for this application is:

> The teacher must be able to enter a record for a student that includes the student's name and five grades. Selecting the Add Student command adds the student record to the end of an existing file named stugrades.txt. The Clear Grades command removes any existing data in the stugrades.txt file so that a new set of student data can be created. The Show Grades command reads each student's name and corresponding set of grades and then displays each name and average grade rounded to 1 decimal place in a message box.

① CREATE A NEW PROJECT

Create a Windows application named Grade Calculator.

② CREATE THE INTERFACE

Refer to the forms below to add, position, and size objects. Use the table below to set properties. Note there are two screens below to better show all the objects:

Object	Name	Text
Form1		Grade Calculator
MenuItem1	mnuFile	File
MenuItem2	mnuAddStudent	Add Student
MenuItem3	mnuClearGrades	Clear Grades
MenuItem4	mnuShowGrades	Show Grades
MenuItem5	mnuExit	Exit
Label1	lblStuNamePrompt	Student Name:
TextBox1	txtStudentName	*empty*
Label2	lblGrade1Prompt	Grade 1:
TextBox2	txtGrade1	*empty*
Label3	lblGrade2Prompt	Grade 2:
TextBox3	txtGrade2	*empty*
Label4	lblGrade3Prompt	Grade 3:
TextBox4	txtGrade3	*empty*
Label5	lblGrade4Prompt	Grade 4:
TextBox5	txtGrade4	*empty*
Label6	lblGrade5Prompt	Grade 5:
TextBox6	txtGrade5	*empty*

③ WRITE THE APPLICATION CODE

a. Display the Code window.

b. Add comments that include your name and today's date.

c. At the very top of the code module, add an **Imports** System.IO statement.

d. Add two global constants and comments for each:

```
'file containing student data
Const strFILENAME As String = "stugrades.txt"

'number of grades entered for each student
Const intNUMGRADES As Integer = 5
```

e. Create a mnuAddStudent_Click event procedure and then add documentation and statements to add a student record to the data file and then clear the text boxes for the next student record:

```
'~~~~~~~~~~~~~~~~~~~~~~~~~~~~~~~~~~~~~~~~~~~~~~~~~~~~~~~~~
'Adds a student name and five (5) grades to a data file. Clears
'text boxes for new record.
'
'post: data file created, if necessary, and opened for adding data
'(append) to the end of existing data. Student name and five (5)
'grades (numeric scores) are added to the end of the file.
'~~~~~~~~~~~~~~~~~~~~~~~~~~~~~~~~~~~~~~~~~~~~~~~~~~~~~~~~~
Private Sub mnuAddStudent_Click(ByVal sender As Object, _
ByVal e As System.EventArgs) Handles mnuAddStudent.Click

    'create new file if necessary and opens file for appending data
    Dim fs As New FileStream(strFILENAME, FileMode.Append, FileAccess.Write)
    Dim TextFile As New StreamWriter(fs)

    'write student name and data to file
    TextFile.WriteLine(Me.txtStudentName.Text)
    TextFile.WriteLine(Me.txtGrade1.Text)
    TextFile.WriteLine(Me.txtGrade2.Text)
    TextFile.WriteLine(Me.txtGrade3.Text)
    TextFile.WriteLine(Me.txtGrade4.Text)
    TextFile.WriteLine(Me.txtGrade5.Text)

    'close stream writer and file stream
    TextFile.Close()
    fs.Close()

    'clear text boxes for new data
    Me.txtStudentName.Text = Nothing
    Me.txtGrade1.Text = Nothing
    Me.txtGrade2.Text = Nothing
    Me.txtGrade3.Text = Nothing
    Me.txtGrade4.Text = Nothing
    Me.txtGrade5.Text = Nothing

End Sub
```

f. Create a mnuShowGrades_Click event procedure and then add documentation and statements to read student information from the data file, compute an average grade, and display this information in a message box:

```
'~~~~~~~~~~~~~~~~~~~~~~~~~~~~~~~~~~~~~~~~~~~~~~~~~~~~~
'Reads student names and intNUMGRADES grades for each and then
'displays the student name and an average score in a message box.
'
'post: Data read from data file and an average grade computed and
'displayed for each student.
'~~~~~~~~~~~~~~~~~~~~~~~~~~~~~~~~~~~~~~~~~~~~~~~~~~~~~
Private Sub mnuShowGrades_Click(ByVal sender As Object, _
ByVal e As System.EventArgs) Handles mnuShowGrades.Click

    Dim fs As New FileStream(strFILENAME, FileMode.Open, FileAccess.Read)
    Dim TextFile As New StreamReader(fs)

    Dim strStudent As String
    Dim intStudent As Integer
    Dim sngTotalScore, sngAverageGrade As Single
    Do While TextFile.Peek > -1                    'check for the end of file
        strStudent = TextFile.ReadLine            'read student name
        sngTotalScore = 0                          'initialize score for each student
        For intStudent = 1 To intNUMGRADES        'read grades
            sngTotalScore = sngTotalScore + Val(TextFile.ReadLine)
        Next intStudent
        sngAverageGrade = Math.Round((sngTotalScore / intNUMGRADES), 1)
        MessageBox.Show(strStudent & " " & sngAverageGrade)
    Loop

    TextFile.Close()
    fs.Close()

End Sub
```

g. Create a mnuClearGrades_Click event procedure and then add documentation and statements to delete the existing data file:

```
'~~~~~~~~~~~~~~~~~~~~~~~~~~~~~~~~~~~~~~~~~~~~~~~~~~~~~
'Deletes the existing data file.
'
'post: strFILENAME deleted.
'~~~~~~~~~~~~~~~~~~~~~~~~~~~~~~~~~~~~~~~~~~~~~~~~~~~~~
Private Sub mnuClearGrades_Click(ByVal sender As Object, _
ByVal e As System.EventArgs) Handles mnuClearGrades.Click

    Dim DataFile As New FileInfo(strFILENAME)
    DataFile.Delete()

End Sub
```

h. Create a mnuExit_Click event procedure and then add a statement to end the application:

```
End
```

④ RUN THE APPLICATION

a. Save the modified Grade Calculator project.

b. Run the application. Test the application by adding two students and their grades and then show the grade averages.

c. Close the Grade Calculator application.

⑤ PRINT THE CODE AND THEN CLOSE THE PROJECT

In this Case Study the Word Guess application created in Chapter 6 will be modified to play a game with a randomly selected word from a file.

specification

The specification for this Case Study is:

A Word Guess II application that allows a user to guess the letters in a secret word. The secret word is randomly selected from a file containing 25 words that each have from 3 to 8 characters. The secret word is represented as a row of dashes on the form, with one dash for each letter. The user is prompted for a letter automatically and can enter a lowercase letter or an uppercase letter as a guess. If the letter is in the secret word, the appropriate dash(es) on the form is replaced by the letter guessed. The user may try to guess the word at any time. If the secret word is guessed, the word is displayed on the form along with the number of guesses made. If the wrong word is guessed, the user loses.

design

The interface design does not need to change from the original Word Guess application. However, the algorithm must take into account selecting a random word:

1. Generate a random number between 1 and 25.
2. Read *random number* number of lines in the secretwords.txt file. The word at line random number is the secret word.
3. Display the same number of dashes as in the secret word.
4. Prompt the user for a letter, but also allow the user to enter a flag if ready to guess the entire word.
5. Increment a guess counter.
6. If a letter was entered determine if the letter is in the secret word and then display the letter entered in the proper position on the form.
7. If the flag was entered, prompt the user for the entire word.
8. Repeat step 1 until the word has been guessed or the user gives up by clicking Cancel in the input box or leaves the input box empty.

The Chapter 6 case study is easily extended to read a word from a file because the original code accommodates a word of an unspecified length. The program is extended by simply adding a function that gets a secret word from a file. To match the specification, the secret word is made all uppercase because the player's guesses are converted to uppercase. The pseudocode for this case study is on the next page.

```
Sub btnPlayGame_Click()
    Const FLAG As Char = "!"
    Static NumGuesses As Integer = 0
    Dim LetterGuess As Char
    Dim WordGuess As String
    Dim LetterPos As Integer
    Dim TempWord As String
    Dim EndGame As Boolean

    Dim SecretWord = RandomSecretWord()
    Dim WordGuessedSoFar = ""
    Dim Length = SecretWord.Length
    WordGuessedSoFar = WordGuessedSoFar.PadLeft(Length, "–")
    Show WordGuessedSoFar in a label

    Get LetterGuess from user, ending game if Cancel is clicked
    Do While LetterGuess <> Flag And WordGuessedSoFar <> SecretWord _
    And Not EndGame
        Increment number of guesses
        Compare each letter of SecretWord to LetterGuess
        If LetterGuess matches a letter in SecretWord Then
            Replace appropriate dash in WordGuessedSoFar with LetterGuess
        If WordGuessedSoFar <> SecretWord Then
            Get LetterGuess from user, ending game if Cancel clicked
    Loop

    If WordGuessedSoFar = SecretWord Then
        Display message with number of guesses
    Else If LetterGuess = FLAG Then
        Show input box prompting for WordGuess
        If WordGuess = SecretWord Then
            Display message with number of guesses
        Else
            Display "you lose" message
    Else
        Display "game over" message
End Sub

Function RandomSecretWord() As String
    WordNum = A random number between 1 and 25
    Dim SecretWord As String
    For TextLine = 1 To WordNum–1
        TextFile.ReadLine(secretwords.txt)
    Next TextLine
    Return TextFile.ReadLine(secretwords.txt)
End Function
```

The interface for this Case Study, shown on the next page, has new
Text for the form and the label and form are wider to accommodate for
longer words. The modified code is below the interface:

Object	Name	Text	TextAlign	Font
Form1		Word Guess II		
Label1	lblSecretWord	*empty*	MiddleCenter	Size 36
Button1	btnPlayGame	Play Game		

Imports System.IO

Public Class Form1
   Inherits System.Windows.Forms.Form

   Windows Form Designer generated code

   Private Sub btnPlayGame_Click(**ByVal** sender **As Object**, **ByVal** e **As** System.EventArgs) _
   Handles btnPlayGame.Click

      Const chrFLAG **As Char** = "!"
      Const strGuessPrompt **As String** = "Enter a letter or " & chrFLAG & " to guess word:"
      Dim intNumGuesses **As Integer** = 0
      Dim chrLetterGuess **As Char**
      Dim strWordGuess **As String**
      Dim intLetterPos **As Integer**
      Dim strTempWord **As String**
      Dim blnEndGame **As Boolean** = False

      'get secret word
      Dim strSecretWord **As String** = RandomSecretWord()
      strSecretWord = strSecretWord.ToUpper   'make all uppercase

      'set same number of dashes as letters in strSecretWord
      Dim strWordGuessedSoFar **As String** = ""
      Dim intLength **As Integer** = strSecretWord.Length
      strWordGuessedSoFar = strWordGuessedSoFar.PadLeft(intLength, "–")
      Me.lblSecretWord.Text = strWordGuessedSoFar   'Initialize game

      'get first guess
      Dim strTempLetterGuess = InputBox(strGuessPrompt, **Me**.Text)
      'Test data entered
      If strTempLetterGuess = **Nothing Then**   'Cancel or empty text box
         blnEndGame = **True**
      Else   'user entered a letter
         chrLetterGuess = strTempLetterGuess
      End If

      Do While chrLetterGuess <> chrFLAG **And** strWordGuessedSoFar <> strSecretWord _
      And Not blnEndGame
         intNumGuesses = intNumGuesses + 1
         For intLetterPos = 0 **To** strSecretWord.Length – 1
           If strSecretWord.Chars(intLetterPos) = Char.ToUpper(chrLetterGuess) **Then**
              'remove dash at position of letter guessed
              strTempWord = strWordGuessedSoFar.Remove(intLetterPos, 1)
              'insert guessed letter
              strWordGuessedSoFar = strTempWord.Insert(intLetterPos, Char.ToUpper(chrLetterGuess))
              Me.lblSecretWord.Text = strWordGuessedSoFar   'Update interface
           End If
         Next intLetterPos

```vbnet
        'get next letter if word hasn't been guessed
        If strWordGuessedSoFar <> strSecretWord Then
            'get user guess
            strTempLetterGuess = InputBox(strGuessPrompt, Me.Text)
            'test data entered
            If strTempLetterGuess = Nothing Then        'Cancel or empty text box
                blnEndGame = True
            Else                                         'user entered a letter
                chrLetterGuess = strTempLetterGuess
            End If
        End If
    Loop

    If strWordGuessedSoFar = strSecretWord Then          'user guessed all letters
        MessageBox.Show("You guessed it in " & intNumGuesses & " guesses!")
    ElseIf chrLetterGuess = chrFLAG Then                 'user tries to guess word
        strWordGuess = InputBox("Enter a word:", Me.Text)
        If strWordGuess.ToUpper = strSecretWord Then
            MessageBox.Show("You guessed it in " & intNumGuesses & " guesses!")
            Me.lblSecretWord.Text = strSecretWord
        Else
            MessageBox.Show("Sorry you lose.")
        End If
    Else                                                 'end game
        MessageBox.Show("Game over.")
    End If

End Sub


'~~~~~~~~~~~~~~~~~~~~~~~~~~~~~~~~~~~~~~~~~~~~~~~~~~~~~~~~~~
'Reads a random word from a file with 25 words stored one word per line.
'
'pre: the file contains one word per line.
'post: a word that was randomly selected is returned.
'~~~~~~~~~~~~~~~~~~~~~~~~~~~~~~~~~~~~~~~~~~~~~~~~~~~~~~~~~~
Function RandomSecretWord() As String

    Dim fs As New FileStream("secretwords.txt", FileMode.Open, FileAccess.Read)
    Dim TextFile As New StreamReader(fs)

    'generate random number
    Dim intWord As Integer = Int(25 * Rnd())

    'read word from file
    Dim strLineOfText As String    'stores a line read from a file
    Dim intLineNum As Integer
    For intLineNum = 1 To intWord - 1
        TextFile.ReadLine()
    Next
    Return TextFile.ReadLine        'return word at position intWord

    TextFile.Close()
    fs.Close()

End Function


End Class
```

Running Word Guess and guessing two correct letters displays:

This Case Study should be tested by entering correct and incorrect characters and correct and incorrect word guesses.

Modify the Word Guess II Case Study to include a File menu with Add Word and New commands. The Add Word command prompts the user with an input box for a new word to add to the secretwords.txt file. The New command prompts the user with an input box for the number of new words and then displays that many more input boxes for getting the words. The new words are used to create a new secretwords.txt file, overwriting the existing words. The Case Study code and comments will need to modified to account for using a secretwords.txt file with an unknown number of words. Hint: The number of words in the file can be counted by counting how many lines can be read from the file. The FileStream Position() method may be used to set the file pointer back to the beginning of the file.

Chapter Summary

A file is a collection of related data stored on a persistent medium such as a hard disk. Files are often used to store data needed by applications. Text files store data as characters. However, an application can be written to convert data read to the expected data type. For example, a file containing numeral characters can be read by an application that includes the Val() function to convert strings to numbers.

The Visual Basic .NET FileInfo class includes properties and methods for creating, copying, and deleting files. The Imports System.IO statement must be included at the top of a program using file classes.

A stream can be thought of as a sequence of characters. A file stream is used for manipulating a file. The file stream keeps track of the file position, which is the point where reading or writing last occurred, and can write to, read from, and close a file to prevent further file access.

The Visual Basic .NET FileStream is used to create a file stream object for a specific file. The stream can access an existing file for reading, for appending data, or can create a new file.

The **StreamReader** class is used to create an object that can read characters from a specific stream. A stream reader object can peek ahead to determine if the end of file has been reached, and can read one character or one line of characters at a time from the stream.

The **StreamWriter** class is used to create an object that can write characters to a specific stream. A stream writer object can write one character or an entire line of characters at a time to the stream.

`abl` TextBox

A TextBox object has properties that can be set to display many lines of text. A text box can be docked in the form window, include scroll bars, and automatically wrap text. A text box that is set to read-only can display text, but will not allow the user to type in the text box.

A KeyPress event procedure can be coded for a text box. A KeyPress event occurs when the user presses a key while the text box has focus. The event procedure can be coded to check for the Enter key so that actions can be taken based on the text box entry. The Visual Basic .NET Keys enumerated type can be used to determine which key was pressed.

OpenFileDialog

An OpenFileDialog control is an component that displays the Open dialog box at run time, but has no graphical element. The OpenFileDialog control has the properties Name and FileName. An OpenFileDialog object name should begin with opn. The ShowDialog() method is used to display the dialog box at run time and the FileName property is used to determine which file the user has selected.

SaveFileDialog

Similar to the OpenFileDialog control is the SaveFileDialog control. The SaveFileDialog control is an component that displays the Save As dialog box at run time, but has no graphical element. The SaveFileDialog control has the properties Name and FileName. A SaveFileDialog object name should begin with sav. The ShowDialog() method is used to display the dialog box at run time and the FileName property is used to determine which file the user has selected or typed.

Vocabulary

End of file A value of –1 read from the file stream.

File A collection of related data stored on a persistent medium.

File position The point in a file stream where reading or writing last occurred.

File stream A file as a sequence of characters.

Line terminator The carriage return and line feed characters at the end of each line in a file.

Persistent Lasting.

Sequential Access File Reading or writing one character after another or one line after another in a file stream.

Stream A sequence of characters.

Visual Basic .NET

FileInfo class Used for creating an object associated with a specific file. Properties include Exists, Length, and FullName. Methods include Create(), CopyTo(), and Delete().

FileMode Visual Basic .NET enumerated type with members that include Open, Create, OpenOrCreate, and Append.

FileStream class Used for creating a stream object for a specific file. File modes include Open, CreateNew, OpenOrCreate, and Append. Properties include Length and Position. Methods include Close().

Imports Statement used to include a namespace in an application.

Keys Visual Basic .NET enumerated type with members that correspond to key names.

[OpenFileDialog] **OpenFileDialog control** Used to add an application component that displays the Open dialog box. Properties include Name and FileName. Methods include ShowDialog().

StreamReader class Used for creating a stream object for reading characters and lines of text from a file. Methods include Peek(), Read(), ReadLine(), and Close().

StreamWriter class Used for creating a stream object for writing characters and lines of text to a file. Methods include Write(), WriteLine(), and Close().

[SaveFileDialog] **SaveFileDialog control** Used to add an application component that displays the Save As dialog box. Properties include Name and FileName. Methods include ShowDialog().

[abl TextBox] **TextBox control** Used to create a control class object that can display multiple lines of text. Properties include Dock, ReadOnly, Multiline, WordWrap, and ScrollBars. Events include KeyPress.

1. List one advantage of having prices of inventory items read from a file as opposed to hard-coding them as constant values in a program.

2. Why should word wrap be allowed in a multiline text box?

3. Labels and text boxes both can display multiple lines of data. What is the advantage of using a text box?

4. Why might a programmer choose to use an OpenFileDialog component or a SaveFileDialog component instead of:
   a) prompting the user for a file name with a text box or input box?
   b) hard-coding the path and file name into the program?

5. A file named sales_tax.txt stores the current sales tax rate.
   a) Write statements to read the value from the file and store it in sngSalesTaxRate.
   b) The sales tax value needs to be changed. To do this during run-time, which file mode should be used and why?

6. Correct the error(s) in the following code:
```
'take info from textbox and save to a file of the users
'choice with a SaveFileDialog object
Me.savSaveFile.ShowDialog()
If strFileName <> Nothing Then        'Cancel not selected
    Dim fs As New FileStream(strFileName, FileMode.Create, FileAccess.Write)
    Dim TextFile As New StreamWriter
    TextFile.WriteLine = Me.txtFileContents.Text
    fs.Close()
End If
```

7. a) Write statements to read data from namefile.txt and then write each line, except for the line containing the string equal to strDeleteThis, to a file named tempfile.txt.
   b) What does the following code accomplish?
```
Dim TF As New FileInfo("namefile.txt")
TF.Delete()
Dim TTF As New FileInfo("tempnamefile.txt")
TTF.CopyTo("namefile.txt")
TTF.Delete()
```

8. CSV (comma separated values) is a common data file format, and files of this format have the file name extension .csv. A CSV file contains lines with two or more fields of data separated by commas.

a) What does the following code accomplish?

```
Dim fs As New FileStream("file.csv", FileMode.Open, FileAccess.Read)
Dim TextFile As New StreamReader(fs)
Dim intP As Integer
Dim strL, strE As String
Dim strInput As String = InputBox("Type in value")
If strInput <> Nothing Then
  Do While TextFile.Peek > –1
    strL = TextFile.ReadLine()
    intP = strL.IndexOf(",")
    strE = strL.Substring(intP + 1, strL.Length – intP – 1)
    If Val(strE) >= 70 Then
      Me.txtFileContents.Text = Me.txtFileContents.Text & strL.Substring(0, intP – 1) & _
        vbTab & strE & vbCrLf
    End If
  Loop
End If
fs.Close()
TextFile.Close()
```

b) Write the statements needed to perform a linear search on the file StudentGrades.csv. Each line of the CSV file has three fields. The first field is a student's last name, the second is a student's first name, and the third is the student's average. Search for a last name that matches strLast and a first name that matches strFirst and then display the message "_____ has an average of _____", otherwise display the message "Student not found." Assume the appropriate FileStream has been created, StudentFile is the name of the StreamReader, and that there can be only one student with the name being searched for.

9. Determine if each of the following is true or false. If false, explain why.
   a) File1.CopyTo(File2) will overwrite the current data in File2.
   b) A path must be specified when creating a new file at run time.
   c) A value of –1 in the file stream indicates the end of the file.
   d) Read() gets the next piece of data up to the next space.
   e) A multiline text box can only display data from a file.
   f) An application can contain a text box which the user cannot type in.
   g) Scroll bars can always be displayed in a multiline text box.
   h) The exact keystrokes of a user typing in a text box can be determined in a KeyPress event procedure.
   i) If the full path is not provided for a file, an application expects the file to be in the Project folder.
   k) Files used in a Visual Basic .NET program must have been created with Visual Basic. NET.
   l) When writing data to a file, the file will not actually be written to if the file stream writer is not closed.
   m) Read() and ReadLine() both return data as string values.
   n) The Append file mode adds data to the beginning of an existing file.

Exercise 1 ———————————————————————————— File Statistics

Create a File Statistics application that prompts the user for a file name. When Enter is pressed, the number of lines and the total number of characters in the typed text file or a message that the file does not exist is displayed. Several text files should be stored in the bin folder of the project folder for testing purposes. The application interface should look similar to:

Advanced Modify the File Statistics application to use the Read() method to report the visible number of characters in the file, ignoring all white space (tabs, carriage returns, line feeds, and spaces):

Exercise 2 ———————————————————————————— Number Statistics

Create a Number Statistics application that includes a File menu with Open and Exit commands. Open should display the Open dialog box to allow the user to select a file containing numeric data. The selected file's contents are then displayed in a text box, and the total and average of the numbers stored in the file can be displayed by clicking buttons, also on the interface. A file of numeric data with one number per line should be created for testing purposes. The application interface should look similar to the following after opening a file and clicking Total and Average:

Exercise 3 ———————————————————————— Mad-Lib

A Mad-Lib story is a story where nouns and verbs in a sentence are randomly replaced with other nouns and verbs, usually with humorous results. Create a Mad-Lib application that reads sentences, nouns, and verbs from separate text files to create a single mad-lib sentence. The following text files are available as data files with this text:

- sentences.txt contains one sentence per line, each with % signs as verb placeholders and # signs as noun placeholders. For example:

  Gloria Martin's job is to % all of the #s.

- verbs.txt contains verbs, one per line. For example:

  run
  display
  eat

- nouns.txt contains nouns, one per line. For example:

  banana
  soprano
  elephants
  vegetable

Hint: Use the StrConv() function, mentioned in the side bar on page 6-11 in the text, to change lower-case nouns to proper case for sentences that begin with nouns. The application interface should look similar to:

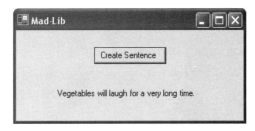

Exercise 4 ———————————————————————— Encode File

Create an Encode File application that encodes text by replacing each letter with a coded version, leaving nonletters unchanged. Use the CodeChar() function to encode each letter:

```
Function CodeChar(ByVal chrPlain As Char) As Char

    Select Case chrPlain
        Case "A" To "Y", "a" To "y"
            Return ChrW(AscW(chrPlain) + 1)
        Case "Z"
            Return "A"
        Case "z"
            Return "a"
        Case Else
            Return chrPlain
    End Select

End Function
```

Include a File menu with New, Open, Encode, Save, Close, and Exit commands. Selecting the Encode command should encode any text in the text box and write the coded text to a file named encoded.txt. The application interface should look similar to the following after opening a file containing a quote, selecting Encode, closing the original file, and then opening encoded.txt:

Exercise 5 —————————————————————— Append Files

Create an Append Files application that prompts the user for the names of two existing files. When the user clicks Append, an input box should be displayed prompting the user for the name of a third file to create from the contents of the two existing files. The third file's contents are then displayed in a text box. Display an appropriate message if either of the first two files do not exist. The application interface should look similar to the following after entering names of files stored in the bin folder of the project folder, clicking Append, and entering a new file name in the input box:

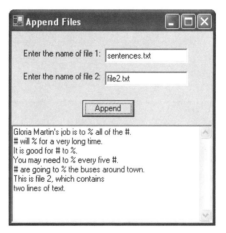

Exercise 6 —————————————————————————————— Quiz Results

Create a Quiz Results application that appends records containing quiz answers to a file named quizanswers.txt. If the file does not exist, one should be created. The records should be written with the student name on one line followed by a single T or F answer on the next five lines. The application should include a File menu with Add Student, Clear Records, Show Results, and Exit command, which allow records to be cleared, and quiz results to be displayed for each student in a message box. The application interface should look similar to the following after entering data for several students and selecting Show Results:

Exercise 7 —————————————————————————————— Replace Text

Create a Replace Text application that replaces all occurrences of a word or phrase in a file with a specified word or phrase. A text file should be stored in the bin folder of the project folder for testing purposes. The application interface should look similar to:

Exercise 8 —————————————————————————— Remove Text

Create a Remove Text application that removes all occurrences of a word or phrase in a file. A text file should be stored in the bin folder of the project folder for testing purposes. The application interface should look similar to:

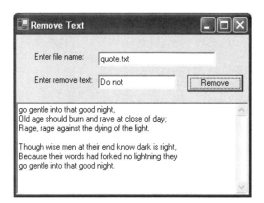

Exercise 9 (advanced) ————————————————— Merge Files

Create a Merge Files application that merges two files of sorted numbers into a third file of sorted numbers. For example, if the two files of sorted numbers are similar to the following and stored in the bin folder of the project folder:

file1.dat	file2.dat
12	4
23	5
34	10
45	20

then the application interface should look similar to:

The application should not use an array to temporarily store numbers, but should merge the two files by taking one element at a time from each and writing it to the new file.

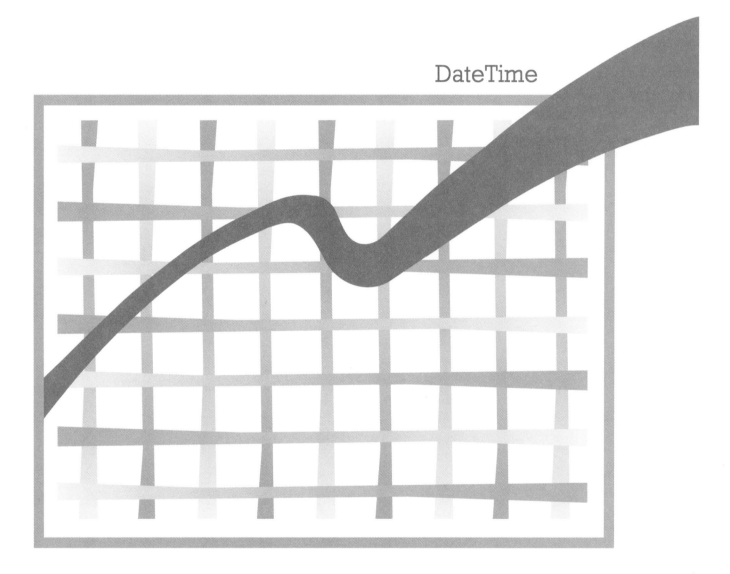

DateTime

Chapter 13 Expectations

After completing this chapter you will be able to:

1. Understand sorting.

2. Implement the bubble sort algorithm.

3. Use the built-in **DateTime** structure to determine the speed of sorts.

4. Implement the selection sort algorithm.

5. Implement the insertion sort algorithm.

6. Implement the binary search algorithm.

$\mathbf{S}$orting and searching algorithms are used in many applications for manipulating and analyzing data. In this chapter you will learn several of these algorithms.

13.1 Bubble Sort

sorting

Sorting is the process of putting items in a designated order, either from low to high or high to low. *Bubble sort* is a basic sorting algorithm that starts at the first element of a list of items and proceeds sequentially to the last, comparing each element with the next. If the first item is greater than the second, they are swapped. Then the second item is swapped with the third, if necessary, and so on until the end of the list is reached. This process is performed on each item in the list to "bubble" up items to their proper position.

For an array of integers, the BubbleSort procedure pseudocode is:

```
Sub BubbleSort(ByRef intArray() As Integer)
  For intItem = 0 To intArray.Length – 1
    For intIndex = 0 To intArray.Length – 2
      If intArray(intIndex) > intArray(intIndex+1) Then
        Swap intArray(intIndex) with intArray(intIndex+1)
      End If
    Next intIndex
  Next intItem
End Sub
```

The Bubble Sort application includes a BubbleSort() procedure to sort a list of randomly generated numbers:

```vb
Private Sub btnSort_Click(ByVal sender As System.Object, _
ByVal e As System.EventArgs) Handles btnSort.Click

    Dim intDataArray(-1) As Integer           'dynamic array

    'user chooses how many elements
    Dim intNumDataItems As Integer = Val(Me.txtNumElements.Text)
    If intNumDataItems > 0 Then
        'Create array of random numbers
        Call GenerateArray(intDataArray, intNumDataItems)

        'display generated array
        Me.lstListArrayElements.Items.Clear()    'clear any existing data
        Call DisplayData(intDataArray, Me.lstListArrayElements, "Original array:")

        'sort array
        Call BubbleSort(intDataArray)

        'Display sorted array in list box
        Call DisplayData(intDataArray, Me.lstListArrayElements, "Sorted array:")
    Else
        MessageBox.Show("Number of elements must be greater than 0.")
        Me.txtNumElements.Text = Nothing       'clear text box
    End If

End Sub


'~~~~~~~~~~~~~~~~~~~~~~~~~~~~~~~~~~~~~~~~~~~~~~~~
'Resizes intArray() to intNumElements and then assigns to
'each element a random integer between 1 and intMAXNUMBER.
'
'pre: intNumElements >= 0
'post: intArray() contains intNumElements elements with
'random integers between 1 and intMAXNUMBER.
'~~~~~~~~~~~~~~~~~~~~~~~~~~~~~~~~~~~~~~~~~~~~~~~~
Sub GenerateArray(ByRef intArray() As Integer, _
ByVal intNumElements As Integer)

    Const intMAXNUMBER As Integer = 100      'greatest value in an element
    ReDim intArray(intNumElements - 1)       'size array

    'assign each array element a random number
    Randomize()
    Dim intIndex As Integer
    For intIndex = 0 To intArray.Length - 1
        intArray(intIndex) = Int(intMAXNUMBER * Rnd()) + 1
    Next intIndex

End Sub


'~~~~~~~~~~~~~~~~~~~~~~~~~~~~~~~~~~~~~~~~~~~~~~~~~~~
'Displays the contents of intArray() in a list box.
'
'post: intArray() items displayed in a list box with a
'title at the top of the list.
'~~~~~~~~~~~~~~~~~~~~~~~~~~~~~~~~~~~~~~~~~~~~~~~~~~~
Sub DisplayData(ByRef intArray() As Integer, _
ByRef lstList As ListBox, ByVal strTitle As String)

    lstList.Items.Add(strTitle)        'title of list
    Dim intIndex As Integer
    For intIndex = 0 To intArray.Length - 1
        lstList.Items.Add(intIndex & vbTab & intArray(intIndex))
    Next intIndex

End Sub
```

```
'~~~~~~~~~~~~~~~~~~~~~~~~~~~~~~~~~~~~~~~~~~~~~
'Sorts intArray() from low to high.
'
'post: intArray() elements are sorted low to high.
'~~~~~~~~~~~~~~~~~~~~~~~~~~~~~~~~~~~~~~~~~~~~~
Sub BubbleSort(ByRef intArray() As Integer)

    Dim intItem, intIndex, intTemp As Integer

    'bubble each element as necessary
    For intItem = 0 To intArray.Length – 1
        'compare element to every other element
        For intIndex = 0 To intArray.Length – 2
            If intArray(intIndex) > intArray(intIndex + 1) Then
                'swap elements
                intTemp = intArray(intIndex)
                intArray(intIndex) = intArray(intIndex + 1)
                intArray(intIndex + 1) = intTemp
            End If
        Next intIndex
    Next intItem

End Sub
```

13.2   The DateTime Structure

One measure of the efficiency of a sorting algorithm is the speed at which it can complete a sort. The Visual Basic .NET **DateTime** structure includes members that can be used for timing:

- **Millisecond** property stores the number of milliseconds of a DateTime variable.

- **Now()** is a shared method that must be used with the **DateTime** structure. Now() returns the current time on the computer.

timing a sort   To time a sort, the start time can be compared to the end time, as in the statements below that time a bubble sort:

```
Dim datStart As New DateTime()
Dim datEnd As New DateTime()

datStart = DateTime.Now          'start time
Call BubbleSort(intDataArray)
datEnd = DateTime.Now            'end time

MessageBox.Show(datEnd.Millisecond – datStart.Millisecond)
```

Review 1

Modify the Bubble Sort application to display a label with the time required for a sort. Test the application with 1000, 3000, and 5000 elements.

13.3　A More Efficient Bubble Sort

The BubbleSort() procedure could be made more efficient by using a Do...Loop instead of a For...Next loop to process items. The For...Next processes every element in the array, even when no more swaps are needed to sort the list. By using a flag and a Do...Loop, processing need only be done until the list is sorted:

```
'~~~~~~~~~~~~~~~~~~~~~~~~~~~~~~~~~~~~~~~~~~~~~~~~~
'Sorts intArray() from low to high.
'
'post: intArray() elements are sorted low to high.
'~~~~~~~~~~~~~~~~~~~~~~~~~~~~~~~~~~~~~~~~~~~~~~~~~
Sub BubbleSort(ByRef intArray() As Integer)

  Dim intIndex, intTemp As Integer
  Dim blnSwapRequired As Boolean = True        'flag

  Do While blnSwapRequired
    blnSwapRequired = False
    For intIndex = 0 To intArray.Length – 2
      If intArray(intIndex) > intArray(intIndex + 1) Then
        'swap elements
        intTemp = intArray(intIndex)
        intArray(intIndex) = intArray(intIndex + 1)
        intArray(intIndex + 1) = intTemp
        blnSwapRequired = True
      End If
    Next intIndex
  Loop

End Sub
```

Note that the blnSwapRequired flag is True upon entering the loop and then immediately made False. If values are swapped, blnSwapRequired is made True to indicate that the list was still not sorted. When one pass can be made through the list without any swaps, the loop is exited.

Review 2　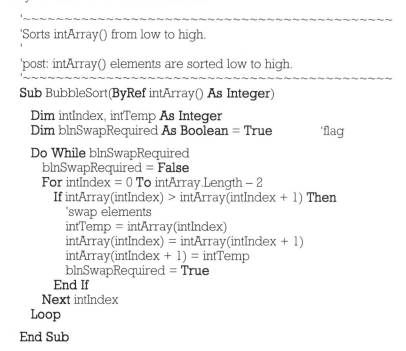

Modify the Bubble Sort application, last modified in Review 1, to include the more efficient BubbleSort() procedure in Section 13.3. Test and time the application with 1000, 3000, and 5000 elements.

An Introduction to Programming Using Microsoft Visual Basic .NET

13.4 Selection Sort

The *selection sort* is an algorithm that starts by finding the lowest item in a list and swapping it with the first. Next, the lowest item among items 2 through the last is found and swapped with item 2, and then the lowest item among items 3 through the last is swapped with item 3. This process is continued until the last item is reached, at which point all the items will be sorted.

For an array of integers, the SelectionSort() procedure pseudocode is:

```
Sub SelectionSort(ByRef intArray() As Integer)
  For intIndex = 0 To LastArrayItem
    LowItemIndex = FIndLowest(intArray(intIndex), intArray(LastArrayItem))
    Swap(intArray(intIndex), intArray(LowItemIndex))
  Next intIndex
End Sub
```

The Selection Sort application below includes the SelectionSort() procedure:

```
Private Sub btnSort_Click(ByVal sender As System.Object, _
ByVal e As System.EventArgs) Handles btnSort.Click

  Dim intDataArray(-1) As Integer              'dynamic array

  'user chooses how many elements
  Dim intNumDataItems As Integer = Val(Me.txtNumElements.Text)
  If intNumDataItems > 0 Then
    'Create array of random numbers
    Call GenerateArray(intDataArray, intNumDataItems)

    'display generated array
    Me.lstListArrayElements.Items.Clear()    'clear any existing data
    Call DisplayData(intDataArray, Me.lstListArrayElements, "Original array:")

    'sort array
    Call SelectionSort(intDataArray)

    'Display sorted array in list box
    Call DisplayData(intDataArray, Me.lstListArrayElements, "Sorted array:")
  Else
    MessageBox.Show("Number of elements must be greater than 0.")
    Me.txtNumElements.Text = Nothing      'clear text box
  End If

End Sub
```

```
'~~~~~~~~~~~~~~~~~~~~~~~~~~~~~~~~~~~~~~~~~~~~~~~~
'Resizes intArray() to intNumElements and then assigns to
'each element a random integer between 1 and intMAXNUMBER.
'
'pre: intNumElements >= 0
'post: intArray() contains intNumElements elements with
'random integers between 1 and intMAXNUMBER.
'~~~~~~~~~~~~~~~~~~~~~~~~~~~~~~~~~~~~~~~~~~~~~~~~
Sub GenerateArray(ByRef intArray() As Integer, _
ByVal intNumElements As Integer)

    Const intMAXNUMBER As Integer = 100    'greatest value in an element
    ReDim intArray(intNumElements - 1)         'size array

    'assign each array element a random number
    Randomize()
    Dim intIndex As Integer
    For intIndex = 0 To intArray.Length - 1
        intArray(intIndex) = Int(intMAXNUMBER * Rnd()) + 1
    Next intIndex

End Sub


'~~~~~~~~~~~~~~~~~~~~~~~~~~~~~~~~~~~~~~~~~~~~~~~~
'Displays the contents of intArray() in a list box.
'
'post: intArray() items displayed in a list box with a
'title at the top of the list.
'~~~~~~~~~~~~~~~~~~~~~~~~~~~~~~~~~~~~~~~~~~~~~~~~
Sub DisplayData(ByRef intArray() As Integer, _
ByRef lstList As ListBox, ByVal strTitle As String)

    lstList.Items.Add(strTitle)       'title of list
    Dim intIndex As Integer
    For intIndex = 0 To intArray.Length - 1
        lstList.Items.Add(intIndex & vbTab & intArray(intIndex))
    Next intIndex

End Sub


'~~~~~~~~~~~~~~~~~~~~~~~~~~~~~~~~~~~~~~~~~~~~~~~~
'Sorts intArray() from low to high.
'
'post: intArray() elements are sorted low to high.
'~~~~~~~~~~~~~~~~~~~~~~~~~~~~~~~~~~~~~~~~~~~~~~~~
Sub SelectionSort(ByRef intArray() As Integer)

    Dim intLowItemIndex, intTemp, intIndex As Integer

    For intIndex = 0 To intArray.Length - 1
        'find element with lowest value
        intLowItemIndex = FindLowest(intArray, intIndex, intArray.Length - 1)
        'swap low item element with element at current index
        intTemp = intArray(intIndex)
        intArray(intIndex) = intArray(intLowItemIndex)
        intArray(intLowItemIndex) = intTemp
    Next intIndex

End Sub
```

An Introduction to Programming Using Microsoft Visual Basic .NET

```
'~~~~~~~~~~~~~~~~~~~~~~~~~~~~~~~~~~~~~~~~~~~~~~~~~~~
'Returns the index of the lowest item in elements intLow
'to intHigh of intArray().
'
'pre: indexes intLow to intHigh are valid for intArray().
'post: Index of the lowest item in range intLow to intHigh returned.
'~~~~~~~~~~~~~~~~~~~~~~~~~~~~~~~~~~~~~~~~~~~~~~~~~~~
Function FindLowest(ByRef intArray() As Integer, _
ByVal intLow As Integer, ByVal intHigh As Integer) As Integer

    'Make first element the lowest
    Dim intLowSoFar As Integer = intLow

    Dim intIndex As Integer
    For intIndex = intLow To intHigh
        If intArray(intIndex) < intArray(intLowSoFar) Then        'new low item
            intLowSoFar = intIndex
        End If
    Next intIndex

    Return intLowSoFar

End Function
```

Note that several of the procedures are similar to those used in the Dynamic Array Demo application in Chapter 9.

Review 3

Modify the Selection Sort application to display a label with the time required for a sort. Test the application with 1000, 3000, and 5000 elements.

13.5   Insertion Sort

More efficient than the bubble or selection sort algorithms is the insertion sort algorithm. An *insertion sort* starts by sorting the first two items in a list. This sort is performed by shifting the first item into the second spot if the second item belongs in the first spot. Next, the third item is properly inserted within the first three items by again shifting items into their appropriate position to make room for the moved item. This process is repeated for the remaining elements.

The insertion sort is illustrated on the next page with an array containing four elements. Step 1 shows the original list, which contains items 40, 10, 30, and 20. Step 2 shows that 40 is shifted to make room for the second item, 10. Next, 30 compared to the value in the previous position (40), 40 is shifted into position 3, 30 is then compared to the value in the previous position (10), and then 30 is placed at position 2. This process repeats for the remaining items.

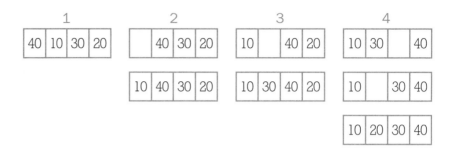

For an array of integers, the InsertionSort procedure pseudocode is:

```
Sub InsertionSort(ByRef intArray() As Integer)
  For intItemIndex = 0 To intArray.Length – 1
    intTemp = intArray(intItemIndex)
    intPreviousItemIndex = intItemIndex – 1
    Do While intArray(intPreviousItemIndex) > intTemp _
    And intPreviousItemIndex > 0
      Shift intArray(intPreviousItemIndex) up one element
      intPreviousItemIndex = intPreviousItemIndex – 1
    Loop
    If intArray(intPreviousItemIndex) > intTemp Then
      Swap the two elements
    Else
      Insert element at appropriate location
    End If
  Next intItem
End Sub
```

The Insertion Sort application below includes the InsertionSort() procedure:

```
Private Sub btnSort_Click(ByVal sender As System.Object, _
ByVal e As System.EventArgs) Handles btnSort.Click

  Dim intDataArray(–1) As Integer                    'dynamic array

  'user chooses how many elements
  Dim intNumDataItems As Integer = Val(Me.txtNumElements.Text)
  If intNumDataItems > 0 Then
    'Create array of random numbers
    Call GenerateArray(intDataArray, intNumDataItems)
```

```
        'display generated array
        Me.lstListArrayElements.Items.Clear()    'clear any existing data
        Call DisplayData(intDataArray, Me.lstListArrayElements, "Original array:")

        'sort array
        Call InsertionSort(intDataArray)

        'Display sorted array in list box
        Call DisplayData(intDataArray, Me.lstListArrayElements, "Sorted array:")
    Else
        MessageBox.Show("Number of elements must be greater than 0.")
        Me.txtNumElements.Text = Nothing       'clear text box
    End If

End Sub


'~~~~~~~~~~~~~~~~~~~~~~~~~~~~~~~~~~~~~~~~~~~~~~~~
'Resizes intArray() to intNumElements and then assigns to
'each element a random integer between 1 and intMAXNUMBER.
'
'pre: intNumElements >= 0
'post: intArray() contains intNumElements elements with
'random integers between 1 and intMAXNUMBER.
'~~~~~~~~~~~~~~~~~~~~~~~~~~~~~~~~~~~~~~~~~~~~~~~~
Sub GenerateArray(ByRef intArray() As Integer, _
ByVal intNumElements As Integer)

    Const intMAXNUMBER As Integer = 100   'greatest value in an element
    ReDim intArray(intNumElements – 1)      'size array

    'assign each array element a random number
    Randomize()
    Dim intIndex As Integer
    For intIndex = 0 To intArray.Length – 1
        intArray(intIndex) = Int(intMAXNUMBER * Rnd()) + 1
    Next intIndex

End Sub


'~~~~~~~~~~~~~~~~~~~~~~~~~~~~~~~~~~~~~~~~~~~~~~~~
'Displays the contents of intArray() in a list box.
'
'post: intArray() items displayed in a list box with a
'title at the top of the list.
'~~~~~~~~~~~~~~~~~~~~~~~~~~~~~~~~~~~~~~~~~~~~~~~~
Sub DisplayData(ByRef intArray() As Integer, _
ByRef lstList As ListBox, ByVal strTitle As String)

    lstList.Items.Add(strTitle)       'title of list
    Dim intIndex As Integer
    For intIndex = 0 To intArray.Length – 1
        lstList.Items.Add(intIndex & vbTab & intArray(intIndex))
    Next intIndex

End Sub
```

```
'~~~~~~~~~~~~~~~~~~~~~~~~~~~~~~~~~~~~~~~~~~~~~~~~
'Sorts intArray() from low to high.
'
'post: intArray() elements are sorted low to high.
'~~~~~~~~~~~~~~~~~~~~~~~~~~~~~~~~~~~~~~~~~~~~~~~~
Sub InsertionSort(ByRef intArray() As Integer)

    Dim intIndex, intPreviousIndex, intTempItem As Integer

    For intIndex = 1 To intArray.Length – 1
        intTempItem = intArray(intIndex)          'store current item
        intPreviousIndex = intIndex – 1
        'compare current item to each previous item until proper location found
        Do While intPreviousIndex > 0 _
        And intArray(intPreviousIndex) > intTempItem
            'shift item up into next element position
            intArray(intPreviousIndex + 1) = intArray(intPreviousIndex)
            'decrease index to compare current item to next previous item
            intPreviousIndex = intPreviousIndex – 1
        Loop

        'element at index 0 is greater than current item
        If intArray(intPreviousIndex) > intTempItem Then
            'shift item in first element up into next element position
            intArray(intPreviousIndex + 1) = intArray(intPreviousIndex)
            'place current item at index 0 (first element)
            intArray(intPreviousIndex) = intTempItem
        Else                    'element at previous index is less than current item
            'place current item at index ahead of previous item
            intArray(intPreviousIndex + 1) = intTempItem
        End If
    Next intIndex

End Sub
```

Note that in the InsertionSort() procedure, the Do…Loop moves up, if necessary, all but the element in the first position. An If…Then statement is then used to move the first position element up if necessary.

Review 4

Modify the Insertion Sort application to display a label with the time required for a sort. Test the application with 1000, 3000, and 5000 elements.

13.6   Binary Search

Linear Search

The linear search is discussed in Chapter 9. Linear searching is much less efficient than binary searching. However, a linear search does not require a sorted list.

Lists are sorted in order to perform a more efficient search. A *binary search* is used with a sorted list of items to quickly find the location of a value. The binary search algorithm can be thought of as a "divide and conquer" approach to searching. It works by examining the middle item of an array sorted from low to high, and determining if this is the item sought, or if the item sought is above or below this middle item. If the item sought is below the middle item, then a binary search is applied to the lower half of the array; if above the middle item, a binary search is applied to the upper half of the array, and so on.

An Introduction to Programming Using Microsoft Visual Basic .NET

For example, a binary search for the value 5 in a list of items 1, 2, 3, 4, 5, 6, and 7 could be visualized as:

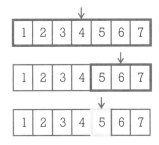

The binary search algorithm is very efficient. For example, an array of 100 elements checks no more than 8 elements in a search, and in an array of one million items no more than 20 items are checked. If a list of the entire world's population were to be searched using this algorithm, less than 40 checks are made to find any one person.

For an array of integers, the BinarySearch() function pseudocode is:

```
Function BinarySearch(ByRef intArray() As Integer, _
ByVal intNumToFind As Integer) As Integer
    Dim intHighIndex As Integer = intArray.Length – 1
    Dim intMidIndex As Integer
    Dim intLowIndex = 0
    Dim blnFound As Boolean = False
    Do While (Not blnFound) And (intLowIndex <= intHighIndex)
        intMidIndex = (intHighIndex + intLowIndex) \ 2
        If intArray(intMidIndex) = intNumToFind Then
            blnFound = True
        ElseIf intArray(intMidIndex) > intNumToFind Then
            intHighIndex = intMidIndex – 1
        Else
            intLowIndex = intMidIndex + 1
        End If
    Loop
    If blnFound Then
        Return intMidIndex
    Else
        Return –1
    End If
End Function
```

The Binary Search application, shown on the next page, generates an array of random numbers and then sorts the numbers using an insertion sort. The user can then enter a number to search for in the text box and click Search to display the index of the number, if found:

Private Sub GenerateAndSearch(ByVal sender As System.Object, _
ByVal e As System.EventArgs) Handles btnGenerate.Click, btnSearch.Click

   Static intDataArray(–1) As Integer
   Dim btnButtonClicked As Button = sender 'Generate or Search button

   Select Case btnButtonClicked.Tag
     Case "Generate Array"   'generate sorted array
       'Create sorted array of random numbers
       Call GenerateSortedArray(intDataArray)

       'Display sorted array in list box
       Me.lstListArrayElements.Items.Clear()
       Call DisplayData(intDataArray, Me.lstListArrayElements, _
       "Sorted array:")

     Case "Search Array"   'search sorted array
       'get number user wants to search for
       Dim intNumToFind As Integer = Val(Me.txtNumToFind.Text)
       Dim intNumFoundIndex As Integer

       'find number
       intNumFoundIndex = BinarySearch(intDataArray, intNumToFind)
       If intNumFoundIndex = –1 Then   'number not found in array
         Me.lblFoundMessage.Text = "Number not found."
       Else   'number found in array
         Me.lblFoundMessage.Text = "Number found at index " & _
         intNumFoundIndex
       End If

   End Select

End Sub

'~~~~~~
'Resizes intArray() to intNUMELEMENTS and then assigns to
'each element a random integer between 1 and intMAXNUMBER.
'
'post: intArray() contains intNUMELEMENTS elements with
'random integers between 1 and intMAXNUMBER that are sorted
'from low to high.
'~~~~~~
Sub GenerateSortedArray(ByRef intArray() As Integer)

   Const intNUMELEMENTS As Integer = 50   'number of array elements
   Const intMAXNUMBER As Integer = 100   'greatest value in an element
   ReDim intArray(intNUMELEMENTS – 1)   'size array

```
'assign each array element a random number
Randomize()
Dim intIndex As Integer
For intIndex = 0 To intArray.Length – 1
   intArray(intIndex) = Int(intMAXNUMBER * Rnd()) + 1
Next intIndex

'sort array
Call InsertionSort(intArray)

End Sub


'~~~~~~~~~~~~~~~~~~~~~~~~~~~~~~~~~~~~~~~~~
'Sorts intArray() from low to high.
'
'post: intArray() elements are sorted low to high.
'~~~~~~~~~~~~~~~~~~~~~~~~~~~~~~~~~~~~~~~~~
Sub InsertionSort(ByRef intArray() As Integer)

   Dim intIndex, intPreviousIndex, intTempItem As Integer

   For intIndex = 1 To intArray.Length – 1
      intTempItem = intArray(intIndex)       'store current item
      intPreviousIndex = intIndex – 1
      'compare current item to each previous item until proper location found
      Do While intPreviousIndex > 0 _
      And intArray(intPreviousIndex) > intTempItem
         'shift item up into next element position
         intArray(intPreviousIndex + 1) = intArray(intPreviousIndex)
         'decrease index to compare current item to next previous item
         intPreviousIndex = intPreviousIndex – 1
      Loop

      'element at index 0 is greater than current item
      If intArray(intPreviousIndex) > intTempItem Then
         'shift item in first element up into next element position
         intArray(intPreviousIndex + 1) = intArray(intPreviousIndex)
         'place current item at index 0 (first element)
         intArray(intPreviousIndex) = intTempItem
      Else                 'element at previous index is less than current item
         'place current item at index ahead of previous item
         intArray(intPreviousIndex + 1) = intTempItem
      End If
   Next intIndex

End Sub


'~~~~~~~~~~~~~~~~~~~~~~~~~~~~~~~~~~~~~~~~~
'Displays the contents of intArray() in a list box.
'
'post: intArray() items displayed in a list box with a
'title at the top of the list.
'~~~~~~~~~~~~~~~~~~~~~~~~~~~~~~~~~~~~~~~~~
Sub DisplayData(ByRef intArray() As Integer, _
ByRef lstList As ListBox, ByVal strTitle As String)

   lstList.Items.Add(strTitle)       'title of list
   Dim intIndex As Integer
   For intIndex = 0 To intArray.Length – 1
      lstList.Items.Add(intIndex & vbTab & intArray(intIndex))
   Next intIndex

End Sub
```

```
'~~~~~~~~~~~~~~~~~~~~~~~~~~~~~~~~~~~~~~~~~~~~~~~~~
'Returns the index of intNumToFind or a –1 if intNumToFind
'not found.
'
'post: index of intNumToFind is returned or –1 returned
'if intNumToFind not found.
'~~~~~~~~~~~~~~~~~~~~~~~~~~~~~~~~~~~~~~~~~~~~~~~~~
Function BinarySearch(ByRef intArray() As Integer, _
ByVal intNumToFind As Integer) As Integer

    Dim intHighIndex As Integer = intArray.Length – 1
    Dim intMidIndex As Integer
    Dim intLowIndex As Integer = 0
    Dim blnFound As Boolean = False

    Do While (Not blnFound) And (intLowIndex <= intHighIndex)
        'check middle element of current range
        intMidIndex = (intHighIndex + intLowIndex) \ 2
        If intArray(intMidIndex) = intNumToFind Then              'found
            blnFound = True
        ElseIf intArray(intMidIndex) > intNumToFind Then
            'look in lower half of current range
            intHighIndex = intMidIndex – 1
        Else
            'look in upper half of current range
            intLowIndex = intMidIndex + 1
        End If
    Loop

    If blnFound Then              'number found in array
        Return intMidIndex
    Else                          'number not found in array
        Return –1
    End If

End Function


Private Sub NewData_TextChanged(ByVal sender As Object, _
ByVal e As System.EventArgs) Handles txtNumToFind.TextChanged, _
btnGenerate.Click

    Me.lblFoundMessage.Text = Nothing

End Sub
```

Review 5

Modify the Binary Search application to display a label with the indexes of items checked in a search. Be sure to clear the label if a new array is generated or a new number is searched for.

Chapter Summary

Sorting is the process of putting items in a designated order, either from low to high or high to low. The bubble sort starts at the first item of a list and proceeds sequentially to the last, comparing each item with the next and swapping items as necessary. The selection sort repeatedly finds the lowest item from a portion of a list and swaps it with the item at index, which is incremented until index is equal to that of the last element. The insertion sort sequentially removes items from a list and adds them back to the list in the appropriate position relative to the previous items in the list.

One measure of efficiency with sorting algorithms is the time it takes the implemented algorithm to sort a list of items. The DateTime structure includes the Millisecond property and the Now() method for determining elapsed milliseconds.

A binary search is a very efficient way to search a sorted list of elements. The binary search takes a "divide and conquer" approach to searching a list of items.

Vocabulary

Binary search An algorithm that searches for an item in a sorted list by repeatedly comparing the middle item in a portion of a list to the search item.

Bubble sort A sorting algorithm that starts at the first item of a list and proceeds sequentially to the last, comparing each item with the next and swapping items as necessary.

Insertion sort A sorting algorithm that sequentially removes an item from a list and adds it back to the list in the appropriate position relative to the previous items in the list.

Selection sort A sorting algorithm that repeatedly finds the lowest item from a portion of a list and swaps it with the item at index, which is incremented until index is equal to that of the last element.

Sorting The process of putting items in a designated order, either low to high or high to low.

Visual Basic .NET

DateTime **structure** Used for timing. Properties include Millisecond. Methods include Now().

1. Let 4, 6, 2, 10, 9 be a set of numbers to be sorted. For each algorithm below, show how the numbers are ordered after each loop iteration of the algorithm.
   a) Bubble
   b) Selection
   c) Insertion

2. Compare and contrast the time that will be required for the bubble, selection, and insertion sorts.

3. What must be done to a list of items before you can apply the Binary Search?

4. List the numbers checked by a binary search when finding 10 in the list 2, 3, 7, 10, 12, 17, 25, 30, 42.

5. The DateTime structure also contains a Seconds property. A very large set of data may require seconds, rather than milliseconds, to order. Write a set of statements that checks the Seconds property of a DateTime variable. If the seconds are 0, then the Milliseconds property should be checked.

6. strCDsOwned is a sorted array. The following procedure uses a binary search algorithm to determine where strInsertNew belongs and insert it in the correct position. Correct the errors.

```
Private Sub Insert(ByRef strCDsOwned() As String, ByVal strInsertNew As String)

    Dim intHighIndex As Integer = strCDsOwned.Length()
    Dim intLowIndex As Integer = 0
    Dim intMidIndex, intSpot, intMove As Integer

    If strInsertNew < strCDsOwned(0) Then
        intSpot = 1
    ElseIf strInsertNew > strCDsOwned(strCDsOwned.Length - 1) Then
        intSpot = strCDsOwned.Length
    Else
        Do While (intLowIndex < intHighIndex)
            intMidIndex = (intHighIndex - intLowIndex) \ 2
            If strCDsOwned(intMidIndex) > strInsertNew Then
                intHighIndex = intMidIndex - 1
            Else
                intLowIndex = intMidIndex + 1
            End If
        Loop
        intSpot = intLowIndex
    End If

    'move everyone down to insert new item
    For intMove = strCDsOwned.Length - 2 To intSpot
        strCDsOwned(intMove) = strCDsOwned(intMove + 1)
    Next intMove
    strCDsOwned(intSpot) = strInsertNew

End Sub
```

7. Determine if each of the following are true or false. If false, explain why.
   a) To arrange data in a specified order is called sorting.
   b) Of the Bubble Sort, Insertion Sort, and Selection sort, the Bubble sort is the most efficient.
   c) Sorting an array by the Bubble sort can be done with one pass through the data.
   d) Selection Sort can be used to order data from largest to smallest.
   e) If *n* items need to be sorted, the Selection Sort will require *n* passes through the data.
   f) The Binary Search can be done on any list of data.
   g) A Binary Search will usually be faster than the Linear Search, discussed in Chapter 9.
   h) datNow = DateTime returns the current date and time.

Exercise 1 ——————————————————————— Alphabetize Names

Create an Alphabetize Names application that allows the user to enter any number of names in input boxes and then displays them sorted alphabetically. The application interface should look similar to:

Exercise 2 ——————————————————————— Sort by Field

Create a Sort by Field application that allows the user to enter first name, last name, and age information for any number of people and then displays the data in a list box sorted by the field selected by the user. Hint: use a structure for storing the data. The application interface should look similar to:

Exercise 3 ——————————————————— Interpolation Search

One variation of binary search is called the *interpolation search*. The idea is to look in a likely spot, not necessarily the middle of the array. For example, if the value sought is 967 in an array that holds items ranging from 3 to 1022, it would be intelligent to look near the end of the sorted array. Mathematically, the position to start searching at is a position 95% of the way down the array, because 967 is about 95% of the way from 3 to 1022. For example, if the array holds 500 elements, the first position to examine is 475 (95% of the way from 1 to 500). The search then proceeds to a portion of the array (either 1 to 474 or 476 to 500) depending upon whether 967 is greater or less than the 475th element.

Create an Interpolation Search application based on the Binary Search application presented in the text.

Exercise 4 ——————————————————— Ternary Search

Create a Ternary Search application, similar to the Binary Search application, that divides the array into three pieces rather than two. Ternary Search finds the points that divide the array into three roughly equal pieces, and then uses these points to determine where the element should be searched for. Add code to time the ternary search to compare it to the binary search.

Exercise 5 (advanced) ——————————————— Slang Dictionary

a) Create a Slang Dictionary application that allows the user to click **Add** to add a word and its definition to a file. Clicking **Search** reads each word and corresponding definition from the file into an array of structures. The first line of the file should contain a number indicating how many definitions are stored in the file. The array of words should then be sorted and searched for the word entered by the user. If the word is found, the word and its definition are displayed, otherwise a message box is displayed indicating the word was not found. The application interface should look similar to:

b) The Slang Dictionary application sorts the file every time **Search** is clicked. Modify the application to be more efficient by storing the sorted status in the second line of the file. For example, when **Add** is clicked the second line should store Unsorted and the new word and definition appended to the file. When **Search** is clicked, the sort status should be checked. If unsorted, then the words should be sorted, the second line changed, and then the file searched. If sorted, only searching need be done.

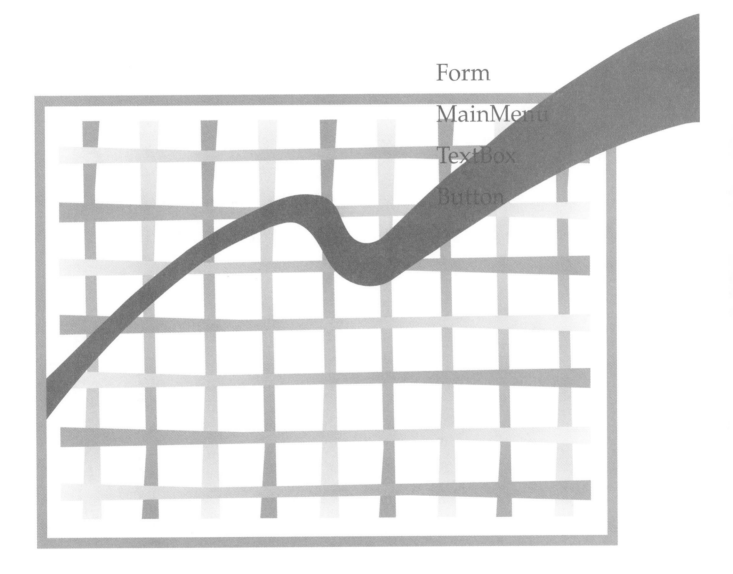

Form

MainMenu

TextBox

Button

Chapter 14 Expectations

After completing this chapter you will be able to:

1. Create an MDI application.

2. Understand the parent form-child form relationship.

3. Add standard Windows application menus to an application.

4. Set MainMenu control object properties so that child form names are displayed in a Window menu.

5. Create an application that enables a user to cut, copy, and paste text between document windows.

6. Create dialog boxes.

Many applications require multiple forms and dialog boxes. The concepts discussed in this chapter are MDI applications, standards for an MDI application, and dialog boxes.

14.1 MDI Applications

multiple-document interface
parent form

An *MDI application* is a multiple-document interface application. This type of Windows application has a parent form and one or more child forms. The *parent form* is a container for the child forms. The MDI application below displays two child forms:

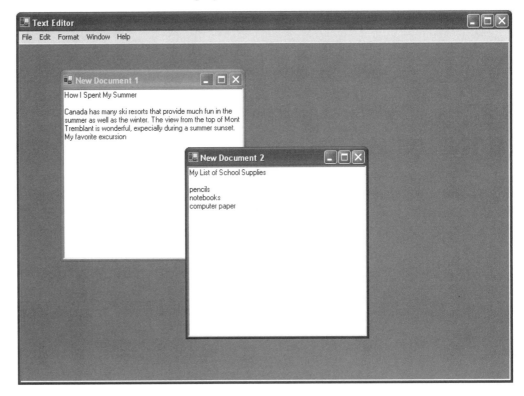

child form

A *child form* functions completely within the parent form and cannot be moved outside the parent form. The child windows can be tiled, cascaded, and dragged to arrange them within the parent form.

14.2 Creating an MDI Application

creating a parent

Any Windows Forms project can be an MDI application by simply setting additional properties for Form1 to make it a parent and then adding child forms to the project and setting their properties at run time. The Form control has properties available in the Properties window at design time for designating it a parent form:

IsMdiContainer

- **IsMdiContainer** is set to True for a parent form.

WindowState

- **WindowState** can be Normal, Minimized, or Maximized. A parent form is typically set to Maximized to fill the entire screen.

The parent form should also include menus and commands, which are discussed later in the chapter, for controlling the child forms.

adding children

A child form is added to an application by adding a new form. To add a new form to an open project, select Add Windows Form from the Project menu. The Add New Item dialog box is displayed with the Windows Form icon selected:

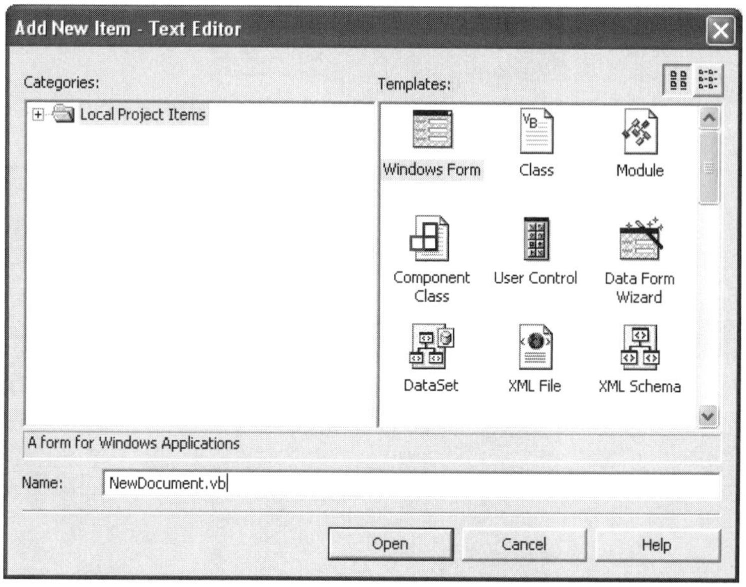

Type a descriptive form name in the Name box (be sure to keep the .vb extension) and then select Open. In this case, NewDocument is the name used for the new child form. The form Design window is displayed in the IDE:

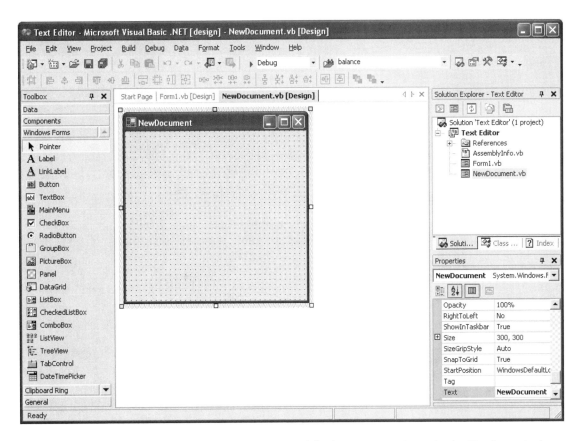

The child form can be modified just as any form in the Design window. Code specific to the child form is added to the application by switching to the child's Code window.

14.3 Using Child Forms

Program code for the parent form in an MDI application typically must include statements that declare a child form, display the child form for user interaction, and close the child form. For example, the following statements instantiate a new form, make the new form a child by assigning it a parent, and then display the child form:

instantiating a form

```
Dim ChildForm As New NewDocument()    'instantiate a new form
ChildForm.MdiParent = Me              'assign a parent
ChildForm.Show()                      'show the child form
```

MdiParent
current form as the parent
showing a child form

The Form control has the property MdiParent, which can be set at run time only. Note this property is set to **Me** when assignment occurs in the parent form. The Form control has a Show() method that is used to display the child form. The first statement declares a variable named ChildForm using NewDocument as the type. As explained in Section 3.9 of this text (page 3–10), a new Visual Basic .NET project includes some automatically generated code. Taking a closer look at the Code window for a form, on the next page, shows the **Inherits** statement that indicates a new form is a derived class:

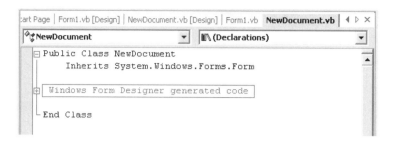

The event and Sub procedures added to the Code window extend the derived class. An object of this class can be instantiated with a **Dim** statement in another Code window of the project. The NewDocument class shown above is a child form added to the project. It can be used in the parent form code to instantiate new forms. The forms displayed at run time are instances of this class.

Close()   A child window is closed with the Close() method. The Form control method for closing the form is:

* **Close()** closes a form. The form cannot be reopened after closing.

closing the active child
ActiveMdiChild

This method can be called from the child code or from the parent code by first determining the active child. To close the active child, the ActiveMdiChild property for the parent form is used. For example, the following statement closes the active child window:

Me.ActiveMdiChild.Close()   'parent form closes active child

Review 1

In this review you will create an MDI application. Form instantiation is also demonstrated with the New command.

① *CREATE A NEW PROJECT*

Create a Windows application named Text Editor.

② *CREATE THE PARENT FORM*

For Form1, set the Text property to Text Editor, the IsMdiContainer to True, and WindowState to Maximized. Refer to the form below to add a MainMenu component. Use the table on the next page to add MenuItem objects and set properties.

Object	Name	Text
MenuItem1	mnuFile	File
MenuItem2	mnuNew	New
MenuItem3	mnuClose	Close
MenuItem4	mnuExit	Exit

③ *ADD A CHILD FORM*

    a. Select Project → Add Windows Form. A dialog box is displayed.

        1. In the Templates list, click Windows Form, if it is not already selected.

        2. In the Name box, type NewDocument.vb.

        3. Select Open. A form named NewDocument.vb is displayed in a Design window. Note the file added to the project as shown in the Solution Explorer window.

    b. Set the Text property of the NewDocument form to New Document.

④ *WRITE THE APPLICATION CODE*

    a. Display the Form1 Design window and then display the Form1 Code window.

    b. Add comments that include your name and today's date.

    c. Create a mnuNew_Click event procedure and then add statements to display a new document window with an appropriate title bar:

```
Dim Doc As New NewDocument()              'create new document window
Doc.MdiParent = Me                        'set parent for document

Static intNextDoc As Integer              'document number
intNextDoc = intNextDoc + 1               'increment document number
Doc.Text = "New Document " & intNextDoc   'show document number in title bar
Doc.Show()                                'show document window
```

    d. Create a mnuClose_Click event procedure and then add a statement to close the active window:

```
Me.ActiveMdiChild.Close()
```

    e. Create a mnuExit_Click event procedure and then add a statement to end the application:

```
End
```

⑤ *RUN THE APPLICATION*

    a. Save the modified Text Editor project and then run the application.

    b. Select File → New. A New Document 1 window is displayed. Drag the window in the Text Editor window to move it.

    c. Select File → New. A New Document 2 window is displayed.

    d. Click the New Document 1 window to make it the active window. Select File → Close. The window is closed.

    e. Close the New Document 2 window.

    f. Quit the Text Editor application.

14.4 Creating a Window Menu

Windows application standards require an application to contain a Window menu with commands for arranging windows and switching between open windows. Commands for arranging open windows are Tile Horizontal, Tile Vertical, and Cascade. To switch between active windows, the name of an open window name is clicked from the list displayed at the bottom of the Window menu, as in the menu:

A Window menu typically contains commands for arranging open windows and for activating a window from a list of open windows

LayoutMdi()

The Form control includes a method for automatically arranging windows in a parent form:

- **LayoutMdi(*Layout Option*)** arranges open windows in a parent form. *Layout Option* includes MdiLayout.Cascade, MdiLayout.TileHorizontal, and MdiLayout.TileVertical.

For example, the following MenuItem event procedure tiles open windows horizontally:

```
Private Sub mnuTileHorizontal_Click(ByVal sender As Object, _
ByVal e As System.EventArgs) Handles mnuTileHorizontal.Click

    Me.LayoutMdi(MdiLayout.TileHorizontal)

End Sub
```

The MainMenu control includes a property that is available in the Properties window at design time for automatically adding open child form names to a menu:

- **MdiList** is set to True to automatically add child form names as they are opened to a menu.

Review 2

In this review you will add a Window menu to the Text Editor application. Open the Text Editor project and display the Form1 Design window.

① ADD A WINDOW MENU

Refer to the form on the next page to add four MenuItem objects to the MainMenu component. Use the table below the form set properties.

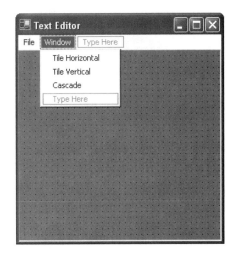

Object	Name	Text	MdiList
MenuItem1	mnuWindow	Window	True
MenuItem2	mnuTileHorizontal	Tile Horizontal	
MenuItem3	mnuTileVertical	Tile Vertical	
MenuItem4	mnuCascade	Cascade	

② WRITE THE APPLICATION CODE

    a. Display the Form1 Code window.

    b. Create a mnuTileHorizontal_Click event procedure and then add a statement to tile opened windows horizontally:

        Me.LayoutMdi(MdiLayout.TileHorizontal)

    c. Create a mnuTileVertical_Click event procedure and then add a statement to tile opened windows vertically:

        Me.LayoutMdi(MdiLayout.TileVertical)

    d. Create a mnuCascade_Click event procedure and then add a statement to cascade opened windows:

        Me.LayoutMdi(MdiLayout.Cascade)

③ RUN THE APPLICATION

    a. Save the modified Text Editor project and then run the application.

    b. Select File → New three times to display three new document windows.

    c. Display the Window menu. Note the form names list at the bottom of the menu with the active window displaying a check mark.

    d. Test each of the Window menu commands.

    e. Quit the Text Editor application.

14.5 Advanced TextBox Methods

abi TextBox

The TextBox control has methods that can be used for editing text in a text box. These methods are:

- **Copy()** copies selected text in the text box to the Windows Clipboard.

- **Cut()** removes selected text from the text box and places it on the Windows Clipboard.

- **Paste()** replaces selected text with text from the Windows Clipboard. If no text is selected, text from the Clipboard is placed at the insertion point.

selecting text   The user selects text by dragging the pointer over any amount of text. Double-clicking text selects a single word. Selected text is shown as highlighted in the text box.

Edit menu   The Copy(), Cut(), and Paste() methods are typically used in Edit menu Click event procedures. For example, the mnuCut_Click event procedure below removes selected text from the active child form. Note that the active child must first be determined:

```
Private Sub mnuCut_Click(ByVal sender As Object, _
ByVal e As System.EventArgs) Handles mnuCut.Click

    Dim ActiveDoc As NewDocument = Me.ActiveMdiChild
    ActiveDoc.txtDocument.Cut()

End Sub
```

Review 3

In this review you will add a text box to the child form of the Text Editor application and add an Edit menu to the Text Editor parent form. Open the Text Editor project, if it is not already displayed.

① *DISPLAY THE NEWDOCUMENT DESIGN WINDOW*

② *MODIFY THE NEWDOCUMENT FORM*

Refer to the form below to add a TextBox object. Set the Name property to txtDocument, Multiline to True, Dock to Fill, and Text to *empty*.

An Introduction to Programming Using Microsoft Visual Basic .NET

③ *ADD AN EDIT MENU TO THE PARENT FORM*

Display the Form1 Design window. Refer to the form below to add four MenuItem objects to the MainMenu component. Use the table below the form to set properties.

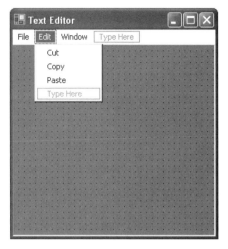

Note: To add the Edit menu between the File and Window menus, right-click the Window menu name and select Insert New from the displayed menu.

Object	Name	Text
MenuItem1	mnuEdit	Edit
MenuItem2	mnuCut	Cut
MenuItem3	mnuCopy	Copy
MenuItem4	mnuPaste	Paste

④ *MODIFY THE APPLICATION CODE*

a. Display the Form1 Code window.

b. Create a mnuCut_Click event procedure and then add statements to move selected text in the active window to the Clipboard:

```
Dim ActiveDoc As NewDocument = Me.ActiveMdiChild
ActiveDoc.txtDocument.Cut()
```

c. Create a mnuCopy_Click event procedure and then add statements to copy selected text to the Clipboard:

```
Dim ActiveDoc As NewDocument = Me.ActiveMdiChild
ActiveDoc.txtDocument.Copy()
```

d. Create a mnuPaste_Click event procedure and then add statements to copy Clipboard text to the insertion point:

```
Dim ActiveDoc As NewDocument = Me.ActiveMdiChild
ActiveDoc.txtDocument.Paste()
```

⑤ *RUN THE APPLICATION*

a. Save the modified Text Editor project and then run the application.

b. Display two new document windows and then type some text into the New Document 1 window.

c. Select some of the typed text and then select Edit ➙ Cut. The selected text removed.

d. Click in the New Document 2 window to place the insertion point. Select Edit ➙ Paste. The text from the Clipboard is inserted.

e. Test the Copy command.

f. Close the document windows and quit the Text Editor application.

14.6 Creating Dialog Boxes

Applications typically include menus with commands that perform actions. However, many commands require information from the user before executing. For example, an Alignment command must be told the type of paragraph alignment before it can execute. An application uses *dialog boxes* to get the information needed to execute a command.

OK Cancel

Dialog boxes have certain features. They cannot be sized, minimized, or maximized. They include at least an OK button and a Cancel button, and they require the user to select one of these buttons before control is given back to the calling form.

Form properties

A dialog box is created for an application by first adding a new form to the project. The Form control has properties available in the Properties window at design time for designating the form a dialog box:

- **ControlBox** is set to False because a dialog box should not offer access to the System menu.

- **MaximizeBox** is set to False because a dialog box should not be sized.

- **MinimizeBox** is set to False because a dialog box should not be sized.

- **FormBorderStyle** is set to FixedDialog to prevent the dialog box from being sized.

> ### Commands with an Ellipsis
>
> A command name usually has an ellipsis (…) after it to indicate that a dialog box will be displayed when the command is selected.

After setting properties, the dialog box can then be customized with objects that get the needed user input. For example, an Alignment dialog box might look similar to:

`ab|` Button

The Button control has a property that must be set for the OK and Cancel buttons in a dialog box:

- **DialogResult** can be set to None, OK, Cancel, Abort, Retry, Ignore, Yes, or No. None is the default. The option should be set to correspond to the Text property of a dialog box button. For example, a Yes button has Text set to Yes and DialogResult set to Yes.

ShowDialog()

The Form control has a method for displaying a dialog box as a modal form:

- **ShowDialog()** displays a form modally.

modal form

A *modal form* does not allow other forms to receive input until it has been removed from the screen. For example, a dialog box displayed as a modal form requires the user to select the OK or Cancel button, which removes the dialog box from the screen, before other forms can receive input.

The code below instantiates a dialog box object and then displays the object as a modal form. No other statements are executed until the user selects either the OK or Cancel buttons in the dialog box. If the user selected OK, the If...Then statement is executed to change the alignment of the text box in the active form:

```
'show dialog box
Dim AlignmentDB As New AlignmentDialogBox()
AlignmentDB.ShowDialog()        'display dialog box

'change alignment of text in active document
Dim ActiveDoc As NewDocument = Me.ActiveMdiChild
If AlignmentDB.DialogResult = DialogResult.OK Then        'OK
    If AlignmentDB.radLeft.Checked Then
        ActiveDoc.txtDocument.TextAlign = HorizontalAlignment.Left
    ElseIf AlignmentDB.radCenter.Checked Then
        ActiveDoc.txtDocument.TextAlign = HorizontalAlignment.Center
    ElseIf AlignmentDB.radRight.Checked Then
        ActiveDoc.txtDocument.TextAlign = HorizontalAlignment.Right
    End If
End If
```

Review 4 ⟳

In this review you will add a Format menu to the Text Editor application and add a dialog box to the project. Open the Text Editor project, if it is not already displayed.

① ADD A DIALOG BOX

a. Select Project → Add Windows Form. A dialog box is displayed.

    1. In the Templates list, click Windows Form, if it is not already selected.

    2. In the Name box, type AlignmentDialogBox.vb.

    3. Select Open. A form named AlignmentDialogBox.vb is displayed in a Design window.

b. Set the Text property of the AlignmentDialogBox form to Alignment.

c. Set the ControlBox, MaximizeBox, and MinimizeBox properties to False.

d. Set the FormBorderStyle to FixedDialog.

e. Refer to the form below to add, position, and size objects. Use the table below the form to set properties.

Object	Name	Text	DialogResult
GroupBox1	grpAlignmentOptions	Choose Alignment	
RadioButton1	radLeft	Left	
RadioButton2	radCenter	Center	
RadioButton3	radRight	Right	
Button1	btnOK	OK	OK
Button2	btnCancel	Cancel	Cancel

② ADD A FORMAT MENU

Display the Form1 Design window. Refer to the form below to add two MenuItem objects to the MainMenu component. Use the table below the form to set properties.

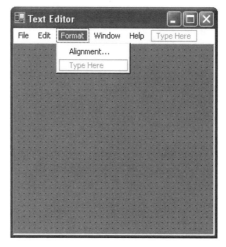

Note: To add the Format menu between the Edit and Window menus, right-click the Window menu name and select Insert New from the displayed menu.

Object	Name	Text
MenuItem1	mnuFormat	Format
MenuItem2	mnuAlignment	Alignment...

③ MODIFY THE APPLICATION CODE

a. Display the Form1 Code window.

b. Create a mnuAlignment_Click event procedure and then add statements to display a dialog box and apply selected alignment:

```
Dim AlignmentDB As New AlignmentDialogBox()
AlignmentDB.ShowDialog()    'display dialog box

'change alignment of text in active document
Dim ActiveDoc As NewDocument = Me.ActiveMdiChild
If AlignmentDB.DialogResult = DialogResult.OK Then          'OK
    If AlignmentDB.radLeft.Checked Then
        ActiveDoc.txtDocument.TextAlign = HorizontalAlignment.Left
    ElseIf AlignmentDB.radCenter.Checked Then
        ActiveDoc.txtDocument.TextAlign = HorizontalAlignment.Center
    ElseIf AlignmentDB.radRight.Checked Then
        ActiveDoc.txtDocument.TextAlign = HorizontalAlignment.Right
    End If
End If
```

④ RUN THE APPLICATION

a. Save the modified Text Editor project and then run the application.

b. Display a new document window and then type several paragraphs of text into the New Document 1 window.

c. Select Format → Alignment. A dialog box is displayed.

  1. Click Center.

  2. Click OK. The text is center aligned.

d. Test the other alignment options.

e. Close the document window and quit the Text Editor application.

14.7 Creating a Help Menu

About command

Windows application standards require an application to contain a Help menu with commands for displaying information about how to use an application. The last command in the Help menu displays a dialog box with copyright, authorship, and version information. This command is referred to as the About command. For example, the About Text Editor... command displays an About dialog box similar to:

The About dialog box is created by adding a form to the project and then setting appropriate form options, adding labels, and an OK button with the appropriate DialogResult property set.

Review 5

In this review you will add a Help menu to the Text Editor application and add another dialog box to the project. Open the Text Editor project, if it is not already displayed.

① ADD A DIALOG BOX

a. Select Project → Add Windows Form. A dialog box is displayed.
   1. In the Templates list, click Windows Form, if it is not already selected.
   2. In the Name box, type AboutDialogBox.vb.
   3. Select Open. A form named AboutDialogBox.vb is displayed in a Design window.
b. Set the Text property of the AboutDialogBox form to About Text Editor.
c. Set the ControlBox, MaximizeBox, and MinimizeBox properties to False.
d. Set the FormBorderStyle to FixedDialog.
e. Refer to the form below to add, position, and size objects. Use the table below the form to set properties.

Object	Name	Text	DialogResult
Label1	lblInfo	*see form*	
Button1	btnOK	OK	OK

② *ADD A HELP MENU*

Display the Form1 Design window. Refer to the form below to add two MenuItem objects to the MainMenu component. Use the table below the form to set properties.

Object	Name	Text
MenuItem1	mnuHelp	Help
MenuItem2	mnuAbout	About Text Editor...

③ *MODIFY THE APPLICATION CODE*

a. Display the Form1 Code window.

b. Create a mnuAbout_Click event procedure and then add statements to display the About dialog box:

```
'show dialog box
Dim AboutDB As New AboutDialogBox()
AboutDB.ShowDialog()
```

④ *RUN THE APPLICATION*

a. Save the modified Text Editor project and then run the application.

b. Select Help → About Text Editor. A dialog box is displayed.

  1. Note the application information and then click OK. The dialog box is removed.

c. Quit the Text Editor application.

d. Quit Visual Studio.

In this Case Study a Bingo application will be created.

specification

The specification for this Case Study is:

> An application that plays a game of Bingo with one or two players. Each player can display any number of cards, with each card being unique. The cards are traditional Bingo cards with columns B, I, N, G, and O, and numbers that range from 1 through 75 with column B containing five numbers ranging from 1 to 15, column I with five numbers from 16 to 30, column N with four numbers from 31 to 45 and a Free Space in the middle of column N, column G with five numbers from 46 to 60, and column O with five numbers from 61 to 75. After a random number is "called," players "mark" their cards. The first player to mark five consecutive numbers has "Bingo!"

design

A MDI application is the best design approach because this game can have more than one player and each player can have more than one card. As with any MDI application, Bingo will have File, Window, and Help menus. A button docked at the bottom of the parent form generates number calls and a label docked on the right of the parent form lists numbers already called:

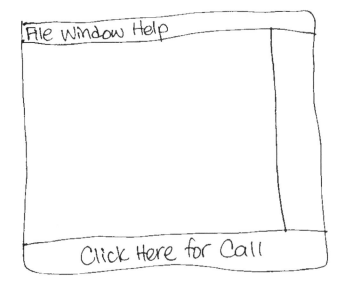

The Bingo cards in the application interface can be generated from a single child form designed with rows and columns of numbers. The player must be able to "mark" the "card," so buttons are the best choice for displaying the numbers. Before an instance of the Bingo form is displayed, a set of randomly generated numbers can be assigned to the Text property of each of the 25 buttons:

B	I	N	G	O
6	16	33	46	64
8	19	36	50	68
11	22	FREE SPACE	52	70
13	25	41	59	72
15	27	44	60	73

FormBorderStyle The player should not be able to size the card. This can be prevented by setting the FormBorderStyle property to FixedSingle. The Maximize button will not be needed on this form either.

This MDI application requires two other forms, a Help dialog box with game instructions and an About dialog box. These could look similar to:

The algorithm for this Case Study can be based on one player with one Bingo card:

1. A Bingo card object is instantiated from the BingoCard child form by selecting New Card from the File menu. Random numbers are generated and assigned to the buttons of the new Bingo card before displaying the card.

2. The player clicks the call button at the bottom of the screen to start the calls. Clicking this button generates a unique random number from 1 through 75 and then displays the number along with the proper row letter. The number called is also added to the label shown on the right side of the interface.

3. If a called number is also on the Bingo card, the user clicks the card so that the number is marked with Xs on both sides (for example, X14X).

4. The player continues to click the call button until five consecutive buttons on the card are marked. At this point the player has Bingo. It is up to the player to determine when the fifth consecutive number is marked on the card. The player can double-check the marked numbers by checking the call list.

5. The player quits the application by selecting Exit from the File menu.

Based on the game algorithm, the menus and their commands for the application can be further refined:

- A New Card command in the File menu contains a submenu with Player 1 and Player 2 commands to instantiate Bingo card objects. The title bar of the new card should state the player and card number. For example, "Player 1 Card 1."

- An Exit command in the File menu to end the application.

- The Window menu contains commands for tiling the cards. There is no need for a Cascade command because players won't be able to see all the numbers on cascaded cards.

- The Help menu contains commands for displaying a Help dialog box with basic game instructions and an About dialog box with application information.

The algorithm for creating a Bingo card also needs further refinement. A Bingo card can be thought of as five columns of five unique random numbers with each column having numbers from a different range. In this case, column B ranges from 1 to 15, column I from 16 to 30, column N from 31 to 45, column G from 46 to 60, and column O from 61 to 75. With this approach, the task of creating a Bingo card can be divided into procedures GenerateBingoCard(), GenerateColumn(), and UniqueNumberArray():

- GenerateBingoCard() declares five arrays of Button objects, one for each row of the card. The array of Button objects is passed by reference to GenerateColumn().

- GenerateColumn() assigns each Button element a value from an array of unique random numbers. The random numbers are generated with UniqueNumberArray().

- UniqueNumberArray() creates an array of unique numbers from 0 to a specified maximum value. The array size and maximum value are specified in the procedure call. A Boolean array with meaningful indexes is used to keep track of which numbers have been generated by storing True in the element with the same index as the generated random number. If the value at the index is already True another number is generated. This process is continued until there are enough unique random numbers to fill the array.

Based on the design, the pseudocode for the parent form appears like:

```
Private Sub mnuPlayer1_Click(sender, e) Handles mnuPlayer1.Click
    Dim BingoCard As New BingoCard()        'form with 25-slot BINGO card layout
    BingoCard.MdiParent = Me
    Static intCardNum As Integer
    intCardNum = intCardNum + 1
    BingoCard.Text = "Player 1 Card " & intCardNum
    Call GenerateBingoCard(BingoCard)        'generate card with random numbers

    BingoCard.Show()
End Sub


Private Sub mnuPlayer2_Click(sender, e) Handles mnuPlayer2.Click
    Dim BingoCard As New BingoCard()        'form with 25-slot BINGO card layout
    BingoCard.MdiParent = Me
    Static intCardNum As Integer
    intCardNum = intCardNum + 1
    BingoCard.Text = "Player 2 Card " & intCardNum
    Call GenerateBingoCard(BingoCard)        'generate card with random numbers

    BingoCard.Show()
End Sub


Private Sub mnuExit_Click(sender, e) Handles mnuExit.Click
    End
End Sub


Private Sub mnuTileHorizontal_Click(sender, e) Handles mnuTileHorizontal.Click
    Me.LayoutMdi(MdiLayout.TileHorizontal)
End Sub


Private Sub mnuTileVertical_Click(sender, e) Handles mnuTileVertical.Click
    Me.LayoutMdi(MdiLayout.TileVertical)
End Sub


Private Sub mnuAbout_Click(sender, e) Handles mnuAbout.Click
    'show dialog box
    Dim AboutDB As New AboutDialogBox()
    AboutDB.ShowDialog()
End Sub


Private Sub mnuHowToPlay_Click(sender, e) Handles mnuHowToPlay.Click
    'show dialog box
    Dim HelpDB As New HelpDialogBox()
    HelpDB.ShowDialog()
End Sub
```

An Introduction to Programming Using Microsoft Visual Basic .NET

```
Sub GenerateBingoCard(ByRef NewCard As BingoCard)
    Dim btnBColumn() As Button = {NewCard.btnBSlot1, NewCard.btnBSlot2, _
    NewCard.btnBSlot3, NewCard.btnBSlot4, NewCard.btnBSlot5}
    Call GenerateColumn(btnBColumn, 1)

    Dim btnIColumn() As Button = {NewCard.btnISlot1, NewCard.btnISlot2, _
    NewCard.btnISlot3, NewCard.btnISlot4, NewCard.btnISlot5}
    Call GenerateColumn(btnIColumn, 16)

    Dim btnNColumn() As Button = {NewCard.btnNSlot1, NewCard.btnNSlot2, _
    NewCard.btnNSlot3, NewCard.btnNSlot4, NewCard.btnNSlot5}
    Call GenerateColumn(btnNColumn, 31)
    NewCard.btnNSlot3.Text = "Free Space"

    Dim btnGColumn() As Button = {NewCard.btnGSlot1, NewCard.btnGSlot2, _
    NewCard.btnGSlot3, NewCard.btnGSlot4, NewCard.btnGSlot5}
    Call GenerateColumn(btnGColumn, 46)

    Dim btnOColumn() As Button = {NewCard.btnOSlot1, NewCard.btnOSlot2, _
    NewCard.btnOSlot3, NewCard.btnOSlot4, NewCard.btnOSlot5}
    Call GenerateColumn(btnOColumn, 61)
End Sub


Sub GenerateColumn(ByRef btnArray() As Button, ByVal intOffset As Integer)
    Dim intNumbers(4) As Integer
    UniqueNumberArray(15, 5, intNumbers)

    Dim intButton As Integer
    For intButton = 0 To btnArray.Length – 1          'set button to a number
        btnArray(intButton).Text = intNumbers(intButton) + intOffset
    Next intButton
End Sub


Sub UniqueNumberArray(ByVal intMaxValue As Integer, _
ByVal intNums As Integer, ByRef intNumArray() As Integer)
    Dim blnNumArray(intMaxValue – 1) As Boolean
    Dim intNum As Integer
    Randomize()
    For intNum = 1 To intNums             'generate intNums unique numbers
        'generate a random number to correspond to an index number
        Dim intIndexToCheck As Integer = Int(Rnd() * intMaxValue)
        Do While blnNumArray(intIndexToCheck)
            'generate random index values until element at index is False
            intIndexToCheck = Int(Rnd() * intMaxValue)
        Loop
        blnNumArray(intIndexToCheck) = True
    Next intNum

    'store selected index values in array
    Dim intIndex As Integer = 0
    For intNum = 0 To blnNumArray.Length – 1
        If blnNumArray(intNum) Then                  'index selected
            intNumArray(intIndex) = intNum           'store index in intNumArray
            intIndex = intIndex + 1                  'increment intNumArray index
        End If
    Next intNum
End Sub
```

```
Private Sub btnNumber_Click(sender, e) Handles btnNumber.Click
    Dim intRange As Integer = 75
    Static blnNumArray(intRange – 1) As Boolean
    Dim intNum As Integer

    Randomize()
    'generate a random number
    Dim intIndexToCheck As Integer = Int(Rnd() * intRange)
    Do While blnNumArray(intIndexToCheck)
        'generate random index values until element at index is False
        intIndexToCheck = Int(Rnd() * intRange)
    Loop
    blnNumArray(intIndexToCheck) = True

    'call out
    Select Case intIndexToCheck
        Case 0 To 14
            Me.btnNumber.Text = "B " & intIndexToCheck + 1
        Case 15 To 29
            Me.btnNumber.Text = "I " & intIndexToCheck + 1
        Case 30 To 44
            Me.btnNumber.Text = "N " & intIndexToCheck + 1
        Case 45 To 59
            Me.btnNumber.Text = "G " & intIndexToCheck + 1
        Case 60 To 74
            Me.btnNumber.Text = "O " & intIndexToCheck + 1
    End Select

    'add call to numbers called list
    Me.lblCalled.Text = Me.lblCalled.Text & Me.btnNumber.Text & vbCrLf
End Sub
```

Pseudocode for the child form, which must mark numbers appears like:

```
Private Sub Button_Click(ByVal sender As Object, ByVal e As System.EventArgs) _
Handles ALL BUTTONS
    Dim btnButtonClicked As Button = sender
    btnButtonClicked.Text = "X" & btnButtonClicked.Text & "X"
End Sub
```

coding   The application interface, additional forms, and code for this Case Study follow. The parent form interface and BingoCard interface are:

An Introduction to Programming Using Microsoft Visual Basic .NET

Object	Name	Text	WindowState
Form1		Bingo	Maximized
MainMenu1			
MenuItem1	mnuFile	File	
MenuItem2	mnuNewCard	New Card	
MenuItem3	mnuPlayer1	Player 1	
MenuItem4	mnuPlayer2	Player 2	
MenuItem5	mnuExit	Exit	
MenuItem6	mnuWindow	Window	
MenuItem7	mnuTileHorizontal	Tile Horizontal	
MenuItem8	mnuTileVertical	Tile Vertical	
MenuItem9	mnuHelp	Help	
MenuItem10	mnuHowToPlay	How To Play...	
MenuItem11	mnuAbout	About Bingo...	

Object	Name	Text	Dock	Font Style	Font Size
Button1	btnNumber	Click Here for Call	Bottom	Bold	18
Label1	lblCalled	*empty*	Right		

Object	Name	Text	FormBorderStyle	MaximizeBox
Form1	BingoCard	Bingo Card	FixedSingle	False

Object	Name	Text	TextAlign	Font Style	Font Size
Label1	lblB	B	MiddleCenter	Bold	14
Label2	lblI	I	MiddleCenter	Bold	14
Label3	lblN	N	MiddleCenter	Bold	14
Label4	lblG	G	MiddleCenter	Bold	14
Label5	lblO	O	MiddleCenter	Bold	14
Button1	btnBSlot1	*empty*			
Button2	btnBSlot2	*empty*			
...					
Button13	btnNSlot3	*empty*			
...					
Button24	btnOSlot4	*empty*			
Button25	btnOSlot5	*empty*			

The Bingo application also contains two dialog boxes, which have FormBorderStyle set to FixedDialog, and MaximizeBox, MinimizeBox, and ControlBox set to False. The dialog box form interfaces and additional properties set are:

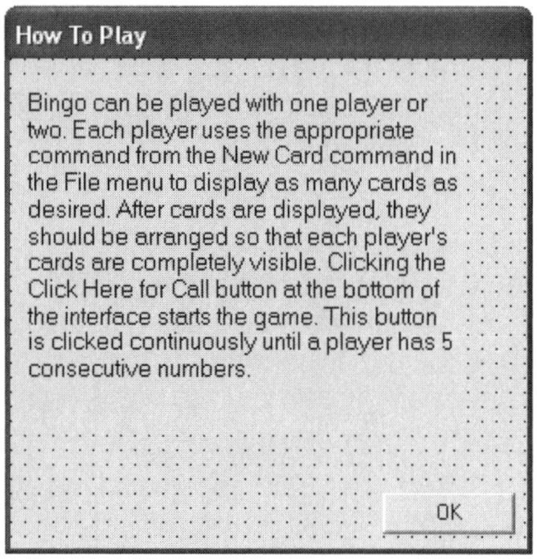

Object	Name	Text	Font Size	DialogResult
Form1	HelpDialogBox	How To Play		
Label1	lblInfo	*see form*	10	
Button1	btnOK	OK		OK

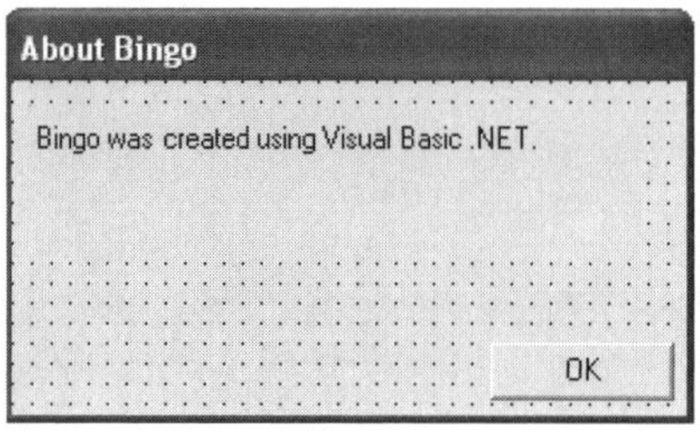

Object	Name	Text	Font Size	DialogResult
Form1	AboutDialogBox	About Bingo		
Label1	lblInfo	*see form*	10	
Button1	btnOK	OK		OK

Form1 code

```
Public Class Form1
    Inherits System.Windows.Forms.Form

Windows Form Designer generated code

'File menu commands~~~~~~~~~~~~~~~~~~~~~~~~~~~~~~~~~~~~~~~~~~~~~~~~~~~~~~

Private Sub mnuPlayer1_Click(ByVal sender As Object, ByVal e As System.EventArgs) _
Handles mnuPlayer1.Click

    Dim BingoCard As New BingoCard()    'form with 25-slot BINGO card layout
    BingoCard.MdiParent = Me

    Static intCardNum As Integer
    intCardNum = intCardNum + 1
    BingoCard.Text = "Player 1 Card " & intCardNum
    Call GenerateBingoCard(BingoCard)    'generate card with random numbers

    BingoCard.Show()

End Sub
```

```
Private Sub mnuPlayer2_Click(ByVal sender As Object, ByVal e As System.EventArgs) _
Handles mnuPlayer2.Click

    Dim BingoCard As New BingoCard()      'form with 25-slot BINGO card layout
    BingoCard.MdiParent = Me

    Static intCardNum As Integer
    intCardNum = intCardNum + 1
    BingoCard.Text = "Player 2 Card " & intCardNum
    Call GenerateBingoCard(BingoCard)     'generate card with random numbers

    BingoCard.Show()

End Sub


Private Sub mnuExit_Click(ByVal sender As Object, ByVal e As System.EventArgs) _
Handles mnuExit.Click

    End

End Sub


'Windows menu commands~~~~~~~~~~~~~~~~~~~~~~~~~~~~~~~~~~~~~~~~~~~~~~~~~~

Private Sub mnuTileHorizontal_Click(ByVal sender As Object, _
ByVal e As System.EventArgs) Handles mnuTileHorizontal.Click

    Me.LayoutMdi(MdiLayout.TileHorizontal)

End Sub


Private Sub mnuTileVertical_Click(ByVal sender As Object, ByVal e As System.EventArgs) _
Handles mnuTileVertical.Click

    Me.LayoutMdi(MdiLayout.TileVertical)

End Sub


'Help menu commands~~~~~~~~~~~~~~~~~~~~~~~~~~~~~~~~~~~~~~~~~~~~~~~~~~~~~

Private Sub mnuAbout_Click(ByVal sender As Object, ByVal e As System.EventArgs) _
Handles mnuAbout.Click

    'show dialog box
    Dim AboutDB As New AboutDialogBox()
    AboutDB.ShowDialog()

End Sub


Private Sub mnuHowToPlay_Click(ByVal sender As Object, ByVal e As System.EventArgs) _
Handles mnuHowToPlay.Click

    'show dialog box
    Dim HelpDB As New HelpDialogBox()
    HelpDB.ShowDialog()

End Sub
```

'other procedures~~~~~~

'~~~~~~
'Generates a bingo card with random numbers.
'
'pre: A typical 5x5 Bingo card layout with a column B containing numbers
'that range from 1 to 15, column I ranging from 16 to 30, column N from 31 to 45,
'column G from 46 to 60, and column O from 61 to 75.
'post: The Text property of each button has a unique random number.
'~~~~~~

Sub GenerateBingoCard(**ByRef** NewCard **As** BingoCard)

   Dim btnBColumn() **As** Button = {NewCard.btnBSlot1, NewCard.btnBSlot2, _
   NewCard.btnBSlot3, NewCard.btnBSlot4, NewCard.btnBSlot5}
   Call GenerateColumn(btnBColumn, 1)

   Dim btnIColumn() **As** Button = {NewCard.btnISlot1, NewCard.btnISlot2, _
   NewCard.btnISlot3, NewCard.btnISlot4, NewCard.btnISlot5}
   Call GenerateColumn(btnIColumn, 16)

   Dim btnNColumn() **As** Button = {NewCard.btnNSlot1, NewCard.btnNSlot2, _
   NewCard.btnNSlot3, NewCard.btnNSlot4, NewCard.btnNSlot5}
   Call GenerateColumn(btnNColumn, 31)
   NewCard.btnNSlot3.Text = "Free Space"

   Dim btnGColumn() **As** Button = {NewCard.btnGSlot1, NewCard.btnGSlot2, _
   NewCard.btnGSlot3, NewCard.btnGSlot4, NewCard.btnGSlot5}
   Call GenerateColumn(btnGColumn, 46)

   Dim btnOColumn() **As** Button = {NewCard.btnOSlot1, NewCard.btnOSlot2, _
   NewCard.btnOSlot3, NewCard.btnOSlot4, NewCard.btnOSlot5}
   Call GenerateColumn(btnOColumn, 61)

End Sub

'~~~~~~
'Sets the text for each button of btnArray() to a number
'ranging from 0 to 14, offset by intOffset.
'
'pre: A typical 5x5 Bingo card layout with a set of 5 numbers from a
'range of 15 in each column.
'post: The Text property of each button in btnArray() has a unique number.
'~~~~~~

Sub GenerateColumn(**ByRef** btnArray() **As** Button, **ByVal** intOffset **As Integer**)

   Dim intNumbers(4) **As Integer**
   UniqueNumberArray(15, 5, intNumbers)

   Dim intButton **As Integer**
   For intButton = 0 **To** btnArray.Length – 1   'set button to a number
     btnArray(intButton).Text = intNumbers(intButton) + intOffset
   Next

End Sub

'~~~~~~
'Returns an array of unique integers ranging from 0 to intMaxValue.
'
'pre: intNumArray() has intNums elements.
'post: intNums unique numbers are stored in intNumArray().
'~~~~~~

Sub UniqueNumberArray(**ByVal** intMaxValue **As Integer**, **ByVal** intNums **As Integer**, _
ByRef intNumArray() **As Integer**)

   Dim blnNumArray(intMaxValue – 1) **As Boolean**
   Dim intNum **As Integer**
   Randomize()

```
        For intNum = 1 To intNums                'generate intNums unique numbers
            'generate a random number to correspond to an index number
            Dim intIndexToCheck As Integer = Int(Rnd() * intMaxValue)
            Do While blnNumArray(intIndexToCheck)
                'generate random index values until element at index is False
                intIndexToCheck = Int(Rnd() * intMaxValue)
            Loop
            blnNumArray(intIndexToCheck) = True
        Next

        'store selected index values in array
        Dim intIndex As Integer = 0
        For intNum = 0 To blnNumArray.Length - 1
            If blnNumArray(intNum) Then               'index selected
                intNumArray(intIndex) = intNum        'store index in intNumArray
                intIndex = intIndex + 1               'increment intNumArray index
            End If
        Next

    End Sub


    '~~~~~~~~~~~~~~~~~~~~~~~~~~~~~~~~~~~~~~~~~~~~~~~~~~~~~~~~~~~~~~~~
    'Displays a number in the range 1 through 75 that is unique to the game run.
    '
    'pre: A typical 5x5 Bingo card layout with numbers ranging from 1 through 75.
    'post: The button displays a new number. The new call is added to a call list.
    '~~~~~~~~~~~~~~~~~~~~~~~~~~~~~~~~~~~~~~~~~~~~~~~~~~~~~~~~~~~~~~~~
    Private Sub btnNumber_Click(ByVal sender As Object, ByVal e As System.EventArgs) _
    Handles btnNumber.Click

        Dim intRange As Integer = 75
        Static blnNumArray(intRange - 1) As Boolean
        Dim intNum As Integer

        Randomize()
        'generate a random number
        Dim intIndexToCheck As Integer = Int(Rnd() * intRange)
        Do While blnNumArray(intIndexToCheck)
            'generate random index values until element at index is False
            intIndexToCheck = Int(Rnd() * intRange)
        Loop
        blnNumArray(intIndexToCheck) = True

        'call out
        Select Case intIndexToCheck
            Case 0 To 14
                Me.btnNumber.Text = "B " & intIndexToCheck + 1
            Case 15 To 29
                Me.btnNumber.Text = "I " & intIndexToCheck + 1
            Case 30 To 44
                Me.btnNumber.Text = "N " & intIndexToCheck + 1
            Case 45 To 59
                Me.btnNumber.Text = "G " & intIndexToCheck + 1
            Case 60 To 74
                Me.btnNumber.Text = "O " & intIndexToCheck + 1
        End Select

        'add call to numbers called list
        Me.lblCalled.Text = Me.lblCalled.Text & Me.btnNumber.Text & vbCrLf

    End Sub

End Class
```

The BingoCard form code:

```
Private Sub Button_Click(ByVal sender As Object, ByVal e As System.EventArgs) _
  Handles btnBSlot1.Click, btnBSlot2.Click, btnBSlot3.Click, btnBSlot4.Click, btnBSlot5.Click, _
  btnISlot1.Click, btnISlot2.Click, btnISlot3.Click, btnISlot4.Click, btnISlot5.Click, _
  btnNSlot1.Click, btnNSlot2.Click, btnNSlot4.Click, btnNSlot5.Click, _
  btnGSlot1.Click, btnGSlot2.Click, btnGSlot3.Click, btnGSlot4.Click, btnGSlot5.Click, _
  btnOSlot1.Click, btnOSlot2.Click, btnOSlot3.Click, btnOSlot4.Click, btnOSlot5.Click

    Dim btnButtonClicked As Button = sender
    btnButtonClicked.Text = "X" & btnButtonClicked.Text & "X"

End Sub
```

testing and debugging   Running Bingo, displaying four cards, and calling a few numbers displays the interface similar to:

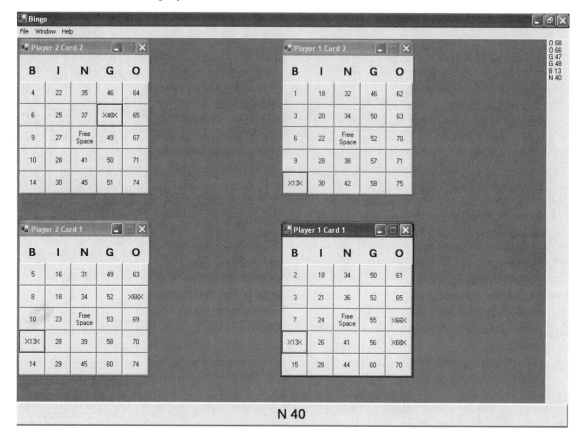

This Case Study should be tested by creating multiple cards and checking for number randomness, clicking each of the slots on a card and verifying that the number "marks" as expected, verifying the call list is updated when the call button is clicked. The Help and About dialog boxes should also be tested.

Review 6

Modify the Bingo Case Study application so that the backcolor of the buttons clicked by a player changes to a green, rather than having Xs displayed around the number.

An MDI application is an application with a parent form and one or more child forms. The parent form is a container for the child forms. The parent typically contains menus with commands for controlling the child forms. Menus usually include at least File, Window, and Help. The File menu includes commands for opening, closing, and creating documents, which are the child forms. The Window menu includes commands for arranging windows and a list of currently open windows, and the Help menu includes a command for displaying information about the application.

Form is a control class that is inherited by forms in a Windows Forms project. As with any class, objects are instantiated in a Dim statement that includes the New keyword. The Form control has IsMdiContainer and WindowState properties for making a form a parent form. A child form is added to a project by selecting Add Windows Form from the Project menu. The Form control has an MdiParent property for making a form a child form, and a Show() method for displaying a form. The Form control Close() method is used to close a form. To close the active child form, the ActiveMdiChild property must be used as well.

The Form control includes the LayoutMdi() method for arranging open windows either tiled horizontally, tiled vertically, or cascaded. The MainMenu control includes the MdiList property that can be set to True so that window names are automatically added to a menu.

abl TextBox

The TextBox control includes Copy(), Cut(), and Paste() methods for editing text in a text box. These methods are especially useful in a MDI application for editing text between open documents.

Applications use dialog boxes to get the information needed to execute some commands. A dialog box is also used to display information about an application, such as the creator's name. This dialog box is called the About dialog box.

A form is designated a dialog box by setting the properties ControlBox, MinimizeBox, MaximizeBox, and FormBorderStyle, and displaying the form as a modal form. A modal form does not allow other forms to receive input until it has been removed from the screen. The Form control ShowDialog() method is used to display a form as a modal form. A dialog box must contain at least OK and Cancel buttons. The Button control includes the DialogResult property that must be set according to the button response.

Child form A form that functions completely within a parent form and cannot be moved outside the parent form.

Dialog box A form presented to the user to get the information needed to execute a command. A dialog box must contain at least an OK and a Cancel button.

MDI Application A multiple-document interface application.

Modal form A form that does not allow other forms to receive input until it has been removed from the screen.

Parent form A container for child forms.

Visual Basic .NET

Add Windows Form command Adds a new form to a project. Found in the Project menu.

🗟 MainMenu **MainMenu control** Used to add an application component that contains menu items. Properties include MdiList.

Form class Used to create a control class object that can be a parent form for the application interface, a child form for application windows, or a dialog box for getting information from the user. Properties include IsMdiContainer, WindowState, MdiParent, ActiveMdiChild, ControlBox, MaximizeBox, MinimizeBox, and FormBorderStyle. Methods include Show(), ShowDialog(), LayoutMdi(), and Close().

abl TextBox **TextBox control** Used to add a TextBox control class object to a form. Methods include Copy(), Cut(), and Paste().

abl Button **Button control** Used to create a Button control class object. Properties include DialogResult.

1. Why is an MDI Parent form referred to as a container form?

2. Why is it important to have menus on a parent form?

3. a) To designate a form a parent form, which property(ies) must be changed? To what?
   b) After adding a new form with the purpose of becoming a child form which property(ies) must be changed? To what? Where is this done?

4. When a command requires information from the user, should a child form or a dialog box be used?

5. a) List the Visual Basic .NET predefined dialog boxes discussed throughout the text.
   b) What is the difference in implementing a predefined dialog box and a dialog box created for a specific application?
   c) List the similarities and differences between dialog boxes and interface forms.

6. What is a modal form? Explain.

7. a) What form properties must be changed to designate the form a dialog box? What should these properties be set to?
   b) When buttons are added to a dialog box, which button property must be set for the button response to properly work? What should this property be set to?

8. What does each procedure accomplish?
   a) **Private Sub** mnuAddChildren_Click(**ByVal** sender **As** System.Object, _
      ByVal e **As** System.EventArgs) **Handles** mnuAddChild.Click

      Dim NewOne **As New** Baby()
      Dim OtherOne **As New** Baby()
      NewOne.MdiParent = **Me**
      OtherOne.MdiParent = **Me**

      NewOne.Text = "Baby: NewOne"
      OtherOne.Text = "Baby: OtherOne"
      NewOne.Show()
      OtherOne.Show()

      End Sub

   b) **Private Sub** btnShow_Click(**ByVal** sender **As** System.Object, **ByVal** e **As** System.EventArgs) _
      Handles btnShow.Click

      Dim X **As** Baby = **Me**.ActiveMdiChild
      Me.txtParent.Text = X.Text

      End Sub

   c) **Private Sub** mnuDisplay_Click(**ByVal** sender **As** System.Object, _
      ByVal e **As** System.EventArgs) **Handles** mnuDisplay.Click

      Me.txtParent.Text = **Me**.ActiveMdiChild.Text
      Dim X **As** Baby = **Me**.ActiveMdiChild
      X.txtStuff.Paste()

      End Sub

9. a) Write code to instantiate and display a new dialog box. The form is named DataForm.vb and the specific dialog box should be named GetDataDB.

   b) The DataForm dialog box has objects: txtName, txtAge, btnOK, and btnCancel. Write statements for the parent form that perform the following when btnOK is clicked: Assign the name from the text box to strName and then if the age entered is less than 18 display the message "Student discount applies." and assign the value 5 to a variable named intStudentDiscount.

10. A dialog box has OK (btnOK) and Cancel (btnCancel) buttons as well as three check boxes: Back Stage Prices (chkBkStage), VIP Refreshments (chkRefresh), and VIP Parking (chkPark). Correct the errors in the following code that should determine the number of selected check boxes and assign decExtraCost appropriately:

```
Const decONE_PRIV As Decimal
Const decTWO_PRIV As Decimal
Const decTHREE_PRIV As Decimal

Dim intNumChks As Integer
Dim decExtraCost As Decimal

SpecPrivDB.ShowDialog()

If SpecPrivDB.DialogResult = OK Then
    If Me.chkBkStage.Checked Then
        intNumChks = intNumChks + 1
    End If
    If Me.chkRefresh.Checked Then
        intNumChks = intNumChks + 1
    End If
    If Me.chkPark.Checked Then
        intNumChks = intNumChks + 1
    End If

    Select intNumChks
        Case 1: decExtraCost = decONE_PRIV
        Case 2: decExtraCost = decTWO_PRIV
        Case 3: decExtraCost = decTHREE_PRIV
    End Select
End If
```

11. Determine if each of the following is true or false. If false, explain why.
    a) A parent form can have only one child form.
    b) There can be only one parent form in a MDI application.
    c) It is possible to close the parent form and leave children forms open.
    d) When a child form is minimized, its icon appears in the parent form, not on the Desktop taskbar.
    e) A parent form can hold different child forms.
    f) MdiList is a Form property that automatically adds the names of open child forms to a menu.
    g) If multiple open child forms are to be entirely visible, then they should be tiled.
    h) A user must respond to a dialog box before work can continue in the parent form.
    i) The DialogResult property is automatically set based on the name of the button.
    j) It is possible to ignore a displayed dialog box and continue to work in a child window.

Exercise 1 ———————————————————————The Vacation Stop

Create The Vacation Stop application that is used to promote the weekly special for a travel agency. The weekly special is displayed in a dialog box that can be displayed in English or French. The application interface should look similar to:

The File menu should contain an Exit command. The Specials menu should contain a Select Language... command, which displays a dialog box prompting the user to select English or French. Clicking English displays a dialog box with the weekly special "Las Vegas, 3 days, $199." Clicking French displays a dialog box with "Las Vegas, 3 jours, 199$." The Help menu should contain an About Vacation Stop... command. The sponges.jpg image file is a data file for this text.

Exercise 2 ⟳ ———————————————————————— Mad-Lib II

Create a Mad-Lib II MDI application that includes the standard Windows application commands and dialog boxes. Refer to Chapter 12 Exercise 3 for information about Mad-Libs. Mad-Lib II should include commands that display:

- a window for adding verbs to a file.
- a window for adding nouns to a file.
- a window for adding sentences to a file. The sentences should contain placeholders for verbs and nouns.
- a window that displays random Mad-Libs using the previously created files.

Be creative with your Mad-Lib II application. Add color to windows, graphics to the Mad-Lib windows, and animations where appropriate.

Exercise 3 ⚙ ——————————————————————— Bingo

Modify the Bingo Case Study to play Math Bingo. In Math Bingo, a math problem is displayed for each call and the result of this math problem is the number to be marked. For this Bingo application, the Case Study should be modified so that:

- the application uses a file named mathprob.dat that stores one math problem per line. This file can be created in a text editor, such as the one discussed in Chapter 12. In this file, the first math problem should evaluate to 1, the second math problem should evaluate to 2, and so on, up to 75.
- the btnNumber_Click() procedure sets the button text to the math problem that corresponds to the selected random number. For example, if 10 is the selected random number, then the tenth math problem in the mathprob.dat file is displayed.

Exercise 4 ⚙ ——————————————————— My Business Accessories

Create a My Business Accessories MDI application that includes the standard Windows application commands and dialog boxes. My Business Accessories should also include commands that display:

- a window for calculating a mortgage using the Pmt() function (similar to the Loan Payment application in Chapter 8 Review 3)
- a window for calculating the cost of financing (similar to the Credit Card Loan application in Chapter 8 Review 4)
- a window for calculating the value of an investment after a specified period (similar to the Watch Your Money Grow application in Chapter 8 Review 5)

Exercise 5 ⚙ ——————————————————————My Accessories

Create a My Accessories MDI application that includes the standard Windows application commands and dialog boxes. My Accessories should also include commands that display:

- a working calculator (the Chapter 7 case study)
- a triangle calculator (the Chapter 11 case study)
- a text editor (the Write File application from Chapter 12 Review 5)
- the Click It! game (the Chapter 10 case study).

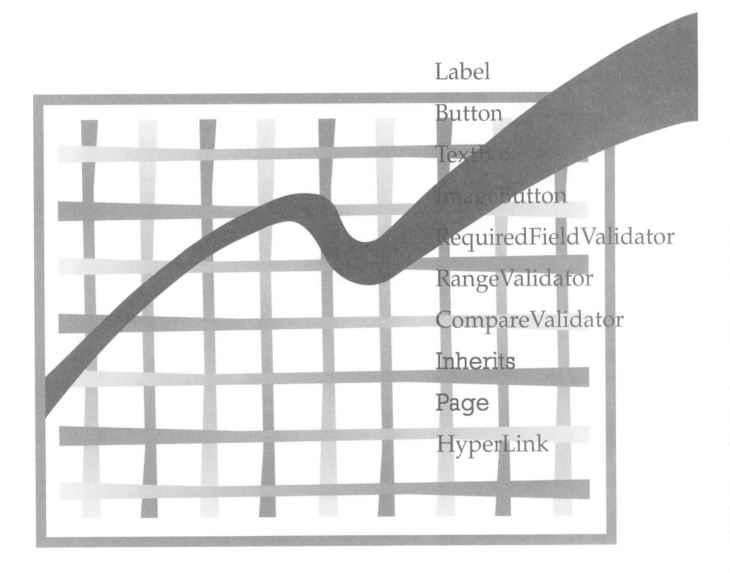

Label

Button

TextBox

ImageButton

RequiredFieldValidator

RangeValidator

CompareValidator

Inherits

Page

HyperLink

Chapter 15 Expectations

After completing this chapter you will be able to:

1. Create an ASP.NET Web application.

2. Understand Web Forms.

3. Use Web Forms controls to create an application interface.

4. Use validation controls in a Web application.

5. Write event procedures for a Web application.

6. Add forms to a web application and use the HyperLink control to link between the forms.

This chapter introduces Web applications. The concepts explained in this chapter include adding objects to a Web Forms page to make an interactive Web application, using validation control objects to check user input on a Web Forms page, and writing event procedures for the Web application.

15.1   Web Applications

Visual Basic .NET can be used to create Web applications. A *Web application* consists of one or more related Web Forms pages and runs in a Web browser, such as Internet Explorer. A Web Forms page is a form that can include objects similar to those used with forms for Windows applications in the previous chapters of this text. These objects are created with Web Forms controls, and enable the user to interact with the application. For example, in the Web application below, a monthly car payment is calculated based on data entered by the user:

Users can interact with a Web application

Web applications are posted to a server so that multiple users have access to the application. *Posting* simply means to place files on a *server*, which is a powerful computer used to manage communications and data sharing. Some servers are used for maintaining an internal network, such as a school network. Posting to an internal server allows users with access to the network to run the application. Posting to a server maintained by an Internet Service Provider (ISP) or a Web host makes the application accessible to users on the World Wide Web.

ISPs and Web Hosts

An ISP (Internet Service Provider) offers access to the Internet for a fee. A Web host is a company that provides servers for posting Web applications.

15.2   Creating a Web Application

Web Forms is the Visual Basic .NET platform for creating Web applications. Web Forms contain *pages* that are the visual user interface. *Web Forms controls* are used to add objects, such as text boxes, to a page to allow interaction with the user. Web Forms controls are based on *ASP.NET (Active Server Pages)*, Microsoft's Web development platform.

To create a Web application, create a new project. The New Project dialog box is displayed:

Web Application Location

The Location of an ASP.NET application refers to the client and host of the application. The client is the user's computer and the host is the computer "serving" the application. An application that will be used and served by the same computer will have location localhost. A different server is designated by providing an IP address or domain name for the location.

An IP address (Internet Protocol address) is a 32-bit binary number that identifies a computer connected to the Internet. An IP address is written as four numbers that range from 0 to 255 separated by a period. For example, 1.120.05.123.

A domain name is descriptive text (i.e., www.lpdatafiles.com) that correlates to an IP address.

Select Visual Basic Projects in the Projects Types list and click the ASP.NET Web Application icon in the Templates list. The Location box is used to specify the location followed by a slash and then the project name. Type localhost for the location to create an application for the current computer. Select OK to create the web.

The Create New Web dialog box is displayed while the Web is being set up on the server:

When the Web is set up, the IDE displays a Web Forms Design window:

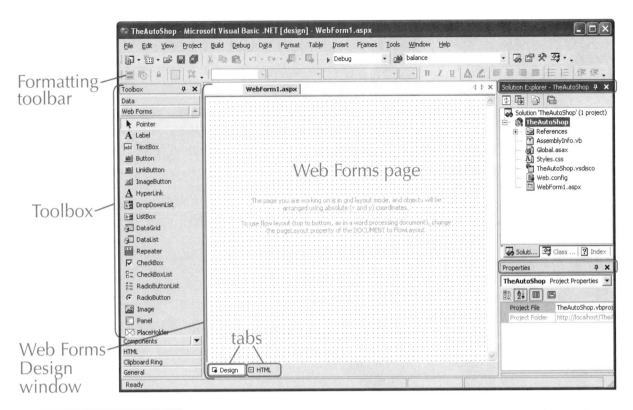

Formatting toolbar

Toolbox

Web Forms Design window

tabs

- The **Formatting toolbar** contains buttons that can be used to format the Web form.

- The **Web Forms Design window** contains the Web Forms page.

- The **Web Forms page** consists of a Web form that can contain Web Forms control objects and HTML.

- The **Solution Explorer window** displays the files for a project. A Web form has a .aspx extension.

- The **Properties window** lists the properties of a selected object.

- The **Design tab** shows the Web form.

- The **HTML tab** displays HTML for the Web form.

- The **Toolbox** contains controls that are used to create objects.

Review 1

In this review you will create a ASP.NET Web application in a project named TheAutoShop.

CREATE A NEW PROJECT

    a. On the toolbar, click the New Project button (⊞▾). The New Project dialog box is displayed.

        1. In the Projects Type list, select Visual Basic Projects if it is not already selected.

        2. In the Templates list, click the ASP.NET Web Application icon.

        3. In the Location box, modify the existing text to read http://localhost/TheAutoShop.

        4. Select OK. A project is created and the WebForm1.aspx Design window is displayed.

    b. Locate the Toolbox with Web Forms controls for creating objects, the Solution Explorer window, and the Properties window.

15.3 Web Forms

A Web application consists of one or more Web forms. A Web form is the visual component of a Web Forms page and has the properties:

- **title** is the text displayed in the title bar of the browser window running the application. This text should be meaningful and descriptive because it is also used when the user adds the page to the Favorites list.

- **Description** is text that describes the contents of the Web application.

- **keywords** are words or phrases that describe the Web application's content. They are words that users may use as search criteria in a Web search engine to locate the site.

- **pageLayout** sets the mode for the Web Forms Design window. This property is discussed in Section 15.4.

- **targetSchema** selects the Web browser that the application will be designed for.

- The **leftMargin**, **rightMargin**, **topMargin**, and **bottomMargin** properties can be set to create space from the browser window to the edge of the Web Forms page.

Search Engines

A search engine is a program that searches a database of Web pages for keywords and then lists hyperlinks to those pages. Search engines include Yahoo!, Google, and HotBot.

META tags   The Description and keyword properties are stored as META tags. *META tags* are HTML tags that are used by search engines to index Web pages. Setting the Description and keywords properties increase the probability that a Web page will be indexed by a search engine. META tags can be viewed by clicking the HTML tab at the bottom of the Web Forms Design window.

15.4 Page Layout Modes

GridLayout   The pageLayout property for a Web Forms page can be set to one of two modes. *GridLayout* mode is the default and allows objects to be precisely positioned and sized. When the page is viewed in a Web browser, the objects will maintain the exact position that was specified.

FlowLayout   *FlowLayout* mode does not have a grid and has an insertion point in the upper-left corner of the Web Forms page. Text can then be typed directly on the form from top to bottom just like a word processor document. When the page is viewed in a Web browser, the objects will size according to the user's screen resolution and browser size. This may produce an undesirable result because the text or objects may wrap differently in the user's browser.

Regardless of the design mode used, the Web application should be tested by displaying it in as many different Web browsers as possible and at different screen resolutions to ensure that all users will be able to view the Web application appropriately. Running a Web application in a Web browser is discussed in Section 15.6.

adding objects

Web Forms controls are used to add objects to a Web form. A Web Forms object is added by clicking a control and then dragging on the form. For example, clicking the Label control in the Toolbox and then dragging on the form adds a new Label object:

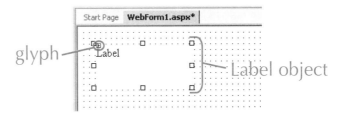

glyph

A *glyph* (▣) appears in the upper-left corner of an object to indicate a server-based control rather than a Windows control. The glyph does not appear when the page is viewed in a Web browser.

properties

A Label

Many of the Web Forms controls are similar to the Windows Forms controls. However, many of the property names are different than the names used with the Windows Forms controls. For example, the Web Forms Label control has the properties:

- **ID** identifies a control for the programmer. It is good programming style to begin Label object names with lbl.

- **Text** is the text displayed in the label.

- **Font** can be expanded by clicking ⊞ to display the Bold, Italic, Name, Size, and Underline properties.

Property values are set by typing or selecting a new value in the Properties window.

ab Button

The Web Forms Button control is similar to the Windows Forms Button, and has the properties:

- **ID** identifies a control for the programmer. It is good programming style to begin Button object names with btn.

- **Text** is the text displayed on the button.

ab TextBox

The Web Forms TextBox control is similar to the Windows Forms TextBox control, and has the properties:

- **ID** identifies a control for the programmer. It is good programming style to begin TextBox object names with txt.

- **Text** is the text displayed in the text box.

Web Forms Controls

Other commonly used Web Forms controls include CheckBox and RadioButton.

The ImageButton control displays an image that can respond to a mouse click from the user. The ImageButton has the properties:

- **ID** identifies a control for the programmer. It is good programming style to begin ImageButton object names with ibt.

- **ImageUrl** contains **...** that is clicked to display the Select Image dialog box:

Select Image

Projects:
//localhost/TheAutoShop

Contents of 'TheAutoShop'

Files of type: Image Files(*.gif;*.jpg;*.jpeg;*.bmp;*.wmf;*.png)

URL type: Document Relative

URL: Browse ...

URL preview:

OK   Cancel   Help

Images to be placed on a Web form should be stored in the project folder. To select an image from the project folder, click the appropriate file name in the Contents of list and then select OK.

15.6   Saving and Running a Web Application

An application should be saved frequently to avoid losing changes. To save a project, select Save from the File menu or click the Save button (🖫) on the toolbar.

To run a Web application, click the Start button (▶) on the toolbar or select Start (F5) from the Debug menu. The IDE remains on the screen, but the Web application is displayed in a Web browser and becomes the active window. The form no longer displays a grid. Control objects cannot be modified, but objects can be tested to see if events, such as clicking a button, produce the desired effect. A Web application can be run at any time for testing at different stages of development.

Review 2 ⟳

In this review you will add objects to TheAutoShop application. Open TheAutoShop project if it is not already open.

① *SET THE WEB FORM PROPERTIES*

a. Click the Web Forms page to select it. Handles are not displayed, but the Properties window displays DOCUMENT in the object list.

b. Set the pageLayout property to GridLayout, if this is not the current setting.

c. Set the title property to: Payment Calculator

d. Set the Description property to: The Auto Shop illustrates how affordable a car is by providing a calculator that will calculate a monthly car payment

e. Set the keywords property to: auto, automotive, car, purchase, calculator, monthly payment

② ADD A WEB FORMS LABEL OBJECT TO THE FORM

a. In the Toolbox, click the Label control and then drag on the form grid. A label is displayed. Note the glyph in the upper-left corner of the object.

b. In the Properties window, set ID to lblBusiness.

c. Set the Text property to The Auto Shop. The label now displays "The Auto Shop."

d. In the Properties window, click the ⊞ next to Font. Font properties are displayed.

   1. Click Bold and select True.

   2. Click Name and select Arial.

   3. Click Size and select Large.

e. Size the label if necessary so that all the text is displayed on one line.

③ ADD ADDITIONAL OBJECTS TO THE WEB FORM

Refer to the form below to add, position, and size objects. Use the table below to set properties.

Object	ID	Text	Font
Label1	lblPurchase	see interface above	Italic
Label2	lblPricePrompt	see interface above	Bold
TextBox1	txtPrice	0	
Label3	lblRatePrompt	see interface above	Bold
TextBox2	txtRate	empty	
Label4	lblTermPrompt	see interface above	Bold
TextBox3	txtTerm	empty	
Button1	btnPayment	see interface above	
Label5	lblPayment	empty	Italic

    a. Save the modified TheAutoShop project and then run the application.

    b. The application is displayed in a browser window. No interaction is possible because code has not been written for this form.

    c. Close the browser window.

15.7   Validation Controls

Validation controls are Web Forms controls for creating objects that check the data entered by the user. For example, a RequiredFieldValidator object checks to see if data has been typed into a designated object. The validator control object is placed where an error message should be displayed if a object being validated is left empty:

> Purchase Price ($): [   ] RequiredFieldValidator

This validator object displays a message if the TextBox object is left empty

RequiredFieldValidator

The RequiredFieldValidator control has the properties:

- **ID** identifies a control for the programmer. It is good programming style to begin RequiredFieldValidator object names with rfv.

- **ControlToValidate** is the object on the form to be checked.

- **ErrorMessage** is the text displayed in the RequiredFieldValidator object if the checked object is empty.

RangeValidator

A RangeValidator object checks a typed value to see if is within a specific range. The RangeValidator control has the properties:

- **ID** identifies a control for the programmer. It is good programming style to begin RangeValidator object names with rgv.

- **ControlToValidate** is the object on the form to be checked.

- **ErrorMessage** is the text displayed in the RangeValidator object if the checked object is empty.

- **MaximumValue** is the upper bound of the range and must contain a value.

- **MinimumValue** is the lower bound of the range and must contain a value.

- **Type** is the data type, such as Integer.

CompareValidator

A CompareValidator object checks the data in one object against that in another. The CompareValidator control has the properties:

- **ID** identifies a control for the programmer. It is good programming style to begin CompareValidator object names with cpv.

- **ControlToCompare** is the object on the form that is compared.

- **ControlToValidate** is the object on the form to be checked.

- **ErrorMessage** is the text displayed in the CompareValidator object if the checked object is empty.

- **Type** is the data type, such as Integer.

Review 3

In this review you will add validation objects to a Web application. Open TheAutoShop project if it is not already open.

① ADD A VALIDATION OBJECT

a. In the Toolbox, click the RangeValidator control and then drag to the right of the Purchase Price text box.

b. In the Properties window, set the:

1. ID property to rgvPurchasePrice.
2. ControlToValidate property to txtPrice.
3. ErrorMessage property to: Please enter a price from 1 to 100000.
4. MaximumValue property to 100000.
5. MinimumValue property to 1.
6. Type property to **Double**.

c. Size the RangeValidator object so that the text is completely displayed on one line.

② ADD ADDITIONAL VALIDATION OBJECTS TO THE WEB FORM

Refer to the form below to add, position, and size objects. Use the steps below to set properties:

The Auto Shop

Purchasing a car is affordable. Calculate your payments:

Purchase Price ($): | 0 | Please enter a price from 1 to 100000.

Interest Rate (%): | | Please enter a rate between 0 and 25.

Term of Loan (years): | | Please enter the term of the loan.

Calculate Monthly Payment

[lblPayment]

a. Next to the Interest Rate text box, add a RangeValidator object and set the ID property to rgvRate, ControlToValidate to txtRate, ErrorMessage as shown in the form, MaximumValue to 25.0, MinimumValue to 0.5, and Type to **Double**.

b. Next to the **Term of Loan** text box, add a RequiredFieldValidator object and set the ID property to rfvTerm, ControlToValidate to txtTerm, ErrorMessage as shown in the form.

③ *RUN THE APPLICATION*

a. Save the modified TheAutoShop application and run the application.

b. In the **Interest Rate** text box, type 45. Leave a 0 in the **Purchase Price** text box, and leave the **Term of Loan** text box empty.

c. Click **Calculate Monthly Payment**. Error messages are displayed.

d. Close the browser window.

15.8 Application Code

In a Web application project, Visual Basic .NET automatically generates code as Web Forms control objects are added. This code is added to initialize objects on the page and set property values.

To display Code view, click the View Code button (⊞) in the Solution Explorer window. The Code window for a new Web application looks similar to:

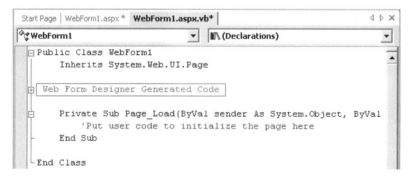

The code that generates a Web form is a class. The **Inherits** statement indicates that the class contains, or has "inherited," all the attributes of the **Page** class. Statements can be added below the **Inherits** statement to extend the class and add functionality to the application.

When an object is added to a Web form, a declaration statement is automatically generated as well. For example, adding a label to a Web form and setting its ID to lblBusiness generates the statement that is circled in blue below:

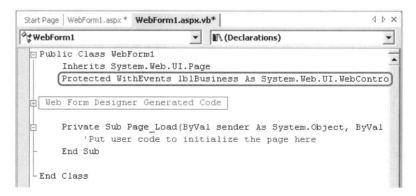

An Introduction to Programming Using Microsoft Visual Basic .NET

A Web application is viewed in a Web browser on the user's computer, but the code that is written for Web Forms control objects is located and executed on the Web server.

15.9 Event Procedures

Event procedures can be written for the control objects on a Web form. In a Web application, event procedures are added and coded the same way they are in a Windows application.

application design

A Web application that will be posted to a Web server should be designed with only simple Click event procedures because the client computer must send information back to the server when an event occurs. The sending of information back to the server increases the time required for the next Web form or page to load. Users will wait about six seconds for a Web page to load. Events such as MouseMove require information to continually be sent to server, which could result in long page loads.

Review 4

In this review you will add an event procedure to TheAutoShop application. Open TheAutoShop project if it is not already open.

① *OPEN THEAUTOSHOP PROJECT*

    a. In the Solution Explorer window, click the View Code button (▦). TheAutoShop Code window is displayed.

    b. Note the code that has been automatically generated.

② *ADD AN EVENT PROCEDURE*

    a. From the Class Name list, select btnPayment.

    b. From the Method Name list, select Click. The btnPayment_Click event procedure has been added to the program code.

    c. Add the statements:

```
Dim sngRate, sngPrincipal As Single
Dim intTerm As Integer
Dim sngPayment As Single

sngPrincipal = Val(Me.txtPrice.Text)
sngRate = Val(Me.txtRate.Text)
intTerm = Val(Me.txtTerm.Text)

sngRate = sngRate / 100                    'convert to a percentage
sngPayment = Pmt(sngRate / 12, intTerm * 12, –sngPrincipal)
Me.lblPayment.Text = "The monthly payment for a loan of " _
    & Format(sngPrincipal, "Currency") & " at " & Format(sngRate, "Percent") _
    & " for " & intTerm & " years is " & Format(sngPayment, "Currency")
```

③ *RUN THE APPLICATION*

    Save the modified TheAutoShop project and then run and test the application with valid and invalid data.

④ *PRINT THE CODE AND THEN CLOSE THE PROJECT*

15.10 Adding a Web Form to a Project

A Web application usually contains multiple forms. To add a new Web form to an open project, select Add Web Form from the Project menu. The Add New Item dialog box is displayed with Web Form selected:

Type a descriptive form name in the Name box (be sure to keep the .aspx extension) and then select Open. A new Web form is displayed in a Design window and the file name is added to the list of project files in the Solution Explorer window.

adding a hyperlink

A HyperLink object can be used to create a link to another Web form in the application or to a Web page that is stored on a Web server. The HyperLink control has the properties:

A HyperLink

- **ID** identifies a control for the programmer. It is good programming style to begin HyperLink object names with hyp.

- **Text** is the hyperlink text. By default this text is displayed as blue and underlined, which should not be changed because blue underlined text is understood by users to be a hyperlink.

- **NavigateUrl** contains the **...** button that is clicked to display the Select URL dialog box:

Project

🔲	Add Web Form...	
🔲	Add Web User Control...	
🔲	Add HTML Page...	
🔲	Add Web Service...	
🔲	Add Component...	
🔲	Add Class...	
🔲	Add New Item...	Ctrl+Shift+A
🔲	Add Existing Item...	Shift+Alt+A
🔲	Copy Project...	
	Web Project	▶
	Exclude From Project	
🔲	Show All Files	
	Add Reference...	
	Add Web Reference...	
	Set as StartUp Project	

Select URL

Projects:
- //localhost/TheAutoShop

Contents of 'TheAutoShop'
- AssemblyInfo.vb
- Styles.css
- Web.config
- Global.asax
- TheAutoShop.vsdisc
- WebForm1.aspx

Files of type: All Files(*.*)

URL type: Document Relative

URL: [ ] Browse ...

URL preview: [ ]

OK   Cancel   Help

To create a hyperlink to a Web page, type the URL (including http://) in the URL box. For example, http://www.lpdatafiles.com. To create a hyperlink to another Web form that is part of the project, select the appropriate .aspx file from the Contents of list.

Review 5 ♻

In this review you will add a Web form to TheAutoShop project. The two Web forms in TheAutoShop project will then be linked using the HyperLink control.

① OPEN THEAUTOSHOP PROJECT

② ADD A WEB FORM

    a. Select Project → Add Web Form. A dialog box is displayed.

        1. In the Templates list, select the Web Form icon if it is not already selected.

        2. In the Name box, modify the existing test to read Store Location.aspx.

        3. Select Open. A blank Web form is displayed in a Design window. Note the Store Location.aspx file name in the Solutions Explorer window.

③ ADD OBJECTS TO THE WEB FORM

    Refer to the form below to add, position, and size objects. Use the table below to set properties.

The Auto Shop 47 Main Street, Delray Beach, FL 33445

We are located beside the AutoMall, take exit 23

Visit us soon!

Back

Object	ID	Text	Font
Label1	lblBusiness	*see interface above*	Bold, Arial, Large
Label2	lblAddress	*see interface above*	
Label3	lblLocation	*see interface above*	
Label4	lblVisit	*see interface above*	Italic

Object	ID	Text	NavigateUrl
Hyperlink	hypBack	Back	WebForm1.aspx

④ *DISPLAY WEB FORM1 AND ADD A HYPERLINK*

    a. Display the Web Form1 Design window.

    b. In the Toolbox, click the HyperLink control and then drag in the upper-right corner of the form grid. A hyperlink is displayed. Move the hyperlink to the upper-right corner of the form.

    c. In the Properties window, set ID to hypLocation.

    d. Set the Text property to Store Location. The hyperlink now displays "Store Location."

    e. In the Properties window, click the ... button in the Navigate Url property. The Select URL dialog box is displayed.

        1. In the Contents of list, select Store Location.aspx.

        2. Click OK. The dialog box is removed.

⑤ *RUN THE APPLICATION*

    a. Save the modified TheAutoShop project and run the application. The application is displayed in a browser window.

    b. Click Store Location. The Store Location Web form is displayed.

    c. Click Back. Web Form1 is again displayed.

    d. Close the browser window.

⑥ *PRINT THE APPLICATION CODE*

⑦ *CLOSE THE PROJECT*

Visual Basic .NET can be used to create Web applications. A Web application consists of one or more related Web forms and runs in a Web browser, such as Internet Explorer. Web applications are usually posted to a server so that the application is accessible to multiple users. Posting can be to an internal server of an internal network or to a Web server so that the application can be run by users on the Internet.

Web Forms is the Visual Basic .NET platform that is used to create Web applications. Web Forms contain pages that are the visual user interface and can include Web Forms control objects, such as text boxes, to allow interaction with the user. Web Forms controls are based on ASP.NET (Active Server Pages), Microsoft's Web development platform.

A Web application is created by creating a new project and selecting Visual Basic Projects in the Projects Types list and clicking the ASP.NET Web Application icon in the Templates list. The Location box is used to specify the location and the name of the project.

The Web Forms Design window is where the Web Forms page is displayed. A Web Forms page has the properties title, Description, keywords, pageLayout, targetSchema, leftMargin, rightMargin, topMargin, and bottomMargin. The Web Forms pageLayout property can be set to GridLayout or FlowLayout mode. GridLayout mode is the default and allows objects to be precisely positioned and sized. FlowLayout mode removes the grid from the Windows Form Design window and places an insertion point in the top left corner of the screen.

Web Forms controls are used to add objects to a Web form. A glyph appears in the upper-left corner of an object to indicate a server-based control rather than a Windows control. Web Forms controls include the HyperLink control, the Button control, the TextBox control, and the ImageButton control.

Validation controls are Web Forms controls that are used to check the data entered by the user to ensure that the data is appropriate. Validation controls include the RequiredFieldValidator control, the RangeValidator control, and the CompareValidator control.

A Web application is run by clicking the Start button on the toolbar or selecting Start. The IDE remains on the screen, but the Web application is displayed in a Web browser and becomes the active window.

The code that generates a Web form is a class derived from the Page class. When an object is added to a Web form, code is automatically generated to declare the control class object. The code with event procedures written for Web Forms controls is located and executed on the Web server.

A Web application usually contains multiple forms. A new Web form is added to an open project by selecting Add Web Form. The HyperLink control can be used to link the Web forms in a project.

ASP.NET (Active Server Pages) Microsoft's Web development platform.

FlowLayout A pageLayout mode that removes the grid from the Windows Forms page and places an insertion point in the top left corner of the screen.

Glyph Appears in the top-left corner of an object to indicate a server-based control.

GridLayout A pageLayout mode that allows objects to be precisely positioned and sized.

META tags HTML tags that are used by many search engines to index Web pages.

Posting Placing files on a server.

Server A powerful computer used to manage communications and data sharing.

Validation controls Web Forms controls that can be used to check the data entered by the user to ensure that the data is appropriate.

Web application An application that consists of one or more related Web forms and runs in a Web browser.

Web Forms The Visual Basic .NET platform for creating Web applications.

Web Forms controls Objects that enable the user to interact with the application.

Add Web Form command Adds a new Web form to an open project. Found in the Project menu.

Button control Used to add a Button control class object to a Web Forms page. Properties include ID and Text. Events include Click.

CompareValidator control Used to add a CompareValidator control class object to a Web Forms page. Properties include ID, Type, ControlToCompare, ControlToValidate, and ErrorMessage.

Hyperlink control Used to add a Hyperlink control class object to a Web Forms page. Properties include ID, Text, and NavigateURL. Events include Click.

ImageButton control Used to add an ImageButton control class object to a Web Forms page. Properties include ID and ImageURL. Events include Click.

Label control Used to add a Label control class object to a Web Forms page. Properties include ID, Text, and Font.

RangeValidator control Used to add a RangeValidator control class object to a Web Forms page. Properties include ID, Type, ControlToValidate, ErrorMessage, MinimumValue, and MaximumValue.

RequiredFieldValidator control Used to add a RequiredFieldValidator control class object to a Web Forms page. Properties include ID, ControlToValidate, and ErrorMessage.

Save command Saves the current project. Found in the File menu. The Save Project button on the toolbar can be used instead of the command.

Start command Runs an application. Found in the Debug menu. The button on the toolbar can be used instead of the command.

TextBox control Used to add a TextBox control class object to a Web Forms page. Properties include ID and Text.

View Code button Displays the Code window. Found in the Solution Explorer window. The Code command from the View menu can be used instead of the button.

Web Form The visual component of a Web Forms page. A Web Form has the properties title, Description, keywords, pageLayout, targetSchema, leftMargin, rightMargin, topMargin, and bottomMargin.

1. How can a user know if a running application is a Web application or a Windows application?

2. Describe the difference between a hyperlink and text in a label in a Web application.

3. Assume a running Web application. When you click a hyperlink, a new page is not displayed as expected. What should be checked?

4. Why is it best to limit events in a Web application to simple ones such as Click events?

5. Why would GridLayout be chosen instead of FlowLayout for the pageLayout property?

6. Imagine a Web application that is a Web site for learning about whales and then has a quiz based on the presented information.
    a) What keywords might you use for this application?
    b) What Description might you use for this application?
    c) Describe in detail the pages you would have for this application, including the key controls and the title of the pages?

7. List the controls introduced in this chapter and include the 3-letter prefix that should be used for their ID as good programming style.

8. A form in a Web application needs the following information:
    First Name, Last Name, Address1, Address2, City, State, Zip, Phone
    Which should have the RequiredFieldValidator assigned to it?

9. For each of the situations below, which control is needed?
    a) Allows the user to input name, address, and number of tickets ordered.
    b) Show a new web page to see the fall sports schedule.
    c) Check to see that the age entered by the user is between 14 and 21.
    d) Check to see that an e-mail address was not left blank.
    e) Check to see that the two password fields contain identical text.

10. For each of the following, indicate True or False. If False, explain why.
    a) Every Web application must include hyperlinks.
    b) What is assigned to the keyword property will be the words that search engines look for.
    c) The targetSchema property allows you to choose which type of web browser you would like to design for.
    d) The Description property is what is utilized when a user adds the application page to their favorites list.
    e) When running a Web application from the IDE you will view it as a Windows application unless you first open up a Web browser.

f) In a Web application, when desired input is not of the appropriate type or is left blank you should use a message box to inform the user.

g) The RequiredFieldValidator, RangeValidator, and CompareValidator are controls which have no graphical element.

h) The RequiredFieldValidator can only be used to check for an empty CheckBox object.

i) The RangeValidator control can be used to determine if input is within an alphabetic range.

Exercise 1 ———————————————————————————— Web Access

Web applications often require users to register at their site. Create a Web Access application that prompts the user for data and determines if the data is valid. If the data is valid, a UserID is generated for the user. The application should look similar to the following after data has been entered and Register has been clicked:

The application interface should include:

- Web Form Description and keyword properties.
- RequiredFieldValidator objects for the First Name and Last Name text boxes.
- A CompareValidator object for the Password and Retype Password text boxes.
- A RangeValidator object for the Age text box. The applicant has to be 18 years or older.

Note that the TextMode property for the Password and Retype Password textboxes should be set to Password.

The generated UserID is formed from the first five characters of the user's last name and the first character of their first name.

Create a Magic Answer application that prompts the user to ask a yes or no question and then responds by randomly displaying one of eight possible answers. The application interface should look similar to the following after the user asks a question:

The application interface should include:

- Web Form Description and keyword properties.
- a RequiredFieldValidator object for the Question text box.

The program code should randomly display one of the following answers when a question is asked:

- Yes
- No
- Probably
- Probably Not!
- Maybe
- Definitely
- You're Dreaming
- What?

Exercise 3 ——————————————————— Pizza Order

Many restaurants allow customers to place takeout orders over the Internet. Create a Pizza Order application that prompts the user for their order, checks that all required delivery data has been entered, and then displays a summary of the order when the order is placed. The application interface should look similar to the following after the user has selected some order options:

The application interface should include:

- Web Form Description and keyword properties.
- a RequiredFieldValidator object for the Name, Address, and Phone text boxes.

The program code should calculate the price as follows:

Regular:	$6.00
Large:	$10.00
one topping:	$1.00 additional
two toppings:	$1.75 additional
three toppings:	$2.50 additional
four toppings:	$3.25 additional

Clicking New Order clears the selected options on the Web Form, selects Regular and removes the current price and order number. The order number should automatically increment when the next order is placed during program execution.

Body Mass Index (BMI) is an assessment used to determine if an individual is underweight, over-weight, or within a healthy weight range. Create a BMI Web application that calculates a user's BMI. The application interface of the Web Form contains a hyperlink to the calculator and should look similar to the following:

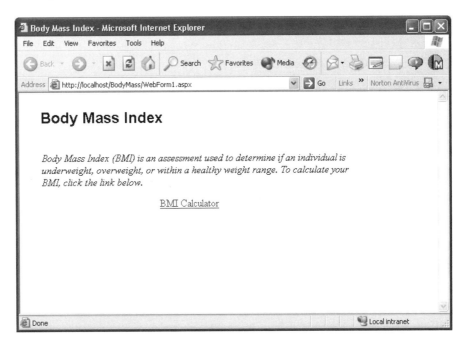

Clicking <u>BMI Calculator</u> should display the application interface of the BMI calculator. The application interface of the BMI Calculator Web Form should look similar to the following after "Calculate" has been clicked:

- The application interface should include a Web Form Description and keyword properties.
- A RequiredFieldValidator object should be used to verify data in the Height and Weight text boxes.
- The program code should use the formula BMI = weight (kg) / [height (m)] ^ 2 to calculate the Body Mass Index.
- Add an additional Measurement Conversion Web Form that the user can reference to convert pounds to kilograms and feet and inches to meters.

Appendix A
Using Help

A.1 Finding a Help Topic

Selecting Help → Index displays the Index window. Selecting Visual Basic and Related in the Filtered by box displays a list of help topics:

Typing a keyword in the Look for box scrolls the list to the closest topic alphabetically, and selects the topic. Clicking a topic may display information in a window in the IDE or may display the Index Results window:

Clicking a topic in the Index Results window displays information in a window in the IDE. Any blue underlined text within the help topic is a link to related information.

Printing a help topic   The topic that is currently displayed is printed by selecting File → Print.

Help

Selecting Help → Help on Help displays information on the many kinds of help available in Visual Basic .NET.

A.2 Using Dynamic Help

Selecting Help → Dynamic Help displays the Dynamic Help window:

The Dynamic Help window displays a list of help topics that are related to the current task being performed within the IDE. In the example above, a Label control was added to a form and then Dynamic Help was selected.

The Dynamic Help window organizes help topics into categories, such as Help, Actions, Getting Started, and Samples. Clicking a link in the Dynamic Help window displays information in a window in the IDE. Any blue underlined text within the help topic is a link to related information.

Printing a help topic

The topic that is currently displayed is printed by selecting File → Print.

An Introduction to Programming Using Microsoft Visual Basic .NET

Program Index

In Order of Appearance

Calculator (Case Study)　4-15
Number Guess (Section 5.1)　5-2
Pizza Order (Case Study)　5-21
Word Guess (Case Study)　6-19
Greetings　7-2
Hot Dog　7-13
Hot Dog II　7-14
Test Calculate() Function　7-23
Calculator II (Case Study)　7-24
Loan Analyzer (Case Study)　8-19
Dice Rolls　9-5
Letter Occurrences　9-6
Dynamic Array Demo　9-9
Tic-Tac-Toe　9-13
Lucy's Cuban Cafe (Case Study)　9-20
Skate!　10-9
Testing Graphics v1　10-13
Testing Graphics v2　10-14
Test Solid Graphics　10-16
Test Curves and Polygons　10-18
Click It! (Case Study)　10-23
Triangle Calculator (Case Study)　11-24
Word Guess II (Case Study)　12-21
Bubble Sort　13-2
Selection Sort　13-5
Insertion Sort　13-8
Binary Search　13-12
Bingo (Case Study)　14-20

Alphabetical

Binary Search　13-12
Bingo (Case Study)　14-20
Bubble Sort　13-2
Calculator (Case Study)　4-15
Calculator II (Case Study)　7-24
Click It! (Case Study)　10-23
Dice Rolls　9-5
Dynamic Array Demo　9-9
Greetings　7-2
Hot Dog　7-13
Hot Dog II　7-14
Insertion Sort　13-8
Letter Occurrences　9-6
Loan Analyzer (Case Study)　8-19
Lucy's Cuban Cafe (Case Study)　9-20
Number Guess (Section 5.1)　5-2
Pizza Order (Case Study)　5-21
Selection Sort　13-5
Skate!　10-9
Test Calculate() Function　7-23
Test Curves and Polygons　10-18
Test Solid Graphics　10-16
Testing Graphics v1　10-13
Testing Graphics v2　10-14
Tic-Tac-Toe　9-13
Triangle Calculator (Case Study)　11-24
Word Guess (Case Study)　6-19
Word Guess II (Case Study)　12-21

Index

−, subtraction   3-19, 4-10
−, pattern matching   6-17
"   4-7
#, pattern matching   6-17
#, assigning a date   4-7
$ 8-4
%   8-4, 8-5
&   8-9, 8-14, 6-13
(Name)   3-6
*, pattern matching   6-17
*, multiplication   3-19, 4-10
, pattern matching   6-17
. accessing a property   3-14, 3-15
. accessing a member   6-10, 9-15, 11-1
.aspx   15-10, 15-13
.aspx.vb   15-10
.bmp   10-6
.dat   12-1
.doc   2-10
.log   12-1
.txt   12-1
.vb   11-3
.vbproj   2-10
?   6-17
[]   6-17
[Design] tab   3-11
^   3-19, 4-10
_, identifier names   4-6
_, line continuation   5-18
+   3-19, 4-10
<   5-1, 6-16
/   3-19, 4-10
\   4-10
'   3-18
🔲   3-3
↖   3-4
False   4-7
▶   15-5
π   4-5, 8-24
True   4-7
<=   5-1, 6-16
<>   5-1, 6-16
<> (angle brackets)   15-3
=   3-14, 3-15, 5-1, 6-16
>   5-1, 6-16
>=   5-1, 6-16
… (ellipsis)   2-6, 14-10
32-bit operating system   6-15

A

ABC Computer   1-4
About command   14-13
Abs()   8-1
absolute value   8-1
access key   2-6, 8-13
access modifier   11-5
accessing elements   9-12
accumulator   6-5
Acos()   8-26
active child   14-4, 14-8
Active Server Pages (ASP.NET)   15-2
actual parameters   7-7
Ada, programming language   1-6
Add Class command   11-3
Add Existing Item command   11-17, 11-18
Add Watch command   4-12
Add Web Form command   15-12
Add Windows Form command   14-2
adding a control   3-5
addition   3-19
address   1-13, 7-8
address bus   1-9
Aiken, Howard   1-3
Airbrush Tool   10-6
algorithm   5-9
alphabetical string compare   6-16
Alt key   8-13
Altair   1-8
ALU   1-9
amortization   8-4
ampersand (&)   8-9, 8-14, 6-13
Analytical Engine   1-2
And   5-12
angle   8-24, 10-13
angle, finding   8-26
angle, sweep   10-13
animation   10-9
annuity   8-3, 8-4
antivirus software   1-15
Apple computer   1-8
application   2-3, 3-1
    design   3-4, 4-14, 15-11
    quitting   2-12
applications software   1-10
arc   10-13
arccosine   8-26

arcsine   8-26
arctangent   8-26
argument   7-4
    array   9-3
    file   12-5, 12-11
    object   7-11
    structure   9-15
    in a procedure call   7-5
arithmetic operators   3-19
array   9-1, 9-16
    0 elements   9-8
    changing size   9-8
    declaration   9-1
    initialization   9-1
    object elements   9-23, 14-17
    parameters   9-3, 9-12
    passing   9-4
    searching   9-8
    structure elements   9-16
    two-dimensional   9-11
Array class   9-2, 9-12
arrow keys   2-9, 3-6
AscW()   6-15
Asin()   8-26
ASP.NET   15-2, 15-10
assignment   3-14, 4-4, 7-18
    variable   4-2
Atan()   8-26
Atanasoff, John   1-4
Atanasoff-Berry Computer   1-4
authorship   14-13
AutoHide button   3-3
AutoList   3-15, 7-13
average score   6-6

B

Babbage, Charles   1-2
background color   10-1, 10-3
background image   10-4
BackgroundImage property   10-4
Backspace key   2-9
backup   2-18
bandwidth   1-10
Bardeen, John   1-6
base 10   1-12
base 16   1-12
base 2   1-12
base class   11-16
Base Class Events   10-19
base unit   1-8, 1-9

An Introduction to Programming Using Microsoft Visual Basic .NET

Baseband 1-11
BASIC 1-6
Berry, Clifford 1-4
bin folder 7-2, 10-6, 12-1, 12-2
binary code 6-15
binary notation 5-2
binary number system 1-4, 1-12
binary search 5-26, 13-10
bit 1-12
bitmap images 10-5
bits 10-6
blinking line 2-9
blocks of code 7-1
BMP 7-2, 10-4, 10-6
body 3-12
Boolean 4-7
   expression 5-1, 5-12, 6-1
   variable 5-1
booting 2-1
borrowing, for a loan 8-3
bottomMargin 15-4
bps 1-10
breakpoint 4-12
Brittain, Walter 1-6
Broadband 1-11
Brush Tool 10-6
bubble sort 13-1
bugs 7-23
bus 1-9
bus topology 1-11
business functions 8-3
Button 7-11
Button control 3-20, 10-4, 14-10, 15-5
ByRef parameter 7-7, 7-11, 9-3, 9-15, 12-5, 12-11
Byron, Ada 1-2, 1-6
byte 1-12
ByVal parameter 7-4, 7-17

C

C 1-6
C++ 1-7
C-10 1-5
cache 1-9
calculator 7-20
Call 7-1, 7-5
calling a procedure 7-1
Cancel button 14-10
capacity, storage media 1-13
carriage return 12-5
carriage return character 12-3
carriage return-linefeed 6-14
Cascade command 14-6
case, of characters 6-11
case, variable 4-6
casting 4-8
CD 2-12
CD Writing Wizard 2-18
CD/DVD drive 1-8, 2-12
CDs, handling 2-13
Census, U.S. 1-3

Char 4-7, 12-6
   elements 9-12
   structure 6-14
character lists 6-17
character ranges 6-17
characters, valid file names 2-10
characters 6-11
Chars(), string 6-10
check box 2-7, 5-17
   determining state 5-17
CheckBox control 5-17, 7-11, 15-5
   variable 7-13
child control 10-1, 10-2
child form 14-2, 14-3
   active 14-4, 14-8
   creating 14-2
   displaying 14-3
chip 1-7
ChrW() 6-15, 12-4, 12-5, 12-6
circle 10-12
class 3-1, 3-5, 3-11, 6-10, 9-15, 10-1, 11-2, 11-16
   declaration 11-4
   derived 11-16, 14-3
   design 11-2
Class module 11-3
Class Name list 3-11, 10-19
Clear() 10-13
Click event procedure 3-11
clicking 2-3
client 15-2
client/server network 1-10
clip art 7-2, 10-6
clock rate 1-9
Close button 2-4, 2-7, 2-12, 3-1, 3-4, 3-7
Close() 12-4, 12-11, 14-4
closing
   documents 2-11
   projects 3-9
   images 10-6
COBOL 1-6
Code command 3-11
Code window 3-3, 3-11, 4-11, 7-2, 10-19, 14-4
code 3-10, 3-18, 4-15, 7-1
   documenting 3-18
   indenting 3-12, 5-3
   level 1 7-23
   level 2 7-24
   printing 3-12
   reuse 11-17
cold boot 2-1
Color dialog box 10-2
color, changing 10-1
color, text 10-1
ColorDialog control 10-3
Colors window 10-5
combo box 8-10
ComboBox control 8-11
command name 3-9
command-line applications 3-1
commands 2-6
comments 3-18, 4-11, 5-4, 7-6

Compare() 6-16
CompareValidator control 15-9
comparing values 5-1
compile 3-7
component 3-8, 10-3, 10-8
component tray 3-8
composite data type 9-1, 9-15
compressed files and folders 2-18
computer 1-5
   first generation 1-4
   fourth generation 1-8
   personal 1-8
   second generation 1-6
   stored program 1-5
   third generation 1-7
computing equal periodic payments 8-4
Concat() 6-13
concatenation 6-13, 8-9
condition 6-1
constants 4-5, 4-6, 7-9, 9-16
   in a class 11-6
constructor 11-13
controls 3-5, 10-2, 11-1
   adding to form 3-5
   validation 15-8
control bus 1-9
control class 3-5, 11-1
   data type 7-11, 9-23
Control key 2-9
control object 3-5, 7-11
   passing 7-11
ControlToCompare 15-9
ControlToValidate 15-8, 15-9
conversion, type 4-8
copy files or folders 2-15, 2-16
Copy() 14-8
copying diskettes 2-18
copying files 12-1
copying files to a CD 2-18
copyright 14-13
CopyTo() 12-1
Cos() 8-24
counter 5-16, 6-8
counting 9-6
CPU 1-5, 1-9
Creat() 12-1
CreateGraphics method 10-12
Ctrl key 2-9, 3-6
currency values 8-4
   processing 8-4
cursor, *See* insertion point
Curve Tool 10-6
curves 10-17
Cut() 14-8

D

dash-dot lines 10-14
dashed line 10-14
dashed line, in button 8-14
DAT file 12-1
data bus 1-9

data hiding   11-5
data tape   2-12
data type   4-6, 7-11, 9-15, 9-23
data type storage requirements 4-6
data types   9-1
data
   in memory   1-13
   input   12-15
   member   11-2, 11-6
   protecting   1-15
   reading   12-15
   storing   9-4
   writing   12-15
datastream   12-3
Date   4-7
DateTime   13-3
debug, history of   1-6
debugging   4-12, 4-17
Decimal   4-7
decimal places   8-2
decision structure   5-1, 5-5
declaration   4-1
   placement   4-8
   variable   4-8
decrement a counter   6-9
default button   2-7
default setting   2-11
degrees   8-24
Delete command   3-9
delete files or folders   2-16
Delete key   2-9
Delete()   12-1
derived class   11-16, 14-3
Description, Web Forms   15-4
design   4-14
Design tab   15-3
Design window   3-3, 10-3, 10-5,
   10-8, 14-3
designing a class   11-2
Desktop   2-1
   appearance   2-1
devices, storage   2-12
dialog box   10-2, 14-10, 14-13
dialog boxes   2-7
Difference Engine   1-2
Dim   4-1, 14-4
dimmed object   8-14
disabled object   8-13, 8-14
Disk Cleanup   2-14
disk drives   2-14
diskette   2-12
   drive   1-8
   copying   2-18
   formatting   2-17
   handling   2-13
displaying a list of items   8-8
division   3-19
   integer   4-10
   modulus   4-10
Do While   6-2
Do...Loop   6-1
dock   3-3
docking an object   12-6

document
   closing   2-11
   printing   2-11
documenting
   code   3-18
   procedures   7-6
dollar amounts, processing   8-4
dollar sign ($)   8-4
domain name   15-2
dot   3-14, 3-15, 6-10, 9-15, 11-1
dots per inch   10-12
dotted lines   10-14
Double   4-7
double-clicking   2-3
double-clicking text   14-8
double-quotation marks   4-7
dpi   10-12
DrawArc()   10-13
DrawClosedCurve()   10-17
DrawCurve()   10-17
DrawEllipse()   10-13
drawing graphics   10-12
drawing surface   10-12
DrawLine()   10-13
DrawLine()   10-17
DrawPolygon()   10-18
DrawRectangle()   10-13
drives, in My Computer   2-14
DVD   2-12
   handling   2-13
dynamic array   9-8

E

E   8-27
e parameter   7-12, 10-19, 12-6
e^x 8-27
Eckert, J. Presper   1-4
Edit menu   14-8
EDSAC   1-5
EDVAC   1-5
Electronic Communications Privacy
Act   1-15
Electronic Freedom of Information
Act   1-15
element   9-1
   accessing   9-12
   passing   9-4
elements, dialog box   2-7
ellipse   10-13
Ellipse Tool   10-6
ellipsis (...)   2-6, 14-10
EMF   7-2, 10-4
encapsulation   11-5
End   3-12
End key   2-9
end of file   12-3, 12-4
End Sub   3-12
ENIAC   1-4
Enter key   2-9, 12-6
enumerated type   9-16
equal sign   3-14, 3-15
equality comparison   5-2

Equals()   6-16
Erase Tool   10-6
ErrorMessage   15-8, 15-9
errors   4-11
Esc key   2-9
Ethernet   1-11
ethical implications   1-14
ethical responsibilities   1-16
event   3-1, 7-12
   handler   3-11
   handler procedures   7-12
   procedure   3-11, 7-1, 15-11
event-driven application   3-1
exception   4-11
execution, stopping   4-12
Exit command   3-9
Exp()   8-27
explicit conversion   4-8
exponent   1-13
exponentiation   3-19
expression, numeric   3-19, 3-20
extension   2-10

F

F11   4-12
factorial   6-9
Fair Credit Reporting Act   1-14
False   6-1
Fast Ethernet   1-11
field member   11-2, 11-6, 11-16
file   2-10, 3-2, 12-1, 12-3
   compressed (zipped)   2-18
   copying   2-15, 2-16
   copying to a CD   2-18
   deleting   2-16
   end of   12-3, end of   12-4
   moving   2-15, 2-16
   opening   2-11
   renaming   2-15
   saving   2-10
   searching for   2-19
   sequential   12-3
File and Folder Tasks   2-15
File command   10-5, 12-1
file mode   12-4, 12-11
file name extension, *See* extension
file position   12-3
file stream   12-3
FileInfo class   12-1
f ile stream   12-3
FileStream class   12-4, 12-10
FillClosedCurve()   10-18
FillEllipse()   10-16
FillPie()   10-16
FillPolygon()   10-18
FillRectangle()   10-16
final coding   7-24
Financial Privacy Act   1-14
financing a car   8-4
finding files and folders   2-19
Fix()   5-7
flag   6-6

floating point   1-13, 4-7, 5-2
floppy diskette
    copying   2-18
    formatting   2-17
FlowLayout mode   15-4
focus   8-13
folder   2-14
    compressed (zipped)   2-18
    copying   2-15, 2-16
    creating   2-17
    deleting   2-16
    moving   2-15, 2-16
    renaming   2-15
    searching for   2-19
Font   15-5
For...Next   6-8, 9-2
forecolor   10-1
ForeColor   10-8
Form   3-4, 14-1
    See also child form, parent form,
    and dialog box
    child   14-1
    class   3-25, 10-27, 14-28
    container   14-1
    control   14-2, 14-3, 14-6, 14-10
    events   10-19
    image   10-4
    modal   14-10
    open   3-10
    parent   14-1
    reusing   11-18
    sizing   3-4
form name in the Solution Explorer
    3-10
Form1 module   11-3
Format()   8-3
Formatting an Interface   3-17
formatting diskettes   2-17
Formatting toolbar   15-3
formatting, numbers   8-3
forms, in a Web application   15-12
Fortran   1-6
fourth generation computers   1-8
freehand drawing   10-6
frequency, counting   9-4
FromFile() method   10-4
function   4-4, 7-17
    testing   7-23
    business   8-3
function procedure   7-17, 11-9
    class   11-9
future value   8-3
FV()   8-4

G

GDI+   10-13
generation of computers
    first   1-4
    fourth   1-8
    second   1-6
    third   1-7
generic procedures   7-11

Get()   11-6, 11-7
GetLength()   9-12
GIF   7-2, 10-6, 15-6
Gigabit Ethernet   1-11
gigabytes   1-13
gigahertz   1-9
global declaration   4-8
glyph   15-5
Google   15-4
graphic   10-4
    See also image, picture
    creating   10-12
graphical object   3-5
Graphics class   10-12
grid   3-5, 9-11, 10-6
GridLayout mode   15-4
group box   3-17, 5-17, 8-14
    hiding   8-14
GroupBox   3-17, 5-17

H

Handles   7-12
handles, sizing   3-4, 10-6
hard disk drive   2-12, 2-14
hard disks   2-12
hardware   1-8
help
    finding   A-1
    in dialog boxes   2-7
Help menu   14-13
hexadecimal   1-12
hiding, objects   8-14
high-level language   1-6
Hoff, Marcian   1-8
Holberton, Francis Betty   1-5
Hollerith, Herman   1-3
Home key   2-9
Hopper, Grace Murray   1-6
HotBot   15-4
HTML   15-3
HTML tab   15-3, 15-4
HTML tags   15-4
HTTP   15-6
hub   1-11
hyperlink   15-12
HyperLink control   15-12
Hypertext Markup Language   15-3
HyperText Transfer Protocol   15-6

I

IBM   1-3
IC   1-7
ICO   7-2, 10-4
Icons   2-2
ID   15-5, 15-5, 15-8, 15-9, 15-12
IDE   3-2, 3-12, 3-15, 4-6, 10-5
IDE, tabs   3-11
If...Then   5-1
If...Then...Else   5-3
If...Then...ElseIf   5-4

image   7-2, 10-4
    See also picture, graphic
    background   10-4
    changing at run time   7-2, 10-4
    creating   10-5
    closing   10-6
    distorted   7-2
    form   10-4
    sizing   7-2
    tiled   10-4
Image class   10-4
Image Editor   10-5
    toolbar   10-5, 10-6
Image property   10-4
ImageButton control   15-6
ImageUrl   15-6
implicit conversion   4-8
Imports   10-2
Imports System.IO   12-2, 12-5, 12-11
indenting code   3-12, 4-11, 5-3
index, array   9-2
index, item   8-8, 8-11
IndexOf()   6-13
infinite loop   6-2
    ending   6-2
information age   1-14
inheritance   10-1, 11-16
Inherits   3-11, 11-16, 14-3, 15-10
initializing a variable   4-1, 4-2
inkjet printer   1-9
input box   6-4
input devices   1-8
input, web application   15-8
InputBox()   6-5
Insert New command   3-9
insertion point   2-9
insertion sort   13-7
Inserts()   6-13
installment loan   8-3, 8-4
instance, form   14-4
instantiating   11-1
    form   14-1
Int()   5-7, 7-17
Integer   4-7
integer division   4-10
integrated circuits (ICs)   1-7
integrated development environ-
    ment   3-2
Intel Corporation   1-8
interest   8-4
interface   2-3
interface, formatting   3-17
internal network   15-2
Internet Explorer   15-1
Internet Protocol address   15-2
Internet Service Provider (ISP)   15-2
inverse trigonometric function   8-26
investment   8-3
Iomega Zip disk   2-12
IsNumeric()   8-1, 8-4
ISP (Internet Service Provider)   15-2
items in a list box   8-8
items, displaying at run time   8-8
iteration   6-1, 6-8

J

Jacquard, Joseph   1-2
Java   1-7
Jobs, Steve   1-8
JPG   7-2, 10-4, 10-6, 15-6

K

Kemeny, John   1-6
keyboard   1-8
keyboard   2-9
keyboard accelerator   2-6
KeyPress event   12-6
keys   2-9
Keys enumerated type   12-6
keyword   4-6
keywords, Web Forms   15-4
Kilby, Jack S.   1-7
kilobytes   1-13
Kurtz, Thomas   1-6

L

Label control   3-5, 3-6, 7-11, 10-4,
     15-5
label, text box prompt   4-3
LAN   1-10
     topologies   1-11
languages, programming 1-6, 3-1
     high-level   1-6
     object-oriented   1-7, 3-1
laser printer   1-9
leftMargin   15-4
Length   6-10, 9-2
letter occurences   9-6
lifetime   5-10
Like   6-17
line   10-12
line feed   12-5
line feed character   12-3
line terminator   12-3
Line Tool   10-6
line
     dash-dot   10-14
     dashed   10-14
     dotted   10-14
linear search   9-8, 13-10
line-continuation character   5-18
list box   8-8
List, in dialog boxes   2-8
ListBox control   8-8
loan   8-3
local declaration   4-8
Local-Area Network   1-10
localhost   15-2
Location box   3-3
LOG file   12-1
Log()   8-27
Log10()   8-27
logic error   4-11, 6-2
logical operator   5-12
logos   10-6

Long   4-7
Look in list   3-10
loop   6-6
looping   6-1
looping structure   6-1, 6-8
lowercase characters   6-11

M

machine language   1-5
Macintosh   1-8
magnetic tape   1-6
mainframe   1-7
MainMenu control   3-8, 14-6
mantissa   1-13
Mark 1   1-3
marquee selection   3-6
Math class   8-1
Mauchly, John   1-4
Maximize button   2-4, 3-4
MaximumValue   15-8
MDI application   14-1
Me   3-15, 7-11, 11-13
media, storage   2-12
megabytes   1-13
megahertz   1-9
members   6-10, 9-15, 11-1, 11-2
     accessibility   11-5
     field   11-6
memory   1-9
     location   4-1, 7-8
menu bar   2-4
menu name   3-9
Menu property   3-9
menu   3-8
     expanding   2-6
     using   2-6
MenuItem object   3-9, 3-11
message box   5-15
message, displaying   5-15
MessageBox class   5-15
META tags   15-4
Metcalfe, Bob   1-11
method   6-11, 11-2, 11-9, 11-13
     base class   11-16
     derived class   11-16
     overloaded   11-14
     protected   11-9
     public   11-9
     redefining   11-16
     shared   6-13
Method Name list   3-11, 10-19
method of design   5-9
microcomputer   1-8
microprocessor   1-8
Millisecond   13-3
milliseconds   10-8
Minimize button   2-4, 3-4
MinimumValue   15-8
Mod   4-10
modal form   14-10
Model 650   1-6
module-level declaration   4-8

modulus division   4-10
monitor   1-8
monthly interest rate   8-3
mortgage loan   8-3, 8-4
motherboard   1-9
mouse   1-8
     click   3-11
     events   10-19
     using   2-3
MouseDown event   10-19
move files or folders   2-15, 2-16
moving an object   3-6
multiple values   9-1
multiple-document interface   14-1
multiplication   3-19
multitasking   2-1
My Computer   2-13

N

Name Property   3-12
name, object   3-6
naming conventions   3-6, 4-7
nanoseconds   1-9
natural logarithm   8-27
NavigateUrl   15-12
nested statement   5-4
netiquette   1-14
network   1-10, 15-2
network architecture   1-10
network interface card   1-10
New   3-3, 12-1, 10-5, 10-12, 10-17,
     11-1, 11-13
New Project button   3-2
node   1-10
Not   5-12
Nothing   4-7
notification area   2-2
Now()   13-3
Noyce, Robert   1-7
number systems   1-12
numbers, formatting   8-3
numbers, generating a range   5-6
numbers, images   5-7

O

Object   7-12
object   3-1, 3-5, 6-10, 7-11, 11-1
     docking   12-6
     height   10-12
     variable   11-1
     width   10-12
     adding to form   3-5
object-oriented programming   1-7,
     11-2, 11-16
object-oriented language   3-1
objects   3-1
     array   9-23
     docking   12-5
     identifying   7-13
OK button   14-10
On/Off   8-3

OOP 1-7, 3-1
Open dialog box 12-8
Open Project button 3-2
open windows, listing 14-6
OpenFileDialog component 12-8
opening a file 2-11
opening a project 3-9
operating system 2-1
operating system software 1-10
operator 3-19
operator precedence 3-19, 4-10
Or 5-12
order of operations 3-19, 4-10
output device 1-9
overflow error 1-13, 6-2
overloaded function 8-27
overloading methods 11-14
Overridable 11-16
Overrides 11-16
overwrite 2-11

P

PadLeft() 6-11
PadRight() 6-11
Page class 15-10
Page Down key 2-9
Page Up key 2-9
pageLayout 15-4
pages 15-2
palette 10-1
paper tape 1-5
parameters 7-4
    array 9-3, 9-12
    method 11-15
    passing 7-4
    reference 7-7
    structure 9-15
    value 7-4
parent control 10-1, 10-2
parent form 14-1, 14-2
    creating 14-2
parentheses 4-10
parentheses in an expression 3-20
Pascal, Blaise 1-1
Pascaline 1-1
passing control objects 7-11
Paste() 14-8
pattern matching 6-17
payment function 8-3
Peek() 12-4
peer-to-peer network 1-10
Pen 10-12
Pen class 10-14
Pencil Tool 10-6
percent sign (%) 8-4, 8-5
percentage rates 8-4
percentages, processing 8-5
peripheral devices 1-8
persistent 12-1
personal computer 1-8
photographs 7-2, 10-6
PI 8-24
picture box 10-4

picture element 10-12
picture 10-4 *See also* image, graphic
PictureBox 7-11
PictureBox control 7-2
PictureBox control 10-9
piracy 1-15
pixel 10-12
Pmt() 8-3
PNG 7-2, 10-4, 15-6
point 10-17
Point structure 10-17
pointing 2-3
polygons 10-17
polymorphism 11-16
post: 7-6
posting 15-2
Pow() 8-27
pre: 7-6
prefix, data type 4-7
present value 8-3, 8-4
Preserve 9-8
preview pane 10-6
prime number 6-3
principal 8-3, 8-4
Print command 3-12
printers 1-9
printing a document 2-11
printing code 3-12
privacy 1-14
Privacy Act 1-14
Private 3-12, 11-5
Private Const 11-6
procedure 3-11, 7-4, 7-17
    call 9-4
    class 11-9
    documenting 7-6
    executing 7-1
    generic 7-11
program 1-5
    stopping execution 4-12
program code 3-10
programming languages
    high-level 1-6
    object-oriented 1-7
project 3-2
    folder 7-2
Project command 3-3, 3-9
Project Types list 3-3
prompt 4-3, 6-5
proper case 6-11
properties 3-4, 3-15
Properties window 3-3, 10-6, 15-3
property, class 11-1, 11-2
    declaration 11-6
    member 11-6
    creating 11-7
property, setting 3-14
Protected 11-5, 11-9, 11-10, 11-16
pseudocode 5-9
pseudorandom 5-7
Public 11-5, 11-9
punched cards 1-2, 1-3
PV() 8-4

Q

Quick Launch toolbar 2-2
quitting an application 2-12
quitting Visual Basic.NET 3-9

R

radians 8-24
Radio button 2-7
radio buttons 3-17
RadioButton 7-11, 15-5
RadioButton control 3-17
RAM 1-9
Random Access Memory 1-9
random numbers 5-6
    generating unique set 14-17
Randomize() 5-7
RangeValidator control 15-8
Rank 9-12
read (data) 1-6
Read Only Memory 1-9
Read() 12-4
ReadLine() 12-4
ReadOnly 11-7
real numbers 1-13
record 12-16
rectangle 10-12
Rectangle Selection Tool 10-6
Rectangle Tool 10-6
Recycle Bin 2-16
red circle 4-12
ReDim 9-8, 9-12
ReDim Preserve 9-8
reel-to-reel tape 1-6
reference parameters 7-7
relational operators 5-1
Remove() 6-11
rename files or folders 2-15
repeat keys 2-9
Replace() 6-13, 8-4
RequiredFieldValidator control
    15-8
resize tab 2-4
retirement plan 8-3, 8-4
Return 7-17
right-clicking 2-3
rightMargin 15-4
ring topology 1-11
Ritchie, Dennis 1-6
Rnd() 5-6, 7-17
Rock Paper Scissors 5-13
ROM 1-9
Round() 8-2
rounding 4-8
    rules 8-2
roundoff error 1-14, 5-2
running an application 3-6
running total 6-5
running, Web application 15-6
run-time error 4-4, 4-11, 6-2,
    7-9, 8-4, 9-2

S

Safety and Freedom through Encryption Act   1-15
Save As   10-6
Save As Dialog box   12-12
Save button   3-6
Save command   3-6, 12-1, 15-6
SaveFileDialog component   12-12
saving a file   2-10
saving, Web application   15-6
scaler   9-1
scanner   1-8
scope   5-10
scope   4-8
screen resolution   10-12
Screen Tip   2-6
scroll bar   2-4, 8-8, 8-10, 12-5
search engine   15-4
Search pane, using   2-20
search   13-10
    array   9-8, 13-10
searching files and folders   2-19
second generation computers   1-6
seed   5-7
Select...Case   5-5, 9-17
Select...Case Is   5-5
selected object   3-4
selection sort   13-5
semantic error   4-11
sender parameter   7-12
sentinel   6-6
sequential file access   12-3
server   15-2
Set()   11-6, 11-7
Shadows   11-16
shapes, creating   10-12
shared method   6-13
Shockley, William   1-6
Short   4-7
shortcuts, in dialog boxes   2-8
Show()   5-15, 14-3
ShowDialog()   10-3, 12-9, 12-12,
    14-10
side effects   7-23
Sign()   8-1
silicon wafers   1-7
Sin()   8-24
Single   4-1, 4-6, 4-7
single quotation mark   3-18
sizing a form   3-4
smart menus   3-8
social implications   1-14
software   1-10
software, antivirus   1-15
SolidBrush Class   10-16
Solution Explorer command   3-11
Solution Explorer window   3-3,
    3-11, 15-3
sort, timing   13-3
sorting   13-1, 13-5
space   12-5
Space()   6-13

spaces, pad string   6-11
spaces, remove from string   6-11
spec   4-14
specification   4-14
Sqrt()   8-1
SRAM   1-9
staetment, dividing   5-18
star topology   1-11
Start button   3-6, 15-6
Start command   3-6, 15-6
start menu   2-2
Start Page   3-2
statement   3-10, 3-18
    See also code
    continuing to next line   5-18
Static   5-10, 5-16
static variable   5-10
status bar   2-4
Step   6-9
Step Into button   4-12
Step Into command   4-12
Stepped Reckoner   1-1
Stop Debugging Command   3-7
storage media   1-9, 2-12
storage media capacity   1-13
stored program computer   1-5
StrConv()   6-11
stream   12-3
StreamReader class   12-4, 12-15
StreamWriter class   12-11, 12-15
String   4-7, 6-10
    compare alphabetically   6-16
    matching   6-17
    pad with character   6-11
    String class   6-10
Strings, with numbers   8-2
structure   6-14, 9-15
    argument   9-15
    parameter   9-15
structure, array   9-16
Style Settings   10-6
Sub procedure   3-12, 7-1
subscript   9-2
substring   6-11
Substring()   6-11
subtraction   3-19
sum   6-5
SuperDisk diskette   2-12
syntax error   4-11
System 360   1-7
system menu   3-4
System.Drawing   10-2

T

tab   12-5
Tab key   3-12, 8-13
tab order   8-13, 8-14
tabs in IDE   3-11
tabulating machine   1-3
Tag property   7-13
tags   15-3
Tan()   8-24

targetSchema   15-4
taskbar   2-2
Templates list   3-3
terminal   1-8
testing   4-17
testing a function   7-23
text box   2-7, 4-3
    label   4-3
text color   10-1
Text property   3-4
Text Tool   10-6
text, highlighted   14-8
text, selecting   14-8
TextAlign options   3-15
TextBox control   4-4, 12-5, 12-6,
    14-8, 15-5
TextChanged event   4-4
textual comparison   6-17
third generation computers   1-7
Tick event   10-8
tic-tac-toe   9-12
Tile Horizontal command   14-6
Tile Vertical command   14-6
timer   10-8
    starting   10-8
    stopping   10-8
Timer control   10-8, 10-9
timing a sort   13-3
title   15-4
title bar   2-4, 3-4
To   5-5, 6-8
ToLower   6-11
ToLower()   6-14
toolbar   10-6
toolbar, Quick Launch   2-2
toolbars   2-4, 2-6
Toolbox   3-3, 3-5, 15-3, 15-5
Toolbox button   3-3
topMargin   15-4
topology   1-10
ToUpper   6-11
ToUpper()   6-14
transistor   1-6
transmission media   1-10
transparent   10-1
trigonometric methods   8-24
Trim   6-11
TrimEnd   6-11, 8-5
TrimStart   6-11
True   6-1
True/False   8-3
truth tables   5-12
Turing, Alan   1-5
two-dimensional array   9-11
    parameters   9-12
TXT file   12-1
Type   15-8, 15-9
type conversion   4-8

U

U.S. Census Bureau   1-3, 1-5
UDTs (user-defined types)   9-16

An Introduction to Programming Using Microsoft Visual Basic .NET

underscore   4-6, 5-18
Unicode   1-13, 6-15, 6-16, 12-5
Uniform Resource Locator   15-6
UNIVAC   1-5
updating a counter   5-16
uppercase characters   6-11
URL   15-6, 15-13
user-defined types (UDTs)   9-16

V

vacuum tube   1-4, 1-6
Val()   4-4, 8-4, 6-5, 12-4, 12-5
valid file names   2-10
validation controls   15-8
value parameter   7-4
variable   4-1, 4-6
   assignment   4-2
   Boolean   5-1
   counter   5-16
   declaration   4-8, 5-10
   object   11-1
   parameters   7-7
   retaining value   5-10
vbCrLf   6-14
vbTab   6-14, 8-9
vector-based graphics   7-2
version information   14-13
video   10-9
View Code button   3-11, 15-10
viewing disk contents   2-13
viewing folders   2-14
virus   1-15
Visual Basic .NET   3-1
von Leibniz, Gottfried Wilhelm 1-1
von Neumann, John   1-5

W

WAN   1-10
warm boot   2-1
Watch window   4-12
Web application   15-1
   running   15-6
   saving   15-6
Web browser   15-4, 15-6
Web colors   10-1
Web development platform   15-2
Web forms   15-2
Web Forms controls   15-1, 15-2, 15-8
Web Forms Design window   15-3
Web Forms page   15-1, 15-3, 15-4
Web host   15-2
Web servers   15-1
Wide-Area Network   1-10
wildcard characters   6-17
Window menu   14-6
window   2-1
   closing   2-4
   expanding and reducing   2-4
Windows application   2-3, 3-1, 8-13

Windows   2-1
   Clipboard   14-8
   Explorer   2-15
   Taskbar   6-2
Windows Form Designer generated code   3-11
Windows metafiles   7-2
Windows NT   6-15
Windows XP   6-15, 10-13
windows   14-1
   arranging child   14-6
   opening child   14-6
WinZip   2-18
wireless network   1-10
WLAN   1-10
WMF   7-2, 10-4
word   1-13
WordPad   2-3
World Wide Web   15-1
Wozniak, Stephen   1-8
write (data)   1-6
Write()   12-11
WriteLine()   12-11, 12-15
write-protect tab   2-18

X

X property   10-20
x-coordinate   10-17

Y

Y property   10-20
Yahoo!   15-4
y-coordinate   10-17
Yes/No   8-3

Z

zipped files and folders   2-18

An Introduction to Programming Using Microsoft Visual Basic .NET